Graduate Leadership

Third Edition, Volume 2

4900 LaCross Road
North Charleston, SC 29406, USA

www.DrMarkGreen.com

Release 1.1, July 10, 2015

Library of Congress
Cataloging-in-Publication
Data is available

Leadership Press
ISBN-13: 978-0692419168
(Leadership Press)
ISBN-10: 0692419160

Dedicated to the Sisters of Divine Providence

Who Model How to Serve People Whose Needs are Being Neglected
Who Educate Within a Broad Vision of Ministry
Who Not Only Teach but Renew People's Faith and
Who Serve Them Constantly Through Works of Mercy

Graduate Leadership
Changes in the Third Edition

The third edition of *Graduate Leadership* contains two major additions and several important improvements.

Empirical Methods

Additional information is contained in chapter 2 that more thoroughly explains the statistics used in meta-analyses. Explanations of multiple regression and meta-analytic multiple regression have been added.

New Meta-Analyses

The findings from nine meta-analyses have been added to the research results provided in chapters 3 through 7. Additionally, the chapter on personality and leadership has been greatly expanded.

Meta-Analytic Regressions

The results of numerous, more advanced, meta-analytic regressions have been included in chapters 3 through 7.

Graphical Presentation of Meta-Analytic Results

The second edition of *Graduate Leadership* presented the results of the meta-analytic literature in tabular form. The third edition provides the meta-analytic results in graphical form.

Graduate Leadership
Acknowledgements

This book doesn't provide any new theories of leadership, propose any new instruments or present any new research results.

Rather, it connects a large amount of empirical research in the area of leadership and provides it in a synthetic and student-oriented manner.

Synthesizing a textbook such as this requires a great deal of support from many people.

It is difficult to compile a textbook about leadership, if one doesn't have good leaders creating an environment that fosters research and teaching.

For the past 21 years, I have been supported by the students, staff, faculty and administration at Our Lady of the Lake University. The university only exists because thousands of Sisters of Divine Providence dedicated their lives to the institution.

In my small window of time at Our Lady of the Lake University, I have been fortunate to observe this dedication from Sisters Ann, Elizabeth Anne, Isabel, Jane Ann, Janet, Madlyn, Margit, Maria and Rose Annelle.

For the past 17 years, my work at Our Lady of the Lake University has been in the Department of Leadership Studies. Dr. Jacquelyn Alexander started the department and its associated doctoral program in leadership studies. Dr. Robert Bisking led the expansion of the program to three campuses. More importantly, Dr. Bisking's leadership helped my colleagues to continue to be graduate faculty primarily focused on collaborative teaching rather than competitive research. Dr. Dwayne Banks is continuing this tradition of being a servant leader, and helping the leadership studies faculty to serve our students in the heritage of the Sisters of Divine Providence.

Within my department, four colleagues have enabled me to make the transition from a department chair to a teacher/ researcher by performing a great deal of administration in addition to their own teaching and research. Dr. Meghan Carmody-Bubb has handled everything related to our San Antonio masters program in leadership. Dr. Phyllis Duncan has handled all of the administration for our doctoral program in San Antonio. Dr. Jared Montoya has handled all of the administration for our masters and doctoral programs in the Rio Grande Valley.

Dr. Esther Gergen has handled all of the administration for our doctoral program in Houston and all of the departmental level administration. The dedication of these colleagues to our students has provided me the time to create this book and the opportunity to migrate from the role of a department chair to that of slightly eccentric but loveable professor who can explain meta-analyses to students but can't tell them how to register for the next semester.

Graduate Leadership
Acknowledgements

A Practitioner-Scholar Program

We describe the focus of the doctoral program in which I teach as a practitioner-scholar model. While overly simplified, the table below conveys this idea. Every day hundreds of thousands of individuals attend leadership training and seminars, or teach others how to become better leaders. Typically, these practitioner-oriented leadership programs are quite applied with minimal discussion of the empirical background behind what is taught. Time is limited, and the focus is to help real or future leaders become better leaders.

Practitioner	Practitioner-Scholar	Scholar
Working Leaders or Individuals Involved in Leadership Training Programs Such as School, Civic, Faith-Based or Workplace Leadership Development	Can Conduct Research Can Understand the Research Others Produce Can Explain Research to Practitioners	Perform Research to Acquire Grants Acquire Grants to Perform Research Contribute Significantly to the Body of Literature

Meanwhile, there are thousands of faculty and doctoral students studying leadership and management at research-oriented institutions of higher learning. This “publish or perish” type of environment emphasizes acquiring grant money to support research. In order to receive grant money, applicants typically need a record of prior research.

A middle area, the practitioner-scholar area of the table above, connotes graduate students who are learning about the empirical research base underlying management and leadership theories, while concomitantly keeping their “day-jobs” as practitioners. These individuals often influence or conduct practitioner-training programs, or serve in leadership positions. They typically perform less research than those toward the scholar end of the spectrum. They are often, however, quite good at “translating” the empirical base in the literature into understandable language that practitioners can use “in the real world,” as the practitioner-scholars are themselves often full-time leaders or leader educators.

For the past 16 years, Dr. Malcolm Ree has served as the primary research and statistics professor in the department in which I teach. He has patiently mentored my colleagues and me in understanding and explaining advanced statistical findings from the literature. He has also guided us through a variety of statistical methods to use for the over 150 dissertations we have directed. I could only compile this book because of his dedication to our students and faculty.

Within the department in which I teach, all of the doctoral faculty are eventually involved in every dissertation. This collaborative activity has assisted me in developing multiple metaphors and analogies that seem to help graduate students to experience “aha” moments. Most of these epiphany-producing techniques have been used in this book. Those “aha” experiences would not have been possible without the assistance of Dr.’s Carmody-Bubb, Duncan, Gergen, Hinojosa, Montoya, Ree, Salter, Sun and Wheeler. Each has contributed a unique way of explaining the empirical/scholar side of leadership to practitioner-scholar students.

Graduate Leadership
Contributors

Staff members Norma Anderson, Anne Gomez, Gloria Urrabazo and Dan Yoxall have each been instrumental in supporting the leadership programs in which I have honed my teaching analogies and metaphors. Ms. Valerie Hernandez provided a significant amount of administrative support for this book.

Seventeen colleagues with mastery of the empirical literature related to leadership assisted in distilling the body of research presented in this textbook. Additionally, professor Steven Wise served as the contributing researcher, assisting all of us in locating and obtaining articles, reports and dissertations that were difficult to obtain through typical academic databases.

Contributing Authors

John W. Blumentritt, PhD

Dr. John Blumentritt is an Assistant Professor in the Department of Security Studies and Criminal Justice at Angelo State University (ASU) in San Angelo, Texas. He served as a pilot in the U.S. Air Force, held various flying, staff and command assignments, and retired at the rank of Colonel.

Dr. Blumentritt earned his BS from ASU and an MS from Michigan State University. He then completed three additional master's degrees related to strategy development and national security from the U.S. Naval War College, School of Advanced Airpower Studies and Air War College. He earned his PhD in 2009 from Our Lady of the Lake University. His dissertation compared senior political and military leadership during the post-cold war environment. Dr. Blumentritt's teaching, public speaking and publishing tend to integrate political science, history and leadership-centric perspectives. He has been featured in the *Reader's Digest* and on the History Channel.

Meghan Carmody-Bubb, PhD

Dr. Meghan Carmody-Bubb earned her PhD in Experimental Psychology from Texas Tech University in 1993. She served in the U.S. Navy as an Aerospace Experimental Psychologist, conducting research in adaptive automation, aircrew training, and advanced technology displays for tactical aircraft. She retired from the Navy Reserves at the rank of Commander.

Dr. Carmody-Bubb is currently an Associate Professor in the Department of Leadership Studies at Our Lady of the Lake University in San Antonio, Texas. She lives in Bulverde, Texas with her husband and three children.

Graduate Leadership

Contributors

Phyllis A. Duncan, PhD

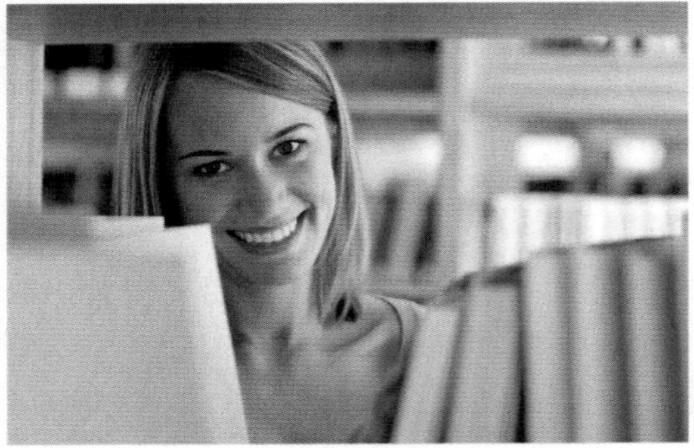

Dr. Phyllis Duncan is an Associate Professor in the School of Business and Leadership at Our Lady of the Lake University. She has held leadership positions in various businesses including CEO, COO and Senior Vice President.

Dr. Duncan holds a Bachelor of Science in Business Administration from the University of the Ozarks, a Master of Business Administration from the University of Arkansas, a Master of Science in Industrial Engineering from Southwest University and a PhD from the University of the Incarnate Word.

Esther S. Gergen, PhD

Dr. Esther Gergen is an Assistant Professor of Leadership Studies in the School of Business and Leadership at Our Lady of the Lake University. Her executive career began with the HEB Grocery Company for which she was a store director. She led several of the San Antonio store locations. Shortly thereafter, she transitioned into the financial services industry by joining Citigroup as a Client Financial Analyst. During her time at Citi, she served in a variety of leadership roles including her final assignment as Director of Credit Sales Strategy.

Dr. Gergen is a native Texan, who was born and raised in El Paso, Texas. She holds a Bachelors degree in Marketing from Texas A&M University, and an MBA and PhD in Leadership Studies from Our Lady of the Lake University. She is currently serving as the Chair of the Department of Leadership Studies at Our Lady of the Lake University.

Florelisa Y. Gonzalez, MBA

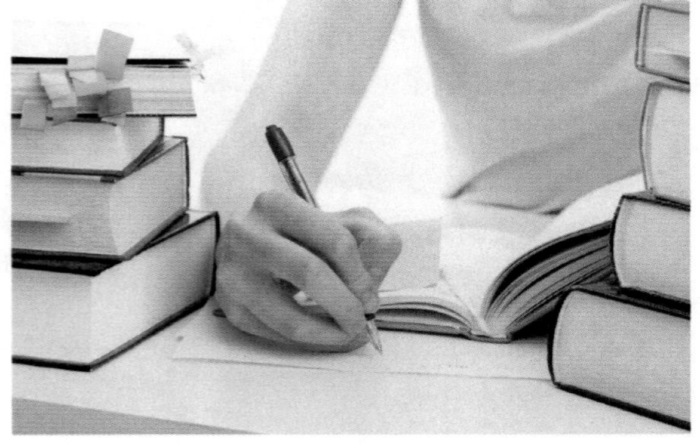

Florelisa Gonzalez is completing her doctoral dissertation in Leadership Studies at Our Lady of the Lake University.

Florelisa holds a Bachelors degree in Business Management from Texas State University and an MBA from Our Lady of the Lake University. She has presented papers at national conferences and co-authored several articles in peer-reviewed journals.

Graduate Leadership
Contributors

Barbara Baggerly-Hinojosa, PhD.

Dr. Barbara Baggerly-Hinojosa is a wife, mother and educator living in the Rio Grande Valley of Texas. She holds a PhD in Leadership Studies from Our Lady of the Lake University. In addition, she holds an Associate of Arts degree in Education from McLennan Community College, a Bachelor of Arts in Interdisciplinary Studies from the University of Texas – Pan American and a Master of Arts in Educational Supervision from the University of Texas – Pan American. Dr. Baggerly-Hinojosa's current research is focused on servant leadership, gender issues in leadership, and spirituality in the workplace.

Dr. Baggerly-Hinojosa is a guest writer for *The Mercedes Enterprise* newspaper, *RgVision* magazine*, Examiner Corpus Christi* and a blogger for oneinabillionconsulting.com. In addition, she has published three books on leadership: *Are You a Ten? The Ten Characteristics of a Servant Leader, The Leadership Collection* and *Eres un Diez*?

David Lauber, PhD

Dr. David Lauber is an instructional/eLearning developer at a Fortune 500 energy company in San Antonio, TX. His career began in training and development as an instructor, transitioning to instructional systems design and web/computer-based training.

Dr. Lauber holds an MBA and PhD in Leadership Studies from Our Lady of the Lake University. Dr. Lauber also holds a BFA in Visual Communications and an M.Ed. in Instructional Technology from American Intercontinental University.

Jared A. Montoya, PhD

Dr. Jared A. Montoya is an Associate Professor of Leadership Studies in the School of Business and Leadership at Our Lady of the Lake University. He began his career working in human resources for Sears Home Central in Provo, UT and later worked as a recruiter for Select Personnel Services in Los Angeles, CA. Prior to pursuing his graduate education, he worked in São Paulo, Brazil as an English teacher to executives from several multinational corporations.

Dr. Montoya was born and raised in Colorado and earned a Bachelors, Masters, and PhD degree from Brigham Young University in Provo, UT where he specialized in Social Psychology. Dr. Montoya's research focuses on gender, culture, multiculturalism and health. He has researched for non-profit organizations, has published in several academic journals and has presented at a number of national conferences.

Graduate Leadership
Contributors

Malcolm James Ree, PhD

Dr. Malcolm Ree is a Professor of Leadership Studies at Our Lady of the Lake University. Dr. Ree holds an M.A. in Psychology and a PhD in Psychometrics and Statistics from the University of Pennsylvania. Dr. Ree has published over 13 book chapters, 60 journal articles, 50 technical reports and 40 conference presentations and papers.

Prior to becoming a college professor, he had a distinguished career as an Air Force researcher holding positions as Senior Scientist, Air Force Research Laboratory, Human Effectiveness Directorate; Past Chairman, (DOD) Psychometric Committee; ASVAB Working Group Chairman; (DOD) Joint Service Selection and Classification Psychometric Committee; First Chairman, Publications Review Panel; Past Chairman, (DOD) Selection and Classification, Technology Task Group and Air Force Representative to the TAPSTEM Scientific Group.

Richard A. Rodriguez, PhD

Dr. Richard Rodriguez has been an educator for over 20 years. He teaches at both the high school and college levels in Texas. At the high school level, Richard teaches in the area of mathematics. At the collegiate level, he teaches in the area of human development.

Dr. Rodriguez holds a BS in Kinesiology from the University of Texas at San Antonio, an M.Ed in Educational Administration from Lamar University and a PhD in Leadership Studies from Our Lady of the Lake University.

Charles Salter, PhD

Dr. Charles Salter is an Assistant Professor of Business Administration at Schreiner University. Dr. Salter holds a PhD in Leadership Studies and an MBA with a concentration in Management and Finance, Series 6, 63 and 65 Securities Licenses, and is a Texas real estate broker. He has served on the board of directors for a healthcare firm and a charitable organization, and has over 32 years of experience in middle and upper management and leadership for three Fortune 500 organizations and in municipal government.

Graduate Leadership
Contributors

Roy Sheneman, PhD

Dr. Roy Sheneman serves as the Senior Human Resource Manager for the VTX1 family of companies headquartered in Raymondville, TX. He speaks at numerous conferences on a variety of organizational and family leadership topics.

Dr. Sheneman holds a BS in Education from the University of Dayton, an MA in Marriage and Family Therapy from the University of Louisiana, Monroe and a PhD in Leadership Studies from the Our Lady of the Lake University. He is a Certified Practitioner of the *Myers-Briggs Type Inventory* (MBTI), the *California Psychological Inventory* (CPI-260), the *Strong's Interest Inventory* and is trained by the Ken Blanchard Companies to deliver the *Situational Leadership II* program.

Yu Sun, PhD

Dr. Yu Sun received her MS in Applied Mathematics in 2007 and PhD in Management Science in 2010 from Donghua University, Shanghai, China. She joined the Department of Mathematics, Wayne State University, Detroit, Michigan in 2007 and received her MA in Mathematical Statistics and PhD in Applied Mathematics in 2012. She is currently an Assistant Professor at Our Lady of the Lake University. Before joining the university, she served as an Assistant Professor in the Quantitative Business Analysis Department at Siena College, Loudonville, NY. Her research interests include mathematics in decision-making, business statistics, operations management, stochastic optimization, quantitative analysis and leadership studies.

Sandra Tibbs, PhD

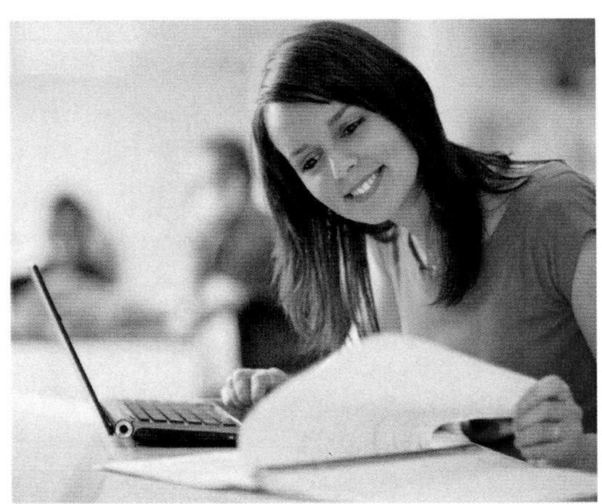

Dr. Sandra Tibbs is the founder of Neverest Solutions, a leadership development consultancy that specializes in training corporate, government and small business executives. Sandra combines her extensive experience in military intelligence training with an understanding of whole brain thinking, neuro leadership and organizational leadership.

Dr. Tibbs holds a BS in Biology, an MS in Organizational Leadership and a PhD in Leadership Studies from Our Lady of the Lake University.

Graduate Leadership

Contributors

Wes Venters, PhD

Dr. Wes Venters is an Air Force officer who has had assignments at the USAF Research Laboratory, Brooks City-Base, San Antonio, TX (Behavioral Scientist), the USAF Headquarters Air Force Recruiting Service, Randolph AFB, TX (Research & Marketing Analyst), the USAF Academy, Colorado Springs, CO (Behavioral Scientist/ Assistant Professor), and the USAF Research Laboratory, Wright-Patterson AFB, OH (Behavioral Scientist). He is currently the Research Team Leader for an Air Force Human Effectiveness Branch that focuses on human insight and trust research studies in the areas of trust in autonomy, trust and suspicion, and social signatures exploitation.

Dr. Venters holds a BS in Social Psychology from Park University, an MA in Counseling (emphasis in MFT) from Webster University and a PhD in Leadership Studies from Our Lady of the Lake University.

F. Irene Waggoner, PhD

Dr. Irene Waggoner has spent the majority of her career within the higher education system, both as faculty and in administration. She currently teaches undergraduate business courses, and masters and doctoral leadership courses. Professionally, she has served in human resources management, talent management and global operations with a Fortune 500 global software company. She holds a Ph.D. in leadership studies, an MBA, a BA in psychology and various certifications. Dr. Waggoner is passionate about life-long learning for both others and herself. Her professional memberships include the Society for Human Resources Management, American Society for Training and Development and World Future Society.

Carol Wheeler, PhD

Dr. Carol Wheeler is an Assistant Professor in the Leadership Studies Department at Our Lady of the Lake University. She teaches graduate level courses in leadership theory, conflict management, strategy and teamwork. Prior to joining Our Lady of the Lake University, Dr. Wheeler taught in the Mays Business School at Texas A&M, focusing on undergraduate leadership courses. She also worked for a number of years in student affairs at various universities.

Dr. Wheeler holds a BS in Agricultural Leadership Development from Texas A&M University, an MS in Higher Education and Student Affairs from Indiana University and a PhD in Leadership Education from Oklahoma State University.

Graduate Leadership
Contributors

Contributing Researcher

Steven Wise, MA, MLIS

Steven Wise is an Associate Professor of Learning Resources and Instruction Librarian for the Sueltenfuss Library at Our Lady of the Lake University. Professor Wise holds a BA and an MA in Political Science from St. Mary's University of San Antonio and an MLIS (Library and Information Science) from the University of Texas at Austin.

Contributing Students

Since 1998, I have taught a first-year leadership sequence to over 400 doctoral students. As part of this teaching, I have explained multiple aspects of leadership ideas in multiple ways. Some of these methods have resulted in happy expressions and small epiphanies from a variety of adult learners. Many of those methods have been used in this book.

Collectively, the dissertation literature reviews that I have directed and read from many of these students add up to over 6,000 pages.

My work with hundreds of doctoral student practitioner-scholars to synthesize the literature related to each student's leadership interest has also given me a range of teaching tools that were used in this book.

There are simply too many alumnae and current doctoral students to mention in this acknowledgement. Their work on each of their individual journeys has assisted me in compiling this book. My hope is that this textbook makes the journey toward understanding the empirical base in organizational leadership a bit easier and much more enjoyable for those students just beginning their journeys.

Final Acknowledgement

My wife of 17 years, Justina, continues to support my academic career in countless ways.

She has grown accustomed to my absences on Saturdays when classes meet, and my recurrent answer of "working on a book" to most of her questions about my day.

I couldn't have compiled this textbook without her love and support.

Graduate Leadership
Table of Contents

Graduate Leadership
Table of Contents

Introduction

The Research Base for Popular Theories of Leadership

Chapter 1
Introduction

A Brief History of Organizational Leadership Theories

A Chronology of Influential Management and Leadership Theories

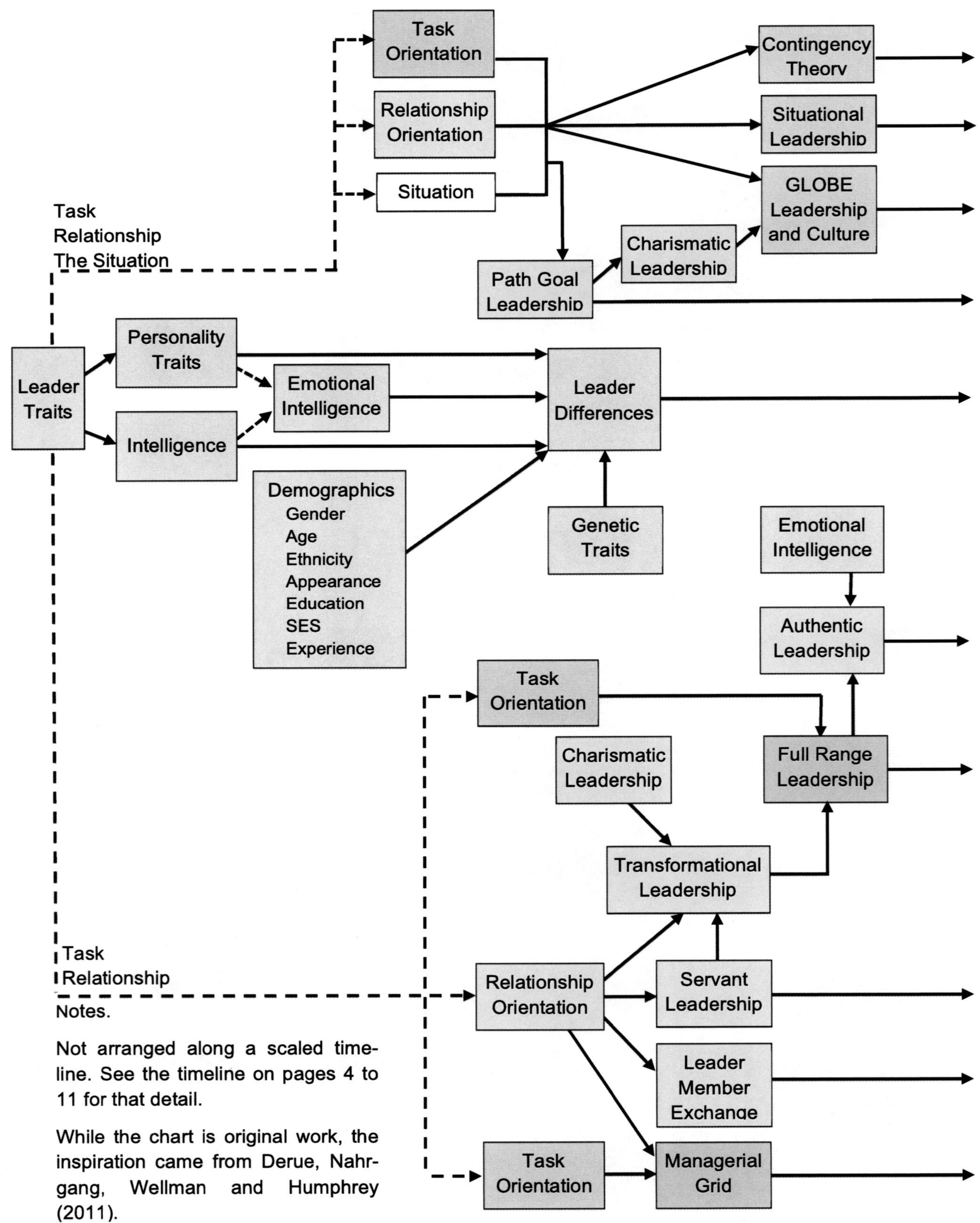

Notes.

Not arranged along a scaled timeline. See the timeline on pages 4 to 11 for that detail.

While the chart is original work, the inspiration came from Derue, Nahrgang, Wellman and Humphrey (2011).

A Brief History of Organizational Leadership Theories

A Chronology of Influential Management and Leadership Theories

Volume 1 of the Third Edition of *Graduate Leadership* reviewed 51 influential theories in the general area of organizational leadership and management. For students who do not have access to that volume, those 51 theories are provided in this volume in tabular form.

Those theories shown in grey are management or leadership ideas that have had some influence on the development of organizational leadership theory.

Those theories shown in beige have had a bit more influence.

Those shown in blue have had a significant influence on the development of leadership theory. These will be reviewed in detail in chapters 3 through 8.

Seven of these highly influential theories are both popular and have a significant quantitative base:

- Chapter 3: Task, Relationship and Situation
- Chapter 4: The Full Range Model of Leadership
- Chapter 5: Personality and Leadership
- Chapter 6: Emotional Intelligence and Leadership
- Chapter 7: Leader-Member Exchange Theory
- Chapter 8: Project GLOBE
- Chapter 10: Authentic Leadership

While servant leadership (chapter 9) currently lacks a significant quantitative research base, several instruments have recently been developed and the likelihood that a quantitative foundation for servant leadership will develop over the next decade is high.

The chart on the opposite page provides a general sense of how earlier theories have influenced later theories along the journey to the eight popular theories that will be reviewed in this volume.

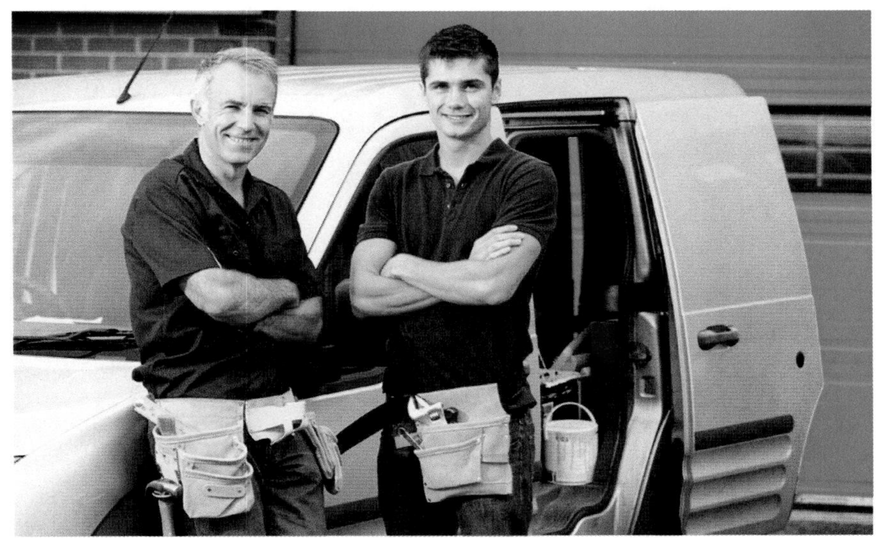

A Brief History of Organizational Leadership Theories

A Chronology of Influential Management and Leadership Theories

Year	Theory	Authors	Comments
The Era of Leadership Traits			
1880's to 1920's	Great Person	Carlyle, Goldberg, Brattin, and Engel (1888)	This early leadership theory lacked an empirical base. The theory advanced that successful leaders were born to greatness.
1911	Scientific Management	Taylor (1911)	Taylor's principles describing specialization of work were related to the changes occurring as a result of the industrial revolution.
1933	Hawthorne Studies	Mayo (1933, 1945)	The Hawthorne studies were designed to measure the impact of workplace environment on productivity. A related finding was that whenever workers were studied, productivity increased.
1938	Executive Functions	Barnard (1938)	Barnard's book on the functions of an executive emphasized more of the relational aspects of management than did the scientific management approach.
1947	Theory of Administrative Behavior in Organizations	Simon (1947) March and Simon (1958)	Rather than allocate all of our time and energy to an optimal solution for a single problem, we search for a decision for most problems that is good enough, called satisficing. Organizations typically run on a collection of decisions that were good enough rather than optimal.
1948	Leader Traits	Stogdill (1948)	Stogdill analyzed 128 published trait studies, but was unable to develop a definitive list.
1949	Principles of Management	Fayol (1949)	Fayol's five functions and 14 principles of management were largely an extension of the scientific management approach. The impact of the labor movement, however, likely influenced a bit more emphasis on fair treatment of all workers.

A Brief History of Organizational Leadership Theories

A Chronology of Influential Management and Leadership Theories

The Era of Leadership Behaviors			
1954	Maslow's Hierarchy	Maslow (1954, 1962, 1965)	Maslow's ideas on self-actualization influenced later writers such as Burns' (1978) and Bass' (1985) conceptualizations of transformational leadership.
1954	Management by Objectives	Drucker (1954)	Management by objectives was an important milestone in the history of management. It emphasized leader/follower participative goal setting.
1955	Ohio State Studies	Fleishman, Harris and Burtt (1955) Hemphill and Coons (1957) Stogdill (1963)	These studies were foundational to most subsequent leadership theories. Several meta-analyses have found both leader task and relationship behaviors to be important in organizational and follower outcomes.
1956	Five Bases of Social Power	French (1956) French and Raven (1959)	This model of leader power has been the subject of nearly 400 peer-reviewed studies.
1957	Personality and Organization	Argyris (1957, 1964, 1973, 1983)	Argyris argued that organizations typically structure followers' roles and direct their work in order to achieve organizational objectives. Followers, on the other hand, generally want to be self-directive and feel fulfilled through exercising initiative and responsibility.
1959	Motivation Hygiene Theory	Herzberg (1959, 1966, 1976)	Herzberg developed a theory on aspects of work that motivate followers versus hygiene factors or dissatisfiers. Dissatisfiers don't motivate followers, but their absence lessens motivation.
1960	Theory X and Theory Y	McGregor (1960, 1966)	A theory X view is that the average follower is lazy, dislikes work, and will try to do as little as possible. A theory Y view is that followers want responsibility.
1960	University of Michigan Studies	Katz and Kahn (1952) Cartwright and Zander (1960) Likert (1961)	These studies were also foundational to most subsequent leadership theories.

A Brief History of Organizational Leadership Theories

A Chronology of Influential Management and Leadership Theories

The Era of Leadership Behaviors			
1961	Management Systems	Likert (1961, 1967) Likert and Likert (1976)	Likert created four types of leadership/management styles: exploitive, authoritative benevolent, authoritative consultative and participative.
1961	Mechanistic and Organic Systems	Burns and Stalker (1961)	Burns and Stalker used the terms mechanistic and organic to describe two different organizational forms and philosophies.
1963	Behavioral Theory of the Firm	Cyert and March (1963)	Cyert and March introduced the idea of problemistic searching in which problem solving is usually triggered by a specific problem and the goal is to solve that one problem.
1964	Managerial Grid	Blake and Mouton (1964, 1965, 1972, 1978)	The managerial (leadership) grid was a highly influential book/theory. The grid describes the leadership dimensions of concern for production and concern for people.
1964	Contingency Theory	Fiedler (1964, 1966, 1967, 1971), Fiedler and Mahar (1979) Fiedler and Chemers, (1974), Fiedler, Chemers and Mahar (1976) Fiedler and Garcia (1987)	Fiedler's contingency model provides eight scenarios, based on: the leader-follower relationship, the structure of the task at hand and how much position power the leader holds.
1965	Technological Determinism	Woodward (1965, 1970)	Woodward argued that the technology an organization used seemed to influence the type of structure the organization created. This idea came to be known as technological determinism, connoting that, to some degree, technology determines organizational structure.
1966	Four-Factor Theory	Bowers and Seashore (1966)	Bowers and Seashore proposed an integrative framework for understanding similarities of earlier leadership research. Their four leadership dimensions were support, goal emphasis, interaction facilitation and work facilitation.

A Brief History of Organizational Leadership Theories

A Chronology of Influential Management and Leadership Theories

1966	Social Psychology of Organizations	Katz and Kahn (1966, 1978)	Katz and Kahn encouraged managers and leaders to envision workplace organizations as open rather than closed systems.
1969	Situational Theory	Hersey and Blanchard (1969, 1977)	Beyond the two leader behavior dimensions of supportive and directive behavior, Hersey and Blanchard theorized that leaders should adjust their styles of leading based on two dimensions related to followers: the follower's capability to do a particular task/job and the follower's commitment to do that task/job.
The Era of Transforming Followers			
1970	Servant Leadership	Greenleaf (1970, 1972, 1974, 1977, 1979)	The idea of leaders being servants of their followers is popular. The theory, however, lacks a deep research base. Several promising instruments to measure servant leadership, however, have recently been developed.
1971	Path-Goal Theory	Evans (1970) House (1971, 1996)	Path-goal theory indicates that leaders should engage in combinations of directive path-goal clarifying, supportive, participative and achievement oriented behaviors in order to assist followers to reach their goals.
1973	Normative Theory	Vroom and Yetton (1973) Vroom and Jago (1978, 1988)	Vroom, Yetton and Jago are known for their work on decision-making. Their theory used seven questions that could lead to five types of leader decision-making approaches. There have been about 10 peer-reviewed articles on the model, but only about two since 1990.
1974	Traits Continued	Stogdill (1974)	Stogdill analyzed 163 new studies related to personality and leadership traits. He grouped the 26 most frequently referenced traits into three categories: leadership skills, relationship with the group and personal characteristics.

A Brief History of Organizational Leadership Theories

A Chronology of Influential Management and Leadership Theories

The Era of Transforming Followers			
1975	Leader Member Exchange Theory	Dansereau, Graen and Haga (1975) Graen and Uhl-Bien (1991,1995)	Leader-member exchange theory points out that leaders form different relationships with different followers within the same work areas – often called out-groups and in-groups. Leaders and followers often go through three developmental stages: stranger, acquaintance and partner.
1977	Charismatic Theory	House (1977, 1992)	House and others developed explanations of the personal characteristics, behaviors and effects on followers that surround charismatic leadership.
1978	Theory Z	Ouchi and Jaeger (1978) Ouchi (1981, 1984)	In 1978, Ouchi contrasted what he described as a typical set of American leadership/work assumptions with those that might be typical Japanese assumptions. He then proposed a hybrid set that he labeled type Z assumptions. This slowly became known as theory Z.
1978	Substitutes for Leadership	Kerr and Jermier (1978)	Kerr and Jermier asked whether certain factors could lessen the need for leadership. They divided possible substitutes into three sources: followers, the tasks being done and the organization.
1978	Transformational Leadership	Burns (1978)	While there have been many contributions to the idea of transformational leadership, the theory was first fully described by Burns in 1978. In transformational leadership, pooled interests of the leaders and followers result in being united in the pursuit of "higher" leader and follower goals.
1981	Six Sigma	Motorola (1981) General Electric (1995)	Six sigma refers to a standard of quality that equates to 3.4 defects per one million opportunities (DPMO). This equates to 99.997% "quality."
1982	In Search of Excellence	Peters and Waterman (1982)	Peters and Waterman reported what they believed were best practices among excellent Fortune 500 companies.

A Brief History of Organizational Leadership Theories

A Chronology of Influential Management and Leadership Theories

The Era of Transforming Followers			
1985	Full Range Model of Leadership	Bass (1985, 1998, 1999) Bass and Avolio (1994, 1995, 1996, 1997, 2002) Bass, Avolio and Jung (1999)	More than 100 peer-reviewed studies have been published on this theory. Meta-analyses have found that the full range model of leadership is related to individual-level performance, group performance, task performance, leader effectiveness, follower satisfaction with leaders, follower job satisfaction, follower motivation and leader job performance.
1986	Total Quality Management	Deming (1986)	Total quality management is a phrase used to describe various quality initiatives suggested by Deming and others. The methods were highly influenced by Japanese manufacturing methods.
1986	Traits Continued	Lord, de Vader and Alliger (1986)	Lord, de Vader and Alliger conducted a meta-analysis of trait research. They found that intelligence, masculinity-femininity, adjustment, dominance, extraversion and conservatism were related to leadership.

A Brief History of Organizational Leadership Theories

A Chronology of Influential Management and Leadership Theories

The Search for the Successor to Transformational Leadership			
1990	Big-Five Personality	McCrae and Costa (1987,1990, 2010)	Generally, extraversion, agreeableness and openness are often associated with effective leadership, and neuroticism and lack of conscientiousness with ineffective leadership.
1990	Emotional Intelligence	Salovey and Mayer (1990) Goleman (1995) Bar-On (1997) Mayer, Salovey, and Caruso (2004)	Mayer, Salovey and Caruso developed a four-dimension model of emotional intelligence that is measured by the MSCEIT. Their four dimensions are perception of emotions, facilitating thought, understanding emotions and managing emotions. Bar-On developed a six-dimension model of Emotional Intelligence that is measured by the EQ-I 2.0. His six dimensions are self-perceptions, self-expression, interpersonal, decision making, stress management and well-being.
1990	Learning Organizations	Senge (1990)	Senge argued that leaders of learning organizations engage in five disciplines: systems thinking, personal mastery, mental models, shared vision and team learning.
1993	Reengineering	Hammer and Champy (1993)	Hammer described reengineering as "the notion of discontinuous thinking - of recognizing and breaking away from outdated rules."
1994	Built to Last	Collins and Porras (1994, 1996)	Based on their analysis of 32 different companies in 16 industries, Collins and Porras developed what they called *Twelve Shattered Myths* related to being a lasting organization.
1996	Competing for the Future	Hamel and Prahalad (1994,1996)	Hamel and Prahalad's article and subsequent best-selling book, was targeted toward senior executives. The book provided ideas about how to think strategically about a rapidly changing world.
2001	Good to Great	Collins (2001)	Collins compared companies that had made a leap from being good to great. As part of the study, Collins described what he called level 5 leaders.

A Brief History of Organizational Leadership Theories

A Chronology of Influential Management and Leadership Theories

2004	The Global Leadership Project GLOBE	Den Hartog, House, Hanges, Ruiz-Quintanilla, Dorfman, Peter Ashkanasy, and Falkus (1999) House and GLOBE Research Team (2004, 2012)	The GLOBE project surveyed 17,370 middle managers from 951 organizations in three industries in 62 societies. Charismatic/value-based, team-oriented and participative leadership were considered important worldwide. Conversely, self-protective leader behaviors were believed to inhibit being an outstanding leader.
2007	Authentic Leadership	Kernis and Goldman, (2003-6), George (2003) George and Sims, (2007) Avolio, Gardner and Walumbwa (2007) Walumbwa, Avolio, Gardner, Wernsing and Peterson (2008)	A leading instrument to measure authentic leadership is the *Authentic Leadership Questionnaire*, by Avolio, Gardner and Walumbwa. They describe authentic leadership as consisting of four components: self-awareness, relational transparency, balanced processing and internalized moral perspective.
2011	Traits Continued	Derue, Nahrgang, Wellman and Humphrey (2011)	Derue, Nahrgang, Wellman and Humphrey performed meta-analytic regressions, using 143 bivariate relationships, to predict leader effectiveness, follower job satisfaction and follower satisfaction with their leader. Their results found that leader behaviors, particularly consideration, transformational leadership, contingent reward and not being passive-avoidant, were more important in predicting leadership outcomes than leader personality, intelligence or gender.
2000's	Genetic Studies	Li, Arvey, Zhang and Song (2011) Chaturvedi, Arvey, Zhangmand and Christoforou (2011) Loehlin, McCrae, Costa and John (1998)	The results of twin studies have estimated that somewhere around 50% of the variance in both personality and transformational leadership can be explained by genetic factors.

Chapter 2
Understanding a Meta-Analysis

A Primer on Reliability, Validity and Meta-Analyses

Introduction

The areas of research and statistics can be daunting to graduate students. This very brief and very high-level primer is not designed to help you pass a graduate course in research or statistics. Rather, it is designed to help you understand the terms and ideas used in chapters 3 through 10. This primer has four sections.

What are instrument reliability and validity?
What is a correlation?
What does a meta-analysis do with correlations?
What is a *Cohen's d* score?
What is a multiple regression?
What is a meta-analytic multiple regression?
What do the terms antecedents, consequences, mediation and commonality connote?

Levels of Complexity

Like most things in life, however, research and statistics have levels of complexity. The answer one gets to a philosophical research question depends on the level of understanding of the individual asking the question.

As a real-life example, imagine that you had a nephew who wanted to be a baseball pitcher. When he was just starting out, his coach would have almost assuredly told him "always try to throw the ball over the plate." At this stage of development, that was the best advice the coach could offer.

A few years later, however, once your nephew could throw a baseball over the plate at will, his coach might begin to provide different advice. The coach might tell your nephew that if he already had two strikes on a hitter, to intentionally throw the next pitch outside the strike zone, in hopes that the nervous hitter would swing and miss.

This is different advice than your nephew received before he had mastered the fundamentals of getting the ball over the plate. The previous coach wasn't deceiving your nephew when he said "always try to throw the ball over the plate." The coach was simply adjusting his guidance to your nephew's level of development.

When your nephew became a high school pitcher, an opposing player may have already hit two home runs that day. Now your nephew's coach might advise him to intentionally walk that hitter.

So, your nephew has been told by his coaches: always try to get the ball over the plate; in some situations don't throw the ball over the plate; and in some situations don't throw the ball over the plate four straight times.

A Primer on Reliability, Validity and Meta-Analyses

Reliability and Validity

Similar to your nephew's journey, there are levels of complexity that can change the specific answer you receive to a statistical question. The information that follows in this primer is designed for graduate students who are at the level of "getting the ball over the plate."

Instrument Concepts

Two main ideas related to instruments are reliability and validity. At their broadest meanings:

Reliability generally refers to the consistency of scores from an instrument. In our non-statistical world if we advise someone who is having car troubles that she should trade in her car for a reliable one, we generally mean one that starts up the same every morning, and gets her to work the same every day.

Validity generally connotes the degree to which an instrument measures what it proposes to measure. Imagine that you worked as an accounting manager. Your boss indicated that this year's bonuses would be based on how well you performed on an instrument that measures knowledge of accounting management.

When you took the "test," however, the questions were about methods used by Antarctic penguins to survive winter. You scored low on the instrument, and didn't get a bonus. You would almost certainly complain that the instrument wasn't a valid measure of knowledge of accounting management.

Like most things in life, however, reliability and validity can be broken down into categories that are more specific. This isn't just an insidious effort by statistics professors to stress graduate students. We do it in many of the areas of our everyday life.

If you were asked, for example, what the word "clothes" meant, you might indicate that clothes are items we wear over our bodies for protection or appearance.

Now picture your closet and think about all of the types of clothing you have. One type of clothing is a shirt. Two types of shirts are short and long-sleeved. Three types of short-sleeved shirts might be polos, button-front and t-shirts – you get the idea.

Just as we can talk more specifically about types of clothes, we can talk more specifically about types of reliability and validity.

A Primer on Reliability, Validity and Meta-Analyses

Reliability

Types of Reliability

Inter-Rater Reliability

In this type of reliability, we are concerned with whether different individuals give consistent ratings on a particular phenomenon.

Let's use a leadership example. Imagine that someone developed a new instrument to measure transformational leadership.

Now imagine that a room of individuals all watched a video of a leader being very transformational during a meeting. Those individuals were then asked to rate the leader who appeared in the video by using the new instrument. If the ratings given by different individuals were widely varied from one another, one worry we would have is whether the instrument had sufficient inter-rater reliability.

Test-Retest Reliability

In this type of reliability, we are concerned with whether scores on a particular instrument remain consistent from one time period to another. Imagine that a leader took a measure of personality and it indicated that she was very extraverted. She re-took the same instrument two weeks later and the instrument indicated the leader was very introverted. Assuming nothing extraordinary, such as a near-death experience, had happened during the two-week period, we would be concerned about the low test-retest reliability of this instrument.

Internal Consistency Reliability

Internal consistency reliability is primarily a statistical analysis of the items *within* an instrument. Let's say that a new instrument had six questions. Each question is believed to measure *leader enthusiasm.* Generally, we would expect a follower to rate a leader similarly on all six questions. This general idea is called being correlated. Imagine a follower was rating a leader on these six questions on a scale of 1 to 5. A score of 1 was very low on enthusiasm and a score of 5 was very high on enthusiasm.

If she circled:

Question 1: 4
Question 2: 5
Question 3: 4
Question 4: 5
Question 5: 4
Question 6: 4

We see that she has consistently rated the leader as enthusiastic.

What if, however, the ratings she gave were:

Question 1: 4
Question 2: 1
Question 3: 3
Question 4: 5
Question 5: 2
Question 6: 4

This time she has rated the leader as high on enthusiasm on questions 1, 4 and 6, low on enthusiasm on questions 2 and 5, and "typical" on question 3. How reliable is this instrument?

While it is somewhat easy to simply visually peruse the data in this second example, what statisticians do is run analyses on large samples. So now, imagine that 100 followers each rated their leader on these six questions. It would be difficult to visually find a pattern in these 600 scores by simply looking at pages and pages of numbers.

We could, however, do all sorts of statistical analyses on those 600 answers. We could compare answers given to each question across the 100 followers, or we could compare "sets" of questions to each other.

One way to compare sets of questions is to get the total score for half of the questions and correlate that to the total score for the other half. This is called a split-half reliability test. Even with only six questions, there are eight possible "spit-half" combinations that could be tested for how well the items are inter-correlated. Three split-half examples are shown below. Remember that each of the examples below is only for one person who took the survey. There would actually be split-half scores for all 100 participants.

Split-Half Example 1		Split-Half Example 2		Split-Half Example 3	
Question 1: 4	Question 2: 5	Question 1: 4	Question 4: 5	Question 1: 4	Question 2: 5
Question 3: 4	Question 4: 5	Question 2: 5	Question 5: 4	Question 5: 4	Question 3: 4
Question 5: 4	Question 6: 4	Question 3: 4	Question 6: 4	Question 6: 4	Question 4: 5
Total: 12	Total: 14	Total: 13	Total: 13	Total: 12	Total: 14

Fortunately, we don't have to do all of this to understand what an article is telling us about the internal reliability of an instrument. While there are several statistical tests to measure internal consistency, a frequently reported statistic is the *Cronbach Alpha*. This is typically a number between 0 and 1. The closer the number is to 1, the more we have a sense that the questions on an instrument are internally consistent.

So, if an article reporting the internal reliability of a leadership instrument reported a *Cronbach Alpha* score of .11, that would be low. Conversely, if the *Cronbach Alpha* score was .81, that would be an indication that the internal consistency was relatively high.

A Primer on Reliability, Validity and Meta-Analyses

Validity

Validity versus Reliability

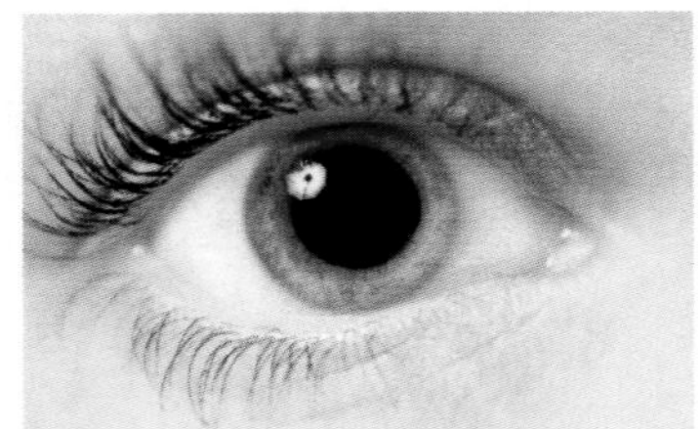

While reliability generally refers to the consistency of an instrument, validity generally connotes the degree to which an instrument measures what it proposes to measure.

To illustrate how these ideas are different, imagine that someone created a *What is Your Leadership Style* questionnaire. The entire instrument, however, consisted of only one question:

Question 1: Which answer best describes your eye color?

a) Green
b) Brown
c) None of the Above

The scoring instructions for the *What is Your Leadership Style* questionnaire indicated that if you answered:

a) Your Eyes Are Green, You Are a Transformational Leader
b) Your Eyes Are Brown, You Are a Transactional Leader
c) Your Eyes Are None of the above, You Are a Passive-avoidant Leader

Regardless of how many times you took this instrument, you should get the same score every time – so it is quite consistent. Of course, however, we don't believe it is valid. We don't believe it is actually measuring leadership style as it claims.

Types of Validity

There are many types of validity. However, a brief discussion of six will provide you with enough background to read chapters 8 though 15. The six types are:

Face Validity

Content Validity

Predictive Validity

Concurrent Validity

Convergent Validity

Discriminant Validity

A Primer on Reliability, Validity and Meta-Analyses

Validity

Face Validity

If someone made you a business offer of some type and after a cursory discussion, the offer seemed legitimate, you might say something such as "on its face, it looks good." This is the idea of face validity.

If we return to our example of *leader enthusiasm*, the questions below have been vetted by the International Personality Item Pool as measuring enthusiasm. We can look at them and likely agree that "on their face" they seem to measure enthusiasm.

a) Look Forward to Each New Day
b) Can't Wait to Get Started on a Project

But what about these questions?

a) Yells "Let's Go People" When Things Are Not Done on Time
b) Wears a Shirt with the Company Logo

On their face, we are a little less sure of what they seem to be measuring.

When an article discussing an instrument talks about its face validity, usually the questions were reviewed by "experts" who agreed that the questions appeared to be measuring the construct they proposed to measure.

Content Validity

Content validity is typically a bit stronger than face validity. In content validity, we first try to determine what facets comprise a construct.

In chapter 5, the big five dimensions of personality were presented. Within each aspect of personality, though, there were subdimensions or facets.

Extraversion
Warmth Gregariousness Assertiveness Activity Excitement Seeking Positive Emotions

Extraversion, for example has six facets. If we were developing a new instrument to measure leader extraversion, and wanted to ensure content validity, we would assemble a panel of experts.

These experts would assess whether we had some questions that seemed to measure warmth, other questions that seemed to measure gregariousness and so forth.

We would also likely use a formal method in which these experts would assign each question to a category they believed the question was measuring.

A Primer on Reliability, Validity and Meta-Analyses
Validity

Predictive and Concurrent Validity

Predictive validity is what it sounds like. Does an instrument that purports to measure something actually predict it in the future? A good example of worrying about predictive validity is in the area of aptitude testing. If one had an instrument that claimed to measure leader potential, we would want high scores on the instrument to correlate with individuals who took the test actually becoming leaders in the future.

In concurrent validity, however, the question is whether the instrument is related to something it should be related to "now." Let's say an instrument indicated it measured leader optimism. It would have concurrent validity if it measured current levels of optimism of leaders who took the instrument.

Convergent Validity

Convergent validity analyzes the degree to which an instrument correlates with existing instruments with which it "should" correlate. Currently, for example, the *Multifactor Leadership Questionnaire* (*MLQ*) measures transformational leadership. Convergent validity would assess the degree to which a new transformational leadership instrument, for example, was related to the existing instrument.

Discriminant Validity

Discriminant validity tests whether an instrument is different from a construct from which it should be different. Let's continue our new instrument example.

Let's assume that we believe that transformational leadership is different from simply being extraverted. We would want an instrument that indicates it measures transformational leadership to be able to discriminate between the construct the instrument claims to be measuring, and a known measure of extraversion.

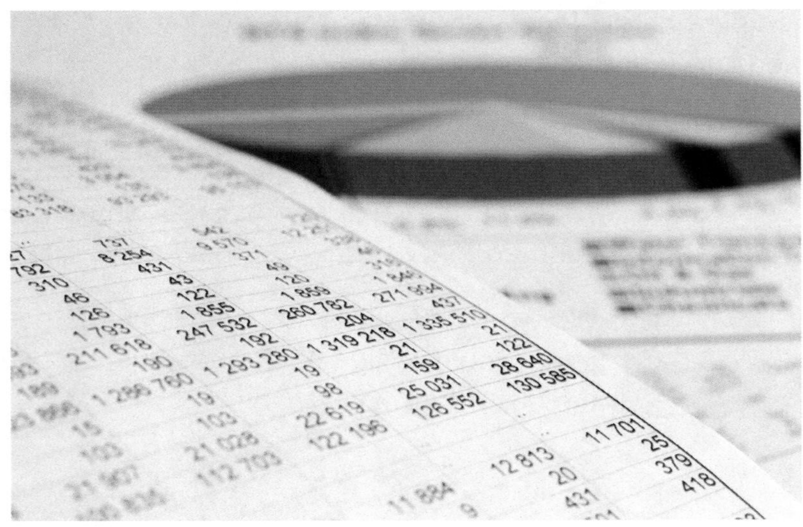

Factor Loadings

As part of discriminant and convergent validity, it is common to run a more advanced set of statistics called factor analysis. In our example of six new questions to measure leader enthusiasm, we indicated we might be worried if our results had some questions with high scores and others with low scores. In our simple example, we just looked at those questions.

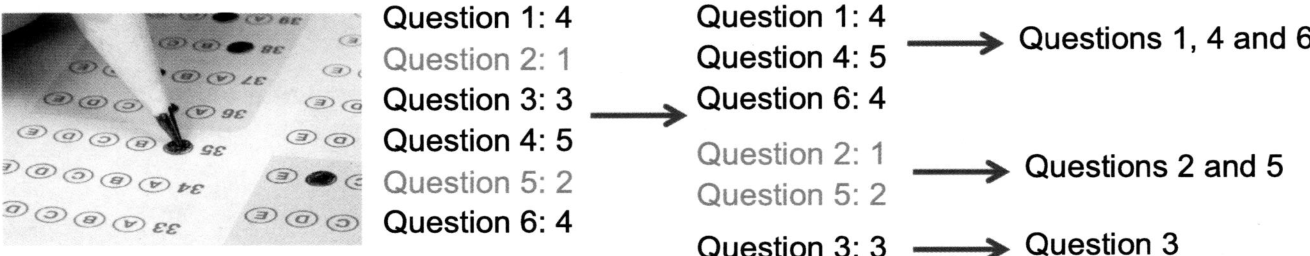

Articles addressing the validity of an instrument will often describe the results of one or more factor analyses. The articles will report factor loadings for various sets of questions, often called factors, scales or components.

Since this primer is only designed to help you get the ball over the plate, we will leave the details of factor loadings to a statistics class. In general, the factor loadings will be a number between -1 and 1. The closer the factor loadings are to -1 or 1,[1] the better we feel that those questions seem to be measuring a similar construct.

Summary of Reliability and Validity

Type	Measures
Inter-Rater Reliability	Do Raters Observing the Same Phenomenon, Rate It Similarly on an Instrument
Test-Retest Reliability	If One Completes an Instrument at Two Different Times, Will the Results Be Similar
Internal Consistency Reliability	Are the Multiple Items on an Instrument That Propose to Measure the Same Construct Inter-Correlated or Consistent with Each Other
Face Validity	Does an Instrument Appear on Its Face to Measure What It Proposes
Content Validity	Does an Instrument Appear to Measure a Construct
Predictive Validity	Does the Instrument Predict What It Proposes to Measure at a Later Time
Concurrent Validity	Does the Instrument Measure What It Proposes to Measure Now
Convergent Validity	Does the Instrument Measure Something Similar to Existing Instruments That Also Measure That Construct
Discriminant Validity	Does the Instrument Measure Something Different, It Discriminates, Between What It Proposes to Measure and a Related but Different Construct
Factor Loading	How Well Instrument Questions Are Related to a Common Measure - Do the Questions Seem to Be Measuring Something Similar

A Primer on Reliability, Validity and Meta-Analyses

Introduction to Correlations

Introduction to Correlations

One of the most fundamental statistical tests is a called a correlation. This word is used because we are analyzing two variables (the "co" part of the word) and we are asking what is the relationship between these two variables - co-relationship. The technical definition of a correlation coefficient is: the (sample) covariance of the variables divided by the product of their (sample) standard deviations.

When we talk about correlations, we often talk about three aspects.

The Direction of the Correlation
The Magnitude of the Correlation
The Confidence We Have in the Correlation

Visualizing a Relationship

We usually discuss three types of relationships: positive relationships, negative relationships and no relationship.

One way to visualize what a correlation is telling us is to look at a type of graph called a scatter plot. Let's assume that followers in an organization each rated their leader on transformational leadership, and also rated their satisfaction with that leader. The table below shows scores for seven followers.

Follower	Rating of Transformational Leadership	Satisfaction with Leader
Sandy	1.98	2.60
Janet	3.88	3.90
Lamar	3.40	2.60
Anthony	3.60	3.40
Michelle	2.35	3.35
Maria	2.65	2.16
Gilbert	1.95	1.28

One way to search for a "pattern" or "trend" in these data is to plot them on a graph. On the scatterplot below, each dot is one of the followers from the table above.

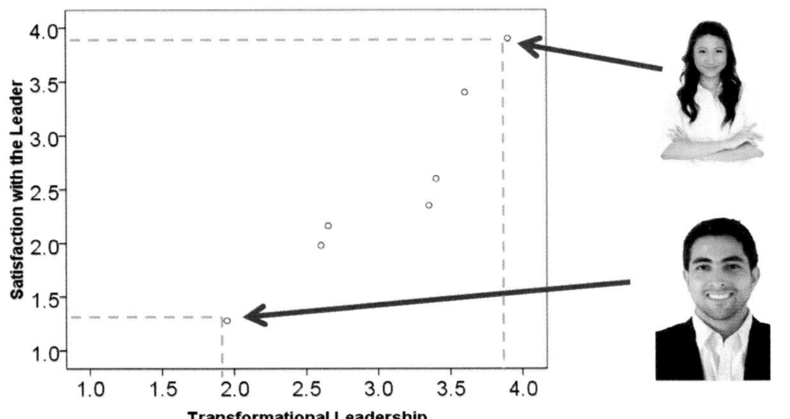

Janet rated her leader as a 3.88 on a transformational leadership assessment. She rated her satisfaction with her leader as a 3.90

Gilbert rated his leader as a 1.95 on a transformational leadership assessment. He rated his satisfaction with his leader as a 1.28

A Primer on Reliability, Validity and Meta-Analyses

The Direction of a Correlation

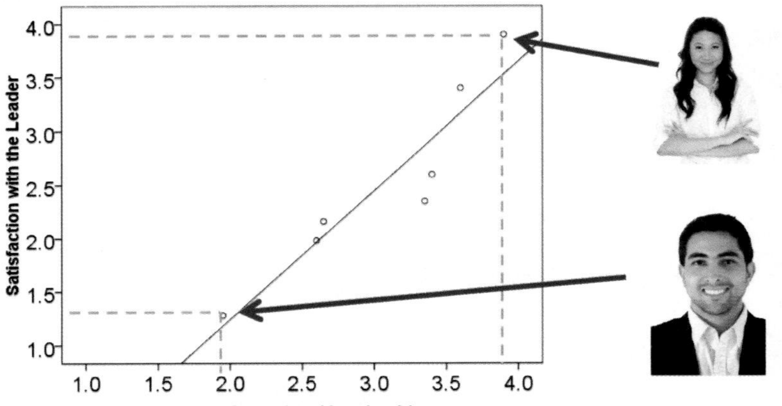

Janet rated her leader as a 3.88 on a transformational leadership assessment. She rated her satisfaction with her leader as a 3.90

Gilbert rated his leader as a 1.95 on a transformational leadership assessment. He rated his satisfaction with his leader as a 1.28

In case you eyes didn't notice the "pattern" or trend in either the data or scatterplot before, notice the general upwards and to the right trend in the followers' responses.

We can see that as ratings of transformational leadership were higher, so was satisfaction with the leader. Or, we could say this the other way, reading the trend from right to left (high to low). As ratings of transformational leadership decreased, so did satisfaction with the leader.

We wouldn't feel too confident in our newfound pattern, however, with only seven followers. If we gave the same surveys to hundreds of followers, the pattern of answers might look more like the scatterplot below. Each dot is still one follower; there are simply lots of follower scores represented.

The Direction of a Correlation

Positive Correlations (Relationships)

Janet rated her leader as a 3.88 on a transformational leadership assessment. She rated her satisfaction with her leader as a 3.90

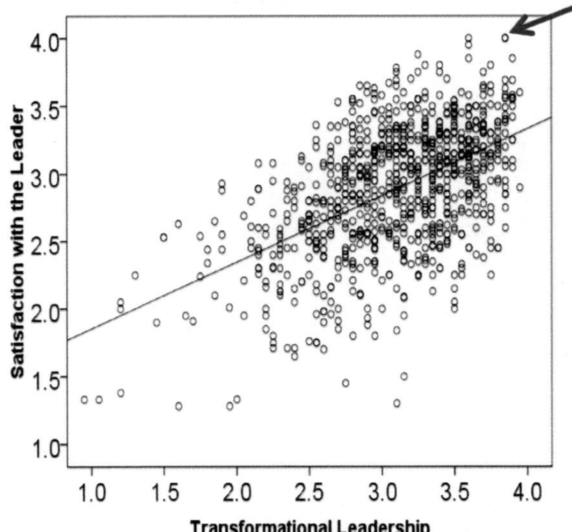

A positive correlation means that as one of the two variables increases the other also increases. In the scatterplot to the left, we again see that, generally, as ratings of transformational leadership were higher, so was satisfaction with the leader

When one first encounters positive and negative correlations, there is a tendency to translate the adjective *positive* into *good*, and the adjective *negative* into *bad*.

A positive correlation is neither "good" nor "bad" in and of itself. The word positive simply means the two variables are related in the same direction.

Negative Correlations (Relationships)

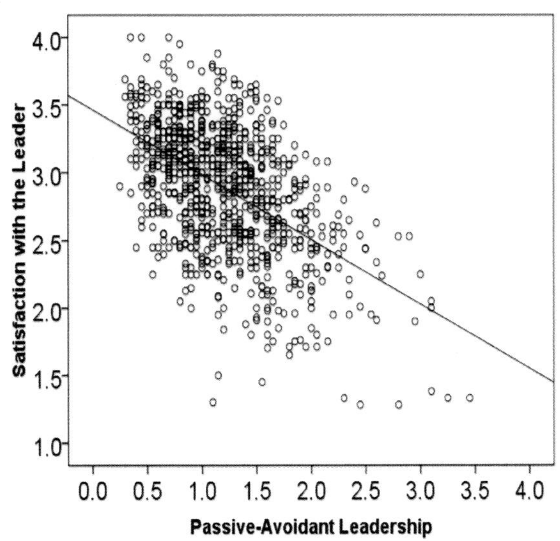

The second possibility is that two variables are correlated but in opposite directions – as one increases, the other decreases. In the scatterplot on the left, as ratings of passive-avoidant leadership decreased, satisfaction with the leader increased. That's describing the pattern from right to left.

If we describe the pattern from left to right, we can say that as passive-avoidant leadership increased, satisfaction with the leader decreased. In either of these descriptions, as one of the variables increased, the other decreased.

Just as a "positive" correlation is neither good nor bad of itself, neither is a "negative" correlation. Here negative connotes that as one variable increases, the other decreases.

No Correlation (Relationship)

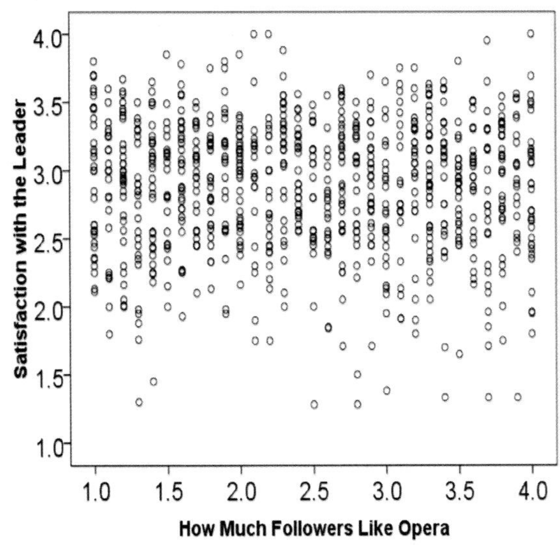

A third possibility is that there is no relationship between the two variables that we feel confident describing. For this example, let's say that we asked the same group of followers how much they liked opera music, and how satisfied they were with their leader. We might find that the answers looked like the scatterplot on the left.

For these data, we would say that we lack confidence to describe any clear pattern or relationship.

The Magnitude of a Correlation

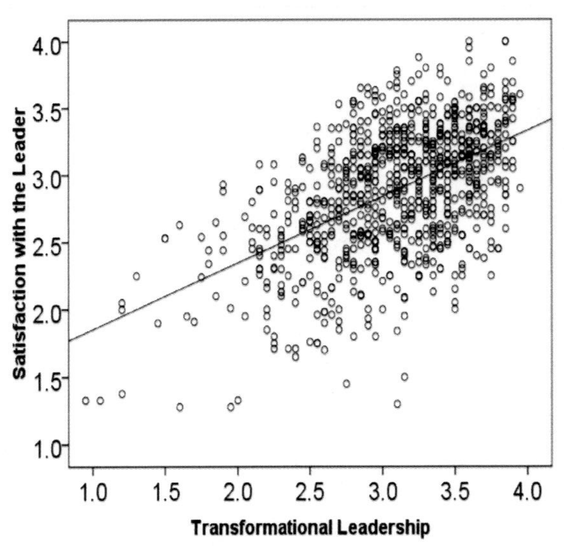

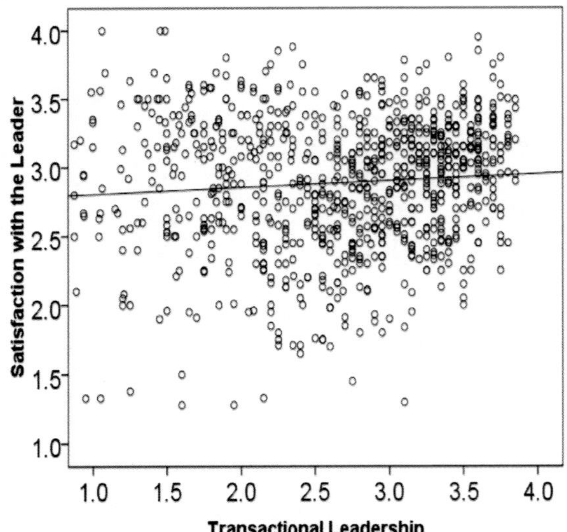

Both scatterplots shown above have a trend we can notice. In the first scatterplot, the more transformational a leader was rated, the more satisfied the follower was with that leader. In the second scatterplot, we have a pattern of the more transactional the leader, the more satisfied the follower was with that leader.

But, you'll notice that the angles, or slopes, of the lines depicting the trends or relationships are different. The acuteness of the line depicting the pattern is a way to envision the magnitude or strength of a correlation.[2]

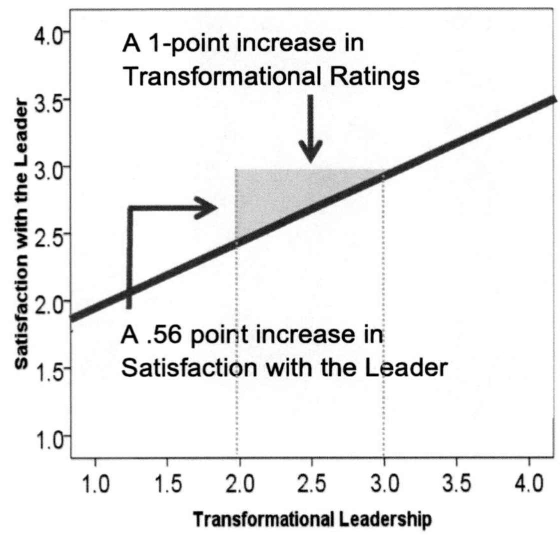

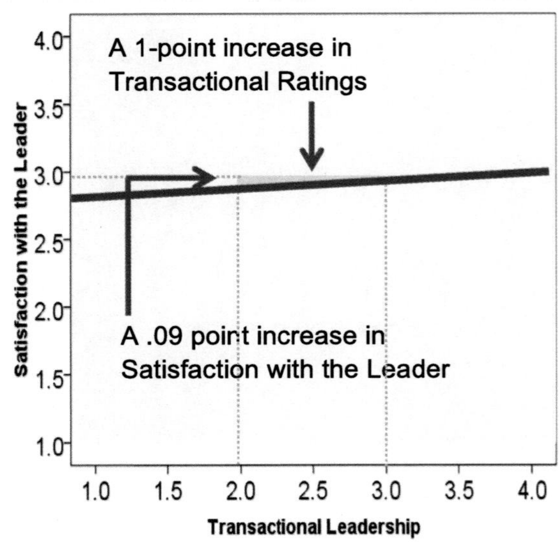

A Primer on Reliability, Validity and Meta-Analyses

The Magnitude of a Correlation

So, both styles of leadership are positively related to follower satisfaction with the leader.

For every 1 point increase in transformational scores, there was a corresponding .56 point increase in satisfaction with the leader.[3]

For transactional leadership, however, the magnitude or strength of the positive correlation was weaker. For every 1 point increase in transactional scores, there was a corresponding .09 point increase in satisfaction with the leader.

Because journal articles can't consume the space required to provide a graphic for every possible relationship tested, there is a number that describes these relationships that is frequently reported called the *Pearson correlation coefficient*. Pearson's correlation coefficient, also known as r, or *Pearson's* r, is a measure of the strength and direction of the linear relationship between two variables.

The table below is the "short-hand" format of a typical journal. The number is the relationship between that particular form of leadership (or love of opera) and the satisfaction with the leader. A quick perusal tells us that transformational leadership is positively related to satisfaction with the leader $r = .56$.

Transactional leadership is also positively related to satisfaction with the leader $r = .09$.

Passive-avoidant leadership is negatively related to satisfaction with the leader $r = -.68$.

	Satisfaction with the Leader
Transformational Leadership	.56**
Transactional Leadership	.09*
Passive-Avoidant Leadership	-.68**
Love of Opera	.01

** $p < .01$, * $p < .05$

But what should we say about the relationship between how much followers love opera and how satisfied they were with their leader. You'll notice that the first three Pearson correlation coefficient numbers reported all have asterisks next to them, with footnotes that indicate ** $p < .01$, * $p < .05$.

But, love of opera doesn't have an asterisk. This is a typical way in which a journal article indicates that we either do or do not have confidence that there is a "pattern," "trend," or now more precisely, a statistical relationship between the two variables. No asterisk typically means we lack confidence in that relationship.[4]

A Primer on Reliability, Validity and Meta-Analyses

The Confidence in a Correlation

This brings us to our third important aspect of correlations – statistical confidence.

The Confidence We Have in the Correlation

In a statistics class, you would receive detailed explanations of statistical confidence, hypotheses testing, regions of rejection and so forth. In our effort to "get the ball over the plate" in understanding what a significant or non-significant correlation connotes, we'll only focus on two aspects:

Sample Size and
How Well the "Pattern," "Trend" or "Relationship" Can Be Described with One Straight Line

Sample Size

Let's return to our starter example in which we had seven followers each rate their leader on transformational leadership and rate how satisfied they were with their leader.

Follower	Rating of Transformational Leadership	Satisfaction with Leader
Sandy	1.98	2.60
Janet	3.88	3.90
Lamar	3.40	2.60
Anthony	3.60	3.40
Michelle	2.35	3.35
Maria	2.65	2.16
Gilbert	1.95	1.28

We recognized what we now would describe as a positive relationship between transformational leadership and satisfaction with the leader. But, how confident should we be with only seven people answering our survey?

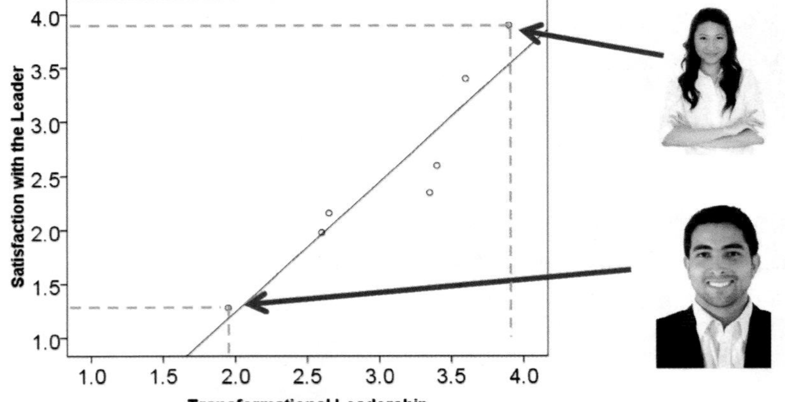

Janet rated her leader as a 3.88 on a transformational leadership assessment. She rated her satisfaction with her leader as a 3.90

Gilbert rated his leader as a 1.95 on a transformational leadership assessment. He rated his satisfaction with his leader as a 1.28

A Primer on Reliability, Validity and Meta-Analyses

The Confidence in a Correlation

Imagine that five other workers handed back their survey packets late and you then added them to your table.

Follower	Rating of Transformational Leadership	Satisfaction with Leader
Sandy	1.98	2.60
Janet	3.88	3.90
Lamar	3.40	2.60
Anthony	3.60	3.40
Michelle	2.35	3.35
Maria	2.65	2.16
Gilbert	1.95	1.28
Francisco	2.12	3.14
Annette	3.83	1.42
Ben	2.21	2.26
Dante	2.85	2.64
Kenya	3.03	1.52

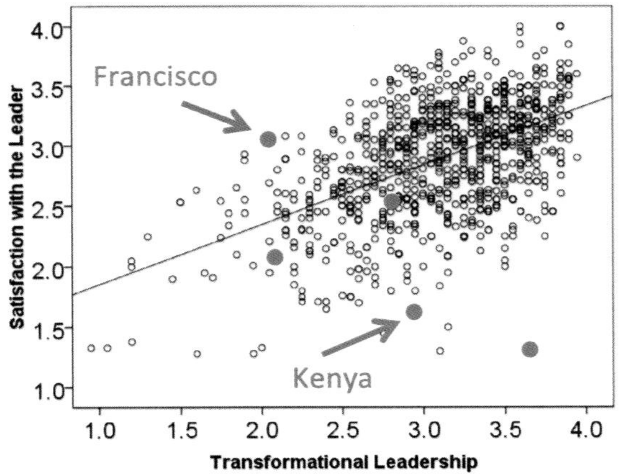

With a small sample size, a few extra data points could impact what we believed was a pattern or relationship in our data. With a large sample, if there is a relationship there, a few extra data points typically won't change our opinion.

So in the scatterplot to the left, we no longer are confident that the relationship is the more transformational the leader the more satisfied the follower.

In the scatterplot on the right, we are likely still confident that the more transformational the leader the more satisfied the follower. The addition of a few extra responses to our questions we asked the followers doesn't change our assessment.

A Primer on Reliability, Validity and Meta-Analyses

The Confidence in a Correlation

How Well the Relationship Can be Described with One Straight Line

The types of relationships we are exploring now are called linear relationships. In a statistics class, however, you might study "non-linear" relationships. Relationships that can be described with curved lines and so forth. For "getting the ball over the plate," however, we'll stick with the question of how confident we should be that there is a "pattern" in the data that we can describe with a straight line.

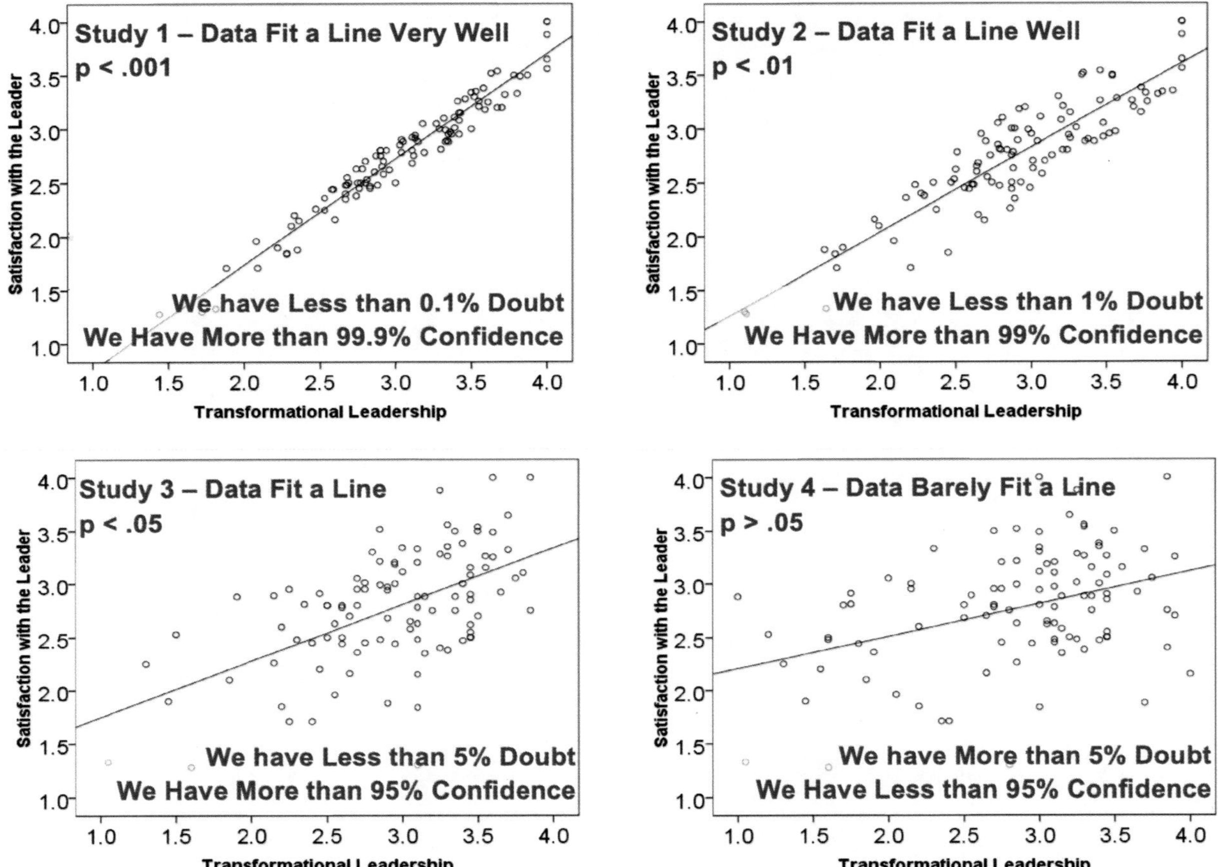

Above are four different scatterplots. Imagine each was a different study reported in a journal. In study 1, we are able to describe the positive relationship between the two variables very well. Conversely, while there *appears* to be a positive relationship between transformational leadership and satisfaction with the leader in study 4, we are less confident in that relationship.[5]

One can spend half of a statistics class just on the idea of *p* values. The technical definition is *the probability of obtaining by chance a result at least as extreme as that observed, even when the null hypothesis is true and no real difference exists.*

A heuristic when one is getting started, however, is to read the *p* value as "doubt" and (1 - the *p* value) as "confidence." That heuristic is shown on the scatterplots.

A Primer on Reliability, Validity and Meta-Analyses

Summary of Correlations

Putting it all Together

In a typical journal article, the research will report three aspects of a correlation.

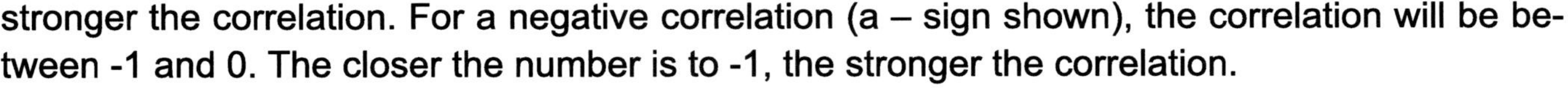

The Direction of the Correlation A "-" sign indicates a negative relationship. As one variable increases, the other decreases. No sign at all indicates a positive relationship, as one variable increases, the other also increases.

The Magnitude of the Correlation For a positive correlation (no sign shown), the correlation will be between 0 and 1. The closer the number is to 1, the stronger the correlation. For a negative correlation (a – sign shown), the correlation will be between -1 and 0. The closer the number is to -1, the stronger the correlation.

The Confidence We Have in the Correlation This is usually indicated in the table footnote, and is often shown with asterisks as in the table below. If $p < .01$ we are more than 99% confident. If $p < .05$ we are more than 95% confident. If there is no asterisk, then $p > .05$, we are less than 95% confident.[6]

Sample Full Range of Leadership Variable	Satisfaction with the Leader	What Does this Mean
Idealized Influence Attributed (IIA)	.38*	We have more than 95% confidence in this relationship $p < .05$ (See the asterisks at the bottom of the table) It is a positive correlation $r = .38$ The higher a follower rated a leader on IIA The more satisfied she/he was with the leader
Individual Consideration (IC)	.63**	We have more than 99% confidence in this relationship $p < .01$ (See the asterisks at the bottom of the table) It is a positive correlation $r = .63$ The higher a follower rated a leader on IC The more satisfied she/he was with the leader
Management By Exception Active (MBEA)	.03	Because there is no asterisk shown, the table is telling us the relationship was not significant $p > .05$ We have more than 5% doubt and less than 95% confidence in this relationship.
Management By Exception Passive (MBEP)	-.37*	We have more than 95% confidence in this relationship $p < .05$ (See the asterisks at the bottom of the table) It is a negative correlation $r = -.37$ The higher a follower rated a leader on MBEP The less satisfied she/he was with the leader
Laissez-Faire (LF)	-.48**	We have more than 99% confidence in this relationship $p < .01$ (See the asterisks at the bottom of the table) It is a negative correlation $r = -.48$ The higher a follower rated a leader on LF The less satisfied she/he was with the leader

** $p < .01$, * $p < .05$

A Primer on Reliability, Validity and Meta-Analyses

Introduction to Meta-Analyses

What Does a Meta-Analysis Do With Correlations?

There are many studies done on aspects of leadership. A challenge is to summarize, or synthesize, this body of literature. One method used to synthesize the literature is called a *meta-analysis*, literally a "study of studies." Imagine that we found the five studies shown below.

Five Studies Reporting Correlations Between Transformational Leadership and Satisfaction with the Leader

Study	Correlation	What Does this Mean
Study 1	.64*	The higher a follower rated a leader on transformational leadership the more satisfied she/he was with the leader, $r = .64$, $p < .05$
Study 2	.43*	The higher a follower rated a leader on transformational leadership the more satisfied she/he was with the leader, $r = .43$, $p < .05$
Study 3	.46*	The higher a follower rated a leader on transformational leadership the more satisfied she/he was with the leader, $r = .46$, $p < .05$
Study 4	.25*	The higher a follower rated a leader on transformational leadership the more satisfied she/he was with the leader, $r = .25$, $p < .05$
Study 5	.41*	The higher a follower rated a leader on transformational leadership the more satisfied she/he was with the leader, $r = .41$, $p < .05$

* $p < .05$

One option is to look over these five positive correlations and conclude *"Generally, the more transformational the leader, the more satisfied the follower is with that leader."*

If, however, someone asked us what the magnitude or strength of the relationship between transformational leadership and satisfaction with the leader was, we'd have to reply *"Well....it seems to range from r = .25 (study 4) to r = .64 (study 1)."*

Study	Correlation
Study 1	.64
Study 2	.43
Study 3	.46
Study 4	.25
Study 5	.41
Average Correlation	.44

Another option is to say:

"The average correlation is .44"

The .44 is a more concise summary of what the literature indicates and boils things down to one number.

We got this average correlation by adding up the five correlations (.64 + .43 + .46 + .25 + .41) and dividing by 5 = .44

But, as we have seen, there are likely more nuances in statistics than what this first effort to meta-analyze these studies gave us.

A Primer on Reliability, Validity and Meta-Analyses

Introduction to Meta-Analyses

After we calculated the average correlation for the five studies, we then began to think about how many followers were represented in each study. Typically, a journal article will use the letter *N* to indicate sample size. We add another column to the table and notice that study 4 had seven times as many participants (*N* = 700) as each of the other four studies (*N* = 100). So now we wonder, "should each study be considered equally important?"

Five Studies Reporting Correlations Between
Transformational Leadership and Satisfaction with the Leader

Study	Correlation	Sample Size
Study 1	.64	N = 100
Study 2	.43	N = 100
Study 3	.46	N = 100
Study 4	.25	N = 700
Study 5	.41	N = 100

Alaska

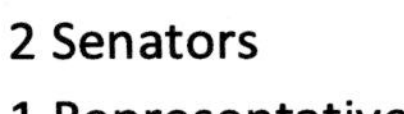

California

2 Senators
53 Representatives

This question is not unusual. We see the two approaches, considering "sample size" versus "counting everything equally" in the number of lawmakers per state in the US government.

Each state gets two senators, regardless of how many people live in the state. In a meta-analysis, this approach would be the approach we took on the previous page. Each study counts equally and we average the correlations.

Each state, however, also gets representatives based on how many people live in the state. California, for example, gets 53 times as many representatives as Alaska. This approach is called a weighted approach, weighting how things are counted based on the number of people represented.

In journal articles, the number of people represented, remember, is called the sample size and is usually represented by the letter *N*.

A weighted average of the correlations in the five studies above would give greater weight to study 4 (*N* = 700) than to studies 1, 2, 3 and 5 (each with an *N* of 100).

A Primer on Reliability, Validity and Meta-Analyses

Weighted Average Correlations

Although calculating the weighted average correlation is a bit more complicated than the table below, the table helps us to visualize what is happening. Studies 1, 2, 3 and 5's correlation were each represented once – similar to Alaska, Rhode Island, Delaware or Montana in the US House of Representatives. Study 4, however, was represented seven times, similar to Alabama, Colorado or South Carolina in the US House of Representatives.

Using the un-weighted method (similar to the US Senate) we would tell others "the average correlation" between transformational leadership and satisfaction with the leader is .44.

Using the weighted method (similar to the US House of Representatives) we would tell others "the weighted average correlation" between transformational leadership and satisfaction with the leader is .34.

Five Studies Reporting Correlations Between
Transformational Leadership and Satisfaction with the Leader

Study	Correlation	Sample Size
Study 1	.64	N = 100
Study 2	.43	N = 100
Study 3	.46	N = 100
Study 4 Counted the First time	.25	N = 100
Study 4 Counted the Second time	.25	N = 100
Study 4 Counted the Third time	.25	N = 100
Study 4 Counted the Fourth time	.25	N = 100
Study 4 Counted the Fifth time	.25	N = 100
Study 4 Counted the Sixth time	.25	N = 100
Study 4 Counted the Seventh time	.25	N = 100
Study 5	.41	N = 100
Weighted Average Correlation	.34	

Our example only had five studies. Many meta-analyses have hundreds of studies, and the sample sizes for the studies also vary much more than our simple example. It will be quite common, to see the weighted, sometime called corrected, average correlation in a meta-analysis.

There is, though, one more level of advanced analysis often reported in a meta-analysis.

A Primer on Reliability, Validity and Meta-Analyses

Estimated True Score Correlations

The Estimated True Population or Estimated True Score Correlation

Many meta-analyses report the weighted or corrected correlation we just reviewed (US House of Representatives model).

It is also common to see another, more complex, statistic reported called the *estimated true population correlation* or sometimes the *estimated true score correlation*.

There is no simple way to explain what is happening when we move from the weighted average correlation to the estimated true score correlation. Remember that we began this chapter learning about various forms of reliability. The estimated true score correlation is accounting for some of the unreliability in the scores used. It also takes into account something called range restriction.

Below is a simple example to help grasp the idea of range restriction. Let's assume study 1 was done primarily on traditional college students. The age range was pretty narrow, or restricted.

The sample in study 1 is quite different than that in study 3 that was done primarily with working adults. Its age range is larger and less restricted.

Study	Correlation	Sample Size	Age Range In Sample
Study 1	.64	N = 100	18 - 24
Study 2	.43	N = 100	35 - 55
Study 3	.46	N = 100	21 - 75

The simple average correlation (US Senate model) calculated an average of each correlation and ignored how many participants each correlation represented. The weighted average correlation (US House of Representatives model) improved on the simple average correlation by taking into account the sample size of each correlation.

The estimated true score correlation is doing what the weighted average correlation does and taking into consideration, the various range restrictions of the samples as well as unreliability that could appear in multiple ways.

The estimated true score correlation is generally considered a better estimate of what the actual relationship between the two variables is "in the real world," or "overall" or "in general."

A Primer on Reliability, Validity and Meta-Analyses

Cohen's d Score

One other twist that occurs in meta-analyses has to do with the types of variables analyzed.

At the broadest level, there are two types: continuous and categorical. So far, we have looked at meta-analyses of continuous variables. There are, however three types of continuous variables.

In addition to the three types of continuous variables, there is a second kind of variable that is called categorical.

Type	Example	Description
Nominal (Categorical)	Leader Gender	There are "discrete" groups. Think of categorical (nominal) data as "either/or." In this case, the leader is *either* female *or* male.
Ordinal (Continuous)	The leader inspires me. 1 Never, 2 Seldom, 3 Often, 4 Always Rating on a Likert Scale	The numbers used are in an order.[7] But… the distance between the numbers isn't necessarily the same idea. A 1-point "distance" between *Always* and *Often* may not be the same idea as a 1-point distance between *Often* and *Seldom.*
Interval (Continuous)	Temperature	Interval and ratio data are similar. Both are numbers, both are in an order, and the interval between each data point is the same. With interval data, however, the number "0" is just a number like any other number. For example, if the temperature outside is 0 degrees, that doesn't mean there is a complete absence of weather – it is still very cold outside. Zero is simply a degree warmer than -1 and a degree colder than +1 degrees.
Ratio (Continuous)	Salary	In ratio data, the number 0 has a special meaning. If our salary is $0, we literally are receiving no money for our work. Here 0 means "none."

A Primer on Reliability, Validity and Meta-Analyses

Cohen's d Score

To envision continuous and categorical data, let's return to our table from the chapter section on correlations. In the table below, rating of transformational leadership and satisfaction with the leader are both continuous variables.

But, the new column shows the gender of the leader (categorical – *either* male *or* female) each follower is rating. Sandy, for example, is rating her boss who is a male, while Janet is rating her boss who is a female.

Follower	Rating of Transformational Leadership (Continuous)	Satisfaction with Leader (Continuous)	Leader's Gender (Categorical)
Sandy	1.98	2.60	Male
Janet	3.88	3.90	Female
Lamar	3.40	2.60	Male
Anthony	3.60	3.40	Female
Michelle	2.35	3.35	Male
Maria	2.65	2.16	Male
Gilbert	1.95	1.28	Female
Francisco	2.12	3.14	Female
Annette	3.83	1.42	Male
Ben	2.21	2.26	Male
Dante	2.85	2.64	Female
Kenya	3.03	1.52	Female

The chart below shows the ratings each leader received on how transformational her/his follower perceived the leader to be.

Leader's Gender	Rating of Transformational Leadership
Male	1.98
Male	2.21
Male	2.35
Male	2.65
Male	3.40
Male	3.83
Mean	2.74
Female	1.95
Female	2.12
Female	2.85
Female	3.03
Female	3.60
Female	3.88
Mean	2.91

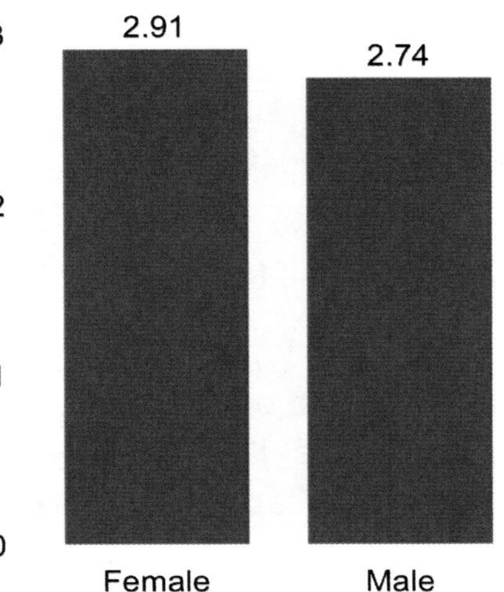

A Primer on Reliability, Validity and Meta-Analyses

Cohen's d Score

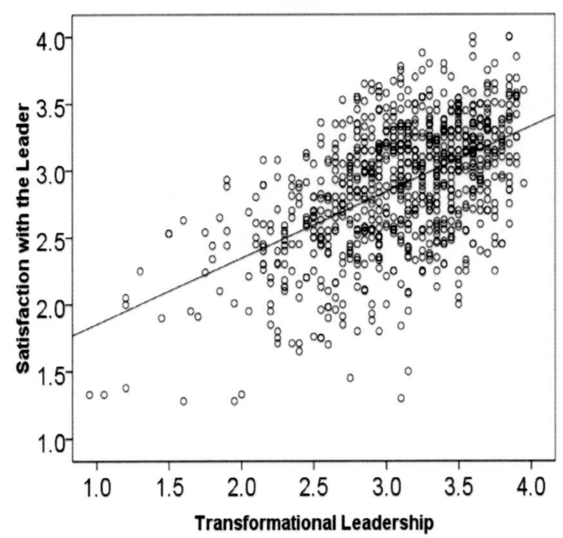

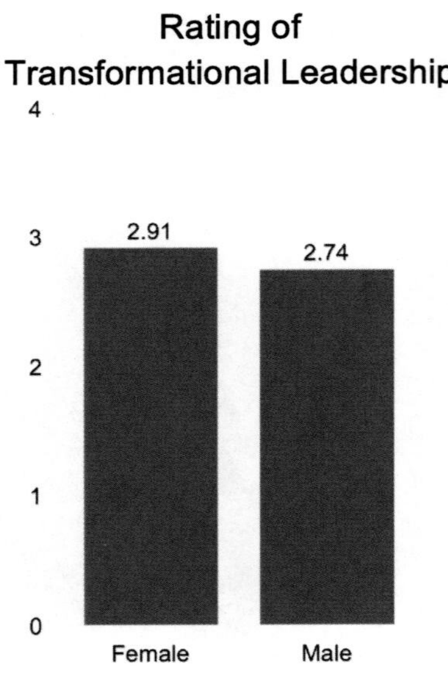

With continuous variables, when we run correlations we discuss patterns such as the more transformational the leader, the more satisfied followers are with the leader.

Generally, with categorical variables we discuss *differences* in the means for the groups. If we ran a statistical test and the female leaders with a mean (average) of 2.91 were more transformational than the male leaders with a mean (average) of 2.74 we would likely use words such as *different* or *than.*

We might say that female leaders were more transformational *than* male leaders. Because the leaders in this study were either male or female, there is no "gradation" between male and female. We can't describe a trend such as "the more female the more transformational."

There are many leadership studies done that include variables such as the leader's gender, leader's education level, the country in which the leader leads and so forth – categorical variables. Fortunately, statisticians have another tool for helping us meta-analyze these types of studies. A frequently reported statistical test is called a *d* score or *Cohen's d*.[8]

Although not originally developed for meta-analyses *Cohen's d* (Cohen, 1988) has proven to be indispensable for the interpretation of what research means. It is also key in specifying how important a result is in terms of application to real-world situations.

A Primer on Reliability, Validity and Meta-Analyses

Cohen's d Score

Technically *Cohen's d* is called a measure of effect size. It answers the practical question of how strong of a correlation or how big of a difference was found. *Cohen's d* is a ratio of difference or relationship divided by the variability of the variable.[9]

A good example of an effect size is a small rowboat with a hole in it.

How much *effect* does the hole have on your trip? If the hole in the boat is 1/32nd of an inch, it will be annoying, but you can occasionally bale out some water and continue fishing. If the hole is 4 inches in diameter, it is time to return to the dock immediately – the hole had a large effect.

But...the effect of the size of the hole also depends on how big the boat is. A 4-inch hole in a boat that is the size of a rowboat is a large effect – head back to shore.

While not desirable, a 4-inch hole in a large cruise ship can likely be managed by a few water pumps until the ship's next port of call – less of an effect. Think of the size of the boat as the "scale" of the boat.

We can see a similar phenomenon in survey results. Below are results of gender differences on three hypothetical measures of transformational leadership. Notice that in each case female leaders were rated, on average, 0.20 points higher than male leaders. But....the scale of the first instrument is from 0 to 4, the second instrument is from 0 to 5, and the third instrument 0 to 100. Because the scales are different, how we react to a 0.20 point difference (the hole in the boat) is different.

Rating of Transformational Leadership

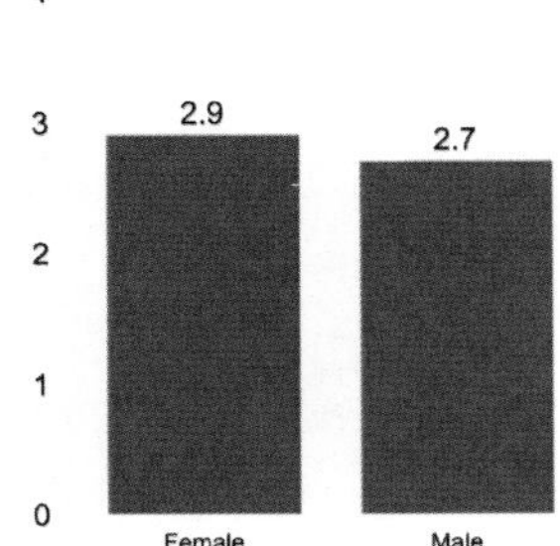

0.20 Difference, 0 to 4 Scale

Rating of Transformational Leadership

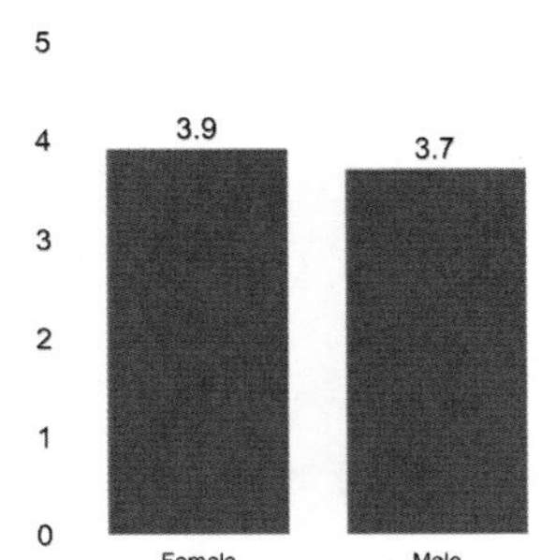

0.20 Difference, 0 to 5 Scale

Rating of Transformational Leadership

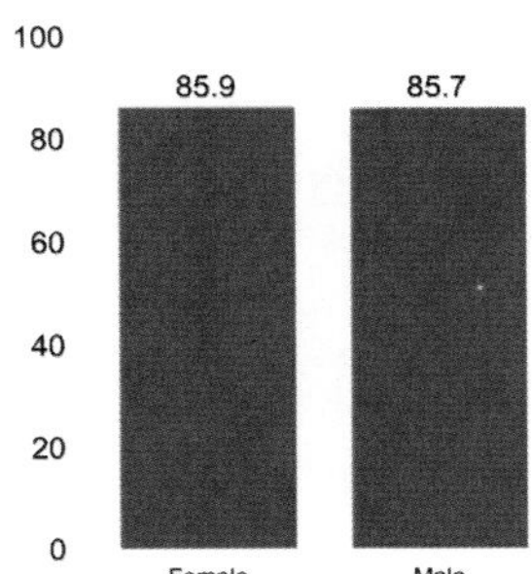

0.20 Difference, 0 to 100 Scale

A Primer on Reliability, Validity and Meta-Analyses

Cohen's d Score

There are at least two ways of interpreting effect size.[10] The first is by comparing the results presented to a standard. Cohen (1988) proposed rules of thumb for interpreting effect sizes.

Effect Size	*d* score
Small	0 to .20
Medium	.21 to .50
Large	> .51

The second way is to compare a reported *Cohen's d* to *Cohen's d* values found in similar studies. Effect sizes can be used to compare across studies and across meta-analyses. But...there is one additional nuance to understand.

Gender and Leadership		
	k	*d*
Transformational	44	0.10
Transactional	21	0.13
Laissez Faire	16	0.16

Imagine that we read an article that performed a meta-analysis for gender and leadership. Gender is a categorical variable so we can't readily run a correlation and say "the more female the more transformational...."[11]

A common statistic reported in meta-analyses of categorical variables is the *d* score. In the table to the left, we see that across 44 studies (*k* = 44) a small effect size (difference) between males and females was found for transformational leadership (*k* = 44, *d* = 0.10).[12]

Gender and Leadership			
	k	*d*	Comment
Transformational	44	0.10	Females Higher
Transactional	21	0.13	Females Higher
Laissez Faire	16	0.16	Males Higher

But who was more transformational, males or females? One option would be to add a comment column next to each *d* score as we have here, but that would consume a lot of room in a journal article.

Gender and Leadership		
	k	*d*
Transformational	44	- 0.10
Transactional	21	- 0.13
Laissez Faire	16	+ 0.16

A positive effect size (*d*) indicates that men had higher scores than women on a given leadership style, and a negative *d* indicates that women had higher scores than men.

A more common practice is to use the "+" and "-" symbols in front of the *d* score, with an explanation in the note below the table. Its important to understand that what a + or – means will vary from article to article, but the table will tell you in the notes section. In this example, a positive *d* score indicates males were rated higher on that aspect of leadership.

Gender and Leadership		
	k	*d*
Transformational	37	+ 0.15
Transactional	19	+ 0.18
Laissez Faire	18	- 0.13

A positive effect size (*d*) indicates that women had higher scores than men on a given leadership style, and a negative *d* indicates that men had higher scores than women.

A different meta-analysis might find similar results, but elect to have a "+" indicate females higher than males and a "-" indicate males higher than females. In this example, a positive *d* score indicates females were higher on that aspect of leadership. Always look at the notes in order to be able to interpret the *d score* results.

A Primer on Reliability, Validity and Meta-Analyses

Publication Bias and The File Drawer Effect

One final note generally related to the body of literature you will review in graduate work relates to two ideas: publication bias and the file drawer effect.[13]

Publication Bias

Scholarly journals usually use the method called peer review to assure competence and accuracy in published studies. Peer review is conducted by a number of referees, often at least three, to gather informed reviews of the paper proposed for publication. After the reviews, the journal editor usually makes the final decision to publish or reject a study.

Even with the best of intentions, many journals are unlikely to devote their limited print space to studies that do not find statistically significant results. This can limit the information available about the relationships among variables. A finding of no significant difference or no significant relationship can be just as important as a finding of a significant difference or a finding of a significant relationship. Many studies with no statistically significant results, however, wind up not being published.

File Drawer Effect

The idea of publication bias is related to journal editors and reviewers. The file drawer effect is related to researchers. Submitting research findings for peer-review can be daunting. If one has a journal article rejected for publication, it is very easy to make self-statements such as "this was a poor article/research."[14]

If researchers believe that some research they performed that, found no significance, will likely be rejected because of perceived publication bias, many researchers say to themselves "Why even submit it?" The connotation is that the researchers file away their results and don't even submit them for peer review.

The biases introduced because of the file drawer effect and perceived publication bias potentially impact effect sizes, such as *Cohen's d*, or weighted correlations. The calculated effect sizes or correlations may be higher than they should be if un-submitted or rejected studies were not included.

Meta-analyses often try to account for the file drawer effect and publication bias in two ways. First, meta-analyses may report both published and unpublished literature. Secondly, many meta-analyses will attempt to estimate what impacts the file drawer effect and publication bias might have had on the results and provide either a range or possible results beyond what the analyzed articles found, or sometimes attempt to adjust the meta-analytic statistic to account for the file drawer effect and/or publication bias.

A Primer on Reliability, Validity and Meta-Analyses

How to Interpret a Meta-Analysis Table

Putting it All Together

Although there will typically be more columns than shown below, when you are first getting started reading a meta-analysis, a table will often include four columns you will want to review.

The table below is a portion of a meta-analysis that analyzed the relationships among different aspects of leadership and follower performance.[15]

k is routinely used to represent how many studies were meta-analyzed.

In the table below, we see that 62 (*k* = 62) studies were located that reported scores for transformational leadership and individual-level performance. There were 50 (*k* = 50) studies located that reported scores for the use of contingent reward and individual-level performance. Finally, there were six studies (*k* = 6) found that reported scores for the use of management by exception passive leadership and individual-level performance.

Relationships of Leadership with Individual-Level Follower Performance

Variable	*k*	*N*
Transformational Leadership	62	16,809
Contingent Reward	50	9,108
Management by Exception Passive	6	555

In a meta-analysis, the column labeled *N* is usually the total sample size represented by those *k* studies.

For the 62 studies that reported correlations between transformational leadership and individual-level performance, study 1 might have had 500 participants, study 2, 100 participants, study 3, 300 participants and so forth.

If we added up all of the participants from those 62 studies, those studies represent 16,809 participants. (*k* = 62, *N* = 16,809).

There were 50 studies found that reported relationships between leader contingent reward and individual-level performance. If we added up all of the participants from those 50 studies, there would be 9,108 of them. (*k* = 50, *N* = 9,108). There were six studies found that reported management by exception passive with a total of 555 participants (*k* = 6, N = 555).

A Primer on Reliability, Validity and Meta-Analyses

How to Interpret a Meta-Analysis Table

The symbols used to represent the weighted or corrected average correlation vary from article to article. What the symbols represent, however, are almost always explained in the note under the table.

In our case, the *r* with the bar above it, sometimes written as r_c connoting corrected for variations in the sample sizes, is the weighted average correlation (US House of Representatives example).

The meta-analytic result for transformational leadership and individual performance (k = 62, N = 16,809, r_c = .22) using the weighted average correlation found that the more transformational the leader was rated, the higher the individual-level of performance.

Relationships of Leadership With Individual-Level Follower Performance

Variable	k	N	$\bar{r}$ or r_c	ρ
Transformational Leadership	62	16,809	.22	.25
Contingent Reward	50	9,108	.20	.22
Management by Exception Passive	6	555	–.05	–.06

k is the number of studies analyzed; N is the total sample size; r_c is the weighted average correlation; ρ is the estimated true score correlation.

The estimated true score correlation is often represented by the symbol ρ. Unfortunately, this is the Greek symbol for rho, and looks similar to an italicized *p* that is frequently used to represent statistical confidence. They are, however, two completely different ideas. Sometimes the table will show a ρ (rho) as it is here, sometimes a ρ (rho) with a bar and other times a ρ (rho) with a hat.

We are generally talking about the same results, the weighted average correlation, then corrected for unreliability and range restriction.

The meta-analytic result for transformational leadership and individual performance (k = 62, N = 16,809, ρ (rho) = .25) using the estimated true score correlation found that the more transformational the leader was rated, the higher the individual-level of performance.

A Primer on Reliability, Validity and Meta-Analyses

How to Interpret a Meta-Analysis Table

Gender and Leadership		
	k	*d*
Transformational	44	- .10
Transactional	21	- .13
Laissez Faire	16	+ .16

A positive effect size (*d*) indicates that men had higher scores than women on a given leadership style, and a negative *d* indicates that women had higher scores than men.

If the meta-analysis uses the *d* score to describe the effect size between the two variables, the note at the bottom of the table will explain how to interpret those results.

In this table, there were 44 studies that reported gender and transformational leadership findings. Females (k = 44, d = -.10) were more transformational than men. There were 21 studies that reported gender and transactional leadership findings. Females (k = 21, d = -.13) were more transformational than men. Finally, there were 16 studies that reported gender and laissez faire leadership findings. Females (k = 16, d = .16) were less laissez faire than men.

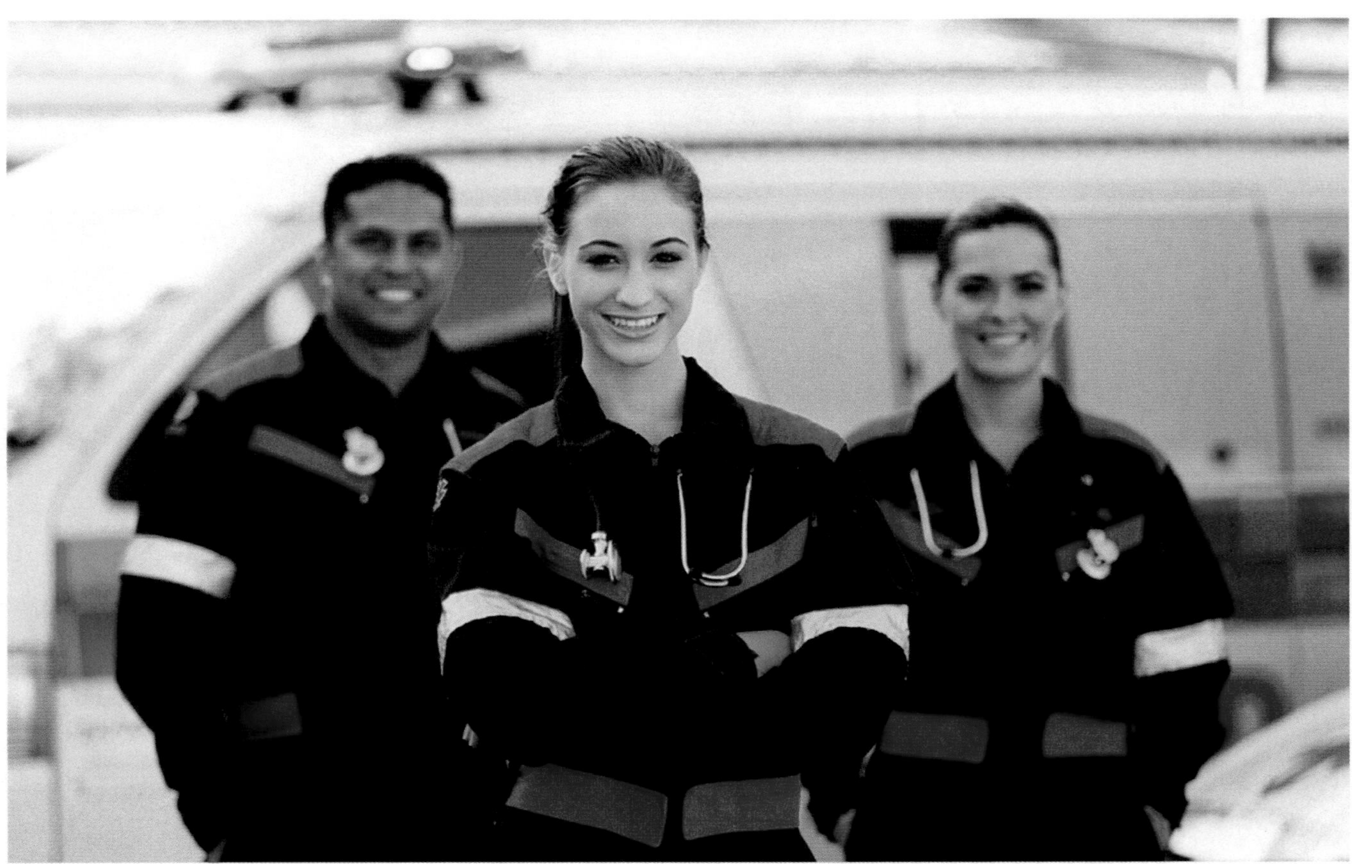

A Primer on Reliability, Validity and Meta-Analyses

How Research Results Will be Presented In Chapters 3 to 10

Chapters 3 through 10 will review popular leadership theories. As part of that review, each chapter will provide you with a synopsis of what the research base indicates about that aspect of leadership and a variety of different outcomes.

Rather than use hundreds of scatter plots to assist you in visualizing the relationships that will be described, those chapters will show the meta-analytic correlations as bars on a chart.[16]

In the first chart below, for example, we see that 13 studies have been published that have analyzed how transformational leaders were and how well followers believed those leaders performed in their jobs.

Those 13 studies collectively represent 2,126 follower ratings of leaders. The overall corrected correlation (the House of Representatives Model) found a weak, positive correlation (.27). The higher a leader was rated on transformational leadership, the higher the leader was rated by her or his followers on job performance.

Example of How Research Results will be Presented in Chapters 3 to 10

Transformational Leadership and Leader Job Performance

Strongly - Correlated	Moderately - Correlated	Weakly - Correlated	Weakly + Correlated	Moderately + Correlated	Strongly + Correlated
-1 to -.50	-.49 to -.30	-.29 to -.10	.10 to .29	.30 to .49	.50 to 1

Outcome	Studies	Followers	
Weakly, Positively Correlated			
Leader Job Performance	13	2,126	.27

Transformational Leadership and Leader Effectiveness

Strongly - Correlated	Moderately - Correlated	Weakly - Correlated	Weakly + Correlated	Moderately + Correlated	Strongly + Correlated
-1 to -.50	-.49 to -.30	-.29 to -.10	.10 to .29	.30 to .49	.50 to 1

Outcome	Studies	Followers	
Moderately, Positively Correlated			
Leader Effectiveness	27	5,415	.48

In the chart above, we see that 27 studies have been published that analyzed how transformational leaders were and how effective followers believed their leaders were. Those 27 studies collectively represent 5,415 follower ratings of their leaders. The overall corrected correlation found a moderate, positive correlation (.48). The higher a leader was rated on transformational leadership, the higher the leader was rated by her or his followers on leader effectiveness.

A Primer on Reliability, Validity and Meta-Analyses

How Research Results Will be Presented In Chapters 3 to 10

The relationship between two variables, however, can also be negative. In the first chart below, we see that 22 studies have been published that analyzed the degree to which leaders engaged in management by exception passive behaviors and how motivated the followers were. Those 22 studies collectively represent 3,441 follower ratings of their leaders.

The overall corrected correlation found a weak, negative correlation between management by exception passive leadership and follower motivation (-.27). The more leaders engaged in management by exception passive behaviors, the lower the followers' motivation.

Management by Exception Passive and Follower Motivation

Strongly - Correlated	Moderately - Correlated	Weakly - Correlated	Weakly + Correlated	Moderately + Correlated	Strongly + Correlated
-1 to -.50	-.49 to -.30	-.29 to -.10	.10 to .29	.30 to .49	.50 to 1

	Outcome	Studies	Followers
Weakly, Negatively Correlated			
-.27	Follower Motivation	22	3,441

Laissez-Faire and Satisfaction with the Leader

Strongly - Correlated	Moderately - Correlated	Weakly - Correlated	Weakly + Correlated	Moderately + Correlated	Strongly + Correlated
-1 to -.50	-.49 to -.30	-.29 to -.10	.10 to .29	.30 to .49	.50 to 1

	Outcome	Studies	Followers
Strongly, Negatively Correlated			
-.58	Follower Satisfaction With Leader	5	838

In the chart above, we see that five studies have been published that analyzed the degree to which leaders engaged in laissez-faire behaviors and how satisfied the followers were with their leaders. Those five studies collectively represent 838 follower ratings of leaders. The overall corrected correlation found a strong, negative correlation (-.58). The more leaders engaged in laissez-faire behaviors the lower the followers' satisfaction with their leaders.

A Primer on Reliability, Validity and Meta-Analyses

Multiple Regression

What is a Multiple Regression?

One frequent use for a multiple regression is to develop prediction models. To envision this, lets assume a business tracks daily data on things such as the temperature outside, the day of the week, the day of the month, yesterday's change in the Dow Jones Industrial Average, interest rates and whether the home sports team won in its last outing. The business also counts the number of customers who enter the store each day.

Multiple Regression for Building a Prediction Model

One of the things the business would like to do is be able to predict the number of customers who might enter the store tomorrow or the next day. In this example, the storeowners would be slowly experimenting with various possible predictors of the number of customers who enter the store. To create this predictive model, a relatively straightforward statistical tool is multiple regression.

There is no guarantee, however, that the data the storeowners have collected are good predictors of the number of customers who enter the store. For example, in the model above, there is no measure of advertising and marketing. The number of customers the day before and week before might also be useful predictors.

Fortunately, when one runs a multiple regression, one of the outputs is a measure of how useful each predictor is. In statistical terms, this is called the strength of the predictor. The symbol typically used to connote strength is R^2. The range of the R^2 can be from 0, meaning the variable doesn't predict the outcome of which we are interested, to 1 that means it is a perfect predictor.

In the area of leadership and workplace outcomes, the R^2 values calculated for each variable allow another use of multiple regression – gauging which of the predictor variables are the strongest predictors.

Multiple Regression for Analyzing the Relative Strength of Predictors

Full Range of Leadership Variable	Satisfaction with the Leader
Idealized Influence Attributed (IIA)	.38*
Individual Consideration (IC)	.63**
Management By Exception Passive (MBEP)	-.37*
Laissez-Faire (LF)	-.48**

** $p < .01$, * $p < .05$

Earlier in this chapter, we reviewed a series of correlations between aspects of the full range model of leadership and satisfaction with the leader.

Now that we understand the ideas of the strength and directions of correlations, we might look at the table to the left and ask, "of the four significant correlations shown, which one is the strongest predictor of satisfaction with the leader?"

While it is tempting to guess based on the strength of each correlation, multiple regression will provide a more accurate assessment.

The correlation table above shows results when aspects of the full range model of leadership were run separately – a correlation for IIA and satisfaction, then a correlation for IC and satisfaction, one for MBEP and satisfaction and, finally, one for LF and satisfaction.

The table below is an example of what a multiple regression that included all four variables "simultaneously" or "head to head" found.

Full Range of Leadership Variable	R^2
Management By Exception Passive (MBEP)	.01*
Idealized Influence Attributed (IIA)	.03*
Laissez-Faire (LF)	.12*
Individual Consideration (IC)	.24*

** $p < .01$, * $p < .05$

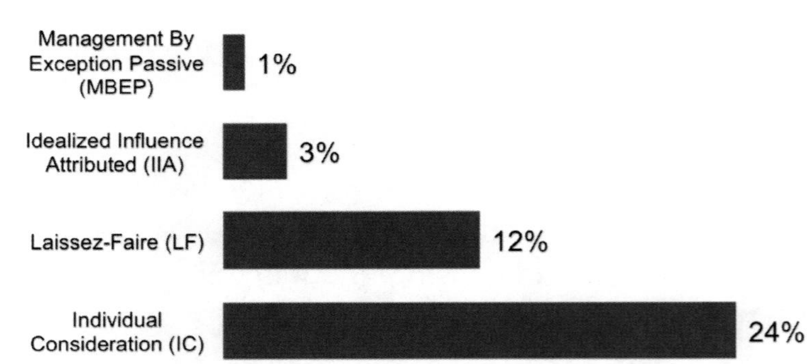

We see that the R^2 value for IC was .24. We can interpret this by saying that "twenty-four percent of the variance in satisfaction with the leader can be explained by the leader's use of individual consideration."

An additional 12% is explained by the leaders' laissez-faire behaviors and so forth. We also see that 60% of the variance in satisfaction with the leader remains "unexplained."

A way to think about this is that there are likely many important variables, such as leader experience, gender, education, personality and so forth, that might also explain satisfaction with the leader, but those were not included in the multiple regression.

Standardized Regression Weights

You will notice in the table below, an additional column has been added that is labeled "standardized regression weight." It is quite common in journal articles to see the beta symbol β used to represent this concept.

The beta weight can provide us another sense of the relative importance of each of the variables in predicting the variance in the dependent variable.

Unlike the R^2, however, the standardized regression weights can be either positive or negative. Because this chapter is targeted at the level of "getting the ball over the plate," we'll leave additional details of the regression equation, unstandardized and standardized regression weights for a statistics class. For now, it is sufficiently helpful to interpret the standardized regression weights as we did correlations.

Full Range of Leadership Variable	R^2	β Standardized Regression Weight
Management By Exception Passive (MBEP)	.01*	β = -.02
Idealized Influence Attributed (IIA)	.03*	β = .05
Laissez-Faire (LF)	.12*	β = -.28
Individual Consideration (IC)	.24*	β = .31

** $p < .01$, * $p < .05$

One finding from the table above is that of the four predictors, individual consideration is the strongest predictor of satisfaction with the leader (R^2 = .24) and management by exception passive is the weakest predictor (R^2 = .01).[17]

Because the standardized regression weights for individual consideration (β = .31) and idealized influence attributed (β = .05) were positive, we can conclude that the higher leaders were rated on these aspects of leadership, the higher the satisfaction with those leaders.

Because the standardized regression weights for laissez-faire (β = -.28) and management by exception passive (β = -.02) were negative, we can conclude that the higher leaders were rated on these aspects of leadership, the lower the satisfaction with those leaders.

Putting it all together, we could say that "the strongest predictor of satisfaction with the leader was individual consideration (R^2 = .24). The more individually considerate leaders were the higher their followers' satisfaction with them (β = .31). Laissez-faire was also a noteworthy predictor (R^2 = .12). The more laissez-faire the leaders, the less satisfied the followers were with their leaders (β = -.28)."

Meta-Analytic Multiple Regression

It is becoming more commonplace to see multiple regressions run with meta-analytic data. Judge, Heller and Mount (2002),[18] for example, conducted a meta-analysis of worker personality and worker job satisfaction. In the table below, the first four columns are the results of meta-analytic calculations for each factor of personality – calculated separately.

For the single personality factor of neuroticism, for example, we see that 92 studies (k) were analyzed, representing 24,527 workers (N). The estimated true population score (Rho) was -.29. The higher the workers' neuroticism, the lower their job satisfaction.

We notice that all five factors are related to workers' satisfaction with their job. But, are some factors stronger predictors than others? The two columns to the right are the result of a meta-analytic regression. Here all five factors were "simultaneously" analyzed. In statistical terms, we would say that job satisfaction was regressed on the five factors of personality.

In the columns to the far right of the table below, we see that three of the five factors, neuroticism, conscientiousness and extraversion were significant predictors of job satisfaction. The additional information a meta-analytic regression provides us might be thought of as follows. "The broad body of literature indicates that all five factors of personality are related to job satisfaction. But.... neuroticism, extraversion and conscientiousness are stronger predictors of job satisfaction than openness and agreeableness."

Meta-Analytic Correlations				Meta-Analytic Regression	
Variable	*k*	*N*	*Rho*	R^2	β
Openness to Experience	50	15,196	.02	.00	
Conscientiousness	79	21,719	.26	.04	.20
Extraversion	75	20,184	.25	.04	.21
Agreeableness	38	11,856	.17	.00	
Neuroticism	92	24,527	-.29	.04	-.20

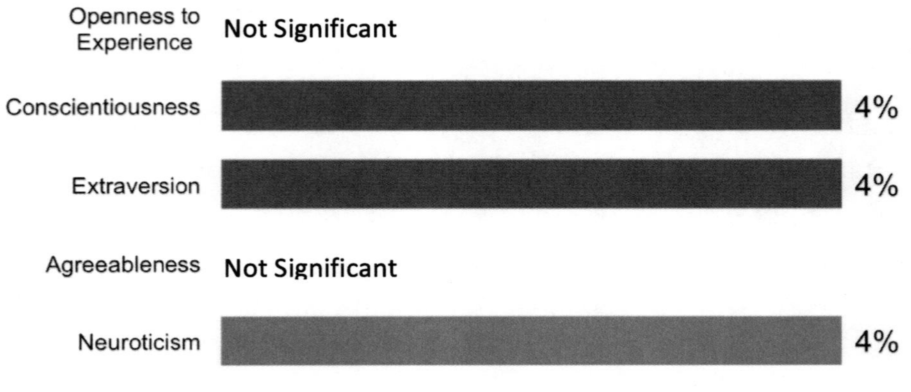

A Primer on Reliability, Validity and Meta-Analyses

Notes

Approximately 21% of U.S. adults hold a bachelors degree. A little over 7% hold a masters degree and less than 1% a doctorate. The charts shown are not percentages earned per year, but estimates of the percentage of adults in the United States holding those degrees.

Earning a graduate degree is a significant accomplishment.[19] Acquiring the ability to read and interpret research on your own is an important skill in becoming part of the 8% or United States adults who hold a graduate degree or the 1% of adults who hold a doctorate degree.

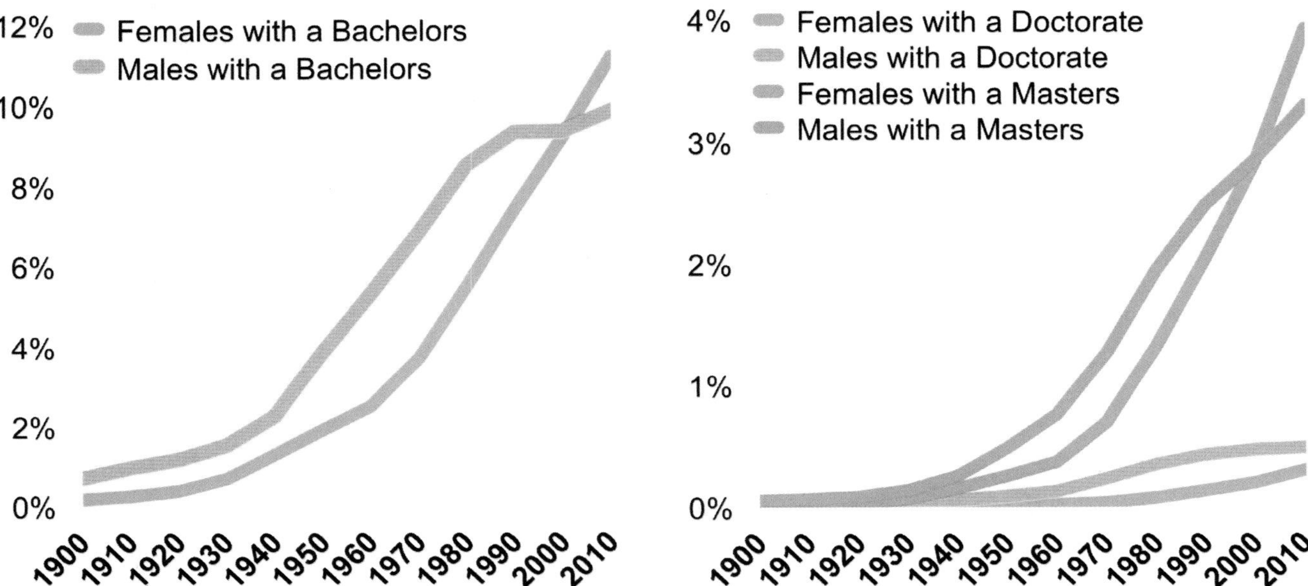

A Primer on Reliability, Validity and Meta-Analyses

Notes

[1] A high negative factor loading often indicates that the question seems to be measuring something similar to a different question, but in an opposite direction. The easiest way to envision this is a question that should be "reverse scored." If question 1 asked about honesty and question 2 asked about dishonesty, we can envision that they are broadly measuring something similar, but in opposite directions. The higher a follower rated a leader on honesty (question 1), theoretically, the lower the follower should rate that leader on dishonesty (question 2). Question 2 would likely have a negative factor loading and question 1 a positive factor loading. If those two questions were used on an instrument, the scoring directions would likely instruct us to "reverse-score" question 2.

[2] These plots were designed for visualizing differences for magnitudes of correlations. One can't simply make a scatterplot and then use the *Line of Best Fit* to get the correlation. We use formulas for correlations. This geometric visual, though, seems to help graduate students grasp the idea of magnitude.

[3] This way of envisioning a correlation requires the scores to be standardized. One can't automatically look at a scatterplot, measure the slope of the line of best fit and deduce that that angle is the correlation coefficient.

[4] There are other measurements for effect size besides *Cohen's d*. You might encounter, for example, *Hedges g* or *Eta-squared η2* in an article. Those are not discussed in this textbook.

[5] Similar to the previous illustration, how confidant we are in a correlation is not deduced by staring at a scatterplot. We use a formula that gives us the level of confidence, the direction and the magnitude of a correlation. Providing this series of gradually more "scattered" scatterplots seems to help graduate students visualize confidence in correlations.

[6] Different articles in different journals report different levels of "doubt" or *p* values.

One article may use *** $p < .001$, ** $p < .01$, * $p < .05$.
A second article might only report * $p < .05$.
A third article might report ** $p < .05$, * $p < .10$.

The table used in this chapter to help you understand reading asterisks and *p* values is generic. Not every article reports *p* values with the same number of asterisks.

[7] You will find different opinions in the scholarly literature on whether a Likert or Likert-like scale is an ordinal or interval type of variable.

[8] The *d* score can be calculated for either categorical or continuous variables. It is common, however, to see the weighted average correlation or estimated true score correlation presented for continuous variables and, often, the *d* score for categorical independent variables.

[9] *Cohen's d* is calculated by subtracting the mean of one group from the mean of a second group, and dividing this difference by the pooled standard deviation $d = (M2 - M1) / s_{pool.}$ Explaining the pooled standard deviation is beyond the scope of this book.

[10] In a meta-analysis, effect size is frequently shown as Cohen's *d*. This will be a number that is usually a decimal fraction such as 0.1, 0.5 or 0.8. However *d* values such as 1.2 or greater can be found on rare occasions.

[11] Some meta-analyses do indeed report weighted mean correlations or true score correlations for categorical variables with only two groups. In the note below the table the meta-analysis will typically indicate that a positive correlation meant that one group (for example females) was higher and a negative correlation that the other group (for example males) was lower.

[12] These data are from Eagly, A. H., Johannesen-Schmidt, M. C., and van Engen, M. L, (2004). Transformational, transactional, and laissez-faire leadership styles: A meta-analysis comparing women and men. *Psychological Bulletin, 129,* 4, 569-91.

[13] Publication bias and the file drawer effect are not unique to meta-analyses. If a graduate student read all of the published articles related to her/his thesis or dissertation topic, she/he too would be impacted by these effects. She/he would not have read the rejected or un-submitted body of research.

[14] Very sound research and an associated article may be rejected by a journal because the topic simply does not fit the focus of the journal.

[15] These results were reported in Wang, G., Courtright, S. H., Colbert, A. E., and Oh, I. S. (2011). Transformational leadership and performance across criteria and levels: A meta-analytic review of 25 years of research. *Group and Organization Management, 36,* 2, 223-270.

[16] The exact boundary between weak, moderate and strong correlations is not universally agreed upon. The definitions used in chapters 8 to 12 are based on Cohen, J. (1992). A power primer. *Psychological Bulletin, 112,* 1, 155-9.

A Primer on Reliability, Validity and Meta-Analyses

Notes

[17] Typically we would refer to this number as a change in the R2 from the previous three predictors and denote it by the symbol ΔR^2.

[18] A more detailed explanation of the meta-analytic regression method employed is available on page 533 of Judge, T. A., Heller, D., & Mount, M. K. (2002). Five-factor model of personality and job satisfaction- A meta-analysis. *Journal Of Applied Psychology*, 87(3), 530-541. doi-10.1037/0021-9010.87.3.530.

To form the correlation matrix that served as input for the multiple regression, the researchers used the meta-analytic estimates of the relationship between the Big Five traits and job satisfaction shown as Judg4 in this chapter. They then used Ones, Viswesvaran, and Reiss's (1996) meta-analytic estimate of the intercorrelations among the Big Five traits. The sample size used for the regressions was equal to the average sample size of all studies in the analysis (Viswesvaran & Ones, 1995): 280. (almost verbatim from page 533 of Judge, Heller and Mount (2002).

[19] From left to right, Dr.'s Richard Suttle, Earnest Thomas, Alicia Gonzalez-Quiroz, Patti Benitez, Debra Lopez and John Blumentritt earning their PhD's in Leadership Studies from Our Lady of the Lake University.

A Primer on Reliability, Validity and Meta-Analyses

Notes

Chapter 3
Task, Relationship and Situation

Task, Relationship and Situation
Introduction

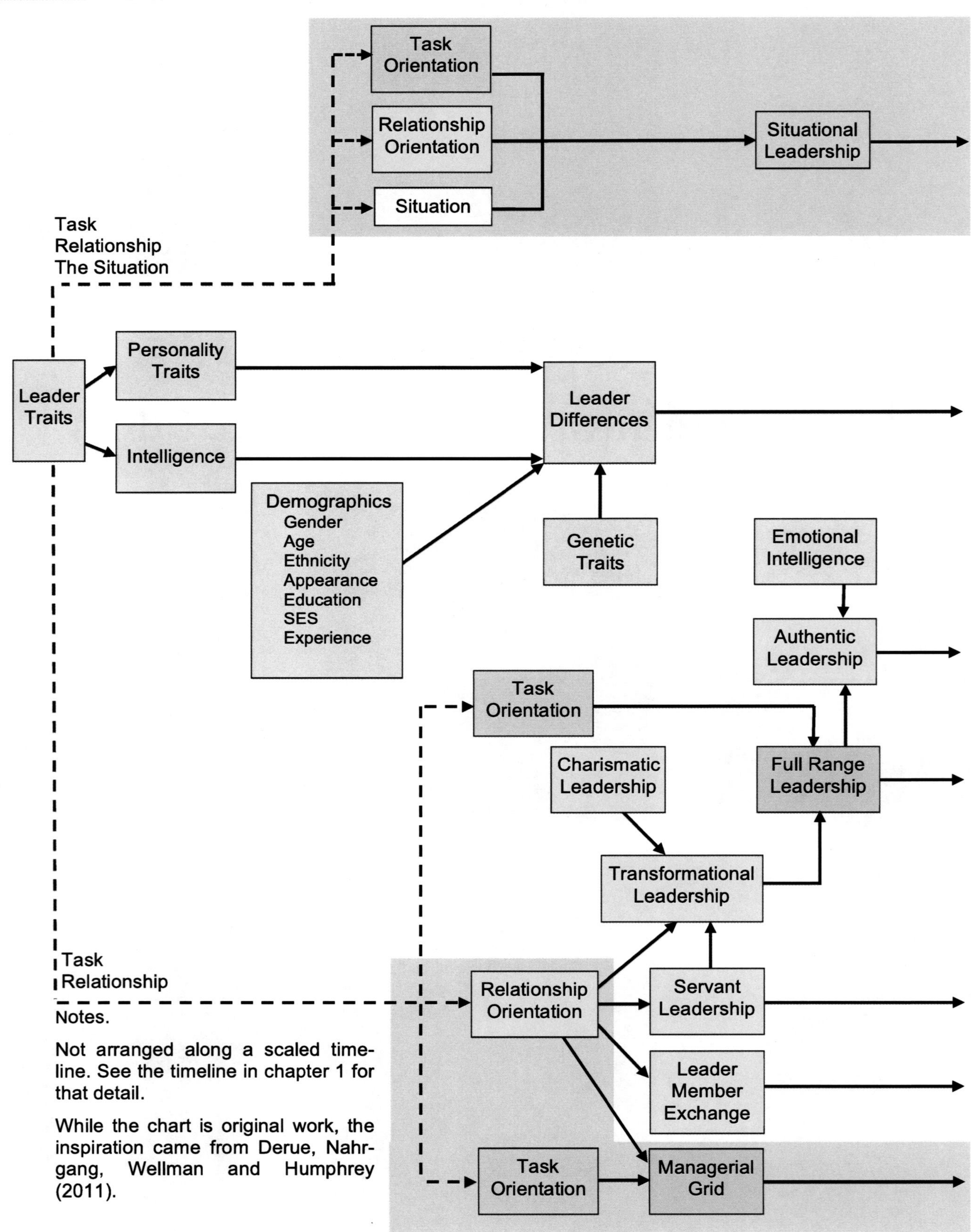

Notes.

Not arranged along a scaled timeline. See the timeline in chapter 1 for that detail.

While the chart is original work, the inspiration came from Derue, Nahrgang, Wellman and Humphrey (2011).

Task, Relationship and Situation

Introduction

The chart on the preceding page reminds us of several things. First, that the dimensions of task orientated and relationship orientated leadership began to take shape after initial efforts to identify general traits of effective leaders were unfruitful.

Second, that task and relationship orientated leadership have served as a foundation for two lines of research. The lower gray box illustrates theories influenced by those two dimensions. The upper box illustrates theories influenced by those two dimensions plus one or more situational dimensions.

The table below summarizes popular theories that include aspects of *Task* and *Relationship*. The four theories shown in beige will each be discussed in separate chapters.

Year	Theory	Task	Relationship
1955	Ohio State Studies	Initiation of Structure	Consideration
1960	University of Michigan	Production Orientation	Employee Orientation
1964	Managerial Grid	Concern for Production	Concern for People
1964	Contingency Theory	Task Orientation	Relationship Orientation
1966	Four-Factor Theory	Goal Emphasis	Support
1969	Situational Leadership	Directive	Supportive
1970	Servant Leadership		Empathy, Healing, Empowering
1971	Path-Goal Theory	Directive, Achievement Oriented	Supportive, Participative
1975	Leader-Member Exchange Theory		Relationship Between Leader and Follower
1985	Full Range Model of Leadership	Contingent Reward, MBE Active	Individual Consideration
2004	Project GLOBE		Team-Oriented, Participative, Humane
2008	Authentic Leadership		Relational Transparency

Task, Relationship and Situation
Introduction

Of the seven theories below, the four-factor theory and situational leadership have very little quantitative research published to assist in assessing the degree to which they seem to work.

While aspects of path-goal theory have been researched, the theory incorporates multiple situational variables, and few studies have been published that simultaneously tested those combinations of variables. Meta-analyses by Wofford and Liska (1993) and Indvik (1986) only found a few studies that included three or more variables, and the results of their meta-analyses gave us limited value in testing the theory.

Contingency theory also has multiple variables associated with it. The instrument associated with contingency theory is the *Least Preferred Co-Worker Scale (LPC)*. Schriesheim, Tepper and Tetrault (1994) meta-analyzed 10 studies that reported *LPC* scores and group performance. Their study supported the theoretical underpinnings for four of the eight "octants," from contingency theory, but did not support the underpinnings behind the other four octants.

There have been however, five meta-analyses on the two primary leadership behaviors measured by versions of the *Leader Behavior Description Questionnaire*. This chapter will focus on that instrument and those meta-analyses.

Year	Theory	Instrument	Research Base
1955	Ohio State	*Leader Behavior Description Questionnaire (LBDQ)*	Over 30 Peer-Reviewed Articles and Over 600 Dissertations Using the *LBDQ*
1960	University of Michigan Studies		Tends to Be Lumped Together with the Ohio State Findings
1964	Managerial Grid	*LBDQ* Typically Used	Nearly 40 Peer-Reviewed Articles Using the Managerial Grid
1964	Contingency Theory	*Least Preferred Co-Worker Scale (LPC)*	Only a Few Studies Done Since 2000
1966	Four-Factor Theory		Very Little Quantitative Research
1969	Situational Leadership		Very Little Quantitative Research
1971	Path-Goal Theory	Primarily *LBDQ*	Meta-Analysis Found Limited Support

Task, Relationship and Situation
Introduction

This leaves us with the following theories that are still popular and have an empirical base:

The Ohio State Studies
The University of Michigan Studies
The Managerial (Leadership) Grid

Because situational leadership is very popular, however, it will also be reviewed.

In addition to those theories, one instrument will be reviewed:

The *Leader Behavior Description Questionnaire XII*

This research comprises the heart of the theories emphasizing *Task, Relationship* and *Situation* that are still relevant.

Task, Relationship and Situation

The Ohio State and Michigan Studies

Changing the Focus of Leadership Research from Traits to Behaviors

Prior to the early 1940's, leadership research tended to focus on the leader. The effort was to identify traits and characteristics that seemed to explain why some people emerged as leaders and others did not, or why some people exceled at leadership while others did not. In 1948, Stogdill compiled a list of leader traits from the existing literature. Those results are shown below. The overall conclusion from that stream of research was that the research on traits simply couldn't be reduced to a simple list.

	+	-
Physical Characteristics		
Activity, Energy	5	
Age	10	
Appearance, Grooming	13	
Height	9	
Weight	7	
Social Background		
Education	22	
Social Status	15	
Mobility	5	
Intelligence and Ability		
Intelligence	23	
Judgment, Decisiveness	9	
Knowledge	11	
Fluency of Speech	13	
Personality		
Adaptability	10	
Alertness	6	
Ascendance, Dominance	11	
Personality (continued)		
Emotional Balance	11	8
Extroversion	5	6
Originality, Creativity	7	
Personal Integrity	6	
Self-Confidence	17	
Strength of Conviction	7	
Task-Related Characteristics		
Achievement Drive	7	
Drive for Responsibility	12	
Persistence	12	
Responsible	17	
Task Orientation	6	
Social Characteristics		
Enlisting Cooperation	7	
Cooperativeness	11	
Popularity, Prestige	10	
Sociability	14	
Social Participation	20	

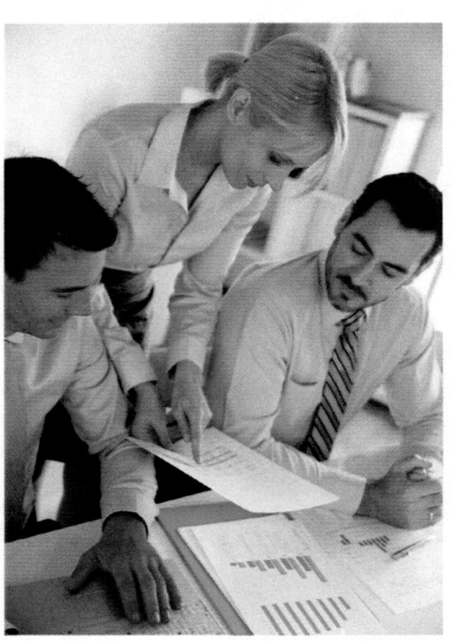

Following the search for traits, researchers at universities such as Ohio State and Michigan began to interview followers and brainstorm on what leaders actually did (behaviors) rather than who leaders were (traits).

Hundreds of leader behaviors were generated. The researchers grouped that long list of behaviors into two broad categories – the ideas of task and relationship.

Researchers at Ohio State called these dimensions initiation of structure and consideration. Researchers at the University of Michigan called these dimensions production orientation and employee orientation.

Task, Relationship and Situation

The Ohio State and Michigan Studies

The Ohio State University Studies

The Ohio State studies viewed initiation of structure and consideration as two separate constructs.

Initiation of Structure **Low ←——————→ High**
Clearly defines own role and lets followers know what is expected

Consideration **Low ←——————→ High**
Regards the comfort, well-being, status and contributions of followers

The University of Michigan Studies

The University of Michigan studies researched similar constructs to those researched at Ohio State, but called them production orientation and employee orientation. Unlike the Ohio State researchers, however, the researchers at the University of Michigan originally conceived of these constructs as opposite ends of a continuum.

Production Orientation
Emphasizes the task or production aspects of the job and getting things done

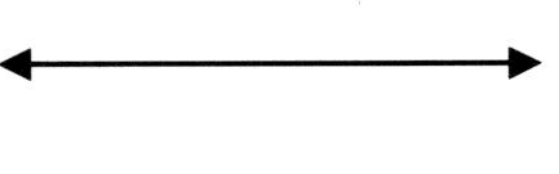

Employee Orientation
Emphasizes a concern for interpersonal relations and the personal needs of followers

Consideration

1,9								9,9
				5,5				
1,1								9,1

Initiation of Structure

If we think about the original two constructs from the Ohio State studies and envision consideration as a vertical, rather than a horizontal scale, the two concepts can form a grid.

Task, Relationship and Situation
The Managerial Grid

The Managerial Grid

The managerial grid placed the ideas of consideration and initiation of structure onto a grid. Rather than call the X-axis *Initiation of Structure*, Blake and Mouton called it *Concern for Production*. They called the Y-axis *Concern for People.*

The managerial grid has gone through several iterations. In 1991, Blake and McCanse published *Leadership Dilemmas - Grid Solutions*. In that book, they called the managerial grid the leadership grid. The managerial (leadership) grid describes four major styles that leaders might use.

Leadership Style	Concern for Production	Concern for People	General View
Impoverished Management	Low	Low	As the name implies, this combination of leader behaviors is most likely "non-leadership."
Authority Compliance Management	High	Low	This style of leadership emphasizes results over people. It can be somewhat effective in short bursts during times of crisis, but as a long-term style tends to produce stress and passive-aggressive behaviors in followers.
Country Club Management	Low	High	While it might seem that followers would like an "anything you want" style of leader, it is generally not effective. Followers like to feel that they are contributing to something "important" and that they are treated equitably. The country club style lacks a sense of direction and quickly results in some followers feeling that other followers are "getting over."
Team Management	High	High	This combination of task and relationship is typically found to be the preferred long-term style of leadership.

Task, Relationship and Situation

Situational Leadership

Situational Leadership

The managerial grid is usually presented as a *descriptive* theory. It describes a leader's preferred leadership style. Hersey and Blanchard's[1] situational leadership is often presented as a *prescriptive* theory. Given information on the follower's *Competence to Perform a Task* and *Commitment to Perform a Task*, the theory *prescribes* leadership behaviors that are believed to be effective.

Leadership Style	Directive Behaviors	Supportive Behaviors	Follower Competence	Follower Commitment
Delegating	Low	Low	High	High
Directing	High	Low	Low	High
Supporting	Low	High	High	Low
Coaching	High	High	Some	Low

The chart below reminds us that situational leadership is still very popular. It has an intuitive appeal that seems to resonate with many leaders.

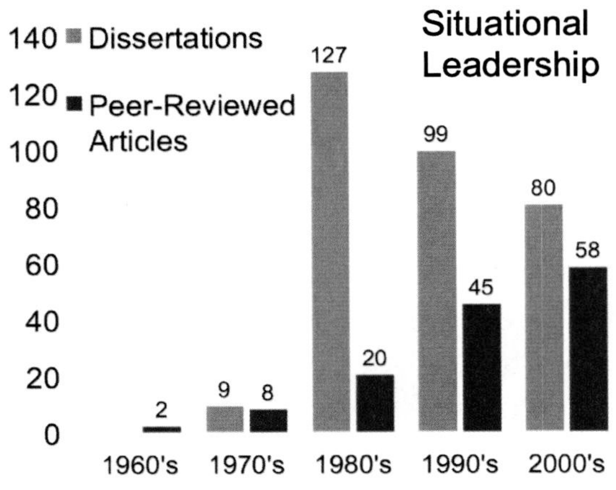

Task, Relationship and Situation

Situational Leadership
The Four Situations

Situational leadership generally consists of four situations.

Situation 1 – A Follower Who is Highly Committed, but not Particularly Competent

An easy way to imagine a follower who is high on commitment but low on competence, is a new worker. Imagine that the woman on the right has just begun her first professional job. She is making enough money to afford a car and an apartment. She likely wants to be employee of the year and to get promoted. But....she still hasn't mastered office politics, the demands of her job and so forth.

Leadership Style 1 – High Directing, Low Support

In this situation, situational leadership suggests that the preferred combination of leader behaviors is to be high on directing and low on supporting behaviors.

At first, this combination sounds a bit ominous. A good way to envision this leadership style is that of a benevolent micro-manager. The worker is already committed, or motivated – so much so that she or he likely annoys workers who have been in the organization for a while. The leader's task for this type of worker is to keep her or him out of trouble by engaging in close supervision until the follower masters the job.

Situation 2 – A Follower Who Is Highly Competent, but not Particularly Committed

One way to envision this situation is a worker who has been somewhat successful in the organization, but who is undergoing personal stress in her or his life. Imagine that the woman on the right has been promoted a few times, and is generally quite competent at her job. Imagine, however, that she has a child who is experiencing serious medical issues. Chances are that, for a period of time, her heart may not be completely in the job, as she is being pulled in multiple directions.

Leadership Style 2 – High Support, Low Directing

Here, situational leadership suggests that the preferred combination of leadership behaviors is to be high on supporting and low on directing behaviors.

This is a situation in which the leader may want to ask the follower if she or he would like to "get a cup of coffee," and then simply listen to the situation that is causing a typically highly committed employee to be distracted. The employee is very competent at her or his job. If the follower's performance is waning, it is not the result of a lack of leader supervision. Rather, it is the result of, what we hope, is a temporary tug of war going on in the life of the follower. Situational leadership advocates supporting the follower to help guide her or him back toward being both highly competent and committed.

Situational Leadership
The Four Situations

Situation 3 – A Follower Who is Highly Committed and Highly Competent

The third situation is an employee who is both really good at her or his job and highly motivated.

These followers are often high on what is called intrinsic, or internal job satisfaction. Intrinsic job satisfaction stems from the feelings of personal growth and achievement experienced as a result of doing one's job well.

Leadership Style 3 – Low Directing, Low Support

In this situation, situational leadership suggests that the preferred combination of leadership behaviors is to be low on directing and low on supporting behaviors. A good way to envision this leadership approach is one of empowering the follower.

The leader engages in roles such as acquiring needed resources for the follower and clarifying broad goals. Unlike the other two situations, however, the leader is neither "micro-managing" nor "asking if the follower wants to grab a cup of coffee." The leader respects the follower's motivation and skills and generally stays out of the way.

Situation 4 – A Follower Who is Moderately Committed and Moderately Competent[2]

More Committed,
Less Competent

A good way to envision the final situation is one that is in between the first two situations. Here we have a follower who has likely been in the organization for a period of time and has gained some competence, but has also gained a bit of jadedness, compared to the eager new follower. The follower in this situation is likely a bit less competent but more committed than the veteran who is going through a difficult time in her or his life.

Leadership Style 4 – High Directing, High Support

This fourth situation calls for a leader to be high on both directing and supporting. While this type of follower needs less supervision than the rookie, she or he still needs a mentor to guide her through the job. Because followers often experience disappointments in their career aspirations, this type of follower likely needs some support. Here the support is likely less frequent than that provided to the follower undergoing a temporary crisis in her or his life. The leader, however, still needs to periodically "check-in" with the follower on how she or he is feeling about the job, career goals and so forth.

Task, Relationship and Situation

Situational Leadership
Examples of the Directing Style

Leading a Follower Who is Highly Committed, but Not Particularly Competent

Situational leadership recommends a directing style of leadership with highly committed, but not particularly competent followers. With this style, the leader pays particular attention to the work that the follower is doing, trying to keep her or him out of trouble

Examples of the Directing Style of Leadership The remainder of this page provides examples of what a leader using the directing style might say to a follower who is high on commitment but low on competence.

Why don't we review how that works here.

Lets walk through what would have happened if you had done it that way.

Please follow these steps, in this order, to ensure a successful outcome.

Let me know when you have finished this section, and we can go over the next steps.

You have such a positive attitude. Let's go over these guidelines to make sure we are on track with what needs to be done next.

Let's review each of the steps and the outcome to see how we can help you improve your performance on this task next time.

We need to increase our accuracy on these reports. Let's look at what happened and determine what training or tools you might need to help improve for next time.

We've tweaked the work processes for this particular task – let me explain.

Everything looks good so far, please keep the team informed on your progress.

Here is a great example of the kind of reports you will be working on.

It is very important to complete these instructions as written in this guideline. Lets go over any questions you might have.

With just a little more time and practice, these processes will soon seem like second-nature.

Here is a checklist of items that you'll need to accomplish today. Please let me know if you have any questions.

Task, Relationship and Situation

Situational Leadership
Examples of the Coaching Style

Leading a Follower Who is Moderately Committed, and Moderately Competent

Situational leadership recommends a coaching style of leadership with moderately committed and moderately competent followers. With this style, the leader pays attention to the work that the follower is doing, but also serves as a mentor or coach.

Examples of the Coaching Style of Leadership The remainder of this page provides examples of what a leader using the coaching style might say to a follower who is moderately committed and moderately competent.

Since one of your career ambitions is to move up to vice president, there will be a few dissenters. Here are some ways you may want to tweak your proposal to accommodate their views.

Please look over this assignment, then let's get back together and decide on next steps.

Looks like you are making good progress on this project. Let the team know if you need any help.

This needs to be completed by the end of the week. Let's work together on the best method to use.

What do you think the best approach will be for the next stage of this project?

Your work on this portion of the project was especially helpful – thanks.

What are your views for improvements on this process?

Would you set up a meeting with the team to discuss your plans on the new directives?

Looks like we got a little pushback from the president. Where do you think we should start on the revisions?

What are your thoughts on the concerns raised by the board today?

I see your arms are crossed and you seem hesitant. Can you share with me what you are thinking?

This project calls for your particular talents and will hone your skills - good results here will get you noticed.

This assignment will be a challenge, but I think you will knock it out of the park.

Why don't you reflect on this division's quandary over the weekend, and let's discuss it on Monday.

Task, Relationship and Situation

Situational Leadership
Examples of the Supporting Style

Leading a Follower Who is not Particularly Committed, but Highly Competent

Situational leadership recommends a supporting style of leadership with a highly competent but not particularly committed follower. With this style, the leader supports the follower. This is typically for an abbreviated period of time while the follower regains her or his commitment.

Examples of the Supporting Style of Leadership The remainder of this page provides examples of what a leader using the supporting style might say to a follower who has low commitment but is highly competent.

I can only imagine what you are going through.

You've always done great here.

You'll get through this, and we'll figure out some way to make it work here in the mean time.

What can we do to make your job easier as you transition through this issue?

Tell me what you think about temporarily rearranging your schedule until this issue has been resolved.

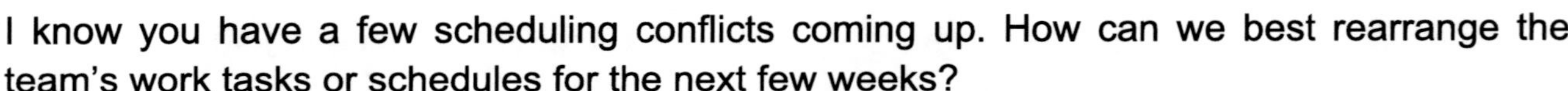

I know you have a few scheduling conflicts coming up. How can we best rearrange the team's work tasks or schedules for the next few weeks?

Here are a few ideas that helped me when I went through a similar experience.

I've noticed you have been a little distracted lately. Would you like to discuss what's going on?

Seems like things have been a bit rough for you lately. Let's talk about what we can do to help reduce some of the stress.

You must miss the old team, but we can certainly use your unique talents to make this team just as successful.

We're all so glad to see you back at work. Would you like some temporary help for the first few days?

Task, Relationship and Situation

Situational Leadership
Examples of the Delegating Style

Leading a Follower Who is Highly Committed and Highly Competent

Situational leadership recommends a delegating style of leadership with a highly committed and highly competent follower. With this style, the leader empowers the follower to continue doing a great job.

Examples of the Delegating Style of Leadership The remainder of this page provides examples of what a leader using the delegating style might say to a follower who has high commitment and is highly competent.

I don't know what we would do without you.

What can I do to help?

Great job. Would you be willing to mentor Jake on a similar project?

Thanks for your excellent presentation. Are you available to present this information to the executive board next week?

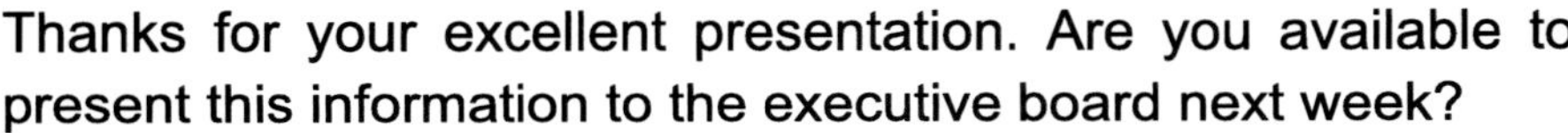

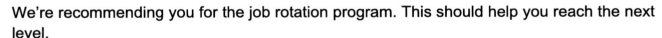

We're recommending you for the job rotation program. This should help you reach the next level.

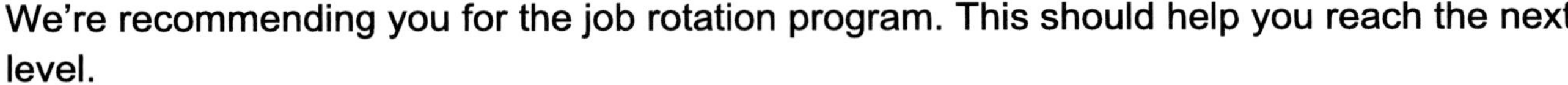

Congratulations – the team lead position is yours.

This product is really taking off. We need you to take charge of the team for the next phase of the launch.

You have strategic and operational responsibility for getting the production line up and running by the end of the year. Can you tell me what you'll need by the end of the month?

This department needs your leadership to implement the new direction set by the incoming president.

Please pull together a team of our best employees to finalize this initiative.

It's a very visible project – let's see what you can do.

We'll need you to help on a strategic plan for this new division.

I need a partner and this stage of the project calls for your brand of expertise.

It's time to turn this enterprise over to you and your team.

We are referring the client to you. You are our subject matter expert in this area.

Task, Relationship and Situation

The Leader Behavior Description Questionnaire

The situational leadership model has instruments, called the *Leader Behavior Analysis II,* the *Leader Action Profile* and the *Leader Effectiveness and Adaptability Description* associated with the theory. No peer-reviewed articles, however, were located that reported validity or reliability[3] for the instruments. Similarly, while there are some self-assessment instruments associated with the managerial grid, none have been analyzed in the peer-reviewed literature.

The instrument most frequently used to measure initiating structure and consideration is the *Leader Behavior Description Questionnaire XII.*

The Leader Behavior Description Questionnaire XII Development

1950 to 1957

Hemphill and colleagues at The Ohio State University brainstormed 1,800 possible leader behaviors, and then selected 150 behaviors they believed could be uniquely assigned to subscales.[4]

Factor Analyses indicated that the questions loaded on two main components: consideration and initiation of structure.

This produced the original *Leader Behavior Description Questionnaire* that had 40 questions and measured these two leader dimensions.

1957 to 1963

Additional work continued to develop more subscales that were related to initiation of structure and consideration, yet were also different. Through additional factor analyses, this research produced the twelve scales of the *LBDQ XII* shown on the next page.

Nine different reliability studies were conducted on groups of army members, highway patrol members, aircraft executives, ministers, community leaders, corporation presidents, labor presidents, college presidents and senators. The Kuder-Richardson measure of internal reliability was calculated for each of these nine samples. Similar to a Cronbach Alpha score, the Kuder-Richardson score ranges from 0 to 1. The closer the score is to 1, the more internally consistent the questions. The Kuder-Richardson scores for each of the 12 subscales for each of the nine samples generally fell between 0.54 and 0.87.[5]

1963 to 1989

The following six versions related to the *LBDQ* were developed.

a) *LBDQ XII Leader* (Stogdill, 1963)
b) *LBDQ XII Ideal Leader* (Stogdill, 1963)
c) *LBDQ XII Self* (Stogdill, 1963)
d) *LBDQ XII Ideal Self* (Stogdill, 1963)
e) *Supervisory Behavior Description Questionnaire* (Fleishman, 1989)
f) *Leader Opinion Questionnaire* (Fleishman, 1989)

Task, Relationship and Situation
The Leader Behavior Description Questionnaire

Components of the *Leader Behavior Description Questionnaire XII*

1. **Representation** – speaks and acts as the representative of the group. (5 items)
2. **Demand Reconciliation** – reconciles conflicting demands and reduces disorder to systems. (5 items)
3. **Tolerance of Uncertainty** – is able to tolerate uncertainty and postponement without anxiety or becoming upset. (10 items)
4. **Persuasiveness** – uses persuasion and argument effectively; exhibits strong convictions. (10 items)
5. **Initiation of Structure** – clearly defines own role, and lets followers know what is expected. (10 items)
6. **Tolerance and Freedom** - allows followers scope for initiative, decision and action. (10 items)
7. **Role Assumption** – actively exercises the leadership role rather than surrendering leadership to others. (10 items)
8. **Consideration** – regards the comfort, well-being, status, and contributions of followers. (10 items)
9. **Production Emphasis** – applies pressure for productive output. (10 items)
10. **Predictive Accuracy** – exhibits foresight and an ability to predict outcomes accurately. (5 items)
11. **Integration** – maintains a closely knit organization; resolves inter-member conflicts. (5 items)
12. **Superior Orientation** – maintains cordial relations with superiors; has influence with them; is striving for higher status. (10 items)

Analysis of the LBDQ-Related Instruments

A review of the LBDQ-related instruments that measure initiating structure and consideration was performed by Judge, Piccolo and Ilies (2004).[6] These authors located 117 journal articles and 13 dissertations that reported a total of 593 correlations computed from 457 independent samples related to consideration and/or initiating structure. The LBDQ-related instruments included in their study were:

The *Leader Behavior Description Questionnaire,* LBDQ (Halpin, 1957)
The *LBDQ Form XII*, LBDQ XII (Stogdill, 1963)
The *Supervisory Behavior Description Questionnaire*, SBDQ (Fleishman, 1989)
The *Leader Opinion Questionnaire*, LOQ (Fleishman, 1989)

The researchers reviewed to what degree initiating structure and consideration were related to the six outcomes of leadership shown below. They also "combined" those six outcomes into one larger analysis in which the combined outcomes were called *leadership criteria*.

a) Follower Job Satisfaction
b) Follower Satisfaction with the Leader
c) Follower Motivation
d) Leader Job Performance
e) Group–Organization Performance
f) Leader Effectiveness.

} Leadership Criteria

When only analyzing the *LBDQ XII*, there were 86 correlations (K = 86, N = 13,110, ρ = .54) meta-analyzed for consideration and leadership criteria. The estimated true score correlation was .54. For the initiating structure scale of the *LBDQ XII*, (K = 86, N = 12,945, ρ = .32) there were also 86 correlations and the estimated true score correlation was .32.

Judge, Piccolo and Ilies concluded:

> Overall, the results provide important support for the validity of initiating structure and consideration in leadership research.[7]
>
> The overall validities did not differ between published and unpublished dissertations and journal articles.
>
> With the exception of consideration in business versus in public sector settings, whether the study was done in a business, college, military or public sector setting didn't seem to impact the average validity of consideration or initiating structure.

Summary

Like most instruments, the *LBDQ XII* has limitations. It is, however, a widely used measure of leadership. There is much more research on the two scales of initiating structure and consideration, than the other 10 scales of the instrument.

The entire *LBDQ XII* questionnaire is 100 questions in length. Given the challenge of convincing followers to answer 100 questions about their leader and the lack of research on the other 10 scales, using just the two scales of initiating structure and consideration is likely a good choice for masters theses or doctoral dissertation research.

As of 2013, the LBDQ-XII was available for use by researchers, free of charge, from the Fisher College of Business at The Ohio State University.[8] The instrument and users' manuals for the various versions of the instrument are available for download.

Task, Relationship and Situation
Research Results

Understanding the Research Results for Initiation of Structure and Consideration

There is a great deal of research on the task and relationship aspects of leadership in the forms of initiation of structure and consideration from the *Leader Behavior Description Questionnaire*. To prepare you for understanding the research results that follow, chapter 2 explained both correlations and meta-analyses. The table below, however, provides a quick review of how the results of the meta-analytic literature will be provided in this chapter.[9]

Example - Leader Initiation of Structure and Follower Motivation

In the example below, 11 studies have been published and meta-analyzed on the relationship between a leader's use of initiation of structure and follower motivation. The notation (B) refers to the meta-analytic study. A list of the studies referenced is provided at the end of this chapter.

The 11 studies meta-analyzed collectively represent 1,067 follower ratings. The meta-analytic finding was a strong, positive correlation (.50). The more initiation of structure a leader used, the higher the follower motivation.

Strongly - Correlated	Moderately - Correlated	Weakly - Correlated
-1 to -.50	-.49 to -.30	-.29 to -.10

Weakly + Correlated	Moderately + Correlated	Strongly + Correlated
.10 to .29	.30 to .49	.50 to 1

Outcome	Studies	Followers	
Follower Motivation (B)	11	1,067	.50

Task, Relationship and Situation
Research Results

Leader Initiation of Structure and Follower Outcomes

Strongly - Correlated	Moderately - Correlated	Weakly - Correlated	Weakly + Correlated	Moderately + Correlated	Strongly + Correlated
-1 to -.50	-.49 to -.30	-.29 to -.10	.10 to .29	.30 to .49	.50 to 1

Outcome	Studies	Followers	
Very Weakly, Positively Correlated			
Satisfaction with Pay (D)	15	2,339	.00
Satisfaction with Promotion Opportunities (D)	14	1,026	.02
Overall Job Satisfaction (C)	42	3,912	.09
Intrinsic Job Satisfaction (C)	55	8,098	.09
Weakly, Positively Correlated			
Satisfaction with the Work Itself (D)	38	5,205	.12
Satisfaction with Co-workers (D)	18	3,757	.12
Job Performance (C)	76	7,030	.16
Follower Job Satisfaction (B)	76	10,317	.22
Strongly, Positively Correlated			
Follower Motivation (B)	11	1,067	.50

	Outcome	Studies	Followers
Moderately, Negatively Correlated			
-.34	Organizational Stress (C)	33	6,205

Research from 367 analyses (effect sizes) that have included 47,889 follower ratings indicates that a leader's use of initiation of structure is weakly, positively correlated with increased follower satisfaction in a variety of work areas.

Initiation of structure is strongly, positively correlated with follow motivation and moderately, negatively correlated with organizational stress.

Task, Relationship and Situation
Research Results

Leader Consideration and Follower Outcomes

Strongly - Correlated	Moderately - Correlated	Weakly - Correlated	Weakly + Correlated	Moderately + Correlated	Strongly + Correlated
-1 to -.50	-.49 to -.30	-.29 to -.10	.10 to .29	.30 to .49	.50 to 1

Outcome	Studies	Followers	
Weakly, Positively Correlated			
Satisfaction with Co-workers (D)	19	2,783	.26
Satisfaction with the Work Itself (D)	45	5,193	.26
Satisfaction with Promotion Opportunities (D)	17	1,762	.27
Satisfaction with Pay (D)	16	1,365	.29
Job Performance (C)	76	7,030	.29
Moderately, Positively Correlated			
Follower Motivation (B)	12	1,041	.40
Follower Job Satisfaction (B)	72	11,374	.46
Strongly, Positively Correlated			
Overall Job Satisfaction (C)	42	3,912	.52
Intrinsic Job Satisfaction (C)	55	8,098	.71

	Outcome	Studies	Followers
Moderately, Negatively Correlated			
-.40	Organizational Stress (C)	33	6,205

Research from 387 analyses (effect sizes) that have included 48,763 follower ratings indicates that leaders' use of consideration is weakly correlated with increased follower satisfaction in a variety of work areas.

Leader consideration is moderately correlated with follower motivation and strongly correlated with overall job satisfaction and intrinsic job satisfaction.

Leader consideration was moderately, negatively correlated with organizational stress.

Task, Relationship and Situation
Research Results

Initiation of Structure and Leader Outcomes

Strongly - Correlated	Moderately - Correlated	Weakly - Correlated	Weakly + Correlated	Moderately + Correlated	Strongly + Correlated
-1 to -.50	-.49 to -.30	-.29 to -.10	.10 to .29	.30 to .49	.50 to 1

Outcome	Studies	Followers	
Moderately, Positively Correlated			
Follower Satisfaction with Supervision (D)	52	8,717	.31
Follower Satisfaction with Leader (B)	49	8,070	.33
Leader Job Performance (B)	22	2,085	.36
Leader Effectiveness (B)	20	1,960	.39
Strongly, Positively Correlated			
Organizational Based, Self Esteem (E)[10]	4	953	.58

Research from 147 studies (effect sizes) that have included 21,785 follower ratings indicates that a leader's use of initiation of structure is moderately correlated with satisfaction with the leader and ratings of leader performance. Initiation of structure is strongly correlated with organizational based self esteem.

Leader Consideration and Leader Outcomes

Strongly - Correlated	Moderately - Correlated	Weakly - Correlated	Weakly + Correlated	Moderately + Correlated	Strongly + Correlated
-1 to -.50	-.49 to -.30	-.29 to -.10	.10 to .29	.30 to .49	.50 to 1

Outcome	Studies	Followers	
Weakly, Positively Correlated			
Leader Job Performance (B)	25	2,330	.25
Moderately, Positively Correlated			
Organizational Based, Self Esteem (E)[11]	9	1,120	.43
Strongly, Positively Correlated			
Leader Effectiveness (B)	20	1,605	.52
Follower Satisfaction with Leader (B)	49	7,871	.78
Follower Satisfaction with Supervision (D)	55	7,640	.80

Research from 158 studies (effect sizes) that have included 20,566 follower ratings indicates that a leader's use of consideration is weakly correlated with leader job performance and strongly correlated with ratings of leader effectiveness and satisfaction with the leader.

Research Results

Leader Initiation of Structure and Team Outcomes

Strongly - Correlated	Moderately - Correlated	Weakly - Correlated	Weakly + Correlated	Moderately + Correlated	Strongly + Correlated
-1 to -.50	-.49 to -.30	-.29 to -.10	.10 to .29	.30 to .49	.50 to 1

Outcome	Studies	Followers	
Weakly, Positively Correlated			
Team Productivity/Quantity (A) Note. N = Number of Teams	6	271	.20
Moderately, Positively Correlated			
Group-Organization Performance (B)	27	2,079	.30
Perceived Team Effectiveness (A) Note. N = Number of Teams	25	1,655	.33

Research from 58 studies (effect sizes) indicates that a leader's use of initiation of structure is both weakly and moderately, positively correlated with multiple team outcomes.

Leader Consideration and Team Outcome

Strongly - Correlated	Moderately - Correlated	Weakly - Correlated	Weakly + Correlated	Moderately + Correlated	Strongly + Correlated
-1 to -.50	-.49 to -.30	-.29 to -.10	.10 to .29	.30 to .49	.50 to 1

Outcome	Studies	Followers	
Weakly, Positively Correlated			
Team Productivity/Quantity (A) *Note. N = Number of Teams*	*24*	1,396	.28
Group-Organization Performance (B)	*27*	2,008	.28
Moderately, Positively Correlated			
Perceived Team Effectiveness (A) [12] *Note. N = Number of Teams*	*55*	3,139	.36
Strongly, Positively Correlated			
Team Learning (A) *Note. N = Number of Teams*	*3*	200	.56

Research from 109 studies (effect sizes) indicates that a leader's use of consideration is weakly, positively correlated with some team outcomes, moderately, positively correlated with perceived team effectiveness and strongly, positively, positively correlated with team learning.

Task, Relationship and Situation
Meta-Analytic Regressions

Meta-Analytic Regressions Related to Initiation of Structure and Consideration
The next five pages summarize the meta-analytic regression research related to initiation of structure and consideration.

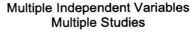

Meta-analyses provided earlier in this chapter analyzed one independent variable at a time. The meta-analytic regressions that follow include multiple independent variables simultaneously.

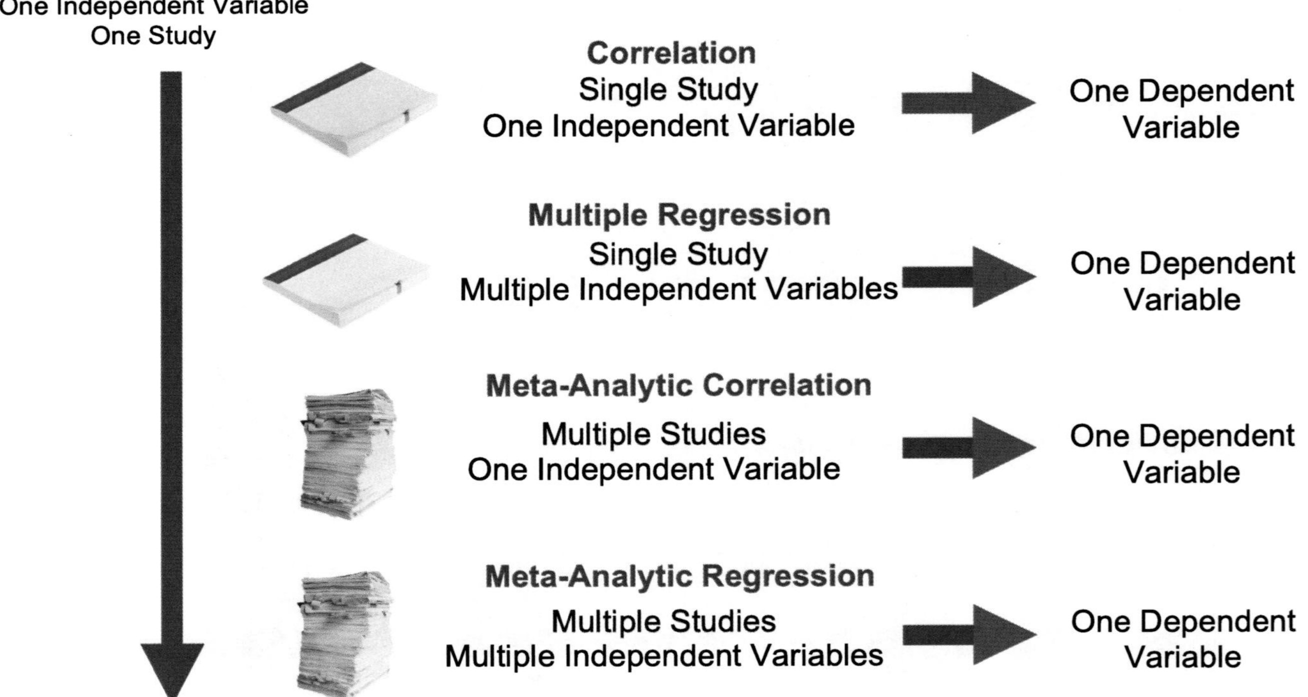

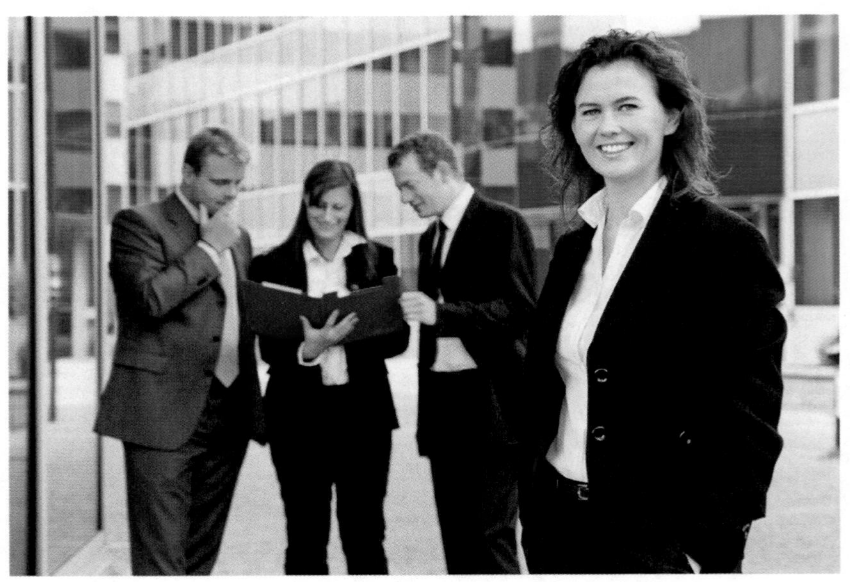

Task, Relationship and Situation

Meta-Analytic Regressions

Leader Consideration, Initiation of Structure and Leader Transformational Behaviors

Piccolo, Bono, Heinitz, Rowold, Duehr and Judge (2012) performed a meta-analysis of 11 studies that included consideration, initiation of structure and transformational leadership as well as measures for follower job satisfaction and assessments of leader effectiveness. One of the findings was that transformational leadership was strongly, positively correlated with consideration (*rho* = .74) and was also strongly, positively correlated with initiation of structure (*rho* = .50).

The authors ran meta-analytic regression analyses to analyze which of the three aspects of leadership were the strongest predictors of follower job satisfaction and leader effectiveness. The relationship numbers shown below are the standardized regression weights.

When analyzed individually, all three aspects of leadership were meta-analytically correlated with follower job satisfaction. When analyzed together in a meta-analytic regression, only consideration and transformational leadership were significant predictors of follower job satisfaction (total R^2 = .21).

Meta-Analytic Regression to Predict Follower Job Satisfaction **(Standardized Regression Weights)**

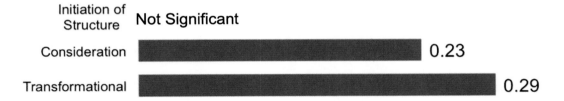

Meta-Analytic Regression to Predict Leader Effectiveness **(Standardized Regression Weights)**

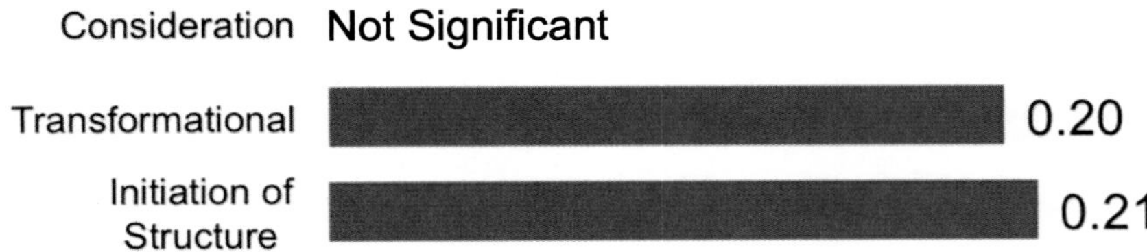

In the meta-analytic regression to predict leader effectiveness consideration was not significant, but both transformational leadership and initiation of structure were positively related to ratings of leader effectiveness (total R^2 = .20).

Task, Relationship and Situation

Meta-Analytic Regressions

Leader Consideration, Initiation of Structure, Full Range Model, Personality, Gender and Intelligence Predicting Leader Effectiveness

Derue, Nahrgang, Wellman and Humphrey (2011) conducted a meta-analytic multiple regression using data from 59 studies. For the multiple regression 14 predictor variables were used:

Leader Gender and Intelligence
The Big Five Domains of Leader Personality
Transformational, Contingent Reward, MBE-Active, MBE-Passive and Laissez-Faire
Initiation of Structure and Consideration

The chart below provides the strength of each variable in predicting leader effectiveness. The number provided is the R^2 value.[13] The total R^2 for all of the variables was .58, and 42% of the variance in leader effectiveness was unexplained when using only these 14 predictors. For those variables with a blue bar, the direction of the relationship was positive. For those variables with a red bar, the direction of the relationship was negative.

Predictors of Leader Effectiveness (R^2 Values)

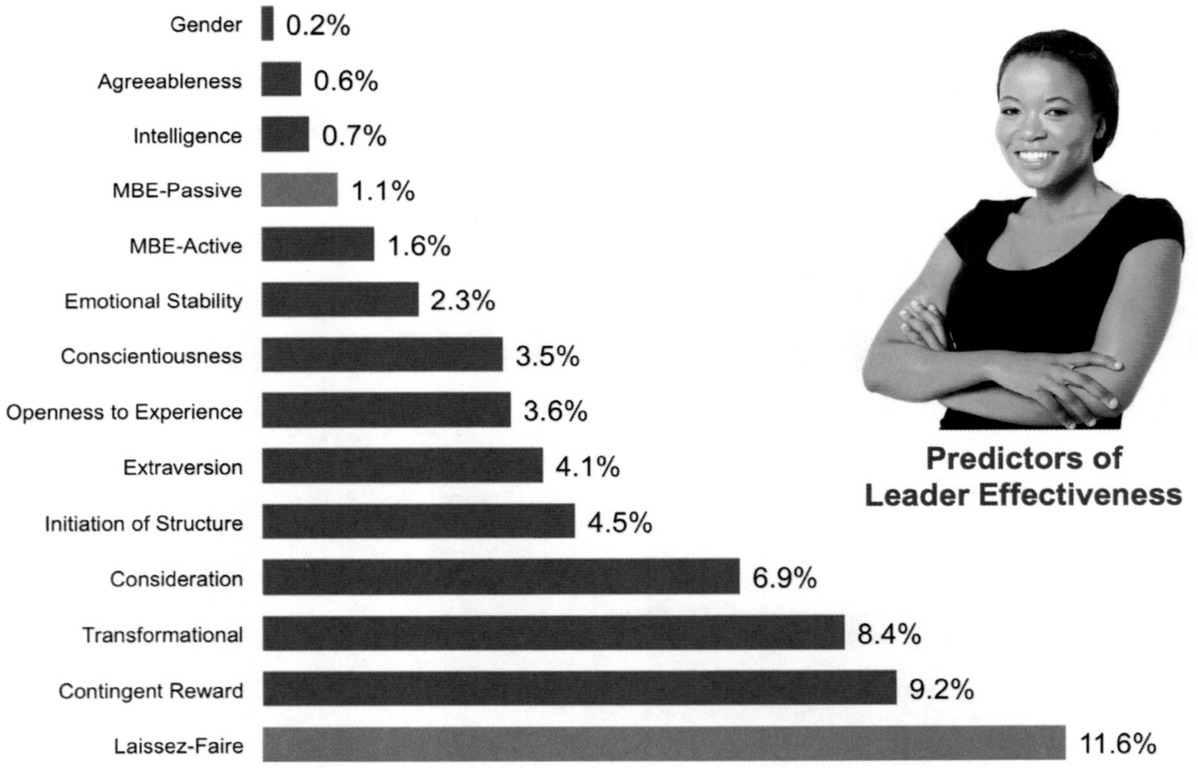

The four strongest predictors of ratings of leader effectiveness were leader consideration, leader transformational behaviors, leader use of contingent reward and leaders not engaging in laissez-faire behaviors.

Task, Relationship and Situation
Meta-Analytic Regressions

Leader Consideration, Initiation of Structure, Full Range Model, Personality and Intelligence Predicting Group Performance

Derue, Nahrgang, Wellman and Humphrey (2011) conducted a meta-analytic multiple regression using data from 59 studies. For the multiple regression 12 predictor variables were used:

Leader Intelligence
The Big Five Domains of Leader Personality
Transformational, Contingent Reward, MBE-Active and MBE-Passive
Initiation of Structure and Consideration

The chart below provides the strength of each variable in predicting group performance. The number provided is the R^2 value. The total R^2 for all of the variables was .31, and 69% of the variance in group performance was unexplained when using only these 12 predictors. For those variables with a blue bar, the direction of the relationship was positive. For those variables with a red bar, the direction of the relationship was negative.

Predictors of Group Performance (R^2 Values)

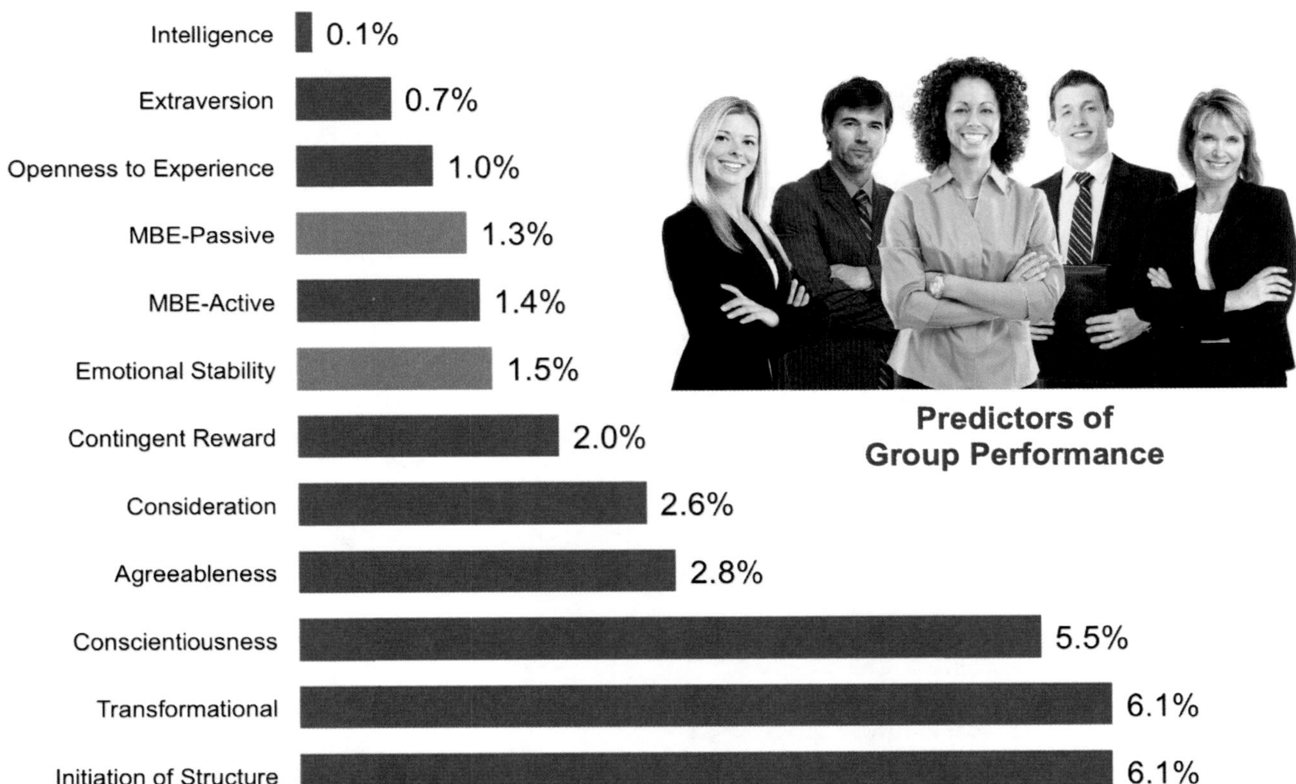

The strongest predictors of group performance were leader conscientiousness, leader transformational behaviors and leader initiation of structure.

Task, Relationship and Situation
Meta-Analytic Regressions

Leader Consideration, Initiation of Structure, Full Range Model, Personality and Gender Predicting Follower Job Satisfaction

Derue, Nahrgang, Wellman and Humphrey (2011) conducted a meta-analytic multiple regression using data from 59 studies. For the multiple regression 13 predictor variables were used:

Leader Gender
The Big Five Domains of Leader Personality
Transformational, Contingent Reward, MBE-Active, MBE-Passive and Laissez-Faire
Initiation of Structure and Consideration

The chart below provides the strength of each variable in predicting follower job satisfaction. The number provided is the R^2 value. The total R^2 for all of the variables was .56 and 44% of the variance in follower job satisfaction was unexplained when using only these 13 predictors. For those variables with a blue bar, the direction of the relationship was positive. For those variables with a red bar, the direction of the relationship was negative.

Predictors of Job Satisfaction (R^2 Values)

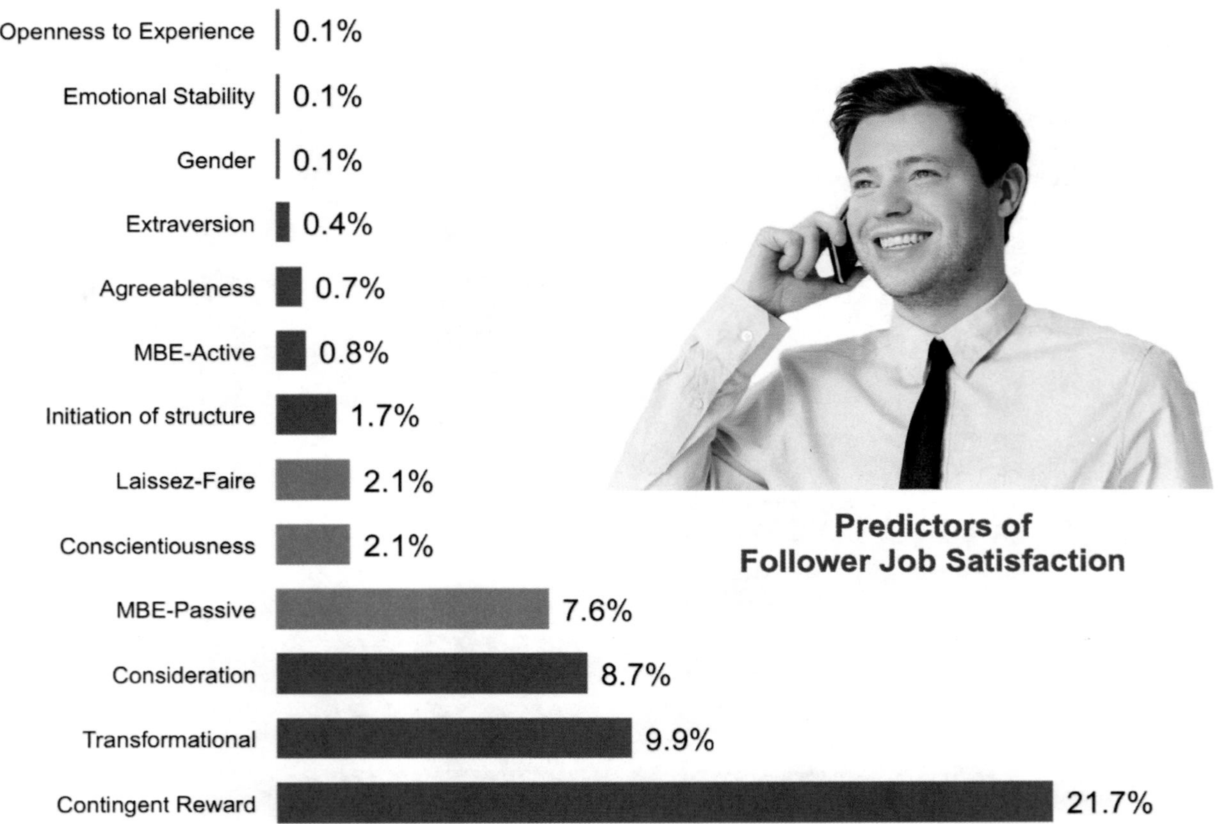

Predictors of Follower Job Satisfaction

When all thirteen variables were used to predict follower job satisfaction, leader use of contingent reward was a much stronger predictor than the remaining variables.

Leader Consideration, Initiation of Structure, Full Range Model, Personality, Gender and Intelligence Predicting Satisfaction with the Leader

Derue, Nahrgang, Wellman and Humphrey (2011) conducted a meta-analytic multiple regression using data from 59 studies. For the multiple regression 13 predictor variables were used:

Leader Gender
The Big Five Domains of Leader Personality
Transformational, Contingent Reward, MBE-Active, MBE-Passive and Laissez-Faire
Initiation of Structure and Consideration

The chart below provides the strength of each variable in predicting satisfaction with the leader. The total R^2 for all of the variables was .92, and 8% of the variance in satisfaction with the leader was unexplained when using only these 13 predictors. For those variables with a blue bar, the direction of the relationship was positive. For those variables with a red bar, the direction of the relationship was negative.

Predictors of Satisfaction with the Leader (R^2 Values)

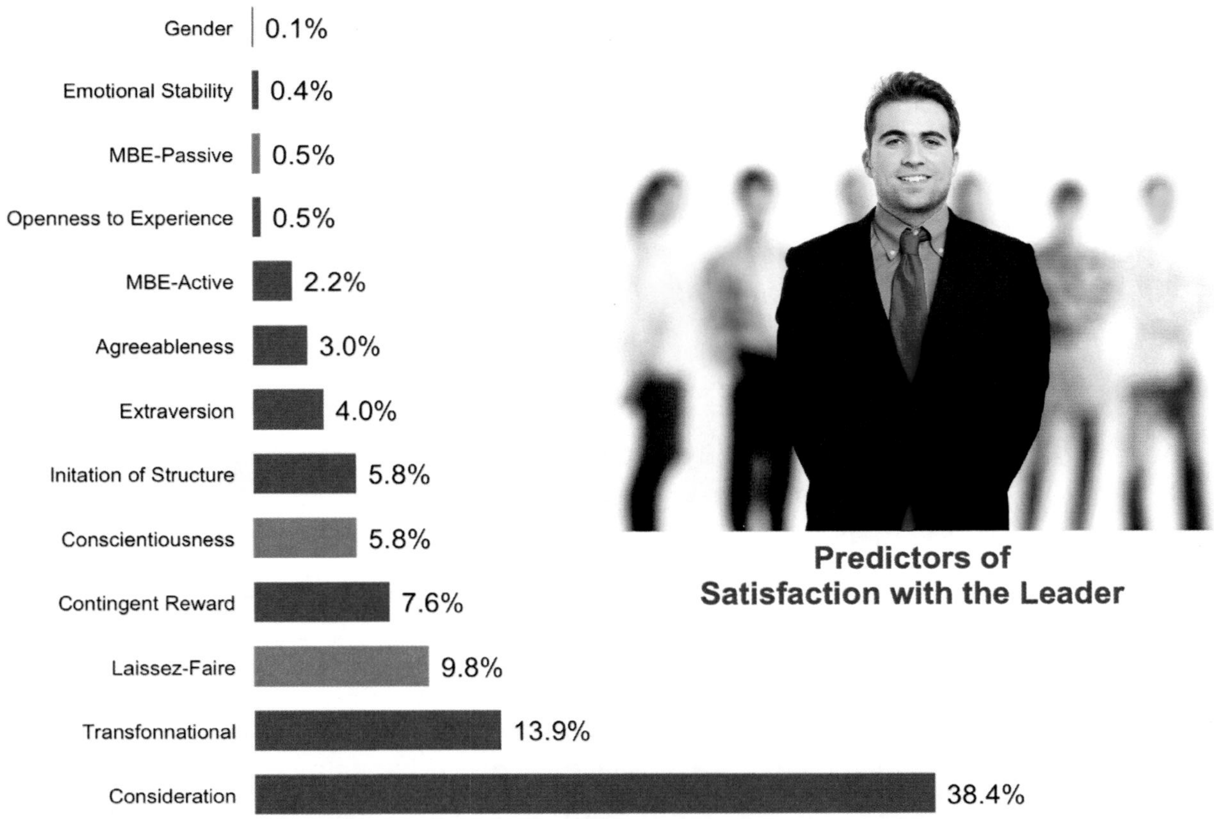

The strongest predictor of satisfaction with the leader was leader consideration. Being transformational and not being laissez-faire were also noteworthy predictors.

Task, Relationship and Situation
Summary

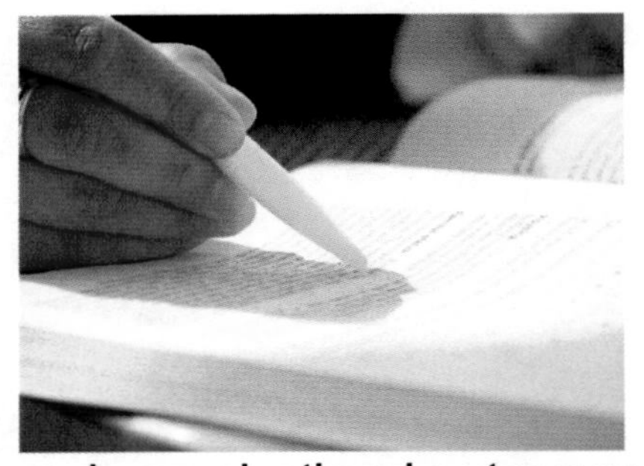

Leader Emphasis on Tasks is Important

Leader Emphasis on Relationships is Really Important

The results of the research on the leader behaviors of task (initiation of structure, production emphasis) and relationship (consideration, relationship orientation, employee orientation) indicate that both are positively related to a range of leader, follower and organizational outcomes. In particular, however, developing a good relationship with our followers is very important.

Situational Leadership

In situational leadership, the idea of caring for our followers can take several forms.

Situation 1 – A Follower Who is Highly Committed, but not Particularly Competent With this type of follower, situational leadership posits that we should be micro-managers and low on relationship behaviors. It's important to view the high directive behaviors, however, as a way of taking care of this type of follower by keeping her or him out of trouble until the follower has mastered the job.

Situation 2 – A Follower Who Is Highly Competent, but not Particularly Committed With this type of follower, situational leadership suggests being high on supportive or consideration behaviors. Here taking care of the follower entails helping her or him to make it through a difficult period and then become re-engaged in the job.

Situation 3 – A Follower Who Is Highly Competent, and Highly Committed At first being low on both directive and supportive behaviors sounds like an absence of leadership. In this situation, however, taking care of the follower connotes giving her or him a great deal of earned respect through empowering behaviors.

Situation 4 – A Follower Who Is Moderately Competent, and Moderately Committed In this situation, situational leadership suggests being high on both task and relationship. The meta-analytic research indicates that both of these leader behaviors are related to followers being satisfied with the leader and work, being motivated and performing well.

Task, Relationship and Situation
Notes

Studies Referenced in the Summaries of Meta-Analyses

A. Kinicki, Stagl, Klein, Goodwin, Salas and Halpin (2006). Measures used were task-focused leadership and person-focused leadership. The statistic reported is the average correlation, weighted by the inverse of effect size sampling error.

B. Judge, Piccolo and Ilies (2004). Measures used were initiating structure and consideration. The statistic reported is the estimated true score correlation.

C. Fisher and Edwards (1988). Measures used were initiating structure and consideration. The statistic reported is the average correlation corrected for sample size, range restriction and unreliability.

D. Kinicki, McKee-Ryan, Schriesheim and Carson (2002). Measures used were initiating structure and consideration. The statistic reported is the weighted average correlation corrected for unreliability.

E. Bowling (2010). Measures used were initiating structure and consideration. The statistic reported is the average weighted correlation coefficient corrected for unreliability

Notes

[1] Hersey, P., & Blanchard, K. H. (1969). Life cycle theory of leadership. *Training & Development Journal*, 23, 26– 34.; Hersey, P., & Blanchard, K. H. (1969). *Management of organizational behavior.* Englewood Cliffs, NJ: Prentice-Hall.

[2] Over the years, the follower combinations for this aspect of situational leadership have had different labels. The somewhat adjective seems to describe this quadrant well for most graduate students.

[3] The *Leader Behavior Analysis II* has been used in two peer-reviewed articles. No peer-reviewed articles were found that used the *Leader Action Profile*, and about 15 using the *Leader Effectiveness and Adaptability Description*. Peer-reviewed articles using the *Leader Effectiveness and Adaptability Description* tended to be studies in nursing and education.

[4] The information from this summary primarily comes from Bass, B. M., and Bass, R. (2008). *The Bass handbook of leadership: Theory, research, and managerial applications*. New York: Free Press; and from Stogdill, R. M. (1963). *Manual for the Leader Behavior Description Questionnaire Form XII.* Columbus: Ohio State University, Bureau of Business Research.

[5] From the LBDQ User's Manual (1963). One outlier, the Senators sample and the scale of Consideration had a Kuder-Richardson score of 0.38. The possible jokes that could be made are legion.

[6] Judge, T. A., Piccolo, R. F. and Ilies, R. (2004). The forgotten ones? The validity of consideration and initiating structure in leadership research. *The Journal of Applied Psychology,* 89, 1, 36-51.

[7] Verbatim from their study

[8] As of 2013 the link for the instrument and manuals was http://fisher.osu.edu/research/lbdq/

If that link doesn't work, most search engines will find the instrument at Ohio State University.

[9] The exact boundary between weak, moderate and strong correlations is not universally agreed upon. The definitions used are based on Cohen, J. (1992). A power primer. *Psychological Bulletin, 112,* 1, 155-9.

[10] Bowling, N. (2010) defined the construct of organization-based self-esteem (OBSE) as "...represents employees' beliefs about their own value and competence as organizational members."

[11] Bowling, N. (2010) defined the construct of organization-based self-esteem (OBSE) as "...represents employees' beliefs about their own value and competence as organizational members."

[12] Table 3 of the Burke article reports this relationship as r = .036, but the article text reports it as r = .36. The latter seems to be correct as the 95% confidence intervals in Table 3 were .301 to .416.

[13] The authors reported epsilon values. For the three charts provided from this study the R^2 values shown were calculate by dividing the relative weight of each predictor (epsilon) by the total R^2.

Task, Relationship and Situation

Notes

Chapter 4
The Full Range Model of Leadership

The Full Range Model of Leadership

Introduction

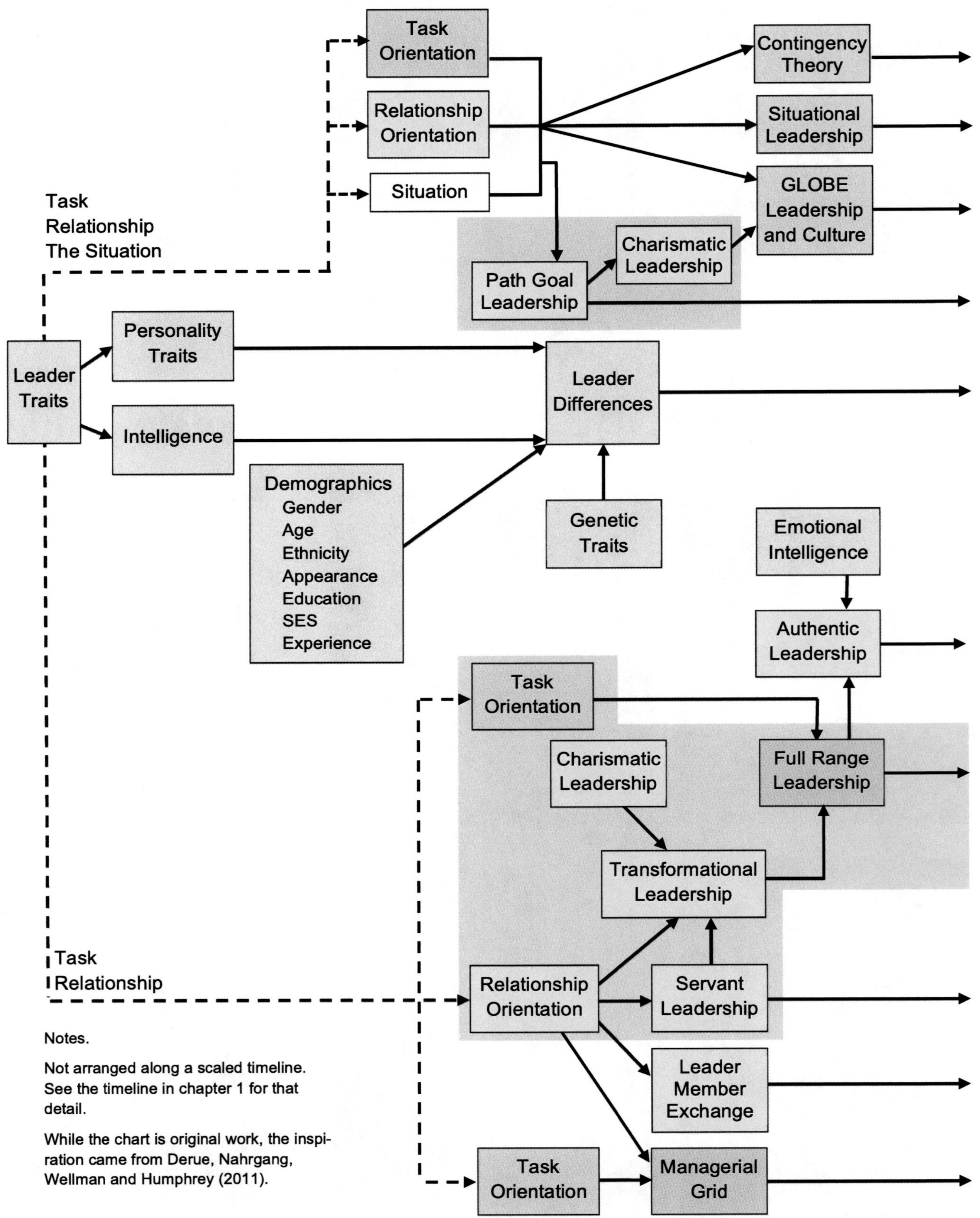

Notes.

Not arranged along a scaled timeline. See the timeline in chapter 1 for that detail.

While the chart is original work, the inspiration came from Derue, Nahrgang, Wellman and Humphrey (2011).

The Full Range Model of Leadership

Introduction

After the search for traits that distinguished between effective and ineffective leaders waned, research shifted to leader behaviors.

On the page on the left, the bottom, shaded area, indicates that charismatic leadership, as well as the idea of relationship oriented behaviors and servant leadership influenced writers' ideas about transformational leadership.

When task oriented behaviors were paired with transformational leadership, a broader range of leadership behaviors was envisioned, currently called the full range model of leadership.

The graph below provides a slightly more synthetic view of some of the important influences on the development of the full-range model of leadership.

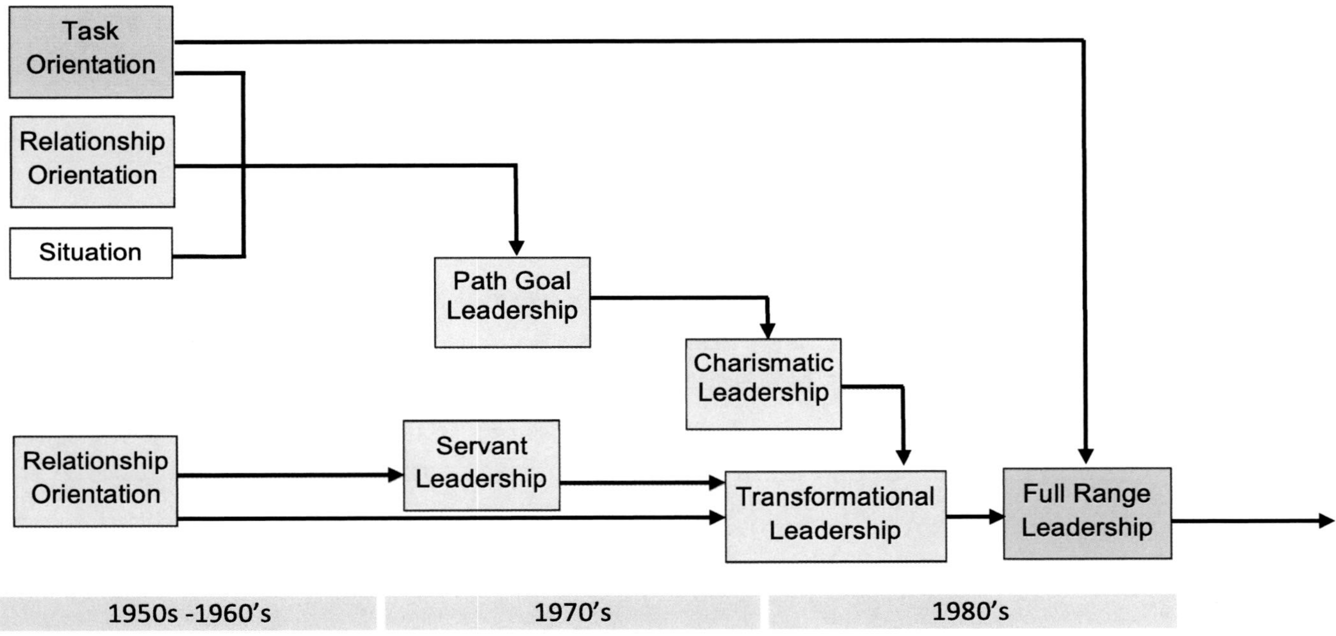

This chapter will review the following theories.

Path-Goal Theory
Charismatic Leadership
Transformational Leadership
The Full Range Model of Leadership

And one instrument:

The *Multifactor Leadership Questionnaire 5X*

Finally, the meta-analytic literature related to transformational/the full range model of leadership will be summarized.

The Full Range Model of Leadership

Antecedents

Path-Goal Theory

Path-Goal Theory

While originally published in 1971, House updated his ideas in 1996 in what he called *The 1996 Path-Goal Theory of Work Unit Leadership*. This theory advanced seven aspects of leadership.[1]

Directive Path-Goal Clarifying Leader Behavior is behavior directed toward providing psychological structure for subordinates.

Supportive Leader Behavior is behavior directed toward the satisfaction of subordinates' needs and preferences.

Participative Leader Behavior is behavior directed toward the encouragement of subordinate influence on decision-making and work unit operations.

Achievement Oriented Behavior is behavior directed toward encouraging performance excellence.

Work Facilitation is behavior that consists of planning, scheduling and organizing work.

Interaction Facilitation is behavior that facilitates collaborative and positive interaction.

Group Oriented Decision Process consists of behaviors such as posing problems, not solutions, identifying mutual interests of group members with respect to solving problems and encouraging all members of the group to participate in a discussion.

Representation and Networking is the ability of work units to acquire resources to perform the tasks for which they are responsible.

Value Based Leader Behavior[2] includes the ability to expect high performance outcomes from others on the basis of firmly held, core beliefs.

While slightly more complex than the flowchart shown, Neider and Schriesheim (1988) provided a model with some of the elements that capture the idea of a leader helping a follower create a path toward a goal.

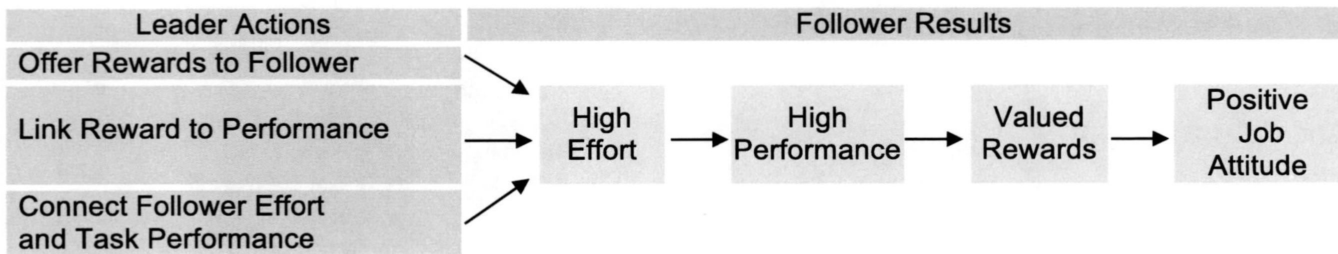

The Full Range Model of Leadership

Antecedents
Charismatic Leadership

Conger and Kanungo developed a popular model of charismatic leadership. Their model contains five behavioral factors. Those five factors are measured by the *Conger-Kanungo Scale of Charismatic Leadership.*

Strategic Vision and Articulation
Sensitivity to the Environment
Sensitivity to Member Needs
Personal Risk
Unconventional Behavior

Conger and Kanungo posited that these five leader behaviors are exhibited across three stages. Their three-stage model is shown below.

	Non-Charismatic Leader	Charismatic Leader[3]
Stage One: Environmental Assessment		
Environmental Sensitivity	Low Sensitivity to: Environmental Opportunities Environmental Constraints Followers' Needs	Heightened Sensitivity to: Environmental Opportunities Environmental Constraints Followers' Needs
Relation to Status Quo	Agree with and Maintain Status Quo	Intolerance with Shortcomings in Status Quo; Search for Change Opportunities
Stage Two: Vision Formulation		
Future Goals	Lack of Vision or Mission Orientation	Strong Vision or Mission Orientation; Shared and Idealized Future Vision
Likableness	Shared Perspective Makes the Executive Likable	Shared Perspective Plus Idealized Vision Makes the Executive Adorable
Articulation	Weak Articulation of Goals and Motivation to Lead	Strong Articulation of Goals and Motivation to Lead (Inspirational)
Stage Three: Implementation		
Behavior	Low Risk; Conventional and Conforming	High Risk; Use of Unconventional Tactics
Trustworthiness	Disinterested Advocacy in Persuasion Attempts	Passionate Advocacy Through Personal Examples; Engaging in Exemplary Acts That Subordinates Interpret as Involving Great Personal Risk and Sacrifice
Expertise	Use of Conventional Means	Use of Unconventional Means and Critiquing of Conventional Means

The Full Range Model of Leadership

Transformational Leadership

Burns

While there have been many contributions to the idea of transformational leadership, the theory was first fully described by Burns in 1978.

In his seminal book, *Leadership*, Burns contrasted leaders who helped transform those they lead to those who tended to engage in quid pro quo relationships.

Burns envisioned transformational and transactional leadership as separate entities. He also tended to write more about political leaders than organizational leaders.[4] Nonetheless, his work formed an important foundation for the development of proceeding theories.

Burns (1978) Transformational versus Transactional Leadership

	Transformational Leadership	Transactional Leadership
Goals	The Leader and Follower Are Presently or Potentially United in the Pursuit of "Higher" Goals	The Leader and Follower Have Separate and Possibly Unrelated Goals
Interests	There is the Achievement of Significant Change That Represents the Collective or Pooled Interests of Leaders and Followers	There is a Bargain to Aid the Individual Interests of Persons or Groups Going Their Separate Ways
Relationship	The Leader Shapes, Alters and Elevates the Motives, Values and Goals of Followers Through the Vital Teaching Role of Leadership	Two Persons May Exchange Goods, Services or Other Things in Order to Realize Independent Objectives
Measures of Success	The End Results of the Transformational Relationship Are "Higher" Goals Such as Liberty, Justice and Equality	The Interactions Comprising the Exchange Have Characteristics Such as Honesty, Responsibility, Fairness and the Honoring of Commitments

The Full Range Model of Leadership

Transformational Leadership
Bass

Bass (1985) built on Burns' work. Bass moved the discussion of transformational leadership to encompass a variety of organizational settings. Bass also envisioned transformational and transactional leadership on a continuum consisting of six components, rather than as two separate entities.

The idea of being a transformational leader was highly influenced by charismatic leadership. Bass, however, replaced charisma with the ideas of idealized influence and inspirational motivation. Bass (1999) explained the reasons charisma was replaced below.[5]

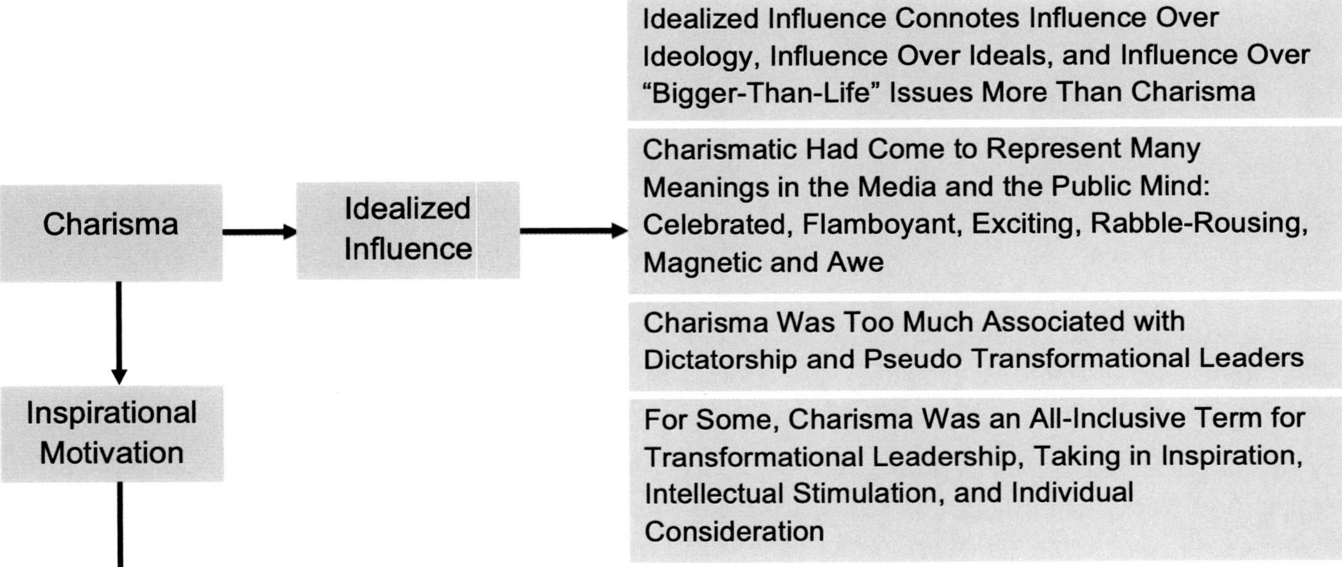

Idealized Influence Connotes Influence Over Ideology, Influence Over Ideals, and Influence Over "Bigger-Than-Life" Issues More Than Charisma
Charismatic Had Come to Represent Many Meanings in the Media and the Public Mind: Celebrated, Flamboyant, Exciting, Rabble-Rousing, Magnetic and Awe
Charisma
Idealized Influence
Charisma Was Too Much Associated with Dictatorship and Pseudo Transformational Leaders
Inspirational Motivation
For Some, Charisma Was an All-Inclusive Term for Transformational Leadership, Taking in Inspiration, Intellectual Stimulation, and Individual Consideration
Inspirational Motivation Was Created Because It Was Believed That a Leader Could Provide Challenge and Meaning Through the Use of Simple Words, Slogans, Symbols and Metaphors to Generate Acceptance of Missions, Without Necessarily Being Charismatic
One Did Not Have to Identify with Charismatic Leaders to Be Aroused by Them about the Importance of a Mission

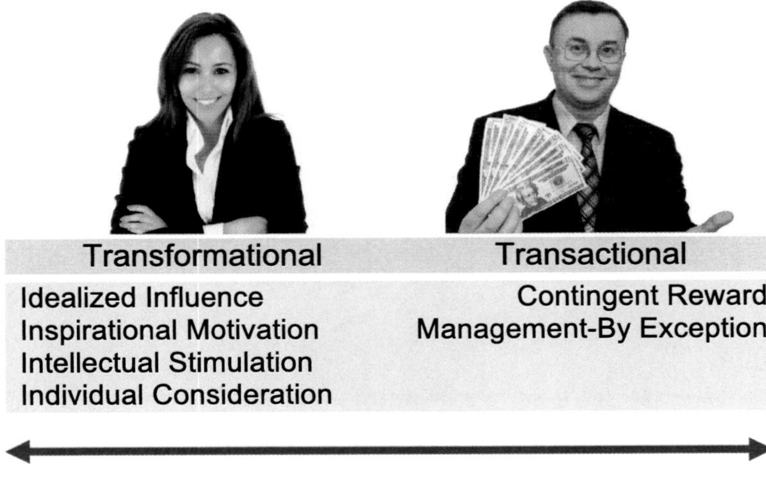

The Full Range Model of Leadership

The Full Range Model of Leadership

Between 1985 and 1990, additional refinements occurred on the continuum of leader behaviors (Hater and Bass, 1988; Avolio and Bass, 1991; Avolio, Waldman, and Yammarino, 1991). By 1991, a nine-component model was developed and was supported by the *Multifactor Leadership Questionnaire 5X*. The model began to experience widespread use following Bass and Avolio's 1994 book, *Improving Organizational Effectiveness through Transformational Leadership.*

Full-Range Model of Leadership, Bass and Avolio (1991)

Transformational	Transactional	Non-Leadership
Inspirational Motivation Idealized Influence Attributed Idealized Influence Behavioral Intellectual Stimulation Individual Consideration	Contingent Reward Management by Exception Active Management by Exception Passive	Laissez-Faire Behaviors

By the late 2000's, several additional studies (Antonakis, Avolio and Sivasubramaniam, 2003; Hinkin and Schriesheim, 2008) found that the management by exception passive scale of the *Multifactor Leadership Questionnaire 5X* loaded more strongly with the laissez-faire scale than the other transactional scales. The model was refined by creating a second-order component called passive-avoidant leadership that consisted of management by exception passive and laissez-faire.

Full-Range Model of Leadership, *Multifactor Leadership Questionnaire* (c. 2009)

Transformational	Transactional	Passive-Avoidant Leadership
Inspirational Motivation Idealized Influence Attributed Idealized Influence Behavioral Intellectual Stimulation Individual Consideration	Contingent Reward Management by Exception Active	Management by Exception Passive Laissez-Faire Behaviors

The Full Range Model of Leadership

The Five "I's of Transformational Leadership

Transformational Leadership involves a leader-follower exchange relationship in which the followers feel trust, loyalty and respect toward the leader and are motivated to do more than originally expected. This is considered the most effective form of leadership within the full range.

Transformational leadership is typically thought of as having five smaller components – often called the five I's as each one begins with the letter "I."

Idealized Influence describes leaders who are admired, respected and trusted. Followers identify with these leaders and they want to emulate them. Leaders who are idealized influences consider followers' needs over their own. They share risks with followers and are consistent in their conduct with underlying ethics, principles and values.[6] There are two forms of idealized influence: behavioral and attributed.

Idealized Influence Attributed can be thought of as believing that someone is a role model based on her or his credentials or reputation.

We might think of someone such as a successful Fortune 500 CEO or governor. We assume they know what they are doing and "attribute" to them role model status, but most of us haven't personally observed their leadership behaviors behind the scenes. We tend to see scripted speeches or ceremonies.

Idealized Influence Behavioral is related to actually observing role modeling behaviors from a leader.

We might observe a leader's behaviors when making difficult decisions and admire her/his ethical foundation and principles. Here we are actually observing leader behaviors rather than simply attributing role model status to the leader.

We can envision idealized influence consisting of five aspects.

Earning Respect
Earning Trust
Walking the Walk
Being a Role Model
Developing a Shared Vision[7]

The Full Range Model of Leadership

The Five "I's of Transformational Leadership

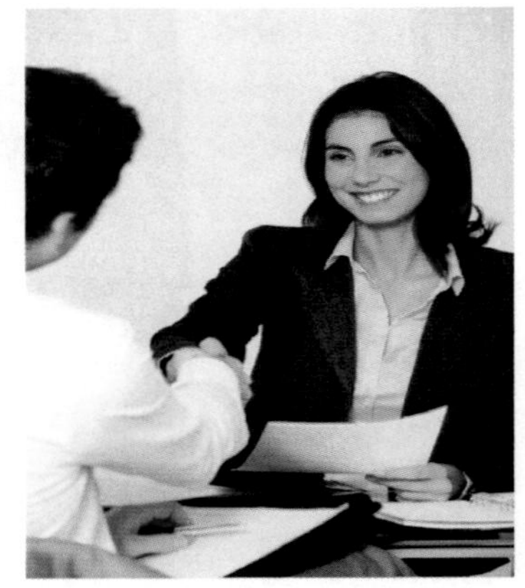

Inspirational Motivation describes leaders who behave in ways that motivate those around them by providing meaning and challenge to their work. These leaders display optimism and arouse enthusiasm. They encourage followers to envision attractive future states, which they can ultimately envision for themselves. We can envision inspirational motivation consisting of four aspects.

- Inspiring Followers
- Creating a Sense of Purpose in Followers' Lives
- Developing Team Spirit
- Painting an Optimistic Future for Followers

Intellectual Stimulation describes leaders who stimulate their followers' efforts to be innovative and creative by questioning assumptions, reframing problems and approaching old situations in new ways. These leaders solicit new ideas and creative solutions from followers without ridicule or public criticism. They include followers in the process of addressing problems and finding solutions. We can envision intellectual stimulation consisting of four aspects.

- Challenging Established Wisdom
- Encouraging Innovation
- Daring to Dream
- Encouraging Diversity

Individual Consideration describes leaders who pay attention to each follower's need for achievement and growth by acting as a coach or mentor. These leaders develop their followers to successively higher levels of potential. They create new learning opportunities and a supportive climate in which followers can grow. These leaders recognize that each follower is unique. We can envision individual consideration consisting of four aspects.

- Making Interpersonal Connections with Followers
- Helping Followers to Grow
- Being Empathetic
- Picking up Followers When They Fall

The Full Range Model of Leadership

Transactional Leadership

Transactional Leadership clarifies expectations and offers recognition when goals are achieved. The clarification of goals and objectives and providing of recognition once goals are achieved should result in individuals and groups achieving expected levels of performance.[8] Transactional leadership can be effective in certain situations but is usually not as effective as transformational leadership. Transactional leadership consists of two components: contingent reward and management by exception active.

Contingent Reward describes leaders who engage in a constructive path-goal transaction of reward for performance. Leaders clarify expectations, exchange promises and resources, arrange mutually satisfactory agreements, negotiate for resources, exchange assistance for effort and provide recommendations for successful follower performance.

We can envision contingent reward as consisting of the following behaviors.

Makes Clear Expectations of Outcomes and Rewards
Exchanges Reward and Recognition for Accomplishments
Actively Monitors Employee's Progress and Provides Supportive Feedback
"If You Do as We Agreed, You'll Get the Reward"[9]

Contingent reward can be effective in situations in which followers believe they can impact their chances for rewards. Sales persons on commission are a good example. When there are less clear connections between follower work and rewards, contingent reward tends to result in shorter-term results than do aspects of transformational leadership.

Management by Exception Active describes leaders who monitor followers' performance and take corrective action if deviations from standards occur. They enforce rules to avoid mistakes.

Many people best envision management by exception active behaviors as micro-management. The leader/manager doesn't truly trust followers and is regularly monitoring them for mistakes.

We can envision management by exception active as consisting of the following behaviors.

Takes Corrective Actions
Enforces Rules, Dislikes Challenges to the Status Quo
Only Hear from the Leader When Something is Wrong
"Uh Oh, Here He/She Comes Again!"

The Full Range Model of Leadership

Passive-Avoidant Leadership

Passive-Avoidant Leadership is generally the absence of leadership. Leaders who engage in passive-avoidant leadership are generally trying to avoid making decisions or taking stands on issues. The best way to envision this type of "leader" is someone who has announced her/his retirement six months into the future, and is avoiding making any decisions for the remainder of her/his tenure. Passive avoidant leadership consists of two components: management by exception passive and laissez-faire.

Management by Exception Passive describes leaders who fail to intervene until problems become serious.

They wait for mistakes to be brought to their attention before they take corrective action.

We can envision management by exception passive consisting of the following behaviors.

Sets Standards, but Waits for Problems to Arise Before Doing Anything
Stresses What People are Doing Wrong
"Uh Oh, Here He/She Comes Again!"

Laissez-Faire describes the absence of leadership. A person in a leadership role who avoids making decisions and carrying out her/his supervisory responsibilities exemplifies it. Laissez-faire leaders are not reactive or proactive, but inactive and passive in their leadership roles.

We can envision laissez-faire consisting of the following behaviors.

Absence of Leadership
Avoids Taking a Stand on Issues
Doesn't Emphasize Results
Refrains from Intervening When Issues Arise
Unaware of Employee Performance
"That Leader Doesn't Even Care if We Do or if We Don't"

The Full Range Model of Leadership

Becoming a More Transformational Leader

Becoming a More Transformational Leader

The next 11 pages will assist you in thinking about some steps that you can take to become more transformational with your followers. The pages will discuss:

How to Be a More Idealized Influence by assisting your followers to understand your attributes, by walking the walk and by building trust.

How to Be More Inspirationally Motivating by creating a sense of purpose in the work your followers do and by inspiring them to do more than they thought they could do.

How to Be More Intellectually Stimulating by assisting your followers to challenge established wisdom and by encouraging diversity.

How to Be More Individually Considerate by helping your followers to grow and by being more empathetic.

The Full Range Model of Leadership

Becoming a Leader with Increased Idealized Influence Attributed

There are subtle differences between idealized influence attributed and behavioral. Idealized influence attributed generally connotes traits that the followers assign to us as leaders. Idealized influence behavioral generally connotes actions that we take as leaders.

Idealized Influence Attributed	Idealized Influence Behavioral
The Leader is Admired and Respected	The Leader Puts Follower's Needs Ahead of Own
The Leader is Confident and Outgoing	The Leader Discusses Important Values and Beliefs
The Leader is Viewed as a Role Model	The Leader Emphasizes the Mission
	The Leader Considers Ethics in Decision-Making

Ideas for Becoming a Leader with More Idealized Influence Attributed

Increase Your Confidence It's easy to say that we should increase our confidence as leaders, but actually doing it is more difficult. One way to display confidence is the manner in which we speak.

Imagine that leader A addressed an issue by saying "For the most part, I believe we are able to do this – assuming we get the right resources and nothing unforeseen occurs."

Leader B addressed the same issue by saying "There is absolutely no doubt in my mind that we have the talent and commitment to do this."

Leader A was using what are often called qualifier words and phrases. Phrases such as "for the most part, assuming… and nothing unforeseen" all tell followers that leader A doesn't actually believe we can do it. This leader wants to ensure that she or he has covered her or himself in case the group doesn't accomplish the goal. Leader B, on the other hand didn't equivocate – this tells followers that leader B is confident.

Be Confident Without Being Arrogant There is an important distinction, however, between being confident and being arrogant. In the example above, the confident leader didn't say "I know I can lead us through this."

The center of attention in the statement "I know I can lead us through this" was the leader's ability. Instead, leader B said, "we have the talent and commitment to do this." This sort of confidence leads to trust, admiration and respect – all aspects of being an idealized influence – attributed.

The Full Range Model of Leadership

Becoming a Leader with Increased Idealized Influence Attributed

Be a Role Model When we first think about being a role model, we likely imagine someone who has received many honors – whether academic, civic or professional.

The image to the left connotes a leader who might be receiving a high honor from an educational institution for a lifetime of work. We see the symbolic medallion around his neck and think “wow, he’s really achieved something.”

This sort of role modeling is called attributed, because we as readers of this book haven’t personally witnessed the acts prompting the award, but, we assume that the leader has legitimately earned the accolade and we attribute to her or him role-model status.

Leaders who serve as role models, however, are everywhere.

The image to the right connotes a caring mother and a helpless new-born. Imagine that this mother will spend decades subverting her own needs for the benefit of the child.

There likely won’t be formal “leadership” award ceremonies for the mother, but, she will role model values and behaviors that will guide the child throughout her life.

Imagine that after over 20 years of role modeling tenacity, honesty and compassion, the infant in the image to the right becomes the woman on the left.

Much of her success can be attributed to the unsung leadership of her mother. During the formative years when competing interests made school seem like a waste of time, her mother almost assuredly repeated regularly “stay in school… make something of your life.”

But the impact of the mother’s role modeling doesn’t end there.

The image to the right portrays the daughter above, some day earning an advanced degree and role modeling tenacity, honesty and compassion to her own daughter.

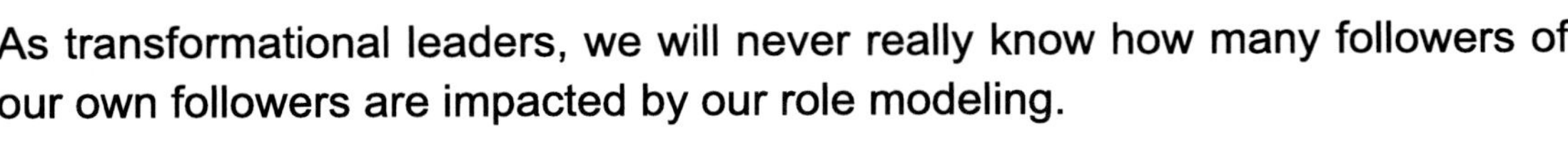

As transformational leaders, we will never really know how many followers of our own followers are impacted by our role modeling.

The Full Range Model of Leadership

Becoming a Leader with Increased Idealized Influence Behavioral

Walking the Walk is one way to increase your idealized influence behaviors.

An old leadership adage is that it's lonely at the top. Part of walking the walk as a leader is being willing to continue a journey when the odds seem insurmountable and when it feels like we are walking alone.

In the image to the left, the woman clearly has a long distance to travel, in harsh conditions, with a hazy objective at the end of the road. Leaders who walk the walk listen to their stakeholders to determine the course that needs to be taken.

These leaders then personally invest in the journey despite the hardships. This type of idealized influence says to followers, "you can follow me, I'm in it for the long haul."

While the image above captures the idea of bravely walking the walk, the image on the right is much more common. Every day leaders represent their followers in meetings at which the leaders must decide whether to focus on their own, personal interests or those of their followers.

Ideas for Walking the Walk

Write it Down Many effective leaders carry a paper or electronic notepad with them. When they indicate to a follower that they will do something, they make a note immediately. Before they leave for the day, these leaders enter that "to do item" into their electronic calendar with a reminder scheduled for a certain date.

Don't Ask Followers to Do Something You Wouldn't Do Although this seems like a cliché, it is an important mental framework for how we view our followers. It is easy to fall prey to the trappings of being the boss. Once that occurs, it's a small step to unconsciously looking down at the work our followers do.

Model, Model, Model If there are behaviors and attitudes we would like our followers to embody, it's important that we embody them first. For example, if we expect patience from our followers, we need to model patience. If we expect our followers to forgive us when we make mistakes, we need to forgive them when they make mistakes.

Show Up Early and Prepared for Meetings and Events It is easy to feel overwhelmed with all of the responsibilities associated with leadership. Unfortunately, those feelings can sometimes translate to a belief that our time is more valuable than our followers' time. Nothing can make our followers believe we don't walk the walk more than this type of dismissive view. One habit to prevent this type of behavior is to ensure that we show up to meetings that we schedule early and well prepared. This tells our followers, that we value both their time and their energy.

The Full Range Model of Leadership

Becoming a Leader with Increased Idealized Influence Behavioral

Building Trust is another way to increase your idealized influence behaviors.

An old adage is that building trust is like building a wall made out of bricks. One builds trust over a long time period, one brick at a time. In the image to the right, we can feel how much work is entailed in building a wall of trust. Each brick must be laid by hand, slowly resting on the solid foundation created by bricks on a lower row.

The image to the left conveys how easily a brick wall can become a pile of rubble. Pulling out a few bricks from the bottom of a wall might cause the entire wall to collapse.

Similarly, one incident of malfeasance or mistrust from a leader can ruin a relationship that took a long time to build.

Ideas for Building Trust

Listen Intently with an Open Mind One of the foundational steps in building trust is to be aware of being judgmental of our followers. It is natural that we will likely bond with different followers at different paces. Listening intently to our followers helps us to better understand their personal challenges as well as their hopes.

Be a Transparent Leader It is very difficult to trust someone who seems to always make political or guarded statements, rather than be forthcoming and transparent. Part of being an idealized influence is taking the risk as a leader to reveal our true selves to our followers. It should be our authentic selves rather than our guarded and masked selves that our followers want to emulate.

Be Transparent with Information This idea of being transparent about ourselves as a leader extends to how we handle information. Followers are able to keenly detect double-speak and phoniness. If we are handling a sensitive topic, there is an important difference between misleading our followers and honestly indicating “I can’t talk about that.”

Respect the Reputation of Your Followers Nothing can pull out a brick of trust and cause a wall to crumble faster than saying harmful things about followers to other followers.

If we want our followers to trust us, we must ensure that they trust that we will keep information that they share with us in confidence.

The Full Range Model of Leadership

Becoming a Leader Who Is More Inspirationally Motivating

Creating a Sense of Purpose is one way to become more inspirationally motivating.

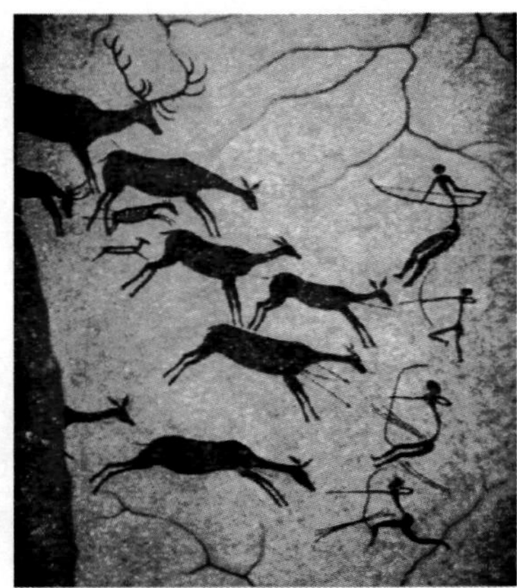

Followers spend a large portion of their lives working. Much of their self-identities are also related to their work lives. Think about a typical dinner party at which you meet new people.

A common question asked is "what do you do?" For most people, included in their response is a description of the work they do.

The image of the hunting party to the right is a cave-painting found in Lascaux, France. The painting is estimated to be over 17,000 years old. We can see that taking pride in our "work" and finding a sense of purpose in those activities seems to be deeply engrained in our DNA.

The image of the choir members captures the idea of finding bliss in one's purpose in life. While the choir members undoubtedly find meaning and purpose in many other activities, we can see the shared joy each member feels through performing her or his best.

One part of the joy the women in the image feel is almost certainly due to their contributions to a musical activity that produces beauty. More importantly, they are experiencing a sense of purpose that is collectively greater than their individual contributions.

Ideas for Creating a Sense of Purpose in Your Followers

Understand Each Follower's Personal Goals and Motivations Industrial robots work dispassionately – people don't. Followers bring to the work place a range of goals and motivations. A vital first step to create a sense of purpose in the lives of our followers is to take the time to understand each follower's goals and motivations.

Connect the Follower's Personal Goals and Motivations to the Vision of the Work Unit or Company It is relatively easy to create posters or PowerPoint sessions with the organization's mission and vision. It requires great leadership, however, to help each follower make the connection of how her or his personal goals can synergistically connect with the organization's mission and vision.

An important way to make this connection is to articulate the organizational vision so that each follower understands how her or his work contributes to that vision.

The Full Range Model of Leadership

Becoming a Leader Who Is More Inspirationally Motivating

Inspiring Followers is another way to become more inspirationally motivating.

While few, if any, work experiences will rise to the level of a rock concert, the image below reminds us that our followers want much more than a paycheck from their jobs. They want to feel connected, both individually to their leader and collectively to their colleagues.

Imagine that the musicians in the image below came on stage and said "Ok folks let's get started… item 1 on the agenda is…." – fans wouldn't be happy. At a less theatrical level, transformational leaders bring a sense of excitement, purpose and, yes, fun to the workplace.

Ideas for Inspiring Followers

Convey a Sense of Purpose in an Exciting Manner Connecting our followers' goals and motivations to the organizational vision is an important first step. Great leaders, however, make that connection with a sense of excitement. Study after study finds that followers consider leader extraversion as a vital part of effective leadership.[10] Extraverted leaders have a sense of energy and share positive emotions such as joy, happiness, love and excitement with their followers.

Share Your Own Dreams and Motivations with Followers It can be difficult to convince our followers to share their dreams and motivations with us. To role model that sharing those personal topics is acceptable, we may need to discuss our own dreams and motivations first. By sharing with our followers our own excitement about the connection between our goals, our motivations and the organizational vision, followers will feel more invested in making their own connections.

Improve Your Public Speaking Skills Many new leaders are hesitant to give rousing talks to followers. Fortunately, becoming a better motivational speaker is something we can all learn. One technique used by many successful leaders is to enroll in brief, public speaking courses such as those offered by Toastmasters.

The Full Range Model of Leadership

Becoming a Leader Who Is More Intellectually Stimulating

Challenging Established Wisdom is one way to become more intellectually stimulating.

Helping followers to challenge established wisdom is one of the most difficult aspects of being a transformational leader. The reason challenging established wisdom is so difficult is quite simple – for most followers, using conventional wisdom has worked out very well.

Take a moment and think about the items that comprise most annual evaluation forms. They tend to be items related to established procedures. Few annual evaluation forms have an item entitled "challenged conventional wisdom."

Consequently, most followers who do what conventional wisdom dictates, tend to receive good evaluations and perhaps even promotions. Since their behaviors were rewarded, they are more likely to engage in similar rather than different workplace behaviors in the future.

This idea is often called operant conditioning, and was made famous by Skinner.[11] Skinner conducted experiments in which a rat was placed in a contraption such as the one above.

If the rat pressed button A, it received food. If the rat pressed button B, the grid on which the rat was standing became briefly electrified. It didn't take long for the rat to learn the message - always press button A, never press button B.

Most followers in organizations have also learned these types of lessons. If they talk about or act on conventional wisdom (button A) they'll be rewarded. If they talk about or act on unconventional wisdom (button b) they may be shocked.

Ideas for Helping Followers Challenge Conventional Wisdom

We will divide a few examples of things you can do to help followers challenge conventional wisdom into two types of activities: logic and future oriented types.

Logic Types of Activities

Ask Why Five Times One logic type of activity is to ask someone "why" five times. For example: an order wasn't processed on time and the leader asks "why weren't we able to process it on time?"

The follower might respond that orders pile up toward the end of the month, and there aren't enough workers to handle them. The leader might then ask "help me understand why we don't have enough workers during those periods?"

The follower might respond that the rule is that everyone works Monday through Friday, 8 – 5. The leader might then ask, "Do you have any idea why that's our rule?" You can see where this is going. This sort of critical thinking can assist followers to challenge established wisdom.

Logic Types of Activities (Continued)

Assign a Meeting's Devil's Advocate A second type of logic activity is often called the devil's advocate.[12] This is the practice of assigning someone during a meeting the role of pointing out the downside of any proposal. At the beginning of the meeting, a leader might say, "ok everyone, today we're thinking about ways to improve X, and I've asked Michelle to play the role of devil's advocate. Even if she thinks a proposal is terrific, her job today is to challenge us all by pointing out the weaknesses of every proposal."

Future Oriented Types of Activities

Starting with a Blank Sheet During the 1990's, the Internet revolution was changing many business models. Hammer coined the term "reengineering" to connote changing organizational processes from paper to digital.[13] One of the activities used to reengineer processes is to lead your team in an exercise in which you imagine that you were going to perform a process or function for the first time. In this exercise, you might pretend your organization has never done the activity before, and ask your team to develop the procedures they would use if they were developing the entire process from scratch.

Imagine Different Future States[14] This activity is often called scenario planning. As a leader, you describe the current scenario in which the group finds itself. You then pose a new scenario. An example might be "what if our current volume doubled, and we couldn't expand our existing warehouse and delivery fleet?" Or, "as robotics become more commonplace, how might affordable robots for repetitive and simple tasks influence..." The exercise is designed to imagine future states, but may engender new ideas for the current state.

Imagine Failure and Work Backwards This activity is, to some degree, the inverse of scenario planning. It also incorporates asking why repeatedly. Here, you challenge your team to imagine complete failure. You might say, "imagine that both of our large customers dropped their contracts with us and switched to our competitor. Why might that have occurred?" After the team brainstorms possible reasons for the failure, you then engage in asking why.

If, for example, a major theme suggested for why the group could lose its two largest customers was "lack of personal contact," then you as the leader would prompt the group to work backwards from there. The question might be "so in this scenario, what would have caused us to have insufficient personal contact?"

The Full Range Model of Leadership

Becoming a Leader Who Is More Intellectually Stimulating

Encouraging Diversity is another way to become more intellectually stimulating.

New leaders often wish that each employee was completely task-oriented and highly consistent. This would allow the leader to treat each follower similarly.

Humans, however, are not automatons with the same goals, needs and foibles. Part of leading, is realizing that each follower brings unique viewpoints, skills and assets to the workplace.

The differences found among employees can be illustrated by the image to the right. The dogs are the extremes within the canine species. The Great Dane can reach 43 inches and 245 pounds. The Chihuahua, on the other hand rarely reaches over 13 inches in height and 12 pounds.

A typical work unit will likely have followers who are as different from each other as a Great Dane and a Chihuahua.

Some followers may be quite extraverted while others may be quite shy. Some may excel at numerical analyses and others at interpersonal relationships.

While it is challenging to do, leaders who are able to recognize the unique gifts of each follower and capitalize on that diversity are typically able to craft high performing work groups.

Ideas for Being a Leader Who Encourages Diversity

While many metaphors exist for how to appreciate the diversity of your followers, the toolbox is a good one.

An old expression is "to a hammer, every problem looks like a nail." This connotes that many leaders attack every problem using the one tool with which they are comfortable, and redefine the problem on which they are working to fit the capabilities of a hammer.

Transformational leaders who encourage diversity in their followers understand that different followers will excel at different problems – just like a hammer can't twist a screw or a screwdriver can't staple two things together.

Having a variety of tools is almost always better for organizations than just having one big hammer.

Becoming a Leader Who Is More Intellectually Stimulating

Encouraging Innovation is another way to become more intellectually stimulating.

Innovation often occurs when two somewhat unrelated ideas are connected to create something new.

Albert Einstein had been working for years without success on his theory of special relativity. Every day Einstein passed a clock tower on his way to the patent office in Bern. One day Einstein imagined a car driving away from the clock tower at the speed of light. If the car was moving at the speed of light, the second hand on the clock tower would appear fixed to passengers in the car. The clock tower's light could not catch up to the car. Within the car, however, the passengers would view the clock on the car's dashboard ticking normally.

Einstein explained that making the association between the clock tower and the speed of light caused a storm to break loose in his mind.

A similar connection of seemingly unrelated artifacts occurred to George de Mestral. After returning from a hike, his pants were covered with burrs. de Mestral looked under a microscope and saw tiny hooks in the burrs that allowed them to cling to tiny loops in the fabric of his pants. From that image, de Mestral had the inspiration to re-create the hook and loop pattern he saw. He called his invention "Velcro," a combination of the words velour and crochet.

Ideas for Helping Followers Increase Innovation

One way to help followers think of new ways to approach problems is to ask them to think of a similar situation in their "non-work." The conversation will likely involve dialogue on very pedestrian topics such as how the follower keeps track of a grocery list or how the follower decides when to put gas in her or his car. These seemingly "unrelated" discussions, however, may lead to an "aha" moment for the problem at work.

This introduction of "unrelated" ideas is a technique that can also be used when brainstorming. Imagine that the woman below is leading a brainstorming session.

At some point her group runs out of ideas – they are stuck. Introducing a few "random" items can often spark an innovative jump. For example, the woman might ask a group member – "what is your favorite food" or "what musical group do you like most?"

Those seemingly unrelated terms are added to the whiteboard list. With luck, someone will make a connection between the new words introduced on the whiteboard and the actual problem on which the group is working – similar to Einstein and the clock tower.

The Full Range Model of Leadership

Becoming a Leader Who Is More Individually Considerate

Helping Followers Grow is one way to become more individually considerate.

Growing up, most of us had at least one special teacher who encouraged, challenged and nurtured us. That teacher, literally, taught us the joy of learning in addition to the actual subject matter of the course.

When you think about that teacher, you likely have an instant, warm feeling in your heart. You also likely say things such as "she pushed me hard, but I always new she was rooting for me to succeed."

Part of being a transformational leader is to help your followers grow both personally and professionally.

Ideas for Helping Followers Grow

Hindsight, Foresight and Insight One popular model for helping followers grow uses the idea of discussing past experiences, called hindsight and projections about change, called foresight.[15] These two discussions can assist a follower in developing insight into what she or he needs to do in order to grow professionally. As a leader, we can help our followers to grow by assisting them to connect the types of ideas discussed in hindsight with thoughts about external and internal changes looming.

Hindsight →	Insight	← Foresight
What Followers Are Good At What Is Most Important to Followers What Keeps Followers Engaged What Type of Work Followers Don't Like to Do How Followers Prefer to Work What Type of Work Followers Find Difficult		External - What Changes Are Occurring in the Industry and Society That Will Effect the Organization Internal - What Changes Are Occurring in the Organization That Will Effect the Work the Follower Will Do in the Future

To make the leap to insight may be frightening. The follower may not feel that she or he has the requisite skills to match the direction the company or industry is heading. To assist the follower, we may need to work on increasing her or his self-confidence.

Increasing Self-Confidence One frequently used tool to assist a follower in building self-confidence is to reinforce previous accomplishments the follower has achieved. For example, we might ask the follower, "what was the most difficult thing you have ever done professionally." Our response will need to both reinforce and challenge the follower.

An example of a response might be "wow, that is really something, I don't think most people could have done that." Our follow-up, however, will need to push the follower toward the future area about which she or he is unsure. We might say, "given that awesome accomplishment, how is preparing for the changes we discussed different?"

The Full Range Model of Leadership

Becoming a Leader Who Is More Individually Considerate

Being Empathetic is another way to become more individually considerate.

Although we use the term empathy in everyday conversation, the concept is actually a bit complicated. Often psychologists distinguish between three related ideas: personal distress, sympathy and empathy to explain a range of emotions that we might experience.

Personal distress is likely an emotion that most of us have felt at one time or another. We have also likely felt sympathy for someone. Feeling empathy, however, is more unusual.

Personal Distress	A selfish motivation to reduce one's own suffering— either by helping the other person or escaping the situation, whichever is less costly[16]
Sympathy	An altruistic motivation to reduce another person's suffering[17]
Empathy	Emotional contagion — the exact matching of another person's emotions[18]

To envision this in a leadership situation, imagine that a follower comes to you and indicates that she or he is overwhelmed with the details of a project and won't make a deadline.

Personal Distress If you feel anxious that you will have to share some of the responsibility, that feeling is personal distress.

Sympathy If you feel bad for the follower and begin to think of ways to help him or her, that feeling is sympathy.

Empathy If you "put yourself in the follower's shoes," processing his or her career stage, outside responsibilities and so forth, and then try to feel the emotions she or he is feeling, that is empathy.

Ideas for Increasing Your Empathetic Leadership

Reflect Back What Your Followers Say A first step to become more empathetic is learning to reflect what your followers are saying. Imagine that the follower who is overwhelmed by a project tells you that she or he is so overwhelmed that she or he is not even sure when the project will be ready. A reflective listener might say something such as "it really sounds like this project has so many moving parts that you're not quite sure what's not finished and what's completed." To us as leaders this may sound pedestrian. To an anxious follower, the message is "my leader heard me!"

Reflect Back What Your Followers Feel To empathize, you will need, however, to search your own memories of feelings that you have experienced. In this situation, perhaps you remember a time when you thought you might be downsized, or perhaps you were experiencing a difficult point in a meaningful relationship. Search for the feelings of despair, helplessness and doom that you felt.

Once you have "re-lived" those emotions, then you can reflect back, not just the follower's words but also her or his feelings. In this case you might affectively respond, "wow, I know that feeling…it feels like you are caught in a tangled forest and no matter how hard you try to orient yourself, more limbs keep hitting you in the face – it feels like you'll never get out of the tangled mess."

The Full Range Model of Leadership

The Multifactor Leadership Questionnaire

The *Multifactor Leadership Questionnaire 5X (MLQ)* contains 36 questions that measure the nine components of the full range model of leadership. it also includes nine outcome questions.

The leadership portion of the instrument consists of 36 questions that measure leadership on a five-point scale.

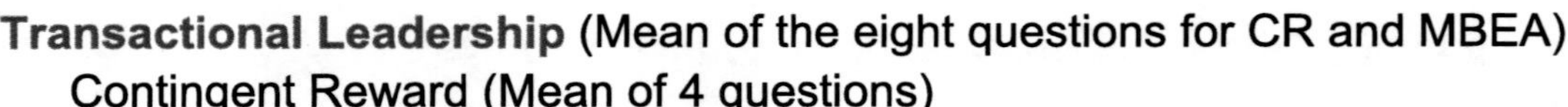

0	1	2	3	4
Not At All	Once in a While	Sometimes	Fairly Often	Frequently, if not always

Leadership Scores

Transformational Leadership (Mean of the 20 questions for the five I's)
- Idealized Attributed (Mean of 4 questions)
- Idealized Behavioral (Mean of 4 questions)
- Inspirational Motivation (Mean of 4 questions)
- Intellectual Stimulation (Mean of 4 questions)
- Individual Consideration (Mean of 4 questions)

Transactional Leadership (Mean of the eight questions for CR and MBEA)
- Contingent Reward (Mean of 4 questions)
- Management by Exception Active (Mean of 4 questions)

Passive-Avoidant Behaviors (Mean of the eight questions for MBEP and LF)
- Management by Exception Passive (Mean of 4 questions)
- Laissez-Faire (Mean of 4 questions)

There are also nine outcome questions that measure the follower's extra effort, rating of how effective the leader is and satisfaction with the leader.

Outcome Scores
- Extra Effort (Mean of 3 questions)
- Effectiveness (Mean of 3 questions)
- Satisfaction with the Leader (Mean of 3 questions)

Details

The MLQ 5X is available in English, German, Italian, Swedish, Spanish, Turkish and Portuguese.

The instrument can be licensed for use at mindgarden.com.

The current version of the MLQ, however, has gone through multiple revisions since 1985. The next nine pages provide a sense of the various versions of the MLQ that have preceded the MLQ 5X.

The Full Range Model of Leadership

Development of The Multifactor Leadership Questionnaire

The Early, Six-Factor Model, 1985, *MLQ Form 1*

Bass and his colleagues (1985) asked 78 executives to describe a leader who had made an impact on whatever they considered important in their leadership roles. The executives were also asked how the best leaders were able to get others to go beyond self-interest to achieve group objectives. The researchers then reviewed the literature on charisma.

Based on the literature on charisma and the responses from the executives, the research team generated 142 items (questions). Eleven experts were able to correctly classify 73 questions as either transformational or transactional with an 80% agreement criterion.

A group of 176 US Army colonels was next asked to rate their own leaders on these 73 questions (the *MLQ Form 1*). A principal components analysis of these data resulted in a six-factor solution shown below.

Transformational		Transactional	Passive-Avoidant
Charisma/Inspirational Individual Consideration	Intellectual Stimulation	Contingent Reward Management by Exception Active	Passive-Avoidant

The Seven-Factor Model, 1990, *MLQ 5R*[19]

After *Form 1* was developed, additional revisions were made. The next major iteration was the 70 question *MLQ 5R*.

Transformational		
10 Items	Idealized Influence	Leaders Engender Trust from and Serve as Role Models for Followers. The Leaders Are Respected and Hold Referent Power (Howell and Avolio, 1993)
7 Items	Inspirational Motivation	Leaders Are Seen as Inspirational, Providing Symbols and Emotional Appeals to Increase Follower Awareness and Understanding Regarding Mutually Desired Goals (Howell and Avolio, 1993)
10 Items	Intellectual Stimulation	Leaders Move Their Followers to Question the "Old Way of Doing Things," Approach Problems from Different Angles and from Alternative Perspectives (Howell and Avolio, 1993)
10 Items	Individualized Consideration	The Leader Recognizes and Elevates Follower Needs and Pushes Them to Higher Levels of Potential and Identifies Ways to Encourage Followers to Improve Their Capabilities and to Take on More Challenging Goals and Opportunities (Howell and Avolio, 1993)
Transactional		
9 items	Contingent Reward	The Leader Clarifies What Is Expected from Followers and What They Will Receive If They Meet Expected Levels of Performance (Bass, 1985) The Leader Provides Rewards If Followers Perform in Accordance with Contracts or Expend the Necessary Effort (Hater and Bass, 1988)
8 items	Active Management by Exception	The Leader Monitors Task Execution for Any Problems That Might Arise and Corrects Those Problems to Maintain Current Performance Levels (Bass, 1985) The Leader Maintains a Vigilance for Mistakes or Deviations and Takes Action If Targets Are Not Met (Hater and Bass, 1988)
Management by Exception Passive/Laissez-Faire		
16 items	MBEP/LF	The Leader Tends to React Only after Problems Have Become Serious Enough to Take Corrective Action and May Avoid Making Any Decisions at All (Bass, 1985) The Leader Preserves the Status Quo and Doesn't Consider Trying to Make Improvements as Long as Things are Going along All Right or According to Earlier Plans (Hater and Bass, 1988)

The Full Range Model of Leadership

Development of The Multifactor Leadership Questionnaire

The Eight-Factor Model
1993, *MLQ 5X*

The current version of the *MLQ*, the *5X* was iteratively developed in the early 1990's. An initial version of the *MLQ 5X* had 80 items (questions).

The items were developed based on the results of a series of factor analyses on the previous version, the *MLQ 5R* as well as factor analyses with an early version of the *MLQ 5X*, called *Form 10*. Additional items were also created based on literature that distinguished charismatic from transformational leadership. Finally, a panel of leadership scholars reviewed the proposed *MLQ 5X* and made recommendations on how to ensure the instrument matched the conceptual model of the full range model of leadership behaviors. All of this item development resulted in an instrument with 80 questions.[20]

During this time frame, work was also ongoing on how charismatic leadership fit into the full range model of leadership and the *MLQ*. About this time, Conger and Kanungo were writing about behavioral and attributed charisma. These ideas were influencing work on the *MLQ*. On *Form 1,* charisma and inspirational motivation were combined into one scale. In the 80-question, eight-factor model of the *MLQ 5X*, charisma was separated from inspirational motivation. Additionally, charisma was split into two aspects: attributed and behavioral.[21]

Attributed and Behavioral Aspects of Charisma

Followers Observe Leader **Behaviors**

Followers **Attribute** Charismatic Status to the Leader

Followers Identify with and Want to Emulate the Leader

Examples of Charismatic Behaviors
Intolerance with Shortcomings in Status Quo; Search for Change Opportunities
Strong Vision or Mission Orientation; Shared and Idealized Future Vision
Strong Articulation of Goals and Motivation to Lead (Inspirational)
High Risk; Use of Unconventional Tactics
Passionate Advocacy Through Personal Examples; Engaging in Exemplary Acts That Subordinates Interpret as Involving Great Personal Risk and Sacrifice

The Full Range Model of Leadership

Development of The Multifactor Leadership Questionnaire

The table below provides the eight factors used in the 80-item *MLQ 5X* plus related definitions of the constructs.

Eight-Factor Model, Early 1990's 80-Item *MLQ 5X*		
Transformational		
8 items	Charisma Attributed	An Attribution Made by Followers Who Observe Certain Behaviors on the Part of the Leader Within Organizational Contexts (Conger and Kanungo, 1986) The Leader is a Role Model for Ethical Conduct That Builds Identification with the Leader and His/Her Articulated Vision (Bass, 1985) The Leader Has a Gift for Seeing What Is Really Important (Hater and Bass, 1988)
10 items	Charisma Behavioral	The Leader Provides Followers with a Clear Sense of Purpose That is Energizing (Bass, 1985) The Leader Instills Pride, Faith, and Respect and Transmits a Sense of Mission (Hater and Bass, 1988)
10 items	Inspirational Motivation	The Leader is Seen as Inspirational; Providing Symbols and Emotional Appeals to Increase Follower Awareness and Understanding Regarding Mutually Desired Goals (Howell and Avolio, 1993)
10 items	Intellectual Stimulation	The Leader Gets Followers to Question the Tried and True Ways of Solving Problems; Encourages Them to Question the Methods They Use (Bass, 1985) The Leader Arouses Followers to Think in New Ways and Emphasizes Problem Solving and the Use of Reasoning Before Taking Action (Hater and Bass, 1988)
9 items	Individualized Consideration	The Leader Delegates Projects to Stimulate Learning Experiences, Provides Coaching and Teaching, and Treats Each Follower as an Individual (Hater and Bass, 1988) The Leader Focuses on Understanding the Needs of Each Follower and Works Continuously to Get Them to Develop to Their Full Potential (Bass, 1985)
Transactional		
9 items	Contingent Reward	The Leader Clarifies What is Expected from Followers and What They Will Receive If They Meet Expected Levels of Performance (Bass, 1985) The Leader Provides Rewards If Followers Perform in Accordance with Contracts or Expend the Necessary Effort (Hater and Bass, 1988)
8 items	Active Management by Exception	The Leader Monitors Task Execution for Any Problems That Might Arise and Corrects Those Problems to Maintain Current Performance Levels (Bass, 1985) The Leader Maintains a Vigilance for Mistakes or Deviations and Takes Action If Targets Are Not Met (Hater and Bass, 1988)
Management by Exception Passive/ Laissez-Faire		
16 items	Passive Avoidant	The Leader Tends to React Only after Problems Have Become Serious Enough to Take Corrective Action and May Avoid Making Any Decisions at All (Bass, 1985) The Leader Preserves the Status Quo and Does Not Consider Trying to Make Improvements as Long as Things are Going Along All Right or According to Earlier Plans (Hater and Bass, 1988)

The Full Range Model of Leadership

Development of The Multifactor Leadership Questionnaire

The Six-Factor Model
Early 1990's, *MLQ 5X*

A next step in the development of the *MLQ* was to conduct confirmatory factor analysis (CFA) on the 80-item version of the *MLQ 5X*. The CFA results found that the data tested did not align well with an eight-factor model. The researchers combined charismatic attributed, charismatic behavioral and inspirational motivation into one scale and then tested a six-factor model.

The researchers were unable to find a satisfactory six-factor solution with the 80 item data set either. Most CFA programs include a feature called modification indexes. In essence, the statistical output suggests which questions should be removed in order to produce a better model fit.

The researchers used this feature and ultimately kept 12 questions for charisma/inspirational, eight questions for passive/avoidant and four questions each for individual consideration, intellectual stimulation, contingent reward and management by exception active. These questions were believed to represent the dimensions of the full range of leadership model, and were the best statistical fit, based on the modification indexes.

This reduced the 80 item version to a 36 item questionnaire.

Multiple confirmatory factor analyses found acceptable fits for this 36 item version. Across five studies the model fits were (*GFI* = .90 to .91, *CFI* = .90 to .91, *RMSEA* = .051 to .056).[22]

Six-Factor Model, Early 1990's 36-Item *MLQ 5X*		
Transformational		
12 items	Charisma/ Inspirational	Provides Followers with a Clear Sense of Purpose That is Energizing; is a Role Model for Ethical Conduct That Builds Identification with the Leader and His/Her Articulated Vision
4 items	Intellectual Stimulation	Gets Followers to Question the Tried and True Ways of Solving Problems; Encourages Them to Question the Methods They Use to Improve Them
4 items	Individualized Consideration	Focuses on Understanding the Needs of Each Follower and Works Continuously to Get Them to Develop to Their Full Potential
Transactional		
4 items	Contingent Reward	Clarifies What is Expected from Followers and What They Will Receive If They Meet Expected Levels of Performance
4 items	Active Management by Exception	Focuses on Monitoring Task Execution for Any Problems That Might Arise and Correcting Those Problems to Maintain Current Performance Levels
Passive Avoidant		
8 items	Passive Avoidant	Tends to React Only after Problems Have Become Serious to Take Corrective Action and May Avoid Making Any Decisions at All

The Full Range Model of Leadership

Development of The Multifactor Leadership Questionnaire

The Nine-Factor Model[23]

Late 1990's to about 2009, *MLQ 5X*

The six-factor model contained 12 items (questions) measuring a broad concept of charisma/ inspirational, and eight items (questions) measuring passive avoidant behaviors.

Concerns were expressed, that these two scales did not adequately capture the "nuances" of the full range model of leadership behaviors. By the late 1990's, a nine-factor model had been developed.

Moving from a 6 to a 9-Factor Model 36-Item *MLQ 5X*		
Transformational		
12 Items Scale Removed	Charisma/ Inspirational	Provides Followers with a Clear Sense of Purpose That Is Energizing; a Role Model for Ethical Conduct That Builds Identification with the Leader and His/her Articulated Vision
4 Items New Scale	Idealized Influence Attributed	These Leaders Are Admired, Respected and Trusted. Followers Identify with and Want to Emulate Their Leaders. They Instill Pride in Followers That, in Turn Results in Followers Respecting the Leader
4 Items New Scale	Idealized Influence Behavioral	These Leaders Earn Credit with Followers by Considering Followers' Needs Over Their Own Needs They Talk about Important Values and Beliefs and Emphasize the Importance of Having a Collective Sense of Mission
4 Items New Scale	Inspirational Motivation	Motivates Those Around Them by Providing Meaning and Challenge to Work Arouses Individual and Team Spirit Envision Attractive Future States that Followers Can Then Envision for Themselves
4 Items Existing Scale	Intellectual Stimulation	Simulates Followers' Effort to Be Innovative and Creative Questions Assumptions, Reframes Problems, Solicits New Ideas
4 Items Existing Scale	Individualized Consideration	Pays Attention to Each Individual's Need for Achievement and Growth Acts as a Coach or Mentor Develops Followers to Successively Higher Levels of Potential
Transactional		
4 Items Existing Scale	Contingent Reward	Clarifies What Is Expected from Followers and What They Will Receive If They Meet Expected Levels of Performance
4 Items Existing Scale	Management by Exception Active	Specifies Standards for Compliance and What Constitutes Ineffective Performance Monitors Task Execution for Any Problems That Might Arise Corrects Those Problems to Maintain Current Performance Levels
4 Items New Scale	Management by Exception Passive	Fails to Interfere until Problems Become Serious Waits for Things to Go Wrong Before Taking Action
Laissez-Faire		
8 Items Scale Removed	Passive Avoidant	Tends to React Only after Problems Have Become Serious to Take Corrective Action and May Avoid Making Any Decisions at All
4 Items Existing Scale	Laissez-Faire	Avoids Getting Involved or Making Decisions When Important Issues Arise Delays Responding to Urgent Questions

The Full Range Model of Leadership

Development of The Multifactor Leadership Questionnaire

The Adjusted Nine-Factor Model
About 2009, *MLQ 5X*

The original scoring for the nine-factor *MLQ 5X* included management by exception passive in the second-order construct of transactional leadership. Based on multiple additional studies in the peer-reviewed literature, toward the end of the first decade of the 2000's the *MLQ 5X* scoring directions were modified. Currently, transactional leadership consists of contingent reward and management by exception active. Passive-avoidant leadership consists of management by exception passive and laissez-faire behaviors.

		Transformational
4 Items	Idealized Influence Attributed	These Leaders Are Admired, Respected and Trusted. Followers Identify with and Want to Emulate Their Leaders. They Instill Pride in Followers That, in Turn Results in Followers Respecting the Leader
4 Items	Idealized Influence Behavioral	These Leaders Earn Credit with Followers by Considering Followers' Needs Over Their Own Needs They Talk about Important Values and Beliefs and Emphasize the Importance of Having a Collective Sense of Mission
4 Items	Inspirational Motivation	Motivates Those Around Them by Providing Meaning and Challenge to Work Arouses Individual and Team Spirit Envision Attractive Future States That Followers Can Then Envision for Themselves
4 Items	Intellectual Stimulation	Simulates Followers' Effort to Be Innovative and Creative Questions Assumptions, Reframes Problems Solicits New Ideas
4 Items	Individualized Consideration	Pays Attention to Each Individual's Need for Achievement and Growth Acts as a Coach or Mentor Develops Followers to Successively Higher Levels of Potential
		Transactional
4 Items	Contingent Reward	Clarifies What Is Expected from Followers and What They Will Receive If They Meet Expected Levels of Performance
4 Items	Management by Exception Active	Specifies Standards for Compliance and What Constitutes Ineffective Performance Monitors Task Execution for Any Problems That Might Arise Corrects Those Problems to Maintain Current Performance Levels
Scale Moved to Passive Avoidant	Management by Exception Passive	Fails to Interfere until Problems Become Serious Waits for Things to Go Wrong Before Taking Action
		Passive Avoidant
4 Items Moved from Transactional	Management by Exception Passive	Fails to Interfere until Problems Become Serious Waits for Things to Go Wrong Before Taking Action
4 Items Existing Scale	Laissez-Faire	Avoids Getting Involved or Making Decisions When Important Issues Arise Delays Responding to Urgent Questions

The Full Range Model of Leadership

Development of The Multifactor Leadership Questionnaire

The chart below provides a sense of the evolution of the *Multifactor Leadership Questionnaire* over the past 30 years.

Brief Evolution of the *MLQ*						
	1985 *MLQ* Form 1	1990 *MLQ* 5R, and Form 10[24]	1993 *MLQ 5X*	c. 1995 *MLQ 5X*	c. 1998 *MLQ 5X*	c. 2009 *MLQ 5X*
Items	73 Items	70 Items	80 Items	36 Items	36 Items	36 Items
Scales	6 Scales	7 Scales	8 Scales	6 Scales	9 Scales	9 Scales
Transformational	CI, IS, IC	II, IM, IS, IC	CA, CB, IS, IC, IM	CI, IS, IC	IIA, IIB, IM, IS, IC	IIA, IIB, IM, IS, IC
Transactional	CR, MBEA	CR, MBEA	CR, MBEA	CR, MBEA	CR, MBEA, MBEP	CR, MBEA
Passive-Avoidant	PA	PA	PA	PA	LF	MBEP, LF
Charisma/ Inspirational (CI)	20 Items			12 Items		
Charisma Attributed (CA)			8 Items			
Charisma Behavioral (CB)			10 Items			
Idealized Influence (II)		10 Items				
Idealized Influence Attributed (IIA)					4 Items	4 Items
Idealized Influence Behavioral (IIB)					4 Items	4 Items
Inspirational Motivation (IM)		7 Items	10 Items		4 Items	4 Items
Intellectual Stimulation (IS)	10 Items	10 Items	10 Items	4 Items	4 Items	4 Items
Individualized Consideration (IC)	10 Items	10 Items	9 Items	4 Items	4 Items	4 Items
Contingent Reward (CR)	9 Items	9 Items	9 Items	4 Items	4 Items	4 Items
Management By Exception Active (MBEA)	8 Items	8 Items	8 Items	4 Items	4 Items	4 Items
Management By Exception Passive (MBEP)					4 Items	4 Items
Laissez-Faire (LF)					4 Items	4 Items
Passive Avoidant (PA)	16 Items	16 Items	16 Items	8 Items		

The Full Range Model of Leadership

Development of The Multifactor Leadership Questionnaire

The chart on the opposite page provides a way to envision changes in the *Multifactor Leadership Questionnaire* over the last three decades.[25]

Charisma, Inspirational Motivation and Idealized Influence

For the *MLQ*, the idea of charisma originally included being inspirational. When inspirational motivation became a separate construct in the instrument, charisma and idealized influence gradually changed places, and were later split into the aspects of attributed and behavioral.

Individual Consideration, Intellectual Stimulation, Contingent Reward and Management by Exception Active

Individual consideration, intellectual stimulation, contingent reward and management by exception active, as scales, have remained consistent throughout the iterations of the *MLQ*.

Passive Avoidant, Management by Exception Active and Laissez-Faire

For the first decade of the *MLQ*, the "ineffective" dimension was passive-avoidant. When the nine-factor model was developed, the passive-avoidant scale was broken into management by exception passive and laissez-faire.

The Full Range Model of Leadership

Development of The Multifactor Leadership Questionnaire

With the exception of the brief period in which the *MLQ 5X* was presented as a six-factor model, we generally see a progression in which the number of items decreased while the number of scales increased.

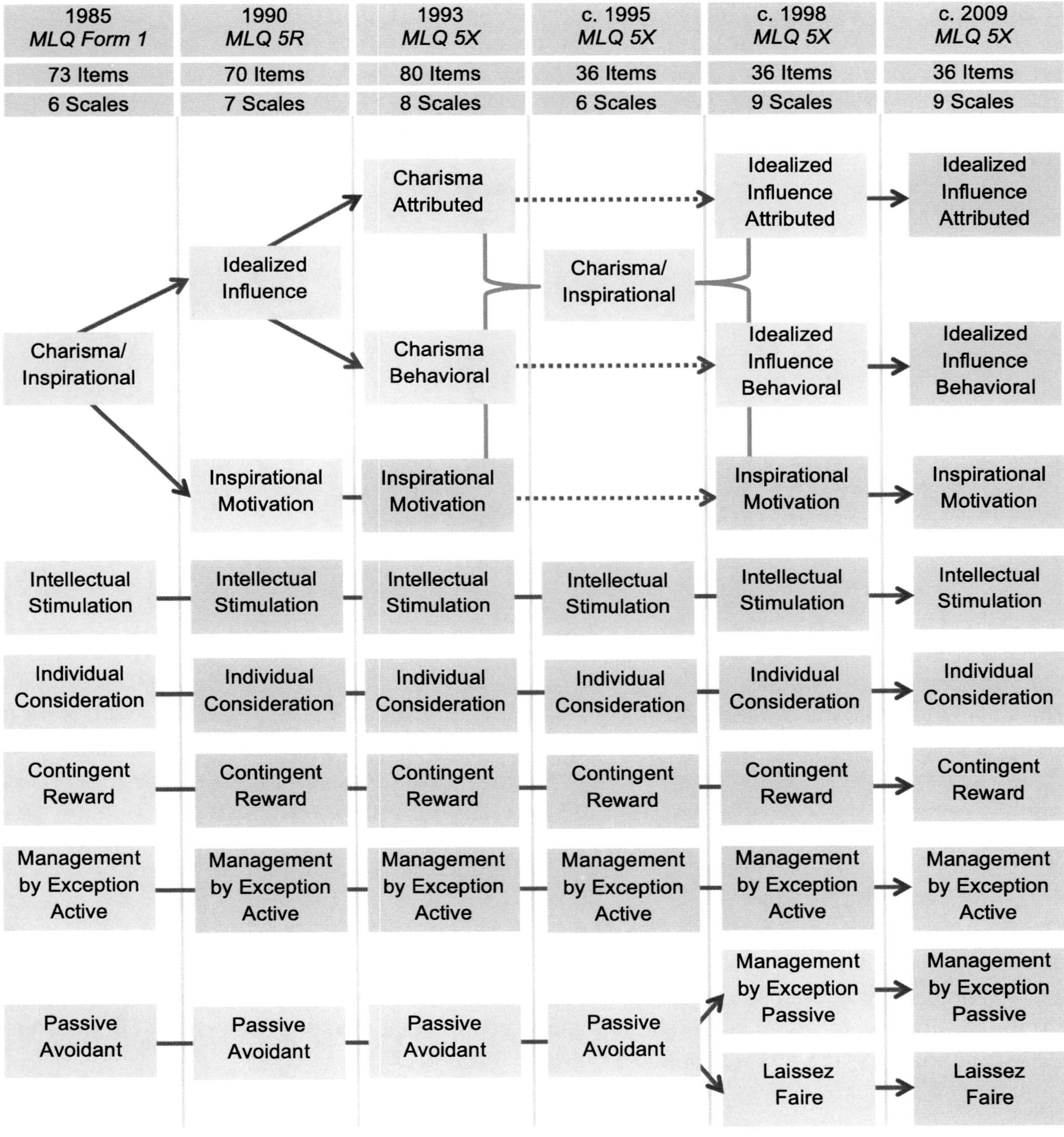

The Full Range Model of Leadership

Reliability and Validity of The Multifactor Leadership Questionnaire

An analysis done using 2004 *MLQ* data provides valuable information about the reliability and validity of the nine-factor *MLQ 5X*. There are, however, multiple possibilities for analyzing who rates whom. The illustration below provides frequent uses of the *MLQ*. Validity and reliability data are provided below the illustration for two of these possibilities: the leader rates her/himself and the follower rates the leader.

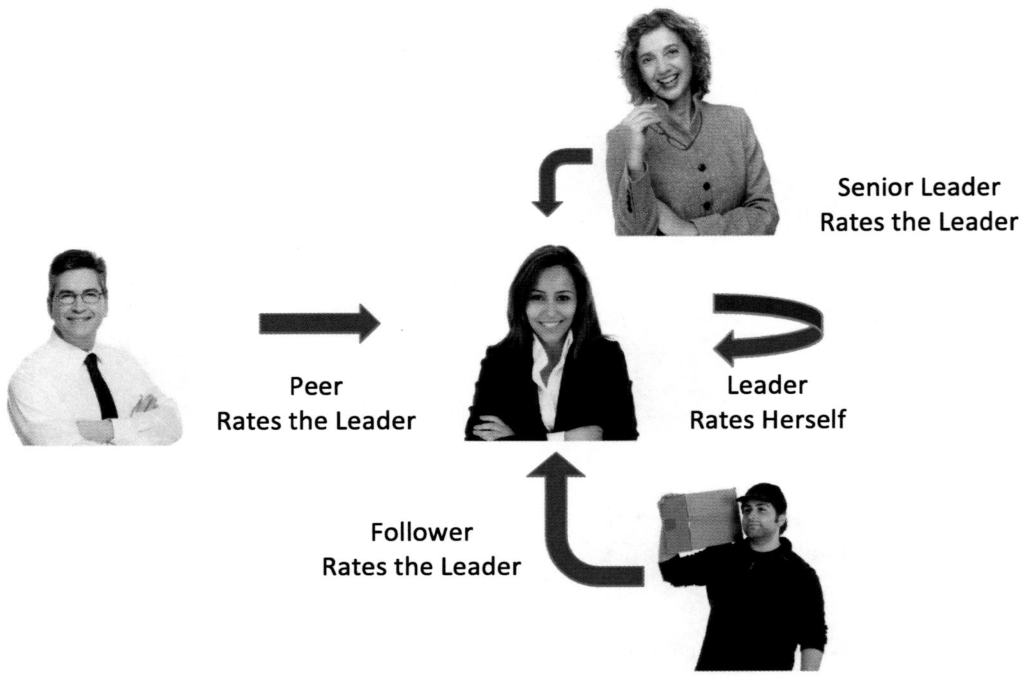

Leader Rates Her/Himself

The CFA results for the 9-factor model (N = 3,755, GFI = .93, CFI = .89, $RMSEA$ = .05) were a better fit than the 3-factor model (N = 3,755, GFI = .81, CFI = .64, $RMSEA$ = .07). Internal reliability scores for the five I's for self-ratings fell in the range of .62 to .76. For transactional leadership the alpha scores fell between .60 and .75. For passive-avoidant behaviors, the alpha scores fell between .60 and .64.

Follower Rates the Leader

The CFA results for the 9-factor model (N = 12,118, GFI = .91, CFI = .91, $RMSEA$ = .05) were also a better fit than the 3-factor model (N = 12,118, GFI = .78, CFI = .77, $RMSEA$ = .08). Internal reliability scores for the five I's for ratings of the participant's leader fell in the range of .70 to .83. For transactional leadership the alpha scores fell between .73 and .74. For passive-avoidant behaviors, the alpha scores fell between .70 and .74.

The Full Range Model of Leadership

Reliability and Validity of The Multifactor Leadership Questionnaire

Antonakis, Avolio and Sivasubramaniam (2003)

A very robust analysis of the *MLQ 5X* was done by Antonakis, Avolio and Sivasubramaniam (2003). For the analysis, the authors obtained data from 1,079 female and 2,289 male followers who rated same-gender leaders through mindgarden.com. Antonakis, Avolio and Sivasubramaniam then conducted a series of confirmatory factor analyses on the data.

The researchers found an adequate fit for the hypothesized 9-factor model ($RMSEA < .08$, $CFI > .90$). Additionally the female group scored significantly higher than did the male group on individual consideration.

To further explore why different factor structures might emerge in different studies, the authors analyzed data from 18 studies. Five studies were independent studies, eight studies had previously been analyzed by Avolio, Bass and Jung (1995) and five studies had previously been analyzed by Avolio, Bass and Jung (1999) for a total sample size of N = 6,525. The studies were coded according to: risk conditions/environmental uncertainty, leader hierarchical level, leader–follower gender and degree of organizational structure.

An important finding was that the authors concluded that the factor structure of the *MLQ 5X* may vary across different combinations of risk conditions/environmental uncertainty, leader hierarchical level, leader–follower gender and degree of organizational structure. They speculated that this might suggest that leaders may operationalize or enact their behaviors differently depending on the context.

Antonakis, Avolio and Sivasubramaniam also indicated that while the pattern of relationships may vary between contextual conditions they tended to be stable within contextual conditions.

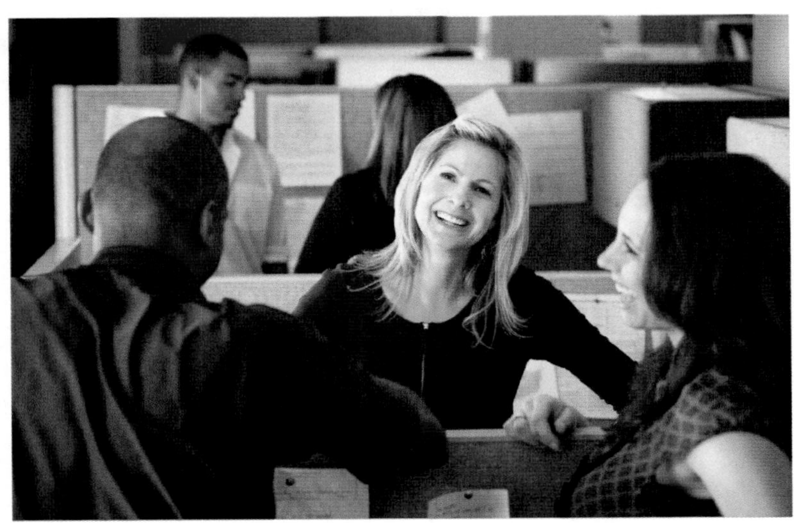

The Full Range Model of Leadership

Research Results

Understanding the Research Results for the Full Range Model of Leadership

There is a great deal of research on the full range model of leadership. To prepare you for understanding the research results that follow, chapter 2 explained both correlations and meta-analyses. The table below, however, provides a quick review of how the results of the meta-analytic literature will be provided in this chapter.[26]

Example - Leader Transformational Leadership and Follower Job Satisfaction

In the example below, 18 studies have been published and meta-analyzed on the relationship between leaders' use of transformational leadership and follower job satisfaction. Those 18 studies collectively represent 5,279 follower ratings. The letter (B) refers to the study that is being referenced. A list of studies is included at the end of this chapter. The meta-analytic finding was a strong, positive correlation (.58). The more transformational leaders were, the higher the followers' job satisfaction.

Strongly - Correlated	Moderately - Correlated	Weakly - Correlated
-1 to -.50	-.49 to -.30	-.29 to -.10

Weakly + Correlated	Moderately + Correlated	Strongly + Correlated
.10 to .29	.30 to .49	.50 to 1

Outcome	Studies	Followers	
Job Satisfaction (B)	18	5,279	.58

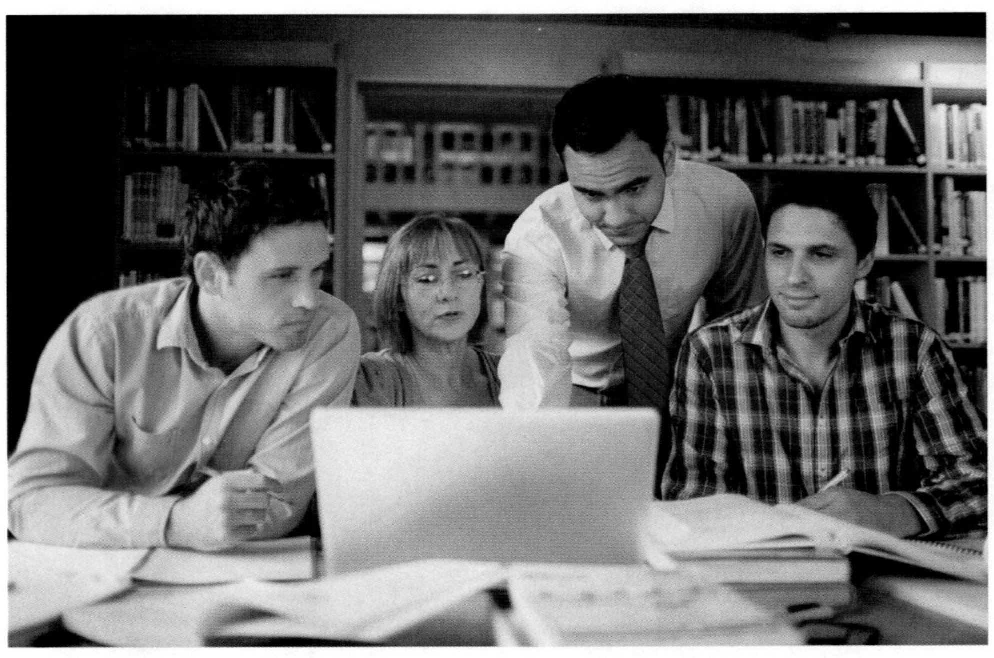

The Full Range Model of Leadership

Research Results

Transformational Leadership and Follower Outcomes

Strongly - Correlated	Moderately - Correlated	Weakly - Correlated	Weakly + Correlated	Moderately + Correlated	Strongly + Correlated
-1 to -.50	-.49 to -.30	-.29 to -.10	.10 to .29	.30 to .49	.50 to 1

Outcome	Studies	Followers	
Uncorrelated			
Follower Continuance Commitment (G)	27	9,417	.00
Weakly, Positively Correlated			
Follower Task Performance (A)	31	7,016	.21
Follower General Performance (A)	13	4,017	.21
Individual-level Performance (A)	62	16,809	.25
Moderately, Positively Correlated			
Follower Normative Commitment (G)	29	9,840	.34
Follower Affective[27] Commitment (G)	102	33,246	.45
Strongly, Positively Correlated			
Follower Motivation (B)	16	4,773	.53
Follower Job Satisfaction (B)	18	5,279	.58

Research from 298 analyses (effect sizes) that have included 90,397 follower ratings indicates that transformational leadership is weakly to moderately, positively correlated with both follower performance and various aspects of commitment. Transformational leadership is strongly, positively correlated with follower motivation and job satisfaction.

The Full Range Model of Leadership

Research Results

Transformational Leadership and Leader Outcomes

Strongly - Correlated	Moderately - Correlated	Weakly - Correlated
-1 to -.50	-.49 to -.30	-.29 to -.10

Weakly + Correlated	Moderately + Correlated	Strongly + Correlated
.10 to .29	.30 to .49	.50 to 1

Outcome	Studies	Followers	
Weakly, Positively Correlated			
Leader Job Performance (B)	13	2,126	.27
Strongly, Positively Correlated			
Leader Effectiveness (B)	27	5,415	.64
Follower Satisfaction With Leader (B)	23	4,349	.71

Research from 63 analyses (effect sizes) that have included 11,890 follower ratings indicates that transformational leadership is weakly, positively correlated with assessments of leaders' job performance. Transformational leadership is strongly, positively correlated with assessments of leaders' effectiveness and with satisfaction with leaders.

Transformational Leadership and Organizational Outcomes

Strongly - Correlated	Moderately - Correlated	Weakly - Correlated
-1 to -.50	-.49 to -.30	-.29 to -.10

Weakly + Correlated	Moderately + Correlated	Strongly + Correlated
.10 to .29	.30 to .49	.50 to 1

Outcome	Studies	Followers	
Weakly, Positively Correlated			
Group or Organization Performance (B)	41	6,197	.26
Team-Level Performance (A)	27	2,408	.27
Moderately, Positively Correlated			
Organizational-Level Performance (A)	34	2,830	.33

Research from 102 analyses (effect sizes) indicates that transformational leadership is weakly, positively correlated with group or organizational performance and team-level performance.

Transformational leadership is moderately, positively correlated with organizational-level performance.

The Full Range Model of Leadership

Research Results

Contingent Reward and Follower Outcomes

Strongly - Correlated	Moderately - Correlated	Weakly - Correlated
-1 to -.50	-.49 to -.30	-.29 to -.10

Weakly + Correlated	Moderately + Correlated	Strongly + Correlated
.10 to .29	.30 to .49	.50 to 1

Outcome	Studies	Followers	
Weakly, Positively Correlated			
Individual-level Performance (A)	50	9,108	.22
Task Performance (A)	17	6,180	.28
Follower Normative Commitment (G)	16	6,506	.28
Moderately, Positively Correlated			
Follower Affective Commitment (G)	51	19,015	.37
Strongly, Positively Correlated			
Follower Motivation (B)	13	3,615	.59
Follower Job Satisfaction (B)	6	1,933	.64

	Outcome	Studies	Followers
Very Weakly, Negatively Correlated			
-.07	Follower Continuance Commitment (G)	16	7,279

Three types of commitment are shown in the research above. Affective commitment is generally the most desirable. In this form of commitment, the follower likes her or his work and is committed to it. Normative commitment is a form of commitment in which the follower is committed out of sense of obligation. The least desirable type of follower commitment is continuance commitment. This form measures the degree to which followers stay at their jobs because they "can't afford to leave."

Research from 169 analyses (effect sizes) that have included 53,636 follower ratings indicates that contingent reward is weakly to moderately, positively correlated with follower performance and commitment, and strongly correlated with follower motivation and affective commitment.

Contingent reward is very weakly, negatively correlated with continuance commitment.

The Full Range Model of Leadership

Research Results

Contingent Reward and Leader Outcomes

Strongly - Correlated	Moderately - Correlated	Weakly - Correlated
-1 to -.50	-.49 to -.30	-.29 to -.10

Weakly + Correlated	Moderately + Correlated	Strongly + Correlated
.10 to .29	.30 to .49	.50 to 1

Outcome	Studies	Followers	
Moderately, Positively Correlated			
Leader Effectiveness (C)	43	7,163	.41
Leader Job Performance (B)	6	684	.45
Strongly, Positively Correlated			
Follower Satisfaction With Leader (B)	14	4,076	.55
Leader Effectiveness (B)	18	886	.55

Research from 81 analyses (effect sizes) that have included 12,809 follower ratings indicates that contingent reward is moderately to strongly, positively correlated with various assessments of leader performance.

Contingent Reward and Organizational Outcomes

Strongly - Correlated	Moderately - Correlated	Weakly - Correlated
-1 to -.50	-.49 to -.30	-.29 to -.10

Weakly + Correlated	Moderately + Correlated	Strongly + Correlated
.10 to .29	.30 to .49	.50 to 1

Outcome	Studies	Followers	
Weakly, Positively Correlated			
Group or Organization Performance (B)	16	3,227	.16
Team-Level Performance (A)	19	1,361	.24

Research from 35 analyses (effect sizes) indicates that contingent reward is weakly, positively correlated with assessments of group or team performance.

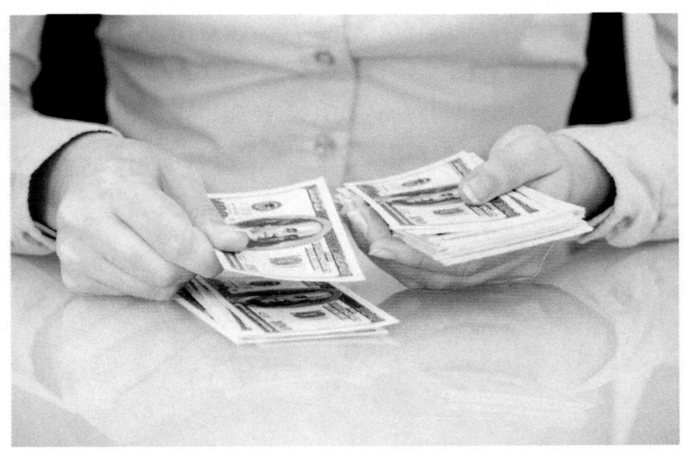

The Full Range Model of Leadership

Research Results

Management by Exception Active and Follower Outcomes

Strongly - Correlated	Moderately - Correlated	Weakly - Correlated	Weakly + Correlated	Moderately + Correlated	Strongly + Correlated
-1 to -.50	-.49 to -.30	-.29 to -.10	.10 to .29	.30 to .49	.50 to 1

Outcome	Studies	Followers	
Very Weakly, Positively Correlated			
Follower Continuance Commitment (G)	12	3,904	.02
Follower Affective Commitment (G)	25	8,845	.08
Weakly, Positively Correlated			
Follower Normative Commitment (G)	13	4,574	.11
Follower Motivation (B)	11	1,879	.14

	Outcome	Studies	Followers
Weakly, Negatively Correlated			
-.12	Task Performance (A)	5	525
-.13	Individual-level Performance (A)	5	525

Research from 65 analyses (effect sizes) that have included 25,655 follower ratings indicates that management by exception active is weakly, positively correlated with various assessments of follower commitment and motivation, but weakly, negatively correlated with individual and team performance.

Management by Exception Active and Leader Outcomes

Strongly - Correlated	Moderately - Correlated	Weakly - Correlated	Weakly + Correlated	Moderately + Correlated	Strongly + Correlated
-1 to -.50	-.49 to -.30	-.29 to -.10	.10 to .29	.30 to .49	.50 to 1

Outcome	Studies	Followers	
Very Weakly, Positively Correlated			
Leader Effectiveness (C)	41	6,948	.05
Weakly, Positively Correlated			
Leader Job Performance (B)	6	684	.13
Leader Effectiveness (B)	14	2,117	.21
Follower Satisfaction With Leader (B)	11	2,272	.24

Research from 72 analyses (effect sizes) that have included 12,021 follower ratings indicates that management by exception active is weakly, positively correlated with assessments of leader performance, satisfaction with the leader and leader effectiveness.

The Full Range Model of Leadership

Research Results

Management by Exception Passive and Follower Outcomes

Strongly - Correlated	Moderately - Correlated	Weakly - Correlated	Weakly + Correlated	Moderately + Correlated	Strongly + Correlated
-1 to -.50	-.49 to -.30	-.29 to -.10	.10 to .29	.30 to .49	.50 to 1

Outcome	Studies	Followers	
Weakly, Positively Correlated			
Follower Continuance Commitment (G)	*10*	3,161	.12

	Outcome	Studies	Followers
Very Weakly, Negatively Correlated			
-.06	Individual-level Performance (A)	6	555
-.08	Task Performance (A)	6	555
Weakly, Negatively Correlated			
-.12	Follower Normative Commitment (G)	12	3,924
-.23	Follower Affective Commitment (G)	23	7,724
-.27	Follower Motivation (B)	22	3,441

Research from 79 analyses (effect sizes) that have included 19,360 follower ratings indicates that management by exception passive is weakly, positively correlated with follower continuance commitment and weakly, negatively correlated with other measures of follower commitment, motivation and performance.

Management by Exception Passive and Leader Outcomes

Strongly - Correlated	Moderately - Correlated	Weakly - Correlated	Weakly + Correlated	Moderately + Correlated	Strongly + Correlated
-1 to -.50	-.49 to -.30	-.29 to -.10	.10 to .29	.30 to .49	.50 to 1

	Outcome	Studies	Followers
Weakly, Negatively Correlated			
-.14	Follower Satisfaction With Leader (B)	23	7,724
-.19	Leader Effectiveness (B)	8	2,627

Research from 31 analyses (effect sizes) that have included 10,351 follower ratings indicates that management by exception passive is weakly, negatively correlated with ratings of leader effectiveness and satisfaction with the leader.

The Full Range Model of Leadership

Research Results

Laissez-Faire and Leader Outcomes

Strongly - Correlated	Moderately - Correlated	Weakly - Correlated	Weakly + Correlated	Moderately + Correlated	Strongly + Correlated
-1 to -.50	-.49 to -.30	-.29 to -.10	.10 to .29	.30 to .49	.50 to 1

Outcome	Studies	Followers	Correlation
Very Weakly, Positively Correlated			
Follower Continuance Commitment (G)	7	3,189	.08

Correlation	Outcome	Studies	Followers
Very Weakly, Negatively Correlated			
-.07	Follower Motivation (B)	6	1,302
Weakly, Negatively Correlated			
-.16	Follower Normative Commitment (G)	8	3,593
Moderately, Negatively Correlated			
-.30	Follower Affective Commitment (G)	15	6,404

Research from 36 analyses (effect sizes) that have included 14,488 follower ratings indicates that laissez-faire behaviors are very weakly, positively correlated with follower commitment. Laissez-faire behaviors are weakly, negatively correlated with follower normative commitment and moderately, negatively correlated with follower affective commitment.

Laissez-Faire and Leader Outcomes

Strongly - Correlated	Moderately - Correlated	Weakly - Correlated	Weakly + Correlated	Moderately + Correlated	Strongly + Correlated
-1 to -.50	-.49 to -.30	-.29 to -.10	.10 to .29	.30 to .49	.50 to 1

Correlation	Outcome	Studies	Followers
Strongly, Negatively Correlated			
-.54	Leader Effectiveness (B)	11	1,920
-.58	Follower Satisfaction With Leader (B)	5	838

Research from 16 analyses (effect sizes) that have included 2,758 follower ratings indicates that laissez-faire behaviors are strongly, negatively correlated with ratings of the leader's effectiveness and satisfaction with the leader.

Meta-Analytic Regressions Related to the Full Range Model of Leadership

The next five pages summarize the meta-analytic regression research related to the full range model of leadership.

Meta-analyses provided earlier in this chapter analyzed one independent variable at a time. The meta-analytic regressions that follow include multiple independent variables simultaneously.

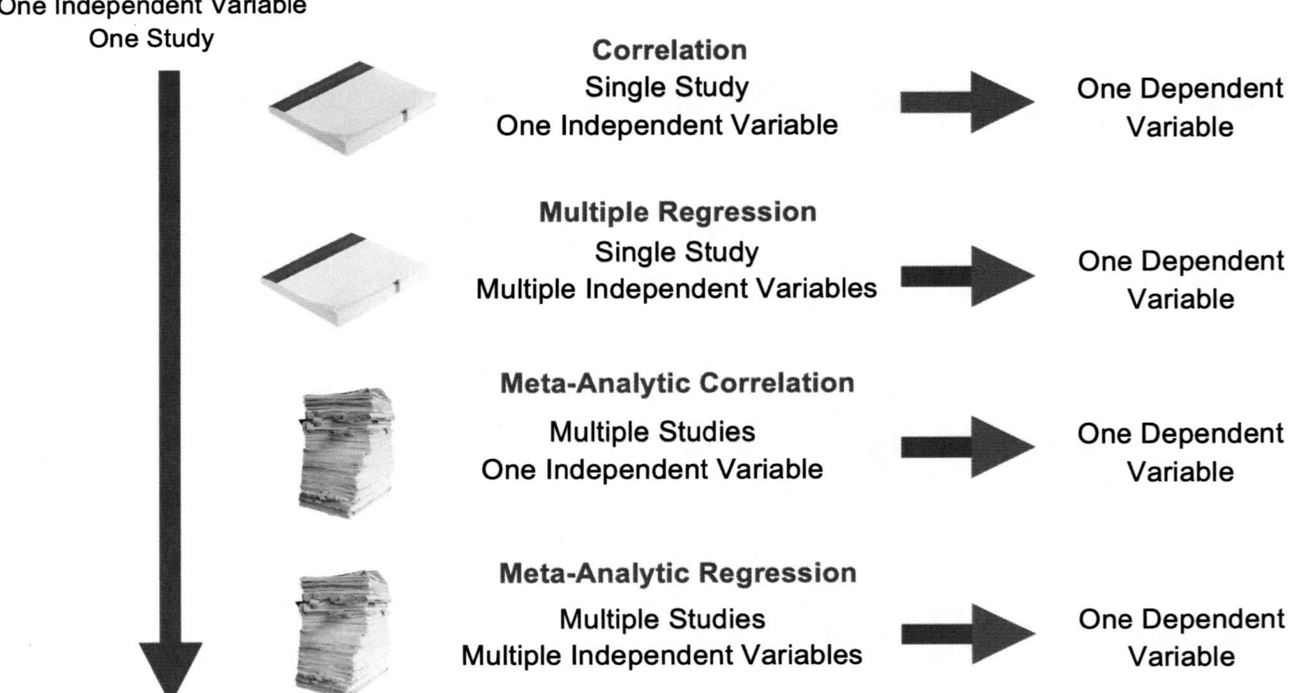

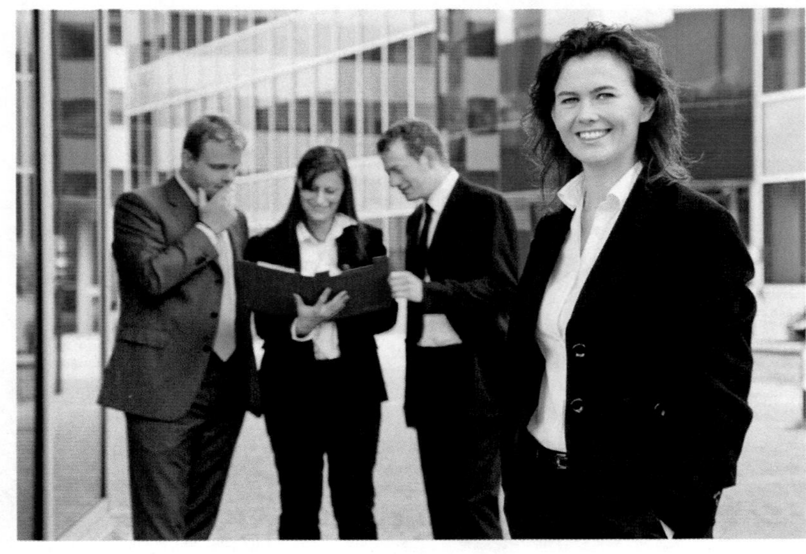

The Full Range Model of Leadership

Meta-Analytic Regressions

Leader Consideration, Initiation of Structure and Leader Transformational Behaviors

Piccolo, Bono, Heinitz, Rowold, Duehr and Judge (2012) performed a meta-analysis of 11 studies that included consideration, initiation of structure and transformational leadership as well as measures for follower job satisfaction and assessments of leader effectiveness. One of the findings was that transformational leadership was strongly, positively correlated with consideration (*rho* = .74) and was also strongly, positively correlated with initiation of structure (*rho* = .50).

The authors ran meta-analytic regression analyses to analyze which of the three aspects of leadership were the strongest predictors of follower job satisfaction and leader effectiveness. The relationship numbers shown below are the standardized regression weights.

When analyzed individually, all three aspects of leadership were meta-analytically correlated with follower job satisfaction. When analyzed together in a meta-analytic regression, only consideration and transformational leadership were significant predictors of follower job satisfaction (total R^2 = .21).

Meta-Analytic Regression to Predict Follower Job Satisfaction **(Standardized Regression Weights)**

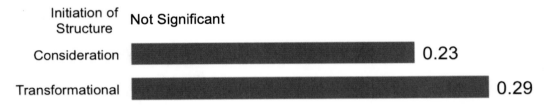

Meta-Analytic Regression to Predict Leader Effectiveness **(Standardized Regression Weights)**

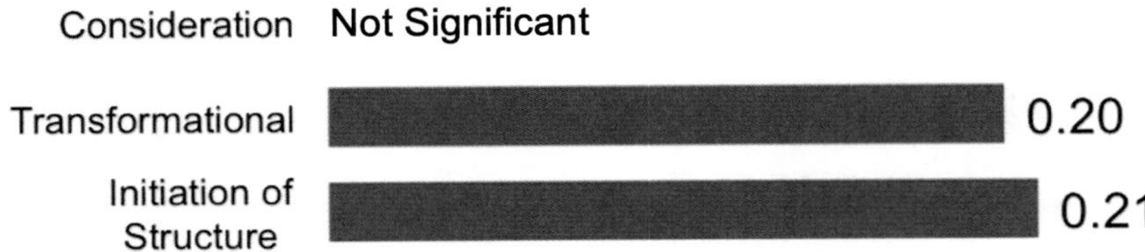

In the meta-analytic regression to predict leader effectiveness consideration was not significant, but both transformational leadership and initiation of structure were positively related to ratings of leader effectiveness (total R^2 = .20).

The Full Range Model of Leadership

Meta-Analytic Regressions

Leader Consideration, Initiation of Structure, Full Range Model, Personality, Gender and Intelligence Predicting Leader Effectiveness

Derue, Nahrgang, Wellman and Humphrey (2011) conducted a meta-analytic multiple regression using data from 59 studies. For the multiple regression 14 predictor variables were used:

Leader Gender and Intelligence
The Big Five Domains of Leader Personality
Transformational, Contingent Reward, MBE-Active, MBE-Passive and Laissez-Faire
Initiation of Structure and Consideration

The chart below provides the strength of each variable in predicting leader effectiveness. The number provided is the R^2 value.[28] The total R^2 for all of the variables was .58, and 42% of the variance in leader effectiveness was unexplained when using only these 14 predictors. For those variables with a blue bar, the direction of the relationship was positive. For those variables with a red bar, the direction of the relationship was negative.

Predictors of Leader Effectiveness (R^2 Values)

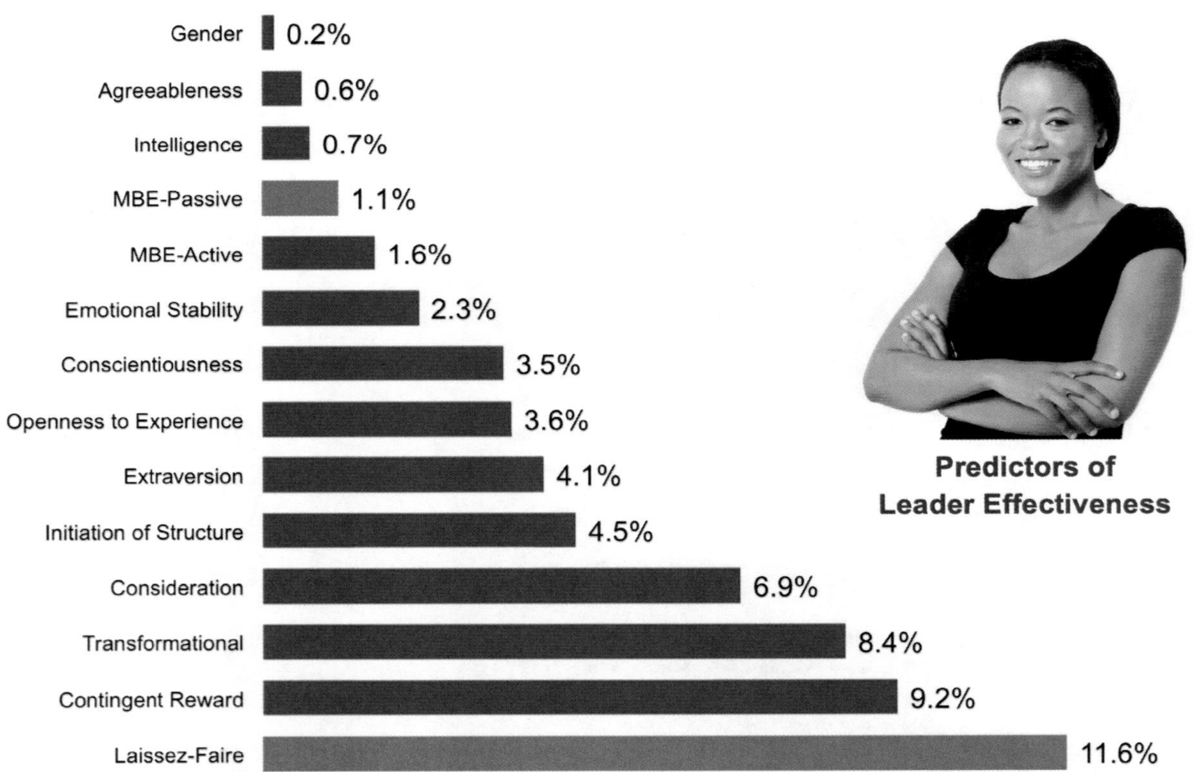

Predictors of Leader Effectiveness

The four strongest predictors of ratings of leader effectiveness were leader consideration, leader transformational behaviors, leader use of contingent reward and leaders not engaging in laissez-faire behaviors.

The Full Range Model of Leadership

Meta-Analytic Regressions

Leader Consideration, Initiation of Structure, Full Range Model, Personality and Intelligence Predicting Group Performance

Derue, Nahrgang, Wellman and Humphrey (2011) conducted a meta-analytic multiple regression using data from 59 studies. For the multiple regression 12 predictor variables were used:

Leader Intelligence
The Big Five Domains of Leader Personality
Transformational, Contingent Reward, MBE-Active and MBE-Passive
Initiation of Structure and Consideration

The chart below provides the strength of each variable in predicting group performance. The number provided is the R^2 value. The total R^2 for all of the variables was .31, and 69% of the variance in group performance was unexplained when using only these 12 predictors. For those variables with a blue bar, the direction of the relationship was positive. For those variables with a red bar, the direction of the relationship was negative.

Predictors of Group Performance (R^2 Values)

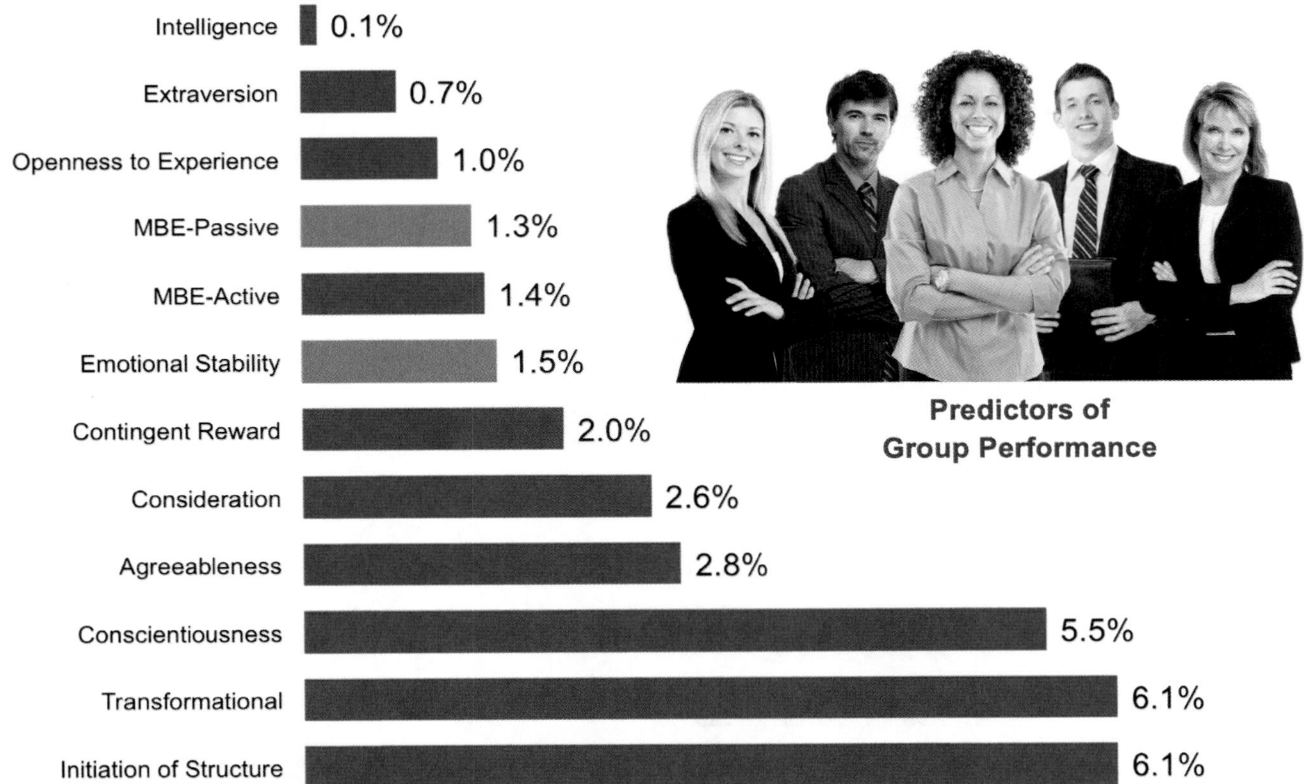

The strongest predictors of group performance were leader conscientiousness, leader transformational behaviors and leader initiation of structure.

The Full Range Model of Leadership

Meta-Analytic Regressions

Leader Consideration, Initiation of Structure, Full Range Model, Personality and Gender Predicting Follower Job Satisfaction

Derue, Nahrgang, Wellman and Humphrey (2011) conducted a meta-analytic multiple regression using data from 59 studies. For the multiple regression 13 predictor variables were used:

Leader Gender
The Big Five Domains of Leader Personality
Transformational, Contingent Reward, MBE-Active, MBE-Passive and Laissez-Faire
Initiation of Structure and Consideration

The chart below provides the strength of each variable in predicting follower job satisfaction. The number provided is the R^2 value. The total R^2 for all of the variables was .56 and 44% of the variance in follower job satisfaction was unexplained when using only these 13 predictors. For those variables with a blue bar, the direction of the relationship was positive. For those variables with a red bar, the direction of the relationship was negative.

Predictors of Job Satisfaction (R^2 Values)

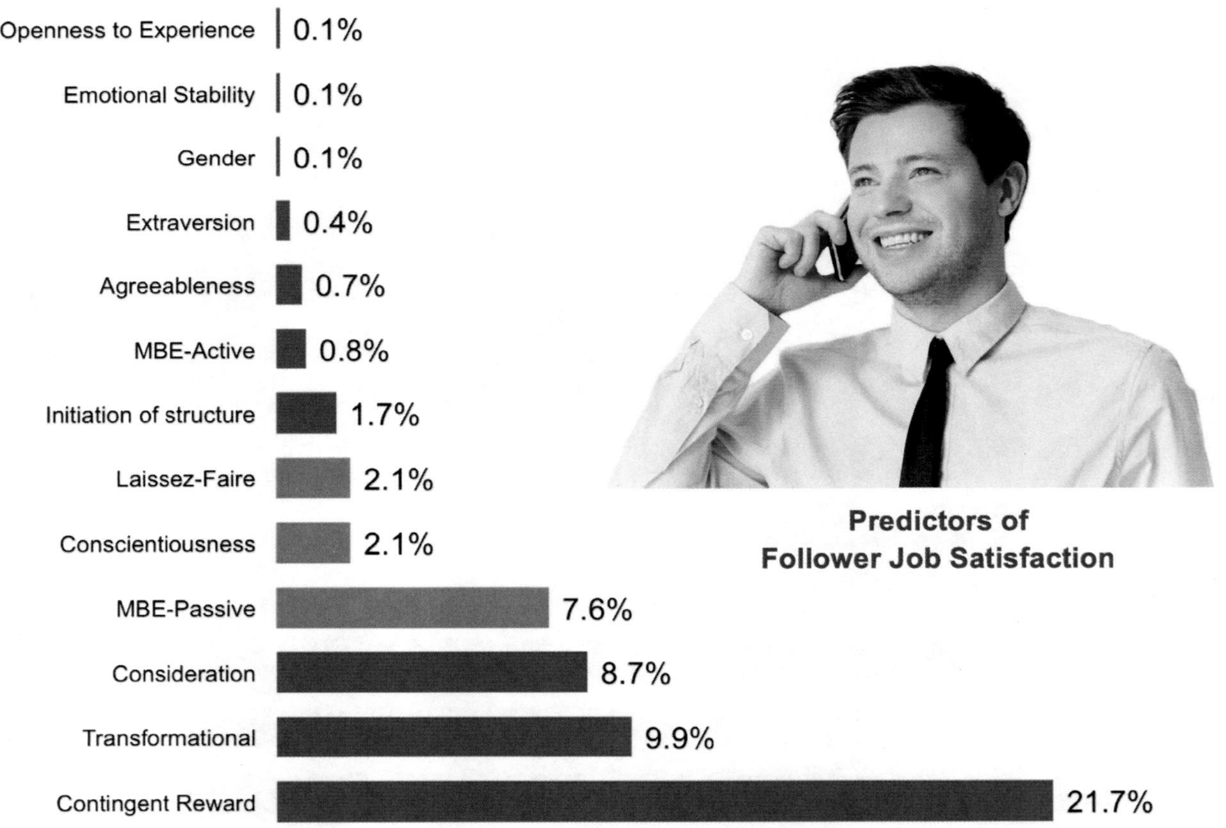

Predictors of Follower Job Satisfaction

When all thirteen variables were used to predict follower job satisfaction, leader use of contingent reward was a much stronger predictor than the remaining variables.

The Full Range Model of Leadership

Meta-Analytic Regressions

Leader Consideration, Initiation of Structure, Full Range Model, Personality, Gender and Intelligence Predicting Satisfaction with the Leader

Derue, Nahrgang, Wellman and Humphrey (2011) conducted a meta-analytic multiple regression using data from 59 studies. For the multiple regression 13 predictor variables were used:

Leader Gender
The Big Five Domains of Leader Personality
Transformational, Contingent Reward, MBE-Active, MBE-Passive and Laissez-Faire
Initiation of Structure and Consideration

The chart below provides the strength of each variable in predicting satisfaction with the leader. The total R^2 for all of the variables was .92, and 8% of the variance in satisfaction with the leader was unexplained when using only these 13 predictors. For those variables with a blue bar, the direction of the relationship was positive. For those variables with a red bar, the direction of the relationship was negative.

Predictors of Satisfaction with the Leader (R^2 Values)

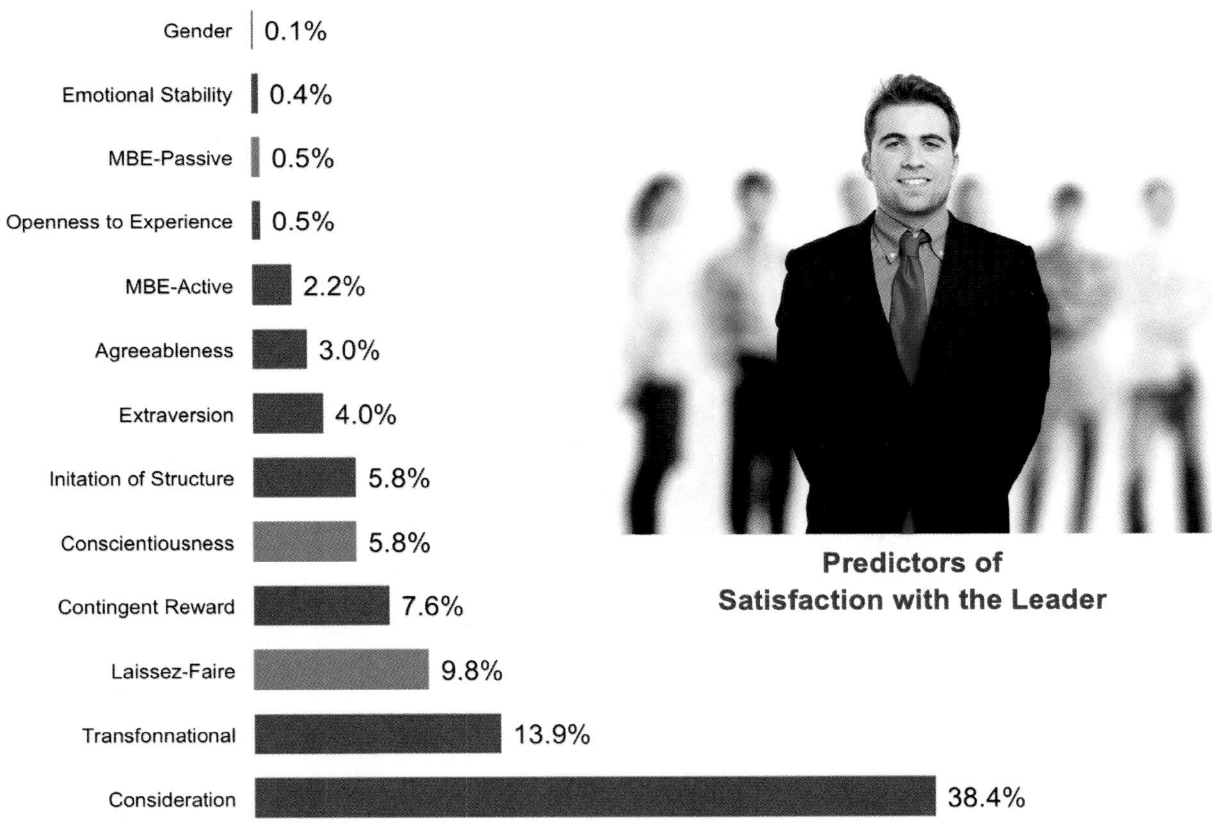

Predictors of Satisfaction with the Leader

The strongest predictor of satisfaction with the leader was leader consideration. Being transformational and not being laissez-faire were also noteworthy predictors.

The Full Range Model of Leadership

Meta-Analytic Regressions

Meta-Analytic Multiple Regression for Leader Personality and the Full Range of Leadership Model

Bono and Judge (2004) conducted several meta-analytic multiple regressions using 384 correlations from 26 independent studies.

For the multiple regressions, all five domains of personality were used as a combined predictor of several of the aspects of the full range model of leadership.

The chart below provides the strength of overall leader personality in predicting leadership style. The number provided is the R^2 value.

Leader Personality and Leadership Style (R^2 Values)

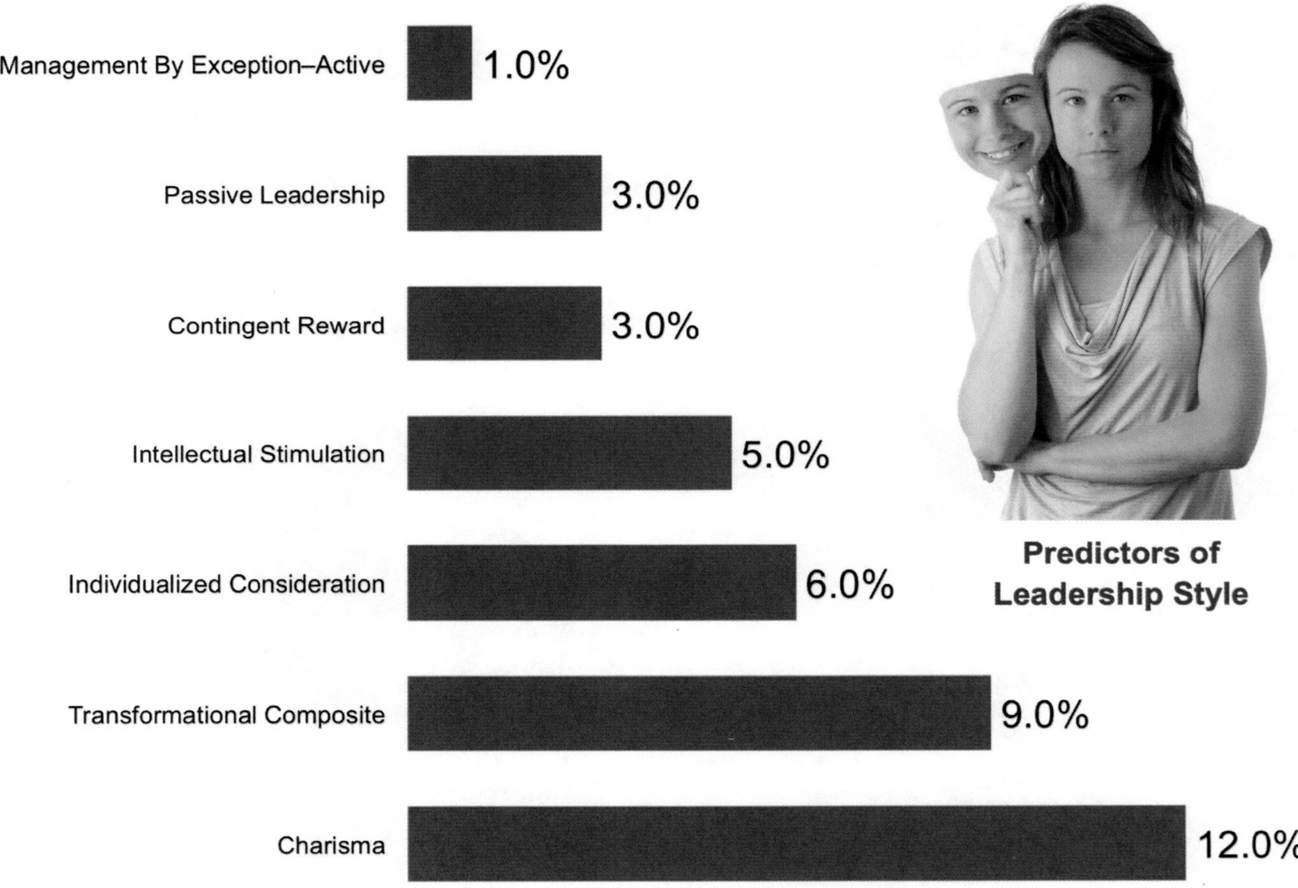

Leaders' personality explained 12% of the variance in how charismatic those leaders were rated. Nine percent of the variance in ratings of transformational leadership can be explained by the five aspects of leader personality.

Meta-Analytic Regressions (Dominance Analysis) for Transformational, Contingent Reward and Follower Task Performance

Wang, Oh, Courtright and Colbe (2011) performed a series of meta-analyses related to the full range model of leadership and aspects of follower performance. As part of the meta-analyses, they analyzed two types of follower performance: task and contextual.

Task performance refers to work behaviors that are described by a formal job description. While not limited to repetitive tasks such as those on an assembly line, task performance relates to aspect of the job that can be readily measured.

The meta-analytic correlations found that both transformational (r_c = .21) and contingent reward behaviors (r_c = .28) are positively related to follower task performance.

Transformational Leadership R = .21 Contingent Reward ΔR = .07

Model 1 R = .28

Contingent Reward R = .28

Model 2 R = .28

In the dominance analysis, two models were tested. In the first model, transformational leadership was entered as the first predictor, followed by contingent reward. Beyond the effect of transformational leadership, the use of contingent reward improved the predictive model – contingent reward augmented transformational leadership for task performance.

In the second model, contingent reward was entered as the first predictor, followed by transformational leadership. The effect of transformational leadership was not significant - transformational leadership did not augment contingent reward for task performance.

The Full Range Model of Leadership

Meta-Analytic Regressions

Meta-Analytic Regressions (Dominance Analysis) for Transformational, Contingent Reward and Follower Contextual Performance

Contextual performance refers to voluntarily motivated work behaviors that go beyond prescribed job roles but contribute to the psychological and social contexts around the job.

In their meta-analytic correlations (Wang, Oh, Courtright and Colbe, 2011) found that both transformational (r_c = .30) and contingent reward behaviors (r_c = .23) are positively related to follower contextual performance.

Transformational Leadership R = .30

Model 1 R = .30

Contingent Reward R = .23

Transformational Leadership ΔR = .07

Model 2 R = .30

In the dominance analysis, two models were tested. In the first model, transformational leadership was entered as the first predictor, followed by contingent reward. The effect of contingent reward was not significant - contingent reward did not augment transformational leadership for contextual performance.

In the second model, contingent reward was entered as the first predictor, followed by transformational leadership. Beyond the effect of contingent reward, the use of transformational leadership improved the predictive model – transformational leadership augmented contingent reward for contextual performance.

The Full Range Model of Leadership

Discussion

Discussion

Similar to the child's game, we want to end this chapter by connecting the dots. In doing so, however, we want to only connect dots that exist and avoid adding our own dots to improve the image.

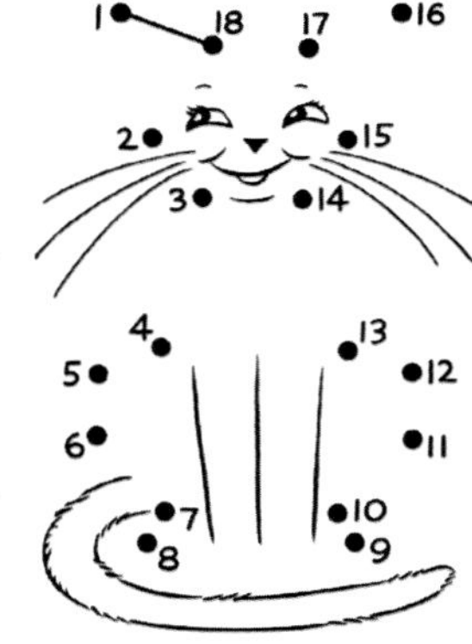

A mistake we don't want to make is "comparing" the strength of two correlations across studies. This can be done, but requires additional, advanced statistical analysis.

The "big picture" observation is that transformational leadership is positively related to a range of follower, organizational and leader outcomes.

Transformational Leadership

Outcome	Correlation
Group or Organization Performance	0.26
Organizational-Level Performance	0.27
Team-Level Performance	0.33
Leader Effectiveness	0.64
Leader Job Performance	0.27
Follower Satisfaction With Leader	0.71
Follower Motivation	0.53
Follower Job Satisfaction	0.58
Follower General Performance	0.21
Follower Task Performance	0.21
Individual-level Performance	0.25
Follower Normative Commitment	0.34
Follower Affective Commitment	0.45

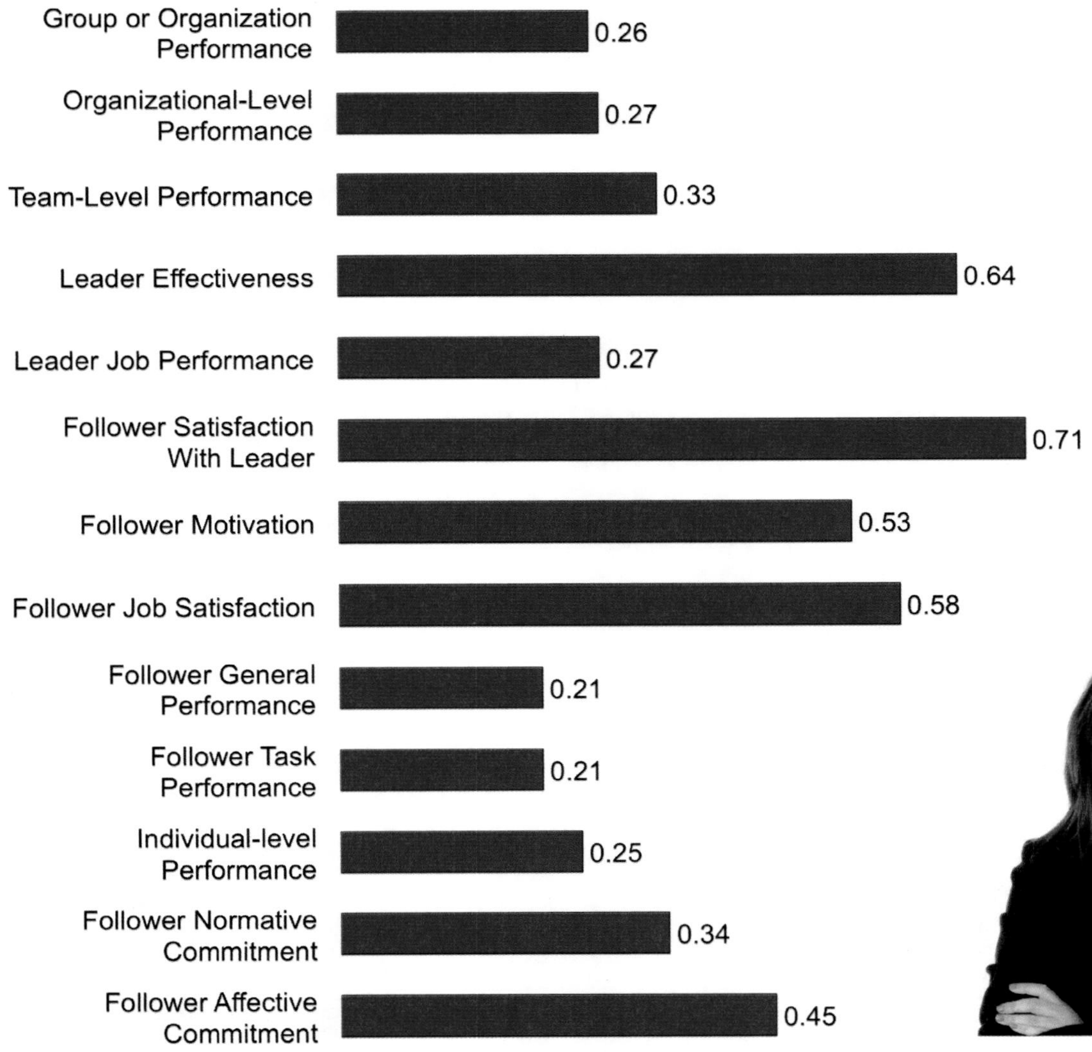

The Full Range Model of Leadership

Discussion

Transactional Leadership

Transactional leadership has mixed results with the outcome variables. Generally, contingent reward is positively related and management by exception active has mixed relationships with a variety of outcomes.

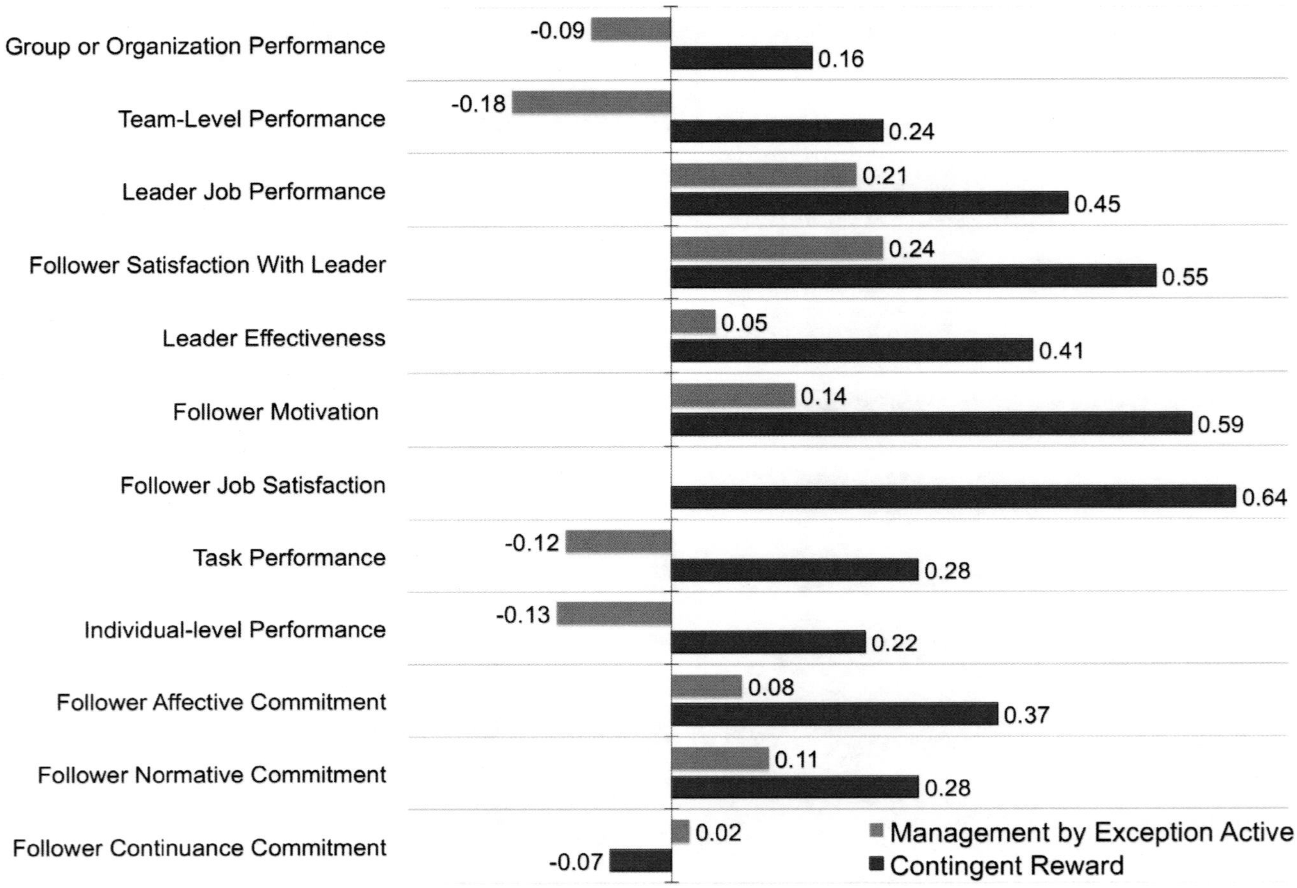

	Management by Exception Active	Contingent Reward
Group or Organization Performance	-0.09	0.16
Team-Level Performance	-0.18	0.24
Leader Job Performance	0.21	0.45
Follower Satisfaction With Leader	0.24	0.55
Leader Effectiveness	0.05	0.41
Follower Motivation	0.14	0.59
Follower Job Satisfaction		0.64
Task Performance	-0.12	0.28
Individual-level Performance	-0.13	0.22
Follower Affective Commitment	0.08	0.37
Follower Normative Commitment	0.11	0.28
Follower Continuance Commitment	0.02	-0.07

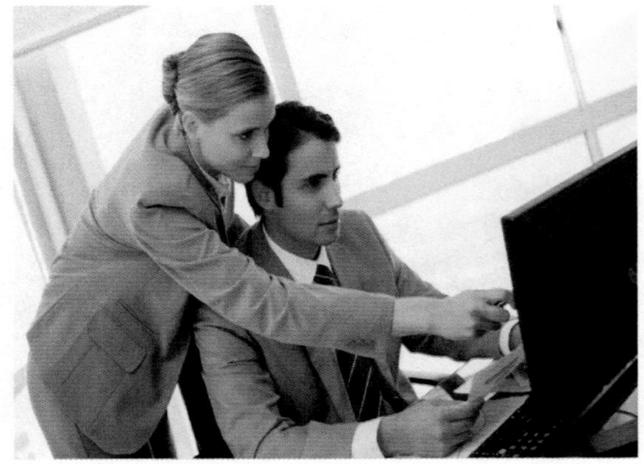

The Full Range Model of Leadership

Discussion

Passive-Avoidant Leadership

Aspects of passive-avoidant leadership are generally negatively related to the outcomes measured in the meta-analyses.

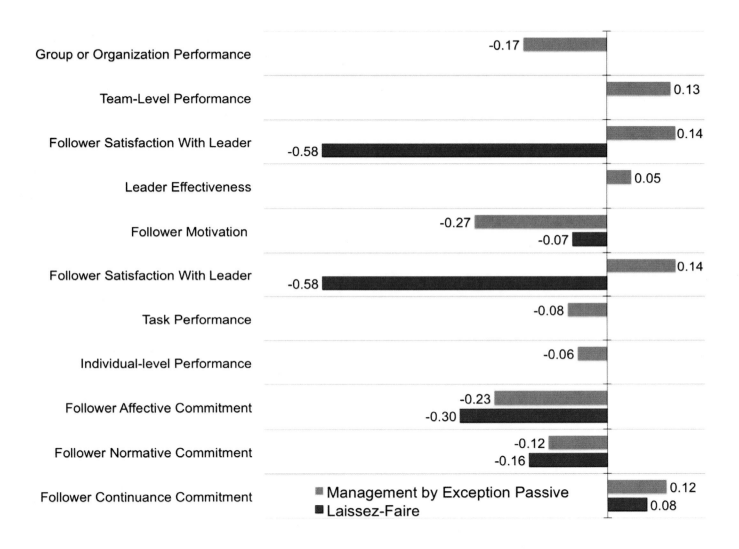

	Management by Exception Passive	Laissez-Faire
Group or Organization Performance	-0.17	
Team-Level Performance	0.13	
Follower Satisfaction With Leader	0.14	-0.58
Leader Effectiveness	0.05	
Follower Motivation	-0.27	-0.07
Follower Satisfaction With Leader	0.14	-0.58
Task Performance	-0.08	
Individual-level Performance	-0.06	
Follower Affective Commitment	-0.23	-0.30
Follower Normative Commitment	-0.12	-0.16
Follower Continuance Commitment	0.12	0.08

The Full Range Model of Leadership

Discussion

Leader Demographics

Female leaders are rated higher on transformational leadership and contingent reward than male leaders. Male leaders are rated higher on management by exception active, management by exception passive and laissez-faire leadership.

The personality dimensions of extraversion, agreeableness, openness to new ideas and conscientiousness are generally positively related to transformational leadership and contingent reward, while negatively related to management by exception active and passive and laissez-faire leadership. Neuroticism has the opposite relationship from the other four aspects of personality.

Finally, emotional intellilgence is positively related to transformational leadership and contingent reward. Emotional intelligence is negatively related to management by exception active, management by exception passive and laissez-faire leadership.

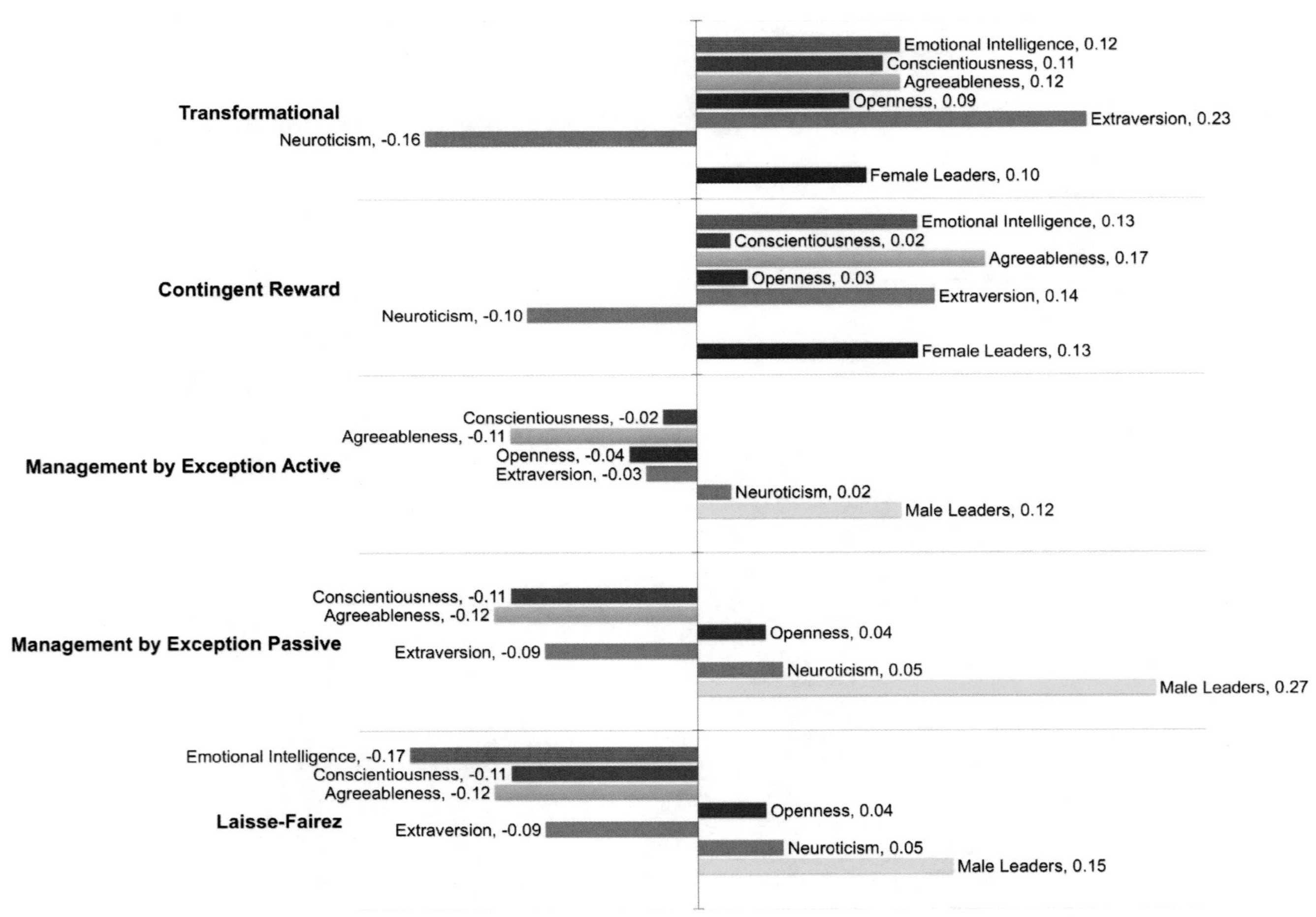

The Full Range Model of Leadership

Discussion

The theoretical underpinnings of the full range model of leadership are that the five "I's" of transformational leadership as well as contingent reward are considered both active and effective aspects of leadership. Management by exception active, management by exception passive and laissez-faire are considered less active and less effective.

The Full Range Model of Leader Behaviors

Transformational	Transactional	Passive-Avoidant
IM, IS, IC, IIA, IIB CR	MBEA MBEP	LF
Active Effective Improved Follower Performance		Passive Ineffective Decreased Follower Performance

The summary of the directionality of the meta-analyses reviewed in this chapter, generally support the idea of a range of effective to ineffective leadership behaviors.

<table>
<tr><th>Variable</th><th>TF</th><th>CR</th><th>MBEA</th><th>MBEP</th><th>LF</th></tr>
<tr><td>Follower Affective Commitment (G)</td><td>+</td><td>+</td><td>+</td><td>-</td><td>-</td></tr>
<tr><td>Follower Normative Commitment (G)</td><td>+</td><td>+</td><td>-</td><td>-</td><td>-</td></tr>
<tr><td>Follower Continuous Commitment (G)</td><td></td><td>-</td><td>+</td><td>+</td><td>+</td></tr>
<tr><td>Individual-Level Performance (A)</td><td>+</td><td>+</td><td>-</td><td>-</td><td></td></tr>
<tr><td>Follower Task Performance (A)</td><td>+</td><td>+</td><td>-</td><td>-</td><td></td></tr>
<tr><td>Follower General Performance (A)</td><td>+</td><td>+</td><td></td><td></td><td></td></tr>
<tr><td>Follower Job Satisfaction (B)</td><td>+</td><td>+</td><td></td><td></td><td></td></tr>
<tr><td>Follower Motivation (B)</td><td>+</td><td>+</td><td>+</td><td>-</td><td>-</td></tr>
<tr><td>Leader Effectiveness (C)</td><td>+</td><td>+</td><td colspan="2">+</td><td></td></tr>
<tr><td>Follower Satisfaction With Leader (B)</td><td>+</td><td>+</td><td>+</td><td>-</td><td>-</td></tr>
<tr><td>Leader Job Performance (B)</td><td>+</td><td>+</td><td>+</td><td></td><td></td></tr>
<tr><td>Leader Effectiveness (B)</td><td>+</td><td>+</td><td>+</td><td>-</td><td>-</td></tr>
<tr><td>Team-Level Performance (A)</td><td>+</td><td>+</td><td>-</td><td>+</td><td></td></tr>
<tr><td>Organizational-Level Performance (A)</td><td>+</td><td>+</td><td></td><td></td><td></td></tr>
<tr><td>Group or Organization Performance (B)</td><td>+</td><td>+</td><td>-</td><td>-</td><td></td></tr>
</table>

Note.

A + indicates a positive relationship.

A - indicates a negative relationship.

A white cell indicates no analysis for that combination of variables, with the exception of follower continuous commitment and TF, for which the correlation was .00.

The Full Range Model of Leadership

Summary

Transformational and Transactional Leadership

Burns envisioned transformational and transactional leadership as separate entities.

Burns posited that transformational leaders are united in their pursuit of higher goals with their followers while transactional leaders have separate and sometimes unrelated goals with their followers.

Bass built on Burns work. Bass envisioned transformational and transactional leadership as a continuum consisting of six components. After various refinements, by 1991 a nine-component model was developed and is currently supported by the *Multifactor Leadership Questionnaire 5X*.

Transformational Leadership is considered the most effective form of leadership within the full range of leader behaviors.

Across 300 analyses representing over 90,000 follower ratings, transformational leadership is weakly, positively correlated with both follower performance and some aspects of commitment. Transformational leadership is moderately correlated with follower motivation, job satisfaction and other aspects of commitment.

There are five components that comprise transformational leadership.

Idealized Influence Attributed and Behavioral describe leaders who followers want to emulate. Leaders who are idealized influences are admired, respected and trusted. There are two forms of idealized influence: behavioral and attributed. Behavioral describes actual observable leader behaviors rather than simply attributing role model status to the leader.

Inspirational Motivation describes leaders who behave in ways that motivate those around them by displaying optimism and arousing enthusiasm.

Intellectual Stimulation describes leaders who solicit new ideas and creative solutions from followers. They stimulate their followers' efforts to be innovative and creative by questioning assumptions, reframing problems and approaching old situations in new ways.

Individual Consideration describes leaders who act as coaches and mentors. They develop their followers to successively higher levels of potential.

The Full Range Model of Leadership

Summary

Transactional Leadership can be effective in certain situations but is usually not as effective as transformational leadership. Transactional leadership consists of two components: contingent reward and management by exception active.

Contingent Reward describes leaders who engage in a constructive path-goal transaction of reward for performance. Leaders make clear expectations of outcomes and rewards. Contingent reward can be effective in situations in which followers believe they can impact their chances for rewards, such as salespeople on commissions.

Across over 150 analyses representing over 50,000 follower ratings, contingent reward is weakly to moderately, positively correlated with follower performance and commitment, and strongly correlated with follower motivation and affective commitment.

Contingent reward is very weakly, negatively correlated to continuance commitment.

Management by Exception Active describes leaders who monitor followers' performance and take corrective action if deviations from standards occur. These behaviors are considered by many people to be micro-managing behaviors.

Across over 65 analyses representing nearly 20,000 follower ratings, management by exception active is weakly, positively correlated with various assessments of follower commitment and motivation, but weakly, negatively correlated with individual and team performance.

.

The Full Range Model of Leadership

Summary

Passive Avoidant Leadership is generally considered the absence of leadership. Passive avoidant leadership consists of two components: management by exception passive and laissez-faire.

Management by Exception Passive describes leaders who fail to intervene until problems become serious.

Across over 30 analyses representing over 10,000 follower ratings, management by exception passive is weakly, negatively correlated with ratings of leader effectiveness and satisfaction with the leader.

Laissez-Faire Behaviors describe the absence of leadership. Laissez-faire leaders avoid making decisions and are inactive and passive in their leadership roles.

Across 16 analyses representing over 2,500 follower ratings, laissez-faire behaviors are strongly, negatively correlated with ratings of the leader's effectiveness and satisfaction with the leader.

Instrument: The Multifactor Leadership Questionnaire 5X The *Multifactor Leadership Questionnaire 5X* contains 36 questions that measure the nine components of the full range model of leadership on a five-point scale.

The Full Range Model of Leadership

Notes

Articles Referenced

A. Wang, Courtright, Colbert and Oh (2011). The statistic reported is the estimated corrected mean correlation.

B. Judge and Piccolo (2004). The statistic reported is the estimated true score correlation.

C. Lowe, Kroeck and Sivasubramaniam (1996). This meta-analysis included 21 published and 16 unpublished studies. The unpublished studies tended to be technical reports from the military, masters theses and doctoral dissertations. The statistic reported is the mean corrected correlation.

D. Harms and Credé (2010). Only the meta-analyses in which the leaders rated themselves on emotional intelligence and someone different rated them on leadership were reported. Correlations based on fewer than five samples were omitted from this table. The statistic reported is the estimated true score correlation.

E. Bono and Judge (2004). The statistic reported is the estimated true score correlation.

F. Eagly, Johannesen-Schmidt and van Engen (2004). The statistic reported is the difference between the leadership style of the male and the female leaders, divided by the pooled standard deviation. A positive effect size indicates that men had a higher score than women on a leadership style, and a negative effect size indicates that women had a higher score.

G. Jackson, Meyer and Wang (2013). The statistic reported is the weighted average corrected correlation.

Notes

[1] The information on the next two pages comes from House, R. J. (1996).

[2] Value based leadership and participative leadership would both become part of the second order dimensions of the project GLOBE study that House guided.

[3] Compiled from Kanungo, R. B. and Conger, J. (1989). Dimensions of executive charisma, *Perspectives*, Vol. 14, No 4, 1-8; and Conger, J. A. and Kanungo, R. N. (1997). Measuring charisma: Dimensionality and validity of the Conger-Kanungo Scale of Charismatic Leadership. *Canadian Journal Of Administrative Sciences 14*(3), 290.

[4] The information for this table was garnered from pp. 425–427 of Burns, J. M. (1978). *Leadership*. New York: Harper and Row. Burns didn't provide a table, but these contrasts are interwoven in those pages.

Notes

[5] Summarized from Bass, B. M. (1999). Two decades of research and development in transformational leadership. *European Journal of Work and Organizational Psychology*, 8 (1), 9–32.

[6] The definitions for all five "I's" come from Bass, B. M., Avolio, B. J., Jung, D. I. and Berson, Y. (2003). Predicting unit performance by assessing transformational and transactional leadership. *Journal of Applied Psychology*, 88 (2), 207–218.

[7] Details about each I come from Green, M. (2012). *Visualizing Transformational Leadership,* Create Space Publishing, Charlotte, NC.

[8] The definitions of CR, MBEA, MBEP and LF come from Bass, B. M. (1985). *Leadership and performance beyond expectations*. New York: Free Press.

[9] Details about CR, MBEA, MBEP and LF come from Barbuto and Brown (2000). http://www.ianrpubs.unl.edu/pages/publicationD.jsp?publicationId=198

[10] Bono, J. E., & Judge, T. A. (2004). Personality and transformational and transactional leadership: a meta-analysis. *The Journal of Applied Psychology, 89,* 5, 901-10.

[11] See for example Ferster, C. B., Skinner, B. F., Harvard University., & United States. (1957). *Schedules of reinforcement: By C.B. Ferster and B.F. Skinner*. New York: Appleton-Century-Crofts; and Skinner, B. F. (1972). *Cumulative record: A selection of papers*. New York: Appleton-Century-Crofts.

[12] This term seems to have originated with the Catholic Church. When someone was being considered for sainthood, a cannon lawyer was assigned the job of arguing against the individual being beatified.

[13] Hammer, M., & Champy, J. (1993). *Reengineering the corporation: A manifesto for business revolution*. New York, NY: HarperBusiness.

[14] These two ideas are from Roberto, M. A. (2005). *Why great leaders don't take yes for an answer: Managing for conflict and consensus*. Upper Saddle River, N.J: Wharton School Pub.

[15] Kaye, B. L., & Giulioni, J. W. (2012). *Help them grow or watch them go: Career conversations employees want*. San Francisco: Berrett-Koehler Publishers, Inc.

[16] Batson, C. D. (1991). *The altruism question: Toward a social psychological answer*. Hillsdale, NJ: Erlbaum.

[17] Eisenberg, N. (2000). Emotion, regulation, and moral development. *Annual Review of Psychology*, 51, 665–697.

[18] Hatfield, E., Cacioppo, J. T., & Rapson, R. L. (1994). *Emotional contagion*. New York, NY: Cambridge University Press.

[19]These definitions come from three sources:

Bass, B. M. (1985). *Leadership and performance beyond expectations*. New York: Free Press.

Hater, J. J. and Bass, B. M. (1988). Superiors' evaluations and subordinates perceptions of transformational and transactional leadership. *Journal of Applied Psychology, 73*, 695-702.

Howell, J. M. and Avolio, B. J. (1991). Predicting consolidated unit performance: Leadership ratings, locus of control and support for innovation. Paper presented at the 51st Annual Meeting of the Academy of Management, Miami, FL.

[20] Avolio, B. J., Bass, B. M. and Jung, D. I. (1999). Re-examining the components of transformational and transactional leadership using the Multifactor Leadership Questionnaire. *Journal of Occupational and Organizational Psychology, 72,* 4, 441-462.

[21] It is unclear why distinguishing between attributed and behavioral was limited to discussions of charismatic leadership. The same two-step distinction could be made for most dimensions of leadership.

[22] These ranges as well as the construct definitions come from Avolio, B. J., Bass, B. M., and Jung, D. I. (1999). Re-examining the components of transformational and transactional leadership using the *Multifactor Leadership Questionnaire*. *Journal of Occupational and Organizational Psychology, 72,*4, 441-462, and four additional replications with 2004 data from Mindgarden.com; Avolio, B. J., Bass, B. M., & Zhu, F. W. W. (2004). *Multifactor Leadership Questionnaire: Manual and sampler set*. Menlo Park, CA: Mind Garden, Inc.

[23] Around 2009, the Mindgarden.com web site changed the suggested scoring of the *MLQ 5X* second-order scores. Prior to 2009, the three scores for contingent reward, management by exception active and management by exception passive were combined to create a transactional leadership score. Laissez-faire was the third "second-order" dimension. Currently, contingent reward and management by exception active are combined to create a transactional leadership score, and management by exception passive and laissez-faire are combined to create a passive-avoidant score. The nine first-order dimensions did not change.

[24] The *MLQ Form 10* was in use at about the same time as the *MLQ 5R*. The *Form 10* contained seven questions that measured charisma, six that measured intellectual stimulation, six that measured individualized correlation, five that measured contingent reward, four for active management by exception and three for passive management by exception.

The description can be found in Howell, J. M. and Avolio, B. J. (1993). Transformational leadership, transactional leadership, locus of control, and support for innovation: Key predictors of consolidated-business-unit performance. *Journal of Applied Psychology, 78,* 6, 891-902.

[25] The chart does not include *Form 10*, that was used only briefly in the early 1990's.

[26] The exact boundary between weak, moderate and strong correlations is not universally agreed upon. The definitions used are based on Cohen, J. (1992). A power primer. *Psychological Bulletin, 112,* 1, 155-9.

[27] Followers with strong affective commitment want to remain in the organization. Those with strong normative commitment feel a duty or obligation to remain. Those with strong continuance commitment believe that they need to remain, typically because they can't financially afford to leave the organization.

[28] The authors reported epsilon values. For the three charts provided from this study the R^2 values shown were calculate by dividing the relative weight of each predictor (epsilon) by the total R^2.

The Full Range Model of Leadership

Notes

Chapter 5
Personality and Leadership

Personality and Leadership

Introduction

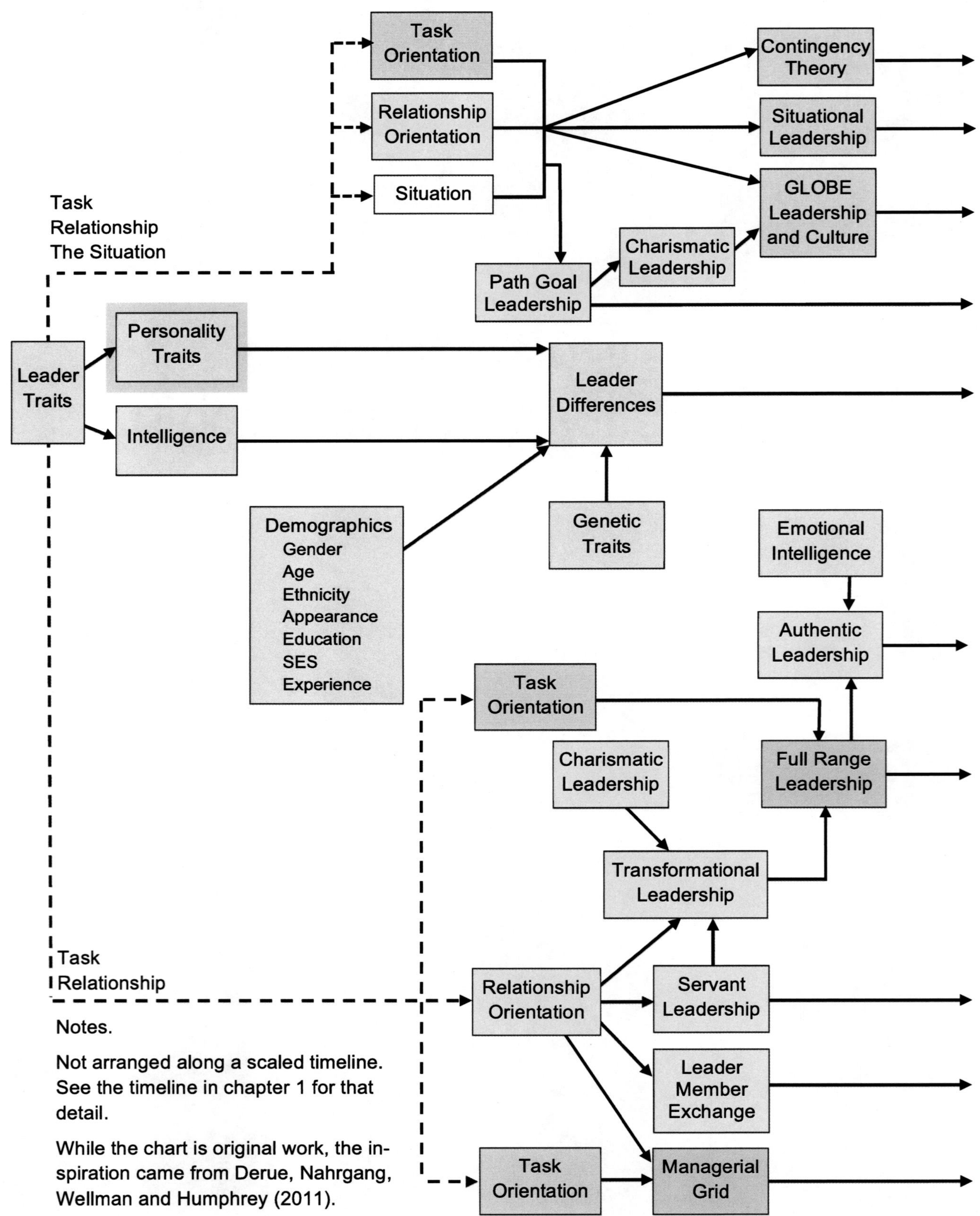

Notes.

Not arranged along a scaled timeline. See the timeline in chapter 1 for that detail.

While the chart is original work, the inspiration came from Derue, Nahrgang, Wellman and Humphrey (2011).

Personality and Leadership

Introduction

Recognizing personality differences among individuals has almost certainly been occurring as long as there have been human beings. The formal study of personality, however, is a relatively new phenomenon.

As we can see, Stogdill had a variety of aspects that he included as *personality* in his 1948 and 1974 assessments of leadership traits.[1]

	1948	1948	1974
	Pos	0/-	Pos
Personality			
Adaptability	10		
Adjustment, normality			11
Aggressiveness			12
Alertness	6		4
Ascendance, dominance	11	6	31
Emotional balance, control	11	8	14
Enthusiasm			3
Extraversion	5	6	1
Independence, nonconformity			13
Objectivity, tough minded			7
Originality, creativity	7		13
Integrity, ethical conduct	6		9
Resourcefulness			7
Self-confidence	17		28
Strength of conviction	7		
Tolerance of stress			9

About the time that Stogdill was performing his first trait study, researchers in the field of psychology were beginning to add more clarity about dimensions of personality.

In 1948, Cattell created a 16-factor model of personality that influenced much of the work on the later five-factor models.

By the time Stogdill performed his second meta-analysis, more focused models of personality were being developed. In 1978, Costa and McCrae developed a three-factor model that, by 1990 had evolved to a model having five high-level domains that can be broken further into 30, more narrow facets of personality.

Personality and Leadership

Models of Personality

Personality has been the subject of enough academic studies that there are over 90 meta-analyses on aspects of personality and "something." One of the lines of personality research is developing models to describe and measure personality.

Many of the models differ in how many factors or domains should be used in order to describe personality. The table below provides a broad visual illustration of what is called a hierarchy of personality models.

Researchers such as Diggman (1997) have argued for two main factors of personality. The alpha factor is somewhat similar to the big five dimensions of agreeableness, conscientiousness, and the inverse of neuroticism. The beta factor is somewhat similar to the big five dimensions of extraversion and openness.

Eysenck's (1997) three-factor model consists of neuroticism, psychoticism and extraversion. Psychoticism is somewhat inversely related to agreeableness and conscientiousness.

The model commonly called the big-five model includes neuroticism, agreeableness, conscientiousness, extraversion and openness. Each of these five domains, however, is frequently broken down into more narrow aspects of personality called facets.

In addition to the two, three and five-factor models illustrated below, Cattell (1989) developed a popular model with 16 factors. Depending on how one views Costa and Mcrae's big-five model, one might feel it is actually a 30 "factor" model as each of the five dimensions contains six facets.

There is also a great deal of research that indicates that, regardless of how many factors a model uses, there is an "overarching" or general factor (called g) that explains a great deal of the common variance among the personality factors.

Much of the research published on personality and leadership uses the five-factor or "big five" model. Consequently, this chapter will limit its review just to that model of personality.

Two-Factor Model	Three-Factor Model	Five-Factor Model	30 Facets of Five-Factor Model	General Factor
Alpha	Neuroticism	Neuroticism	N1, N2, N3, N4, N5, N6	g
	Psychoticism	Agreeableness	A1, A2, A3, A4, A5, A6	
		Conscientiousness	C1, C2, C3, C4, C5, C6	
Beta	Extraversion	Extraversion	E1, E2, E3, E4, E5, E6	
		Openness	O1, O2, O3, O4, O5, O6	

Personality and Leadership

Extraversion

The domain of extraversion is comprised of six facets: warmth, gregariousness, assertiveness, activity, excitement seeking and positive emotions.[2]

Domain	Higher	Lower
Extraversion	Like People Prefer Large Groups and Gatherings Assertive, Active, and Talkative Like Excitement and Stimulation Cheerful in Disposition	Reserved but Not Necessarily Unfriendly Independent Rather Than a Follower Even Paced Rather Than Sluggish Prefer to be Alone
Facet	**Higher**	**Lower**
Warmth	Interest in and Friendliness Towards Others Affectionate	Formal, Reserved Distant in Manner
Gregariousness	Preference for the Company of Others	Loners Who Generally Do Not Seek Social Stimulation
Assertiveness	Social Ascendancy and Forcefulness of Expression	Prefer to Keep in the Background Prefer to Let Others Do the Talking
Activity	Rapid Pace of Living Sense of Energy Need to Keep Busy	Relaxed Tempo More Leisurely
Excitement Seeking	Need for Excitement and Stimulation	Little Need for Thrills
Positive Emotions	Tendency to Experience Positive Emotions Such as Joy, Happiness, Love and Excitement	Less Exuberant and High Spirited

Personality and Leadership

Openness

The domain of openness is comprised of six facets: fantasy, aesthetics, feelings, actions, ideas and values.

Domain	Higher	Lower
Openness	Curious about Both Inner and Outer Worlds Willing to Entertain Novel Ideas and Unconventional Values	Prefer Familiar to the Novel Somewhat Muted Emotional Responses Narrower Scope and Lower Intensity of Interests Tend to be More Socially and Politically Conservative
Facet	**Higher**	**Lower**
Fantasy	Receptivity to the Inner World of Imagination Daydream as a Way of Creating an Interesting World for Themselves	More Prosaic and Applied Prefer to Keep Their Minds on Task
Aesthetics	Appreciation of Art and Beauty Are Moved by Art	Less Interested in Art and Beauty
Feelings	Openness to Inner Feelings and Emotions More Differentiated States of Happiness and Unhappiness	Somewhat Muted Affect Less Importance Placed on Feelings Find it Somewhat Difficult to Experience, Express and Describe Emotions
Actions	Willingness to Try Different Activities and Places	Preference for Stability, Routine and Tried-and-True
Ideas	Intellectually Curious Enjoy Philosophical Arguments	Limited Curiosity More Narrowly Focused Interests
Values	Readiness to Re-Examine Own Social, Political and Religious Values	Value Authority Honor Tradition More Conservative

Personality and Leadership

Agreeableness

The domain of agreeableness is comprised of six facets: trust, straightforwardness, altruism, compliance, modesty and tender-mindedness.

Domain	Higher	Lower
Agreeableness	Fundamentally Altruistic Sympathetic to Others and Eager to Help Them Believe That Others Will Be Equally Helpful in Return	Disagreeable or Antagonistic Toward People Skeptical of Others' Intentions Competitive Rather Than Cooperative
Facet	**Higher**	**Lower**
Trust	Belief in the Sincerity and Good Intentions of Others	More Cynical and Skeptical Tend to Assume Others May Be Dishonest or Dangerous
Straightforwardness	Frankness in Expression Sincere and Ingenuous	More Willing to Manipulate Others Through Flattery, Craftiness or Deception
Altruism	Show an Active Concern for the Welfare of Others Shown by Generosity and Willingness to Assist Others in Need	More Self-Centered More Reluctant to Get Involved Helping Others with Their Problems
Compliance	Defer to Others During Interpersonal Conflict More Meek, Mild and Forgiving	More Aggressive Prefer to Compete Rather Than Cooperate Willing to Express Anger
Modesty	Tend to Play Down Own Achievements and Be Humble	Believe They Are Superior to Others Others May Consider Them Conceited or Arrogant
Tender-Mindedness	Attitude of Sympathy for Others Moved by Others' Needs	More Hardheaded Consider Themselves Realists Who Make Rational Decisions

Personality and Leadership

Conscientiousness

The domain of conscientiousness is comprised of six facets: competence, order, dutifulness, achievement striving, self-discipline and deliberation.

Domain	Higher	Lower
Conscientiousness	High Degree of Organization, Persistence, Control and Motivation in Goal Directed Behavior	More Lackadaisical in Working Toward Goals
Facet	**Higher**	**Lower**
Competence	Capable, Sensible, Prudent and Effective Well-Prepared to Deal with Life	Lower Opinion of Their Abilities Admit They Are Often Unprepared or Inept
Order	Neat, Tidy, Well-Organized	Unable to Get Organized Describe Themselves as Unmethodical
Dutifulness	Emphasis Placed on Importance of Fulfilling Moral Obligations	More Casual about Ethical Principles May Be Somewhat Undependable
Achievement Striving	Need for Personal Achievement and Sense of Direction	Less Driven to Succeed Often Content with Lower Levels of Achievement
Self-Discipline	Capacity to Begin Tasks and Follow Through to Completion Despite Boredom or Distraction	Have Difficulty Doing Things Even Though They Want to Do Them Procrastinate and Become Easily Discouraged
Deliberation	Tendency to Think Things Through Before Acting or Speaking	Hasty, Often Speak or Act Without Thinking Spontaneous, Make Snap Decisions

Personality and Leadership

Neuroticism

The domain of neuroticism is comprised of six facets: anxiety, angry hostility, depression, self-consciousness, impulsiveness and vulnerability (to stress).

Domain	Higher	Lower
Neuroticism	Identifies Individuals Who Are Prone to Psychological Distress	Emotionally Stable Usually Calm, Even-Tempered and Relaxed Able to Face Stress Without Becoming Upset
Facet	**Higher**	**Lower**
Anxiety	Apprehensive, Fearful, Worrisome, Nervous and Tense	Calm and Relaxed Don't Dwell on Things That Might Go Wrong
Angry Hostility	Tendency to Experience Anger and Related States Such as Frustration and Bitterness	Easy-Going and Slow to Anger
Depression	Tendency to Experience Feelings of Guilt, Sadness, Despondency and Loneliness	Less Likely to Experience Feelings of Guilt, Sadness, Despondency and Loneliness
Self-Consciousness	Shy or Social Anxious Uncomfortable Around Others Prone to Feelings of Inferiority	Less Disturbed by Social Situations Comfortable Around Others
Impulsiveness	Tendency to Act on Cravings and Urges Rather Than Delaying Gratification	Higher Tolerance for Frustration More Able to Control Cravings and Urges
Vulnerability (to Stress)	General Susceptibility to Stress Become Dependent, Hopeless or Panicked in Stressful Situations	Perceive Themselves as Capable of Handling Stressful Situations

Personality and Leadership

The NEO-PI

The Development of the *NEO-PI-R*

Instruments measuring the big five personality traits have gone through several iterations. The traits themselves are referred to as the big five dimensions. The dimensions are further broken down into facets. The terms big five and five factor model (FFM) are both used to describe this approach to measuring personality.

1967 Norman's (1967) and Goldberg's (1981, 1982, 1990) Work

In 1967, Norman laid a foundation for the big five traits by creating a long list of descriptive personality terms he placed into 75 categories. Later, Goldberg (1990) generated 1,710 trait adjectives to describe Norman's 75 categories. The first five factors produced from a factor analysis of participants' ratings of the trait adjectives pointed to a big five model.

Extraversion or Surgency	Talkative, Assertive, Energetic
Agreeableness	Good-Natured, Cooperative, Trustful
Conscientiousness	Orderly, Responsible, Dependable
Emotional Stability	Calm, Not Neurotic, Not Easily Upset
Culture or Openness	Intellectual, Imaginative, Independent-Minded

1979 (Sometimes called The Big Two)

Wiggins developed a questionnaire-based personality assessment measuring two of the eventual big five factors. This questionnaire was an adjective-based trait description survey that respondents utilized to self-rate their personalities. At that time, extraversion was called dominance or agency and low neuroticism was called nurturance or communion.

1988 Circumplex Model, 1995 FFM (*Interpersonal Adjective Scales*)

By 1988, Wiggins had developed a model with eight personality types. An individual could be primarily high or low on dominance, high or low on nurturing (the four types shown in beige) or a combination of those two dimensions (the four types shown in light blue).

	High Dominance *Assured-Dominant*	Low Dominance *Unassured-Submissive*
High Nurturing *Warm-Agreeable*	*Gregarious-Extraverted*	*Unassuming-Ingenuous*
Low Nurturing *Cold-Hearted*	*Arrogant-Calculating*	*Aloof-Introverted*

In 1995, Wiggins added the other three big five personality traits to his adjective-based questionnaire and migrated his assessment to measure extraversion, neuroticism, agreeableness, openness and conscientiousness.

Personality and Leadership

The NEO-PI

1978 (The NEO System)

In 1978, Costa and McCrae began creating a series of questionnaires that made use of phrases associated with an individual's behavior to describe personality traits. This Instrument, the *NEO*, only measured three domains of personality: neuroticism, extraversion and openness. The early versions did, however have six facets for each of the three domains.

1983, 1985, (*NEO-PI*), 1990 (*NEO-PI-R*)

In 1983 and 1985, versions of the instrument were produced that included the domains of conscientiousness and agreeableness. The 1983 and 1985 versions had facet scores for neuroticism, extraversion and openness but only domain scores for conscientiousness and agreeableness. In 1990, facet scores for conscientiousness and agreeableness were developed. This resulted in an instrument measuring five domains, and six facets within each domain. This five domain, 30-facet instrument was called the *NEO-PI-R*.

1992 (*NEO-FFI* Short Version)

In 1992, after practitioner concerns about the length of time required to take the long version of the *NEO-PI-R*, Costa and McCrae developed a shortened 60-item version, consisting of the 12 items that loaded best on each of the big five factors. *The NEO-FFI* short version provides five domain scores but doesn't provide facet scores.

2005 (*NEO-PI-3*)

Costa and McCrae's latest iteration of the *NEO-PI* is the *NEO-PI-3* (2005). This revision replaced 37 of the 240 items on the questionnaire that were considered to have weak psychometric properties.

1978 *NEO*	1983, 1985 *NEO-PI*	1990 *NEO-PI-R*	1992 *NEO-FFI*	2005 *NEO-PI-3*
Neuroticism Six Facets	Neuroticism Six Facets	Neuroticism Six Facets	Neuroticism No Facets	Neuroticism Six Facets
Extraversion Six Facets	Extraversion Six Facets	Extraversion Six Facets	Extraversion No Facets	Extraversion Six Facets
Openness Six Facets	Openness Six Facets	Openness Six Facets	Openness No Facets	Openness Six Facets
	Conscientiousness No Facets	Conscientiousness Six Facets	Conscientiousness No Facets	Conscientiousness Six Facets
	Agreeableness No Facets	Agreeableness Six Facets	Agreeableness No Facets	Agreeableness Six Facets

Internal Reliability

In an analysis of scores from their normative sample of 500 men and 500 women, Costa and McCrae (1991) reported Cronbach Alpha scores for the five high-level domains between .86 and .92.

Domain	Cronbach Alpha
Extraversion	.89
Openness	.87
Agreeableness	.86
Conscientiousness	.90
Neuroticism	.92

The range of Cronbach Alpha scores for the six facets within each domain are shown below.

Domain	Range of Cronbach Alpha Scores for the Six Facets	Test-Retest Correlations[3]
Extraversion	.63 to .77	.92
Openness	.58 to .76	.93
Agreeableness	.56 to .79	.92
Conscientiousness	.62 to .75	.93
Neuroticism	.68 to .81	.91

Test-Retest Reliability

The test-retest reliability correlations are shown in the table above.

Exploratory Factor Analysis

An exploratory factor analysis using the principal component method with *Varimax* rotation found that the 30 facets of personality loaded as hypothesized on the five higher-order domains. For example, the six facets of extraversion - warmth, gregariousness, assertiveness, activity, excitement seeking and positive emotions, each loaded on extraversion. The lowest factor loading was for assertiveness at .44 and the highest was for positive emotions at .74.[4]

Domain	Range of Factor Loadings for the Six Facets That Comprise each Domain
Extraversion	.44 to .74
Openness	.49 to .75
Agreeableness	.55 to .77
Conscientiousness	.57 to .75
Neuroticism	.49 to .81

Personality and Leadership

The NEO-PI

Discriminant and Convergent Validity

Costa and McCrae have tested the *NEO-PI-* (*R* or *3*) with a battery of other instruments. Each of the 30 facets has been correlated with similar constructs from the following 11 instruments:

Myers-Brigg Type-Indicator
Buss-Durkee Hostility Inventory
Guilford-Zimmerman Temperament Survey
Revised Interpersonal Adjectives Scales
Self-Directed Search
State-Trait Personality Inventory
Minnesota Multiphasic Personality Inventory
Profile of Mood States
Personality Research Form
Revised California Personality Inventory
Sensation Seeking Scale

Broadly speaking, five scales from different instruments shown above were correlated for each facet of the *NEO-PI* (R or 3). This resulted in 150 correlations – five correlations per facet for 30 facets. The correlations all generally fell between .30 to .70 or -.30 to -.70[5] for all 150 convergent/discriminant correlational tests.

For example, the *NEO-PI* facet of extraversion, called warmth, was correlated at $r = -.68$ with the introverted-aloof scale of the *Revised Interpersonal Adjectives Scales.* Warmth was positively correlated at $r = .64$ with the affiliation scale of the *Personality Research Form.*

Norms

Most of the instruments used in leadership-related studies don't provide normative data. What this means is that one generally can't look at a leader's score on something such as consideration from the *Leader Behavior Description Questionnaire XII* or inspirational motivation from the *Multifactor Leadership Questionnaire 5X* and declare, "you are a considerate leader," or "you are an inspirationally motivating leader." We are able to find patterns between leadership scores and outcomes or differences among leaders, but there are no agreed-upon norms to use to assign labels to leaders.

The *NEO-PI* (R and 3) have norms for age groups, gender, and multiple cultures. These norms allow a researcher to feel comfortable making a statement such as "leader A was in the 90th percentile for extraversion, while leader B was in the 10th percentile. Leader A is very extraverted and leader B very introverted."

Acquiring the *NEO-PI-R* or *NEO-PI-3*

As of 2014, the various versions of the NEO instruments were available commercially at PAR, Inc., 16204 North Florida Avenue, Lutz, FL 33549 www.parinc.com

Personality and Leadership
Research Results

Understanding the Research Results for Personality

There is a great deal of research on the full range model of leadership. To prepare you for understanding the research results that follow, chapter 2 explained both correlations and meta-analyses. The table below, however, provides a quick review of how the results of the meta-analytic literature will be provided in this chapter.[6]

Example – Leader Openness to New Experiences and Leader Charisma

In the example below, nine studies have been published and meta-analyzed on the relationship between a leader's openness to new experiences and ratings of how charismatic followers rated those leaders. Those nine studies collectively represent 1,706 follower ratings. The letter (D) refers to the study that is being referenced. A list of studies is included at the end of this chapter. The meta-analytic finding was a weak, positive correlation (.22). The more open to new experiences the leaders were, the higher the leaders were rated on charismatic leadership.

Strongly - Correlated	Moderately - Correlated	Weakly - Correlated	Weakly + Correlated	Moderately + Correlated	Strongly + Correlated
-1 to -.50	-.49 to -.30	-.29 to -.10	.10 to .29	.30 to .49	.50 to 1

Outcome	Studies	Followers	
Charisma (D)	9	1,706	.22

The following 15 pages will summarize the meta-analytic literature related to aspects of personality with which leaders in the workplace are often concerned. The summaries will be provided in four sections.

Leader Personality and Ratings of Leadership

Follower (Employee) Personality and Follower (Employee) Workplace Attitudes

Follower (Employee) Personality and Follower (Employee) Organizational Attitudes

Follower (Employee) Personality and Follower (Employee) Performance

Personality and Leadership

Research Results

Leader Personality and Ratings of Leadership

The next five pages summarize the research related to leader personality and ratings of leadership. Generally, this body of research associates scores on personality ratings that leaders complete on themselves with leadership ratings that their followers (or others) complete.[7]

Leader Completes a Personality Assessment

Follower(s) Rate Their Leader on Leadership

Personality and Leadership

Research Results

Leader Openness and Leadership

Strongly - Correlated	Moderately - Correlated	Weakly - Correlated	Weakly + Correlated	Moderately + Correlated	Strongly + Correlated
-1 to -.50	-.49 to -.30	-.29 to -.10	.10 to .29	.30 to .49	.50 to 1

Outcome	Studies	Participants	
Very Weakly, Positively Correlated			
Contingent Reward (D)	6	1,469	.03
Passive Leadership (D)	7	1,564	.04
Transformational Leadership (D)	19	3,887	.09
Weakly, Positively Correlated			
Managerial Performance (G)	44	8,678	.10
Intellectual Stimulation (D)	8	1,828	.11
Individual Consideration (D)	8	1,828	.11
Charisma (D)	9	1,706	.22
Leader Emergence (K)	20	(N not provided)	.24
Leader Effectiveness (K)	17	(N not provided)	.24

Strongly - Correlated	Moderately - Correlated	Weakly - Correlated	Weakly + Correlated	Moderately + Correlated	Strongly + Correlated
-1 to -.50	-.49 to -.30	-.29 to -.10	.10 to .29	.30 to .49	.50 to 1

	Outcome	Studies	Participants
Very Weakly, Negatively Correlated			
-.04	Management by Exception Active (D)	6	1,469

Research from 144 analyses (effect sizes) that have included over 20,000 follower ratings indicates that leader openness to new experiences is generally weakly, positively correlated with various aspects of the full range model of leadership. Leader openness is also weakly, positively correlated with leader effectiveness and becoming (emerging as) a leader.

Leader openness to new experiences is weakly, negatively correlated with ratings of management by exception.

Noteworthy meta-analytic correlations are weak, positive correlations between leaders' openness to new experiences and those leaders' charismatic behavior (r_c = .22)[8] and openness to new experiences and leader effectiveness (*rho* = .24).

Personality and Leadership
Research Results

Leader Conscientiousness and Leadership

Strongly - Correlated	Moderately - Correlated	Weakly - Correlated		Weakly + Correlated	Moderately + Correlated	Strongly + Correlated
-1 to -.50	-.49 to -.30	-.29 to -.10		.10 to .29	.30 to .49	.50 to 1

Outcome	Studies	Participants	Correlation
Very Weakly, Positively Correlated			
Contingent Reward (D)	6	1,469	.02
Intellectual Stimulation (D)	8	1,828	.03
Charisma (D)	8	1,605	.05
Weakly, Positively Correlated			
Transformational Leadership (D)	6	1,469	.11
Individualized Consideration (D)	8	1,828	.14
Leader Effectiveness (K)	18	(N not provided)	.16
Managerial Performance (G)	60	11,325	.25
Moderately, Positively Correlated			
Leader Emergence (K)	17	(N not provided)	.33

Strongly - Correlated	Moderately - Correlated	Weakly - Correlated		Weakly + Correlated	Moderately + Correlated	Strongly + Correlated
-1 to -.50	-.49 to -.30	-.29 to -.10		.10 to .29	.30 to .49	.50 to 1

Correlation	Outcome	Studies	Participants
Very Weakly, Negatively Correlated			
-.02	Management by Exception Active (D)	6	1,469
Weakly, Negatively Correlated			
-.11	Passive Leadership (D)	7	1,564

Research from 153 analyses (effect sizes) that have included over 24,162 follower ratings indicates that leader conscientiousness is generally weakly, positively correlated with various aspects of the full range model of leadership.

Leader conscientiousness is weakly, negatively correlated with ratings of management by exception active and passive leadership.

The most noteworthy meta-analytic correlations were the relationships between conscientiousness and managerial performance (*rho* = .25) and conscientiousness and emergence as a leader (*rho* = .33).

Personality and Leadership

Research Results

Leader Extraversion and Leadership

Strongly - Correlated	Moderately - Correlated	Weakly - Correlated	Weakly + Correlated	Moderately + Correlated	Strongly + Correlated
-1 to -.50	-.49 to -.30	-.29 to -.10	.10 to .29	.30 to .49	.50 to 1

Outcome	Studies	Participants	
Weakly, Positively Correlated			
Contingent Reward (D)	5	1,215	.14
Intellectual Stimulation (D)	7	1,574	.18
Individual Consideration (D)	7	1,574	.18
Managerial Performance (G)	67	12,602	.21
Charisma (D)	9	1,706	.22
Transformational Leadership (D)	20	3,692	.23
Leader Effectiveness (K)	23	(N not provided)	.24
Leadership Perceptions (A)	13	1,701	.26
Moderately Correlated			
Leader Emergence (K)	37	(N not provided)	.33

Strongly - Correlated	Moderately - Correlated	Weakly - Correlated	Weakly + Correlated	Moderately + Correlated	Strongly + Correlated
-1 to -.50	-.49 to -.30	-.29 to -.10	.10 to .29	.30 to .49	.50 to 1

	Outcome	Studies	Participants
Very, Negatively Correlated			
-.03	Management by Exception Active (D)	5	1,215
-.09	Passive Leadership (D)	6	1,310

Research from 144 analyses (effect sizes) that have included 26,589 follower ratings indicates that leader extraversion is generally weakly, positively correlated with various aspects of the full range model of leadership.

The most noteworthy meta-analytic correlations were the relationships between extraversion and managerial performance (*rho* = .21), extraversion and transformational leadership (r_c = .23), extraversion and leader effectiveness (*rho* = .24), extraversion and leadership perceptions (r_c = .26) and extraversion and emergence as a leader (*rho* = .33).

Personality and Leadership

Research Results

Leader Agreeableness and Leadership

Strongly - Correlated	Moderately - Correlated	Weakly - Correlated	Weakly + Correlated	Moderately + Correlated	Strongly + Correlated
-1 to -.50	-.49 to -.30	-.29 to -.10	.10 to .29	.30 to .49	.50 to 1

Outcome	Studies	Participants	
Very Weakly, Positively Correlated			
Leader Emergence (K)	23	(N not provided)	.05
Weakly, Positively Correlated			
Managerial Performance (G)	55	9,864	.10
Transformational Leadership (D)	20	3,916	.12
Intellectual Stimulation (D)	8	1,828	.14
Individual Consideration (D)	8	1,828	.17
Contingent Reward (D)	7	1,622	.17
Charisma (D)	9	1,706	.21
Leader Effectiveness (K)	19	(N not provided)	.21

Strongly - Correlated	Moderately - Correlated	Weakly - Correlated	Weakly + Correlated	Moderately + Correlated	Strongly + Correlated
-1 to -.50	-.49 to -.30	-.29 to -.10	.10 to .29	.30 to .49	.50 to 1

	Outcome	Studies	Participants
Weakly, Negatively Correlated			
-.12	Management by Exception Active (D)	6	1,469
-.12	Passive Leadership (D)	7	1,564

Research from 162 analyses (effect sizes) that have included 23,797 follower ratings indicates that leader agreeableness is generally weakly, positively correlated with various aspects of the full range model of leadership and weakly, positively correlated with ratings of leader effectiveness.

Noteworthy meta-analytic correlations were the relationships between agreeableness and charisma (r_c = .21) and agreeableness and leader effectiveness (*rho* = .21).

Personality and Leadership

Research Results

Leader Neuroticism and Leadership

Strongly - Correlated	Moderately - Correlated	Weakly - Correlated	Weakly + Correlated	Moderately + Correlated	Strongly + Correlated
-1 to -.50	-.49 to -.30	-.29 to -.10	.10 to .29	.30 to .49	.50 to 1

Outcome	Studies	Participants	
Very Weakly, Positively Correlated			
Management by Exception Active (D)	7	1,532	.02
Passive Leadership (D)	8	1,627	.05

Strongly - Correlated	Moderately - Correlated	Weakly - Correlated	Weakly + Correlated	Moderately + Correlated	Strongly + Correlated
-1 to -.50	-.49 to -.30	-.29 to -.10	.10 to .29	.30 to .49	.50 to 1

	Outcome	Studies	Participants
Very Weakly, Negatively Correlated			
-.09	Managerial Performance (G)	63	11,591
Weakly, Negatively Correlated			
-.10	Individual Consideration (D)	9	1,772
-.10	Contingent Reward (D)	7	1,532
-.13	Intellectual Stimulation (D)	9	1,772
-.16	Transformational Leadership (D)	18	3,380
-.17	Charisma (D)	10	1,650
-.22	Leader Effectiveness (K)	30	(N not provided)
-.24	Leader Emergence (K)	18	(N not provided)

Research from 179 analyses (effect sizes) that have included 24,856 follower ratings indicates that leader neuroticism is generally weakly, negatively correlated with effective aspects of the full range model of leadership and very weakly, positively correlated with ineffective aspects of the full range model of leadership.

Leader neuroticism is also negatively correlated with leader emergence (*rho* = -.22) and ratings of leader effectiveness (*rho* = -.24).

Personality and Leadership

Research Results

Follower (Employee) Personality and Work Related Attitudes

The next five pages summarize personality research of a different type. Rather than analyze the personality of leaders, this type of research analyzes how employee personality is related to employee work related attitudes.

In this type of research, the employees typically complete two different assessments – a personality assessment and an assessment of their attitudes about some aspect of work.

Workers Complete
a Personality Assessment and
a Work Related Attitudes Assessment

Personality and Leadership

Research Results

Follower (Employee) Openness and Work Related Attitudes

Strongly - Correlated	Moderately - Correlated	Weakly - Correlated	Weakly + Correlated	Moderately + Correlated	Strongly + Correlated
-1 to -.50	-.49 to -.30	-.29 to -.10	.10 to .29	.30 to .49	.50 to 1

Outcome	Studies	Participants	
Very Weakly, Positively Correlated			
Promotion (H)	5	4,942	.01
Follower Intent to Quit (E)	12	3,730	.01
Job Satisfaction (B)	50	5,196	.02
Objective Performance (G)	25	4,401	.03
Supervisor Ratings (G)	116	18,535	.07
Weakly, Positively Correlated			
Follower Turnover (H)	5	4,942	.10
Career Satisfaction (H)	12	3,730	.12
Career Satisfaction (I)	7	10,962	.12
Goal-Setting Motivation (C)	50	5,196	.18
Self-Efficacy Motivation (C)	25	4,401	.20
Personal Accomplishment (E)	116	18,535	.22

Strongly - Correlated	Moderately - Correlated	Weakly - Correlated	Weakly + Correlated	Moderately + Correlated	Strongly + Correlated
-1 to -.50	-.49 to -.30	-.29 to -.10	.10 to .29	.30 to .49	.50 to 1

	Outcome	Studies	Participants
Very Weakly, Negatively Correlated			
-.01	Emotional Exhaustion (E)	17	5,380
-.02	LMX Relationship (L)	5	1,249
-.05	Belief Supervisor is Abusive (M)	5	2,571
-.06	Depersonalization (E)	13	3,937
-.08	Expectancy Motivation (C)	5	567

Research from 468 analyses (effect sizes) that have included 98,274 ratings indicates that worker openness is weakly, positively related to motivation, satisfaction and a sense of accomplishment.

Openness to new experiences is very weakly negatively related to worker attitudes such as emotional exhaustion and depersonalization.

Personality and Leadership

Research Results

Follower (Employee) Conscientiousness and Work-Related Attitudes

Strongly - Correlated	Moderately - Correlated	Weakly - Correlated	Weakly + Correlated	Moderately + Correlated	Strongly + Correlated
-1 to -.50	-.49 to -.30	-.29 to -.10	.10 to .29	.30 to .49	.50 to 1

Outcome	Studies	Participants	Correlation
Very Weakly, Positively Correlated			
Promotion (H)	4	4,428	.06
Weakly, Positively Correlated			
Career Satisfaction (I)	6	10,566	.12
LMX Relationship (L)	9	2,075	.20
Self-Efficacy Motivation (C)	14	3,483	.22
Personal Accomplishment (E)	16	4,615	.22
Expectancy Motivation (C)	11	1,487	.23
Job Satisfaction (B)	79	21,719	.26
Goal-Setting Motivation (C)	18	2,211	.28

Strongly - Correlated	Moderately - Correlated	Weakly - Correlated	Weakly + Correlated	Moderately + Correlated	Strongly + Correlated
-1 to -.50	-.49 to -.30	-.29 to -.10	.10 to .29	.30 to .49	.50 to 1

Correlation	Outcome	Studies	Participants
Weakly, Negatively Correlated			
-.14	Belief Supervisor is Abusive (M)	12	4,368
-.16	Follower Intent to Quit (E)	13	4,315
-.18	Follower Turnover (H)	17	1,631
-.19	Emotional Exhaustion (E)	22	8,237
-.26	Depersonalization (E)	16	5,926

Research from 237 analyses (effect sizes) that have included 75,061 ratings indicates that worker conscientiousness is weakly, positively related to job satisfaction, motivation and a sense of accomplishment.

Worker conscientiousness is weakly, negatively related to turnover, emotional exhaustion and depersonalization.

Personality and Leadership

Research Results

Follower (Employee) Extraversion and Work-Related Attitudes

Strongly - Correlated	Moderately - Correlated	Weakly - Correlated	Weakly + Correlated	Moderately + Correlated	Strongly + Correlated
-1 to -.50	-.49 to -.30	-.29 to -.10	.10 to .29	.30 to .49	.50 to 1

Outcome	Studies	Participants	
Weakly, Positively Correlated			
Expectancy Motivation (C)	6	663	.10
Career Satisfaction (I)	6	10,566	.14
Goal-Setting Motivation (C)	5	498	.15
LMX Relationship (L)	11	2,919	.16
Promotion (H)	4	4,428	.18
Job Satisfaction (B)	75	20,184	.25
Moderately, Positively Correlated			
Self-Efficacy Motivation (C)	7	2,067	.33
Personal Accomplishment (E)	20	6,777	.36

Strongly - Correlated	Moderately - Correlated	Weakly - Correlated	Weakly + Correlated	Moderately + Correlated	Strongly + Correlated
-1 to -.50	-.49 to -.30	-.29 to -.10	.10 to .29	.30 to .49	.50 to 1

	Outcome	Studies	Participants
Very Weakly, Negatively Correlated			
-.03	Belief Supervisor is Abusive (M)	6	2,879
-.04	Follower Turnover (H)	18	1,608
Weakly, Negatively Correlated			
-.12	Follower Intent to Quit (E)	25	7,231
-.26	Emotional Exhaustion (E)	25	10,981
-.26	Depersonalization (E)	19	8,408

Research from 227 analyses (effect sizes) that have included 79,209 ratings indicates that worker extraversion is weakly, positively correlated with job and career satisfaction and moderately correlated with motivation and a sense of personal accomplishment.

Extraversion is also weakly, negatively correlated with intentions to quit, emotional exhaustion and depersonalization.

Personality and Leadership

Research Results

Follower (Employee) Agreeableness and Work-Related Attitudes

Strongly - Correlated	Moderately - Correlated	Weakly - Correlated	Weakly + Correlated	Moderately + Correlated	Strongly + Correlated
-1 to -.50	-.49 to -.30	-.29 to -.10	.10 to .29	.30 to .49	.50 to 1

Outcome	Studies	Participants	
Weakly, Positively Correlated			
Career Satisfaction (I)	5	4,634	.11
Self-Efficacy Motivation (C)	6	1,099	.11
Expectancy Motivation (C)	5	875	.13
Job Satisfaction (B)	38	11,856	.17
LMX Relationship (L)	9	2.290	.19
Personal Accomplishment (E)	13	3,775	.23

Strongly - Correlated	Moderately - Correlated	Weakly - Correlated	Weakly + Correlated	Moderately + Correlated	Strongly + Correlated
-1 to -.50	-.49 to -.30	-.29 to -.10	.10 to .29	.30 to .49	.50 to 1

	Outcome	Studies	Participants
Very Weakly, Negatively Correlated			
-.05	Promotion (H)	4	4,428
Weakly, Negatively Correlated			
-.13	Follower Intent to Quit (E)	10	4,315
-.14	Belief Supervisor is Abusive (M)	9	3,679
-.15	Emotional Exhaustion (E)	18	7,855
-.22	Follower Turnover (H)	15	1,532
-.29	Goal-Setting Motivation (C)	4	373
Moderately, Negatively Correlated			
-.35	Depersonalization (E)	13	5,236

Research from 149 analyses (effect sizes) that have included 49,659 ratings indicates that worker agreeableness is weakly, positively correlated with job satisfaction as well as a sense of personal accomplishment.

Agreeableness is also weakly, negatively correlated with intentions to quit and emotional exhaustion. Agreeableness is moderately, negatively correlated with depersonalization.

Personality and Leadership

Research Results

Follower (Employee) Neuroticism and Work-Related Attitudes

Strongly - Correlated	Moderately - Correlated	Weakly - Correlated	Weakly + Correlated	Moderately + Correlated	Strongly + Correlated
-1 to -.50	-.49 to -.30	-.29 to -.10	.10 to .29	.30 to .49	.50 to 1

Outcome	Studies	Participants	
Weakly, Positively Correlated			
Belief Supervisor is Abusive (M)	12	4,198	.12
Follower Turnover (H)	19	1,824	.16
Follower Intent to Quit (E)	41	15,075	.29
Moderately, Positively Correlated			
Depersonalization (E)	26	10,837	.40
Strongly, Positively Correlated			
Emotional Exhaustion (E)	31	13,047	.50

Strongly - Correlated	Moderately - Correlated	Weakly - Correlated	Weakly + Correlated	Moderately + Correlated	Strongly + Correlated
-1 to -.50	-.49 to -.30	-.29 to -.10	.10 to .29	.30 to .49	.50 to 1

	Outcome	Studies	Participants
Weakly, Negatively Correlated			
-.11	Promotion (H)	5	4,575
-.11	LMX Relationship (L)	6	1,456
-.29	Job Satisfaction (B)	92	24,527
-.29	Goal-Setting Motivation (C)	19	2,780
-.29	Expectancy Motivation (C)	11	1,770
-.29	Personal Accomplishment (E)	26	8,913
Moderately, Negatively Correlated			
-.35	Self-Efficacy Motivation (C)	32	6,730
-.36	Career Satisfaction (H)	6	10,566

Research from 326 analyses (effect sizes) that have included 106,298 ratings indicates that worker neuroticism is weakly, negatively correlated with job satisfaction, motivation and a sense of personal accomplishment. Neuroticism is moderately, negatively correlated with self-efficacy motivation and career satisfaction.

Neuroticism is also moderately, positively correlated with feelings of depersonalization and strongly, positively correlated with emotional exhaustion.

Personality and Leadership
Research Results

Follower (Employee) Personality and Organizational Attitudes

The chart below and the charts on the next five pages summarize a third type of personality research. This type of research analyzes how employee personality is related to employee attitudes about the larger organization of which they are part.

In this type of research, the employees typically complete two different assessments – a personality assessment and an assessment of their attitudes about their organization.

Workers Complete
a Personality Assessment and
an Organizational Attitudes Assessment

Personality and Leadership

Research Results

Follower (Employee) Openness and Organizational Outcomes

Strongly - Correlated	Moderately - Correlated	Weakly - Correlated	Weakly + Correlated	Moderately + Correlated	Strongly + Correlated
-1 to -.50	-.49 to -.30	-.29 to -.10	.10 to .29	.30 to .49	.50 to 1

Outcome	Studies	Participants	
Weakly, Positively Correlated			
Organizational Citizenship Behavior (F)	38	7,405	.14
Organizational Citizenship Change Oriented (F)	19	3,761	.14
Teamwork (G)	10	2,079	.16
Organizational Citizenship Individual Directed (F)	10	2,049	.18
Organizational Citizenship Organizational Directed (F)	7	1,311	.19

Research from 84 analyses (effect sizes) that have included 16,605 ratings indicates that employee openness is weakly, positively correlated with various forms of organizational citizenship and teamwork.

Personality and Leadership

Research Results

Follower (Employee) Conscientiousness and Organizational Outcomes

Strongly - Correlated	Moderately - Correlated	Weakly - Correlated	Weakly + Correlated	Moderately + Correlated	Strongly + Correlated
-1 to -.50	-.49 to -.30	-.29 to -.10	.10 to .29	.30 to .49	.50 to 1

Outcome	Studies	Participants	
		Weakly, Positively Correlated	
Organizational Citizenship Change Oriented (F)	17	2,629	.10
Organizational Citizenship Organizational Directed (F)	20	4,025	.17
Organizational Citizenship Behavior (F)	71	14,355	.18
Organizational Citizenship Individual Directed (F)	28	6,347	.21
Teamwork (G)	38	3,064	.27

Research from 117 analyses (effect sizes) that have included 30,420 ratings indicates that employee conscientiousness is weakly, positively correlated with various forms of organizational citizenship and teamwork.

Personality and Leadership

Research Results

Follower (Employee) Extraversion and Organizational Outcomes

Strongly - Correlated	Moderately - Correlated	Weakly - Correlated	Weakly + Correlated	Moderately + Correlated	Strongly + Correlated
-1 to -.50	-.49 to -.30	-.29 to -.10	.10 to .29	.30 to .49	.50 to 1

Outcome	Studies	Participants	
Very Weakly, Positively Correlated			
Organizational Citizenship Organizational Directed (F)	9	2,017	.02
Organizational Citizenship Behavior (F)	34	6,700	.09
Weakly, Positively Correlated			
Organizational Citizenship Individual Directed (F)	13	3,129	.10
Organizational Citizenship Change Oriented (F)	6	1,144	.13
Teamwork (G)	48	3,719	.18

Research from 110 analyses (effect sizes) that have included 16,709 ratings indicates that employee extraversion is weakly, positively correlated with various forms of organizational citizenship and teamwork.

Personality and Leadership
Research Results

Follower (Employee) Agreeableness and Organizational Outcomes

Strongly - Correlated	Moderately - Correlated	Weakly - Correlated	Weakly + Correlated	Moderately + Correlated	Strongly + Correlated
-1 to -.50	-.49 to -.30	-.29 to -.10	.10 to .29	.30 to .49	.50 to 1

Outcome	Studies	Participants	r
Weakly, Positively Correlated			
Organizational Citizenship Behavior (F)	47	10,308	.14
Organizational Citizenship Organizational Directed (F)	15	4,598	.14
Organizational Citizenship Individual Directed (F)	19	5,608	.18
Moderately, Positively Correlated			
Teamwork (G)	47	10,308	.34

Strongly - Correlated	Moderately - Correlated	Weakly - Correlated	Weakly + Correlated	Moderately + Correlated	Strongly + Correlated
-1 to -.50	-.49 to -.30	-.29 to -.10	.10 to .29	.30 to .49	.50 to 1

r	Outcome	Studies	Participants
Very Weakly, Negatively Correlated			
-.03	Change Oriented Citizenship (F)	8	1,396

Research from 134 analyses (effect sizes) that have included 31,966 ratings indicates that employee agreeableness is weakly, positively correlated with various forms of organizational citizenship and teamwork.

Employee agreeableness was moderately, positively correlated with a sense of teamwork.

A very weak negative correlation was also found between follower agreeableness and change oriented citizenship.

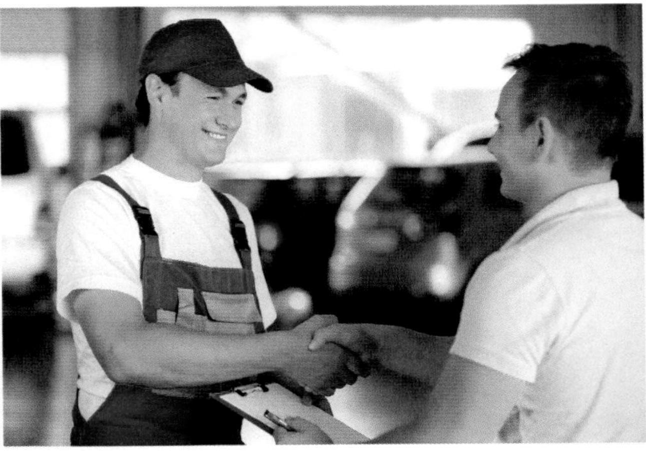

Personality and Leadership

Research Results

Follower (Employee) Neuroticism and Organizational Outcomes

Strongly - Correlated	Moderately - Correlated	Weakly - Correlated
-1 to -.50	-.49 to -.30	-.29 to -.10

Weakly + Correlated	Moderately + Correlated	Strongly + Correlated
.10 to .29	.30 to .49	.50 to 1

	Outcome	Studies	Participants
Very Weakly, Negatively Correlated			
-.08	Organizational Citizenship Change Oriented (F)	7	1,732
Weakly, Negatively Correlated			
-.12	Organizational Citizenship Behavior (F)	36	8,629
-.12	Organizational Citizenship Organizational Directed (F)	10	2,139
-.14	Organizational Citizenship Individual Directed (F)	13	3,073
-.22	Teamwork (G)	41	3,558

Research from 107 analyses (effect sizes) that have included 19,131 ratings indicates that employee neuroticism is weakly, negatively correlated with various forms of organizational citizenship and teamwork.

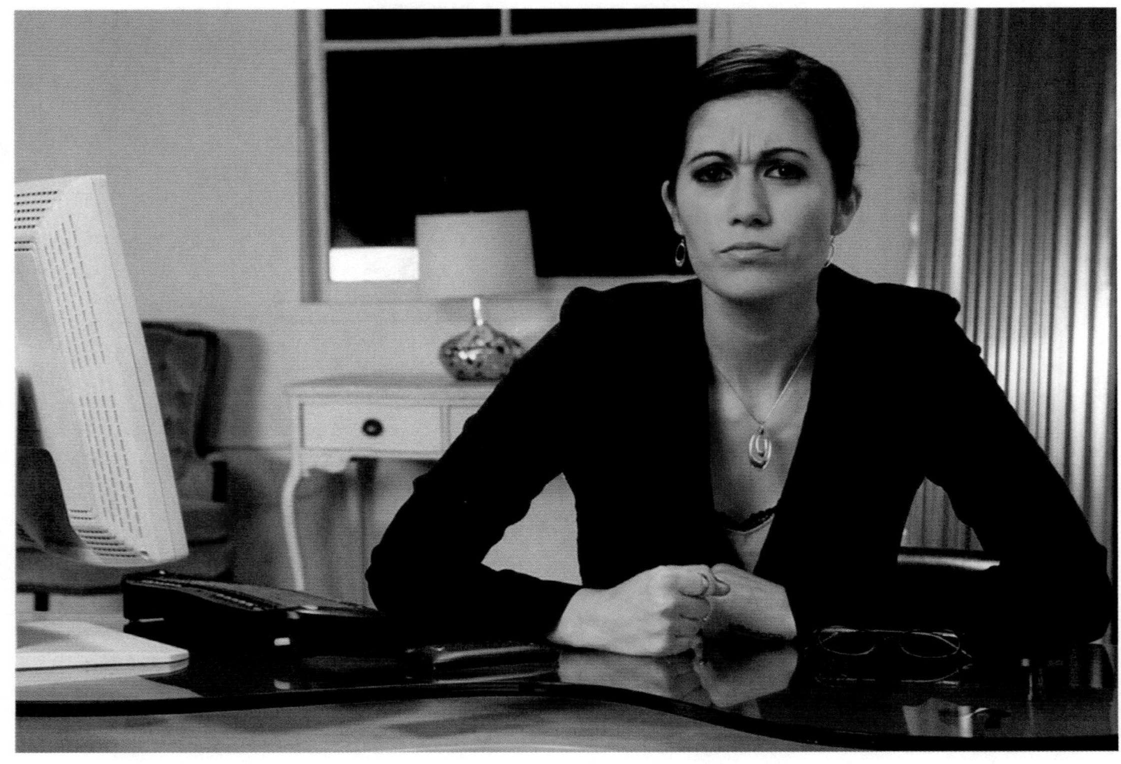

Personality and Leadership

Research Results

Follower (Employee) Personality and Follower (Employee) Performance

The charts on the next five pages summarize a fourth type of personality research. This type of research analyzes how employee personality is related to employee performance.

In this type of research, the employees typically complete a personality assessment then there is some measure of the employees' performance. In some studies, the leader does the performance assessments. In other studies, however, the employees self-assess how well they believe they perform.

Workers Complete
a Personality Assessment and
Some Measure of Performance is Collected

Personality and Leadership

Research Results

Follower (Employee) Openness and Performance

Strongly - Correlated	Moderately - Correlated	Weakly - Correlated	Weakly + Correlated	Moderately + Correlated	Strongly + Correlated
-1 to -.50	-.49 to -.30	-.29 to -.10	.10 to .29	.30 to .49	.50 to 1

Outcome	Studies	Participants	
Very Weakly, Positively Correlated			
Promotion (I)	5	4,942	.01
Objective Performance (G)	25	4,401	.03
Work Performance of Police (G)	16	1,688	.03
Salary (I)	7	6,800	.04
Work Performance of Skilled or Semi-skilled Workers (G)	32	6,055	.05
Overall Work Performance (G)	143	23,225	.07
Supervisor Ratings of Work Performance (G)	116	18,535	.07
Overall Work Performance (G)	143	23,225	.07
Weakly, Positively Correlated			
Work Performance of Managers (G)	44	8,678	.10
Leader Emergence (K)	20	(N not provided)	.24
Leader Effectiveness (K)	17	(N not provided)	.24
Moderately, Positively Correlated			
Training Performance (G)	18	3,177	.33

Research from 537 analyses (effect sizes) that have included 88,984 ratings indicates that employee openness is weakly, positively correlated with multiple measures of performance and moderately, positively related to training performance.

Personality and Leadership

Research Results

Follower (Employee) Conscientiousness and Performance

Strongly - Correlated	Moderately - Correlated	Weakly - Correlated	Weakly + Correlated	Moderately + Correlated	Strongly + Correlated
-1 to -.50	-.49 to -.30	-.29 to -.10	.10 to .29	.30 to .49	.50 to 1

Outcome	Studies	Participants	
Very Weakly, Positively Correlated			
Promotion (I)	4	4.428	.06
Salary (I)	6	6,286	.07
Weakly, Positively Correlated			
Objective Performance (G)	35	6,905	.23
Work Performance of Professionals (G)	6	767	.24
Work Performance of Managers (G)	60	11,325	.25
Work Performance of Sales Persons (G)	36	4,141	.25
Work Performance of Police (G)	22	2,369	.26
Overall Work Performance (G)	239	48,100	.27
Training Performance (G)	20	3,909	.27
Work Performance of Skilled or Semi-skilled Workers (G)	44	7,682	.27
Moderately, Positively Correlated			
Supervisor Ratings of Work Performance (G)	185	33,312	.31

Research from 657 analyses (effect sizes) that have included 118,510 ratings indicates that employee conscientiousness is weakly, positively correlated with multiple measures of performance and moderately, positively correlated with supervisor ratings of work performance.

Personality and Leadership

Research Results

Follower (Employee) Extraversion and Performance

Strongly - Correlated	Moderately - Correlated	Weakly - Correlated
-1 to -.50	-.49 to -.30	-.29 to -.10

Weakly + Correlated	Moderately + Correlated	Strongly + Correlated
.10 to .29	.30 to .49	.50 to 1

Outcome	Studies	Participants	
Very Weakly, Positively Correlated			
Work Performance of Skilled or Semi-skilled Workers (G)	44	6,830	.06
Weakly, Positively Correlated			
Salary (I)	7	6,610	.10
Work Performance of Sales Persons (G)	35	3,806	.11
Work Performance of Police (G)	20	2,074	.12
Supervisor Ratings of Work Performance (G)	164	23,785	.13
Objective Performance (G)	37	7,101	.13
Overall Work Performance (G)	222	39,432	.15
Promotion (I)	4	4,428	.18
Work Performance of Managers (G)	67	12,602	.21
Training Performance (G)	21	3,484	.28

Research from 610 analyses (effect sizes) that have included 99,114 ratings indicates that employee extraversion is weakly, positively correlated with multiple measures of performance.

Personality and Leadership

Research Results

Follower (Employee) Agreeableness and Performance

Strongly - Correlated	Moderately - Correlated	Weakly - Correlated	Weakly + Correlated	Moderately + Correlated	Strongly + Correlated
-1 to -.50	-.49 to -.30	-.29 to -.10	.10 to .29	.30 to .49	.50 to 1

Outcome	Studies	Participants	
Very Weakly, Positively Correlated			
Work Performance of Sales Persons (G)	27	3,551	.01
Work Performance of Professionals (G)	10	965	.06
Weakly, Positively Correlated			
Work Performance of Managers (G)	55	9,864	.10
Overall Work Performance (G)	206	36,210	.13
Supervisor Ratings of Work Performance (G)	151	22,193	.13
Work Performance of Police (G)	18	2,015	.13
Work Performance of Skilled or Semi-skilled Workers (G)	44	7,194	.13
Training Performance (G)	24	4,100	.14
Objective Performance (G)	28	4,969	.17

	Outcome	Studies	Participants
Very Weakly, Negatively Correlated			
-.05	Promotion (I)	4	4,428
\Weakly, Negatively Correlated			
-.10	Salary (I)	6	6,286

Research from 563 analyses (effect sizes) that have included 91,061 ratings indicates that employee agreeableness is weakly, positively correlated with multiple measures of performance.

Employee agreeableness is very weakly, negatively correlated with promotion and weakly, negatively correlated with salary.

Personality and Leadership

Research Results

Follower (Employee) Neuroticism and Performance

Strongly - Correlated	Moderately - Correlated	Weakly - Correlated
-1 to -.50	-.49 to -.30	-.29 to -.10

Weakly + Correlated	Moderately + Correlated	Strongly + Correlated
.10 to .29	.30 to .49	.50 to 1

	Outcome	Studies	Participants
Very Weakly, Positively Correlated			
-.05	Work Performance of Sales Persons (G)	30	3,664
-.06	Work Performance of Professionals (G)	8	926
-.09	Training Performance (G)	25	3,753
-.09	Work Performance of Managers (G)	63	11,591
Weakly, Positively Correlated			
-.10	Objective Performance (G)	32	6,219
-.11	Promotion (I)	5	4,575
-.12	Work Performance of Police (G)	22	2,275
-.12	Salary (I)	7	6,443
-.13	Overall Work Performance (G)	224	38,817
-.13	Supervisor Ratings of Work Performance (G)	167	23,687

Research from 583 analyses (effect sizes) that have included 101950 ratings indicates that employee neuroticism is weakly correlated with multiple measures of performance, promotion and salary.

Personality and Leadership

Meta-Analytic Regressions

Meta-Analytic Regressions Related to Leader Personality and Ratings of Leadership

The next seven pages summarize the meta-analytic regression research related to leader personality and ratings of leadership. Generally, this body of research associates scores on personality ratings that leaders completed on themselves with leadership ratings that their followers completed.[9]

Earlier meta-analyses provided in this chapter analyzed one dimension of personality at a time. The meta-analytic regressions include all measures of personality simultaneously. A few of the meta-analytic regressions include all five dimensions of personality plus some additional independent (predictor) variables.

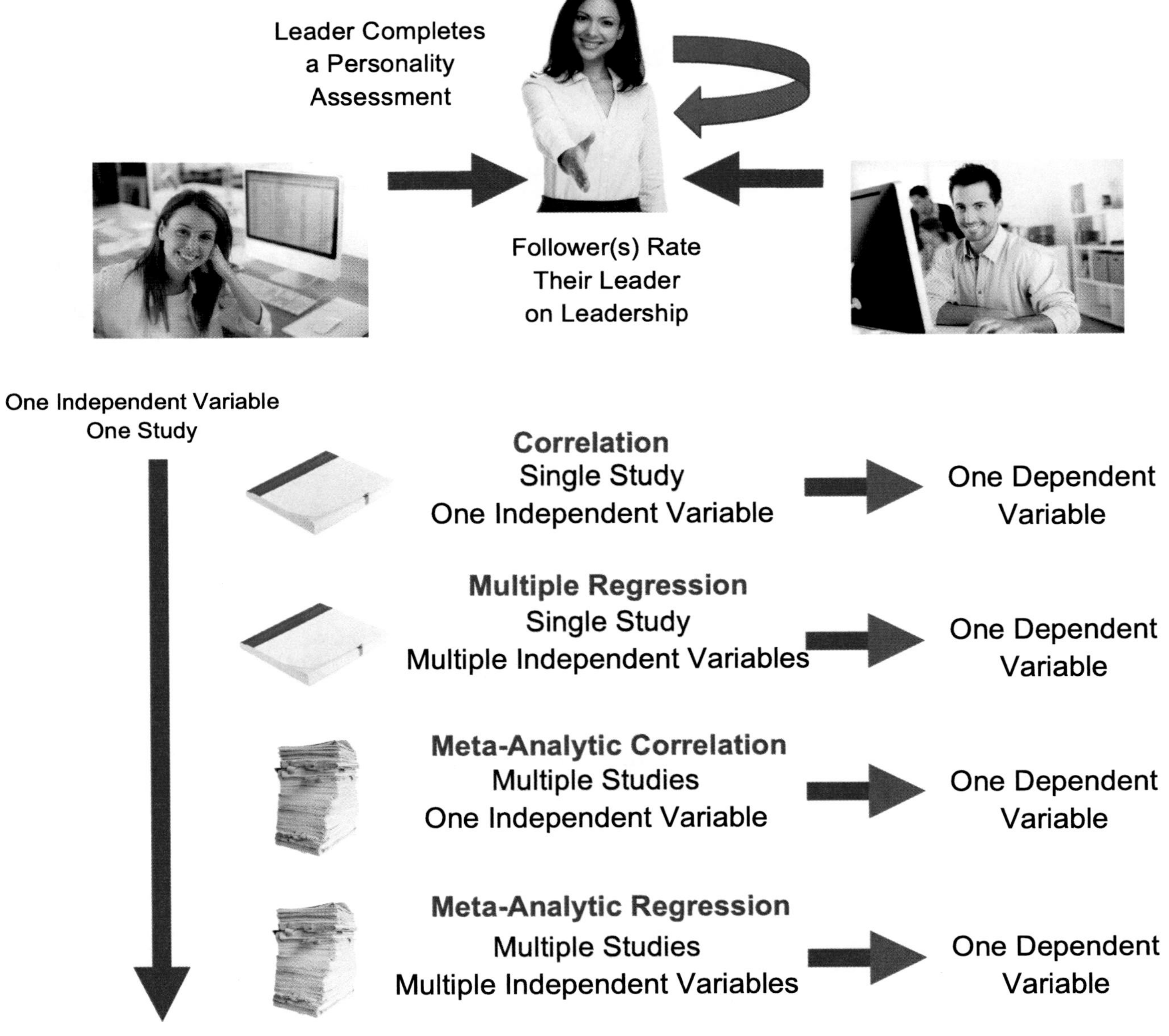

Personality and Leadership

Meta-Analytic Regressions

Meta-Analytic Multiple Regression for Leader Personality and the Full Range of Leadership Model

Bono and Judge (2004) conducted several meta-analytic multiple regressions using 384 correlations from 26 independent studies.

For the multiple regressions, all five domains of personality were used as a combined predictor of several of the aspects of the full range model of leadership.

The chart below provides the strength of overall leader personality in predicting leadership style. The number provided is the R^2 value.

Leader Personality and Leadership Style (R^2 Values)

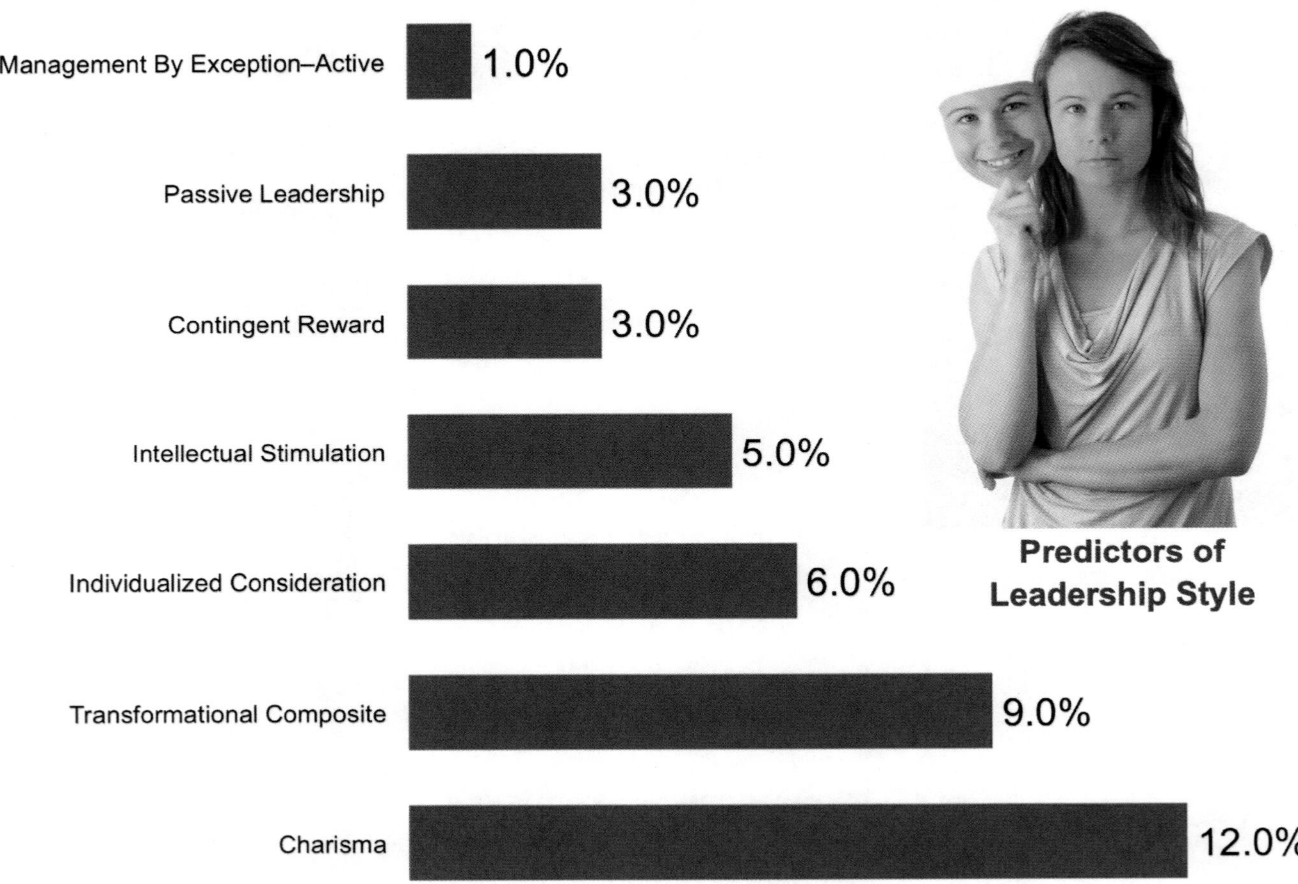

Leaders' personality explained 12% of the variance in how charismatic those leaders were rated. Nine percent of the variance in ratings of transformational leadership can be explained by the five aspects of leader personality.

Personality and Leadership

Meta-Analytic Regressions

Meta-Analytic Multiple Regression for Leader Personality and Leader Emergence

Judge, Bono, Ilies and Gerhardt (2002) conducted a meta-analytic multiple regression using 127 correlations between leader personality and emergence as a leader. They described leader emergence as whether (or to what degree) an individual is viewed as a leader by others, who typically have only limited information about that individual's performance (p. 767).

Leader Personality and Leader Emergence (Standardized Regression Weights)

Agreeableness, -0.14

Conscientiousness, 0.36

Conscientiousness (β = .36) and extraversion (β = .30) are moderately related to the extent that individuals emerge as a leader. Openness was weakly, positively related to leader emergence (β = .21).

Leader agreeableness (β = -.14) and leader neuroticism (β = -.09) were both weakly, negatively related to leader emergence.

Personality and Leadership

Meta-Analytic Regressions

Meta-Analytic Multiple Regression for Leader Personality and Leader Effectiveness

Judge, Bono, Ilies and Gerhardt (2002) also conducted a meta-analytic multiple regression using 95 correlations between leader personality and leader effectiveness. They described leader effectiveness as a leader's performance in influencing and guiding the activities of his or her unit toward achievement of its goals (p. 767).

Leader Personality and Leader Effectiveness (Standardized Regression Weights)

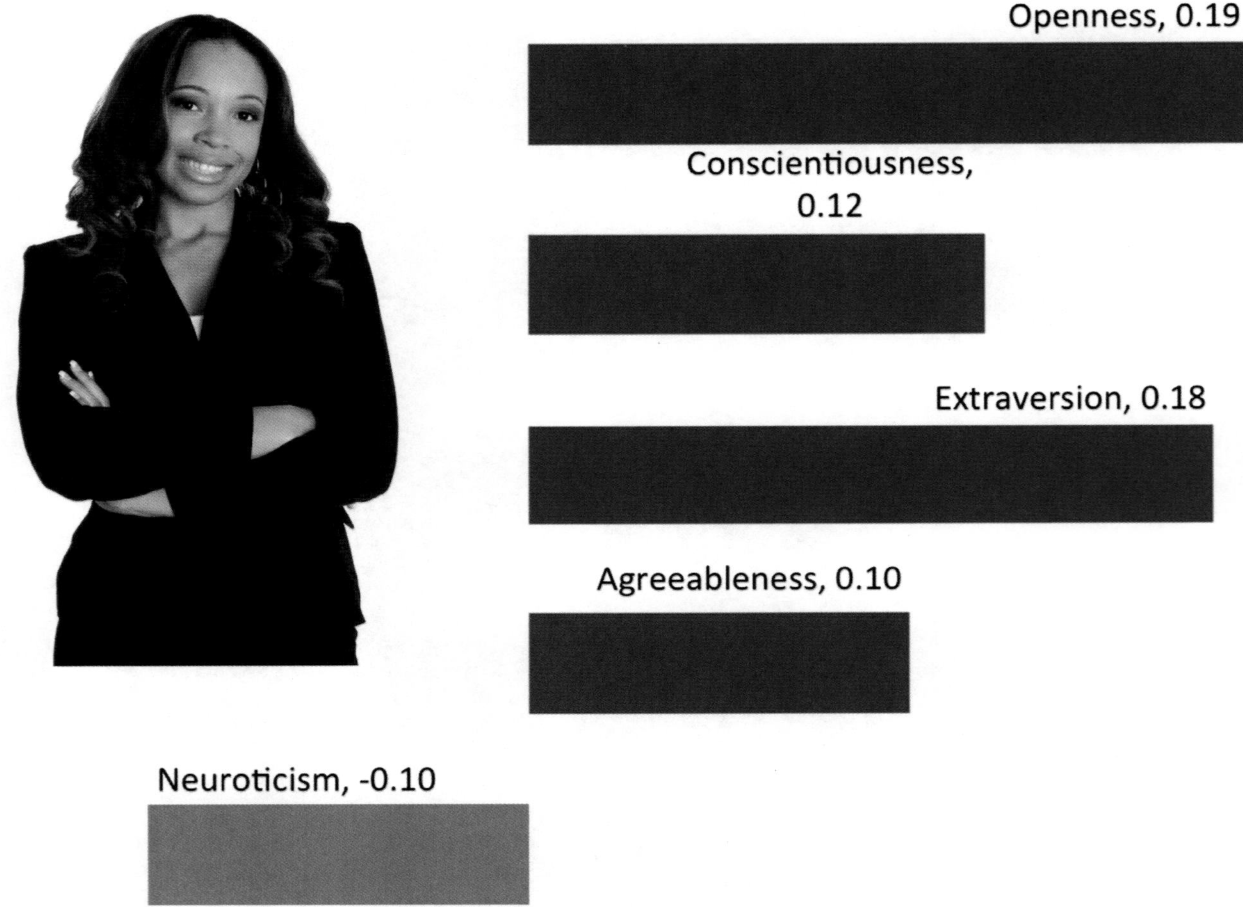

Leader openness (β = .19), extraversion (β = .18) and conscientiousness (β = .12) were noteworthy predictors of ratings of leader effectiveness.

Leader agreeableness (β = .10) was weakly, positively related to leader effectiveness, while leader neuroticism (β = -.10) was weakly, negatively related to leader effectiveness.

Personality and Leadership
Meta-Analytic Regressions

Leader Consideration, Initiation of Structure, Full Range Model, Personality, Gender and Intelligence Predicting Leader Effectiveness

Derue, Nahrgang, Wellman and Humphrey (2011) conducted a meta-analytic multiple regression using data from 59 studies. For the multiple regression 14 predictor variables were used:

Leader Gender and Intelligence
The Big Five Domains of Leader Personality
Transformational, Contingent Reward, MBE-Active, MBE-Passive and Laissez-Faire
Initiation of Structure and Consideration

The chart below provides the strength of each variable in predicting leader effectiveness. The number provided is the R^2 value.[10] The total R^2 for all of the variables was .58, and 42% of the variance in leader effectiveness was unexplained when using only these 14 predictors. For those variables with a blue bar, the direction of the relationship was positive. For those variables with a red bar, the direction of the relationship was negative.

Predictors of Leader Effectiveness (R^2 Values)

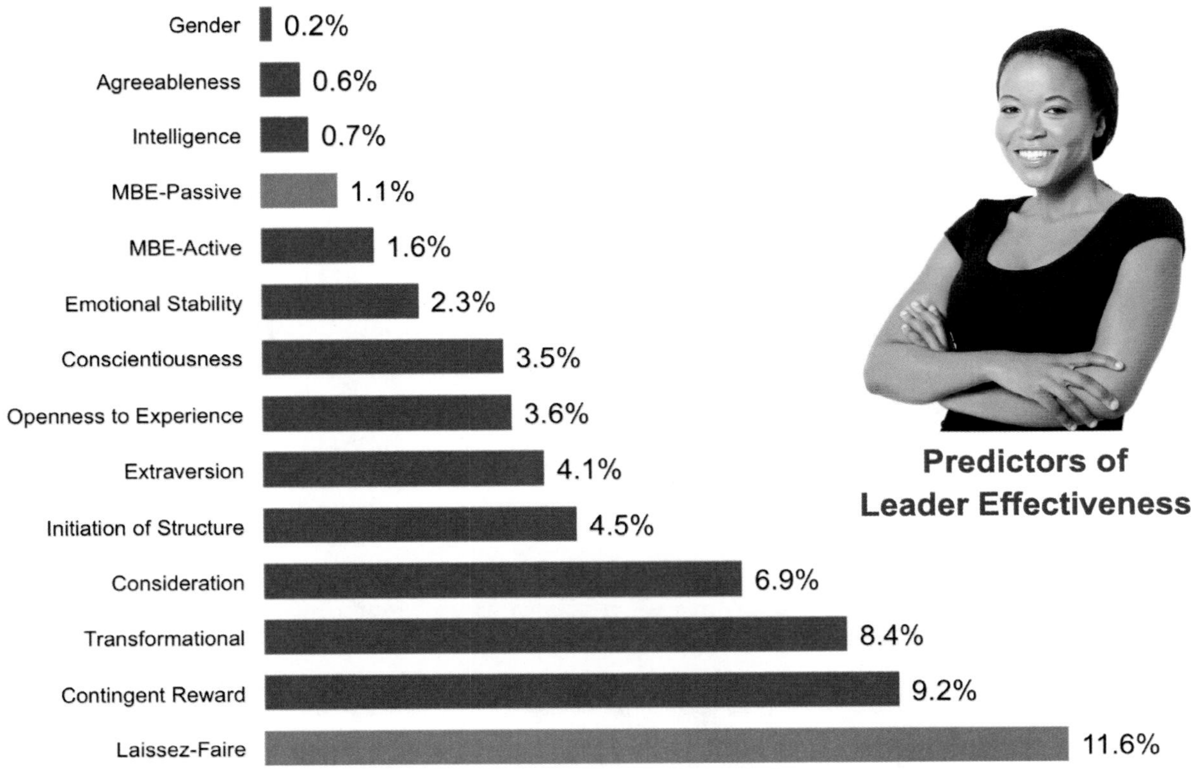

Predictors of Leader Effectiveness

The four strongest predictors of ratings of leader effectiveness were leader consideration, leader transformational behaviors, leader use of contingent reward and leaders not engaging in laissez-faire behaviors.

Personality and Leadership

Meta-Analytic Regressions

Leader Consideration, Initiation of Structure, Full Range Model, Personality and Intelligence Predicting Group Performance

Derue, Nahrgang, Wellman and Humphrey (2011) conducted a meta-analytic multiple regression using data from 59 studies. For the multiple regression 12 predictor variables were used:

Leader Intelligence
The Big Five Domains of Leader Personality
Transformational, Contingent Reward, MBE-Active and MBE-Passive
Initiation of Structure and Consideration

The chart below provides the strength of each variable in predicting group performance. The number provided is the R^2 value. The total R^2 for all of the variables was .31, and 69% of the variance in group performance was unexplained when using only these 12 predictors. For those variables with a blue bar, the direction of the relationship was positive. For those variables with a red bar, the direction of the relationship was negative.

Predictors of Group Performance (R^2 Values)

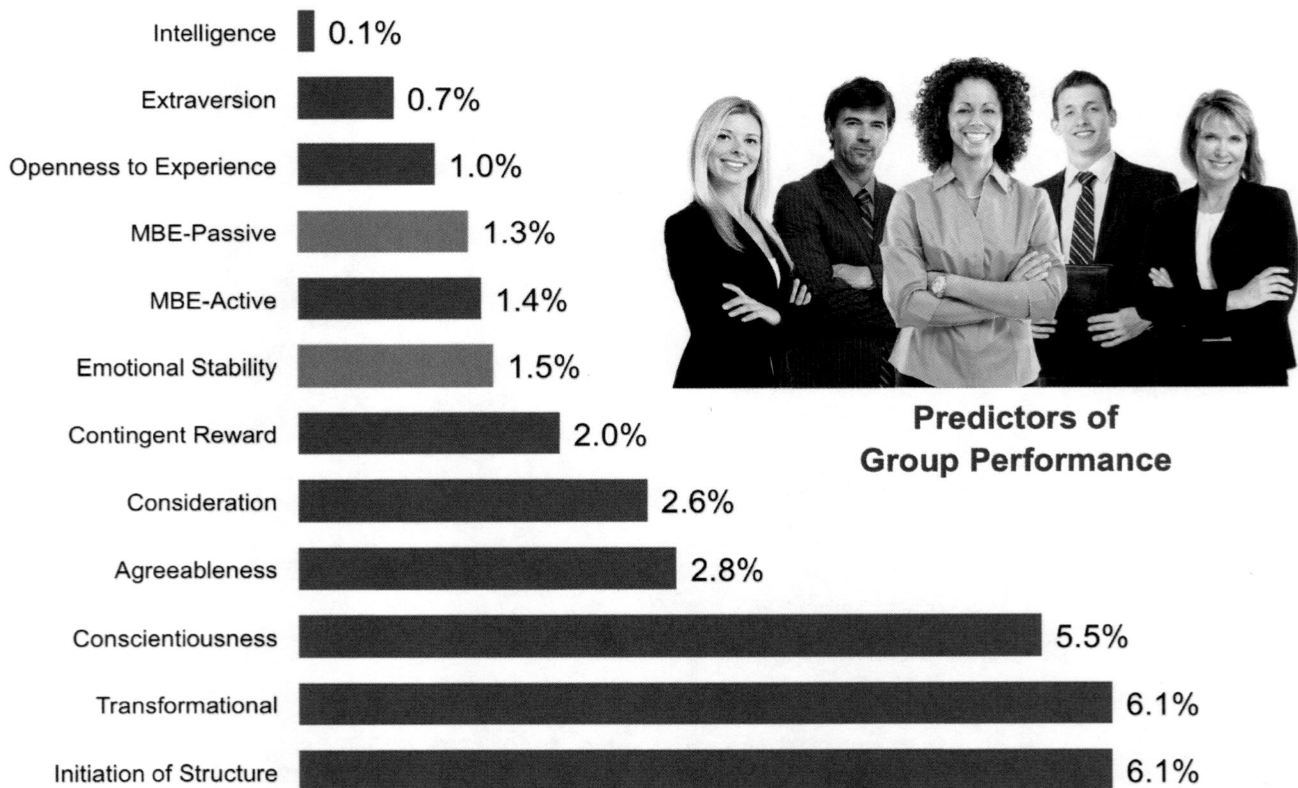

The strongest predictors of group performance were leader conscientiousness, leader transformational behaviors and leader initiation of structure.

Personality and Leadership

Meta-Analytic Regressions

Leader Consideration, Initiation of Structure, Full Range Model, Personality and Gender Predicting Follower Job Satisfaction

Derue, Nahrgang, Wellman and Humphrey (2011) conducted a meta-analytic multiple regression using data from 59 studies. For the multiple regression 13 predictor variables were used:

Leader Gender
The Big Five Domains of Leader Personality
Transformational, Contingent Reward, MBE-Active, MBE-Passive and Laissez-Faire
Initiation of Structure and Consideration

The chart below provides the strength of each variable in predicting follower job satisfaction. The number provided is the R^2 value. The total R^2 for all of the variables was .56 and 44% of the variance in follower job satisfaction was unexplained when using only these 13 predictors. For those variables with a blue bar, the direction of the relationship was positive. For those variables with a red bar, the direction of the relationship was negative.

Predictors of Job Satisfaction (R^2 Values)

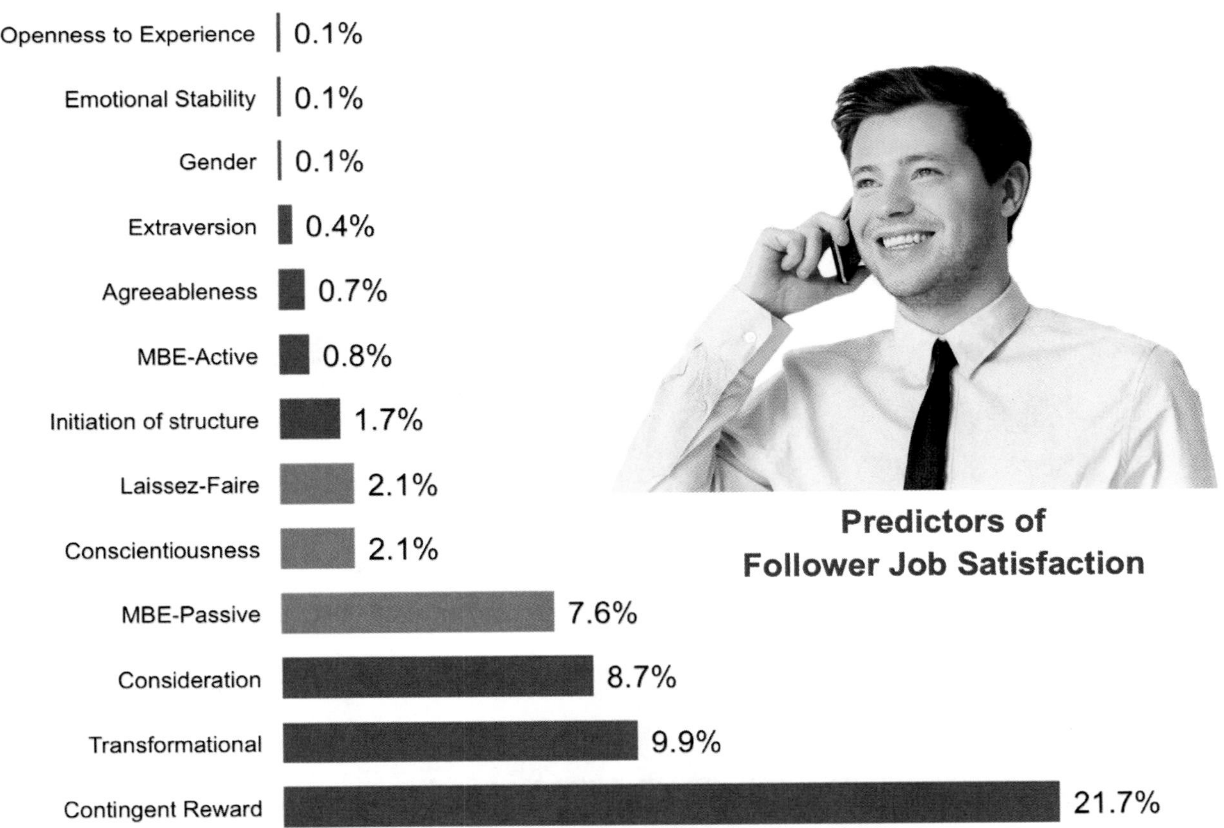

When all thirteen variables were used to predict follower job satisfaction, leader use of contingent reward was a much stronger predictor than the remaining variables.

Personality and Leadership

Meta-Analytic Regressions

Leader Consideration, Initiation of Structure, Full Range Model, Personality, Gender and Intelligence Predicting Satisfaction with the Leader

Derue, Nahrgang, Wellman and Humphrey (2011) conducted a meta-analytic multiple regression using data from 59 studies. For the multiple regression 13 predictor variables were used:

Leader Gender
The Big Five Domains of Leader Personality
Transformational, Contingent Reward, MBE-Active, MBE-Passive and Laissez-Faire
Initiation of Structure and Consideration

The chart below provides the strength of each variable in predicting satisfaction with the leader. The total R^2 for all of the variables was .92, and 8% of the variance in satisfaction with the leader was unexplained when using only these 13 predictors. For those variables with a blue bar, the direction of the relationship was positive. For those variables with a red bar, the direction of the relationship was negative.

Predictors of Satisfaction with the Leader (R^2 Values)

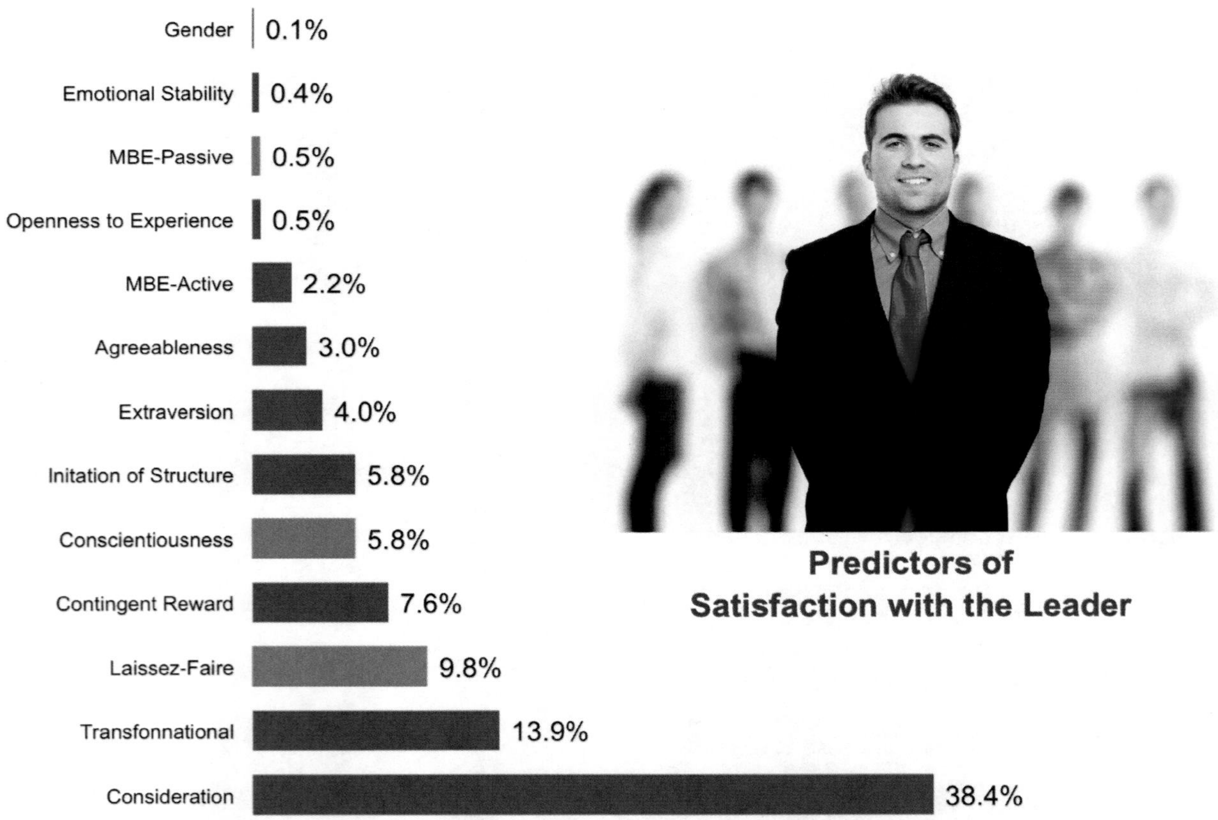

The strongest predictor of satisfaction with the leader was leader consideration. Being transformational and not being laissez-faire were also noteworthy predictors.

Personality and Leadership
Meta-Analytic Regressions

Meta-Analytic Regressions for Follower (Employee) Personality and Work Related Attitudes

The next four pages summarize meta-analytic regressions performed for follower personality and workplace related attitudes.

Workers Complete
a Personality Assessment and
a Work Related Attitudes Assessment

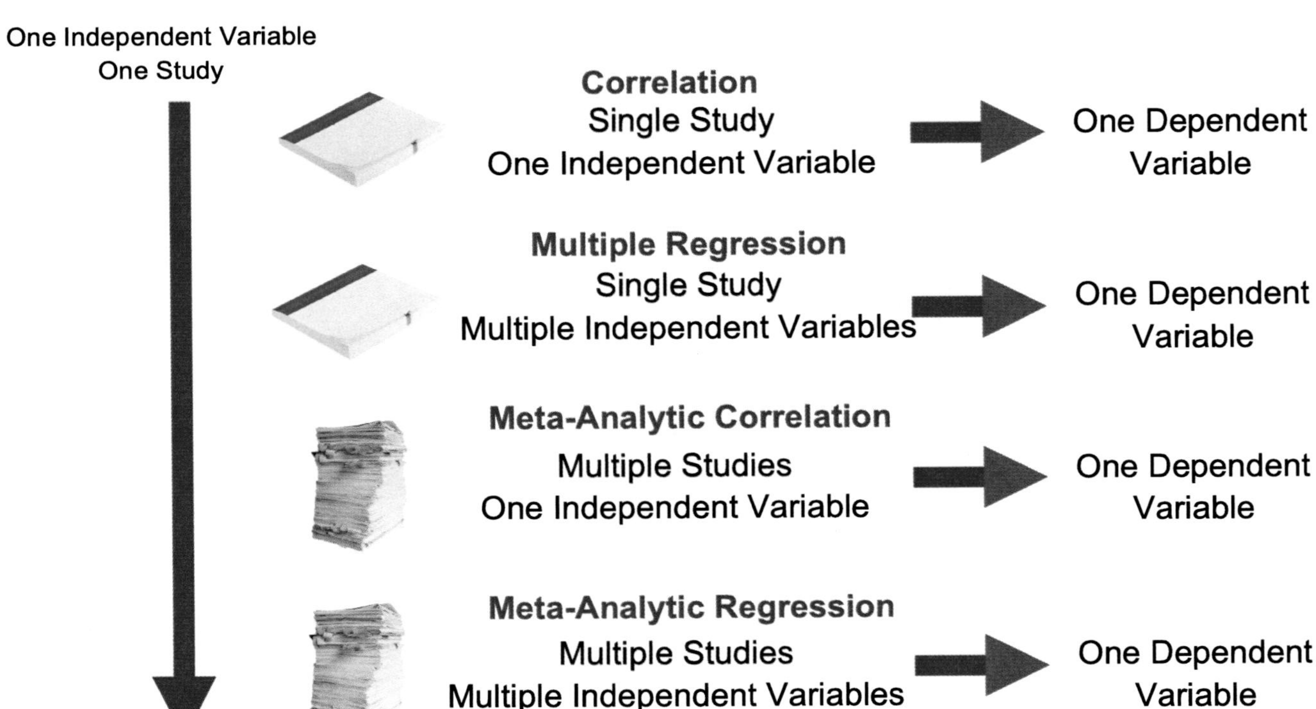

Meta-Analytic Multiple Regression for Follower Personality and Job Satisfaction

Judge, Heller and Mount (2002) conducted a meta-analytic regression for worker personality and job satisfaction.

Follower Personality and Follower Job Satisfaction (Standardized Regression Weights)

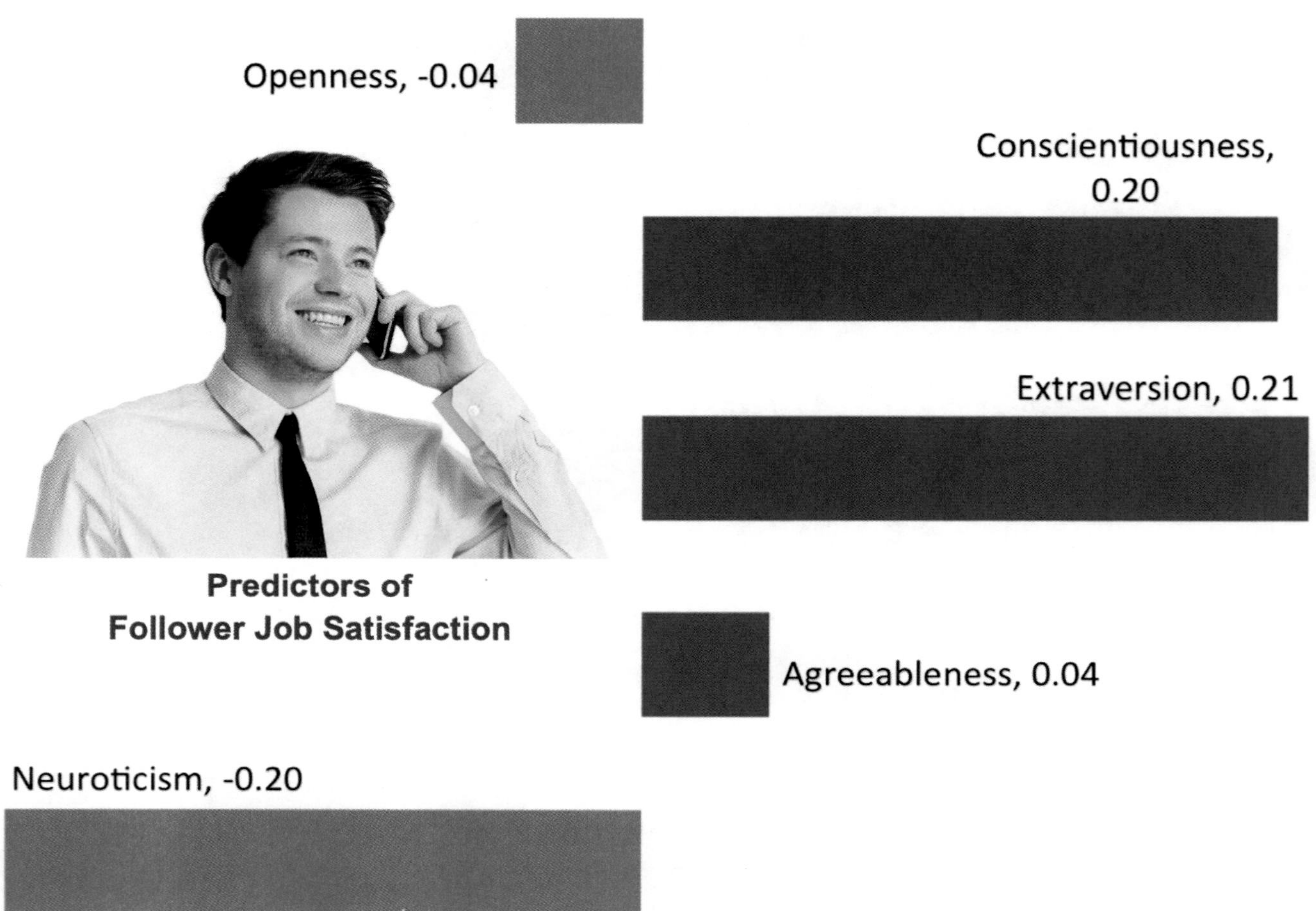

Extraversion (β = .21), conscientiousness (β = .20) and neuroticism (β = -.20) were each significant predictors in the multiple regression. The standardized regression weights for openness and agreeableness are provided, but the authors concluded that neither of these domains were significant predictors in the regression.

Personality and Leadership

Meta-Analytic Regressions

Meta-Analytic Multiple Regression for Follower Personality and Follower Emotional Exhaustion

Alarcon, Eschleman and Bowling (2009) conducted a meta-analytic multiple regression using 113 correlations between follower personality and follower emotional exhaustion.

Follower Personality and Follower Emotional Exhaustion (Standardized Regression Weights)

Predictors of Follower Emotional Exhaustion

Follower neuroticism (β = .45) was the strongest predictor of followers feeling emotionally exhausted. Extraversion (β = -.19) was inversely related to emotional exhaustion.

Openness (β = .09) was weakly, positively related and conscientiousness (β = -.08) and agreeableness (β = -.01) were both weakly, negatively related to emotional exhaustion.

Personality and Leadership

Meta-Analytic Regressions

Meta-Analytic Multiple Regression for Follower Personality and Follower Feelings of Depersonalization

Alarcon, Eschleman and Bowling (2009) also conducted a meta-analytic multiple regression using 80 correlations between follower personality and follower depersonalization.

Openness, 0.03

Conscientiousness, -0.13

Extraversion, -0.17

Agreeableness, -0.22

Predictors of Follower Feelings of Depersonalization

Neuroticism, 0.29

Follower neuroticism (β = .29) was the strongest predictor of followers feeling depersonalized. Agreeableness (β = -.22), extraversion (β = -.17) and conscientiousness (β = -.17) were inversely related to emotional followers feeling depersonalized.

Personality and Leadership

Meta-Analytic Regressions

Meta-Analytic Multiple Regression for Follower Personality and Follower Feelings of Personal Accomplishment

Alarcon, Eschleman and Bowling (2009) also conducted a meta-analytic multiple regression using 89 correlations between follower personality and follower feelings of personal accomplishment.

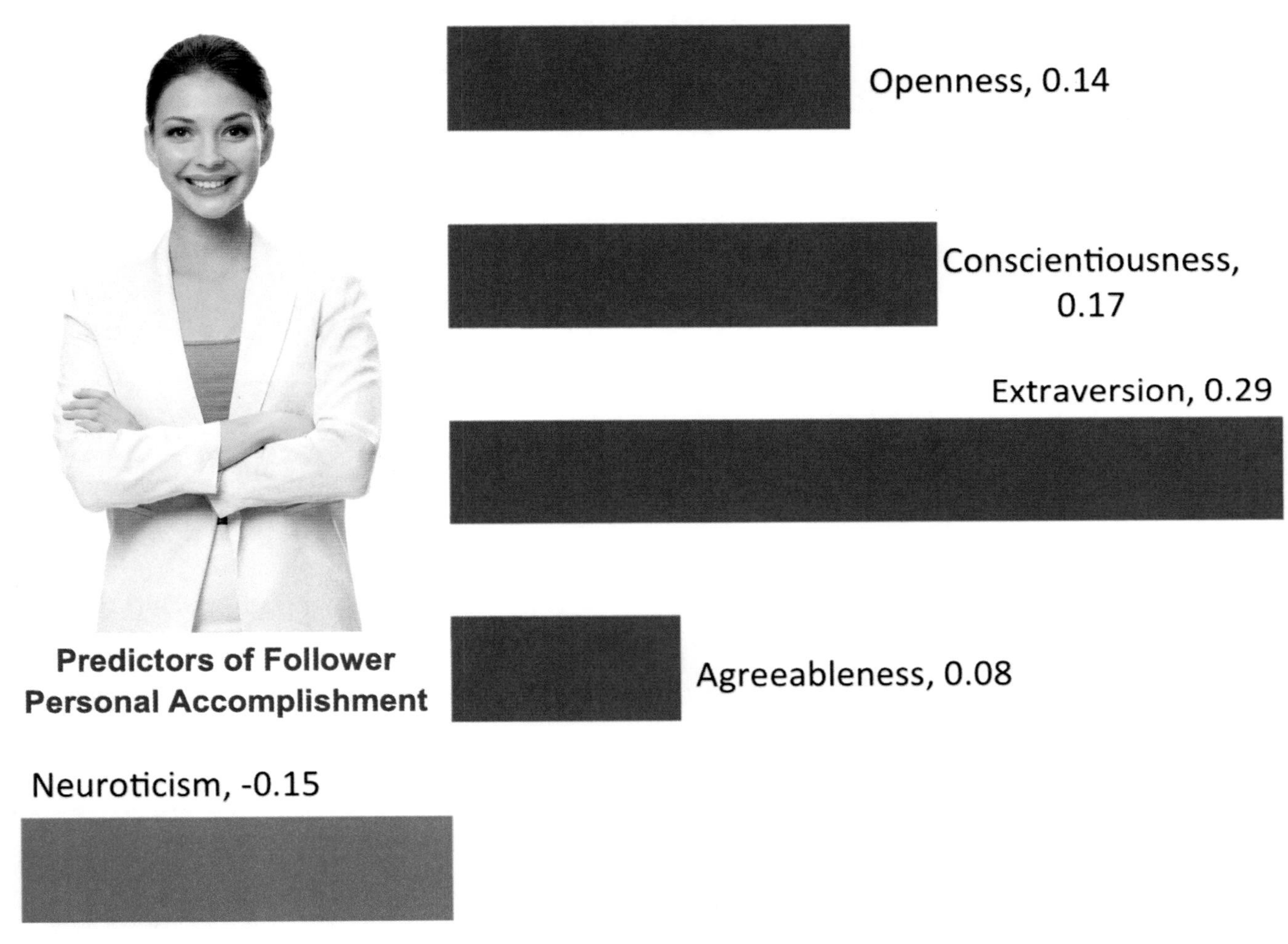

Follower extraversion (β = .29) was the strongest predictor of follower feelings of personal accomplishment. Conscientiousness (β = .17) and openness (β = .14) were also noteworthy predictors. Neuroticism (β = -.15) was inversely related to feelings of personal accomplishment.

Personality and Leadership

Summary

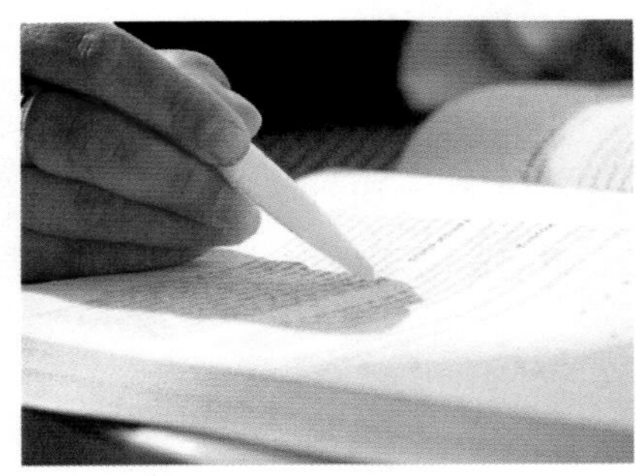

The table below is the conceptual model for the full range model of leadership. The leader behaviors of inspirational motivation, intellectual stimulation, individual consideration, idealized influence attributed, idealized influence behavioral and contingent reward are believed to be active, effective and improve follower performance. Conversely, the behaviors of management by exception active, management by exception passive and laissez-faire are believed to be passive, ineffective and to result in decreased follower performance.

The Full Range Model of Leader Behaviors

Transformational		Transactional			Passive-Avoidant
IM, IS, IC, IIA, IB	CR		MBEA	MBEP	LF
Active Effective Improved Follower Performance					Passive Ineffective Decreased Follower Performance

When we examine the relationships among the meta-analytic correlations between leader personality and the full range model of leadership behaviors, we notice that the direction of the relationship generally "switches" after contingent reward. This generally matches the model behind the full range model of leadership.

With openness, conscientiousness, extraversion and agreeableness, we find positive relationships for the cells shown in light blue, and negative relationships for those in beige.

For neuroticism, we find negative relationships for the cells in light blue and positive relationships for the cells in beige.

Variable	Transformational Leadership	Charisma (IM, II)	Intellectual Stimulation	Individualized Consideration	Contingent Reward	Management by Exception Active	Passive
Openness	.09	.22	.11	.11	.03	-.04	.04
Conscientiousness	.11	.05	.03	.14	.02	-.02	-.11
Extraversion	.23	.22	.18	.18	.14	-.03	-.09
Agreeableness	.12	.21	.14	.17	.17	-.11	-.12
Neuroticism	-.16	-.17	-.13	-.10	-.10	.02	.05
	Active Effective					Passive Ineffective	

Personality and Leadership

Summary

Meta-Analytic Regressions

Meta-Analytic Regression for the Full Range Leadership Model - Charisma, Transformational Behaviors and Individual Consideration

In their meta-analytic regression, Bono and Judge (2002) found that leader personality was the strongest predictor of charismatic leadership, transformational leadership and individual consideration.

Meta-Analytic Regression for Leader Emergence – Conscientiousness and Extraversion

In their meta-analytic regression, Judge, Bono, Ilies and Gerhardt (2002) found that leader conscientiousness and extraversion were the strongest predictors of who emerges as a leader.

Meta-Analytic Regression for Leader Effectiveness – Openness and Extraversion

In their meta-analytic regression, Judge, Bono, Ilies and Gerhardt (2002) found that leader openness and extraversion were the strongest predictors of ratings of leader effectiveness.

Personality and Leadership

Summary

Meta-Analytic Regressions Including Leader Personality, Full Range Model of Leadership, Leader Gender, Leader Intelligence and Leader use of Initiation of Structure and Consideration – Leader Behaviors Matter more than Leader Personality (Derue, Nahrgang, Wellman and Humphrey, 2011)

Leader Effectiveness – (low) Laissez-Faire, Contingent Reward, Transformational, Consideration, Initiation of Structure and Extraversion

For leader effectiveness, leader extraversion was the strongest personality predictor. Low laissez-faire, contingent reward, transformational, consideration and initiation of structure, however, were stronger predictors of leader effectiveness than extraversion.

Follower Job Satisfaction – Contingent Reward, Transformational, Consideration, (low) MBE-Passive and Conscientiousness

For follower job satisfaction, leader conscientiousness was the strongest personality predictor. Contingent reward, transformational, consideration and low MBE-Passive, however, were stronger predictors of follower job satisfaction than conscientiousness.

Satisfaction with the Leader – Consideration, Transformational, (low) Laissez-Faire, Contingent Reward and Conscientiousness

For follower satisfaction with the leader, leader conscientiousness was the strongest personality predictor. Consideration, transformational, (low) laissez-faire and contingent reward, however, were stronger predictors of satisfaction with the leader than conscientiousness.

Personality and Leadership

Notes

Studies Referenced

A. Lord, De Vader and Alliger (1986) The statistic reported is the true r.

B. Judge, Heller and Mount (2002) The statistic reported is the estimated true score correlation.

C. Judge and Ilies (2002) The statistic reported is the estimated true score correlation.

D. Bono and Judge (2004) The statistic reported is the estimated population correlation.

E. Alarcon, Eschleman and Bowling (2009) The statistic reported is the average-weighted correlation coefficient corrected for unreliability in both the predictor and criterion.

F. Chiaburu, Oh, Berry, Li and Gardner (2011) The statistic reported is the mean true-score correlation corrected for unreliability and range restriction.

G. Barrick, Mount and Judge (2001) The statistic reported is the estimated true correlation at the construct level.

H. Zimmerman (2008) The statistic reported is the estimated true-score correlation corrected for unreliability in the predictor and criterion.

I. Ng, Eby, Sorensen and Feldman (2005) The statistic reported is the sample size weighted corrected correlation.

J. Bruk-Lee, Khoury, Nixon, Goh and Spector (2009) The statistic reported is the weighted average correlation.

K. Judge, Bono, Ilies and Gerhardt (2002). The statistic reported is the estimated corrected correlation.

L. Dulebohn, Bommer, Liden, Brouer and Ferris (2012) The statistic reported is the population estimate.

M. Mackey, Frieder, Brees and Martinko (2015). The statistic reported is the correlation for population estimate corrected for attenuation due to measurement error and sampling error variance.

Notes

[1] Stogdill, R. M. (1948). Personal factors associated with leadership: A survey of the literature.

[2] The explanations for each of the big five personality types are based on: McCrae, R. R. and Costa, P. T., Psychological Assessment Resources, Inc. (2010). *NEO inventories for the NEO Personality Inventory-3 (NEO-PI-3), NEO Five-Factor Inventory-3 (NEO-FFI-3), NEO Personality Inventory-Revised (NEO PI-R): Professional manual.* Lutz, FL: PAR.

[3] Based on Kurtz, J. E. and Parrish, C. L. (2001). Semantic response consistency and protocol validity in structured personality assessment: The case of the *NEO-PI-R. Journal of Personality Assessment, 76,* 2, 315-32.

[4] The information for this table as well as the following page came from McCrae, R. R. and Costa, P. T., Psychological Assessment Resources, Inc. (2010). *NEO inventories for the NEO Personality Inventory-3 (NEO-PI-3), NEO Five-Factor Inventory-3 (NEO-FFI-3), NEO Personality Inventory-Revised (NEO PI-R): Professional manual.* Lutz, FL: PAR.

[5] As an example, the NEO facet of anxiety was negatively correlated (r = -.60) with emotional stability measured by the *Guilford-Zimmerman Temperament Survey.*

The NEO facet of anxiety was positively correlated (r = .55) with anxiety measured by the *State-Trait Personality Inventory.*

[6] The exact boundary between weak, moderate and strong correlations is not universally agreed upon. The definitions used are based on Cohen, J. (1992). A power primer. *Psychological Bulletin, 112,* 1, 155-9.

[7] Many of the meta-analyses include some studies in which the leader completed both a personality assessment and then rated her or himself as a leader.

[8] In this case, charismatic leadership is the combination of idealized influence and inspirational motivation.

[9] Many of the meta-analyses include some studies in which the leader completed both a personality assessment and then rated her or himself as a leader.

[10] The authors reported epsilon values. For the three charts provided from this study the R^2 values shown were calculate by dividing the relative weight of each predictor (epsilon) by the total R^2.

Notes

Chapter 6
Emotional Intelligence and Leadership

Emotional Intelligence and Leadership

Introduction

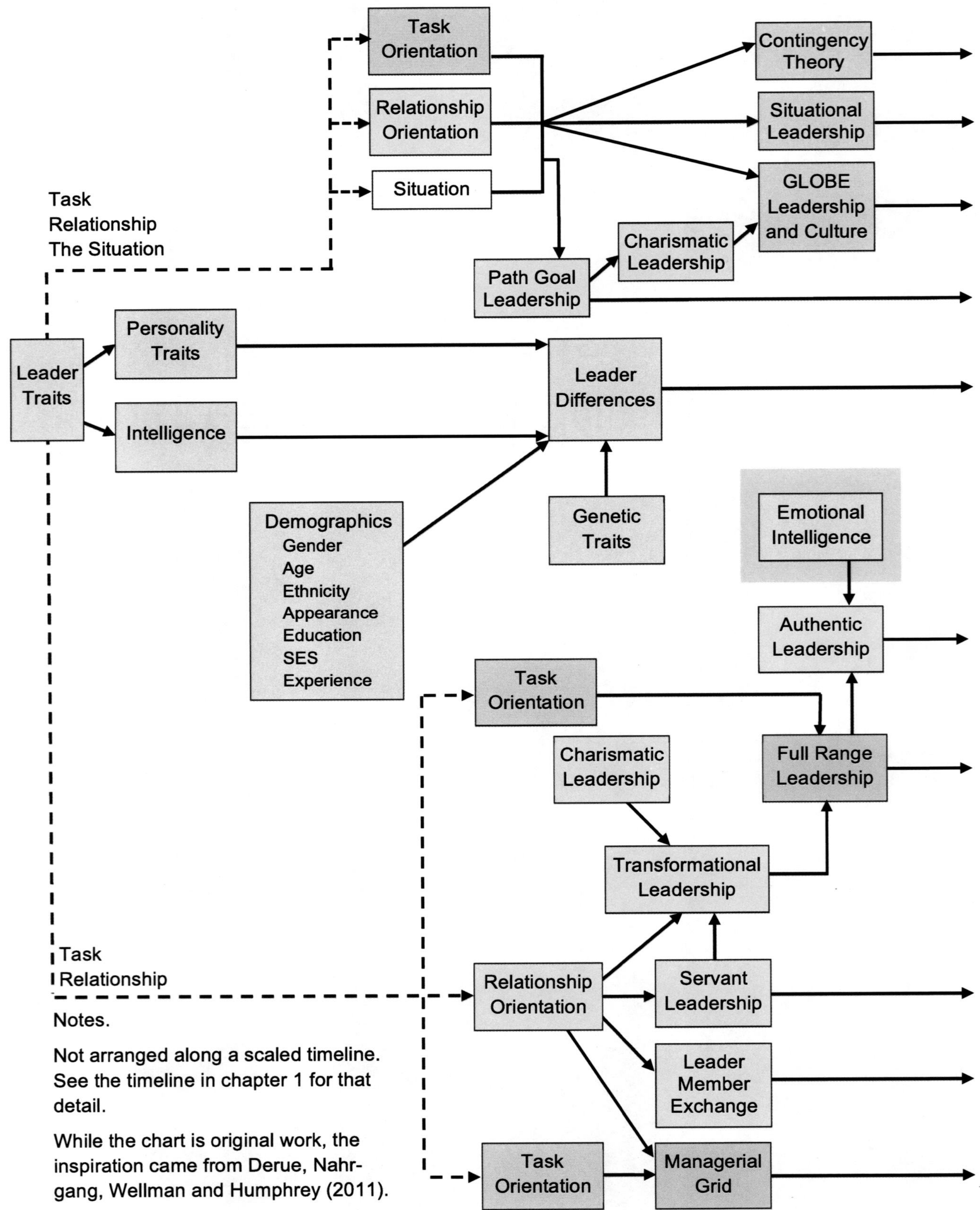

Notes.

Not arranged along a scaled timeline. See the timeline in chapter 1 for that detail.

While the chart is original work, the inspiration came from Derue, Nahrgang, Wellman and Humphrey (2011).

Emotional Intelligence and Leadership

Introduction

Intelligence

Although we use the word intelligent in everyday conversation, it is an area of study that has a deep history, with a concomitant number of theories.

At a high level, researchers often measure different aspects of intelligence. Examples include verbal ability, math ability and spatial ability.

There is also a belief that underlying various measures of intelligence is a general factor of intelligence, often called *g*.

Personality

Personality has also been an area that has a deep research history, with a concomitant number of theories. One of the most popular theories is the big five model of personality.

Like intelligence, there is also a belief that underlying various measures is a general factor of personality.

Extraversion	Agreeableness	Openness to New Experiences	Conscientiousness	Neuroticism
Warmth Gregariousness Assertiveness Activity Excitement Seeking Positive Emotions	Trust Straight Forwardness Altruism Compliance Modesty Tendermindedness	Fantasy Aesthetics Feelings Actions Ideas Values	Competence Order Dutifulness Achievement Striving Self-Discipline Deliberation	Anxiety Hostility Depression Self-Consciousness Impulsiveness Vulnerability

Emotions

We all use terms such as “he’s emotional” or “I was overcome with emotions.” Like other areas of academic study, the study of emotions has many theories, models and classifications.

Emotions that are often called basic emotions include happiness, surprise, fear, sadness, disgust and anger.

Somewhere at the intersections among traditional intelligence or cognitive ability, personality and emotions is the emerging research area called emotional intelligence.

Emotional Intelligence and Leadership
Ability and Mixed Models

Inventories versus Tests

When we consider various measures that leaders and followers might complete, an important distinction is the difference between an inventory or questionnaire, and a test. The easiest way to envision a test is something such as the SAT that many students took to apply to college or the GRE for graduate school. These are tests because there are correct and incorrect answers for each question.

Something such as a big five personality inventory, however, doesn't have "correct and incorrect" answers. It's not a test. These types of measures are often called inventories, measures, questionnaires and so forth.

Ability Models of Emotional Intelligence (Test)

One approach to emotional intelligence (EI) envisions EI as either a form of intelligence or overlapping with intelligence. The predominant ability model is that of Mayer, Salovey and Caruso. Their model posits EI as "the ability to carry out accurate reasoning about emotions and the ability to use emotions and emotional knowledge to enhance thought."[1]

Their test to measure EI ability is the *MSCEIT 2*. The *MSCEIT 2* uses "correct and incorrect" answers. The correct answers have been determined by expert judges.

Because the *MSCEIT 2* is a test rather than an inventory, it is typically more highly correlated with traditional measures of intelligence than are other types of EI assessments. Likewise, it is typically less correlated with traditional measures of personality than are other types of EI assessments.

Mixed Models of Emotional Intelligence (Inventory)

A different approach to EI is often called a mixed models approach. This approach envisions EI as a combination of factors. The predominant mixed model approach is that of Bar-On.

Bar-On envisions EI as cross-section of interrelated emotional and social competencies, skills and facilitators that determine how effectively we understand and express ourselves, understand others, relate with them and cope with daily demands. [2]

Measures using this approach are not tests per se, as there are no purely correct or incorrect answers. Mixed models of EI tend to be less correlated with intelligence and more correlated with personality than the ability based models.

Emotional Intelligence and Leadership

Ability and Mixed Models

The two most popular models of emotional intelligence are shown below.

Ability Model

Mayer, Salovey and Caruso Four Dimension Model Measured by the *MSCEIT 2*

Perceiving Emotions

The ability to perceive emotions in oneself and others as well as in objects, art, stories, music and other stimuli

Facilitating Emotions

The ability to generate, use, and feel emotion as necessary to communicate feelings or employ them in other cognitive processes

Understanding Emotions

The ability to understand emotional information, to understand how emotions combine and progress through relationship transitions, and to appreciate such emotional meanings

Managing Emotions

The ability to be open to feelings, and to modulate them in oneself and others so as to promote personal understanding and growth

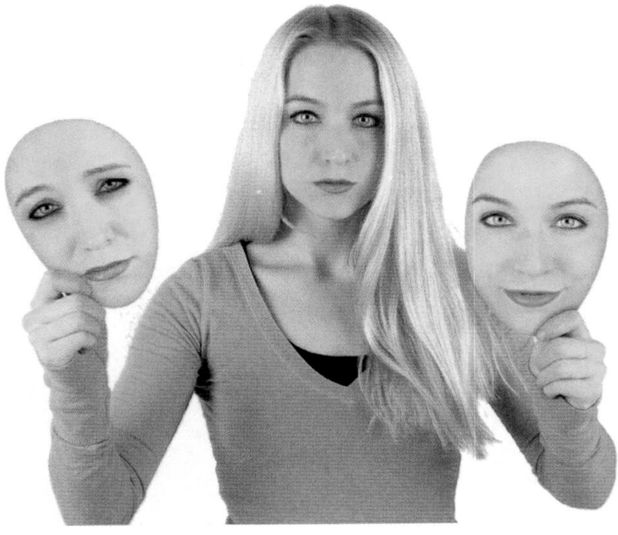

Mixed Model

Bar-On Six Dimension Model Measured by the *EQ-i* 2

Self-Perceptions

Self-Regard To accurately perceive, understand and accept oneself

Self-Actualization To strive to achieve personal goals and actualize one's potential

Emotional Self-Awareness To be aware of and understand one's emotions

Self-Expression

Emotional Expressions To openly express one's feelings, verbally and non-verbally

Assertiveness To effectively and constructively express one's emotions and oneself

Independence To be self-reliant and free of emotional dependency on others

Interpersonal

Empathy To be aware of and understand how others feel

Social Responsibility To identify with one's social group and cooperate with others

Interpersonal Relationships To establish mutually satisfying relationships and relate with others

Decision Making

Problem-Solving To effectively solve problems of a personal and interpersonal nature

Reality-Testing To objectively validate one's feelings and thinking with external reality

Impulse Control To effectively and constructively control emotions

Stress Management

Flexibility To adapt and adjust one's feelings and thinking to new situations

Stress Tolerance To effectively and constructively manage emotions

Optimism To be positive and look at the brighter side of life

Well-Being Indicator

Happiness To feel content with oneself, others and life in general

Emotional Intelligence and Leadership

The Mayer–Salovey–Caruso Emotional Intelligence Test (MSCEIT) 2

The *Mayer–Salovey–Caruso Emotional Intelligence Test (MSCEIT) 2*
The *MSCEIT 2* measures four related abilities.[3]

Perceiving Emotions	The Ability to Recognize How You and Those Around You Are Feeling
Facilitating Emotions	The Ability to Generate Emotions, and to Use Emotions in Cognitive Tasks Such as Problem-Solving and Creativity
Understanding Emotions	The Ability to Understand Complex Emotions and Emotional "Chains" How Emotions Transition from One Stage to Another
Managing Emotions	The Ability to Intelligently Integrate Emotions in Yourself and Others to Devise Effective Strategies That Help You Achieve Positive Outcomes

The four abilities that are measured by the *MSCEIT 2* are sometimes also referred to as branches.

Each of the four branches/abilities, in turn, has two subsections called test sections.

Ability	Test Sections	Question Types
Perceiving Emotions Accurately Identify Faces Identify Subtle Emotions in Faces	Faces	Identify Subtle Emotions in Faces
	Pictures	Identify Emotions in Complex Landscapes and Designs
Facilitating Emotions Generate an Emotion and Solve Problems with That Emotion	Facilitation	Knowledge of How Moods Impact Thinking
	Sensations	Relate Various Feeling Sensations to Emotions
Understanding Emotions Understand the Causes of Emotions	Changes	Multiple Choice Questions about How Emotions Change Over Time
	Blends	Multiple Choice Emotion Vocabulary Definitions
Managing Emotions Stay Open to Emotions and Blend with Thinking	Emotion Management	Indicate Effectiveness of Various Solutions to Internal Problems
	Emotional Relations	Indicate Effectiveness of Various Solutions to Problems Involving Other People

Emotional Intelligence and Leadership

The Mayer–Salovey–Caruso Emotional Intelligence Test (MSCEIT) 2

Internal Reliability

The *MSCEIT 2* reports two sets of reliability data. The first, called "expert" is based on scores from twenty-one scholars and researchers with specialties in emotion.

The "general" score is based on a sample of approximately 2,000 participants.

The *MSCEIT 2* overall split-half reliability was .93 for general and .91 for expert consensus scoring.[4]

Split-Half Reliability Scores	General	Experts
Overall *MSCEIT 2*	.93	.91
Perceiving Emotions	.91	.90
Faces	.80	.82
Pictures	.88	.87
Facilitating Emotions	.79	.76
Facilitation	.64	.63
Sensations	.65	.55
Understanding Emotions	.80	.77
Changes	.70	.68
Blends	.66	.62
Managing Emotions	.83	.81
Emotion Management	.69	.64
Emotional Relations	.67	.64

Confirmatory Factor Analysis

A confirmatory factor analysis (CFA) with a general sample of 1,985 participants found support for the four-factor model hypothesized for the *MSCEIT 2* of perceiving emotions, facilitating emotions, understanding emotions and managing emotions.

The factor loadings for the four components were between .53 and .77.
(X^2 = 94.28, *df* = 15, *NFI* = .97; *TLI* = .96; *RMSEA* = .05).[5]

Emotional Intelligence and Leadership
The Mayer–Salovey–Caruso Emotional Intelligence Test (MSCEIT) 2

Convergent Validity

Brackett and Mayer (2003) reported that the *Mayer–Salovey–Caruso Emotional Intelligence Test* was correlated with the *Emotional Quotient Inventory* at .21 and with the Schutte *Self Report Emotional Intelligence Test* at .18.

Discriminant Validity

The *MSCEIT* was correlated with the *Army Alpha Vocabulary Test* at .36, *Verbal SAT* scores at .32, *Armed Services Vocational Aptitude Battery-General* at .27 and the *Air Force Qualifying Test* at .32.

The *MSCEIT 2* ability and total scores were weakly correlated with the big five measures of personality, ranging from no significance (gray cells) to .24 for managing emotions and agreeableness.[6]

	Total EI		Perceiving Emotions	Facilitating Emotions	Understanding Emotions	Managing Emotions
Neuroticism	-.09	-.08	-.08	-.07	.00	-.07
Extraversion	.06	.11	.05	.06	.01	.11
Openness	.17	.25	.09	.11	.18	.15
Agreeableness	.21	.28	.17	.10	.08	.24
Conscientiousness	.11	.03	.04	.10	.04	.13
Psychological Well-Being	.28					
Subjective Well-Being	-.05					
Verbal SAT	.32					

Predictive Validity

Van Rooy and Viswesvaran (2004) meta-analyzed eight studies that used the *Mayer–Salovey–Caruso Emotional Intelligence Test* and some measure of performance. The measures of performance included employment, academic and "other" measures of performance. The true score correlation between scores on the *MSCEIT* and performance was .19 (k = 8, N = 1,368, ρ *(rho)* = .19).[7]

Harms and Credé (2010) meta-analyzed four studies in which followers rated their leader on transformational leadership and the leaders completed the *MSCEIT*. The true score correlation was .05 (k = 4, N = 441, ρ *(rho)* = .05).

Acquiring the *MSCEIT 2*

As of 2014, the *MSCEIT 2* was available for purchase from Multi-Health Systems, Inc., (MHS) of Toronto, Canada http://www.mhs.com

Emotional Intelligence and Leadership

The Emotional Quotient Inventory 2

EQ-i 2.0

The Bar-On Model

Bar-On based his model on the belief that emotional-social intelligence is a cross section of interrelated emotional and social competencies, skills and facilitators that determine how effectively we understand and express ourselves, understand others and relate with them, and cope with daily demands.

From about 1990 until 2012, The *Emotional Quotient Inventory (EQ-i)* was the instrument used to measure Bar-On's mixed model of emotional intelligence. Around 2013, an updated version of the *EQ-I* was released called the *EQ-i* 2.0.

The EQ-i 2.0 contains 133 items in the form of short sentences and employs a 5-point response scale with a textual response format ranging from "very seldom or not true of me" (1) to "very often true of me or true of me" (5).

Development of the Emotional Quotient Inventory (*EQ-i*)

Face Validity

Bar-On originally developed 15 dimensions of emotional intelligence. Using those dimensions and existing literature, Bar-On and a group of experienced healthcare practitioners generated approximately 1,000 items (questions) that might measure these dimensions.

Exploratory Factor Analyses

Test items were administered to 3,831 North American adults. Through a series of exploratory factor analyses (EFA) using varimax rotation, the 1,000 items were eventually reduced to 133 items believed to load on 15 primary scales. The results, however, produced a 13-factor rather than a 15-factor solution.

In the 13-factor solution, the current subscale of assertiveness loaded with the current subscale of independence as one component called assertiveness/independence.

Additionally in the 13-factor solution the current subscales of self-regard, happiness, optimism and self-actualization loaded on multiple components.

Confirmatory Factor Analyses

Bar-On next ran two confirmatory factor analyses (CFA). One CFA was run for the combination of self-regard, happiness, optimism and self-actualization and a second for the combination of assertiveness and independence.

It is important to note that these CFA's were not run on all 133 items, but rather on the 34 questions that measured aspects of self-regard, happiness, optimism and self-actualization and as a second CFA on the 14 questions that measured assertiveness and independence.

When a CFA was run on just the 34 questions measuring self-regard, happiness, optimism and self-actualization, the questions loaded on the four components hypothesized. Similarly, the CFA ran on the 14 questions that measured assertiveness and independence produced the two-factor solution hypothesized.

Bar-On elected to treat self-regard, happiness, optimism, self-actualization, assertiveness and independence as six separate factors (subscales). Bar-On's rationale was that this treatment struck the correct, delicate balance between theory and empirical research results.[8]

Using the five hypothesized second-order scales of intrapersonal, interpersonal, adaptability, stress management and general mood, Bar-On ran a confirmatory factor analysis to determine the degree to which these five second-order scales loaded on a single *EQ-i* scale. The CFA supported this fit (*GFI* = .97, *CFI* = .98). The factor loadings for intrapersonal, interpersonal, adaptability and stress management fell in the range of .83 to .90. The factor loading for general mood was .65.[9]

Internal Reliability

Bar-On has reported overall internal consistency coefficients in the range of .60 to .89 in studies of the 15 subscales across nine international samples. The average Cronbach Alpha scores from these studies ranged from .69 to .85. The overall mean Cronbach Alpha scores across all scales, across all studies was .76.[10]

In a university student sample, Dawda and Hart (2000) found the Cronbach Alpha for the overall *EQ-i* score was 0.96. The Cronbach Alpha scores for the subscales ranged from .69 to .93.

Gowing (2001) reported that the average correlation among *EQ-i* subscales was .50. Brackett and Mayer (2003) found inter-correlations in the range of .32 to .75.

Test-Retest Reliability

Bar-On (2004) reported test retest reliability of the *EQ-i* as .72 for males and .80 for females at a six-month interval. Schutte, Malouff, Haggerty, Cooper and Golden (1998) reported a test-retest statistic of .78.

Emotional Intelligence and Leadership

The Emotional Quotient Inventory 2

EQ-i 2.0

Convergent Validity

Mayer, Caruso and Salovey (2000) reported that the correlation between the *EQ-i* and the *Multifactor Emotional Intelligence Scale* (MEIS) was .36. Brackett and Mayer (2003) reported that the *EQ-i* was correlated with the *Mayer–Salovey–Caruso Emotional Intelligence Test 2.0* at .21 and with the *Schutte Self Report Emotional Intelligence Test* at .43.

Discriminant Validity

One of the primary criticisms of the *EQ-i* is discriminant validity. On the one hand, Bar-On posits that emotional intelligence is a cross section of interrelated emotional and social competencies, skills and facilitators. On the other hand, the total *EQ-i* score has been correlated at .72 with emotional stability measured by the 1970 *Cattell 16PF*; at -.57 with neuroticism measured by the *NEO-PI*; and at -.77 with anxiety measured by the 1993 *Cattell 16PF*.

EQ-i Correlations In a North American Sample[11]			
Emotional Stability	.72	Apprehension	-.55
Social Boldness	.51	Tension	-.44
Dominance	.38	Abstractedness	-.37
Openness to Change	.33	Vigilance	-.36
Rule-Consciousness	.24	Privateness	-.28
Perfectionism	.21	Sensitivity	Not significant
Warmth	.20	Self-Reliance	Not significant
Reasoning	Not significant	Liveliness	Not significant

	Total *EQ-i*[12]	Male Students[13]	Female Students
Neuroticism	-.57	-.62	-.72
Extraversion	.37, .46	.52	.56
Openness	.16	-.12	.17
Agreeableness	.27	.43	.43
Conscientiousness	.48	.51	.33
Depression		-.57	-.62
Anxiety	-.77		
Tough-Mindedness	-.11		
Independence	.44		
Self-Control	.36		
Gen Cognitive Ability	.08		
Psych Well-Being	.58		
Subj Well-Being	.35		
Verbal SAT	-.03		
WAIS[14]	.12		

Emotional Intelligence and Leadership
The Emotional Quotient Inventory 2
EQ-i 2.0

Predictive Validity

Van Rooy and Viswesvaran (2004) meta-analyzed 13 studies that used the *Emotional Quotient Inventory* and some measure of performance. The measures of performance included employment, academic and "other" measures of performance. The true score correlation between the *EQ-i* and performance was .20 (k = 13, N = 3,046, ρ *(rho)* = .20).[15]

Harms and Credé (2010) meta-analyzed four studies in which followers rated their leader on transformational leadership and the leaders completed the *EQ-i*. The true score correlation was .20 (k = 4, N = 267, ρ *(rho)* = .20).

Acquiring the *EQ-i* or *EQ-i 2.0*

As of 2014, the *EQ-i* or *EQ-i 2.0* were available for purchase from Multi-Health Systems, Inc., (MHS) of Toronto, Canada http://www.mhs.com

Emotional Intelligence and Leadership

The Emotional Quotient Inventory 2

EQ-i 2.0

Emotional Quotient Inventory *EQ-i* and *EQ-i* 2.0 Scales and Subscales

As of 2013, the *EQ-i* had migrated from a five-dimension to a six-dimension model called the *EQ-i* 2.0. The table below helps explain the changes.

EQ-i	***EQ-i* 2.0**
Intrapersonal	**Self-Perceptions**
Self-Regard To accurately perceive, understand and accept oneself	**Self-Regard** To accurately perceive, understand and accept oneself
Self-Actualization To strive to achieve personal goals and actualize one's potential	**Self-Actualization** To strive to achieve personal goals and actualize one's potential
Emotional Self-Awareness To be aware of and understand one's emotions	**Emotional Self-Awareness** To be aware of and understand one's emotions
	Self-Expression
	Emotional Expressions To openly express one's feelings, verbally and non-verbally
Assertiveness To effectively and constructively express one's emotions and oneself	**Assertiveness** To effectively and constructively express one's emotions and oneself
Independence To be self-reliant and free of emotional dependency on others	**Independence** To be self-reliant and free of emotional dependency on others
Interpersonal	**Interpersonal**
Empathy To be aware of and understand how others feel	**Empathy** To be aware of and understand how others feel
Social Responsibility To identify with one's social group and cooperate with others	**Social Responsibility** To identify with one's social group and cooperate with others
Interpersonal Relationship To establish mutually satisfying relationships and relate well with others	**Interpersonal Relationship** To establish mutually satisfying relationships and relate well with others
Adaptability	**Decision Making**
Problem-Solving To effectively solve problems of a personal and interpersonal nature	**Problem-Solving** To effectively solve problems of a personal and interpersonal nature
Reality-Testing To objectively validate one's feelings and thinking with external reality	**Reality-Testing** To objectively validate one's feelings and thinking with external reality
Flexibility To adapt and adjust one's feelings and thinking to new situations	**Impulse Control** To effectively and constructively control emotions
Stress Management	**Stress Management**
Impulse Control To effectively and constructively control emotions	**Flexibility** To adapt and adjust one's feelings and thinking to new situations
Stress Tolerance To effectively and constructively manage emotions	**Stress Tolerance** To effectively and constructively manage emotions
	Optimism To be positive and look at the brighter side of life
General Mood	**Well-Being Indicator**
Optimism To be positive and look at the brighter side of life	**Happiness** To feel content with oneself, others and life in general
Happiness To feel content with oneself, others and life in general	

Emotional Intelligence and Leadership
Research Results

Understanding the Research Results for Emotional Intelligence

There is a great deal of research on emotional intelligence. To prepare you for understanding the research results that follow, chapter 2 explained both correlations and meta-analyses. The table below, however, provides a quick review of how the results of the meta-analytic literature will be provided in this chapter.[16]

Example - Follower Emotional Intelligence and Follower Job Performance

In the example below, 22 studies have been published and meta-analyzed on the relationship between followers' emotional intelligence and followers' job performance. The notation (E) refers to the meta-analytic study. A list of the studies referenced is provided at the end of this chapter.

The 22 studies meta-analyzed collectively represent 2,593 follower ratings. The meta-analytic finding was a moderate, positive correlation (.32). The higher followers' emotional intelligence, the higher followers' job performance.

Strongly - Correlated	Moderately - Correlated	Weakly - Correlated
-1 to -.50	-.49 to -.30	-.29 to -.10

Weakly + Correlated	Moderately + Correlated	Strongly + Correlated
.10 to .29	.30 to .49	.50 to 1

Outcome	Studies	Followers	
Job Performance (E)	22	2,593	.32

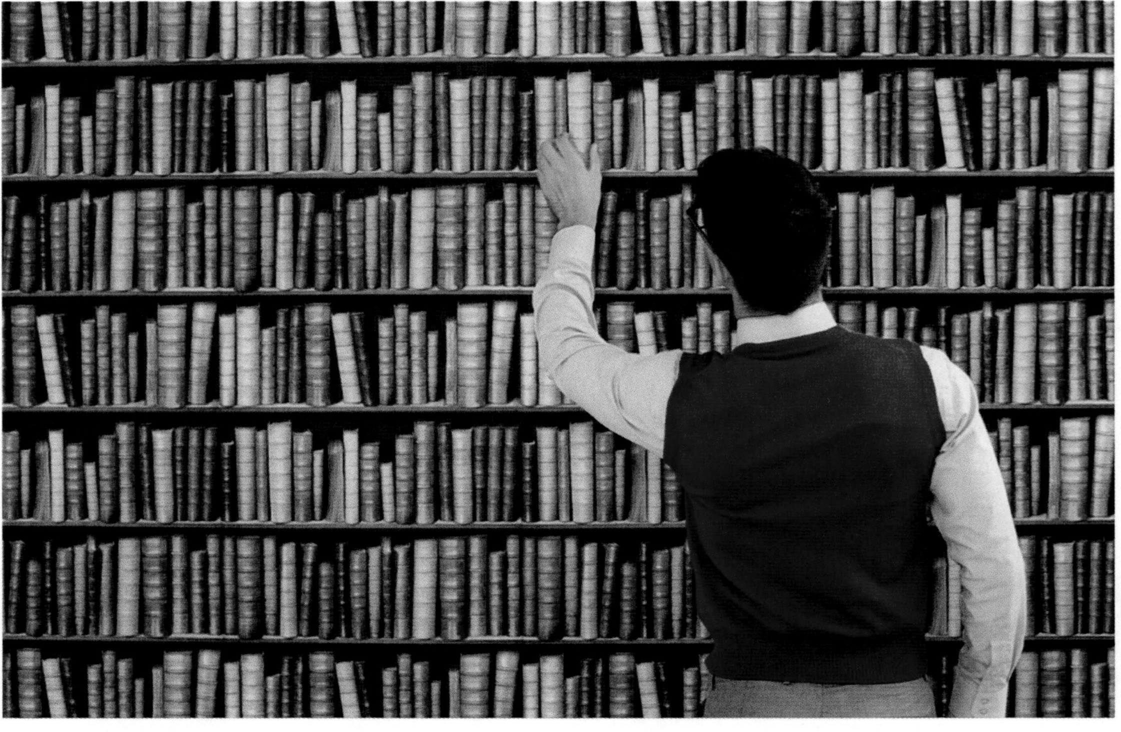

Emotional Intelligence and Leadership

Research Results

Follower Emotional Intelligence and Follower Outcomes

Strongly - Correlated	Moderately - Correlated	Weakly - Correlated
-1 to -.50	-.49 to -.30	-.29 to -.10

Weakly + Correlated	Moderately + Correlated	Strongly + Correlated
.10 to .29	.30 to .49	.50 to 1

Outcome	Studies	Participants	
		Weakly, Positively Correlated	
Academic Performance (B)*	11	1,370	.10
Overall Performance (B)**	8	1,368	.19
Overall Performance (B)***	13	3,046	.20
Overall Performance (B)*	59	9,522	.23
Employment Performance (B)*	19	2,652	.24
Job Performance (G)**	9	700	.24
Job Performance (G)*	43	5,795	.28
Job Performance (G)****	27	3,961	.28
		Moderately, Positively Correlated	
Job Performance (E) *	22	2,593	.32
Other Performance (B)*	34	6,327	.34

*All EQ Instruments, **MSCEIT, ***EQ-I **** EQ-I, AES, ECI, EIS, GENOS

Research from 245 analyses (effect sizes) that have included 37,334 ratings indicates that follower emotional intelligence is weakly to moderately, positively correlated with multiple forms of performance.

Emotional Intelligence and Leadership

Research Results

Follower Emotional Intelligence, Follower Personality and Intelligence

Strongly - Correlated	Moderately - Correlated	Weakly - Correlated	Weakly + Correlated	Moderately + Correlated	Strongly + Correlated
-1 to -.50	-.49 to -.30	-.29 to -.10	.10 to .29	.30 to .49	.50 to 1

All Models

Outcome	Studies	Participants	
		Weakly, Positively Correlated	
Cognitive Ability (E)*	54	10,519	.16
Openness (E)*	58	18,170	.27
		Moderately, Positively Correlated	
Conscientiousness (E)*	60	18,462	.32
Extraversion (E)*	60	18,450	.33
Agreeableness (E)*	59	18,302	.34
Emotional Stability (E)*	60	18,416	.39

*All EQ Instruments, **MSCEIT, ***EQ-I **** EQ-I, AES, ECI, EIS, GENOS

Research from 351 analyses (effect sizes) that have included 102,319 ratings indicates that emotional intelligence is weakly, positively correlated with cognitive ability and openness. Emotional intelligence is moderately, positively correlated with conscientiousness, extroversion, agreeableness and emotional stability (the reverse of neuroticism).

Strongly - Correlated	Moderately - Correlated	Weakly - Correlated	Weakly + Correlated	Moderately + Correlated	Strongly + Correlated
-1 to -.50	-.49 to -.30	-.29 to -.10	.10 to .29	.30 to .49	.50 to 1

Ability Model

Outcome	Studies	Participants	
		Weakly, Positively Correlated	
Extroversion (H)**	25	4,684	.11
Conscientiousness (H)**	22	4,401	.11
Openness (H)**	22	4,684	.18
Agreeableness (H)**	22	3,998	.26
Openness (E)**	26	8,479	.29
		Moderately, Positively Correlated	
Agreeableness (E)**	26	8,479	.31
Extroversion (E)**	26	8,479	.32
Conscientiousness (E)**	27	8,566	.38
Emotional Stability (E)**	26	8,479	.40

*All EQ Instruments, **MSCEIT, ***EQ-I **** EQ-I, AES, ECI, EIS, GENOS

Research from 247 analyses (effect sizes) that have included 64,845 ability model ratings indicates that emotional intelligence is weakly to moderately, positively correlated with measures of personality. Not shown in graphical form is a negative relationship with neuroticism (k = 25, N = 4,596, r_c = -.16)

Emotional Intelligence and Leadership
Research Results

Follower Emotional Intelligence, Follower Personality and Intelligence

Strongly - Correlated	Moderately - Correlated	Weakly - Correlated
-1 to -.50	-.49 to -.30	-.29 to -.10

Weakly + Correlated	Moderately + Correlated	Strongly + Correlated
.10 to .29	.30 to .49	.50 to 1

Mixed Model

Outcome	Studies	Participants	
Very Weakly, Positively Correlated			
Cognitive Ability (H)****	25	6,655	.06
Weakly, Positively Correlated			
Cognitive Ability (E)	19	2,880	.11
Openness (E)	30	5,552	.29
Moderately, Positively Correlated			
Conscientiousness (H)****	30	6,149	.38
Agreeableness (H)****	30	5,992	.38
Conscientiousness (E)	31	5,591	.38
Openness (H)****	25	6,655	.39
Agreeableness (E)	30	5,386	.43
Extraversion (E)	30	5,552	.46
Extroversion (H)****	33	6,655	.49
Strongly, Positively Correlated			
Emotional Stability (D)	30	5,552	.53

*All EQ Instruments, **MSCEIT, ***EQ-I **** EQ-I, AES, ECI, EIS, GENOS

Mixed Model

	Outcome	Studies	Followers
Strongly, Negatively Correlated			
-.54	Neuroticism (H)****	33	6,829

*All EQ Instruments, **MSCEIT, ***EQ-I **** EQ-I, AES, ECI, EIS, GENOS

Conversely, 346 analyses (effect sizes) that have included 69,448 mixed-model ratings of emotional intelligence found that mixed-models scores are generally moderately, positively correlated with personality and strongly, positively correlated with emotional stability (the reverse of neuroticism).

Emotional Intelligence and Leadership

Research Results

Leader Emotional Intelligence and Ratings of Leadership

In the meta-analyses related to leader emotional intelligence, and how leaders lead, there is an important distinction in the type of data collected. In the type below, the leaders complete an emotional intelligence assessment on themselves, and other individuals, such as their followers, assess their leadership style.

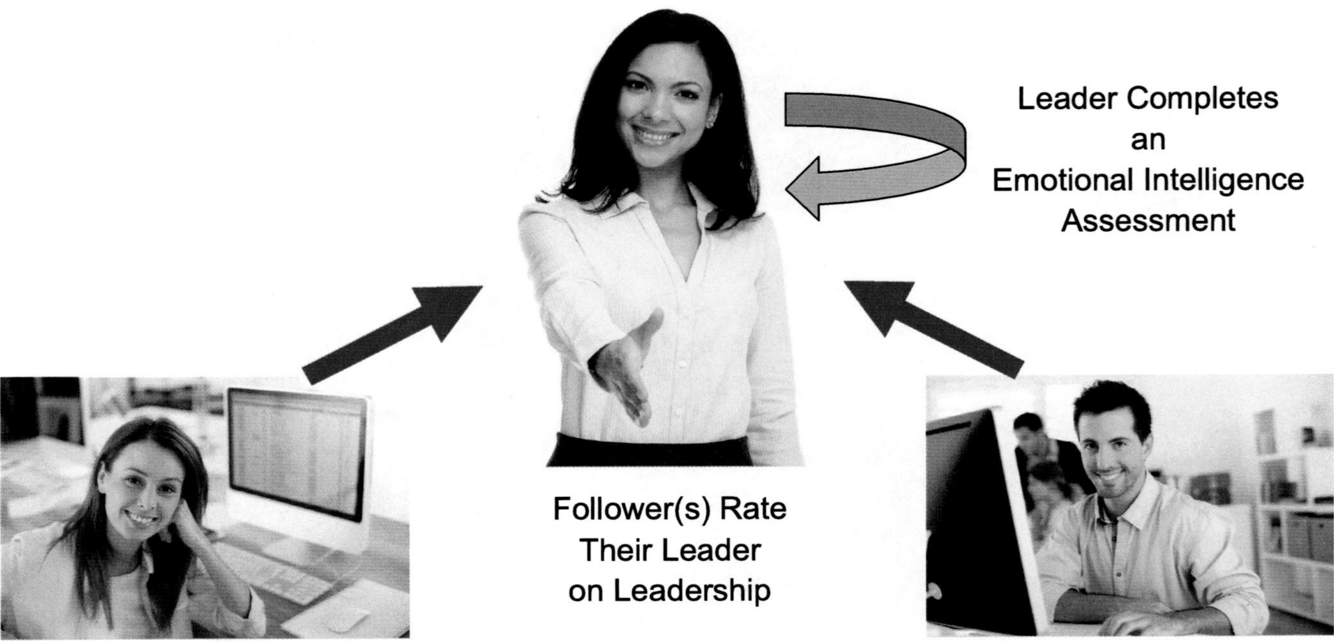

In the second type of research, the leaders self assess both their emotional intelligence as well as how they believe they lead.

The strength of the relationships between leader emotional intelligence and leadership style vary a great deal depending on how the two scores were collected.

Emotional Intelligence and Leadership

Research Results

Leader Emotional Intelligence and Follower Ratings of Leadership

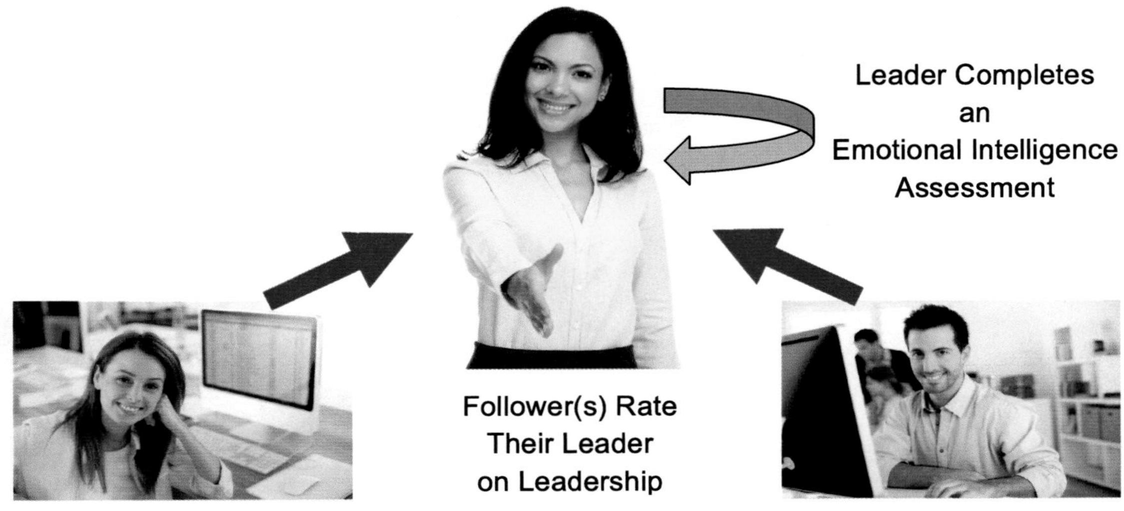

Strongly - Correlated	Moderately - Correlated	Weakly - Correlated	Weakly + Correlated	Moderately + Correlated	Strongly + Correlated
-1 to -.50	-.49 to -.30	-.29 to -.10	.10 to .29	.30 to .49	.50 to 1

Outcome	Studies	Participants	
Very Weakly, Positively Correlated			
Transformational Leadership (D)**	4	441	.05
Weakly, Positively Correlated			
Idealized Influence (overall) (D)*	7	730	.10
Individual Consideration (D)*	7	730	.10
Intellectual Stimulation (D)*	7	730	.10
Transformational Leadership (D)*	22	2,661	.12
Contingent Reward (D)*	6	622	.13
Inspirational Motivation (D)*	7	730	.14
Transformational Leadership (D)***	4	267	.20

*All EQ Instruments, **MSCEIT, ***EQ-i

	Outcome	Studies	Followers
Weakly, Negatively Correlated			
-.17	Laissez-Faire (D) **	8	617

Research from 72 analyses (effect sizes) that have included 7,528 ratings indicates that, when others, such as followers, rate how leaders lead, those ratings are weakly correlated with leader emotional intelligence.

Emotional Intelligence and Leadership

Research Results

Leader Emotional Intelligence and Leader Self-Ratings of Leadership

Leader Completes a Leadership Assessment

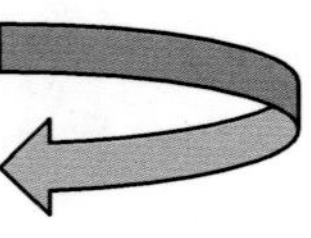

Leader Completes an Emotional Intelligence Assessment

Strongly - Correlated	Moderately - Correlated	Weakly - Correlated	Weakly + Correlated	Moderately + Correlated	Strongly + Correlated
-1 to -.50	-.49 to -.30	-.29 to -.1	.1 to .29	.30 to .49	.50 to 1

Outcome	Studies	Participants	
Weakly, Positively Correlated			
Transformational Leadership (D)**	10	1,066	.24
Moderately, Positively Weakly Correlated			
Contingent Reward (D)*	12	1,272	.35
Idealized Influence (Attributed) (D)*	15	1,576	.38
Intellectual Stimulation (D)*	17	1,815	.40
Idealized Influence (Overall) (D)*	17	1,815	.42
Inspirational Motivation (D)*	17	1,814	.43
Individual Consideration (D)*	17	1,815	.45
Strongly, Positively Correlated			
Transformational Leadership (D)*	47	4,994	.56
Transformational Leadership (B)***	6	640	.67

*All EQ Instruments, **MSCEIT, ***EQ-i

	Outcome	Studies	Followers
Weakly, Negatively Correlated			
-.10	Management by Exception (Active) (D)***	10	871
-.22	Management by Exception (Passive) (D)***	10	871
Moderately, Negatively Correlated			
-.37	Laissez-Faire (D)***	13	1,204

Research from 191 analyses (effect sizes) that have included 19,753 ratings indicates that, when leaders self-assess how they lead, those ratings are moderately to strongly correlated with leader emotional intelligence.

Correlational Differences Based on Who Rates Whom

An important observation related for emotional intelligence and transformational leadership is that the strength of the correlations found between the two constructs varies a great deal, depending on who rates whom. The upper graphs are meta-analytic correlations found when the leaders rate themselves on both instruments. The leaders assess their own emotional intelligence, but also assess their own transformational behaviors.

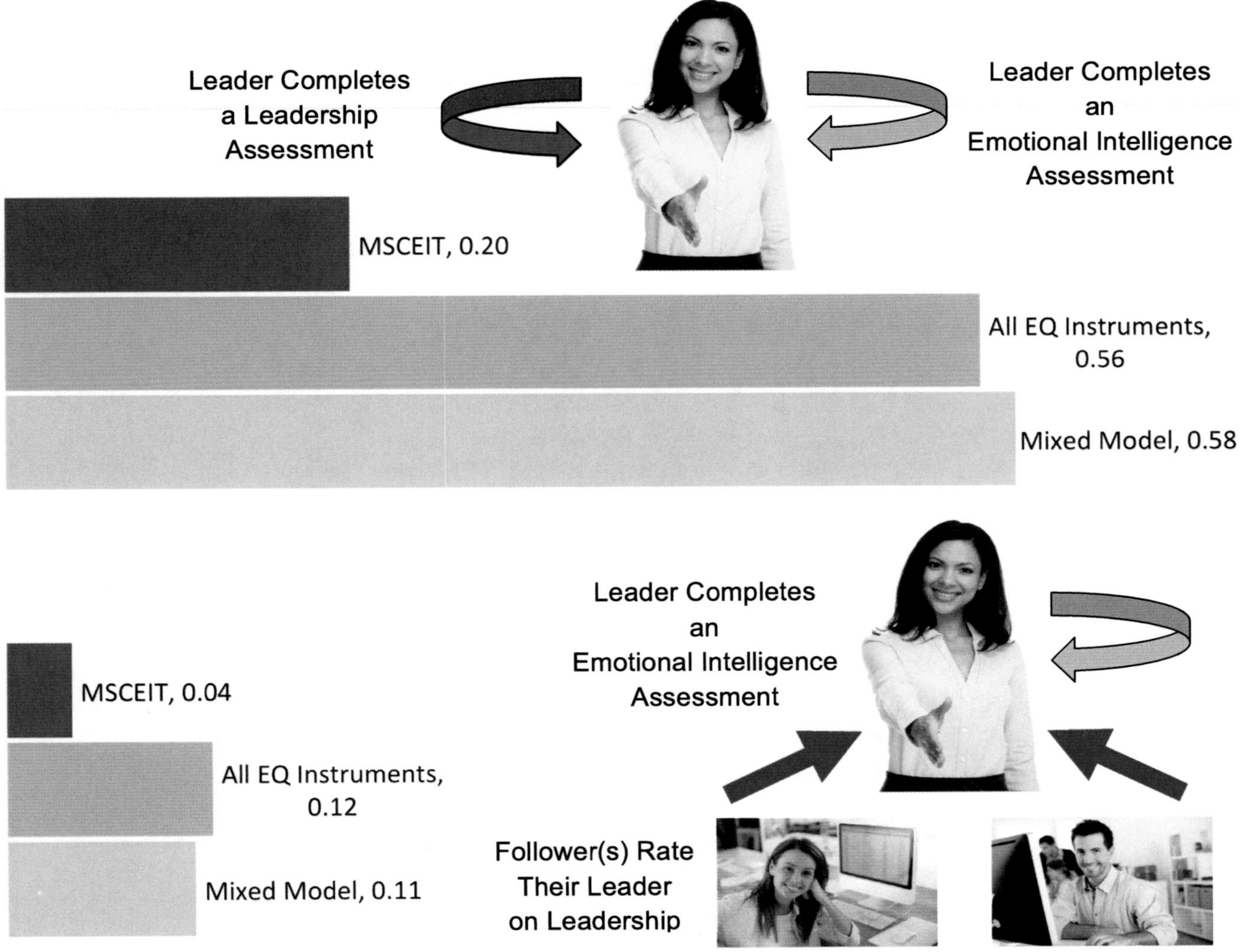

The meta-analytic correlations between leader emotional intelligence and leader transformational behaviors are dramatically weaker when the leaders assess their emotional intelligence, but other individuals assess how transformational those leaders are.

Emotional Intelligence and Leadership
Research Results

Gender and Ethnicity Differences in Emotional Intelligence

Strongly - Correlated	Moderately - Correlated	Weakly - Correlated
-1 to -.50	-.49 to -.30	-.29 to -.10

Weakly + Correlated	Moderately + Correlated	Strongly + Correlated
.10 to .29	.30 to .49	.50 to 1

Outcome	Studies	Participants	
Very Weakly Correlated			
Ability Model (E)	20	5,542	.01 Females Higher
Mixed Model (E)	19	8,942	.01 Females Higher
Overall EI (E)	47	16,383	.07 Females Higher

The meta-analyses above indicate that there are very small differences in measures of emotional intelligence between males and females. Females, as a group, score slightly higher on emotional intelligence than males.

Strongly - Correlated	Moderately - Correlated	Weakly - Correlated
-1 to -.50	-.49 to -.30	-.29 to -.10

Weakly + Correlated	Moderately + Correlated	Strongly + Correlated
.10 to .29	.30 to .49	.50 to 1

Outcome	Studies	Participants	
Weakly Correlated			
Overall EI (E)	7	1,991	.19 Whites Higher
Mixed Model (E)	4	1,555	.22 Whites Higher
Moderately Correlated			
Ability Model (E)	2	305	.31 Blacks Higher

The meta-analytic results for ethnic differences reported by Joseph and Newman (2010) are based on a small number of studies. Joseph and Newman compared black and white participants, but did not include other ethnic groups in their analyses. White participants scored higher on mixed model assessments of emotional intelligence (k = 4) while black participants scored higher on ability model assessments of emotional intelligence (k = 2).

Emotional Intelligence and Leadership

Research Results

Other Relationships For Emotional Intelligence

Strongly - Correlated	Moderately - Correlated	Weakly - Correlated	Weakly + Correlated	Moderately + Correlated	Strongly + Correlated
-1 to -.50	-.49 to -.30	-.29 to -.10	.10 to .29	.30 to .49	.50 to 1

Outcome	Studies	Participants	
		Weakly, Positively Correlated	
Constructive Conflict Resolution and Understanding Own Emotions (G)	16	4,401	.13
Constructive Conflict Resolution and Understanding Others' Emotions (G)	16	4,684	.13
Physical Health (A)	5	N not provided	.22
Constructive Conflict Resolution (G)	12	4,684	.29
Mental Health (A)	33	N not provided	.29
		Moderately, Positively Correlated	
Psychosomatic Health (A)	6	N not provided	.31
Mental Health (C)	46	19,815	.34

Strongly - Correlated	Moderately - Correlated	Weakly - Correlated	Weakly + Correlated	Moderately + Correlated	Strongly + Correlated
-1 to -.50	-.49 to -.30	-.29 to -.10	.10 to .29	.30 to .49	.50 to 1

	Outcome	Studies	Followers
Weakly, Negatively Correlated			
-.10	Alcohol Consumption (F)	11	2,271
-.18	Overall Alcohol Use (F)	11	2,271
Moderately, Negatively Correlated			
-.32	Alcohol related Problems (F)	11	2,271

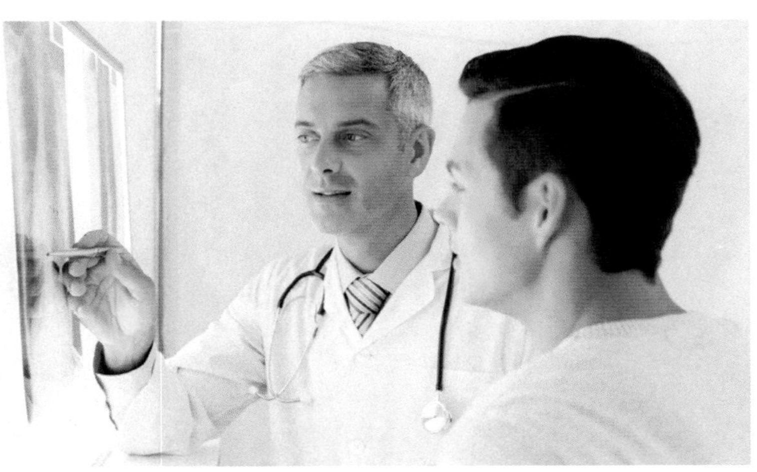

Emotional Intelligence and Leadership

Meta-Analytic Regressions

Meta-Analytic Regressions Related to Emotional Intelligence, Personality and Cognitive Ability

The next three pages summarize the meta-analytic regression research related to emotional intelligence, personality and cognitive ability.

Meta-analyses provided earlier in this chapter analyzed one independent variable at a time. The meta-analytic regressions that follow include multiple independent variables analyzed incrementally.

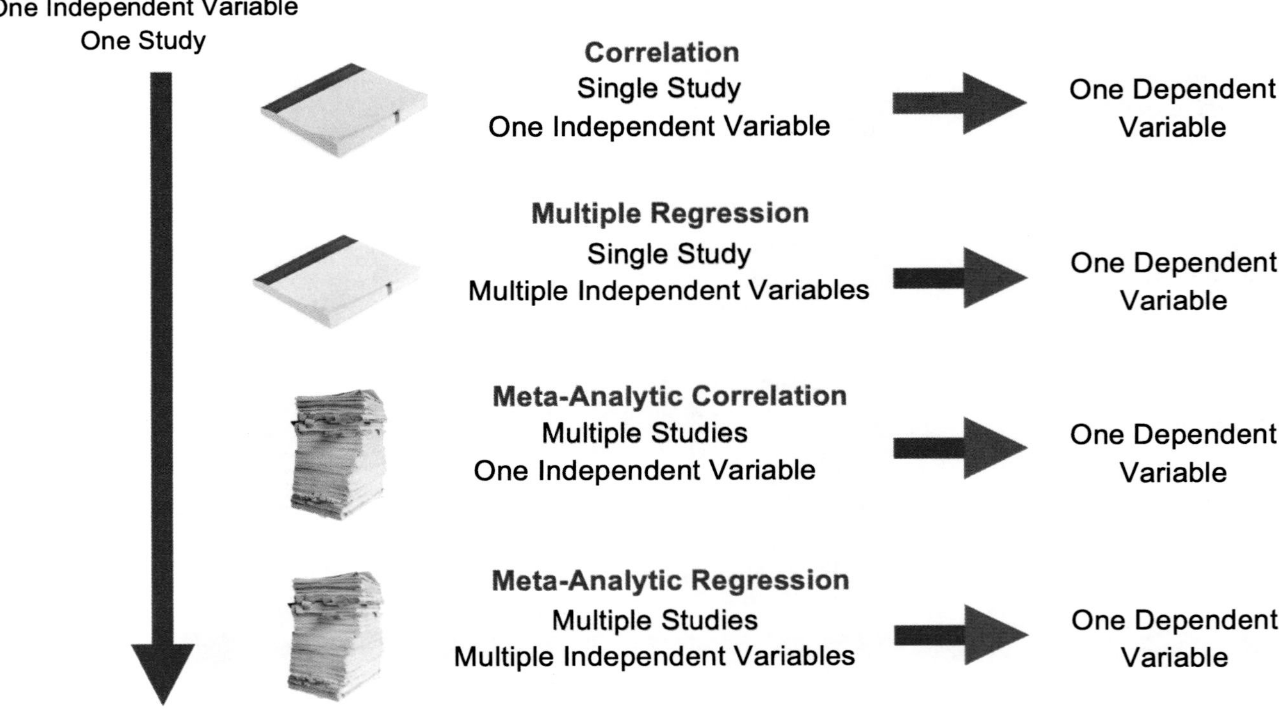

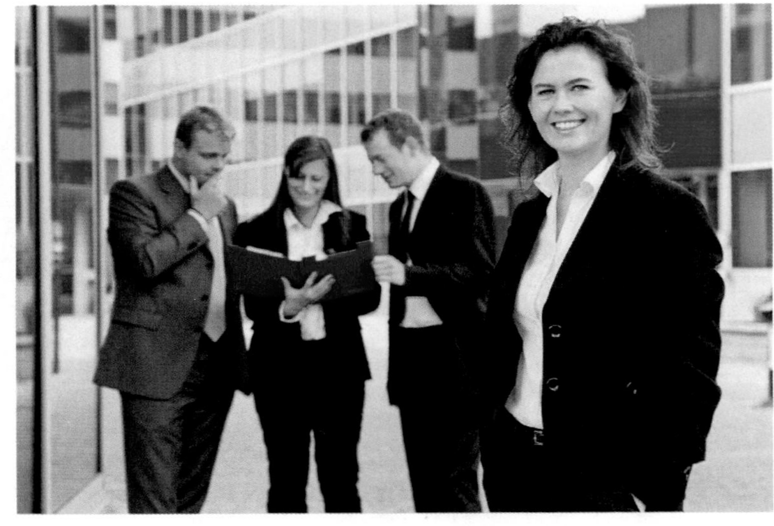

Emotional Intelligence and Leadership

Meta-Analytic Regressions

Incremental Validity of Emotional Intelligence Beyond Cognitive Ability and Personality in Predicting Follower Job Performance

Oboyle, Humphrey, Pollack, Hawver and Story (2010) conducted a meta-analytic regression to explore how much additional variance emotional intelligence explained for job performance, beyond what was already explained by worker cognitive ability and personality. Worker cognitive ability and personality explained most of the variance in job performance.

Emotional intelligence ratings using the MSCEIT explained an additional 0.4% of the variance in job performance (ΔR^2 = .004). Emotional intelligence ratings using mixed model instruments (EQ-I, AES, ECI, EIS, ENOS) explained an additional 0.7% of the variance in job performance (ΔR^2 = .068).

In either case, worker emotional intelligence was only able to improve the ability to predict job performance very slightly beyond the workers' cognitive ability and personality.

Follower Cognitive Ability and Personality Explained 42% of the Variance in Job Performance

Follower Cognitive Ability and Personality, 42%

← Follower Emotional Intelligence (MSCEIT) Explained an Additional 0.4% of the Variance in Job Performance

Follower Cognitive Ability and Personality Explained 49% of the Variance in Job Performance

Personality, 49%

Follower Cognitive Ability and Personality, 49%

← Follower Emotional Intelligence (EQ-I, AES, ECI, EIS, GENOS) Explained An Additional 0.7% of the Variance in Job Performance

Emotional Intelligence and Leadership

Meta-Analytic Regressions

Dominance Analysis for Emotional Intelligence, Cognitive Ability and Personality in Predicting Follower Job Performance

Oboyle, Humphrey, Pollack, Hawver and Story (2010) also conducted a meta-analytic regression to explore how much additional variance emotional intelligence explained for job performance, beyond what was already explained by worker cognitive ability and personality separately. Emotional intelligence explained an additional 3 to 6% of the variance in job performance beyond follower cognitive ability and follower personality.

Follower Cognitive Ability and
Personality Explained 40% of the Variance in Job Performance

Follower Cognitive Ability, 31%	Personality 9%		← Follower Emotional Intelligence (MSCEIT) Explained an Additional 3% of the Variance in Job Performance

Follower Cognitive Ability and
Personality Explained 42% of the Variance in Job Performance

Follower Cognitive Ability, 34%	Personality 8%		← Follower Emotional Intelligence (EQ-I, AES, ECI, EIS, GENOS) Explained an Additional 6% of the Variance in Job Performance

Emotional Intelligence and Leadership

Meta-Analytic Regressions

Incremental Validity of Emotional Intelligence Beyond Cognitive Ability and Personality in Predicting Follower Job Performance

In a similar meta-analytic regression, Joseph and Newman (2010) also conducted a meta-analytic regression to explore how much additional variance emotional intelligence explained for job performance, beyond what was already explained by worker cognitive ability and personality. They categorized emotional intelligence into three types: performance based, ability (MSCEIT, MEIS, WLEIS, EIS and WEIP) and mixed model (all other EI instruments). The self-assessed ability model assessments improved the predictive power by 2.3%. The self-assessed mixed model assessments improved the predictive power by 14.2%.

Follower Cognitive Ability and Personality Explained 20.9% of the Variance in Job Performance

Follower Cognitive Ability and Personality, 20.9%

Follower Emotional Intelligence (Self-Rated Ability Model) Explained an Additional 2.3% of the Variance in Job Performance

Follower Cognitive Ability and Personality Explained 20.9% of the Variance in Job Performance

Follower Cognitive Ability and Personality, 20.9%

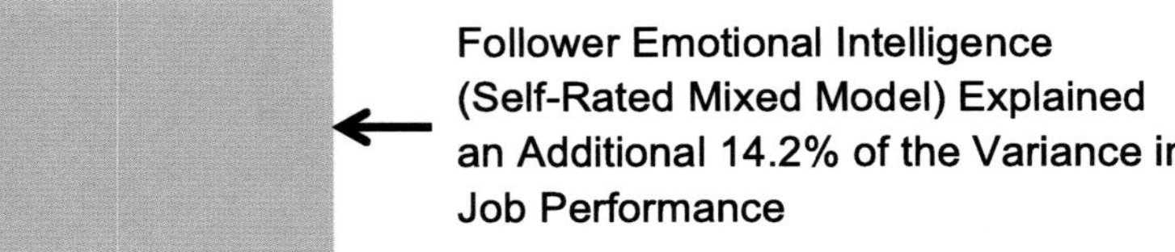
Follower Emotional Intelligence (Self-Rated Mixed Model) Explained an Additional 14.2% of the Variance in Job Performance

Emotional Intelligence and Leadership

Summary

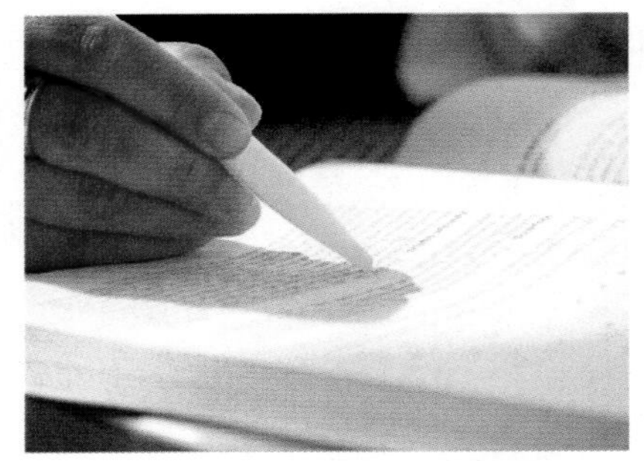

Emotional intelligence is a relatively new construct. Consequently, there are multiple views of what comprises emotional intelligence. The two most frequently referenced models are ability and mixed.

The ability approach to emotional intelligence (EI) envisions EI as either a form of intelligence or overlapping with intelligence. The predominant ability model is that of Mayer, Salovey and Caruso. Their model posits EI as "the ability to carry out accurate reasoning about emotions and the ability to use emotions and emotional knowledge to enhance thought."[17]

Their test to measure EI ability is the *MSCEIT 2*. The *MSCEIT 2* uses "correct and incorrect" answers. The correct answers have been determined by expert judges.

Because the *MSCEIT 2* is a test rather than an inventory, it is typically more highly correlated with traditional measures of intelligence than are other types of EI assessments. Likewise, it is typically less correlated with traditional measures of personality than are other types of EI assessments.

A different approach to EI is often called a mixed models approach. This approach envisions EI as a combination of factors. The predominant mixed model approach is that of Bar-On.

Bar-On envisions EI as cross-section of interrelated emotional and social competencies, skills and facilitators that determine how effectively we understand and express ourselves, understand others, relate with them and cope with daily demands.[18]

Measures using this approach are not tests per se, as there are no purely correct or incorrect answers. Mixed models of EI tend to be less correlated with intelligence and more correlated with personality than the ability based models.

Results from studies that measure leader emotional intelligence and leader transformational behaviors can vary a great deal depending on who rates whom.

In studies in which leaders complete both a measure of emotional intelligence and also rate themselves on transformational leadership, the meta-analytic correlation is strong (r_c = .56).

In studies in which leaders complete a measure of emotional intelligence but their followers rate them on transformational leadership the meta-analytic correlation is weak (r_c = .12).

Worker emotional intelligence is moderately related to job performance. Meta-analytic regressions using worker personality and worker cognitive ability prior to including worker emotional intelligence have found that worker emotional intelligence improves the models by a range of .04% to 14%, depending on which measure of emotional intelligence is used.

Emotional Intelligence and Leadership
Notes

Studies Referenced in the Summaries of Meta-Analyses

A. Schutte, Malouff, Thorsteinsson, Bhullar and Rooke (2007) The statistic reported is the weighted r.
B. Van Rooy and Viswesvaran (2004) The statistic reported is the *p.*
C. Martins, Ramalho and Morin (2010) The statistic reported is the weighted *r.*
D. Harms and Crede (2010) The statistic reported is the *p.*
E. Joseph and Newman (2010) The statistic reported is the *p^.*
F. Peterson, Malouff and Thorsteinsson (2011) The statistic reported is the *r.*
G. Schlaerth, Ensari and Christian (2013) The statistic reported is the Mean Fisher's *z-score* (allows for bias correction).
H. Oboyle, Humphrey, Pollack, Hawver and Story (2010) The statistic reported is the weighted mean correlation.

Notes

[1] Mayer, J. D., Roberts, R. D. and Barsade, S. G. (2008). Human abilities: Emotional intelligence. *Annual Review of Psychology*, 59, 507–536. p. 511.

[2] Bar-On, R. (2006). The Bar-On model of emotional-social intelligence (ESI). *Psicothema*, 18

[3] The data for the two tables on this page are a blend of information from two sources: Mayer, J. D., Salovey, P., Caruso, D. R. and Sitarenios, G. (2003). Measuring emotional intelligence with the *MSCEIT* V 2.0. *Emotion*, 3, 97–105.

Caruso, D. (Date Unknown) *All About the Mayer-Salovey-Caruso Emotional Intelligence Test (MSCEIT)* downloaded from:

http://www.calcasa.org/sites/default/files/msceit_white_paper.pdf

[4] These data come from Mayer, J. D., Salovey, P., Caruso, D. R. and Sitarenios, G. (2003). Measuring emotional intelligence with the *MSCEIT V 2.0. Emotion*, 3, 97–105.

The researchers indicate that split-half reliabilities are reported at the total test, area and branch score levels due to item heterogeneity. Coefficient alpha reliabilities are reported at the subtest level due to item homogeneity.

[5] Mayer, J. D., Salovey, P., Caruso, D. R. and Sitarenios, G. (2003). Measuring emotional intelligence with the *MSCEIT V 2.0. Emotion*, 3, 97–105.

[6] Data come from Mayer, J. D., Salovey, P. and Caruso, D. R. (2004). Emotional intelligence: Theory, findings, and implications. *Psychological Inquiry*, 15(3), 197-215. The big five personality and *MSCEIT* table reflects the weighted mean correlations across five studies.

The second set of personality and total *MSCEIT* score data were measured using the NEO-PI-R (1992) Brackett, M. and Mayer, J. (2003). Convergent, discriminant, and incremental validity of competing measures of emotional intelligence. *Personality and Social Psychology Bulletin*, 29(9), 1147-1158.

[7] ρ was defined as true or operational validity, computed by correcting observed mean for criterion unreliability.

[8] Bar-On, R. (2000).*The Emotional Quotient Inventory (EQ-i): Technical manual*. Toronto, Canada: Multi-Health Systems, Inc.

[9] Ibid

[10] Ibid

[11] Ibid

[12] Extraversion, anxiety, tough-mindedness, independence and self-control were measured by the Cattel (1993) *Sixteen Personality Factor Questionnaire.* General cognitive ability was measured by the *Wonderlic Cognitive Ability Test* (1992).

Data are from Newsome, S., Day, A. L. and Catano, V. M. (2000). Assessing the predictive validity of emotional intelligence. *Personality and Individual Differences*, 29(6), 1005–1016.

[13] Personality was measured by the *NEO-PI*. Depression was measured by the *Beck Depression Inventory*.

Data are from Dawda, D. and Hart, S. D. (2000). Assessing emotional intelligence: reliability and validity of the Bar-On *Emotional Quotient Inventory* (*EQ-i*) in university students. *Personality and Individual Differences*, 28, 797–812.

[14] *Wechsler Adult Intelligence Scale* (Bar-On, 2000).

[15] ρ true or operational validity, computed by correcting observed mean for criterion unreliability.

[16] The exact boundary between weak, moderate and strong correlations is not universally agreed upon. The definitions used are based on Cohen, J. (1992). A power primer. *Psychological Bulletin, 112,* 1, 155-9.

[17] Mayer, J. D., Roberts, R. D. and Barsade, S. G. (2008). Human abilities: Emotional intelligence. *Annual Review of Psychology*, 59, 507–536. p. 511.

[18] Bar-On, R. (2006). The Bar-On model of emotional-social intelligence (ESI). *Psicothema*, 18 13-25.

Chapter 7
Leader-Member Exchange Theory

Leader-Member Exchange Theory

Introduction

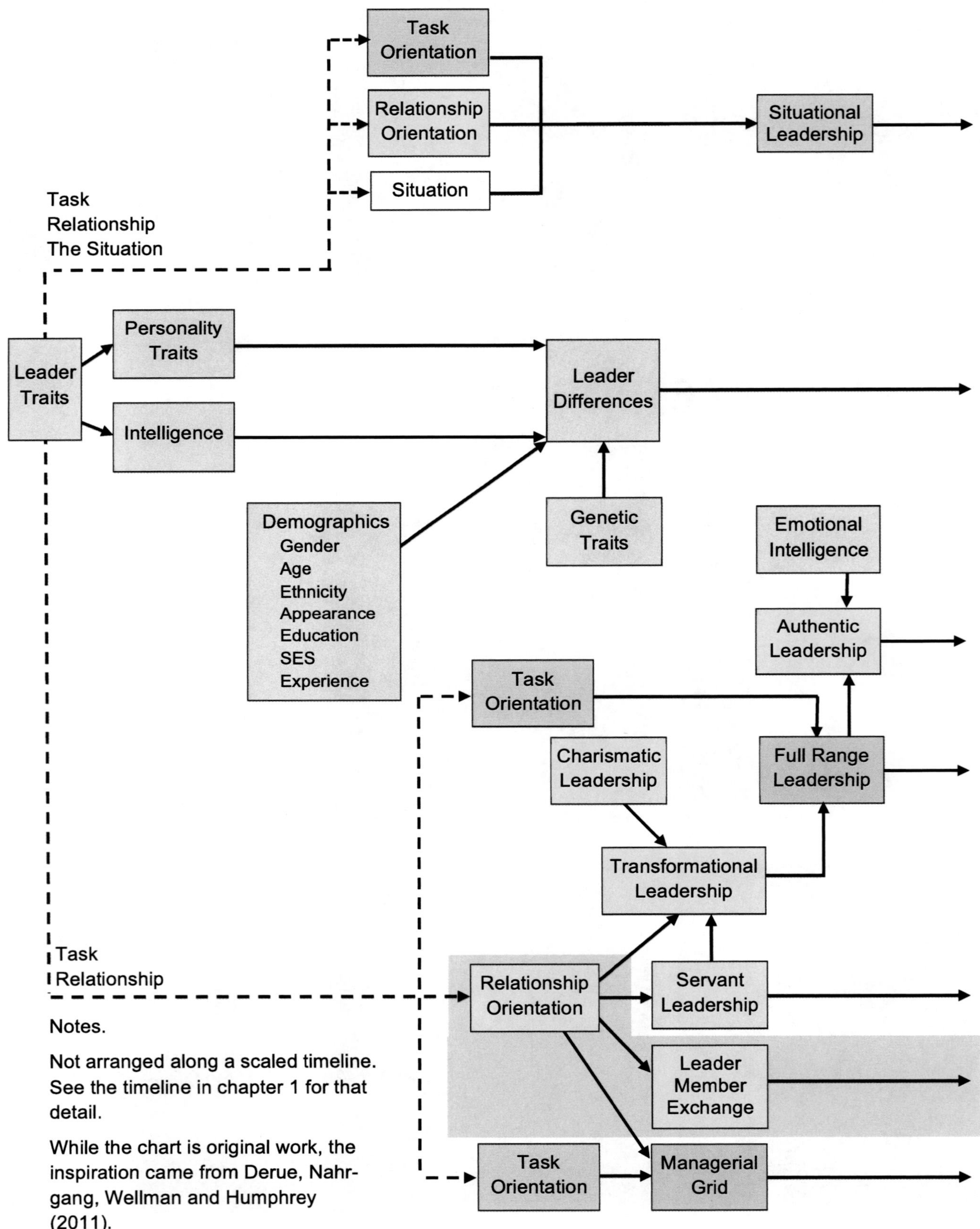

Notes.

Not arranged along a scaled timeline. See the timeline in chapter 1 for that detail.

While the chart is original work, the inspiration came from Derue, Nahrgang, Wellman and Humphrey (2011).

Leader-Member Exchange Theory

Introduction

Leader-member exchange theory primarily focuses on the relationship between the leader and the follower. To some degree, this is similar to the idea of consideration from the early studies at Ohio State that was discussed in chapter 3. It is also similar to the idea of individual consideration included in the full range model of leadership discussed in chapter 4.

The developers of leader-member exchange theory, however, have found that leaders often engage in different levels of relationship behaviors with different followers. Additionally, the researchers of leader-member exchange theory have developed a three-stage model to describe different stages through which the leader and follower might progress.

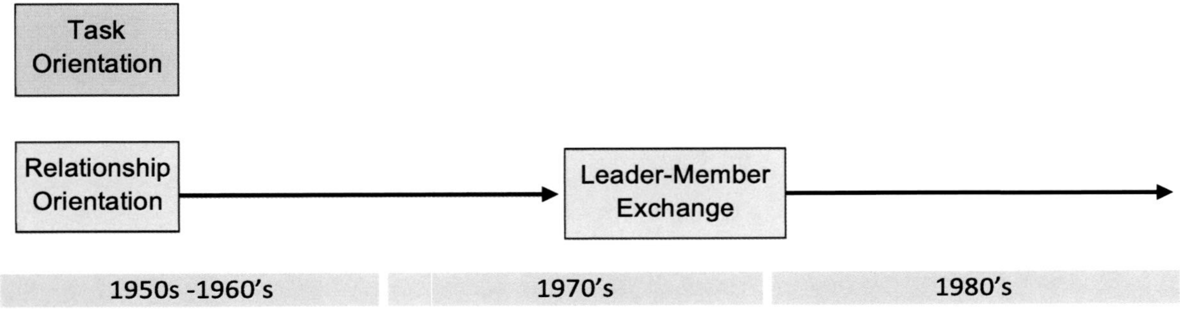

Leader-Member Exchange Theory

In Groups and Out Groups

In Groups and Out Groups

Although it "makes sense," researchers studying leader-member exchange (LMX) theory have found that the quality of the relationships that leaders form with followers differs from follower to follower. Based on these research findings, LMX researchers coined the terms in group and out group.

Followers who believe that they are in their leaders' out group, often cite a lack of trust and open communication as reasons they feel left out.

Out Group

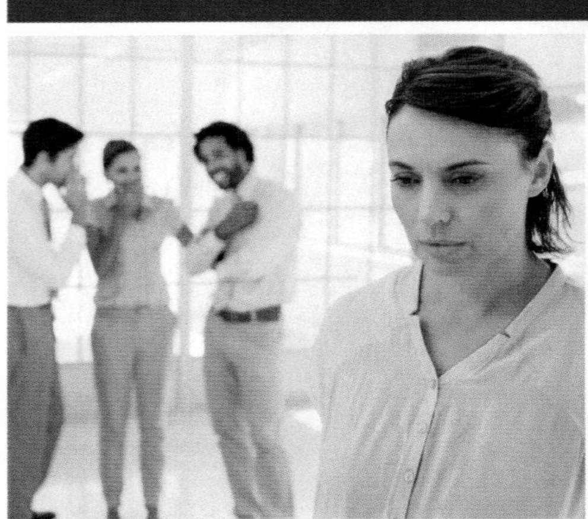

I Am Unsure Where I Stand with My Leader
I Am Unsure Whether My Leader Is Satisfied with Me
My Leader Doesn't Understand My Job Challenges
My Leader Doesn't Recognize My Potential
My Leader Doesn't Use His/Her Power to Help Me Solve Problems
My Leader Doesn't "Have My Back"
I Only Learn about New Organizational Decisions When They are Announced Publicly
I Never Hear the "Inside" Details about Happenings in the Organization

On the other hand, followers who feel that their leader is "looking out for them" as a mentor or partner, tend to also feel that they have a greater understanding of why various organizational decisions have been made.

In Group

I Know Where I Stand with My Leader
I Know Whether My Leader Is Satisfied with Me
My Leader Understands My Job Challenges
My Leader Recognizes My Potential
My Leader Uses His/Her Power to Help Me Solve Problems
My Leader "Has My Back"
My Leader Often Tells Me about Decisions That Will be Announced Later
My Leader Shares "Inside" Details about How Organizational Decisions Were Made

Leader-Member Exchange Theory

Styles of Followers

Styles of Followers

A related idea to in groups and out groups is Kelley's[1] (1992) model of types of followers. His model is based on two dimensions.

The first dimension is the degree to which a follower is able to engage in independent, critical thinking. The second dimension is how involved the follower is in the activities of the organization. The table below connects Kelley's five types of followers to the LMX idea of in groups and out groups.

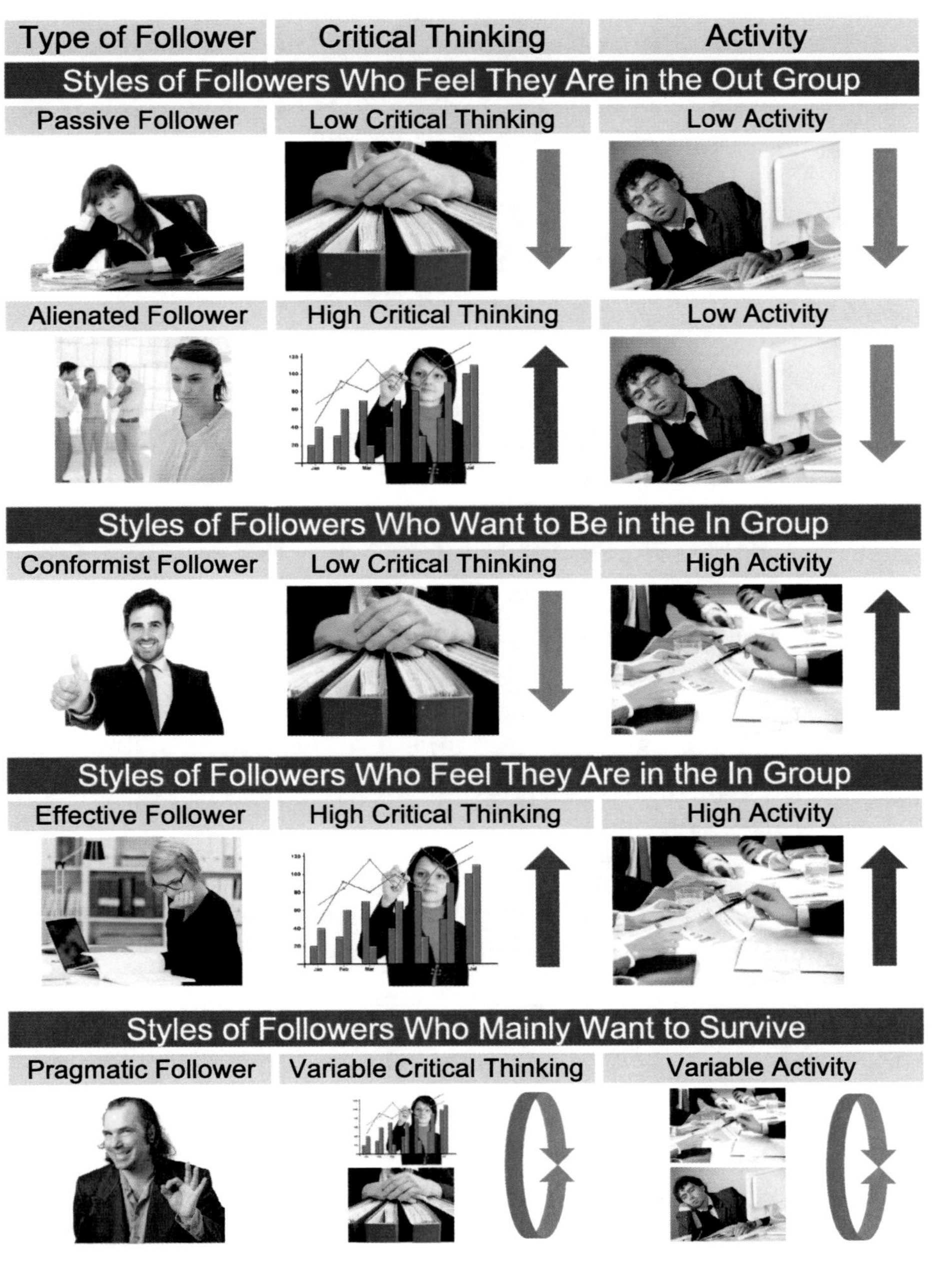

Type of Follower	Critical Thinking	Activity
Styles of Followers Who Feel They Are in the Out Group		
Passive Follower	Low Critical Thinking	Low Activity
Alienated Follower	High Critical Thinking	Low Activity
Styles of Followers Who Want to Be in the In Group		
Conformist Follower	Low Critical Thinking	High Activity
Styles of Followers Who Feel They Are in the In Group		
Effective Follower	High Critical Thinking	High Activity
Styles of Followers Who Mainly Want to Survive		
Pragmatic Follower	Variable Critical Thinking	Variable Activity

Leader-Member Exchange Theory

Stranger, Acquaintance and Mature Partner

Stages of the Leader-Follower Relationship

Leader-member exchange theory posits three phases through which a leader and a follower's relationship may progress as they move from the leader's out group to in group.

Stranger **Acquaintance** **Mature Partner**

The Stranger Phase

In the stranger phase, the leader and follower use highly scripted roles in their relationship.

A helpful image for this stage is a leader and a new follower finding themselves on an elevator together. Most likely, the conversation will be about business, such as "How do you think we'll do on that new proposal…."

A critical aspect of this phase of the leader-follower relationship is that neither the follower nor the leader knows to what degree she or he can trust each other.

At this stage of development, the relationship is typically somewhat formal. Consequently, the leader and follower generally stay comfortably within their perceived roles.

We say that at the stranger phase the quality of the conversations between the leader and follower is generally poor, as the conversations tend to be structured and mostly work-related.

Leader-Member Exchange Theory

Stranger, Acquaintance and Mature Partner

The Acquaintance Phase

In the acquaintance phase, the leader and follower begin to share a bit of mutual trust, and also begin to communicate on aspects of their own lives in addition to work. An important transitional milestone for moving from stranger to acquaintance is a "test." This isn't a pre-designed test. Rather, workplace situations arise that test the relationship.

As an example, imagine that a leader received a project on a Friday with a deadline of Monday. The leader might ask a follower who is at the stranger phase if she or he could help out on Saturday. If the follower was able to contribute, she or he passed a trust type of test.

Reciprocally, the follower, at some point will likely make a somewhat large mistake – an honest, but large mistake. If the leader shouldered part of the responsibility, rather than "throw the follower under the bus," then the leader would also have passed a test of trust.[2]

Because the level of trust between the leader and follower has improved, typically the quality of their conversations also improves. The leader and follower begin to trust each other with small amounts of personal information. Typically at the acquaintance phase the follower begins to believe that she or he is fitting in at the organization and begins to care a bit more about group goals and needs than she or he did at the stranger phase.

Becoming an Alienated Follower

An important aspect of leader-member exchange theory, however, is that if, after a reasonable period of time, the leader and follower fail to move from stranger to acquaintance, the follower will almost certainly believe she or he is in the leader's out group. This is often when some followers become what Kelley calls alienated.

The Mature Partner Phase

In the mature partner phase, the leader and follower are actually "looking out for each other." The leader, for example, would be willing to recommend the follower for various promotions, even though, selfishly, the leader would be losing a valuable team member.

The follower, on the other hand, is much more likely to give the leader honest advice. In the mature partner phase, the follower might say to the leader, "you really don't want to do that, here is why...." That level of relationship is quite different from the nervous elevator conversation during the stranger phase.

Leader-Member Exchange Theory

Moving From Stranger to Mature Partner
Communication, Authenticity and Humility

Moving the Leader-Member Relationship from Stranger to Mature Partner
There are many techniques that leaders can use to move the leader-member relationship forward. Three techniques are using open-ended questions, being authentic and being humble.

Using Open-Ended Questions An example of a closed question is "Are you on top of the project?" What other answer does a follower perceive the leader wants to hear, other than "yes?"

A slightly more open-ended question might be "How is the project going?" This question allows for a richer answer from the follower. The follower might answer something such as "It's going pretty well, but there are some challenges."

Although this question is more open than the first question, the follower likely still feels some pressure to give the leader a positive response.

An open-ended question that would more likely move the leader-member relationship toward maturity might be something such as: "You've got a complex project on your hands and it seems like you are working hard on it. Help me better understand the things that are going well for you and the challenges your experiencing."

Being More Authentic A second way to improve the leader-member relationship is to be more authentic in our interactions with our followers. Chapter 12 will cover the specific theory of authentic leadership.

Three aspects of authentic leadership, however, that are very important to improving the leader-member relationship are relational transparency, self-awareness and balanced processing.

Relational Transparency means that, as leaders, we don't hide things from our followers. An old cliché is "I say what I mean and I mean what I say." This captures the idea of being transparent.

Self-Awareness It is somewhat difficult, however, to be transparent if we are not self-aware. The idea of self-awareness connotes taking time to analyze why we react as we do to certain situations. For example, if we become upset during a meeting, improving our self-awareness would prompt us to analyze why we felt that particular emotion – what was the trigger?

Balanced Processing A third aspect of being authentic is called balanced processing. This involves listening to a variety of different input from our followers prior to making a decision.

A natural tendency is to listen to followers with whom we have a mature partner relationship. Being a leader who is high on balanced processing also entails soliciting ideas from and seriously listening to followers who are at the stranger phase.

Leader-Member Exchange Theory

Moving From Stranger to Mature Partner
Communication, Authenticity and Humility

Demonstrating Humility Often, when we think of humility, we envision someone who might be introverted and lacks self-confidence. One can, however, be an outgoing, exciting, fun-to-be around type of leader and still be humble. Often humility for outgoing leaders takes the form of being able to laugh at ourselves.

Sometimes followers only see the scripted, formal roles in which we engage as leaders. Remaining inside this narrow view of leadership makes it difficult for a follower to move from stranger to mature partner.

Effective leaders who engage in humility do many things, but three important aspects are using we rather than I statements, giving followers credit and being willing to tell followers about situations in which we as leaders made mistakes.

Use We Rather than I Statements Begin to listen intently in meetings you attend. Chances are you will notice that leaders who you admire tend to use the pronoun "we" while those you don't admire say "I" frequently.

As an example, a poor leader might say, "I want this done by the end of the week." This statement comes across as a dispassionate order. An effective leader might say, "I really believe we can get this done by the end of the week – you all are amazing."

Give Followers Credit Followers notice if we take credit for hard work that they have done. Good leaders give credit to followers when its obvious they contributed. Great leaders give credit to followers regardless. As an example, imagine that a great leader had thought of a new strategy completely on her or his own. At an award ceremony the great leader might say "There is no way I could have had the time to think about all of the pieces for this strategy without the incredible work of my team. It's only because of their dedication that I had time to work on this strategy – the credit really goes to them."

Tell Our Followers About Our Mistakes Great leaders can often be somewhat intimidating to followers who are at the stranger phase. An important skill for ensuring that new followers feel more comfortable with improving the leader-follower relationship is to demonstrate humility by telling our followers about some of the mistakes that we have made.

To envision this, imagine that a follower was working on a frustrating and tedious report. A great leader might confide, "When I was doing your job, we had all of these strange codes for the reports. Some days I would have so many yellow post it notes with codes on my monitor that I couldn't see the screen…"

Leader-Member Exchange Theory

Moving from Stranger to Mature Partner
The Passive Follower

Increasing our ability to ask open-ended questions, to be more authentic and to be more humble are good, general ideas for increasing the quality of the leader-member relationship. How we move from stranger to mature partner, however, likely varies somewhat depending on the type of follower who we are leading. Below and on the next four pages are examples of steps that can be used for each type of follower.

Leading the Passive Follower Toward Mature Partnership

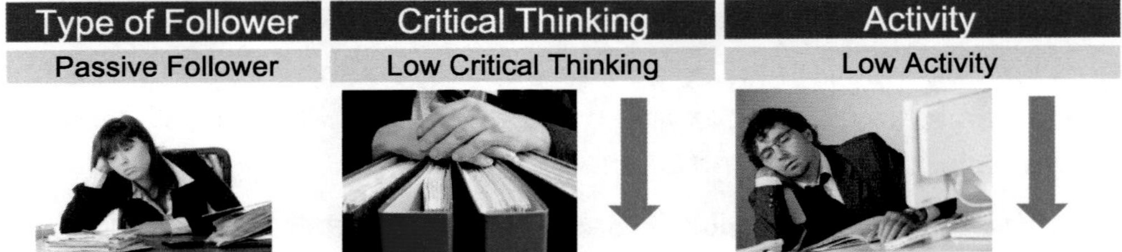

The passive follower most likely lacks self-confidence in her or his current role. Kelley describes this type of follower as low on both critical thinking and action. What we as leaders might view as initiative, this type of follower likely views as a frightening risk.

The passive follower likely has had an authority figure in the past who criticized her or him for mistakes. Subliminally, this type of follower may have vowed "never again."

Of the three tools discussed earlier: open-ended questions, authenticity and humility, humility is an important behavior to move a passive follower toward a mature partner.

Since this type of follower is, generally, avoiding making mistakes, it is important that we share with her or him mistakes that we have made.

Reassuring the follower that, despite our mistakes, we have continued to have a great career, role models engagement, even if that engagement isn't always perfect.

Equally important, however, is to provide positive reinforcement to this type of follower when she or he moves from passivity toward effectiveness.

A risk that we as leaders might view as simple for ourselves, may well be a big deal to a passive follower. When we are successful in getting the passive follower to step out of her or his comfort zone and try something new, we then need to publicly praise the follower.

Leader-Member Exchange Theory

Moving from Stranger to Mature Partner
The Conformist Follower

Leading the Conformist Follower Toward Mature Partnership

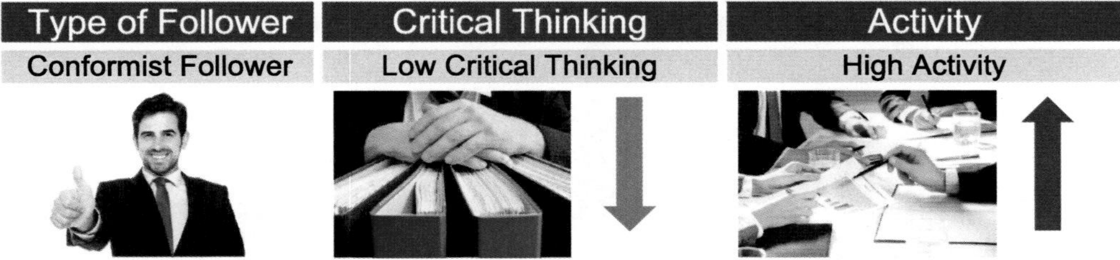

Conformist followers prefer to stay within their comfort zones and be repeatedly successful, rather than experiment with different techniques in the workplace. The critical thinking required to try different scenarios in the workplace is less important to the conformist follower than repeatedly making the leader happy.

Part of reaching the mature partner stage of leader-member exchange theory, however, is for the follower to be able to symbiotically "look out for the boss." Although the conformist follower will almost assuredly be anxious to join the leader's in group, without improved critical thinking skills, this type of follower will struggle to reach the maturity phase and become an effective follower. To better understand critical thinking, a helpful model is Bloom's revised taxonomy.[3]

Higher Order Critical Thinking Skills		
Level	**Behaviors**	**Effective Follower**
Creating	Create, Design, Develop, Plan, Produce	
Evaluating	Evaluate, Critique, Experiment, Test	
Analyzing Information	Compare, Contrast, Outline	
Lower Order Critical Thinking Skills		
Level	**Behaviors**	**Conformist Follower**
Using Information	Implement, Carry Out, Use, Execute	
Understanding Concepts	Describe, Explain, Identify, Paraphrase	
Remembering Information	Recall, Repeat, Reproduce	

You'll notice that the conformist follower is likely very good at executing what the leader asks her or him to do, but likely struggles with higher order thinking skills. An important leadership activity to assist in moving this type of follower toward effectiveness and mature-partnership is the use of open-ended questions.

In particular, the use of open-ended questions should slowly both challenge and assist the follower to improve her or his critical thinking.

As an example, if a leader asked a conformist follower "how is the project going," the conformist follower would likely respond with something such as "I'm all over it boss." An open-ended follow-up question should be at the higher order thinking level, such as "can you compare this project to the last one...how is it different and how is it similar?"

Leader-Member Exchange Theory

Moving from Stranger to Mature Partner

The Alienated Follower

Leading the Alienated Follower Toward Mature Partnership

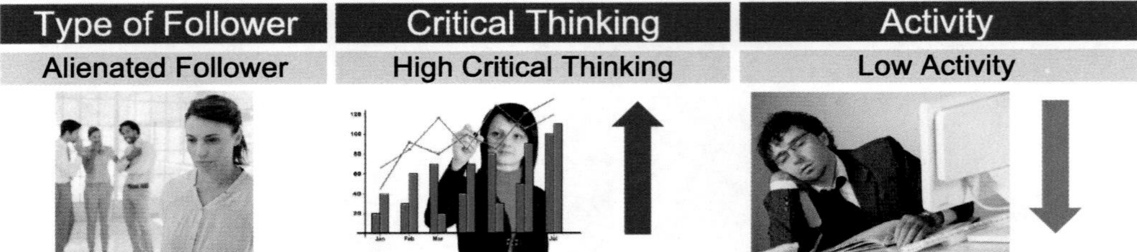

Type of Follower
Alienated Follower
Critical Thinking
High Critical Thinking
Activity
Low Activity

Kelley believes that most alienated followers were, at one time, effective followers. This type of follower possesses the critical thinking skills to be an effective follower. Somewhere, somehow, though, this follower became cynical. Rather than use her or his critical thinking skills for active contributions to the organization, the alienated follower uses those skills to criticize what is happening – typically without offering solutions. Kelley believes there are two primary reasons that effective followers become alienated.

Unmet Expectations have occurred in this type of follower's past. Most likely, the follower believes that she or he worked extremely hard on a project or in a particular role. Subliminally, the follower was expecting something – a promotion, a raise, even public recognition – and that expectation was unfulfilled.

Lack of Trust Because the expectations that the follower believed she or he deserved weren't fulfilled, the follower no longer trusts the leaders or organization to deliver on perceived promises. This lack of trust combines with critical thinking ability to create the alienated follower. The result is regular jadedness and complaints.

Getting the Perceived Injustice into the Open A first step to lead the alienated follower toward mature-partnership and effectiveness is to address the source of the alienation. This is somewhat easy if the perceived injustice happened with a different leader. If it occurred while you were this follower's leader, you will need to work hard at two things.

Establish a Safe Conversation Space If the perceived injustice occurred while the alienated follower was working for you, you will need to mentally prepare to hear criticism. You will also need to create a conversation space in which the alienated follower feels comfortable "unloading." As an example, you might say, "I don't always pay attention to everything I wish I did. My sense is that, somehow, I've failed you as a leader, and for that I'm sorry. Can you help me better understand what I missed?"

Reestablish Trust Assuming that the conversation went well, an additional part of leading the alienated follower back toward mature partner is to rebuild trust. At the end of the conversation you will likely need to reinforce that you very much want to have the alienated follower in your in group, and will do what you can to rebuild her or his trust.

Leader-Member Exchange Theory

Moving from Stranger to Mature Partner
The Effective Follower

Taking Over as a Leader of an Already Effective Follower

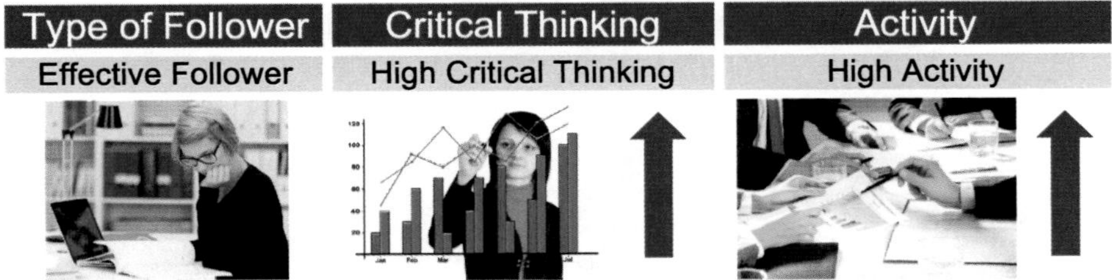

If you have a mature partnership relationship with a follower, or you are actively working at moving a passive, conformist, alienated or pragmatic follower toward effectiveness and mature-partnership, congratulations. What should a leader who takes over a new team or department, however, do with a follower who was in the previous leader's in group?

Almost assuredly, this follower will be in a bit of a hurry to work her or his way into your in group as well. Fortunately, this follower possesses critical thinking abilities and is active in helping to improve the organization. Here are a few aspects of moving from the stranger to mature-partner stage with an effective follower.

Treat the Effective Follower as a Partner The effective follower likely knows a great deal about the organization. It is important to convey a sense of partnership with this type of follower.

Share information and Context Part of this partnership is sharing information. It's important, however, not to simply share facts, but to also help the effective follower to understand the "back-story" or context of the information. In order for an effective follower who is a mature partner to assist you as a leader, the follower needs to understand the environment in which decisions are being made.

Help the Mature Partner Grow Out of the Job This type of follower typically has the potential to move into your or a similar sort of leadership position.

A mental model that is helpful for working with a mature partner follower is that you are grooming her or him to take over your job.

Leader-Member Exchange Theory

Moving from Stranger to Mature Partner
The Pragmatic Survivor

Leading the Pragmatic Survivor Toward Mature Partnership

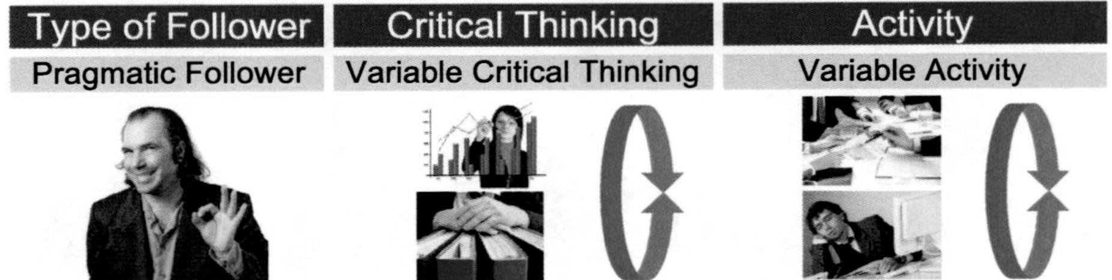

Kelley describes the pragmatic follower as an individual who is able to adopt the other four follower styles, "as needed." The passive follower tries to avoid trouble by going unnoticed. The conformist follower tries to avoid trouble by keeping the leader happy. The pragmatic follower, however, will do whichever works in a particular situation. Kelley suggests three possible reasons pragmatic survivors emerge.

Frequent Changes in Leaders One possible reason pragmatic followers emerge is having a relatively frequent turnover in leaders. These frequent changes contribute to some followers acting like chameleons.

Organizational Uncertainty If there are rumors of downsizing, mergers or restructuring, the type of follower prone to be a pragmatic survivor worries about her or his future to the point that she or he enters survival mode.

Poor Leaders Kelley posits that leaders who play games or politics with their followers can expect the same in return. He believes that pragmatic followers also emerge when leaders put emotional distance between themselves and their followers.

Leading the Pragmatic Follower Toward Effectiveness

Your first encounters with a pragmatic follower will likely resemble those of the conformist. Unlike the conformist, however, you may notice that the pragmatic follower tends to avoid any situation for which she or he might be held responsible. If the pragmatic follower is responsible for something, she or he will likely create a long paper trail in order to cast blame for failures on someone else. To assist this type of follower in moving toward both regular critical thinking and action, you should take two important steps.

Help the Pragmatic Follower Find a True Purpose To assist the pragmatic follower, you will need to challenge this follower to find something that excites her or him besides simply surviving. To consistently take the risks involved with the actions of an effective follower, the pragmatic follower needs to find a passion.

Help the Pragmatic Follower to Trust You Once the follower finds a true passion other than surviving, you will need to ensure that the pragmatic follower knows that if she or he takes an action that isn't completely successful, you will stand behind her or him. Leaders who didn't do this in the past have contributed to the pragmatic survivor's strategies.

Leader-Member Exchange Theory

Moving from Stranger to Mature Partner
Summary of Sample Actions

Summary of Types of Followers and Sample Actions

The table below summarizes the examples provided on the previous five pages.

Type of Follower	Critical Thinking	Activity	Leader Behaviors
Passive Follower	Low Critical Thinking	Low Activity	Leader Behaviors Demonstrate humility to let this follower know that it's okay to take a risk
Conformist Follower	Low Critical Thinking	High Activity	Leader Behaviors Help the conformist follower develop better critical thinking abiites by using questions that lead her or him to higher order thinking
Alienated Follower	High Critical Thinking	Low Activity	Leader Behaviors Get the perceived injustice into the open Re-establish trust
Effective Follower	High Critical Thinking	High Activity	Leader Behaviors Treat the effective follower as a partner Help the effective follower grow out of her or his job
Pragmatic Follower	Variable Critical Thinking	Variable Activity	Leader Behaviors Help the pragmatic follower find a true purpose Help the pragmatic follower trust you

Leader-Member Exchange Theory

LMX Instruments

Instruments

Instruments to measure leader-member exchange theory have gone through several developmental iterations.

1975 (Sometimes called the *LMX-2*)

In their article that "started" the idea of leader-member exchange, Dansereau, Graen and Haga measured four dimensions, one of which was called *Negotiating Latitude*.

Negotiating latitude was defined as the extent to which a leader is willing to consider requests from a follower concerning role development. This was measured by two questions:

a) How flexible do you believe your supervisor is about evolving changes in your job activity structure?
b) Regardless of how much formal authority your supervisor has built into his position, what are the chances that he would be personally inclined to use his power to help you solve problems in your work?

1980 (Sometimes called the *LMX-4*)

In 1980, Liden and Graen added two items to negotiating latitude.

c) To what extent can you count on your supervisor to 'bail you out,' at his expense, when you really need him?
d) How often do you take your suggestions regarding your work to your supervisor?

1982 (Sometimes called the *LMX-5*)

In 1982, a fifth question was added to negotiating latitude.

e) How would you characterize your working relationship with your supervisor?

1984 (First Iteration of the *LMX-7*)

Scandura and Graen used three items from the *LMX-5* and added four new questions to create the *LMX-7*.

1985 (Sometimes called the *LMX-17*)

Graen and Scandura added 10 items to the 1984 version of the *LMX-7* and created the *LMX-17*.

1995 (Second Iteration of the *LMX-7*)

Graen and Uhl-Bien modified some of the language in the 1984 version of the *LMX-7* and converted the response options on the instrument into a 5-point Likert scale.

Leader-Member Exchange Theory

LMX Instruments

1998 *LMX-MDM* (12 Items)

Liden and Maslyn created a 12-item version of the LMX called the *Multidimensional Measure of LMX* (*LMX-MDM*). This instrument is still in use today and was designed to measure four constructs: affect, loyalty, contribution and professional respect.

2008 *LMX-MDM* (13 Items)

Mardanov, Heischmidt and Henson added a 13th item to the 1998, 12-item *LMX-MDM*.

Which Instruments Are Being Used?

Joseph, Newman and Sin (2011) reported that between 1999 and 2010, approximately 65 studies (66%) involving leader-member exchange theory used the *LMX-7*, and approximately 18 studies (19%) used the *LMX-MDM*.

LMX-7 Factor Loadings

Although there is some discussion that the seven questions on the *LMX-7* might measure multiple constructs, most researchers use just one score for the *LMX-7*. Three recent studies have measured the degree to which the seven questions on the *LMX-7* load on a single component.

Schriesheim and Cogliser (2002) found that all seven questions loaded on a single component with factor loadings for each question between .47 and .78 (N = 350).

Collins (2007) also found that all seven questions loaded on a single component with factor loadings for each question between .67 and .81 (N = 1,016).

In a later analysis, Schriesheim and Cogliser (2009) again found that all seven questions loaded on a single component with factor loadings between .50 and .72 (N = 479).

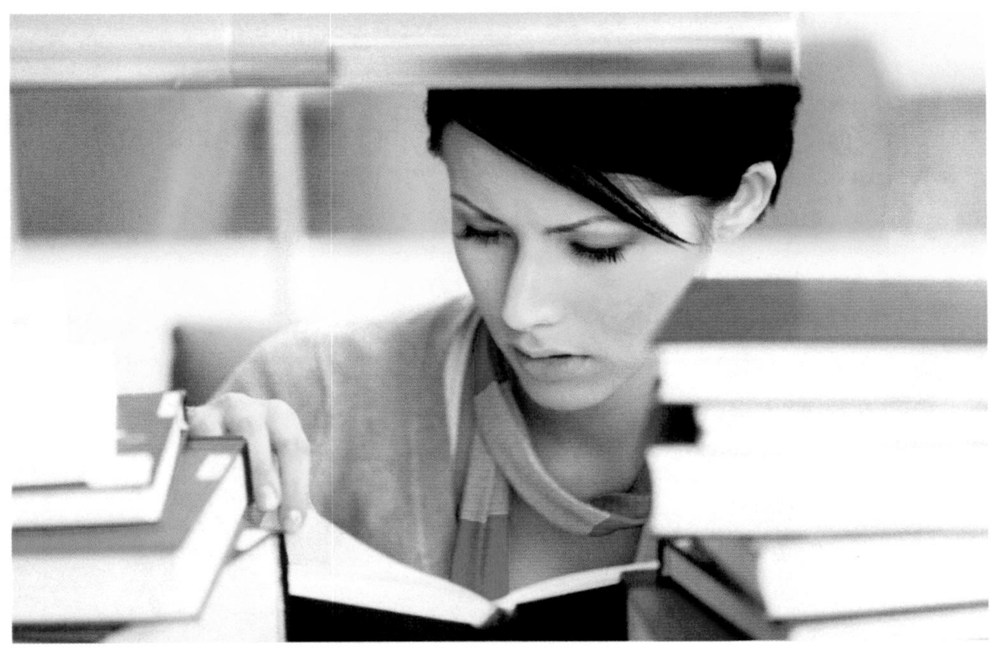

Research on the *LMX-MDM*

Development

In their developmental work on the *LMX-MDM,* Liden and Maslyn (1998) first generated 120 possible questions deemed to have content validity by a panel of faculty and doctoral students. After a second round of content validity review, 42 items were selected for further testing.

Factor Analyses

Liden and Maslyn (1998) conducted three exploratory factor analyses (EFA) and found 11 items that loaded on four components with factor loadings greater than .70. These four components were labeled *Affect, Loyalty, Contribution* and *Professional Respect*. A confirmatory factor analysis (CFA) supported the 4-factor model with a *Goodness of Fit Index* of .96.

Eisenberger, Karagonlar, Stinglhamber, Neves, Becker, Gonzalez-Morales and Steiger-Mueller (2010) conducted a confirmatory factor analysis on 43 questions taken from the *Supervisor's Organizational Embodiment*, Eisenberger et al. (2010); Meyer and Allen's *Affective Commitment Questionnaire (1990);* Williams and Anderson's *Subordinates' In-Role Performance* (1991)*; Subordinates' Extra-Role Performance* questions take from Eisenberger et al. (2001) and van Dyne, Graham, and Dienesch (1994); three questions created to measure supervisor's expressed favorable attitudes by Eisenberger et al. (2010); and 12 questions from the *LMX-MDM*.

Ten of the *LMX-MDM* questions loaded on a single factor with factor loadings higher than .46. Two questions had factor loadings lower than .36.

Dana, Newman and Sin (2011) performed a hierarchical confirmatory factor analysis using the sample-weighted average Pearson correlation coefficients calculated from six samples (*N* = 1,358). They found that all four of the lower-order facets of the *LMX-MDM* were strongly inter-correlated with correlations ranging from .49 to .68. All four facets also loaded onto a single factor with loadings ranging from .67 to .86 per facet (*RMSEA* = .05, *CFI* = 1.00).

Leader-Member Exchange Theory

LMX Instruments

Internal Reliability

Liden and Maslyn (1998) reported that internal consistency reliabilities, measured by coefficient alphas were above .70 for affect, loyalty and professional respect, but were .57 and .60 for contribution in two different samples tested.

Eisenberger, Karagonlar, Stinglhamber, Neves, Becker, Gonzalez-Morales and Steiger-Mueller (2010) reported that the Cronbach Alpha calculated for the 12 *LMX-MDM* questions was .87.

Convergent Validity

Liden and Maslyn (1998) found that the scales of the *LMX-MDM* were correlated with the *LMX-7* as follows: affect (.71), loyalty (.71), contribution (.55) and professional respect (.70).

Discriminant Validity

Liden and Maslyn (1998) found that the four dimensions of the *LMX-MDM* were only weakly correlated with the Satisfaction with Supervisor scale of the *Job Descriptive Index:* affect (.12), loyalty (.25), contribution (.00) and professional respect (.00).

Eisenberger, Karagonlar, Stinglhamber, Neves, Becker, Gonzalez-Morales and Steiger-Mueller (2010) found support for a six-factor solution that discriminated among supervisor's organizational embodiment, affective commitment, in-role performance, extra-role performance, supervisor's favorable attitudes, and the 12 questions from the *LMX-MDM* (*RMSEA* = .05. *CFI* = .91). The *LMX-MDM* questions loaded on a different component than the other instruments. This lends some support that the *LMX-MDM* seems to be measuring something different from the other five instruments.

Using the *LMX-7* and *LMX-MDM*

As of 2014, researchers should request permission to use the *LMX-7* from Dr. Mary Uhl-Bien at the University of Nebraska-Lincoln. The instrument can be found in Graen, G. B., and Uhl-Bien, M. (1995). Relationship-based approach to leadership: Development of leader–member exchange (LMX) theory of leadership over 25 years: Applying a multi-level, multi-domain perspective. *Leadership Quarterly*, 6(2), 219– 247.

As of 2014, researchers should request permission to use the *LMX-MDM* from Dr. Robert C. Liden at the University of Illinois, Chicago. The instrument can be found in Liden, R. C., and Maslyn, J. M. (1998). Multi-dimensionality of leader–member exchange: An empirical assessment through scale development. *Journal of Management*, 24, 43–72.

Leader-Member Exchange Theory

Research Results

Understanding the Research Results for Leader-Member Exchange Theory

There is a great deal of research on leader-member exchange theory. To prepare you for understanding the research results that follow, chapter 2 explained both correlations and meta-analyses. The table below, however, provides a quick review of how the results of the meta-analytic literature will be provided in this chapter.[4]

Example – Leader-Member Relationship and Overall Follower Performance

In the example below, 37 studies have been published and meta-analyzed on the relationship between the quality of the leader-member relationship and overall follower performance. The notation (F) refers to the article referenced. A list of articles is included at the back of the chapter. Those 37 studies collectively represent 5,560 follower ratings. The meta-analytic finding was a moderate, positive correlation (.31). The better the leader-follower relationship, the higher the follower performance.

Strongly - Correlated	Moderately - Correlated	Weakly - Correlated
-1 to -.50	-.49 to -.30	-.29 to -.10

Weakly + Correlated	Moderately + Correlated	Strongly + Correlated
.10 to .29	.30 to .49	.50 to 1

Outcome	Studies	Followers	
Overall Performance (F)	37	5,560	.31

Leader-Member Exchange Theory

Research Results

Leader-Member Exchange and Follower Outcomes

Strongly - Correlated	Moderately - Correlated	Weakly - Correlated
-1 to -.50	-.49 to -.30	-.29 to -.10

Weakly + Correlated	Moderately + Correlated	Strongly + Correlated
.10 to .29	.30 to .49	.50 to 1

Outcome	Studies	Followers	
Weakly, Positively Correlated			
Objective Performance (E)	8	982	.10
Performance Measured (G) Objectively (F)	8	912	.10
Trait Conscientiousness (D)	8	1,708	.13
Task Performance (A)	7	2,298	.13
Competence (E)	15	3,880	.26
Satisfaction with Pay	8	1,418	.27
Performance Ratings (E)	30	4,218	.28
Moderately, Positively Correlated			
Overall Performance (F)	8	982	.31
Normative Commitment (G)	13	3,043	.33
Job Performance (G)	108	25,322	.34
Individual Citizenship Behavior (C)	8	912	.38
Performance Measured Subjectively (F)	8	1,708	.40
Affective Commitment (G)	21	8,118	.41
Overall Satisfaction (E)	7	2,298	.46
Overall Organizational Commitment (G)	58	14,208	.47
General Job Satisfaction (G)	88	22,520	.49
Strongly, Positively Correlated			
Job Satisfaction (D)	33	6,887	.50
Procedural justice (G)	30	7,211	.55
Empowerment (G)	11	4,296	.67
Satisfaction with Supervisor (G)	32	11,195	.68

Leader-Member Exchange Theory

Research Results

Leader-Member Exchange and Follower Outcomes (continued)

Strongly - Correlated	Moderately - Correlated	Weakly - Correlated
-1 to -.50	-.49 to -.30	-.29 to -.10

Weakly + Correlated	Moderately + Correlated	Strongly + Correlated
.10 to .29	.30 to .49	.50 to 1

	Outcome	Studies	Followers
Weakly, Negatively Correlated			
-.13	Counterproductive Work Behavior (A)	13	616
-.17	Actual Turnover (E)	9	1,345
-.28	Turnover Intentions (E)	6	1,074
Moderately, Negatively Correlated			
-.33	Role Conflict (E)	14	5,480
-.42	Role Ambiguity (E)	18	5,813

Research from 569 analyses that have included 138,444 follower ratings indicates that the quality of the leader-member relationship is positively correlated with a range of follower outcomes such as job performance, job satisfaction, feelings of empowerment and satisfaction with one's supervisor.

The quality of the leader-member relationship is negatively correlated with counterproductive work behavior, turnover intentions, role conflict and role ambiguity.

Leader-Member Exchange Theory

Research Results

Leader-Member Exchange and Leader Outcomes

Strongly - Correlated	Moderately - Correlated	Weakly - Correlated
-1 to -.50	-.49 to -.30	-.29 to -.1

Weakly + Correlated	Moderately + Correlated	Strongly + Correlated
.1 to .29	.30 to .49	.50 to 1

Outcome	Studies	Followers	Correlation
Moderately, Positively Correlated			
Role Clarity (E)	14	4,105	.34
Leader Performance Ratings (E)	12	1,909	.41
Trust in One's Supervisor (A)	4	1,171	.48
Strongly, Positively Correlated			
Perceived Organizational Support (A)	14	4,105	.54
Satisfaction with Supervision (E)	12	1,909	.62

Correlation	Outcome	Studies	Followers
Weakly, Negatively Correlated			
-.26	Role Conflict (E)	12	3,728

Research from 68 analyses that have included 16,927 follower ratings indicates that the quality of the leader-member relationship is positively correlated with ratings of how satisfied followers are with their leaders, how much they trust their leaders and how well they believe their leaders perform.

The quality of the leader-member relationship is negatively correlated with leader-member role conflict.

Leader-Member Exchange Theory

Research Results

Leader-Member Exchange and Organizational Outcomes

Strongly - Correlated	Moderately - Correlated	Weakly - Correlated	Weakly + Correlated	Moderately + Correlated	Strongly + Correlated
-1 to -.50	-.49 to -.30	-.29 to -.1	.1 to .29	.30 to .49	.50 to 1

Outcome	Studies	Followers	Correlation
Moderately, Positively Correlated			
Organizational Citizenship Behavior (C)	21	4,119	.31
Organizational Citizenship Behavior (D)	15	3,311	.32
Organizational Commitment (E)	17	3,006	.35
Organizational Citizenship Behavior (F)	6	1,082	.36
Overall Citizenship Behavior (C)	50	9,324	.37
Organizational Citizenship Behavior (A)	10	2,850	.40
Strongly, Positively Correlated			
Organizational Commitment (A)	21	8,038	.64
Trust in One's Organization (A)	4	2,926	.79

Correlation	Outcome	Studies	Followers
Strongly, Negatively Correlated			
-.58	Perceptions of Organizational Politics (B)	11	4,640

Research from 155 analyses that have included 39,296 follower ratings indicate that the quality of the leader-member relationship is positively correlated with ratings of organizational citizenship, organizational commitment and trust in the organization and negatively correlated with perceptions of organizational politics.

Leader-Member Exchange Theory

Summary

Leader-member exchange theory focuses on the relationship between the leader and the follower. The developers of LMX theory have found that leaders often engage in different levels of relationship behaviors with different followers.

Followers who believe that they are part of their leaders' out group cite a lack of trust and open communication as reasons they feel left out. On the other hand, followers who feel that they are a part of their leaders' in group believe their leaders share "inside" details with them and that their leader is looking our for them.

LMX theory posits three phases through which a leader and follower's relationship may progress as they move from the leaders' out group to in group.

During the stranger phase, the relationship between a leader and a follower is typically somewhat formal. The leader and follower generally stay comfortably within their perceived roles. During this stage, neither the follower nor leader knows to what degree she or he can trust each other.

In the acquaintance phase, the leader and follower begin to share a bit of mutual trust, and begin to communicate on aspects of their personal lives. At this point, the level of trust and quality of conversations between the leader and follower has improved.

The mature partner phase consists of the leader and follower "looking out for each other." During this phase, the leader would be willing to recommend the follower for various promotions, even though, selfishly, the leader would be losing a valuable team member. The follower, on the other hand, is much more likely to give the leader honest advice.

Techniques that leaders can use to move the relationship from the stranger phase to the mature partner phase include using open-ended questions, being authentic and being humble. While these techniques help move the relationship forward, how we move from stranger to mature partner varies depending on the type of follower we are leading.

Leader-Member Exchange Theory
Summary

The passive follower lacks self-confidence in his or her current role. When a leader is successful in getting the passive follower to step out of her or his comfort zone and try something new, the leader then needs to publicly praise the follower.

The conformist follower prefers to stay within her or his comfort zone and be repeatedly successful, rather than experiment with different techniques in the workplace. An important leadership activity to assist in moving a conformist type of follower toward effectiveness is to use open-ended questions.

The alienated follower possesses the critical thinking skills to be an effective follower, but is prone to be cynical. Rather than use her or his critical thinking skills to actively contribute to the organization, the alienated follower criticizes what is happening, typically without offering solutions. An important step in leading the alienated follower toward mature-partnership and effectiveness is to address the source of the alienation.

The effective follower is high on both critical thinking abilities and active behaviors. This is the type of follower who we would generally like in organizations. It is important to empower the effective follower by treating her or him as a partner and by grooming her or him for higher levels of leadership in the organization.

Kelley describes the pragmatic follower as an individual able to adopt the other four styles, "as needed." The passive follower tries to avoid trouble by going unnoticed. The conformist follower tries to avoid trouble by keeping the leader happy. The pragmatic follower, however, will do whichever works in a particular situation. Actions to assist the pragmatic follower include helping the pragmatic follower find a true purpose and to trust you.

Leader-Member Exchange Theory
Notes

Studies Referenced

A. Colquitt, Scott, Rodell, Long, Zapata, Conlon and Wesson (2013) The statistic reported is the corrected population correlation.
B. Atinc, Darrat, Fuller and Parker (2010) The statistic reported is the weighted mean correlation corrected for measurement error in both the predictor and criterion.
C. Ilies, Nahrgang and Morgeson (2007) The statistic reported is the true score correlation.
D. Lapierre and Hackett (2007) The statistic reported is the average corrected correlation.
E. Gerstner and Day (1997) The statistic reported is the mean sample-weighted correlation.
F. Jensen, Olberding and Rodgers (1997) The statistic reported is the corrected r value.
G. Dulebohn, Bommer, Liden, Brouer and Ferris (2012) The statistic reported is the population estimate.

Notes

[1] Kelley, R. E. (1992). *The power of followership: How to create leaders people want to follow, and followers who lead themselves*. New York: Doubleday/Currency.

Other popular books on followership include:

Kellerman, B. (2008). *Followership: How followers are creating change and changing leaders*. Boston, Mass: Harvard Business School Press.

Riggio, R. E., Chaleff, I., & Lipman-Blumen, J. (2008). *The art of followership: How great followers create great leaders and organizations*. San Francisco, CA: Jossey-Bass.

[2] The in-group table is a compilation from:

Graen, G. B. and Cashman, J. (1975). A role-making model of leadership in formal organizations: A developmental approach. In J. G. Hunt & L. L. Larson (Eds.), *Leadership frontiers* (pp. 143– 166). Kent, OH: Kent State University Press.

Graen, G. B., Novak, M. and Sommerkamp, P. (1982). The effects of leader-member exchange and job design on productivity and satisfaction: Testing a dual attachment model. *Organizational Behavior and Human Performance*, 30, 109-131.

Graen, G. B. and Uhl-Bien, M. (1995). Relationship-based approach to leadership: Development of leader–member exchange (LMX) theory of leadership over 25 years: Applying a multi-level, multi-domain perspective. *Leadership Quarterly,* 6(2), 219– 247.

Leader-Member Exchange Theory

Notes

[3] Bloom's original taxonomy was from:

Bloom, B. S., Engelhart, M. D., & Committee of College and University Examiners. (1956). *Taxonomy of educational objectives: The classification of educational goals.* London: Longmans.

The revised taxonomy is from:

Anderson, L. W., & Krathwohl, D. R. (2001). *A taxonomy for learning, teaching, and assessing: A revision of Bloom's taxonomy of educational objectives*. New York: Longman.

[4] The exact boundary between weak, moderate and strong correlations is not universally agreed upon. The definitions used in chapters 8 to 12 are based on Cohen, J. (1992). A power primer. *Psychological Bulletin, 112,* 1, 155-9.

Chapter 8
Project GLOBE

Project GLOBE

Introduction

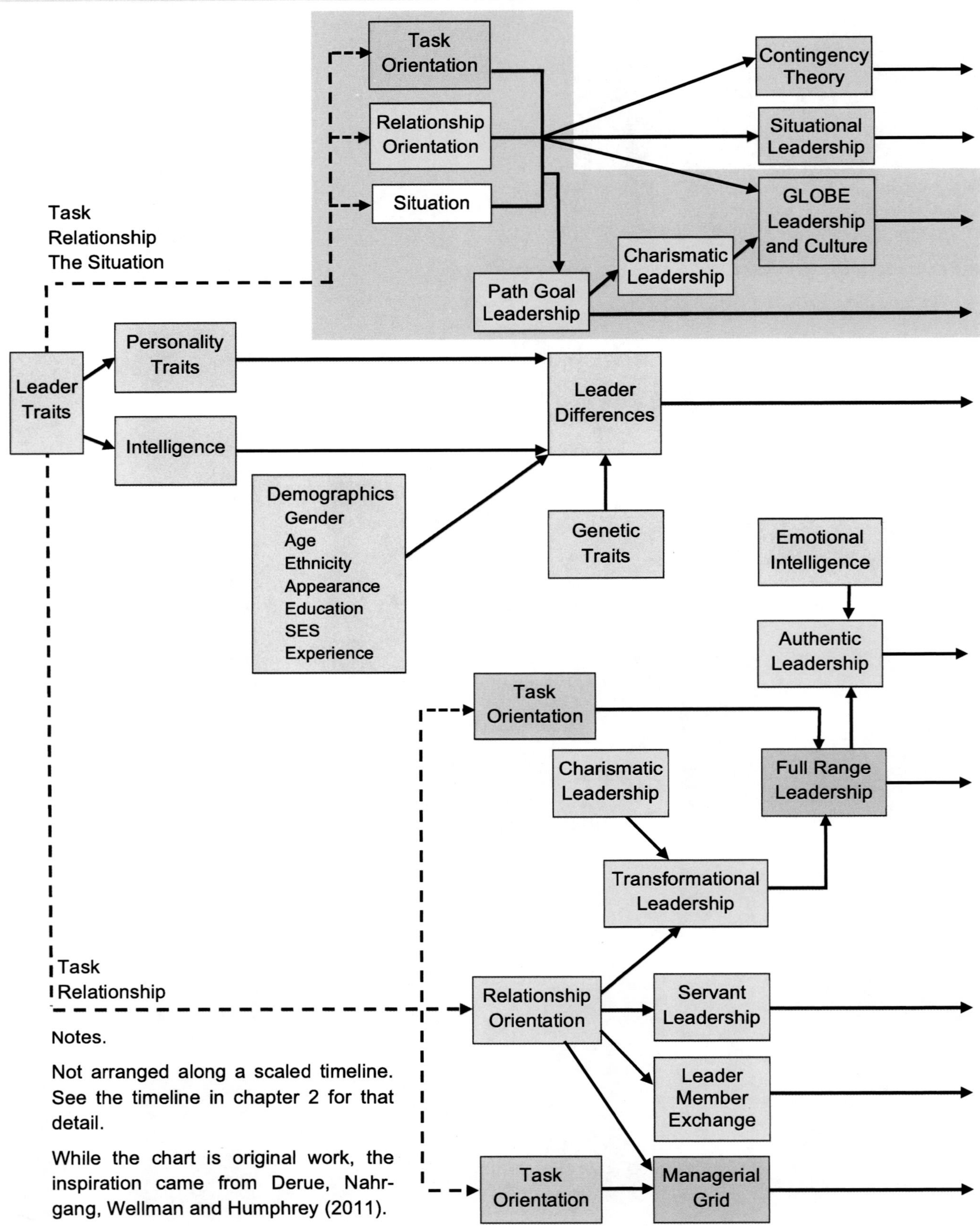

Notes.

Not arranged along a scaled timeline. See the timeline in chapter 2 for that detail.

While the chart is original work, the inspiration came from Derue, Nahrgang, Wellman and Humphrey (2011).

Project GLOBE

Introduction

The shaded area to the left illustrates that House's path-goal theory of leadership influenced his writings on charismatic leadership. Some of that work on charismatic leadership, in turn, influenced his and others' work on project GLOBE.

Project GLOBE was a multi-decade study of attitudes about culture and leadership around the world.

Phase 1 of the study developed instruments to measure both culture and leadership.

Phase 2 administered those instruments to middle managers around the world.

Phase 3 measured how CEO's around the world lead.

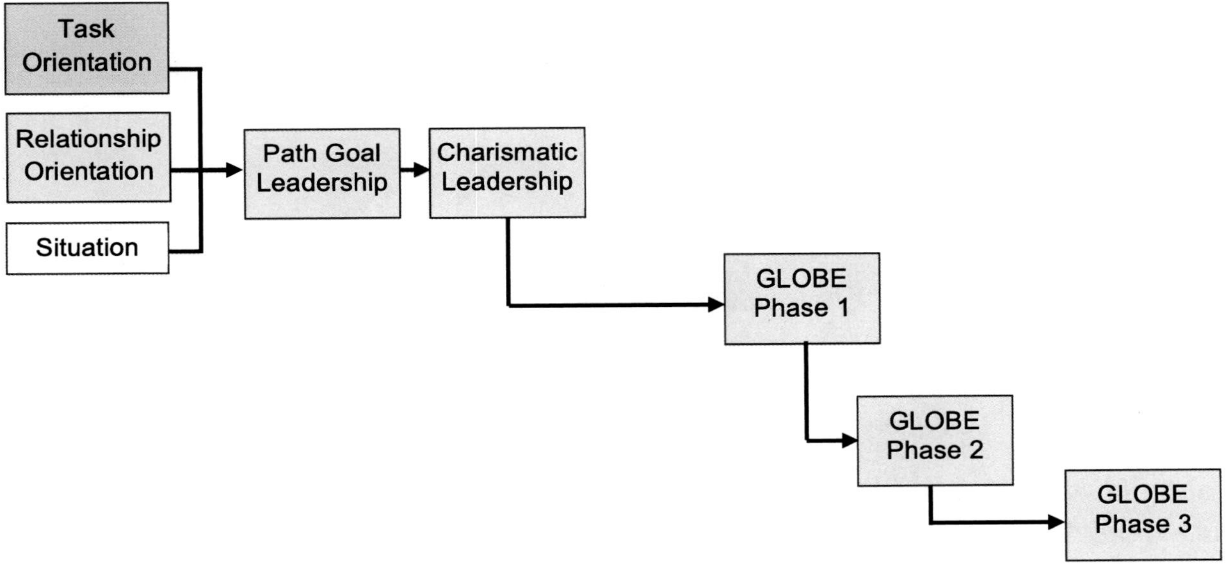

1950s -1960's	1970's	1980's	1990's	2000's	2010's

Project GLOBE – Phase 2

Implicit Leadership

Implicit Leadership, or Leadership Prototypes[1]

Often when we think about measuring leadership, we envision followers or other stakeholders assessing how their leaders actually lead. For example, the followers around the table in the image to the left might assess the leader on how transformational she is, how much emphasis she places on taking care of business and taking care of followers, or even what her personality might be.

A different type of leaderhip research is to ask people, "what makes someone an outstanding leader?"

In this case, the participants aren't assessing an actual leader. Rather, they are describing their stereotypes, prototypes, or implicit assumptions about leadership. The GLOBE study took this approach.

Cultural Leadership Prototypes

The GLOBE study also measured how culture impacted participants' implicit ideas about outstanding leadership.

To assess these cultural relationships as well as differences among global societies, the study surveyed 17,300 middle managers from 951 organizations. The participants were middle managers in the food processing, financial services or telecommunications services industries in 62 societies around the world.

Dimensions of Leadership and Culture

Before surveying these middle managers, the research team developed nine measures of culture, and 21 measures of leadership. Those 21 measures of leadership were called "first order" dimensions or factors. Those 21 first order factors, in turn, were able to be grouped into six second order global implicit leadership dimensions.

Cultural Dimensions	
Power Distance	Assertiveness
Uncertainty Avoidance	Gender Egalitarianism
Humane Orientation	Future Orientation
Institutional Collectivism	Performance Orientation
In-Group Collectivism	

Second Order Leadership Dimensions
Charismatic/Value Based
Team-Oriented
Participative
Humane-Oriented
Autonomous
Self-Protective

Project GLOBE – Phase 2

Dimensions of Leadership

Charismatic/Value-Based Leadership

Charismatic/value-based leadership includes the ability to inspire, to motivate, and to expect high performance outcomes from others on the basis of firmly held, core beliefs. These leaders are visionary, inspirational, engage in self-sacrifice, demonstrate integrity, are decisive and performance-oriented.

First Order Factors	Leader Attribute Items
Charismatic 1: Visionary	Foresight, Prepared, Anticipatory, Plans Ahead
Charismatic 2: Inspirational	Enthusiastic, Positive, Morale Booster, Motive Arouser
Charismatic 3: Self-Sacrifice	Risk Taker, Self-Sacrificial, Convincing
Integrity	Honest, Sincere, Just, Trustworthy
Decisive	Willful, Decisive, Logical, Intuitive
Performance-Oriented	Improvement-Oriented, Excellence-Oriented, Performance-Oriented

Team-Oriented Leadership

Team-oriented leadership emphasizes effective team building and implementation of a common purpose or goal among team members. Team-oriented leaders are collaborative integrators, who are diplomatic, benevolent, administratively competent and procedural.

First Order Factors	Leader Attribute Items
Team 1: Collaborative Team Orientation	Group-Oriented, Collaborative, Loyal, Consultative
Team 2: Team Integrator	Communicative, Team-Builder, Informed, Integrator
Diplomatic	Diplomatic, Worldly, Win/Win Problem-Solver Effective Bargainer
Malevolent (Reverse Scored)	Hostile, Dishonest, Vindictive, Irritable (Reverse Scored)
Administratively Competent	Orderly, Administratively Skilled, Organized, Good Administrator

Project GLOBE – Phase 2

Dimensions of Leadership

Participative Leadership

Participative leadership reflects the degree to which managers and leaders involve others in making and implementing decisions.

First Order Factors	Leader Attribute Items
Autocratic (Reverse Scored)	Autocratic, Dictatorial, Bossy, Elitist
Non-Participative (Reverse Scored)	Non-Delegator, Micro-Manager, Non-Egalitarian Individually-Oriented

Humane-Oriented Leadership

Humane-oriented leadership reflects supportive and considerate leadership but also includes compassion and generosity.

First Order Factors	Leader Attribute Items
Modesty	Modest, Self-Effacing, Patient
Humane Orientation	Generous, Compassionate

Autonomous Leadership

Autonomous leadership refers to independent and individualistic leadership attributes.

First Order Factor (Same)	Leader Attribute Items
Autonomous	Individualistic, Independent, Autonomous, Unique

Project GLOBE – Phase 2

Dimensions of Leadership

Self-Protective Leadership

Self-protective leadership focuses on ensuring the safety and security of the individual and group through status enhancement and face saving.

First Order Factors	Leader Attribute Items
Self-Centered	Self-Centered, Non-Participative, Loner, A-Social
Status Conscious	Status-Conscious, Class Conscious
Conflict Inducer	Normative, Secretive, Intra-Group Competitor
Face Saver	Indirect, Avoids Negatives, Evasive
Procedural	Ritualistic, Formal, Habitual, Procedural

Although countries varied in the degree to which they believed these six second order global implicit leadership dimensions contributed to being an outstanding leader, the grand means for the participants across the study found that charismatic/value-based leadership, team-oriented leadership and participative leadership were endorsed universally. The questionnaire was phrased as follows.

1 = This behavior or characteristic **greatly inhibits** a person from being an outstanding leader.
2 = This behavior or characteristic **somewhat inhibits** a person from being an outstanding leader.
3 = This behavior or characteristic **slightly inhibits** a person from being an outstanding leader.
4 = This behavior or characteristic **has no impact** on whether a person is an outstanding leader.
5 = This behavior or characteristic **contributes slightly** to a person being an outstanding leader.
6 = This behavior or characteristic **contributes somewhat** to a person being an outstanding leader.
7 = This behavior or characteristic **contributes greatly** to a person being an outstanding leader.

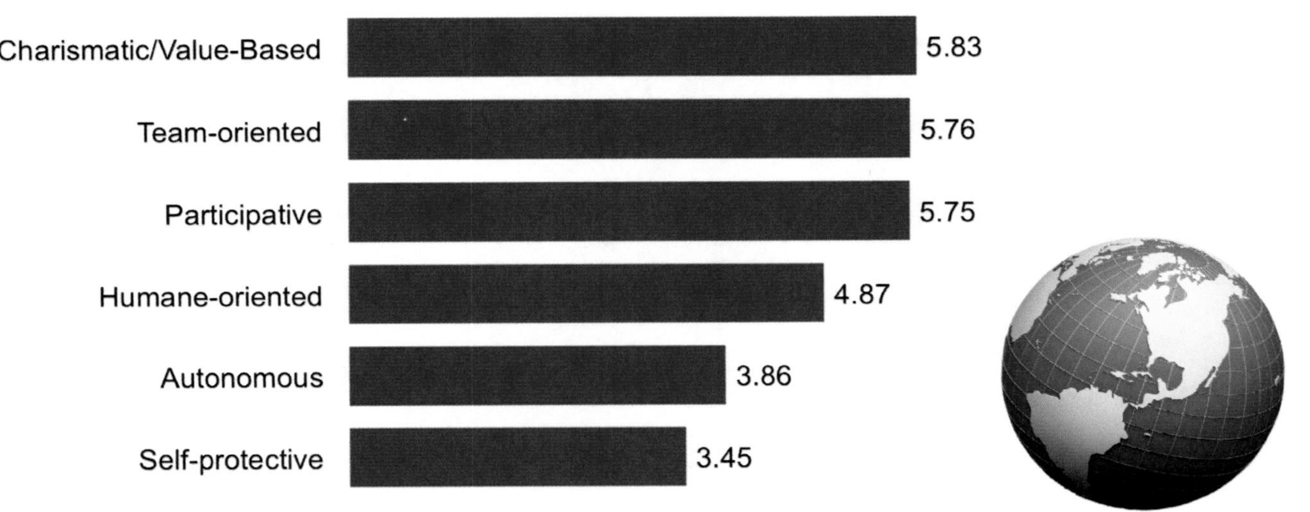

Project GLOBE – Phase 2

Dimensions of Leadership

Universal Leader Attributes

The first two charts below show a more specific set of leader behaviors that were universally considered positive, or negative, across 60 societies in the GLOBE study.[2]

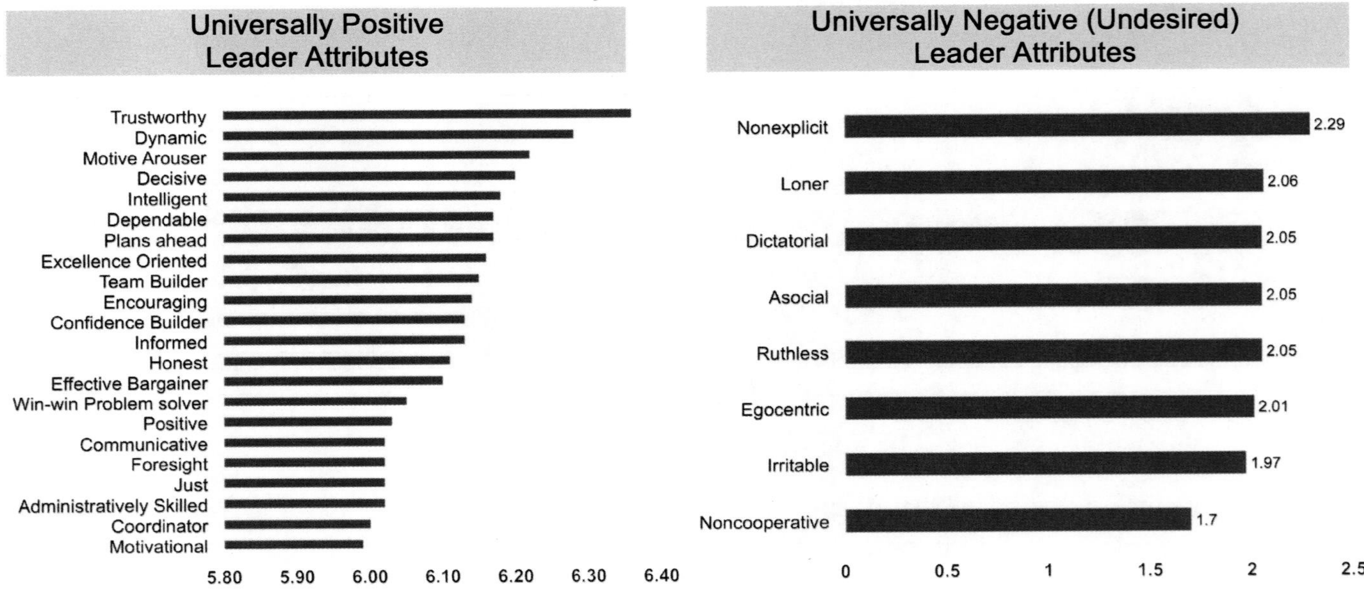

The chart below shows leader attributes that varied quite a bit across cultures. The blue bars extend from the highest to lowest mean societal rating for each attribute. The beige line is the mean across all societies. For example, the leader attribute of *Being a Provocateur*, ranged from a mean of 1.38 in one society to 6.00 in another. The overall mean was 2.42.

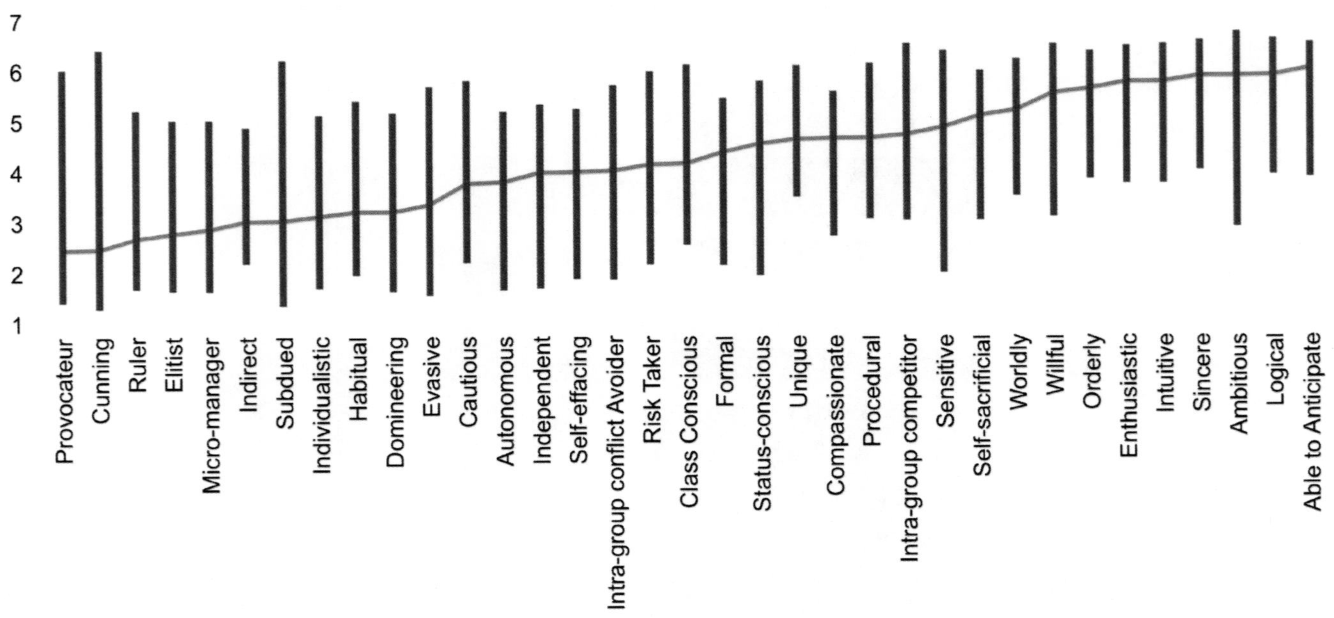

Project GLOBE – Phase 2

Dimensions of Leadership

The chart below shows the 21 first order factor mean scores for the United States. The United States means are shown in beige and the global means are shown in blue.

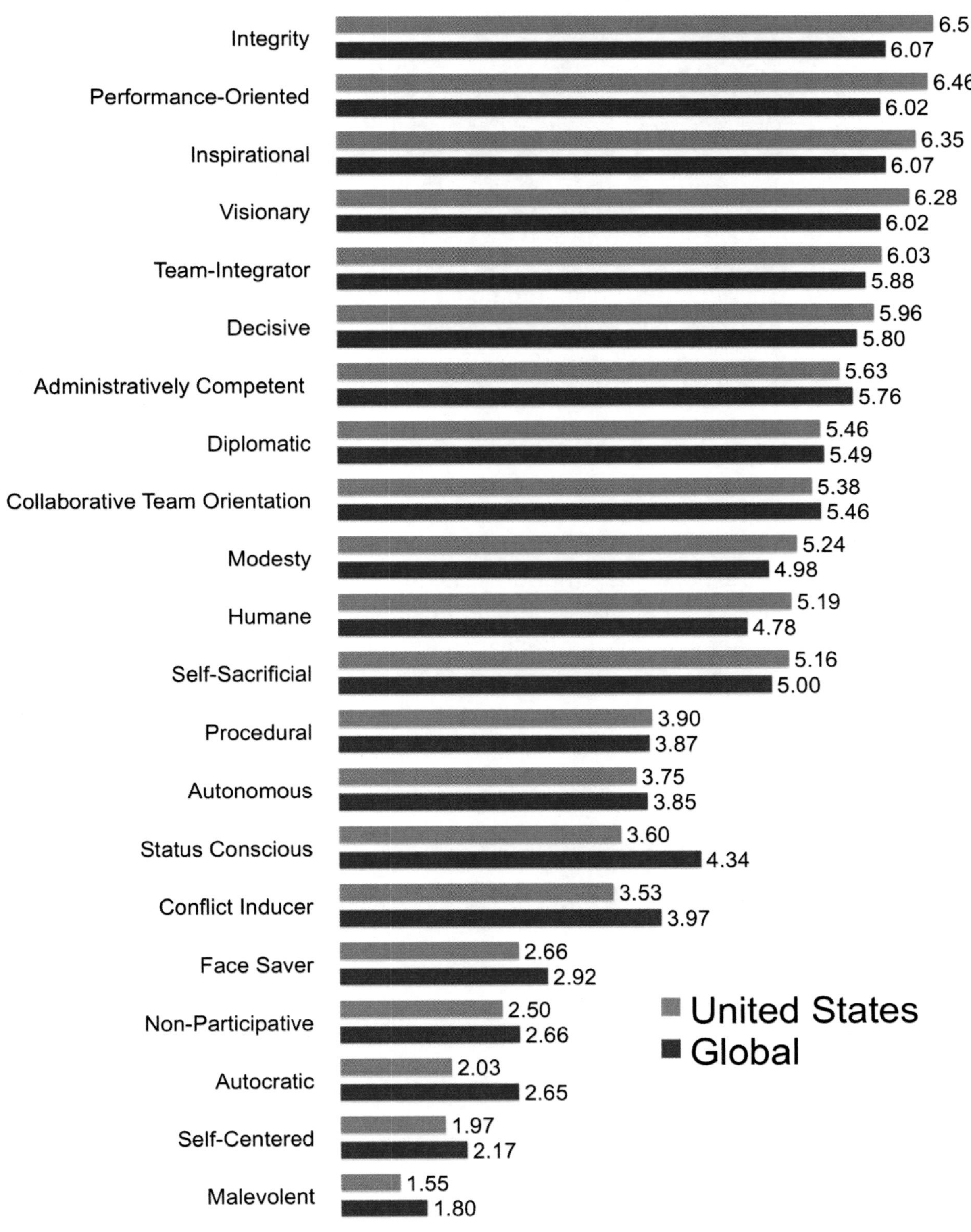

Project GLOBE – Phase 2

Dimensions of Culture

While the broad idea of "cultural differences" is intuitive to us, measuring cultural differences is much more complicated.

The study of cultural influences in leadership can be traced to the late 1960's and early 1970's when cross-cultural psychology emerged as a distinct area of study. The interest in culture during this era reflected the spirit of the times that prompted scholars to consider the sociocultural context when evaluating individual differences.[3] Beginning in 1967, Geert Hofstede, an employee of the International Business Machines (IBM) Corporation conducted a series of studies that lead him to lay the foundational framework for cross-cultural research in organizations. His pioneering investigations sparked a large amount of cultural research, across several disciplines, for the next few decades.

Although Hofstede was not alone in conducting cross-cultural studies, his large-scale surveys were the first to compare cultural values in multiple countries. His position at IBM provided him with access to over 100,000 respondents, from over 50 countries around the world and gave him the opportunity to identify commonalities and differences from one culture to another. The surveys, given in the native language of the participants, focused on attitudes and values in several domains. The results revealed important differences in national values that multinational organizations began to consider as they expanded abroad.[4] The findings from these studies have had a profound impact on business, management and leadership.

Hofstede initially concluded that countries could be classified along four cultural dimensions: power distance, uncertainty avoidance, individualism and masculinity. He later added a fifth dimension called future orientation. Hofstede reported scores and rankings for each country, which allowed practitioners and researchers alike to anticipate prevalent attitudes and behaviors in a given culture. An understanding of these dimensions alongside a country's classification may lead to more fluid cross-cultural interactions.

Project GLOBE – Phase 2

Dimensions of Culture

Hofstede's Five Dimensions of Culture

Low **High**

Power Distance reflects the degree of inequality in a society by measuring dependency on superiors. It indicates how much subordinates accept and expect unequal distribution of power in an organization. Cultures with larger power distances tend to endorse more authoritarianism and to incorporate an unequal workplace organizational hierarchy.

Uncertainty Avoidance is manifest as individuals in a society experience anxiety or feel threatened upon encountering unknown or ambiguous situations. People from cultures with higher scores on this dimension prefer highly organized policies and procedures in the workplace.

Individualism measures the extent to which individuals identify with and favor their unique self and adopt an "I" personal identity compared to those who identify with and favor the group and adopt a "we" personal identity. Collectivist societies tend to favor group cohesion and loyalty among extended family units and the greater community. Individualist societies tend to be loose-knit groups that favor the self and immediate family.

Masculinity is present in a society when there are marked differences between gender roles such that men are expected to express strength, assertiveness, and striving for material gain whereas women are expected to be kind, nurturing and wholesome. High masculine societies tend to favor males in the workplace, endorse more assertiveness and emphasize earning money over leisure.

Long-Term Orientation is the extent to which individuals maintain a perspective in which they anticipate future rewards. Cultures that score high on this dimension tend to conserve resources and are very pragmatic in family and organizational decisions. Those scoring low on this dimension (high on short-term orientation) are concerned with obtaining quick results and maintaining social status.

Project GLOBE – Phase 2

Dimensions of Culture

GLOBE's Nine Dimensions of Culture

In order to measure culture, the GLOBE project built on Hofstede's (1980, 2001)[5] work. The GLOBE ideas of power distance, uncertainty avoidance, gender egalitarianism and future orientation are similar to Hofstede's constructs. The GLOBE researchers developed two types of collectivism: in-group collectivism (informal) and institutional collectivism (formal). The researchers also created three new dimensions of culture: humane-orientation, assertiveness and performance orientation.

These nine cultural dimensions were measured four times: a) at the level of organizations, b) at the level of society, c) as the culture currently is (as is) and d) how you wish the culture was (should be).

	Organizational Level		Societal Level	
What the Culture is "As Is"	Power Distance Uncertainty Avoidance Humane Orientation Institutional Collectivism In-Group Collectivism	Assertiveness Gender Egalitarianism Future Orientation Performance Orientation	Power Distance Uncertainty Avoidance Humane Orientation Institutional Collectivism In-Group Collectivism	Assertiveness Gender Egalitarianism Future Orientation Performance Orientation
What Would You Like the Culture to Be "Should Be"	Power Distance Uncertainty Avoidance Humane Orientation Institutional Collectivism In-Group Collectivism	Assertiveness Gender Egalitarianism Future Orientation Performance Orientation	Power Distance Uncertainty Avoidance Humane Orientation Institutional Collectivism In-Group Collectivism	Assertiveness Gender Egalitarianism Future Orientation Performance Orientation

Low **High**

Power Distance is the Degree to Which Members of an Organization or Society Expect and Agree That Power Should Be Stratified and Concentrated at Higher Levels of an Organization or Government

Uncertainty Avoidance is the Extent to Which a Society, Organization or Group Relies on Social Norms, Rules and Procedures to Alleviate the Unpredictability of Future Events

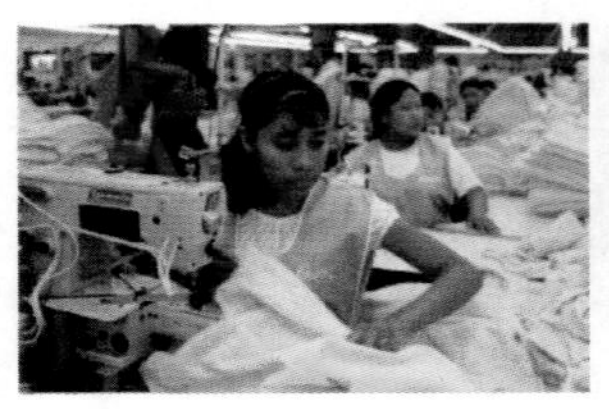

Humane Orientation is the Degree to Which a Collective Encourages and Rewards Individuals for Being Fair, Altruistic, Generous, Caring and Kind to Others

Project GLOBE – Phase 2

Dimensions of Culture

Low	High	
		**Institutional Collectivism** is the Degree to Which Organizational and Societal Institutional Practices Encourage and Reward Collective Distribution of Resources and Collective Action
		**In-Group Collectivism** is the Degree to Which Individuals Express Pride, Loyalty and Cohesiveness in Their Organizations or Families
	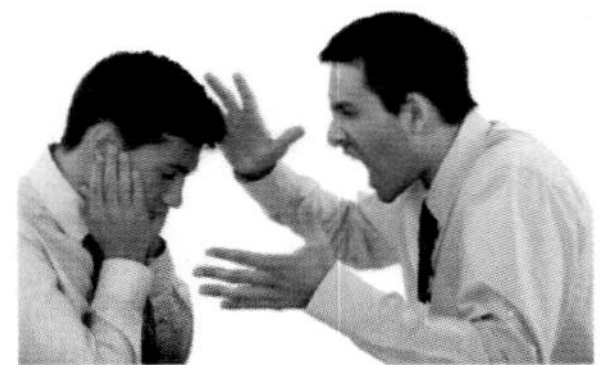	**Assertiveness** is the Degree to Which Individuals are Assertive, Dominant and Demanding in Their Relationships with Others
		**Gender Egalitarianism** is the Degree to Which a Collective Minimizes Gender Inequality
		**Future Orientation** is the Extent to Which a Collective Encourages Future Oriented Behaviors Such as Delaying Gratification, Planning and Investing in the Future
		**Performance Orientation** is the Degree to Which a Collective Encourages and Rewards Group Members for Performance Improvement and Excellence

Project GLOBE – Phase 2

Dimensions of Culture
Power Distance

Power Distance

Power distance is the degree to which members of an organization or society expect and agree that power should be stratified and concentrated at higher levels of an organization or government.

Characteristics of Societies with Lower Power Distance[6]	Characteristics of Societies with Higher Power Distance
Have large middle classes	Differentiated into classes on several criteria
Power bases are transient and sharable (e.g., skill, knowledge)	Power bases are stable and scarce (e.g., land ownership)
Power is seen as a source of corruption, coercion and dominance	Power is seen as providing social order, relational harmony and role stability
High upward social mobility	Limited upward social mobility
Information is shared	Information is localized
All the groups enjoy equal involvement, and democracy ensures parity in opportunities and development for all	Different groups (e.g., women) have different involvement, and democracy does not ensure equal opportunities
Strong native historical influences and long standing independence of the society	Strong non-native historical influences and recent independence of the society
Civil liberties are strong and public corruption low	Civil liberties are weak and public corruption high
Mass availability of tools, resources, and capabilities for independent and entrepreneurial initiatives, as reflected in wide educational enrollment	Only a few people have access to resources, skills, and capabilities, contributing to low human development and life expectancies
Mature growth rates of consumption and high per capita purchasing power	High growth rates of consumption and high need for resource coordination
Need for specialized technology, adapted to each user	Mass use of technology, which supports general power distance reduction

Project GLOBE – Phase 2

Dimensions of Culture

Power Distance

Observing Power Distance in the Workplace[7]

Examples of Workplaces with Lower Power Distance	Examples of Workplaces with Higher Power Distance
Few If Any Reserved Parking Spaces	Separate Parking Spaces for Leaders and Followers
Leaders and Followers Tend to Eat in the Same Facility	Separate Eating Spaces for Leaders and Followers
Cubicle Style Offices with Open and Visible Entry Ways Across Buildings for All	Traditional Offices in Separate Buildings for Executive and Non-Executive Employees
Individuals Mentored by Executives Based on Area of Expertise and Demonstrated Ability	Individuals Pre-Selected for Executive Positions Based on Hierarchical Connections

The Relationships among Power Distance Preference and Implicit Leadership[8]

Most of the variance[9] found for power distance preference and leadership preferences was found at the societal level of the GLOBE study, rather than at the organizational level.

	Organizational Level		Societal Level	
	R^2	HLM Coefficient	R^2	HLM Coefficient
Charismatic/Value Based			17.7%	-.57
Team-Oriented				
Participative	1.6%	-.32	28.4%	-.85
Humane-Oriented			5.5%	-.34
Autonomous				
Self-Protective	1.3%	.25	37.3%	.87

Because this book is about organizational leadership, we will focus on the findings at the organizational level. While the R^2 values are small when analyzed in conjunction with the societal relationships, the organizational level finding was:

As the desire for power distance in organizations increased, participative leadership was considered less important (β = -.32) and self-protective leadership was considered more important (β = .25) to being an outstanding leader.

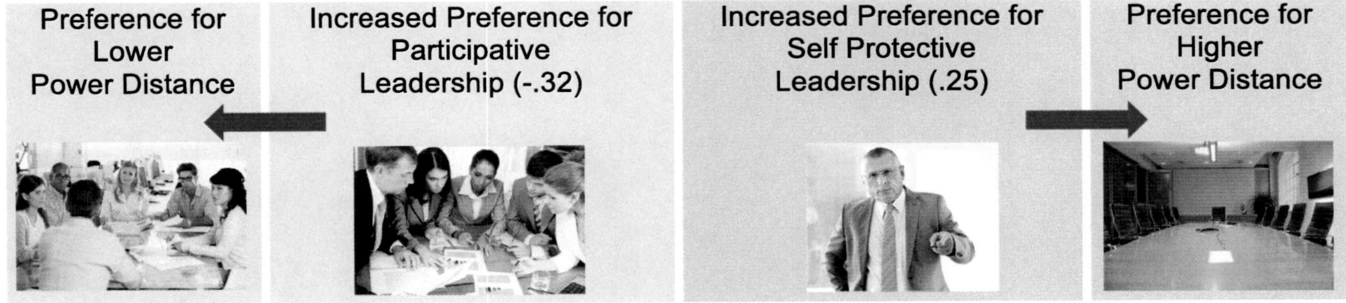

Project GLOBE – Phase 2

Dimensions of Culture
Uncertainty Avoidance

Uncertainty Avoidance

Uncertainty avoidance refers to the extent to which members of collectives seek orderliness, consistency, structure, formalized procedures and laws to cover situations in their daily lives.

Characteristics of Societies with Lower Uncertainty Avoidance	Characteristics of Societies with Higher Uncertainty Avoidance
Have a tendency to be more informal in their interactions with others	Have a tendency toward formalizing their interactions with others
Rely on the word of others they trust rather than contractual arrangements	Document agreements in legal contracts
Are less concerned with orderliness and the maintenance of records, often do not document the conclusions drawn in meetings	Tend to be orderly, keeping meticulous records, documenting conclusions drawn in meetings
Rely on informal interactions and informal norms rather than formal policies, procedures and rules	Rely on formal policies and procedures, establishing and following rules and verifying communications in writing
Are less calculating when taking risks	Take more moderate, calculated risks
Facilitate new product development especially in the initiation phase, through higher risk taking and minimal planning or control	Inhibit new product development but facilitate the implementation stage through risk aversion and tight controls
Show less resistance to change	Show stronger resistance to change
Show less desire to establish rules to dictate behavior	Show stronger desire to establish rules allowing predictability of behavior
Show more tolerance for breaking rules	Show less tolerance for breaking rules

Project GLOBE – Phase 2

Dimensions of Culture
Uncertainty Avoidance

Observing Uncertainty Avoidance in the Workplace

Examples of Workplaces with Lower Uncertainty Avoidance	Examples of Workplaces with Higher Uncertainty Avoidance
Envision Generally Accepted Norms as a Good Starting Point for Planning	Follow Generally Accepted Norms with Flexibility for the Planning of Resources and Deadlines
Are Likely More Organic, with Reliance on the Judgment of Workers	Are Likely More Mechanistic, with Reliance on Standard Operating Procedures
Celebrations and Rewards Emphasize Innovation and Change Efforts	Celebrations and Rewards Emphasize Worker Longevity
Have More Meetings with Brainstorming	Have More Meetings with Planned Agendas

The Relationships among Uncertainty Avoidance Preference and Implicit Leadership

Most of the variance found for uncertainty avoidance preference and leadership preferences was found at the societal level of the GLOBE study, rather than at the organizational level.

As the desire for uncertainty avoidance in organizations increased, participative leadership was considered less important and team-oriented, humane-oriented and self-protective leadership were considered more important to being an outstanding leader.

	Organizational Level		Societal Level	
	R^2	HLM Coefficient	R^2	HLM Coefficient
Charismatic/Value Based			5.3%	-.20
Team-Oriented	3.9%	.17	21.1%	.12
Participative	1.8%	-.13	32.0%	-.49
Humane-Oriented	6.7%	.23	14.2%	.32
Autonomous				
Self-Protective	5.7%	.26	63.6%	.63

Project GLOBE – Phase 2

Dimensions of Culture
Humane Orientation

Humane Orientation

Humane orientation refers to the degree to which individuals in organizations or societies encourage and reward individuals for being fair, altruistic, friendly, generous, caring and kind to others.

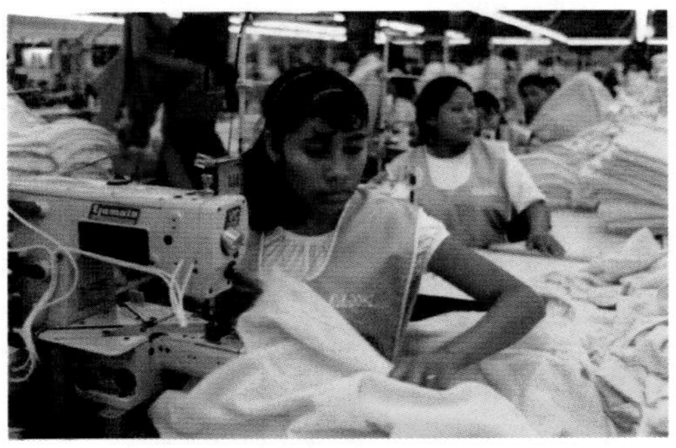

Characteristics of Societies with Lower Humane Orientation	Characteristics of Societies with Higher Humane Orientation
See self-interest as important	Others are important (e.g., family, friends, community, and strangers)
Have more psychological and pathological problems	Have fewer psychological and pathological problems
Value pleasure, comfort, and self-enjoyment	Value altruism, benevolence, kindness, love, and generosity
Motivated by power and material possessions	Have a need for belonging and affiliation
Welfare state guarantees social and economic protection of individuals	Personal and family relationships induce protection for the individuals
Have a lack of support for others; predominance of self-enhancement	Close circle receives material, financial, and social support; concern extends to all people and nature
The state provides social and economic support for individuals' well-being	Others are responsible for promoting the well-being of individuals, the state is not actively involved
The state sponsors public provisions and sectors	The state supports the private sector and maintains a balance between public and private domains
Public policymakers consider child labor practices as somewhat less important	Public policymakers establish sanctions against child labor practices
Members of society are less sensitive to all forms of racial discrimination	Members of society are more sensitive to all forms of racial discrimination

Project GLOBE – Phase 2

Dimensions of Culture
Humane Orientation

Observing Humane Orientation in the Workplace

Examples of Workplaces with Lower Humane Orientation	Examples of Workplaces with Higher Humane Orientation
Positions of Recognition or Distinction for Individuals with Desired Performance or Rank	Have Well Established Affinity Groups or Associations among Employees (i.e. Networking Groups)
Use Punitive Corrective Action for Employees Not Meeting Standards	Establish Support or Mentorship Groups for Employees Not Meeting Standards
Financial Focus on Internal Needs	Fundraise for Community Causes
Meet Minimal OSHA or HR standards	Exceed Minimal OSHA or HR standards

The Relationships among Humane Orientation Preference and Implicit Leadership

The variance for humane orientation preference and leadership preferences was found at both the societal and organizational level of the GLOBE study.

As the desire for humane orientation in organizations increased, autonomous leadership was considered less important and charismatic/value-based, team-oriented, participative and humane-oriented leadership were considered more important to being an outstanding leader.

	Organizational Level		Societal Level	
	R^2	HLM Coefficient	R^2	HLM Coefficient
Charismatic/Value Based	5.6%	.37		
Team-Oriented	12.2%	.35		
Participative	3.2%	.32	16.1%	.62
Humane-Oriented	19.5%	.56		
Autonomous	4.1%	-.29		
Self-Protective			21.4%	-.20

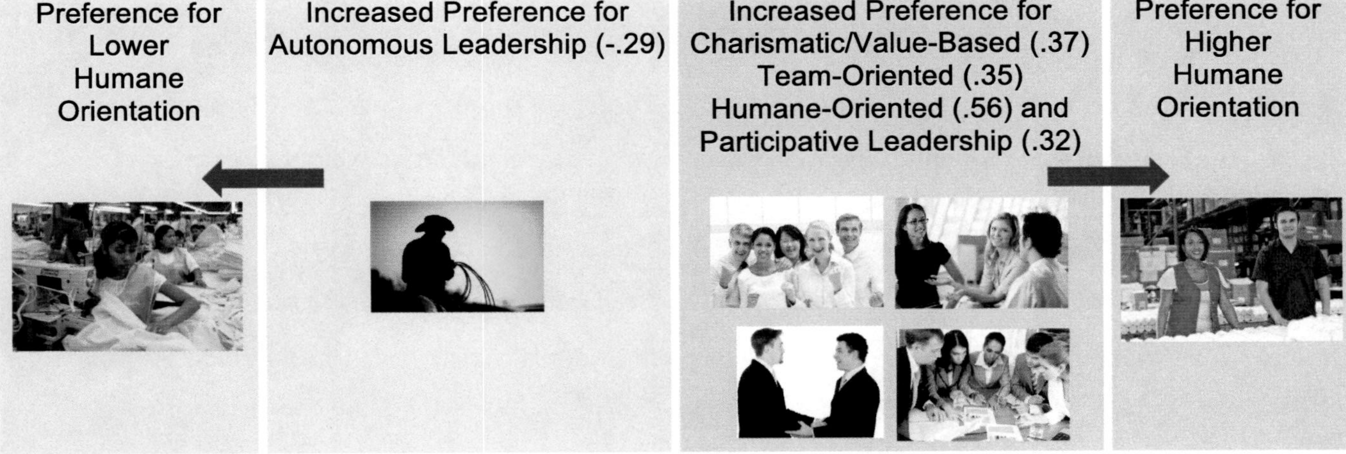

Project GLOBE – Phase 2

Dimensions of Culture
Institutional Collectivism

Institutional Collectivism

Institutional collectivism refers to the degree to which organizational and societal institutional practices encourage and reward collective distribution of resources and collective action.

Features of Societies with Lower Institutional Collectivism	Features of Societies with Higher Institutional Collectivism
Individuals look after themselves or their immediate families	Individuals are integrated into strong cohesive groups
The self is viewed as autonomous and independent of groups	The self is viewed as interdependent with groups
Individual goals take precedence over group goals	Group goals take precedence over individual goals
Attitudes and personal needs are important determinants of behavior	Duties and obligations are important determinants of social behavior
People emphasize rationality	People emphasize relatedness with groups
Ecologies are hunting and gathering, or industrial and wealthy	Ecologies are agricultural, and countries are often developing
There is a faster pace of life	There is a slower pace of life
There are higher heart-attack rates	There are lower heart-attack rates
There is higher subjective well-being	There is lower subjective well-being
There are more nuclear family structures	There are more extended family structures
Love is assigned greater weight in marriage decisions	Love is assigned less weight in marriage decisions
There are higher divorce rates	There are lower divorce rates
Communication is more direct	Communication is more indirect
Individuals are more likely to engage in activities alone	Individuals are more likely to engage in group activities

Project GLOBE – Phase 2

Dimensions of Culture
Institutional Collectivism

Observing Institutional Collectivism in the Workplace

Examples of Workplaces with Lower Institutional Collectivism	Examples of Workplaces with Higher Institutional Collectivism
Utilize Resources Only Within Designated Departments and Functional Areas	Share Resources Across Departments and Functional Areas
Set Goals and Objectives for Each Functional Area with Only Departmental Input	Collaborate on Goals and Objectives with Employees Across Functional Areas
Are Accountable Only at the Functional Level	Are Accountable at the Organizational Level
More Likely to Give Bonuses to an Individual	More Likely to Give Bonuses to a Team

The Relationships among Institutional Collectivism Preference and Implicit Leadership

The variance for institutional collectivism preference and leadership preferences was found at both the societal and organizational levels of the GLOBE study.

As the desire for institutional collectivism in organizations increased, charismatic/value-based, team-oriented, participative and humane-oriented leadership were considered more important to being an outstanding leader.

	Organizational Level		Societal Level	
	R^2	HLM Coefficient	R^2	HLM Coefficient
Charismatic/Value Based	5.9%	.35		
Team-Oriented	6.6%	.20		
Participative	0.9%	.20		
Humane-Oriented	4.1%	.22		
Autonomous			11.4%	-.35
Self-Protective			8.4%	.38

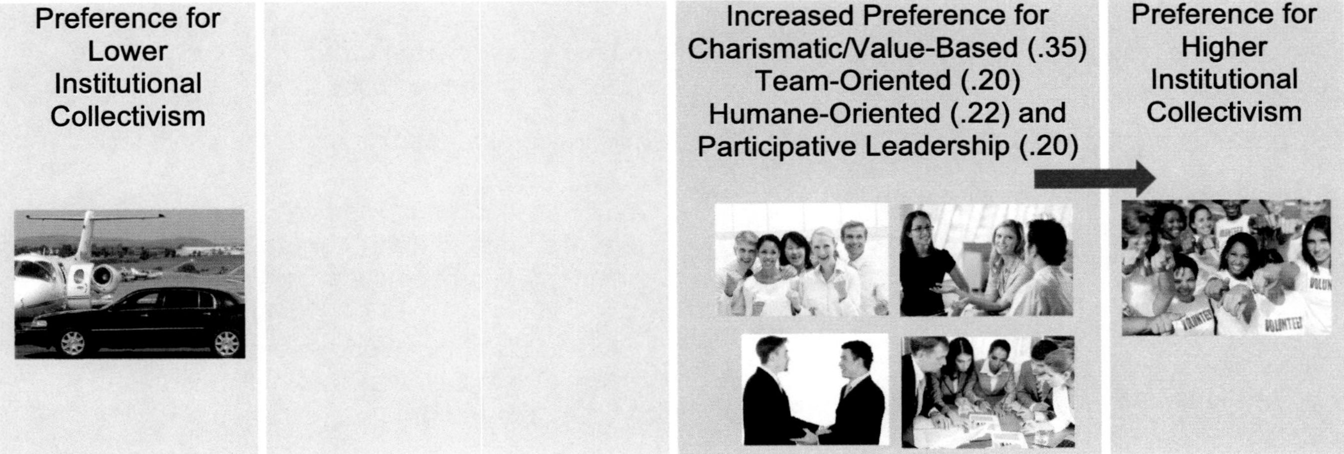

Project GLOBE – Phase 2

Dimensions of Culture
In-Group Collectivism

In-Group Collectivism

In-group collectivism refers to the degree to which individuals express pride, loyalty and cohesiveness in their organizations or families.

Features of Organizations with Lower In-Group Individualism	Features of Organizations with Higher In-Group Collectivism
Members assume that they are independent of the organization and believe it is important to bring their unique skills and abilities to the organization	Members assume that they are highly interdependent with the organization and believe it is important to make personal sacrifices to fulfill their organizational obligations
Employees develop short-term relationships, and change companies at their own discretion	Employees tend to develop long-term relationships with employers from recruitment to Retirement
Organizations are primarily interested in the work that employees perform and not their personal or family welfare	Organizations take responsibility for employee welfare
Important decisions tend to be made by individuals	Important decisions tend to be made by groups
Selection focuses primarily on employees' knowledge, skills and abilities	Selection can focus on relational attributes of employees
Jobs are designed individually to maximize autonomy	Jobs are designed in groups to maximize the social and technical aspects of the job
Selection is emphasized more than training	Training is emphasized more than selection
Compensation and promotions are based on an equity model, in which an individual is rewarded in direct relationship to his or her contribution to task success	Compensation and promotions are based on what is equitable for the group and on considerations of seniority and personal needs
Motivation is individually oriented and is based on individual interests, needs, and capacities	Motivation is socially oriented and is based on the need to fulfill duties and obligations and to contribute to the group

Project GLOBE – Phase 2

Dimensions of Culture
In-Group Collectivism

Observing In-Group Collectivism in the Workplace

Examples of Workplaces with Lower In-Group Collectivism	Examples of Workplaces with Higher In-Group Collectivism
Allow Functional Area Heads to Make Decisions Based on their Knowledge or Authority	Make Functional Area Decisions Via a Democratic Process
Little Coordination of Symbols or Group-Wear	Wear Unifying Symbols Such as Group Polo Shirts
Individuals Within Functional Areas Arrive and Sit Separately at Organizational Meetings	Functional Areas Arrive and Sit Together at Organizational Meetings

The Relationships among In-Group Collectivism Preference and Implicit Leadership

The variance found for in-group collectivism preference and leadership preferences was found at both the organizational and societal levels of the GLOBE study.

As the desire for in-group collectivism in organizations increased, charismatic/value-based, team-oriented, participative and humane-oriented leadership were considered more important to being an outstanding leader.

	Organizational Level		Societal Level	
	R^2	HLM Coefficient	R^2	HLM Coefficient
Charismatic/Value Based	11.8%	.69	10.3%	.41
Team-Oriented	12.4%	.47		
Participative	1.2%	.01		
Humane-Oriented	10.1%	.52		
Autonomous				
Self-Protective			49.2%	

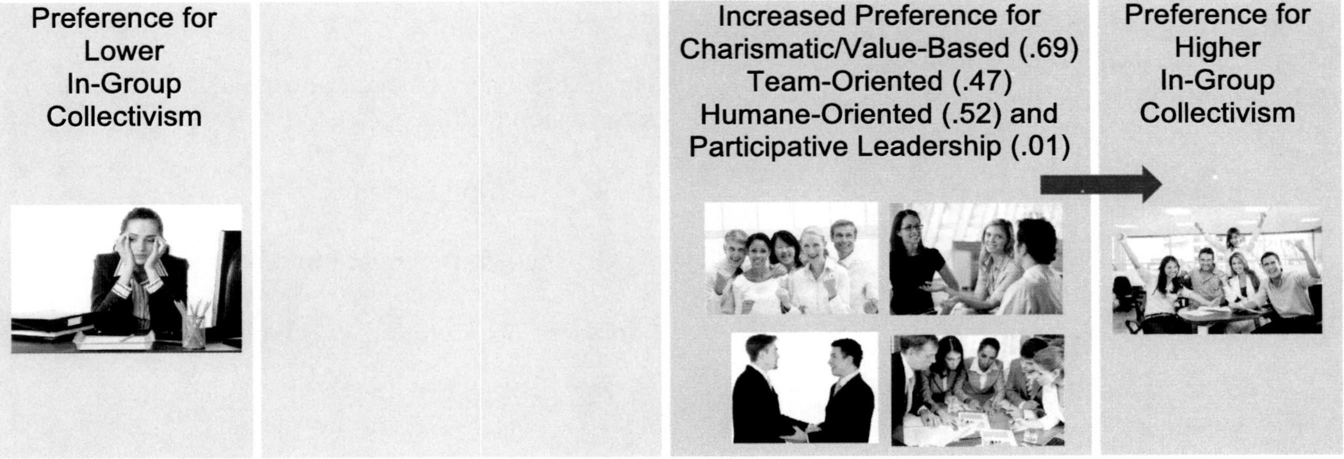

Project GLOBE – Phase 2

Dimensions of Culture
Assertiveness

Assertiveness
Assertiveness refers to the degree to which individuals in organizations or societies are assertive, confrontational and aggressive in social relationships.

Characteristics of Societies with Lower Assertiveness	Characteristics of Societies with Higher Assertiveness
View assertiveness as socially unacceptable and value modesty and tenderness	Value assertive, dominant, and tough behavior for everyone in society
Have sympathy for the weak	Have sympathy for the strong
Value cooperation	Value competition
Associate competition with defeat and punishment	Believe that anyone can succeed if he or she tries hard enough
Value people and warm relationships	Value success and progress
Speak indirectly and emphasize "face-saving"	Value direct and unambiguous communication
Value ambiguity and subtlety in language and communications	Value being explicit and to the point in communications
Value detached and self-possessed conduct	Value expressiveness and revealing thoughts and feelings
Have far more negative connotations with the term aggression (e.g., aggression leads only to negative outcomes)	Have relatively positive connotations for the term aggression (e.g., aggression helps to win)
Have an unjust-world belief	Have a just-world belief
Value harmony with the environment rather than control	Try to have control over the environment
Stress equality, solidarity and quality of life	Stress equity, competition and performance
Emphasize tradition, seniority and experience	Have a "can-do" attitude
Emphasize integrity, loyalty, and cooperative spirit	Emphasize results over relationships

Project GLOBE – Phase 2

Dimensions of Culture

Assertiveness

Observing Assertiveness in the Workplace

Examples of Workplaces with Lower Assertiveness	Examples of Workplaces with Higher Assertiveness
Assign Leadership Roles to Individuals Who Are Cooperative or Have Good Working Relationships	Assign Leadership Roles to Individuals Who Are Competitive
Prefer Delaying of Action or Decisions Until Missing Information is Obtained	Prefer Making Decisions and "Keep on Moving"
Meetings are Run in an Orderly Manner	Arguments During Meetings Are Acceptable

The Relationships among Assertiveness Preference and Implicit Leadership

Most of the variance found for assertiveness preference and leadership preferences was found at the organizational level of the GLOBE study.

As the desire for assertiveness in organizations increased, team-oriented and participative leadership were considered less important and humane-oriented and autonomous leadership were considered more important to being an outstanding leader.

	Organizational Level		Societal Level	
	R^2	HLM Coefficient	R^2	HLM Coefficient
Charismatic/Value Based				
Team-Oriented	7.4%	-.14		
Participative	2.1%	-.13		
Humane-Oriented	12.3%	.27	6.6%	.23
Autonomous	5.9%	.23		
Self-Protective				

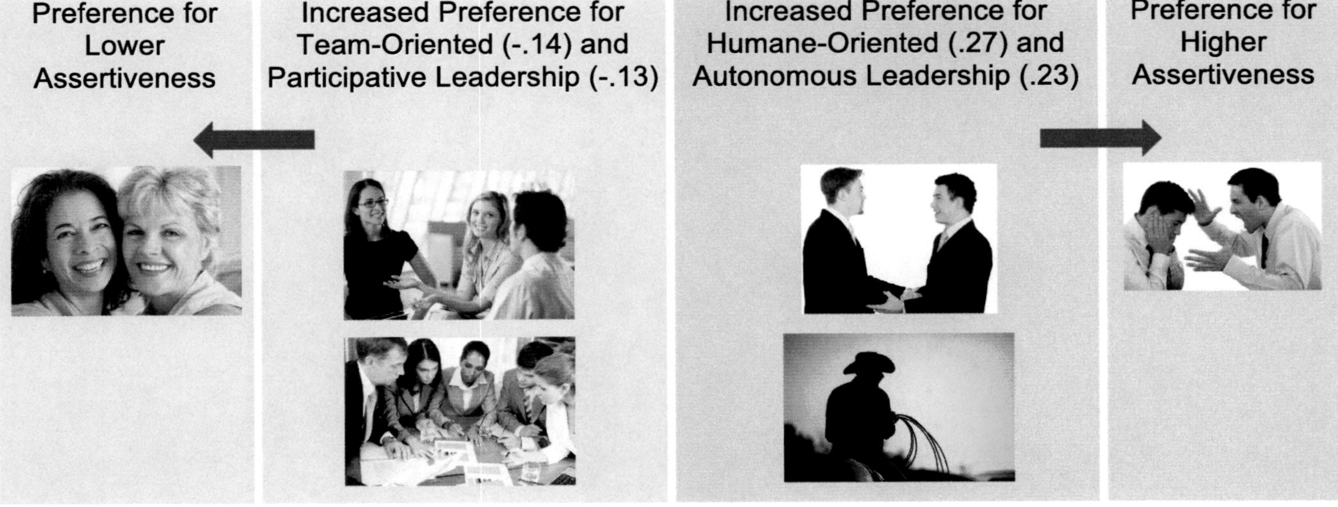

Project GLOBE – Phase 2

Dimensions of Culture
Gender Egalitarianism

Gender Egalitarianism

Gender egalitarianism refers to the degree to which an organization or a society minimizes gender role differences while promoting gender equality.

Characteristics of Societies with Lower Gender Egalitarianism	Characteristics of Societies with Higher Gender Egalitarianism
Have fewer women in positions of authority	Have more women in positions of authority
Accord women a lower status in society	Accord women a higher status in society
Afford women no or a smaller role in community decision making	Afford women a greater role in community decision making
Have a lower percentage of women participating in the labor force	Have a higher percentage of women participating in the labor force
Have more occupational sex segregation	Have less occupational sex segregation
Have lower female literacy rates	Have higher female literacy rates
Have a lower level of education of females relative to males	Have similar levels of education of females and males

Project GLOBE – Phase 2

Dimensions of Culture
Gender Egalitarianism

Observing Gender Egalitarianism in the Workplace

Examples of Workplaces with Lower Gender Egalitarianism	Examples of Workplaces with Higher Gender Egalitarianism
Pay Higher Salaries to Men Than Women in Similar Positions of Responsibility or Job Roles	Provide Salary Equalization for Men and Women in Similar Positions of Responsibility or Job Roles
Frown on Women Being Assertive and Men Being Nurturing in Meetings	Are Tolerant of Assertiveness and/or Nurturance from Both Men and Women in Meetings

The Relationships among Gender Egalitarianism Preference and Implicit Leadership

Most of the variance found for gender egalitarianism preference and leadership preferences was found at the societal level of the GLOBE study.

As the desire for gender egalitarianism in organizations increased, self-protective leadership was considered less important and participative leadership was considered more important to being an outstanding leader.

	Organizational Level		Societal Level	
	R^2	HLM Coefficient	R^2	HLM Coefficient
Charismatic/Value Based			21.7%	.41
Team-Oriented				
Participative	1.7%	.21	39.7%	.65
Humane-Oriented				
Autonomous				
Self-Protective	1.6%	-.20	42.4%	-.62

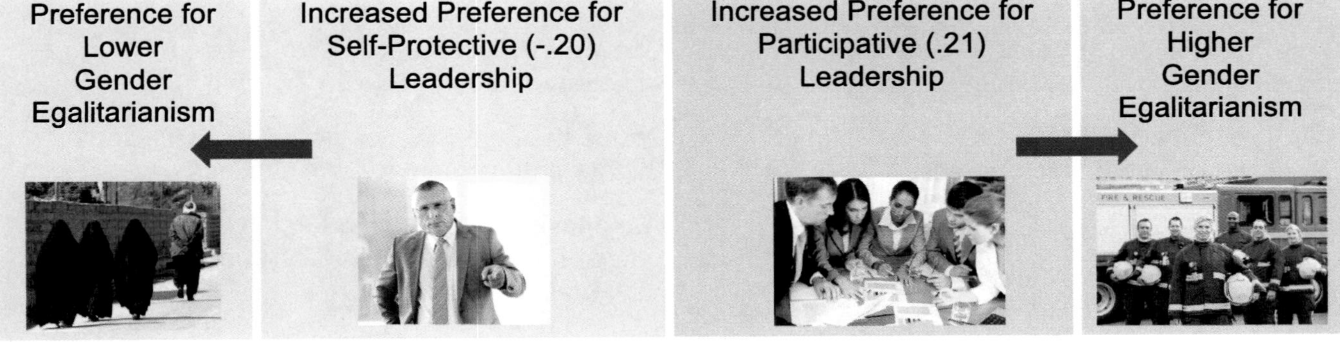

Project GLOBE – Phase 2

Dimensions of Culture
Future Orientation

Future Orientation

Future orientation refers to the degree to which individuals in organizations or societies engage in future-oriented behaviors such as planning, investing in the future and delaying individual or collective gratification.

Characteristics of Societies with Lower Future Orientation	Characteristics of Societies with Higher Future Orientation
Have lower levels of economic success	Achieve economic success
Have a propensity to spend now, rather than to save for the future	Have a propensity to save for the future
Have individuals who are psychologically unhealthy and socially maladjusted	Have individuals who are psychologically healthy and socially well adjusted
Have individuals who are less intrinsically motivated	Have individuals who are more intrinsically motivated
Have organizations with a shorter strategic orientation	Have organizations with a longer strategic orientation
Have inflexible and maladaptive organizations and managers	Have flexible and adaptive organizations and managers
See materialistic success and spiritual fulfillment as dualities, requiring trade-offs	View materialistic success and spiritual fulfillment as an integrated whole
Value instant gratification and place higher priorities on immediate rewards	Value the deferment of gratification, placing a higher priority on long-term success
Emphasize leadership that focuses on repetition of reproducible and routine sequences	Emphasize visionary leadership that is capable of seeing patterns in the face of chaos and uncertainty

Project GLOBE – Phase 2

Dimensions of Culture
Future Orientation

Observing Future Orientation in the Workplace

Examples of Workplaces with Lower Future Orientation	Examples of Workplaces with Higher Future Orientation
Create Short-term Strategic Plans (1-3 Year Timeframe)	Create Long-term Strategic Plans (Beyond the 3-5 Year Timeframe)
Focus on Maximum Use of Resources to Meet Current Needs	Encourage Stewardship of Resources
Embark on Spontaneous Group Activities	Only Undertake Planned Group Activities
Celebrate "The Good Ol' Days"	Believe the Best Days Lie Ahead

The Relationships among Future Orientation and Implicit Leadership

The variance found for future orientation preference and leadership preferences was found at both the societal and organizational levels of the GLOBE study.

As the desire for future orientation in organizations increased, charismatic/value-based, team-oriented, participative and humane-oriented leadership were considered more important to being an outstanding leader.

	Organizational Level		Societal Level	
	R^2	HLM Coefficient	R^2	HLM Coefficient
Charismatic/Value Based	6.7%	.42		
Team-Oriented	7.2%	.28		
Participative	1.0%	.14		
Humane-Oriented	4.3%	.27	5.9%	.35
Autonomous				
Self-Protective			19.1%	.27

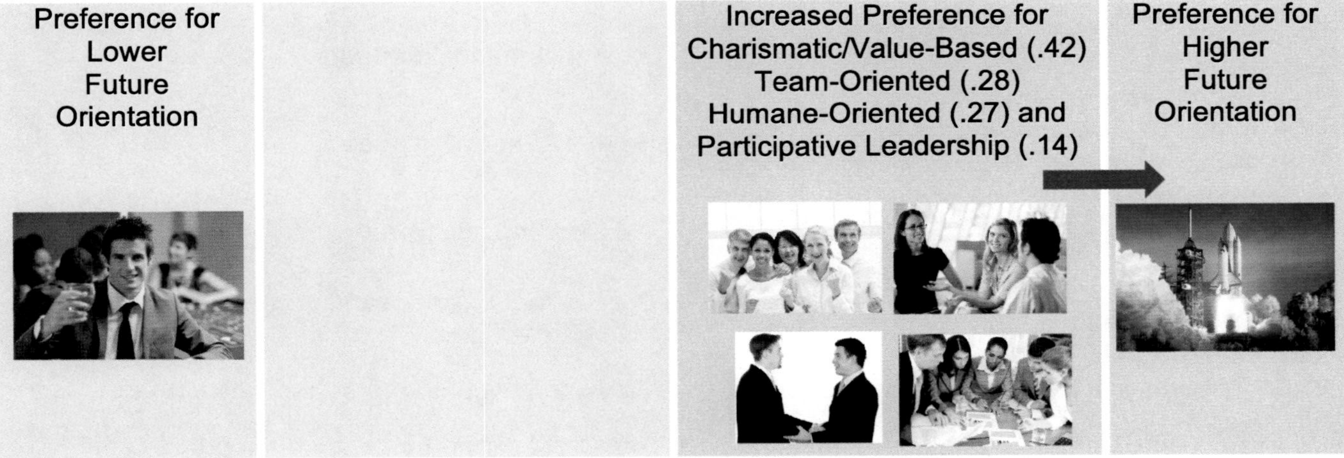

Project GLOBE – Phase 2

Dimensions of Culture
Performance Orientation

Performance Orientation

Performance orientation refers to the degree to which an organization or society encourages and rewards group members for performance improvement and excellence.

Characteristics of Societies with Lower Performance Orientation	Characteristics of Societies with Higher Performance Orientation
Value societal and family relationships	Value training and development
Emphasize loyalty and belongingness	Emphasize results more than people
Have high respect for quality of life	Reward performance
Emphasize seniority and experience	Value assertiveness, competitiveness and materialism
Have performance appraisal systems that emphasize integrity, loyalty and cooperative spirit	Have performance appraisal systems that emphasize achieving results
Value harmony with the environment rather than control	Believe that individuals are in control
View feedback and appraisal as judgmental and discomforting	View feedback as necessary for improvement
View assertiveness as socially unacceptable	Value and reward individual achievement
Regard being motivated by money as inappropriate	Expect demanding targets
View merit pay as potentially destructive to harmony	Have a "can-do" attitude
Value "attending the right school" as an important success criterion	Value taking initiative
Emphasize tradition	Believe that anyone can succeed if he or she tries hard enough
Value who you are more than what you do	Value what you do more than who you are
Pay particular attention to age in promotional decisions	Attach little importance to age in promotional decisions

Project GLOBE – Phase 2

Dimensions of Culture
Performance Orientation

Observing Performance Orientation in the Workplace

Examples of Workplaces with Lower Performance Orientation	Examples of Workplaces with Higher Performance Orientation
Construct Compensation and Reward Systems Based on Availability of Resources	Construct Compensation and Reward Systems Based on Accomplishment of Objectives
Set General Objectives Without Structured or Formal Methods of Measuring Their Accomplishment	Set Specific Objectives and Corresponding Consequences or Accountability for Each Objective

The Relationships among Performance Orientation and Implicit Leadership

The variance found for performance orientation preference and leadership preferences was found at both the societal and organizational levels of the GLOBE study.

As the desire for performance orientation in organizations increased, charismatic/value-based, team-oriented, participative and humane-oriented leadership were considered more important to being an outstanding leader.

	Organizational Level		Societal Level	
	R^2	HLM Coefficient	R^2	HLM Coefficient
Charismatic/Value Based	16.8%	.60	11.2%	.48
Team-Oriented	10.4%	.31		
Participative	2.5%	.25	5.8%	.47
Humane-Oriented	6.3%	.25		
Autonomous				
Self-Protective				

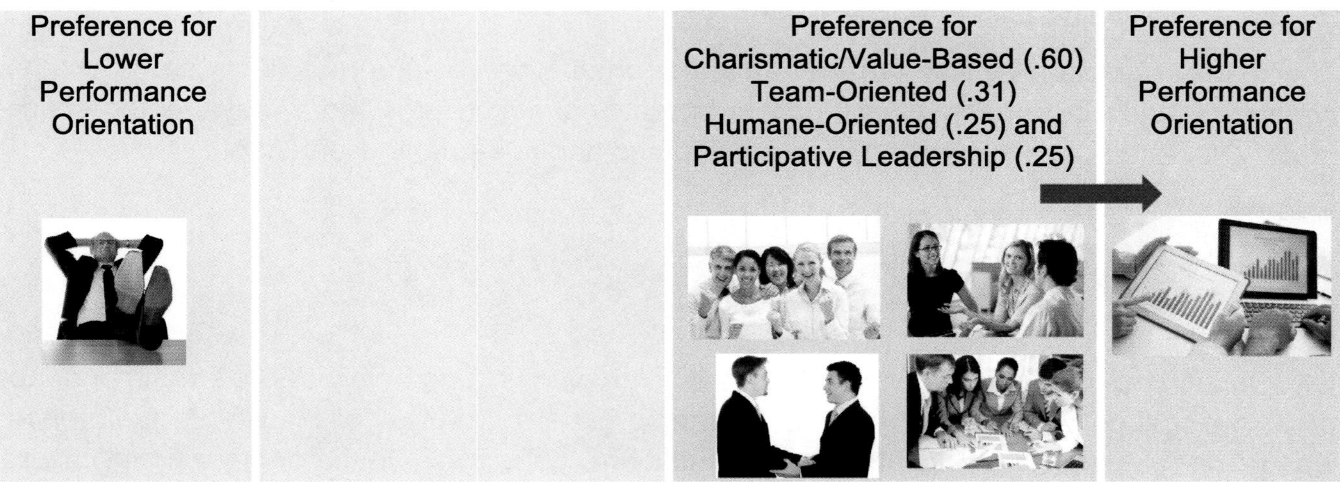

Project GLOBE – Phase 2

Summary of Culture and Leadership

Summary of the Relationships among Cultural and Leadership Preferences

Columns 2 - 7 provide the HLM coefficients for the relationship between *organizational level* cultural preferences and leadership preferences. Column 1 is the US *societal* means.[10]

United States Societal Cultural Preferences	Charismatic/ Value-Based	Team Oriented	Participative	Humane Oriented	Autonomous	Self Protective
Performance Orientation (*M* = 6.14)	Higher (.60)	Higher (.31)	Higher (.25)	Higher (.25)		
In-Group Collectivism (*M* = 5.77)	Higher (.69)	Higher (.47)	Higher (.01)	Higher (.52)		
Humane Orientation (*M* = 5.53)	Higher (.37)	Higher (.35)	Higher (.32)	Higher (.56)	Lower (-.29)	
Future Orientation (*M* = 5.31)	Higher (.42)	Higher (.28)	Higher (.14)	Higher (.27)		

In the United States, participants generally desired cultures to be both performance (*M* = 6.14) and future oriented (*M* = 5.31), with an emphasis on humane (*M* = 5.53) and collective (in-group) (*M* = 5.77) aspects. For these cultural preferences, we see a concomitant preference for charismatic/value-based, team-oriented, participative and humane-oriented leadership.

The more participants wanted performance orientation, in-group collectivism, humane-orientation and future orientation in the organizational culture, the more they wanted charismatic/value-based, team-oriented, participative and humane-oriented leadership.

Institutional Collectivism (M = 4.17)	Higher (.35)	Higher (.20)	Higher (.22)	Higher (.20)

GLOBE participants from the United States didn't have a strong opinion about the importance of institutional collectivism (*M* = 4.17). The same pattern, however of leadership preferences was found. The more participants wanted institutional collectivism in the organizational culture, the more they wanted charismatic/value-based, team-oriented, participative and humane-oriented leadership.

Project GLOBE – Phase 2

Summary of Culture and Leadership

GLOBE participants from the United States didn't want power distance (*M* = 2.85) in their societies. As the desire for power distance increased, the tolerance or preference for self-protective leadership also increased, while the desire for participative leadership decreased. Said the opposite way, as the desire for power distance decreased, the tolerance for self-protective leadership also decreased, while the desire for participative leadership increased.

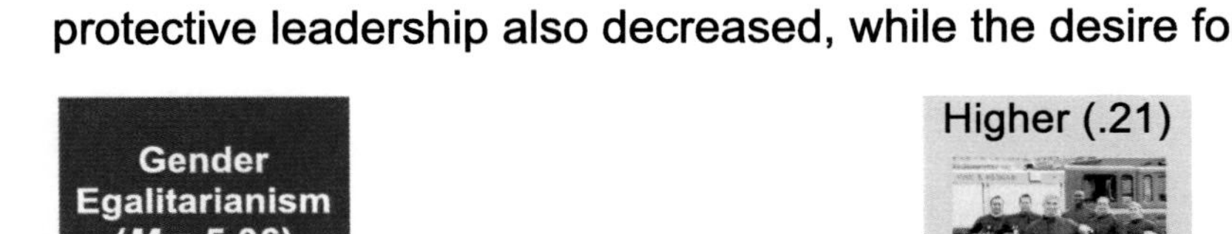

The opposite pattern was found for gender egalitarianism (*M* = 5.06). As the desire for gender equality in organizations increased, the tolerance for self-protective leadership decreased, while the desire for participative leadership increased.

GLOBE participants from the United State didn't have a strong opinion about the importance of uncertainty avoidance (*M* = 4.00) or assertiveness (*M* = 4.32). The preferences for leadership and these two dimensions of culture had multiple relationships in different directions.

Project GLOBE – Phase 2

Summary of Culture and Leadership

United States Societal Culture Scores

The GLOBE study measured organizational culture from two perspectives: what the culture was, and what participants believed the culture should be. The chart below provides those scores for the United States. The scores for assertiveness, institutional collectivism and uncertainty avoidance fell in the range of *neither agree nor disagree.* The United States' mean scores endorsed performance orientation, in-group collectivism, humane orientation, future orientation, gender egalitarianism and low power distance.

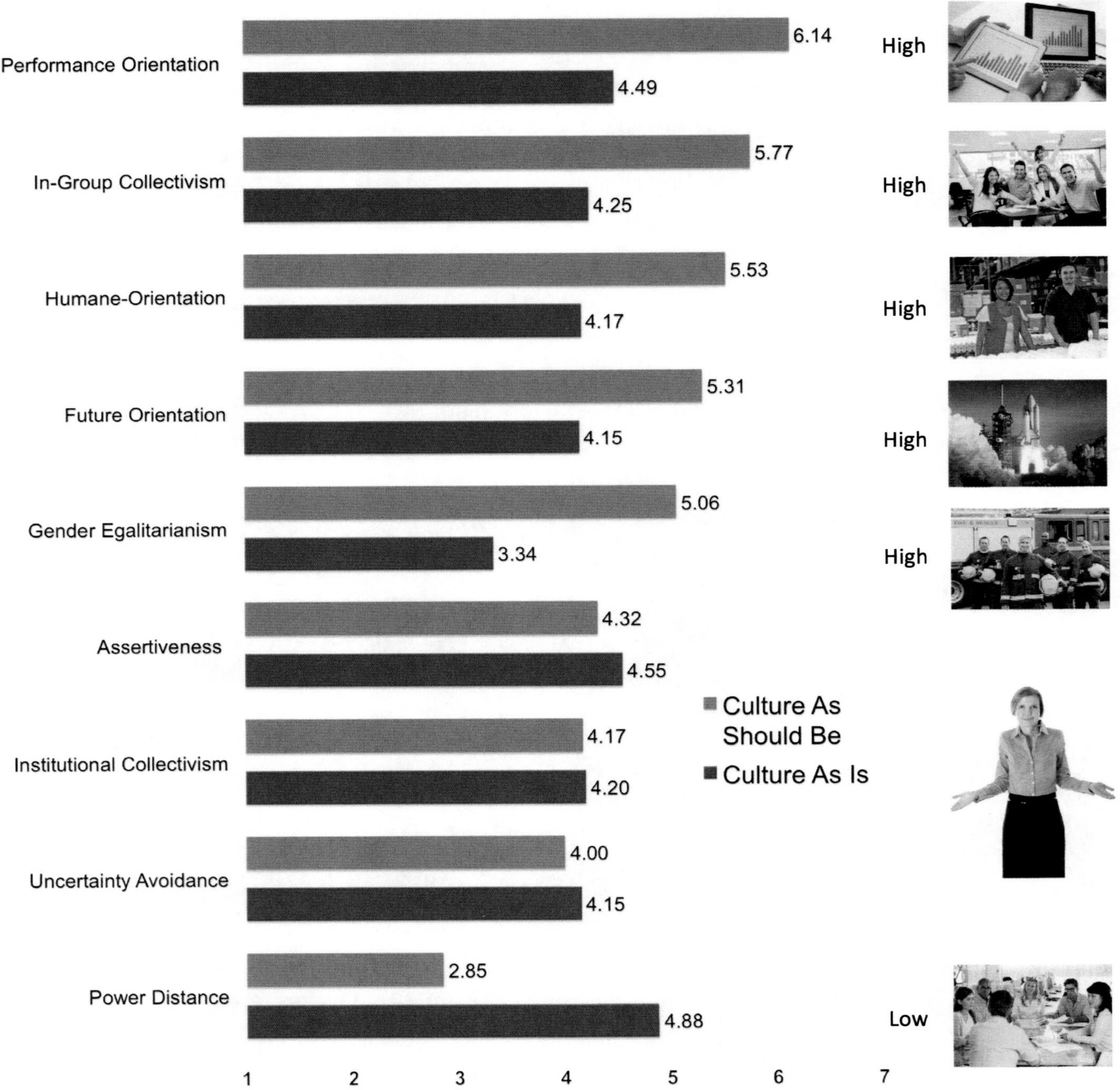

Project GLOBE – Phase 3

CEO Leadership

The primary focus of the second phase of the GLOBE project was what middle managers believed constituted outstanding leadership. These participants didn't rate actual leaders, but, the idea of outstanding leadership.[11]

A primary focus of the third phase of the GLOBE project was to have senior leaders (called the *Top Management Team*) rate the CEO of their organization on actual leadership behaviors. The top management team also rated their own commitment, extra effort and team solidarity. Additionally, the relationships among CEO leadership and the organization's sales performance and industry dominance, relative to similar types of organizations were analyzed.

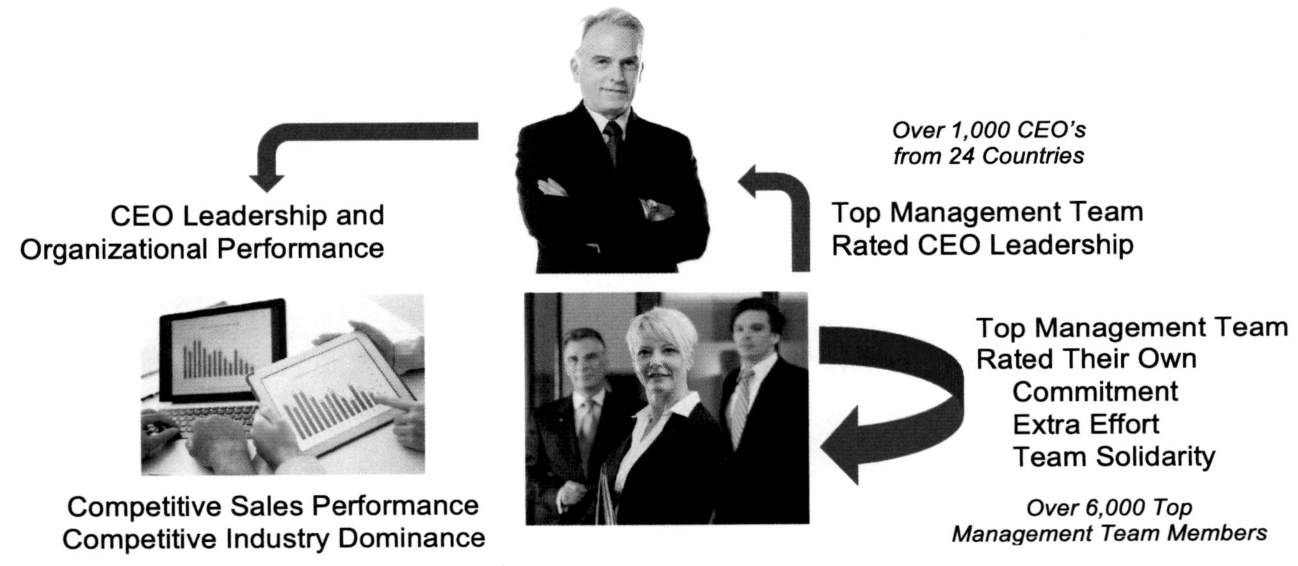

The lead researchers for the third phase of the GLOBE project invited researchers from the 62 societies that participated in the second phase of the GLOBE project. Twenty-four countries had a sufficient number of companies agree to participate in the study. The table below shows the geographic distribution of the organizations that participated.[12]

Participating Countries in Phase 3	Number of Organizations
Austria	40
Azerbaijan	40
Brazil	37
China	97
Estonia	49
Fiji	24
Germany	29
Greece	51
Guatemala	40
India	113
Mexico	42
Netherlands	53

Participating Countries in Phase 3	Number of Organizations
Nigeria	47
Peru	29
Romania	44
Russia	40
Slovenia	40
Solomon Islands	20
Spain	35
Taiwan	40
Turkey	39
Tonga	16
United States	44
Vanuatu	6

Project GLOBE – Phase 3

CEO Leadership

The organizations in the study were heterogeneous along a variety of dimensions.

Ownership of Organization	Number of Organizations Participating	Percentage of Organizations
Founder/Family Owned	485	54.3%
Investor Owned	271	30.4%
Government Owned	87	9.7%
Public/Private Partnership	50	5.6%

Age of Organization	Number of Organizations Participating	Percentage of Organizations
Under 10 years	270	31.4%
10 to 19 years	197	22.9%
20 years and more	392	45.6%

Type of Organization	Number of Organizations Participating	Percentage of Organizations
Products	238	29.8%
Services	340	42.6%
Products and Services	220	27.6%

Project GLOBE – Phase 3

CEO Leadership

The industries represented by the organizations in the study ranged from manufacturing and construction to scientific and health care.

The largest percentage of organizations came from the manufacturing sector, followed by retail trade, finance, insurance and information services.

Industry Sector	Number of Organizations Participating	Percentage of Organizations
Manufacturing	325	38.9%
Retail Trade	74	8.9%
Finance and Insurance	64	7.7%
Information	62	7.4%
Wholesale Trade	49	5.9%
Construction	39	4.7%
Professional, Scientific, and Technical Services	36	4.3%
Accommodation and Food Services	32	3.8%
Transportation and Warehousing	32	3.8%
Health Care and Social Assistance	22	2.6%
Arts, Entertainment, and Recreation	17	2.0%
Real Estate and Rental and Leasing	15	1.8%
Educational Services	14	1.7%
Agriculture, Forestry, Fishing, and Hunting	13	1.6%
Other Services (Except Public Administration)	11	1.3%
Public Administration	10	1.2%
Administrative, Support, Waste Management and Remediation Services	9	1.1%
Mining	8	1.0%
Utilities	3	0.4%
Management of Companies and Enterprises	1	0.1%

Project GLOBE – Phase 3

CEO Leadership

The global means for ratings of CEO leadership are not particularly surprising. As a group, the CEO's tended to be performance oriented, visionary, diplomatic, decisive, ethical, administratively competent and inspirational.

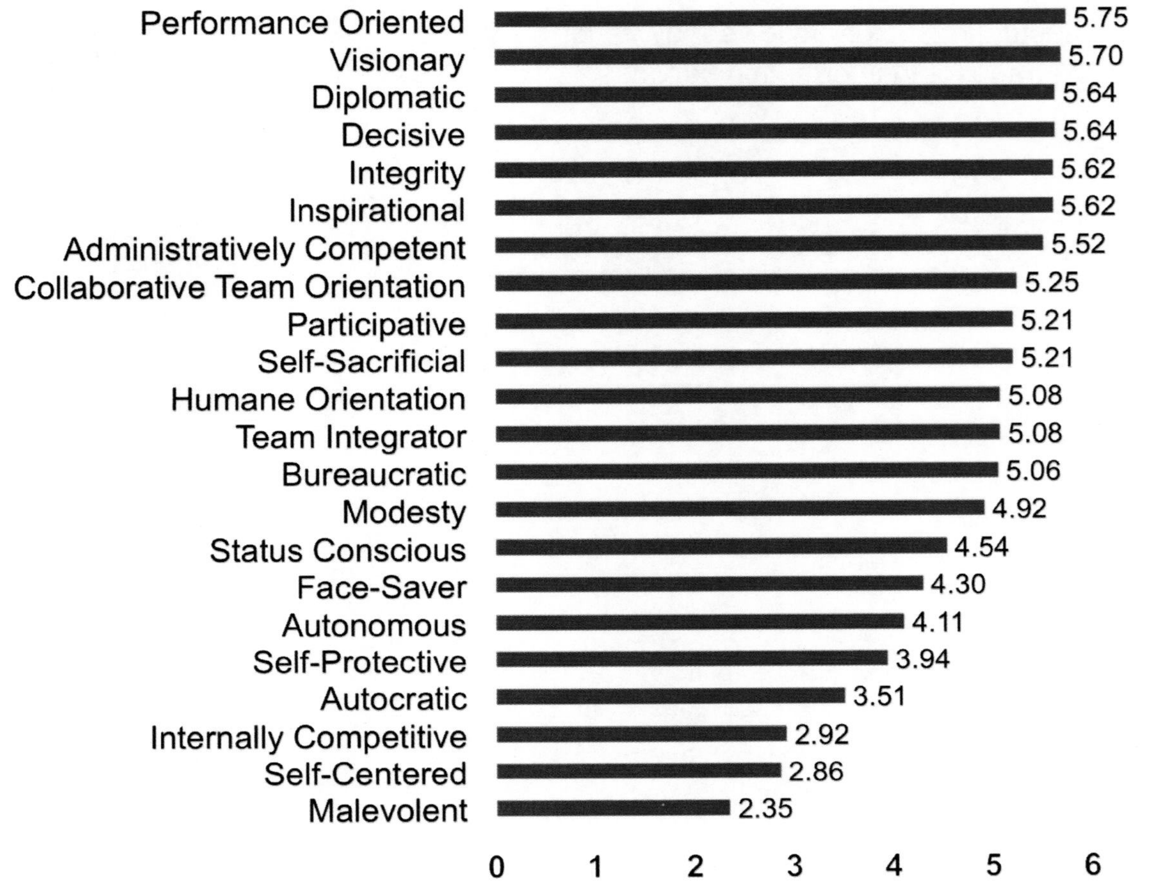

Project GLOBE – Phase 3

CEO Leadership

Generally, United States CEO's were rated less charismatic and autonomous than the global mean. Conversely, United States CEO's were rated more participative, team oriented and humane oriented than the global mean.[13]

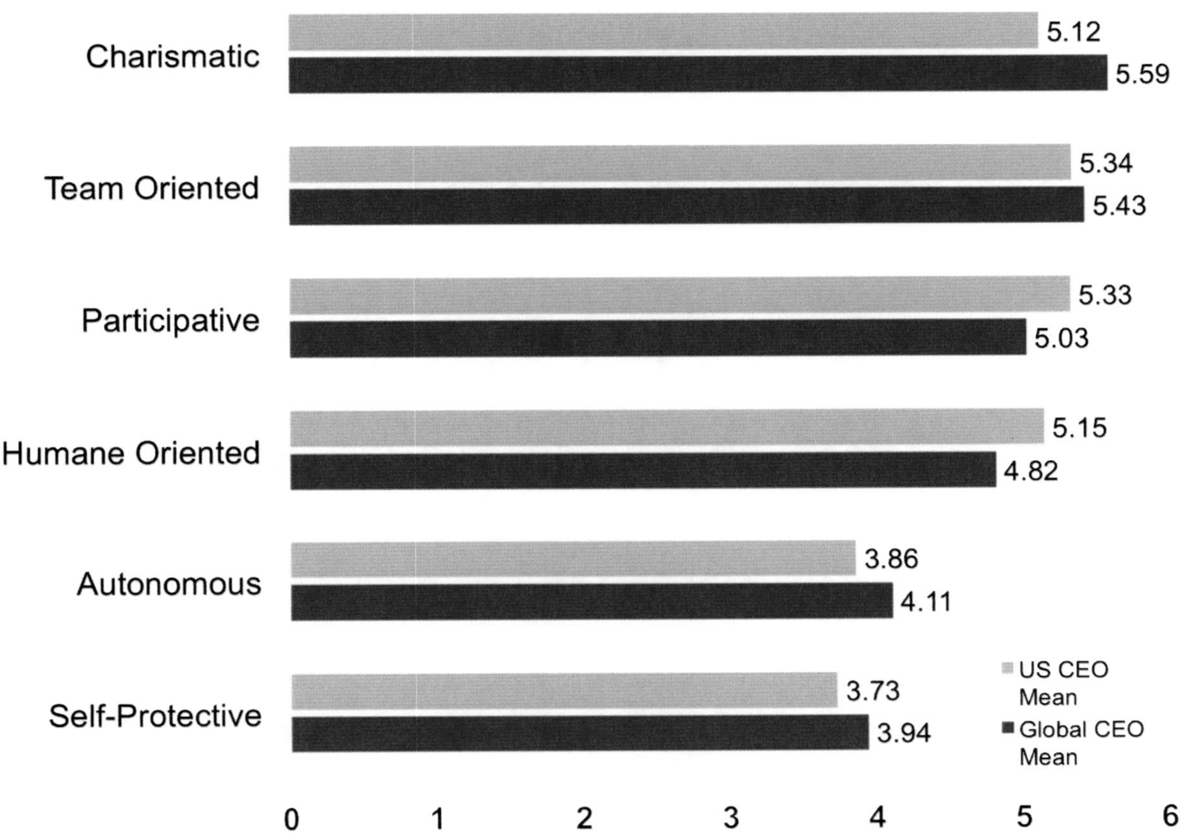

Project GLOBE – Phase 3

CEO Leadership

The chart below compares the global means for how important middle managers felt the first order dimensions of leadership were in the second phase of the GLOBE study paired with the rating of CEO's from the third phase.

Several cautionary notes are in order. First, the data for phase 2 were collected in the late 1990's to early 2000's and the data on CEO leadership were collected in the late 2000's. Additionally, the raters of the CEO's were different participants than the raters of what constituted outstanding leadership in the second phase of the GLOBE study. Finally, the phase 2 participants were rating "ideal" or "desired" characteristics while those in phase 3 were rating actual leaders. Few of us as leaders will ever reach our own definitions of ideal behaviors, never mind those of our followers. The means shown, however, are based only on the phase 2 countries that were also represented in the phase 3 CEO research.

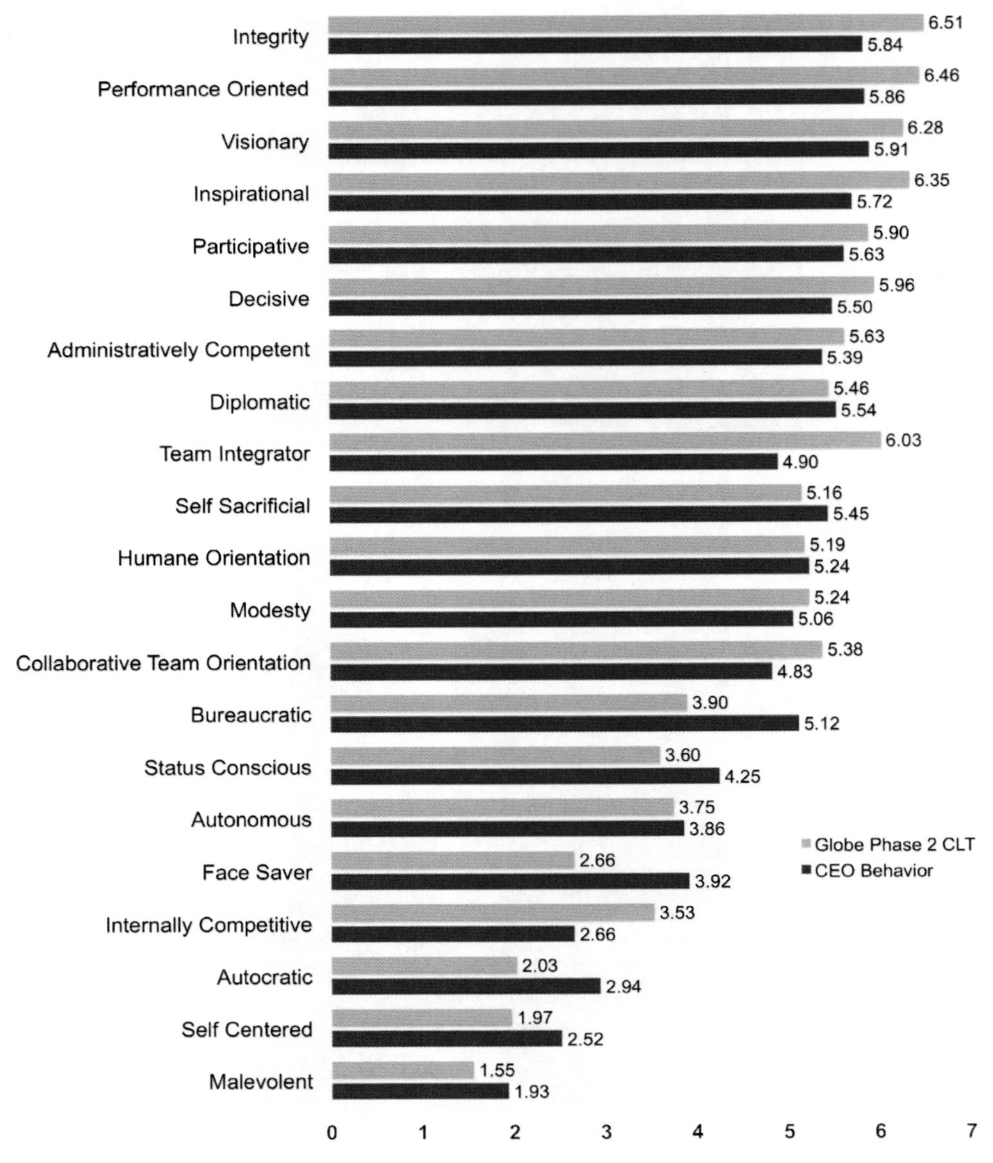

Project GLOBE – Phase 3

CEO Leadership

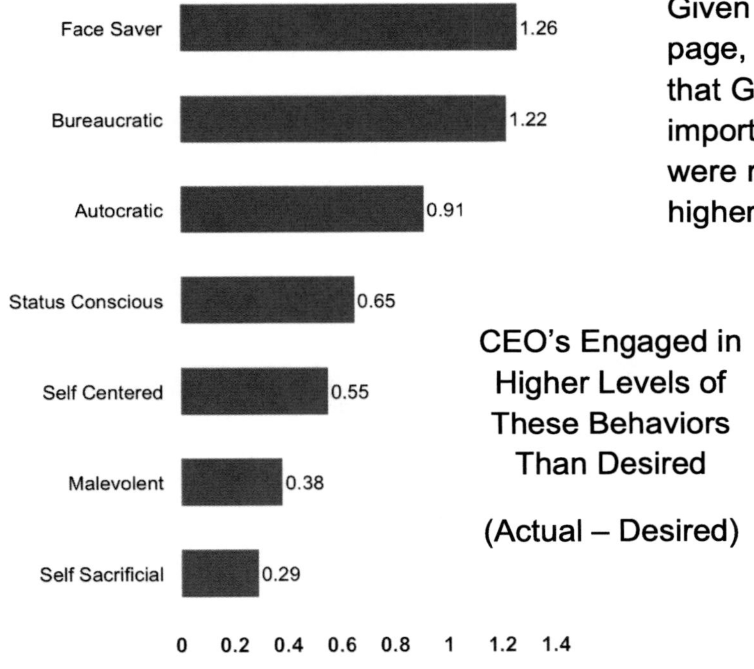

Given the caution explained on the previous page, the graph on the left focuses on areas that GLOBE phase 2 participants rated as less important than how GLOBE phase 3 CEO's were rated. Stated simply – CEO's engaged in higher levels of these behaviors than desired.

CEO's Engaged in Higher Levels of These Behaviors Than Desired

(Actual – Desired)

The graph to the right highlights areas that GLOBE phase 2 participants rated as more important than how GLOBE phase 3 CEO's were rated. Stated simply – CEO's engaged in lower levels of these behaviors than desired.

CEO's Engaged in Lower Levels of These Behaviors Than Desired

(Actual – Desired)

Visionary, -0.37

Decisive, -0.46

Collaborative Team Orientation, -0.55

Performance Oriented, -0.6

Inspirational, -0.63

Integrity, -0.67

Internally Competitive, -0.87

Team Integrator, -1.13

-1.2 -1 -0.8 -0.6 -0.4 -0.2 0

Project GLOBE – Phase 3

Outcome Measures

Internal Outcome Measures

In addition to having the *Top Management Team* rate their CEO's, the members of the top management team also rated their own commitment, extra effort and sense of team solidarity. These outcome measures were considered internal measures. A fourth, composite variable was calculated from the three scores below, and was called top management team dedication.[14]

Top Management Team
Rated Their Own
Commitment
Extra Effort
Team Solidarity

Outcome Variable	Items
Extra Effort	Contributing to the Organization Willingness to Make Personal Sacrifices Intensity of Effort Does the CEO Stimulate My Effort
Commitment	Expecting to Stay with the Organization Optimism about the Organization's Future
Team Solidarity	How Well People Work Together How Well Top Managers Work Together Agreement with the CEO Vision
Top Management Team Dedication	Combination of Extra Effort Commitment Team Solidarity

External Outcome Measures

In addition to the three internal outcome measures, the third phase of project GLOBE measured two external measures. Members of the top management team who identified either finance or accounting as their job functional area, completed the questions below.

Competitive Sales Performance	Competitive Industry Dominance
Sales performance: Please indicate the number that best reflects this organization's performance compared to your major competitors.	To what extent does this organization dominate its industry?
1. __ About 30% or more below major competitors 2. __ Between 20 and 30% below major competitors 3. __ Between 10 and 20% below major competitors 4. __ About the same 5. __ Between 10 and 20% above major competitors 6. __ Between 20 and 30% above major competitors 7. __ Above 30% more than major competitors	1. Very little or not at all 2. Modestly 3. Moderately 4. To a great extent 5. Almost completely

Project GLOBE – Phase 3

CEO Leadership
Leadership and Outcomes

The relationships between the ratings the members of the top management teams gave to CEO's and the self-assessments of each team member's commitment, extra effort and team solidarity are not particularly surprising.

Neither is the composite score of those three, called *Top Management Team Dedication*.

The next three graphs provide the correlation coefficients for CEO leadership ratings and outcomes. We see that CEO behaviors such as being self-centered, autocratic, internally competitive and malevolent are inversely related to desired outcomes among their top management team.

Negatively Correlated Leadership Behaviors

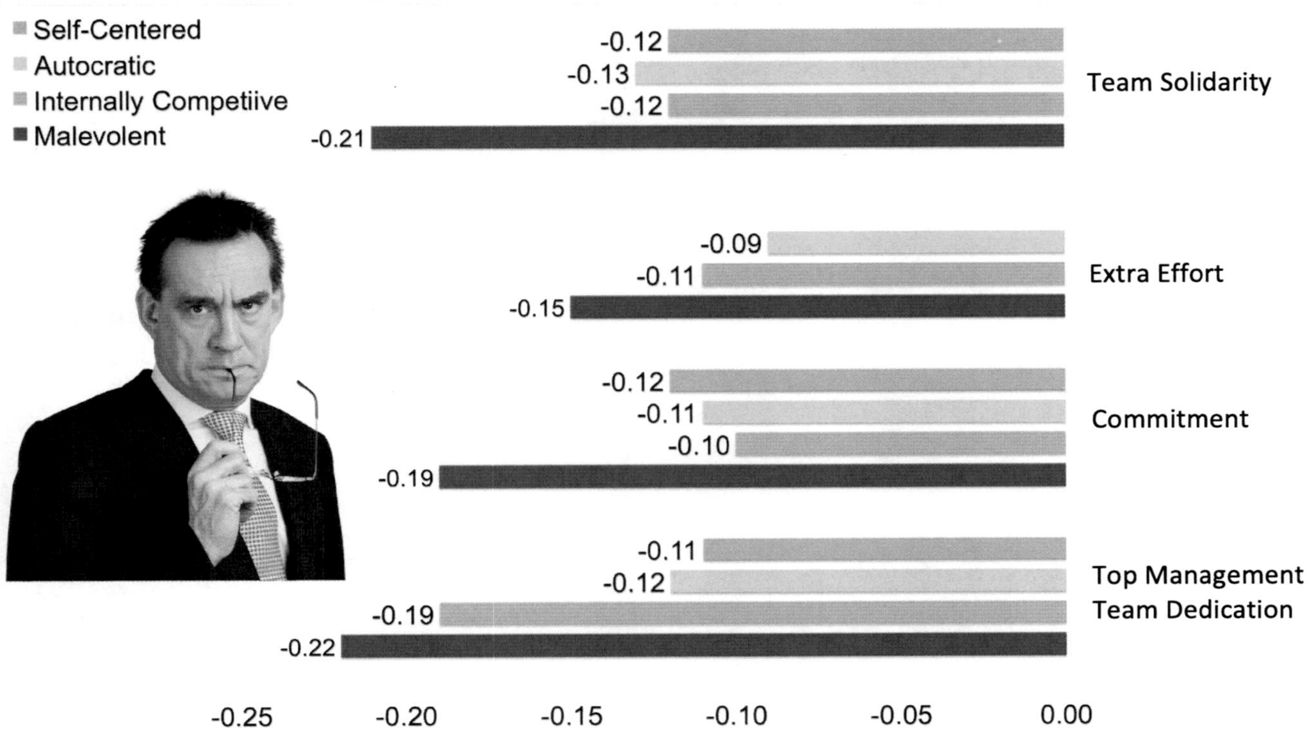

Project GLOBE – Phase 3

CEO Leadership

Leadership and Outcomes

We also see that CEO behaviors such as being inspirational, having integrity and being visionary are positively related to desired top management team outcomes.

Positively Correlated Leadership Behaviors

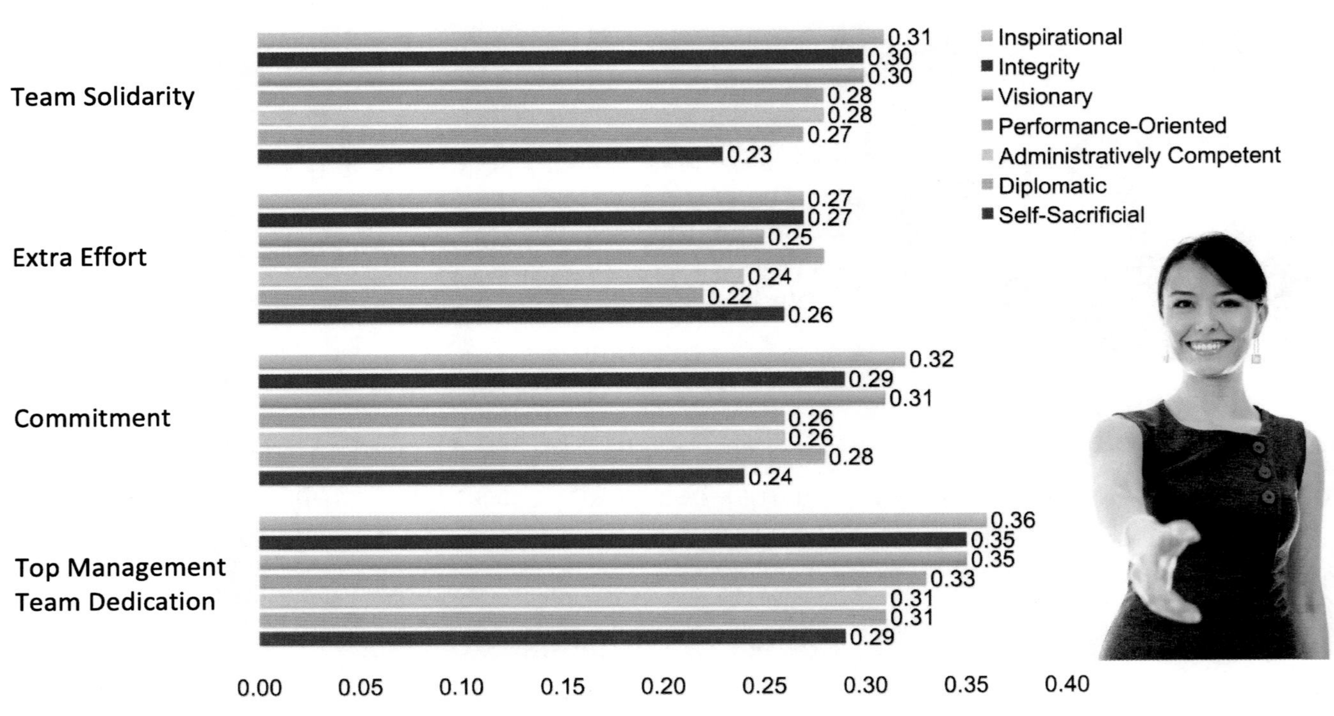

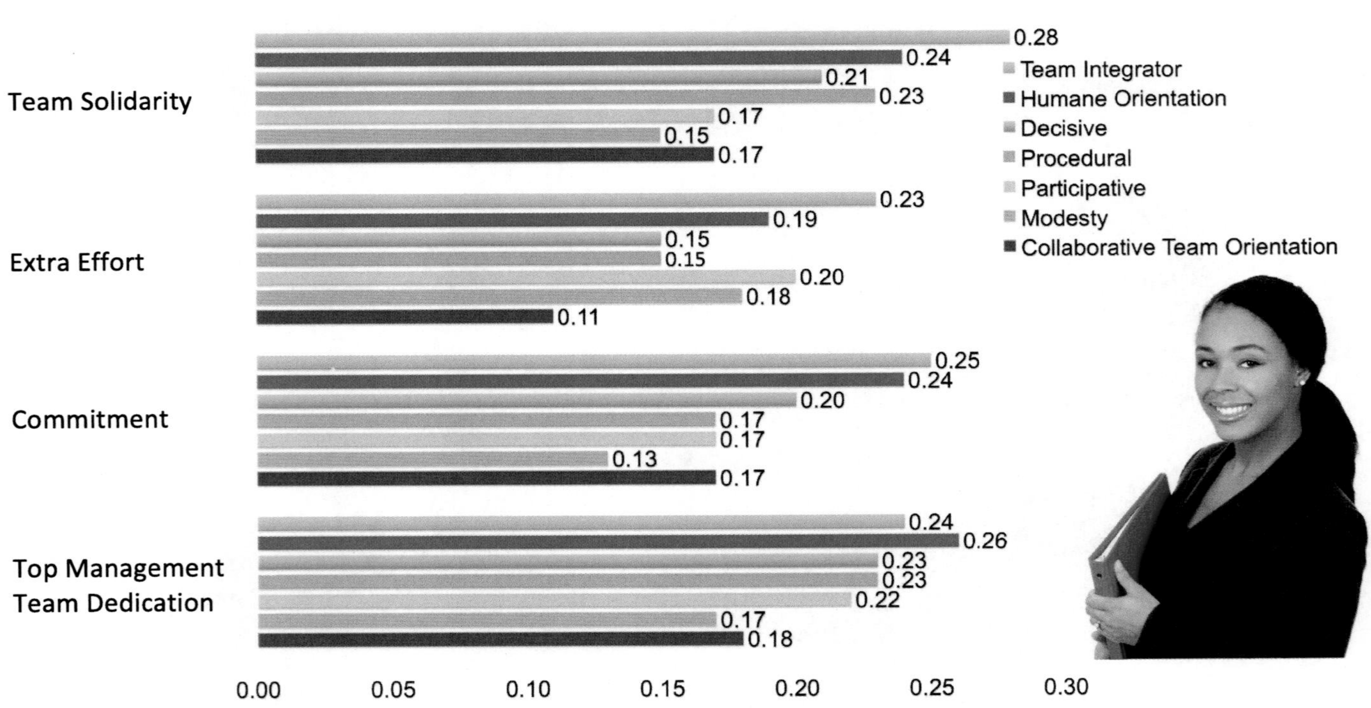

Project GLOBE – Phase 3

CEO Leadership
Leadership and Outcomes

The graphs below illustrate the correlations between the ratings of CEO leadership and the top management teams' dedication scores. This score consisted of the combination of commitment, extra effort and team solidarity. We see that CEO behaviors such as being inspirational, having integrity and vision are moderately, positively correlated with top management teams' dedication scores. We also see negative correlations between behaviors such as being malevolent, internally competitive and autonomous, and top management teams' dedication scores.

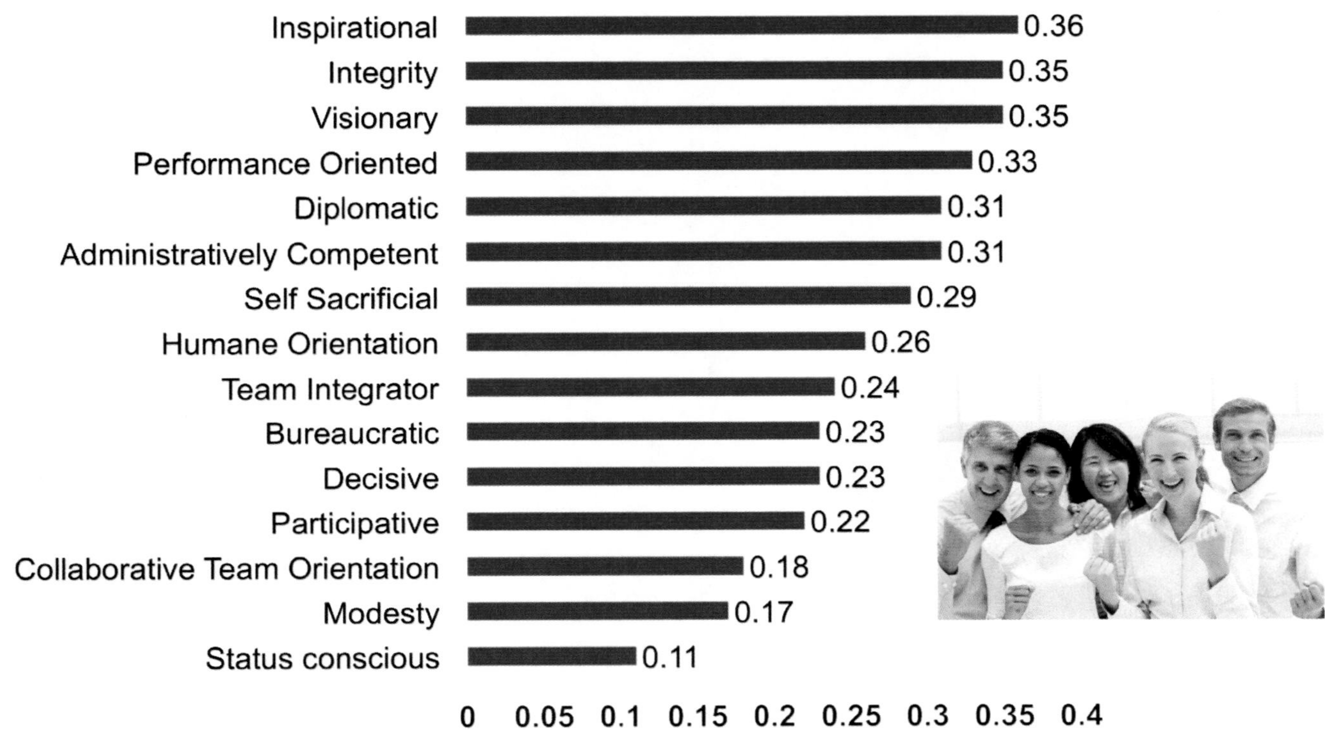

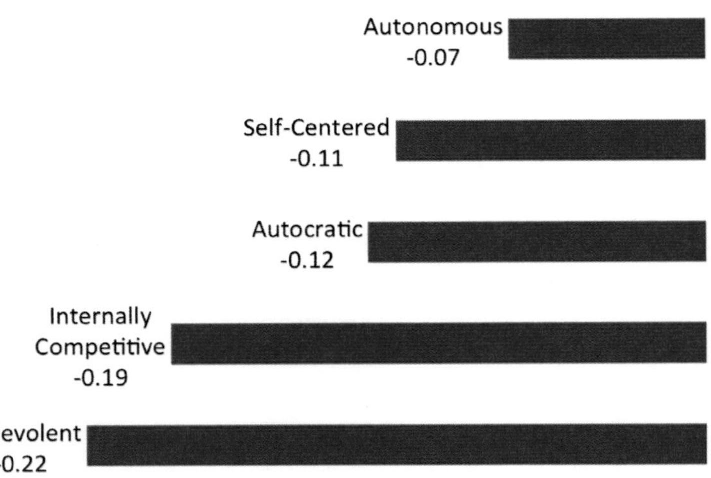

Project GLOBE – Phase 3

CEO Leadership

Leadership and External Outcomes

Each organization's *Sales Performance* and *Competitive Industry Dominance* were measured by assessments on the questions below. The questions were answered by top management team members who identified either finance or accounting as their job functional area.

Competitive Sales Performance	Competitive Industry Dominance
Sales performance: Please indicate the number that best reflects this organization's performance compared to your major competitors.	To what extent does this organization dominate its industry?
1. __ About 30% or more below major competitors 2. __ Between 20 and 30% below major competitors 3. __ Between 10 and 20% below major competitors 4. __ About the same 5. __ Between 10 and 20% above major competitors 6. __ Between 20 and 30% above major competitors 7. __ Above 30% more than major competitors	1. Very little or not at all 2. Modestly 3. Moderately 4. To a great extent 5. Almost completely

Leader behaviors such as being visionary, administratively competent and team oriented were positively related to the company's sales performance.

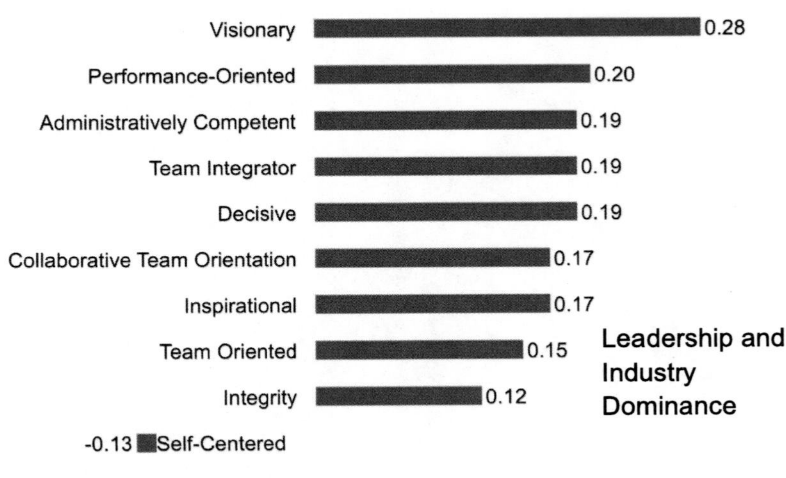

Leader behaviors such as being visionary, administratively competent and team oriented were also positively related to the company's industry dominance. One behavior, being self-centered was inversely related.

Project GLOBE – Phase 3

CEO Leadership

Leadership and Competitive Performance

The researchers also created a composite variable from the variables of competitive sales performance and competitive industry dominance. This variable was called *Competitive Performance*.

Leader behaviors such as being visionary, a team integrator and administratively competent were all related to organizational competitive performance.

Leadership Behaviors and Competitive Performance

Visionary	0.29
Team Integrator	0.26
Administratively Competent	0.24
Decisive	0.23
Inspirational	0.19
Diplomatic	0.16
Integrity	0.16
Performance Oriented	0.16
Collaborative Team Orientation	0.14
Self Sacrificial	0.13
Modesty	0.13

0.00 0.05 0.10 0.15 0.20 0.25 0.30

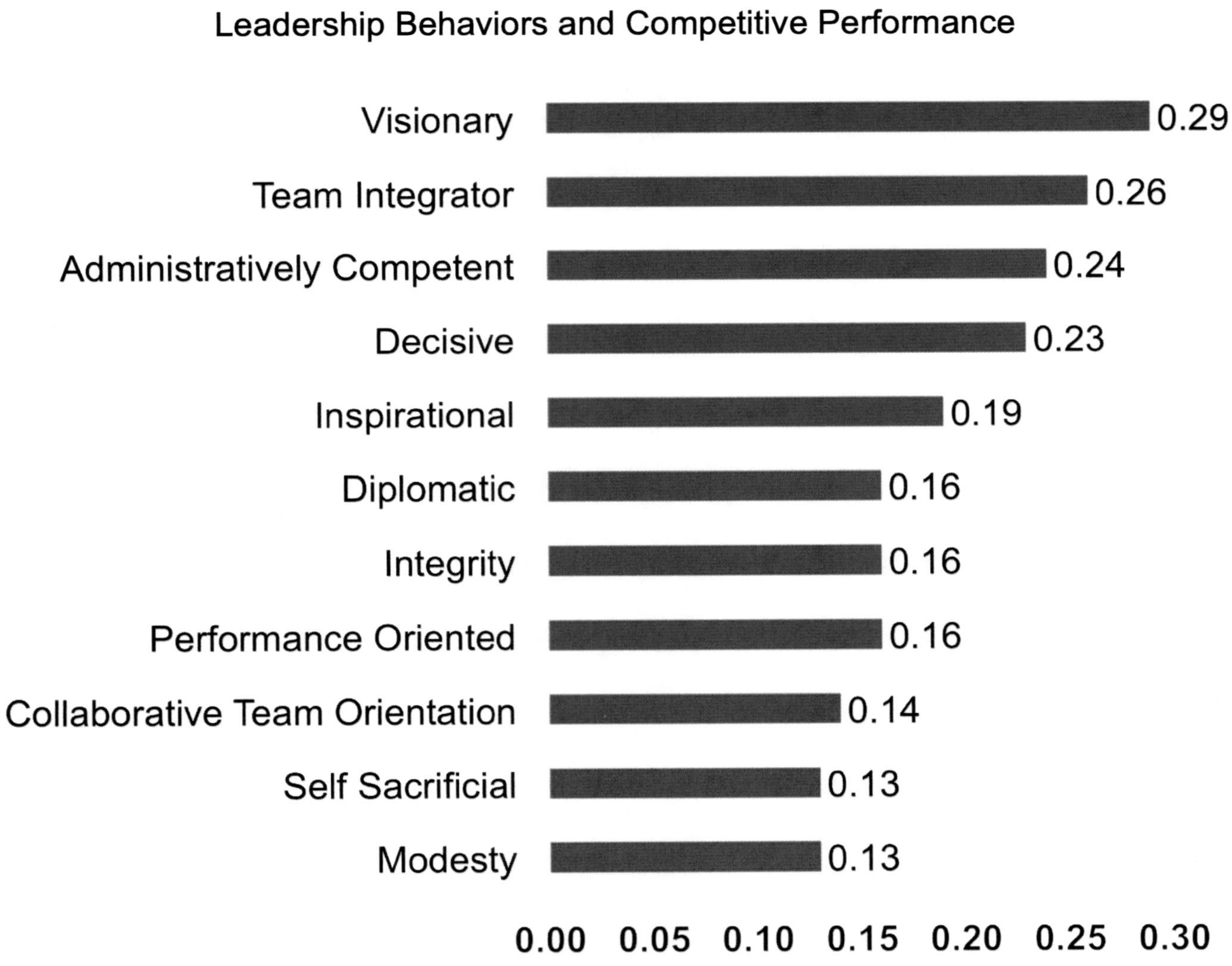

Project GLOBE – Phase 3

CEO Leadership
Superior and Inferior CEO's

Of the 1,015 CEO's studied, 263 CEO's were approximately 1 standard deviation (SD) above all of the other CEO's on top management team dedication and 213 CEO's were approximately 1 SD below the mean. There were 321 organizations that reported organizational competitive performance. There were 99 CEO's who were +1 SD and there were 86 who were -1 SD. Finally, there were 42 CEO's one SD above and 29 one SD below the mean on both top management team dedication and organizational competitive performance. Those 42 CEO's were labeled "Super Superior CEO's" and the other 29 "Super Inferior CEO's."

	Superior CEO's	Inferior CEO's
Top Management Team Dedication	263 CEO's	213 CEO's
Organizational Competitive Performance	99 CEO's	86 CEO's
Top Management Team Dedication And Organizational Competitive Performance	42 Super Superior CEO's	29 Super Inferior CEO's

Project GLOBE – Phase 3

CEO Leadership

Superior and Inferior CEO's

The graph below highlights important trends for the 29 *Super Inferior* and 42 *Super Superior CEO's*. The x-axis is the portion of a standard deviation that, as a group, these *Super Inferior* and Su*per Superior CEO's* varied from the mean of all CEO's in the study. The dependent variable was a composite of overall outcomes – top management team dedication and competitive firm performance.

29 Super Inferior CEO's

42 Super Superior CEO's

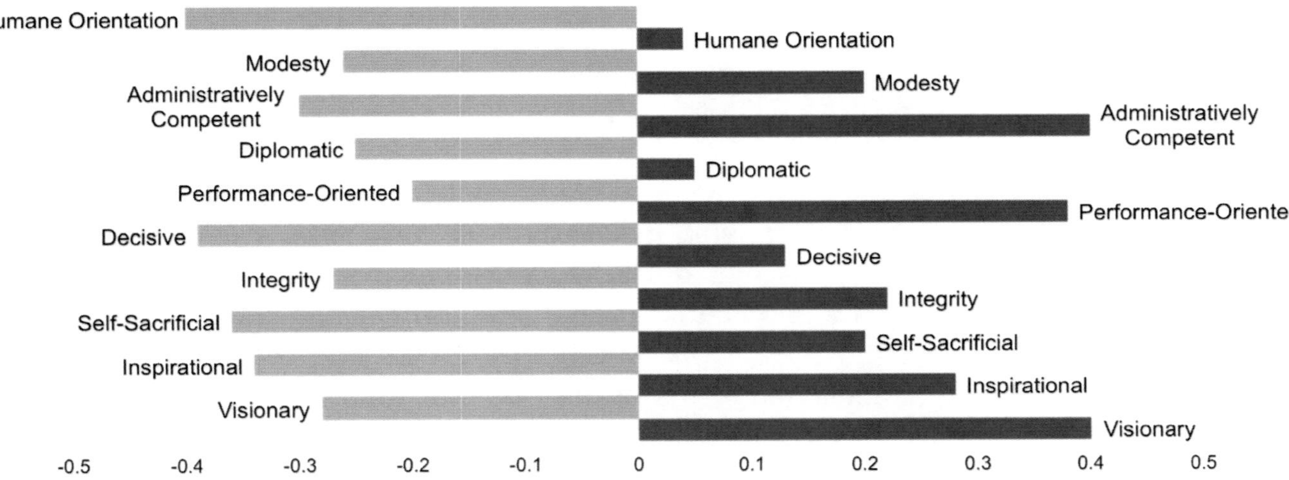

Standard Deviation from the Mean of All CEO's

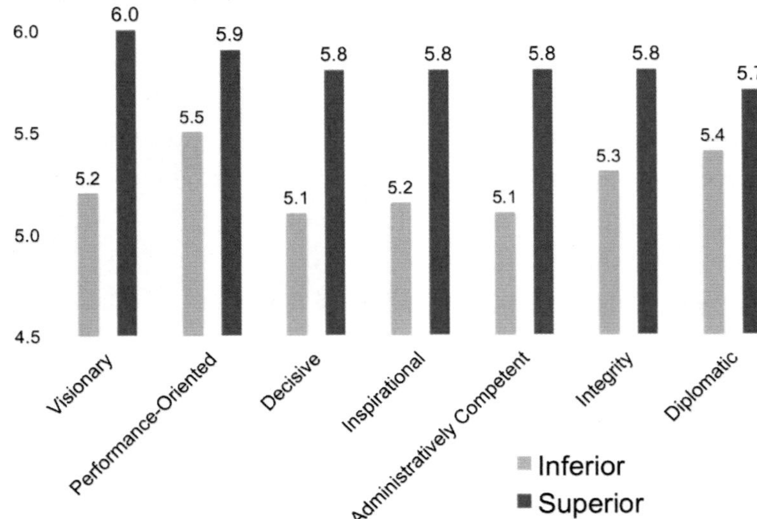

The graph on the left provides the means of the 29 *Super Inferior* and 42 *Super Superior CEO's*. The GLOBE researchers labeled these seven dimensions – *Mission Critical* aspects of leadership.

These dimensions are related to organizational outcomes, and the *Super Superior CEO's* were rated higher on these aspects than the *Super Inferior CEO's.*

Project GLOBE

Phase 2 - Instrument

The next five pages describe the instrument developed for the second phase of the GLOBE study.[15]

Phase 1 – Item Development

Step 1

Culture Scales

The researchers conducted interviews and focus groups in multiple countries. They then developed a series of "tangible" items such as written policies, as well as "intangible" items such as cultural norms and values. For each construct, four versions of the item (question) were written, one for "as is" and one for "should be" culture. Each "as is" and "should be" item was written for the organizational level and the societal level. A total of 371 culture items were written at this stage of development.

Leadership Scales

The researchers wrote 382 items that they believed reflected a variety of traits, skills, abilities and personality characteristics related to leadership emergence and effectiveness.

Q-Sort, Backward and Forward Translations

PhD students and 38 country coordinators conducted a Q-sort in which they attempted to place each question into an a priori category that the question was believed to measure. Items that were categorized 80% of the time into the correct category were retained. However, questions that contained words or phrases that country coordinators indicated were ambiguous or difficult to translate into a particular language used in the study were either re-written or dropped. Finally, backward and forward translation procedures were performed to develop versions of the items in languages germane for administering the survey in multiple countries. At the end of this step, approximately 50% of the items were retained for further testing.

Step 2

The items developed after step 1 were distributed to 877 individuals in 28 countries. The researchers ran a series of exploratory factor analyses, reliability analyses and aggregation analyses on the data collected. The factor analyses on the culture items found seven culture scales that were unidimensional. The seven culture scales were confirmed with four versions of each scale: as is, should be, organizational level and societal level.

The factor analyses on the leadership data found 16 first-order dimensions that, in turn loaded on four second-order dimensions.

Step 3

The items developed during step 1 were next administered to 1,066 individuals from 15 different countries than those that participated in step 2. Factor analyses including confirmatory factor analyses were conducted on these data, and the results generally replicated the results from step 1. Collectivism, however, was honed to include two types of collectivism: institutional and in-group. This resulted in 16 first-order leadership scales and eight first-order culture scales.

Phase 2 – Administration Globally

In phase 2, the leadership and culture questions were administered to 17,370 middle managers from 62 societies. The number of middle managers participating ranged from 27 to 1,790 per country with a mean of 251 participants per country. Among the 62 societies, 951 different organizations were represented. As a method of more accurately capturing societal cultural attitudes, the participating organizations were not multinational organizations.

The organizations came from one of three types of industries. Food processing organizations represented a somewhat traditional labor industry. Financial organizations represented a somewhat traditional service industry. Telecommunications organizations represented a more modern or emerging industry.

After collecting these data, factor analyses identified five additional first-order leadership scales, raising the number of first-order scales from 16 to 21. The number of second-order scales increased from four to six.

Additional factor analysis also found that the original component of gender egalitarianism produced a better fit when it was scored as two components: gender egalitarianism and assertiveness. This resulted in nine cultural dimensions.

The mean comparative fit indexes for the leadership and culture scales are shown below.

Mean Comparative Fit Indexes for Culture and Leadership Scales

	Overall	As Is Culture	Should Be Culture
Organizational		.93	.94
Societal		.89	.95
Leadership	.92		

Project GLOBE

Phase 2 - Instrument

The internal reliability, measured by the Cronbach Alpha, and the inter-rater reliability for each of the leadership dimensions are shown below.

	Internal Consistency (Cronbach Alpha)	Inter-Rater Reliability (Intraclass Correlation)
Charismatic	**.95**	**.98**
First Order Ranges	.68 - .93	.88 - .92
Team Oriented	**.93**	**.96**
First Order Ranges	.64 - .88	.86 - .93
Participative	**.85**	**.95**
First Order Ranges	.71 - .79	.91 - .92
Humane Oriented	**.76**	**.93**
First Order Ranges	.61 - .66	.90
Autonomous	**.59**	**.87**
Self Protective	**.93**	**.98**
First Order Ranges	.71 - .85	.88 - .95

Instrument Sections

Section 1 measures what is typically called "as is" culture. The directions guide the participant as follows:

> *In this section, we are interested in your beliefs about what the norms, values, and practices are in the organization in which you work as a manager. In other words, we are interested in the way your organization is—not the way you think it should be.*

Section 1 has 31 questions, answered on a seven-point scale. The labels representing the seven-point scale vary by question.

1	2	3	4	5	6	7
Strongly Disagree			Neither Agree Nor Disagree			Strongly Agree

Section 3 measures what is typically called "should be" culture. The directions guide the participant as follows:

> *In this section, we are interested in your beliefs about what the norms, values, and practices should be in the organization in which you work as a manager.*

Section 3 has 41 questions, answered on the same seven-point scale as section 1.

Project GLOBE

Phase 2 - Instrument

Sections 2 and 4 are the implicit leadership sections. The instructions for both sections are as follows:

> *You are probably aware of people in your organization or industry who are exceptionally skilled at motivating, influencing, or enabling you, others, or groups to contribute to the success of the organization or task. In this country, we might call such people "outstanding leaders."*
>
> *On the following pages are several behaviors and characteristics that can be used to describe leaders. Each behavior or characteristic is accompanied by a short definition to clarify its meaning.*
>
> *Using the above description of outstanding leaders as a guide, rate the behaviors and characteristics on the following pages. To do this, on the line next to each behavior or characteristic, write the number from the scale below that best describes how important that behavior or characteristic is for a leader to be outstanding.*

Sections 2 and 4 each contain 56 leadership characteristics participants rate using the following scale.

1 = This behavior or characteristic **greatly inhibits** a person from being an outstanding leader.
2 = This behavior or characteristic **somewhat inhibits** a person from being an outstanding leader.
3 = This behavior or characteristic **slightly inhibits** a person from being an outstanding leader.
4 = This behavior or characteristic **has no impact** on whether a person is an outstanding leader.
5 = This behavior or characteristic **contributes slightly** to a person being an outstanding leader.
6 = This behavior or characteristic **contributes somewhat** to a person being an outstanding leader.
7 = This behavior or characteristic **contributes greatly** to a person being an outstanding leader.

Section 5 contains 27 demographic questions.

Availability

The *GLOBE National Culture, Organizational Culture and Leadership Scales* is available in two versions. The sections 2 and 4 leadership instructions are the same in both versions.

In the version called the *Alpha Questionnaire* the as is and should be culture questions are asked about "*Your Work Organization*."

In the version called the *Beta Questionnaire* the as is and should be culture questions are asked about "*Your Society*."

As of 2014, New Mexico State University provided scoring instructions and English, Spanish (Columbia) and French versions of the Alpha and Beta questionnaires.

http://business.nmsu.edu/programs-centers/globe/instruments/

As of 2014, the instrument was free for research use.

Project GLOBE
Phase 3 - Instrument

Leadership Scales

For the phase 3 CEO research, the researchers began with the 112 implicit leadership questions from the GLOBE phase 2 instrument. Generally, these questions were "tweaked" where needed to describe the type of actions that would be associated with these constructs in *actual leaders*. In some cases, new questions were generated. The table below illustrates phase 2 and 3 questions that were essentially the same question, as well as two examples of new questions.

Phase	Question
2	Visionary = Has a vision and imagination of the future
3	Clearly articulates his/her vision of the future
2	Enthusiastic = Demonstrates and imparts strong positive emotions for work
3	Demonstrates and imparts strong positive emotions for work
2	Intra-group conflict avoider = Avoids disputes with members of his or her group
3	Avoids disputes with members of his or her group
3 (New)	Will reconsider decisions on the basis of recommendations of those who report to him/her
3 (New)	Communicates his/her performance expectations for group members

In all, 142 items were generated for the 21 first-order dimensions of leadership. From this initial pool of items, a modified Q-sort was conducted to determine the final set of items to be used for the leadership behavior scales. Raters placed the questions into the first-order category they believed the question measured. Following the Q-sort procedure, these items were then subjected to a series of statistical analyses. Of the initial 142 leadership behavioral items, 118 items were retained and used in the phase 3 research.

Project GLOBE

Phase 3 - Instrument

Exploratory Factor Analyses

Approximately six top management team member ratings per CEO were averaged (aggregated) to get the mean leadership rating of each CEO. The researchers conducted 21, pooled within-country exploratory factor analyses. To do this, they first standardized the average CEO/organizational aggregated leadership scores. Eleven of the 21 scales loaded on two factors and 10 loaded on a single factor.

For eight of the scales that loaded on two factors, the correlations between the two factors were in the range of .35 to .53. The most problematic scales were status conscious, self sacrificial and face saver. The researchers also conducted two types of factor analyses to analyze how well the aggregated CEO ratings fit each dimension of leadership. The Double-Scaled Euclidian Fit Index and the Kernel Smooth Distance Fit Index were calculated. Cronbach Alpha scores were also calculated for each of the leadership dimensions. The dimensions of status conscious, internally competitive and face saver had low Cronbach Alpha scores. The dimension of status conscious also had a low fit index score.

Outcome Scales

The researchers first reviewed the constructs of worker motivation and commitment, social identification, and trust and cooperation. Eleven items were generated to measure these ideas and an expert panel was able to successfully classify 10 of the 11 questions into the categories of extra effort, commitment and team solidarity. The Cronbach Alpha scores and fit indexes are shown at the bottom of this table.

	Internal Consistency (Cronbach Alpha)	Double-Scaled Euclidian Fit Index	Kernel Smooth Distance Fit Index
	> .80	> .90	> .90
Visionary, Inspirational, Integrity, Autocratic, Team Integrator, Administratively Competent, Participative, Malevolent, Performance-Oriented			
	> .70	> .90	> .85
Collaborative Team Orientation, Diplomatic, Humane Orientation, Self-Centered, Procedural, Decisive			
	> .55	> .85	> .80
Self-Sacrificial, Modesty			
	> .45	> .85	> .80
Face Saver			
	.22 to .31	.62 to .89	.50 to .94
Status Conscious, Internally Competitive			
Commitment	0.83	0.93	0.90
Extra Effort	0.76	0.90	0.84
Team Solidarity	0.81	0.93	0.91

Project GLOBE

Summary

GLOBE Phase 2 and 3 Means

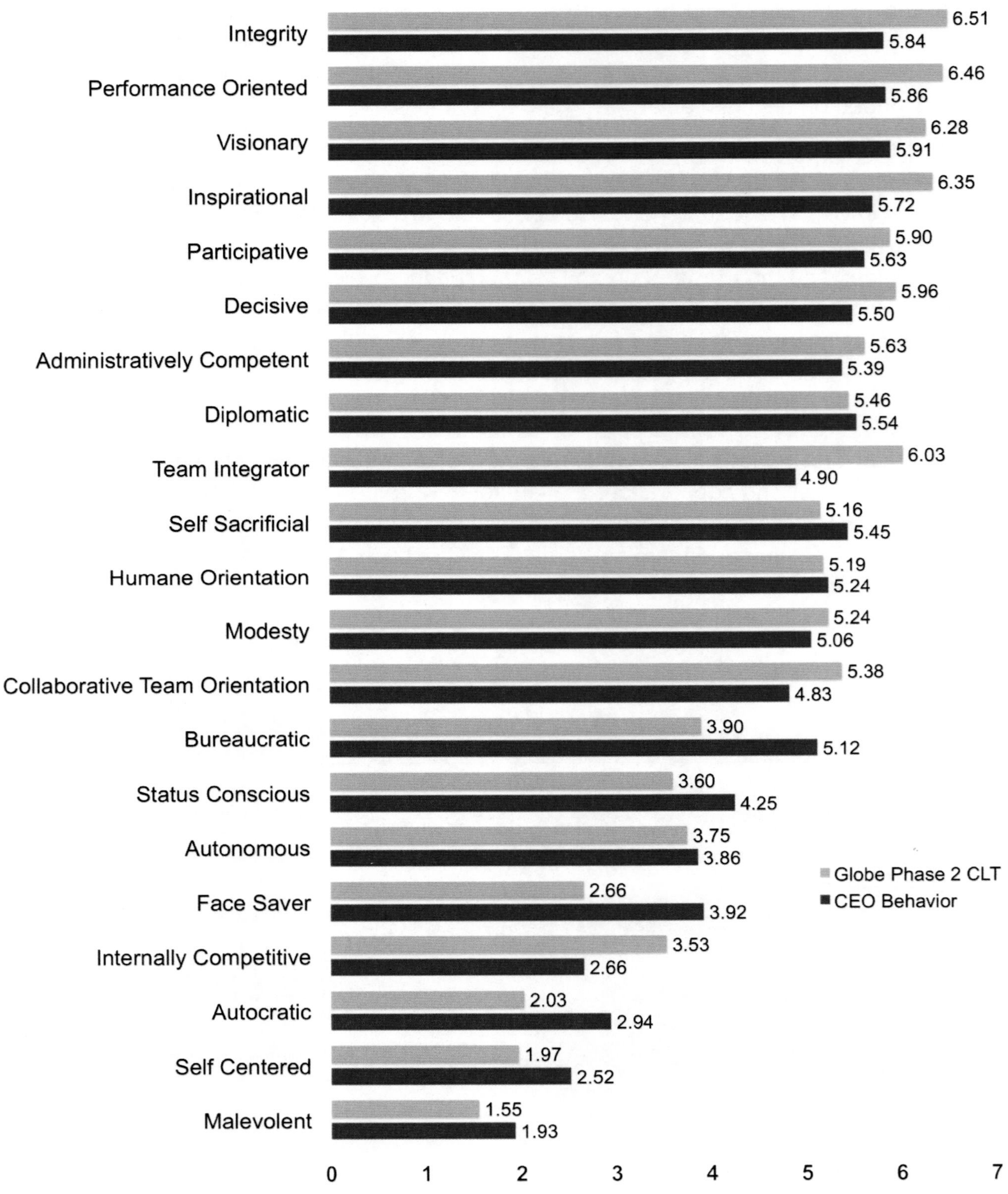
Integrity
6.51
5.84
Performance Oriented
6.46
5.86
Visionary
6.28
5.91
Inspirational
6.35
5.72
Participative
5.90
5.63
Decisive
5.96
5.50
Administratively Competent
5.63
5.39
Diplomatic
5.46
5.54
Team Integrator
6.03
4.90
Self Sacrificial
5.16
5.45
Humane Orientation
5.19
5.24
Modesty
5.24
5.06
Collaborative Team Orientation
5.38
4.83
Bureaucratic
3.90
5.12
Status Conscious
3.60
4.25
Autonomous
3.75
3.86
Face Saver
2.66
3.92
Internally Competitive
3.53
2.66
Autocratic
2.03
2.94
Self Centered
1.97
2.52
Malevolent
1.55
1.93
0
1
2
3
4
5
6
7
Globe Phase 2 CLT
CEO Behavior

Project GLOBE

Summary

Although the volume of empirical data from the two phases of the GLOBE project is staggering, the chart on the preceding page speaks volumes. Based on 17,000 middle manager and 6,000 top management team assessments, the results might readily be paraphrased in four statements.

1. **Trust** "Ensure we can trust you."

2. **Participative Motivation** "Inspire us with your vision by allowing us to participate in that process. Don't autocratically tell us your vision."

3. **Altruism** "Walk the walk by being self-sacrificial and avoiding face-saving, self-centered and status-conscious behaviors."

4. **Humane Performance** "We want to have pride in our work. Be performance oriented and decisive, however, without losing your modesty, diplomacy and sense of humanity."

Project GLOBE

Notes

[1] These definitions for the six and 21 aspects of leadership are contained in various places in House, R. J., and Global Leadership and Organizational Behavior Effectiveness Research Program. (2004). *Culture, leadership, and organizations: The GLOBE study of 62 societies*. Thousand Oaks, Calif: Sage Publications.

[2] These data are based on House et al.'s, 1999 article in *The Leadership Quarterly*. Hartog, D. N. den, House, R.J., Ruiz-Quintanilla, S.A., Dorfman, P. W., and Koopman, P. L. (1999). Culture specific and cross-culturally generalizable implicit leadership theories: Are attributes of charismatic/transformational leadership universally endorsed? *The Leadership Quarterly*, 10, 219-256.

Similar data are not provided in the 2004 book. House, R. J., Global Leadership and Organizational Behavior Effectiveness Research Program. (2004). *Culture, leadership and organizations: The GLOBE study of 62 societies*. Thousand Oaks, Calif: Sage Publications.

These data are on a slightly smaller sample of than those reported in the 2004 book. The data came from 15,022 middle managers from 60 different societies/cultures. The number of respondents by country ranged from 27 to 1,790 with an average per country of 250 respondents. The middle managers represent a total of 779 different local (i.e., non-multinational) organizations from one of three industries (financial industry, food industry, and telecommunication industry).

[3] Mankowski, E. S., Galvez, G. and Glass, N. (2011). Interdisciplinary linkage of community psychology and cross-cultural psychology: History, values and an illustrative research and action project on intimate partner violence. *American Journal of Community Psychology, 47*(1/2), 127-143.

[4] Hofstede, G. (2001). *Culture's consequences: Comparing values, behaviors, institutions, and organizations across nations, 2nd edition*. Thousand Oaks, CA: Sage Publications, Inc.

[5] Hofstede, G. (1980). *Culture's consequences: International differences in work-related values*. London: Sage; Hofstede, G. (2001) and Hofstede, G. (2001). *Culture's consequences: Comparing values, behaviors, institutions, and organizations across nations, 2nd edition*. Thousand Oaks, CA: Sage Publications, Inc.

[6] All nine of the "lower tend to" and "higher tend to" tables in this chapter were compiled from House, R. J., Global Leadership and Organizational Behavior Effectiveness Research Program. (2004). *Culture, leadership, and organizations: The GLOBE study of 62 societies*. Thousand Oaks, Calif: Sage Publications.

[7] None of the "observing in the workplace" tables are from the GLOBE study. These examples for readers of this book were developed by several of the contributing authors.

[8] The data reported for all nine "Leadership and Culture" tables in this chapter are taken from the corresponding culture chapter in House, R. J., Global Leadership and Organizational Behavior Effectiveness Research Program. (2004). *Culture, leadership, and organizations: The GLOBE study of 62 societies.* Thousand Oaks, Calif: Sage Publications.

The GLOBE study conducted hierarchical linear modeling (HLM) for dimensions of leadership and culture. This method identifies the total amount of variance in the cultural (dependent) variable accounted for by leadership preference at the individual, organizational, industrial (food service, finance, telecommunication) and societal levels. The R^2 data are the percentage of variance accounted for at either the organizational or societal level. The HLM coefficients are the single cluster dimension coefficients for the cultural values scores from Table 21.10.

[9] In chapter 7, we reviewed the idea of a correlation. In a regression, the R^2 is the correlation (the r) multiplied by itself (squared), and then multiplied by 100. We generally use the R^2 value to discuss the "variance" in scores.

While more complicated than this example, lets assume we ran a multiple regression to predict how satisfied followers were with their jobs in an organization. We included in our regression their nine scores of how they rated the organizational culture (as is culture).

The regression model resulted in collectivism culture being assigned an R^2 of .25.

We could make a statement such as "Twenty-five percent of the variance in follower job satisfaction can be explained by their rating of the organization's collectivist culture."

To try to understand this, imagine that a colleague looked at the scores for job satisfaction and remarked, "wow, do these scores vary a lot. Some workers are a 1, others are a 3 and others are a 5, they're all over the range of job satisfaction scores."

You could explain that "twenty-five percent of that variance in job satisfaction is related to their attitudes about the collectivist culture." (R^2 = .25).

[10] While the GLOBE study provided HLM coefficients for the organizational level preferences and leadership preferences, it did not provide the organizational level mean cultural preferences for each country, only the societal level means.

Project GLOBE

Notes

[11] The data for this section is contained in House, R. J. and Global Leadership and Organizational Behavior Effectiveness Research Program. (2014). *Strategic leadership across cultures: The GLOBE study of CEO leadership behavior and effectiveness in 24 countries.*

[12] The GLOBE phase 3 data come from: House, R. J. and Global Leadership and Organizational Behavior Effectiveness Research Program. (2014). *Strategic leadership across cultures: The GLOBE study of CEO leadership behavior and effectiveness in 24 countries*. Thousand Oaks, California: SAGE Publications, Inc.

[13] No statistical test was reported concerning confidence levels for these differences.

[14] The actual questions are provided in House, R. J. and Global Leadership and Organizational Behavior Effectiveness Research Program. (2014). *Strategic leadership across cultures: The GLOBE study of CEO leadership behavior and effectiveness in 24 countries*. Thousand Oaks, California: SAGE Publications, Inc.

[15] The methodology used to develop the phase 2 instrument is described in House, R. J., Global Leadership and Organizational Behavior Effectiveness Research Program. (2004). *Culture, leadership, and organizations: The GLOBE study of 62 societies*. Thousand Oaks, Calif: Sage Publications.

The methodology used to develop the phase 3 instrument is described in House, R. J., and Global Leadership and Organizational Behavior Effectiveness Research Program. (2014). *Strategic leadership across cultures: The GLOBE study of CEO leadership behavior and effectiveness in 24 countries*. Thousand Oaks, California: SAGE Publications, Inc.

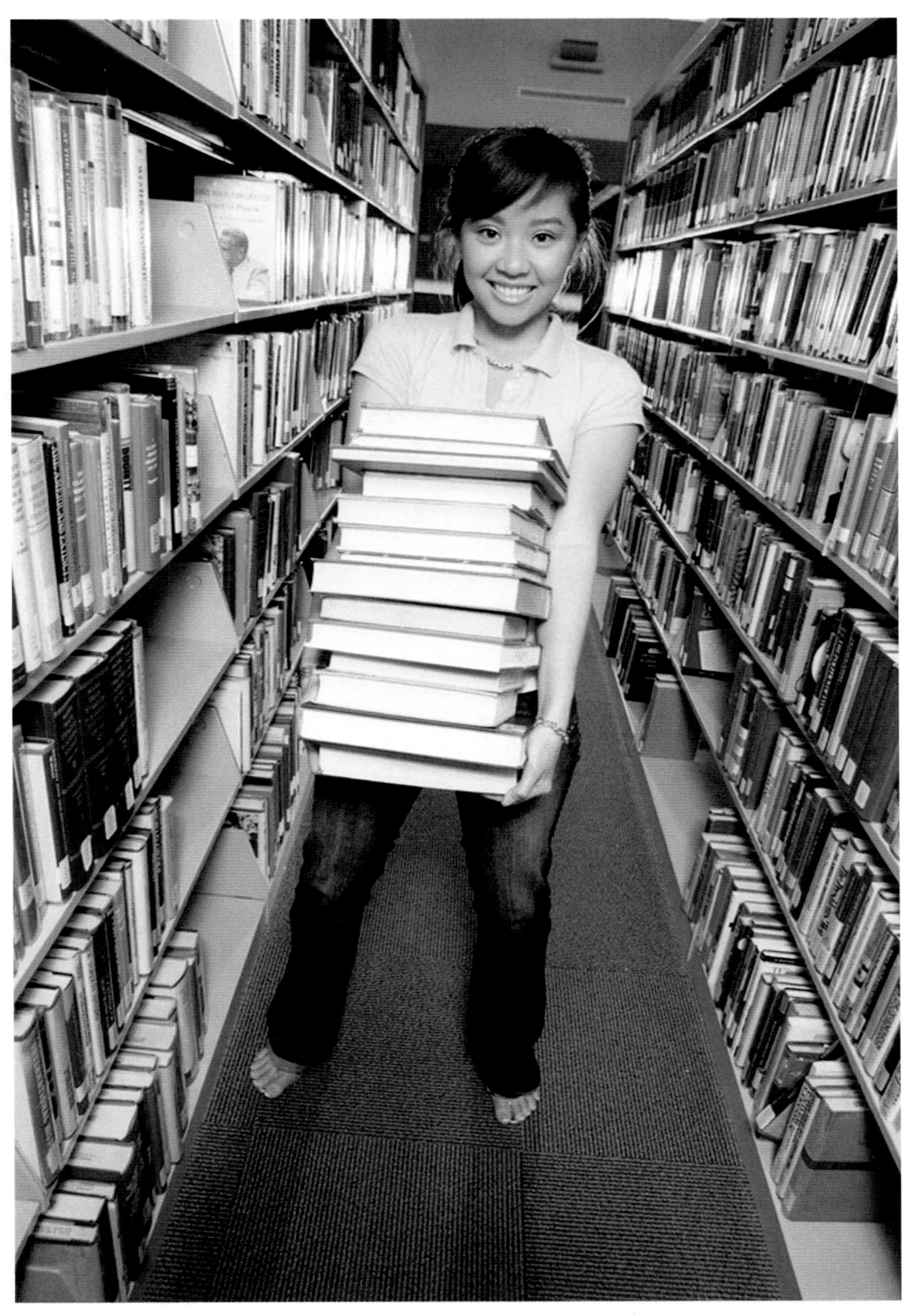

Chapter 9
Servant Leadership

Servant Leadership

Introduction

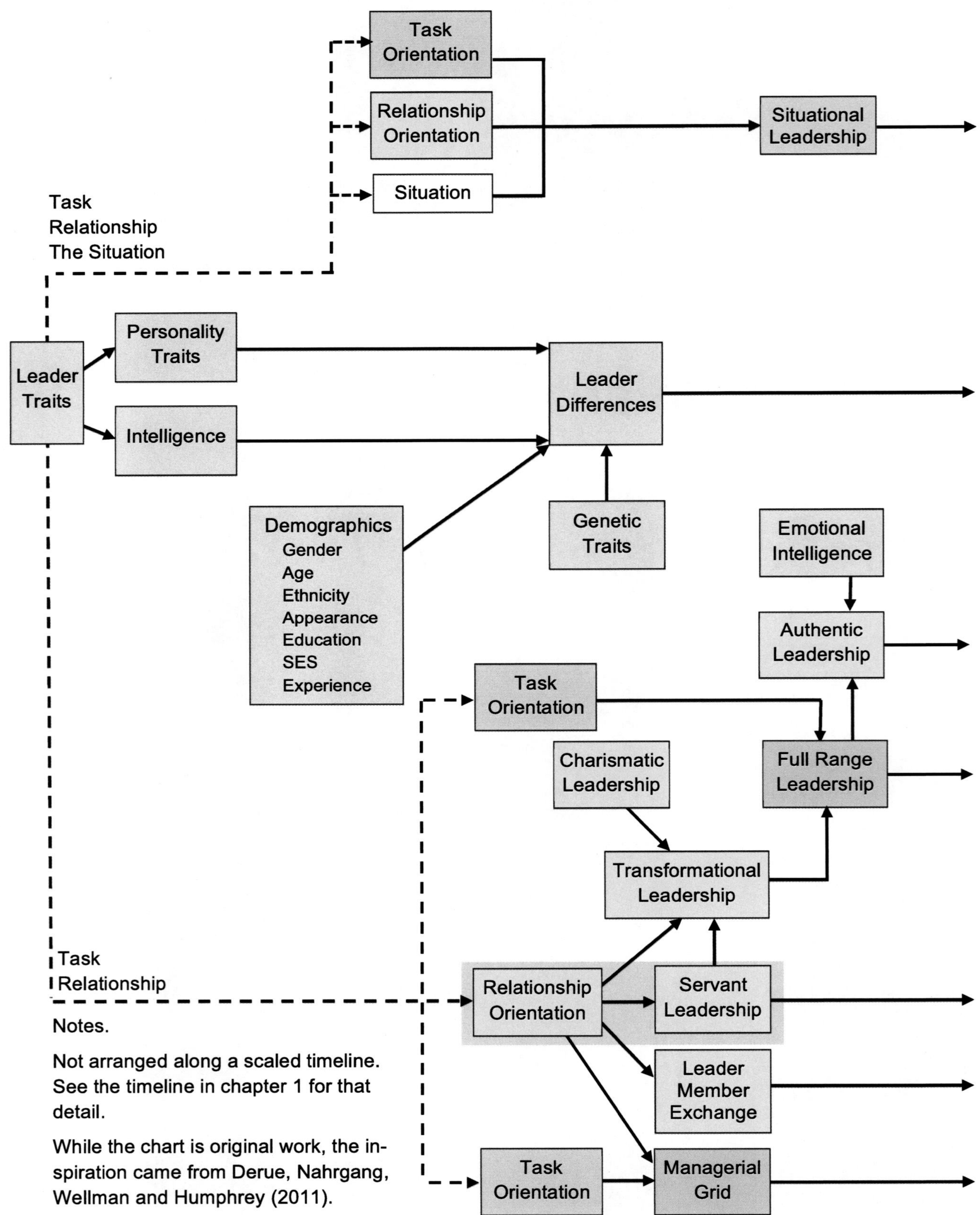

Notes.

Not arranged along a scaled timeline. See the timeline in chapter 1 for that detail.

While the chart is original work, the inspiration came from Derue, Nahrgang, Wellman and Humphrey (2011).

Servant Leadership

Introduction

If one were asked, "Do you believe in freedom?" an instinctual response might be "yes." If a finer point were put on the question, such as "Do you believe in the freedom to take whatever you want from a store without paying?" the response might be different.

What is occurring, is that a broad-sweeping philosophy is being tested against the constraints of the "real world." In this case, the philosophies of freedom and responsibility are intersecting. This more specific application would require a more specific definition of "freedom."

At the philosophical level, the idea of being a servant leader to followers is appealing. When one begins to pose real world questions such as:

What, specifically, does servant leadership entail?
How do we know if someone is high or low on servant leadership?
Does servant leadership actually work?

We are moving from a philosophy to a theory that needs measureable components. To measure those components, we then need reliable and valid assessments.

Up until the mid-2000's, servant leadership was a popular philosophy but generally lacked a testable set of constructs. A step toward a more concrete definition occurred in 1995 with Spears' 10 aspects of servant leadership. In the 2000's, several researchers built on those aspects and others' writings to develop models and instruments to measure servant leadership. This chapter will provide details on six instruments as well as a summary of the limited empirical base for servant leadership.

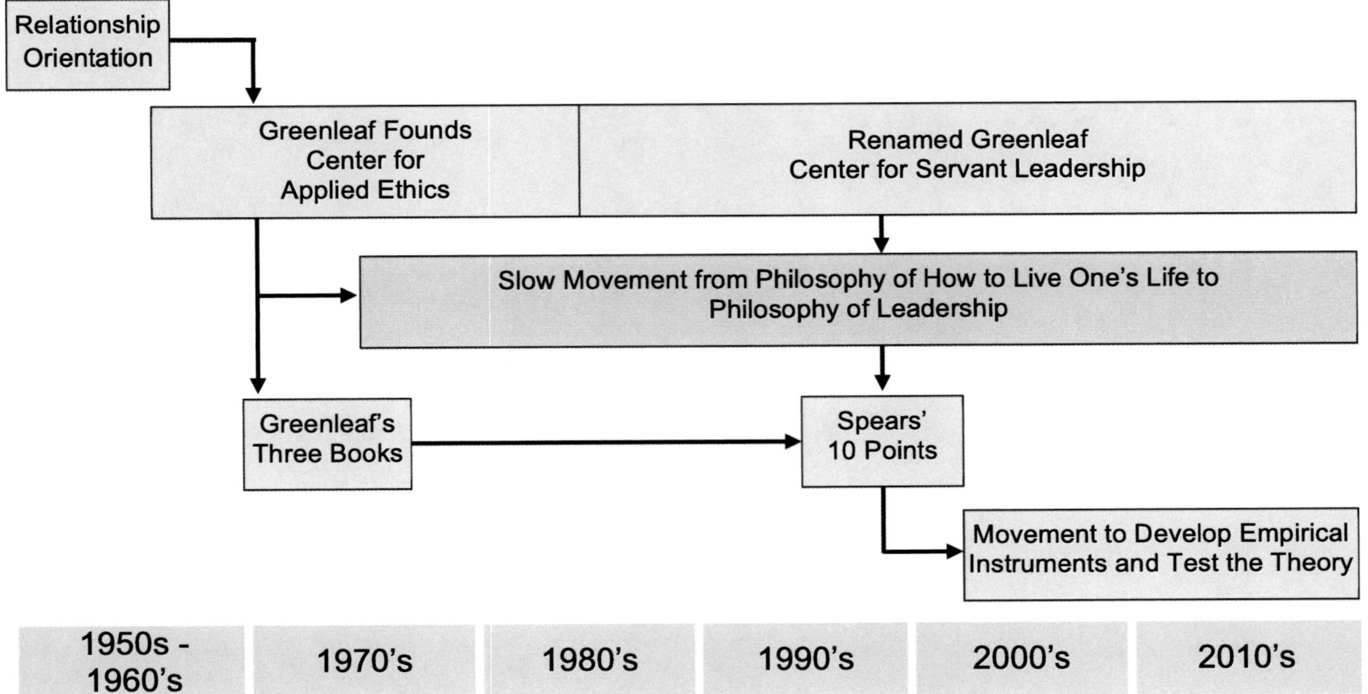

Servant Leadership

Introduction

Greenleaf was a manager at AT&T for 40 years. Over that time, he developed a philosophy that leaders should be servants to their followers. Much of his philosophy was provided in three works.

The Servant as Leader (1970)
The Institution as Servant (1972)
Trustees as Servants (1974)

In his first book, *The Servant as Leader*, he coined the expression servant leader. He explained a servant leader as follows:

> "The servant leader is a servant first... It begins with the natural feeling that one wants to serve, to serve first. Then conscious choice brings one to aspire to lead.
>
> That person is sharply different from one who is a leader first, perhaps because of the need to assuage an unusual power drive or to acquire material possession.
>
> The leader-first and the servant-first are two extreme types. Between them, there are shadings and blends that are part of the infinite variety of human nature.

> The difference manifests itself in the care taken by the servant-first to make sure that other people's highest priority needs are being served.
>
> The best test, and difficult to administer, is:
>
> Do those served grow as persons?
>
> Do they, while being served, become healthier, wiser, freer, more autonomous and more likely themselves to become servants?
>
> And, what is the effect on the least privileged in society? Will they benefit or at least not be further deprived?"

Servant Leadership

Introduction

In *The Institution as Servant* (1972) Greenleaf explained what is often called his "credo."

> "This is my thesis: caring for persons, the more able and the less able serving each other, is the rock upon which a good society is built.
>
> And, what is the effect on the least privileged in society? Will they benefit or at least not be further deprived?"

The graphs below indicate that interest in servant leadership exploded in the 2000's. Despite the number of dissertations, peer-reviewed articles and books on servant leadership however:

There is no widely agreed upon model of servant leadership.
There is no widely used instrument to measure servant leadership.
There have not been a sufficient number of studies with a consistent model/instrument to conduct meta-analyses on servant leadership.

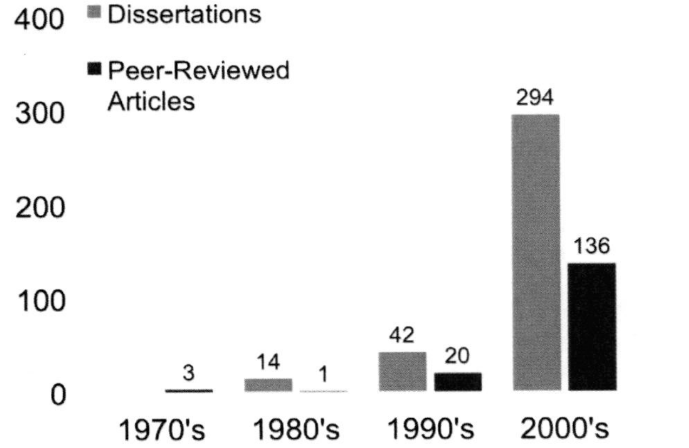

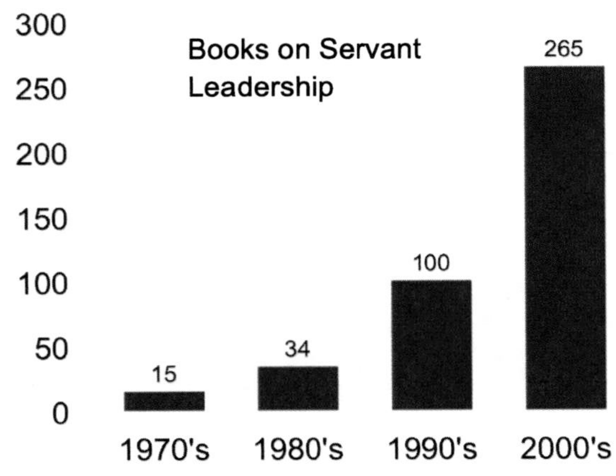

The remainder of this chapter will provide you with:

A summary of 11 frequently referenced models of servant leadership.
A summary of four instruments that indicate they measure servant leadership.
A summary of empirical studies on servant leadership.

Servant Leadership

Philosophy, Theory, Measurement and Research

Moving from a Philosophy to a Theory with a Research Base

When we consider evidence of leadership, its important to consider what differentiates evidence from a personal opinion or philosophy. In the models below, we see a progression from an idea or philosophy, to a theory with defined components, to a way to measure those components, to research on those components.

Servant Leadership Example

Philosophy		Theory		Measurement Model		Research
Serve followers	➡	Serving followers consists of the following observable behaviors…..	➡	Observable behaviors related to serving followers can be measured by….	➡	Using a measurement model, research has found….

Medical Example

Philosophy		Theory		Measurement Model		Research
Exercise will make you healthier	➡	Three hours of cardiovascular exercise per week will lower your blood pressure	➡	Six, 30 minutes sessions of exercise in which your heart rate was greater than 120 beats per minute	➡	Participants who exercised six times per week by keeping their heart rate greater than 120 beats per minute for 30 minutes per session lowered their blood pressure, on average, 10 points more than those who did not exercise

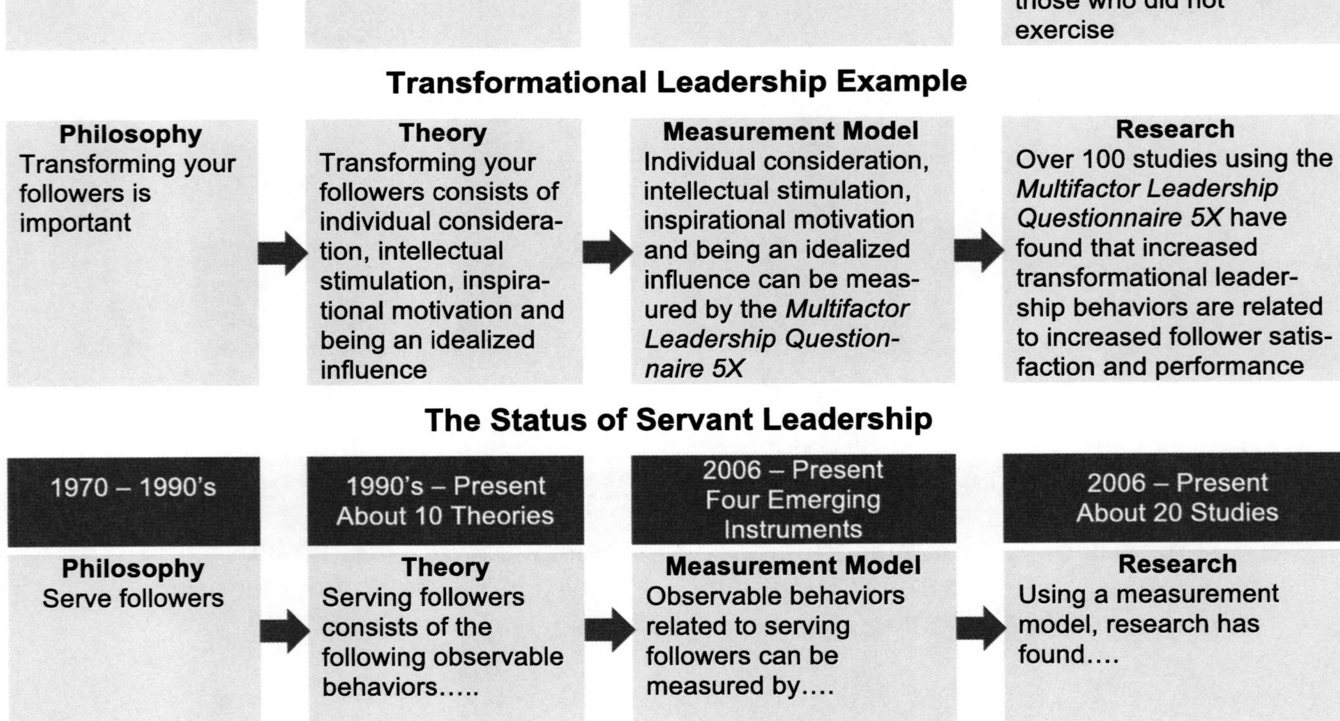

Transformational Leadership Example

Philosophy		Theory		Measurement Model		Research
Transforming your followers is important	➡	Transforming your followers consists of individual consideration, intellectual stimulation, inspirational motivation and being an idealized influence	➡	Individual consideration, intellectual stimulation, inspirational motivation and being an idealized influence can be measured by the *Multifactor Leadership Questionnaire 5X*	➡	Over 100 studies using the *Multifactor Leadership Questionnaire 5X* have found that increased transformational leadership behaviors are related to increased follower satisfaction and performance

The Status of Servant Leadership

1970 – 1990's		1990's – Present About 10 Theories		2006 – Present Four Emerging Instruments		2006 – Present About 20 Studies
Philosophy Serve followers	➡	**Theory** Serving followers consists of the following observable behaviors…..	➡	**Measurement Model** Observable behaviors related to serving followers can be measured by….	➡	**Research** Using a measurement model, research has found….

Servant Leadership

Philosophy, Theory, Measurement and Research

Early Theories of Servant Leadership, 1995 to 1999

Philosophy		Theory
Serve followers	→	Serving followers consists of the following observable behaviors
1970 – 1990's		1995 to 1998

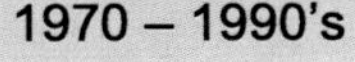

Over the past 40 years, a variety of authors have contributed to the development of models of servant leadership. None of these models, however, seem to have been widely accepted as "the model" of servant leadership.

In a 2013 review of the literature regarding servant leadership, Parris and Peachey found that the Greenleaf quotations on the previous pages and the two models shown below proposed by Spears (1995, 1998) and Laub (1999) were the most frequent foundations for discussing servant leadership in the peer-reviewed literature. To some degree, however, these sources are the most frequently cited because they were advanced prior to more recent models.

Spears (1995, 1998)		
Listening Empathy Healing Awareness	Persuasion Conceptualization Foresight	Stewardship Helping People Grow Community Building

Laub (1999)[1]		
Valuing People Building Community	Providing Leadership Developing People	Displaying Authenticity Sharing Leadership

Servant Leadership

Philosophy, Theory, Measurement and Research

Early Theories of Servant Leadership, 2000 to 2004

Philosophy		**Theory**
Serve followers	➡	Serving followers consists of the following observable behaviors
1970 – 1990's		2000 to 2004

Four additional models of servant leadership that are referenced in the scholarly literature emerged between 2000 and 2004.

Bass (2000)		
Setting An Example Encouraging Influence	Trust Inspiring Vision	Credibility Service

Russell and Stone (2002)		
Love Altruism Trust	Service Honesty	Modeling Appreciation of Others

Patterson (2003)		
Love Altruism Trust	Service Vision	Humility Empowerment

Ehrhart (2004)[2]		
Forming Relationships with Subordinates Empowering Subordinates	Helping Subordinates Grow and Succeed Behaving Ethically Putting Subordinates First	Having Conceptual Skills Creating Value for Those Outside the Organization

Servant Leadership

Philosophy, Theory, Measurement and Research

Emerging Theories with Instruments to Measure Servant Leadership, 2006 - Present

Philosophy		**Theory**		**Measurement Model**
Serve followers	→	Serving followers consists of the following observable behaviors	→	Observable behaviors related to serving followers can be measured by....
1970 – 1990's		1990's – Present About 10 Theories		2006 – Present Four Emerging Instruments

The authors below have each developed instruments to measure servant leadership. Each instrument has an associated peer-reviewed article that describes the development, reliability and validity of the instrument. Additional details about these instruments are provided at the end of this chapter.

Barbuto and Wheeler (2006)		
Altruistic Calling Wisdom	Emotional Healing Organizational Stewardship	Persuasive Mapping

Liden, Wayne, Zhao and Henderson (2008)		
Emotional Healing Creating Value for the Community	Helping Subordinates Grow and Succeed Conceptual Skills	Putting Subordinates First Behaving Ethically Empowering

Sendjaya, Sarros and Santora (2008)		
Voluntary Subordination Authentic Self	Covenantal Relationship Responsible Morality	Transcendental Spirituality Transforming Influence

van Dierendonck and Nuijten (2011)		
Empowerment Standing Back Authenticity	Interpersonal Acceptance Accountability Humility	Courage Stewardship

Servant Leadership

Consolidating Aspects of Servant Leadership

Consolidating Aspects of Servant Leadership

When we look at the most widely referenced model of servant leadership (Spears, 1998) and the four emerging models that have instruments with which to measure servant leadership, we understandably see a great deal of overlap among the models.

The compilations below and on the opposite page group the 34 components from those five models into higher-level constructs.

One of the first observations is that many aspects of servant leadership are similar to concepts contained in both the transformational leadership aspects of the full range model of leadership and in authentic leadership. The table below groups 17 of the components from Spears and the four emerging servant leadership instruments into areas we regularly discuss as part of the full range model of leadership or authentic leadership.

Elements of Servant Leadership Found in Other Popular Leadership Theories

Elements of Servant Leadership Found in Other Popular Leadership Theories
Intellectual Stimulation (Full Range Model of Leadership)
Conceptual Skills (Liden, Wayne, Zhao and Henderson, 2008) Conceptualization (Spears, 1998) Courage (to Think Differently) (van Dierendonck and Nuijten, 2011) Foresight (Spears, 1998) Persuasion (Spears, 1998) Persuasive Mapping (Barbuto and Wheeler, 2006) Wisdom (Barbuto and Wheeler, 2006)
Individual Consideration (Full Range Model of Leadership)
Empathy (Spears, 1998) Helping People Grow (Spears, 1998) Helping Subordinates Grow and Succeed (Liden, Wayne, Zhao and Henderson, 2008) Interpersonal Acceptance (van Dierendonck and Nuijten, 2011) Listening (Spears, 1998)
Idealized Influence – Ethics (Full Range Model of Leadership)
Behaving Ethically (Liden, Wayne, Zhao and Henderson, 2008) Responsible Morality (Sendjaya, Sarros and Santora, 2008)
Authenticity (Authentic Leadership)
Authentic Self (Sendjaya, Sarros and Santora, 2008) Authenticity (van Dierendonck and Nuijten, 2011) Awareness (Spears, 1998)

Servant Leadership

Consolidating Aspects of Servant Leadership

Elements of Servant Leadership Somewhat Unique From Other Popular Leadership Theories

Seventeen of the aspects from Spears and the four emerging instruments don't readily map to areas of the full range model of leadership or authentic leadership. They can be grouped however into the six categories below. We notice that two aspects – spirituality and altruism - are primarily characteristics or behaviors related to the leader. Two aspects – healing and empowerment – are generally related to the relationship between the leader and a follower(s). The final two aspects – stewardship and building community - are related to the leader and larger groups rather than individual followers.

Related to the Leader	Related to the Follower	Related to the Community
Spirituality Altruism	Healing Empowerment	Stewardship Building Community

Elements of Servant Leadership Somewhat Unique From Other Popular Leadership Theories
Spirituality
Altruistic Calling (Barbuto and Wheeler, 2006) Covenantal Relationship (Sendjaya, Sarros and Santora, 2008) Transcendental Spirituality (Sendjaya, Sarros and Santora, 2008)
Altruism
Putting Subordinates First (Liden, Wayne, Zhao and Henderson, 2008) Voluntary Subordination (Sendjaya, Sarros and Santora, 2008) Humility (van Dierendonck and Nuijten, 2011) Standing Back (van Dierendonck and Nuijten, 2011)
Healing
Emotional Healing (Barbuto and Wheeler, 2006) Emotional Healing (Liden, Wayne, Zhao and Henderson, 2008) Healing (Spears, 1998)
Empowerment
Empowering (Liden, Wayne, Zhao and Henderson, 2008) Empowerment (van Dierendonck and Nuijten, 2011)
Stewardship
Accountability (van Dierendonck and Nuijten, 2011) Organizational Stewardship (Barbuto and Wheeler, 2006) Stewardship (Spears, 1998, van Dierendonck and Nuijten, 2011)
Community
Creating Value for The Community (Liden, Wayne, Zhao and Henderson, 2008) Community Building (Spears, 1998)

Servant Leadership

Unique Aspects of Servant Leadership

Becoming a Better Servant Leader

The following six pages will discuss ways to increase your servant leadership behaviors. The pages will provide a bit of detail on each of the unique aspects of servant leadership described on the previous page, and offer some practical suggestions.

Spirituality is related to the servant leader's belief that there is something greater than her or himself.

Altruism refers to placing the needs of our followers ahead of our own.

Healing refers to assisting our followers to recover from harmful experiences that they may have endured at the hands of poor leaders or organizations.

Empowerment refers to ensuring our followers have the skills needed to do their work and, where possible, some degree of freedom in choosing how to do their work.

Stewardship refers to holding something in a trust relationship for the future. When we think about being a servant leader, being a steward includes valuing the resources of the organization as well as valuing our followers.

Building Community refers to building an organization in which followers engage in helping behaviors with others and taking pride in the organization.

Servant Leadership

Leader Aspects
Leader Spirituality

Spirituality

Defining Spirituality Despite decades of research and debate, the definition of spirituality is still a bit amorphous. While more detailed than below, McSherry and Cash, (2004), offered a way to envision a range of viewpoints regarding spirituality.[3] The table below nicely captures that, to some followers, the idea of being spiritual is connected to a set of religious beliefs or practices. Other followers, however, likely conceive of spirituality in terms of self-actualization or feelings of transcendence.[4]

Different Conceptions of Spirituality			
Theistic	Religious	Existential	Mystical
Belief in a Supreme Being or Deity	Belief in a Supreme Being or Deity with Religious Practices and Rituals	Finding Meaning, Purpose and Fulfillment in All of Life's Events	A Relationship with the Transcendent

Spiritual Leadership Within the field of leadership, a popular model of spiritual leadership has been advanced by Fry. His model contains two aspects.[5]

Creating a vision wherein leaders and followers experience a sense of calling in that life has meaning, purpose and makes a difference.

Establishing a social/organizational culture based on the values of altruistic love whereby leaders and followers have a sense of membership, feel understood and appreciated, and have genuine care, concern and appreciation for both self and others.

Ideas for Becoming a More Spiritual Leader

Think About What is Greater than Yourself Your conceptualization of spirituality likely incorporates some of the aspects shown in the table above. One commonality among those conceptualizations of spirituality is a belief that there is something larger or something more important than we are. It is easy to become distracted by petty workplace politics and squabbles. Part of increasing our spirituality as leaders is to regularly stop and re-direct our thoughts from the immediate frustrations we may have in a leadership role to our thoughts about how our leadership role fits into the greater purpose of our lives.

Look Backwards to Gain Perspective One exercise for re-directing your thoughts toward a more spiritual plane is to imagine that you are at your retirement ceremony after all of your working years are over. Imagine yourself sitting at a table prior to receiving your retirement plaque.

What will you remember proudly? Almost assuredly, it will be toward more spiritual accomplishments such as the friendships you made, the followers and customers you served and so forth. After you imagine accomplishments that are greater than yourself, your immediate leadership challenges will likely pale in comparison.

Servant Leadership

Leader Aspects
Leader Altruism

Altruism

There has been debate for millennia on whether humans are ever truly altruistic. A common distinction in that debate compares a theory called egoism with that of altruism. The theory of egoism argues that even what appear to be selfless acts that help someone else, are actually motivated by self-centered drives such as receiving praise for the act, avoiding guilt or simply feeling good about helping someone.

True altruism, on the other hand, would a) help someone, b) acknowledge that the individual who is doing the helping likely enjoys praise and the avoidance of guilt, but c) argue that those self-benefits were secondary to the pure, primary motivation of helping someone else.[6]

Egoism	
Behavior	Benefit Another
Ultimate Goal	Benefit Self
Examples of Primary Motivation	Receive Public Praise Feel Good About Ourselves Avoid Feeling Guilty
Secondary Motivation	Benefit Another

Altruism	
Behavior	Benefit Another
Ultimate Goal	Benefit Another
Primary Motivation	Benefit Another
Examples of Secondary Motivation	Receive Public Praise Feel Good About Ourselves Avoid Feeling Guilty

A second aspect of altruism is that multiple studies have found a connection between empathy and altruism.

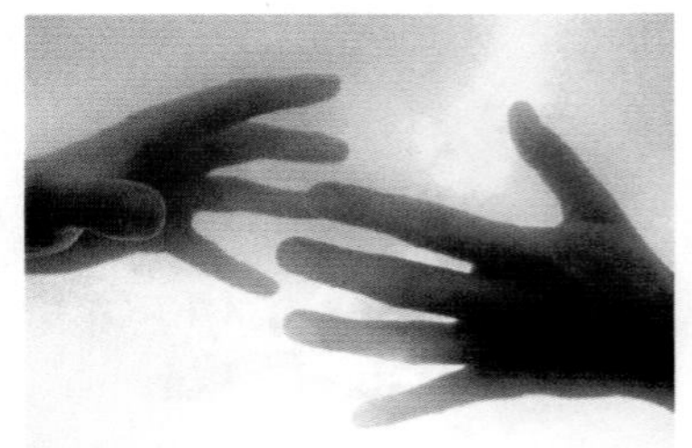

What seems to occur is that behavior that is closer to pure altruism rather than egoism, is usually preceded by feeling the plight or pain of someone else. This feeling evokes empathy, which in turn evokes an altruistic act.[7]

Ideas for Becoming a More Altruistic Leader

Value Benevolence Over Bonuses This simple cliché cuts to the heart of altruism as a leader. An altruistic leader will focus on high-quality work, customer satisfaction and long-term service to followers and the organization ahead of a possible quick bonus.

Reframe Our Rewards It is a challenging idea to put others' needs ahead of our own. In a leadership capacity, this becomes easier to do if we truly understand the life events of our followers.

The more we are able to feel both their joys and sorrows the easier it becomes for us to reframe what we consider as a "reward" for being a leader from our own financial reward to the reward of helping others.

Servant Leadership

Leader-Follower Aspects
Healing Followers

Healing Followers

Our followers' work lives and personal lives are integrated. If the ability to perform well is missing in one area of our followers' lives, it will likely affect their ability to perform well in other areas.

For example, if a follower is dealing with a personal problem, that problem may affect how the follower performs at work.

Helping followers to heal is a much more demanding task than simply being considerate of their needs. Often followers feel damaged in the workplace because of previous downsizings, or previous self-centered or inept leaders. Those followers may have feelings such as anxiety, mistrust, having been betrayed or just a general numbness.

Ideas for Healing Followers

One model for how to heal our followers was provided by Lindenfield (2008).[8] That model has five steps.

A Five-Step Model for Healing Followers, Lindenfield (2008)	
Step 1 Exploration	A first step to assist a follower to heal is to help the follower explore which personal or job related pain she or he may be carrying as excess baggage.
Step 2 Expression	A second step is to help the follower to express the emotions that she or he explored in step 1. As an example, if we assisted a follower in realizing that she or he felt betrayed after being downsized at her or his last company, getting the follower to express the feeling such as "it felt like every promise they made to me was a lie – I felt cheated," would be a great step toward expressing the painful emotions.
Step 3 Comfort	A third step is to assist the follower in experiencing the catharsis that identifying and expressing the painful emotion can achieve.
Step 4 Compensation	A fourth step is to assist the follower in planning how to create an "insurance" policy to prevent the sort of damaging emotions that were explored and expressed in steps 1 and 2. An example might be to help the follower consider what future knowledge and skills she or he can develop to help prevent that feeling again.
Step 5 Perspective	The final step is to assist the follower in "stepping back" and recognizing how the painful experience and the follower's reaction to that experience fit in to the bigger picture of the follower's life. Hopefully, this final step will assist the follower in gaining some closure and completing the healing.

Servant Leadership

Leader-Follower Aspects
Empowering Followers

Empowering Followers

Although we use the word empowerment regularly, what comprises empowerment is a bit more fleeting. A popular model of empowerment was developed by Spreitzer (1995).[9] His model consists of four aspects that collectively comprise empowerment.[10]

Finding Meaning in Our Work	
Do followers care about doing the work?	One aspect of feeling empowered is to place meaning on personal work goals. The value that a follower places on those goals is based on her or his own ideals and standards.
Feeling Competent In Our Work	
Do followers believe they are capable of doing the work?	Competency relates to a follower's beliefs in his or her capability to perform work activities with skill and mastery.
Feeling a Sense of Self-Determination in Our Work	
Do followers believe they have the ability to determine how they do the work?	Self-determination relates to a follower's sense of having a choice in initiating and regulating actions and work behaviors. It includes being able to make their own decisions on how they do their work, how fast they work and how hard they work.
Feeling That Our Work Makes an Impact	
Do followers believe they have the ability to impact things that affect their work?	Impact is the degree to which a follower can influence strategic, administrative or operating outcomes at work.

Ideas for Empowering Followers

Meaning and Competence Ideas for how to help our followers find meaning in their work, and helping them to grow in their jobs were covered in chapters 9 and 10.

Self-Determination Some follower jobs lend themselves better to empowered self-determination than others. For followers who do routine, repetitive work, self-determination is likely akin to feeling that their leaders listen to their suggestions. For those for whom there is some flexibility in how they accomplish processes, emphasizing self-determination requires us to re-focus our leadership attention slightly away from monitoring the processes our followers use and a bit more toward monitoring the outcomes they achieve.

Impact One way to help followers feel that they make an impact is to connect for followers how what they do impacts the goods or services the organization produces.

Imagine that there are grounds keepers in an organization that provides clients with financial advice. At first glance, grounds keeping and financial advice to clients may seem unrelated.

Its important to help the grounds keepers to understand that the work they do has many impacts. For example, it lessens the liability of lawsuits and creates a positive image to clients when they decide whether the financial services company looks "legitimate" and so forth.

Servant Leadership

Community Aspects

Stewardship

Stewardship

We often think of being a steward as holding something in trust for the future. A more elaborate explanation of managerial/leadership stewardship has been advanced by Davis, Schoorman and Donaldson (1997).[11] Several of the differences they proposed between what is called agency theory and stewardship theory are shown below. When perusing the chart, it is somewhat easy to understand why servant leadership advocates a stewardship versus an agency view of work and leadership.

	Agency Theory	Stewardship Theory
Simplified Difference	People try to maximize what is best for them	People want to be a part of something lasting and larger than themselves
View of Human Behavior	Work is a bargain between what maximizes our self-interests and what maximizes the interests of the organization	We seek self-actualization by creating a relationship between the success of the organization and our own satisfaction
Maslow's Psychological Needs Emphasized	We are largely motivated by lower order needs such as economic security and feelings of safety	We are largely motivated by higher order needs such as the desires for self-esteem and self-actualization
Source of Motivation	Largely extrinsic – motivated by rewards	Largely intrinsic – motivated be a sense of accomplishment
Source of Commitment	We are committed at work in exchange for pay and benefits	We are committed at work because we believe in and accept the goals of the organization
Primary Management Philosophy	Shorter-term with an emphasis on policies and procedures as control mechanisms	Longer-term with an emphasis on trust and making things better
Cultural Differences	Tendency to reward individual behaviors (individualism) Well-defined hierarchical roles (high power distance)	Tendency to reward group behaviors (collectivism) Flat organization with more organic roles (low power distance)

Ideas for Increasing Your Stewardship

Work Efficiently and Effectively It is relatively easy to envision a CEO engaging in stewardship by developing a 5 to 10 year strategic plan. Envisioning stewardship at lower levels of the organization is slightly different. At lower levels of an organization, modeling the idea that we are stewards of organizational resources and time is important. This is more akin to real-time stewardship rather than long-range stewardship.

Create Development Plans for Our Followers As leaders we are often able to see the impact that we have on our followers. What we don't see as easily, is the impact that our followers who become leaders will have on their followers. Eventually those followers of our previous followers will also become leaders. This sort of "pass it forward" stewardship begins with assisting our followers with career development plans.

Servant Leadership

Community Aspects
Building Community

Building Community

What Greenleaf referred to as building community, is often also referred to in the peer-reviewed literature as organizational citizenship. Podsakoff (2000, 2009)[12] summarized organizational citizenship concepts into seven categories. Four of those categories are quite related to the idea of building community.

Aspects of Organizational Citizenship and Community	
Helping Behaviors	Voluntarily helping others with, or preventing the occurrence of work related problems
Sportsmanship	A willingness to tolerate the inevitable inconveniences and impositions of work without complaining
Organizational Loyalty	Promoting the organization to outsiders, protecting and defending it against external threats and remaining committed to it even under adverse conditions
Civic Virtue	A willingness to participate actively in organizational governance such as attending meetings, engaging in policy debates, expressing one's opinion about what strategy the organization ought to follow and so forth A willingness to monitor the organization's environment for threats and opportunities such as keeping up with changes in the industry that might affect the organization A willingness to look out for the organization's best interests even at great personal cost

Ideas for Increasing Your Abilities to Build Community

Develop a Community Oriented Culture Shein[13] is a well-known author who writes about leadership and organizational culture. Some of the techniques that Schein suggests that leaders can use to create a community-oriented culture are stories, symbols and rituals.

Stories Most organizations have stories about their founders, or significant moments in the history of the organization. In order to develop a more community-oriented culture, the organizational stories we tell as leaders should emphasize how the organization pulled together to overcome difficult times.

Symbols Things such as the departmental or organizational logos, the physical layout of the workplace and even the artwork placed on walls all symbolically both capture and influence the organization's culture. Symbols that are community oriented tell a much different story than those that emphasize individualism.

Rituals Most organizations have rituals. These can range from formal rituals such as promotion or retirement ceremonies to informal ones such as a generally understood ritual that everyone goes to lunch together on a particular day each week. Rituals that emphasize teamwork and community shape the culture differently than those that emphasize competition and individual achievement.

Servant Leadership

Measuring Servant Leadership

Instruments to Measure Servant Leadership

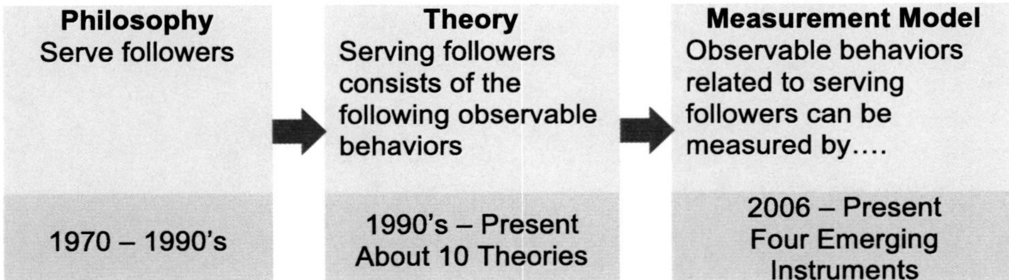
Philosophy
Serve followers
1970 – 1990's
Theory
Serving followers consists of the following observable behaviors
1990's – Present
About 10 Theories
Measurement Model
Observable behaviors related to serving followers can be measured by....
2006 – Present
Four Emerging Instruments

Six instruments that indicate they measure servant leadership, for which their development has been described in the peer-reviewed/dissertation literature, will be reviewed.

Instrument	Author(s)
Organizational Leadership Assessment	Laub (1999)
Servant Leadership Scale	Ehrhart (2004)
Servant Leadership Questionnaire	Barbuto and Wheeler (2006)
Servant Leadership Scale	Liden, Wayne, Zhao and Henderson (2008)
Servant Leadership Behavior Scale	Sendjaya, Sarros and Santora (2008)
Servant Leadership Survey	van Dierendonck and Nuijten (2011)

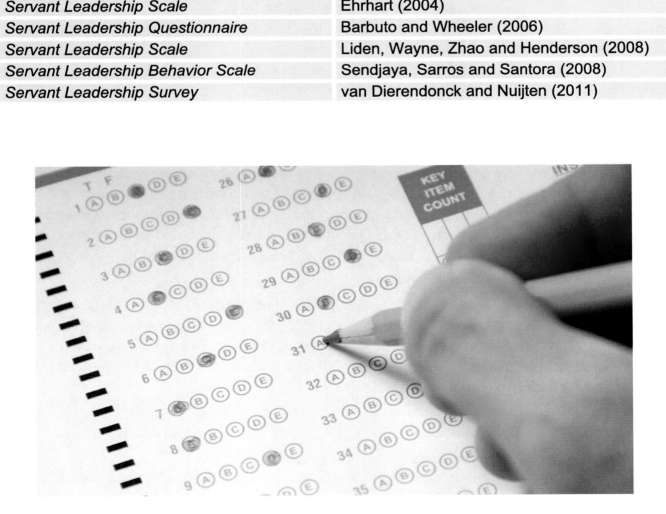

KEY
ITEM
COUNT

Servant Leadership

The Organizational Leadership Assessment

(Servant) Organizational Leadership Assessment, **Laub (1999)**

The *Organizational Leadership Assessment* measures six aspects of servant leadership.[14]

Laub (1999)	
Valuing People	By Believing in People By Serving Other's Needs Before His or Her Own By Receptive, Non-Judgmental Listening
Developing People	By Providing Opportunities for Learning and Growth By Modeling Appropriate Behavior By Building Up Others Through Encouragement and Affirmation
Building Community	By Building Strong Personal Relationships By Working Collaboratively with Others By Valuing the Differences of Others
Displaying Authenticity	By Being Open and Accountable to Others By a Willingness to Learn from Others By Maintaining Integrity and Trust
Providing Leadership	By Envisioning the Future By Taking Initiative By Clarifying Goals
Sharing Leadership	By Facilitating a Shared Vision By Sharing Power and Releasing Control By Sharing Status and Promoting Others

Development of the Organizational Leadership Assessment

Laub developed the *Organizational Leadership Assessment* for his doctoral dissertation. He first developed a pool of questions based on his review of the literature on servant leadership. He then had between 14 and 25 experts who had written on or taught servant leadership at the university level participate in a three step *Delphi* process in order to add to the original pool of items and then rate those items' importance. At the conclusion of the third iteration of the *Delphi* process, 74 potential items had been developed.

Eighty items were then tested with 828 participants. Laub performed a series of exploratory factor analyses (EFA) on these data. Laub found that 27 items loaded on a single component called *Organizational Assessment* and 53 items loaded on a single component called *Leadership Assessment.*[15] After the EFA, the instrument was reduced from 74 to 60 questions to decrease the time it took to complete the instrument.

Internal Reliability

Laub reported Cronbach Alpha scores for each subscale in the range of .90 to .93.

Acquiring the *Organizational Leadership Assessment*

As of 2014, researchers interested in using the *Organizational Leadership Assessment* should contact Dr. Laub at the OLA Group.

Servant Leadership

The Servant Leadership Scale

The *Servant Leadership Scale,* Ehrhart, 2004

The *Servant Leadership Scale* is based on seven aspects of servant leadership.

Ehrhart (2004)	
Forming Relationships with Subordinates Empowering Subordinates Helping Subordinates Grow and Succeed	Behaving Ethically Putting Subordinates First Having Conceptual Skills Creating Value for Those Outside the Organization

Development of the *Servant Leadership Scale*

Based on his review of the literature, Ehrhart hypothesized the seven aspects of servant leadership shown in the table above. He developed 14 questions based on those seven aspects.

Discriminant Validity

Ehrhart administered the *Servant Leadership Scale*, the *LMX-7* and the *MLQ 5X* to 254 employed university students. He conducted a confirmatory factor analysis (CFA) that included all three measures. The results of the CFA found that the three instruments loaded on three different factors (X^2 = 429, *df* = 167, *CFI* = .95, *SRMR* = .04, *RMSEA* = .08).

This lent some support that the *Servant Leadership Scale* seemed to measure something different from transformational leadership or leader-member exchange relationships. The average of the correlations between the *Servant Leadership Scale* dimensions and the *LMX-7* was .61, and was .61 for idealized influence, .53 for inspirational motivation, .53 for intellectual stimulation and .56 for individualized consideration obtained from the *Multifactor Leadership Questionnaire 5X*.

Acquiring the *Servant Leadership Scale*

As of 2014, researchers should contact Dr. Ehrhart at San Diego State University, to acquire permission to use the instrument.

The questions for the *Servant Leadership Scale* can be found in Ehrhart, M. G. (2004). Leadership and procedural justice climate as antecedents of unit level organizational citizenship behavior. *Personnel Psychology*, 57(1), 61–94.

Servant Leadership

The Servant Leadership Questionnaire

The *Servant Leadership Questionnaire*, Barbuto and Wheeler (2006)
The *Servant Leadership Questionnaire* measures five aspects of servant leadership.

Altruistic Calling	Describes a Leader's Deep-rooted Desire to Make a Positive Difference in Others' Lives A Generosity of the Spirit Consistent with a Philanthropic Purpose in Life
Emotional Healing	Describes a Leader's Commitment to and Skill in Fostering Spiritual Recovery from Hardship or Trauma Leaders Using Emotional Healing are Highly Empathetic and Great Listeners
Wisdom	Is a Combination of Awareness of Surroundings and Anticipation of Consequences Leaders are Adept at Picking Up Cues from the Environment and Understanding Their Implications
Persuasive Mapping	Is the Extent to which Leaders Use Sound Reasoning and Mental Frameworks Leaders are Skilled at Mapping Issues and Conceptualizing Greater Possibilities and are Compelling When Articulating These Opportunities
Organizational Stewardship	Describes the Extent that Leaders Prepare an Organization to Make a Positive Contribution to Society Through Community Development, Programs and Outreach Organizational Stewardship Involves an Ethic or Value for Taking Responsibility for the Well-being of the Community

Development of the *Servant Leadership Questionnaire*
Barbuto and Wheeler began with a conceptual model using the 10 characteristics of servant leadership proposed by Spears (1995). They then added an 11th item they labeled *Calling*.

Spears		Barbuto and Wheeler
Listening	Empathy	Calling (The Natural Desire to Serve Others)
Healing	Awareness	
Persuasion	Conceptualization	
Foresight	Stewardship	
Helping People Grow	Community Building	

Face Validity
The authors generated between five and seven potential questions for each of the eleven characteristics. They then asked 11 experts to categorize 56 potential questions into the category the question proposed to measure. After an iteration involving the re-writing of four questions, the experts were able to correctly place the questions into the correct category with more than 80% accuracy.

Servant Leadership

The Servant Leadership Questionnaire

Internal Reliability

Servant Leadership Questionnaire
Altruistic Calling
Emotional Healing
Wisdom
Persuasive Mapping
Organizational Stewardship

The 56-item version of the questionnaire was then tested with 388 raters (followers). A series of exploratory factor analyses (EFA) using *Varimax* and *Oblique* rotations resulted in a five-factor model, rather than the 11-factor model originally hypothesized. Twenty-three questions loaded on the five components with factor loadings higher than .50.

A confirmatory factor analysis (CFA) was next conducted on the 23 questions produced by the EFA. The CFA was conducted on data from 80 leaders. The CFA generally supported the five-factor model (X^2 = 1,410, *CFI* = .96, *RFI* = .95, *RMSEA* = .10).

Mahembe and Engelbrecht (2013) reported Cronbach Alpha Scores between .87 and .93 for the five subscales. The results of a confirmatory factor analysis found a good fit for the first-order factors (*CFI* = .99, *RFI* = .98, *RMSEA* = .06).

Convergent Validity

The 388 raters (followers) completed the seven leader-member exchange questions from the *LMX-7.* The five subscales of the *Servant Leadership Questionnaire* were correlated with the overall *LMX-7* score in the range of .55 to .73.

Discriminant Validity

The 388 raters (followers) also completed 16 transformational leadership questions from the *Multifactor Leadership Questionnaire 5X*. The five subscales of the *Servant Leadership Questionnaire* were correlated with the overall transformational score in the range of .25 to .34.

Predictive Validity

Barbuto and Wheeler also ran correlations for the three "outcome" scores from the *Multifactor Leadership Questionnaire 5X.* The rater (follower) ratings of servant leadership were weakly correlated with follower extra effort scores (.16 to .27) and moderately correlated with follower satisfaction with the leader (.23 to .44) and leader effectiveness (.27 to .55).

Acquiring the *Servant Leadership Questionnaire*

The *Servant Leadership Questionnaire* is copyrighted by Dr. Barbuto and Future Leadership.

As of 2014, researchers should contact Dr. Barbuto at California State University, Fullerton to acquire permission to use the instrument.

The *Servant Leadership Questionnaire* is included in Barbuto Jr., J. E., and Wheeler, D. W. (2006). Scale Development and Construct Clarification of Servant Leadership. *Group & Organization Management*, 31(3), 300-326.

Servant Leadership

The Servant Leadership Scale

The *Servant Leadership Scale*, Liden, Wayne, Zhao and Henderson (2008)
The *Servant Leadership Scale* measures seven dimensions of servant leadership.

Emotional Healing	The Act of Showing Sensitivity to Others' Personal Concerns
Creating Value for The Community	A Conscious, Genuine Concern for Helping the Community
Conceptual Skills	Possessing Knowledge of the Organization and Tasks at Hand Effectively Supporting and Assisting Others, Especially Immediate Followers
Empowering	Encouraging and Facilitating Others, Especially Immediate Followers, in Identifying and Solving Problems Determining When and How to Complete Work Tasks
Helping Subordinates Grow and Succeed	Demonstrating Genuine Concern for Others' Career Growth and Development by Providing Support and Mentoring
Putting Subordinates First	Using Actions and Words to Make It Clear to Others (Especially Immediate Followers) That Satisfying Their Work Needs is a Priority
Behaving Ethically	Interacting Openly, Fairly, and Honestly with Others

Development of the *Servant Leadership Scale*
Liden, Wayne, Zhao and Henderson[16] began with a conceptual model that included nine characteristics of servant leadership.

Emotional Healing	Empowering	Behaving Ethically
Creating Value for The Community	Helping Subordinates Grow and Succeed	Relationships
Conceptual Skills	Putting Subordinates First	Servanthood

Face Validity

The authors reviewed earlier servant leadership instruments created by Page and Wong (2000), Ehrhart (2004) and Barbuto and Wheeler (2006).

The authors then created 85 potential questions to measure the nine characteristics from their conceptual model.

Servant Leadership

The Servant Leadership Scale

Exploratory Factor Analysis

An exploratory factor analysis (EFA) was run on responses to the 85 questions from 285 undergraduate students. The EFA found seven distinguishable factors, with scale reliabilities of: conceptual skills (α = .86), empowering (α = .90), helping subordinates grow and succeed (α = .90), putting subordinates first (α = .91), behaving ethically (α = .90), emotional healing (α = .89) and creating value for the community (α = .89). The authors kept the four questions from each factor that had the highest factor loadings to create a 28-item version of the instrument. Relationships and servanthood failed to load on a single factor and were eliminated from the instrument.

Emotional Healing	Empowering	Behaving Ethically
Creating Value for The Community	Helping Subordinates Grow and Succeed	~~Relationships~~
Conceptual Skills	Putting Subordinates First	~~Servanthood~~

Confirmatory Factor Analysis

Following the exploratory factor analysis, a confirmatory factor analysis (CFA) was conducted with data obtained from 182 individuals (followers) who rated their superiors (leaders). The authors tested multiple models using CFA and concluded that the seven-factor model was better than the alternatives tested (X^2 = 549, *df* = 329, *CFI* = .98, *SRMR* = .05, *RMSEA* = .06).

Convergent Validity

All seven servant leadership dimensions correlated moderately to strongly with transformational leadership (.43 to .79) and the leader-member exchange global score from the *LMX-MDM* (.48 to .75).

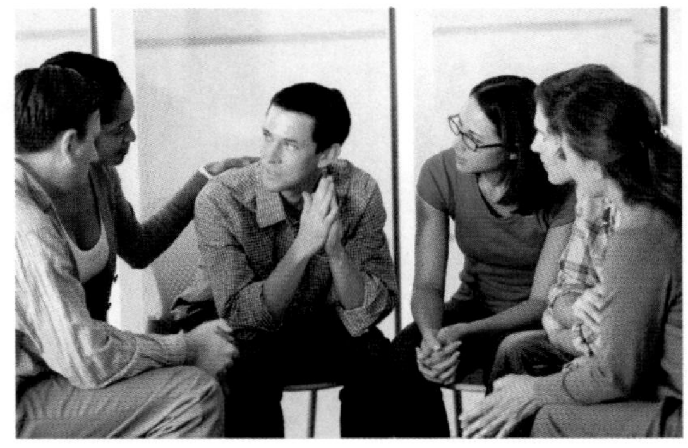

Predictive Validity

The seven dimensions were weakly to moderately correlated with the affective commitment scale of the *Organizational Commitment Questionnaire (*.18 to .45)

Acquiring the *Servant Leadership Scale*

As of 2014, researchers should request permission to use the *Servant Leadership Scale* from Dr. Robert C. Liden at the University of Illinois at Chicago.

The instrument can be found in Liden, R., Wayne, S., Zhao. H. and Henderson, D. (2008). Servant leadership: Development of a multidimensional measure and multi-level assessment. *Leadership Quarterly*, 19(2), 161-177.

Servant Leadership

Servant Leadership Behavior Scale

The *Servant Leadership Behavior Scale*, Sendjaya, Sarros and Santora (2008)
The *Servant Leadership Behavior Scale* measures six dimensions of servant leadership.[17]

Scale	Consists of	Definition
Voluntary Subordination	Being a Servant Acts of Service	A Willingness to Take Up Opportunities to Serve Others Whenever There is a Legitimate Need Regardless of the Nature of the Service, the Person Served or the Mood of the Servant Leader
Authentic Self	Humility Integrity Accountability Security Moral action Vulnerability	Consistent Display of Humility, Integrity and Accountability, Security and Vulnerability A Willingness to Work Quietly Behind the Scenes, Spend Time on Small Things and Make Seemingly Inconsequential Decisions Unrewarded and Unnoticed
Covenantal Relationship	Collaboration Equality Availability Acceptance	Engaging with and Accepting Others for Who They Are, Not for How They Make Servant Leaders Feel
Responsible Morality	Moral Reasoning Moral Action	Ensuring That Both the Ends They Seek and the Means They Employ are Morally Legitimized, Thoughtfully Reasoned and Ethically Justified
Transcendental Spirituality	Interconnectedness Sense of Mission Religiousness Wholeness	Attuned to the Idea of Calling in Seeking to Make a Difference in the Lives of Others Through Service, from Which One Derives the Meaning and Purpose of Life
Transforming Influence	Trust Mentoring Modeling Vision Empowerment	Positively Transforming Others in Multiple Dimensions (e.g. Emotionally, Intellectually, Socially and Spiritually) into Servant Leaders Themselves

Development of the *Servant Leadership Behavior* Scale

Face Validity

The authors interviewed 15 senior executives about what servant leadership entailed. The authors then performed content analysis of the responses and identified 22 possible dimensions of servant leadership. Based on the literature on servant leadership and the results of the content analysis, the authors reduced the original 22 possible dimensions to six dimensions of servant leadership. One hundred and one possible questions were generated for these six dimensions.

Servant Leadership
Servant Leadership Behavior Scale

Content Validity
Fifteen content experts were obtained from a mailing list of the International Leadership Association. The content experts were individuals who taught or conducted research in servant leadership. The authors then calculated content validity ratios for each of the 101 possible items that were rated by the 15 content experts. The content validity ratio is a number that ranges from -1 (meaning none of the experts believed a question was essential to servant leadership) to +1 (meaning all of the experts believed a question was essential to servant leadership). Based on this analysis, 73 items were retained from the original 101 questions.

Confirmatory Factor Analysis
Sendjaya, Sarros and Santora next ran a series of confirmatory factor analyses (CFA) for each of the six subscales. The final CFA was able to reduce the number of questions within each scale while concomitantly improving the model fit.

After the final CFA, the voluntary subordination scale was reduced to seven questions, authentic self to six questions, covenantal relationship to six questions, responsible morality to five questions, transcendental spirituality to four questions and transforming influence to seven questions. In these reduced question sets, the Goodness of Fit Indices were all above .97 and the RMSEA's ranged from .00 to .07. The Cronbach Alpha for each scale ranged from .72 to .93.

Acquiring the *Servant Leadership Behavior Scale*
The *Servant Leadership Behavior Scale* is copyrighted by Dr. Sen Sendjaya. As of 2014, researchers who want to use the *Servant Leadership Behavior Scale* should contact Dr. Sendjaya at Monash University to request permission to use the instrument.

Servant Leadership

The Servant Leadership Survey

The *Servant Leadership Survey*, van Dierendonck and Nuijten (2011)
The *Servant Leadership Survey* measures eight dimensions of servant leadership.

Empowerment	Is a Motivational Concept Focused on Enabling People and Encouraging Personal Development
Accountability	Is Holding People Accountable for Performance They Can Control
Standing Back	Is About the Extent to Which a Leader Gives Priority to the Interests of Others First and Gives Them the Necessary Support and Credits.
Humility	Is the Ability to Put One's Own Accomplishments and Talents in a Proper Perspective
Authenticity	Is Closely Related to Expressing the "True Self," Expressing Oneself in Ways That are Consistent with Inner Thoughts and Feelings
Courage	Is Daring to Take Risks and Trying out New Approaches to Old Problems
Interpersonal Acceptance	Is the Ability to Understand and Experience the Feelings of Others, Understand Where People Come from and the Ability to Let Go of Perceived Wrongdoings and Not Carry a Grudge into Other Situations
Stewardship	Is the Willingness to Take Responsibility for the Larger Institution and Go for Service Instead of Control and Self-interest

Development of the *Servant Leadership Survey*
The instrument underwent three stages in its development.

Stage 1
In the first stage, 688 volunteers completed an early version of the survey that had 99 items. Based on those data, the authors conducted an exploratory factor analysis (EFA) that found fourteen factors with eigenvalues greater than 1. An iterative set of exploratory factor analyses using *Varimax* and *Oblimin* rotation eventually produced a six-factor model based on 28 items. At this stage of development, neither *Humility* nor *Stewardship* loaded on a unique single component. The authors added 11 additional questions designed to measure those hypothesized dimensions. This resulted in 39 possible questions.

Stage 2
The authors next asked an additional 263 individuals to complete the 39-question instrument. Based on those responses, the authors conducted a confirmatory factor analysis (CFA). Following the initial CFA, nine questions were removed. The reduced 30-question model produced a good fit for an 8-factor model (X^2 = 623, *df* = 377, *CFI* = .93, *TLI* = .92, *SRMR* = .05, *AIC* = 19354, *RMSEA* = .05).

Stage 3

The authors next asked an additional 236 individuals to complete the 30-question survey. The authors repeated a CFA with these data and again found support for an 8-factor model (X^2 = 600, *df* = 397, *CFI* = .94, *TLI* = .93, *SRMR* = .06, *AIC* = 17148, *RMSEA* = .05).

The combined sample of all three studies demonstrated Cronbach Alpha scores of .89 for empowerment (7 items), .81 for accountability (3 items), .76 for standing back (3 items), .91 for humility (5 items), .82 for authenticity (4 items), .69 for courage (2 items), .72 for forgiveness (3 items) and .74 for stewardship (3 items).

Convergent Validity

Seven of the eight scales from the *Servant Leadership Survey* were correlated in the range of .47 to .85 with the seven scales of the *Servant Leadership Scale (*Liden, Wayne and Henderson 2008*)*. The accountability scale of the *Servant Leadership Survey* was either uncorrelated or correlated at .20 or below for the seven scales of the *Servant Leadership Scale*.

Five of the eight scales were highly correlated with leader-member exchange *LMX-7* scores in the range of .38 to .85. Three of the *Servant Leadership Survey* scales were also highly correlated with the subscales of Rafferty and Griffin's (2004) measure of transformational leadership. Six of the *Servant Leadership Survey* scales were also highly correlated with the *Brown Ethical Leadership Survey* (2005).

Acquiring the *Servant Leadership Survey*

The *Servant Leadership Survey* is copyrighted by Van Dierendonck and Nuijten. In their 2011 article, the authors indicated that the *Servant Leadership Survey* may freely be used for scientific purposes.

The instrument can be found in van Dierendonck, D. and Nuijten, I. (2011). The servant leadership survey: development and validation of a multidimensional measure. *Journal of Business and Psychology*, 26(3), 249-267.

Research on Servant Leadership

Parris and Peachey (2013) performed a systematic literature review of empirical articles on servant leadership. They found 39 peer-reviewed, empirical articles published between 2004 and 2011. The authors used three different appraisal tools from Letts, Wilkins, Law, Stewart, Bosch and Westmorland (2007)[18], the Institute for Public Health Sciences (2002)[19] and Stoltz, Uden and Willman (2004)[20] to assess the quality of these 39 studies.

Twenty-two of the 39 empirical studies were classified as high-quality studies using the standards below. Of those 22 high-quality studies, four were qualitative and 18 were quantitative. The areas in which the research on servant leadership primarily occurred were: leadership (*N* = 9), education (N = 7), business (*N* = 6), psychology (*N* = 6) and nursing (*N* = 3).

High Quality Qualitative Study Criteria	High Quality Quantitative Study Criteria
Purpose Stated Clearly, Relevant Background Literature Reviewed, Design Appropriate	Clearly Focused Study, Sufficient Background Provided, Well Planned, Method Appropriate
Identified Researcher's Theoretical or Philosophical Perspective, Relevant and Well-described Selection of Participants and Context	Measures Validated, Applicable and Adequate
Procedural Rigor in Data Collection Strategies and Analysis	Number of Participants, Data Analysis Sufficiently Rigorous
Evidence of the Four Components of Trust-worthiness (Credibility, Transferability, Dependability and Confirmability)	Adequate Statistical Methods
Results Are Comprehensive and Well Described	Findings Clearly Stated

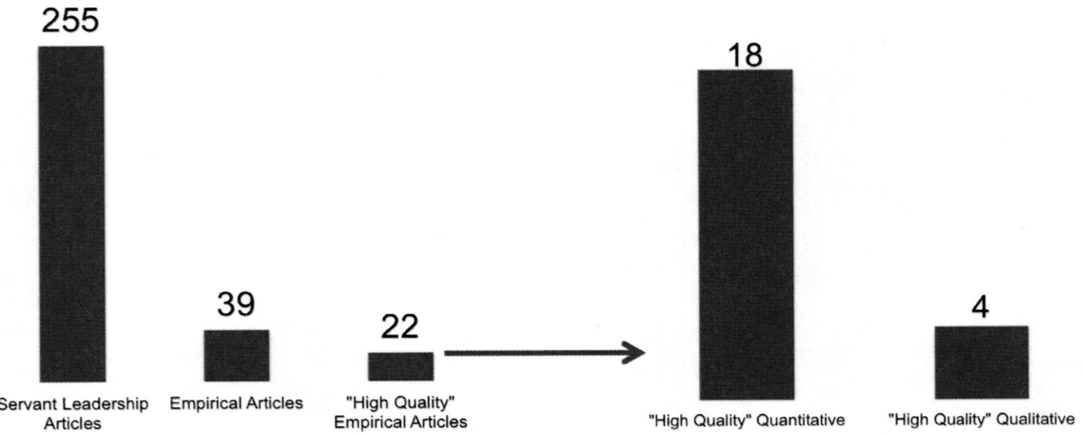

Servant Leadership

Research on Servant Leadership

Research on Servant Leadership

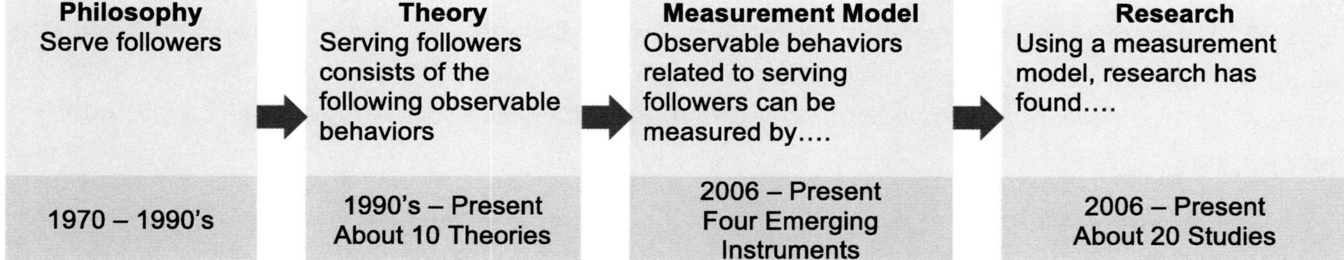

Philosophy
Serve followers
1970 – 1990's
Theory
Serving followers consists of the following observable behaviors
1990's – Present
About 10 Theories
Measurement Model
Observable behaviors related to serving followers can be measured by....
2006 – Present
Four Emerging Instruments
Research
Using a measurement model, research has found....
2006 – Present
About 20 Studies

As of 2014, there were not yet any meta-analyses on servant leadership. The graphs that follow provide details for the high quality, quantitative studies of servant leadership identified by Parris and Peachey (2013) plus two additional studies that have been published in the peer-reviewed literature since their review.

The research that will be summarized can be thought of along three streams of research.

How servant leadership is related to ratings given to leaders

How servant leadership is related to follower outcomes

How servant leadership is related to organizational outcomes

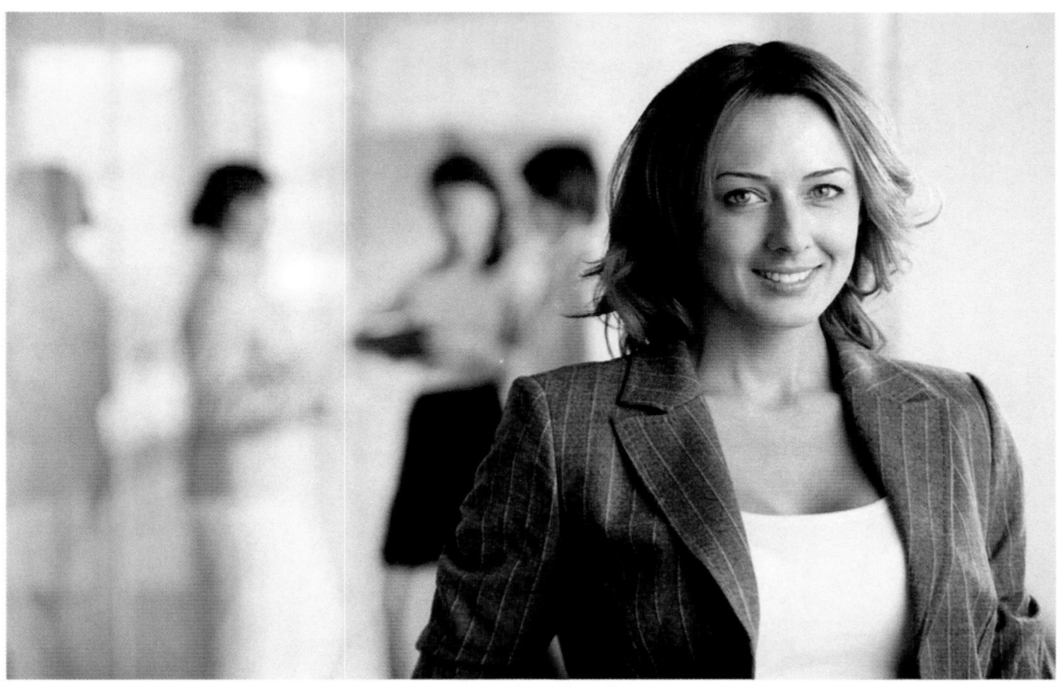

Servant Leadership
Research Results

Understanding the Research Results for Servant Leadership

There have not yet been meta-analyses on servant leadership. There are, however, results from 20 empirical studies of servant leadership. To prepare you for understanding the research results that follow, chapter 2 explained both correlations and meta-analyses. The table below, however, provides a quick review of how the results for individual studies will be provided in this chapter.[21]

Example - Servant Leadership and Follower Job Satisfaction

In the example below, one of the studies published was on the relationship between leaders' servant leadership behaviors and followers' job satisfaction. There were 501 followers who rated their leaders on servant leadership and their own job satisfaction. The notation (M) indicates the study referenced. A list is provided at the end of the chapter. The finding was a strong, positive correlation (.52). The more servant leader behaviors were used, the higher the follower job satisfaction.

Strongly - Correlated	Moderately - Correlated	Weakly - Correlated
-1 to -.50	-.49 to -.30	-.29 to -.10

Weakly + Correlated	Moderately + Correlated	Strongly + Correlated
.10 to .29	.30 to .49	.50 to 1

Outcome	Followers	
Job Satisfaction (M)	501	.52

Servant Leadership

Research Results

Servant Leadership and Follower Outcomes

Strongly - Correlated	Moderately - Correlated	Weakly - Correlated	Weakly + Correlated	Moderately + Correlated	Strongly + Correlated
-1 to -.50	-.49 to -.30	-.29 to -.10	.10 to .29	.30 to .49	.50 to 1

Outcome	Followers	
Weakly, Positively Correlated		
Customer Orientation (M)	501	.17
Commitment to Supervisor (F)	815	.19
Outcome Performance (M)	501	.24
Moderately, Positively Correlated		
Creative Behavior (L)	250	.37
Job Satisfaction (I)	187	.37
Self-Efficacy (F)	815	.39
Overall Need Satisfaction (I)	187	.42
Nurse Job Satisfaction (K)	210	.47
Customer Orientation (O)	530	.49
Strongly, Positively Correlated		
Job Satisfaction (M)	501	.52
Extrinsic Satisfaction (J)	595	.57
Intrinsic Satisfaction (J)	595	.59
Interpersonal Trust (T)	137	.66
Job Satisfaction (J)	595	.67
Organizational Commitment (S)	563	.83

	Outcome	Followers
Weakly, Negatively Correlated		
-.18	Job Stress (M)	501
-.21	Turnover Intentions (R)	425
Moderately, Negatively Correlated		
-.30	Burnout (O)	530
-.32	Turnover Intentions (O)	530
-.32	Disengagement (R)	92

Research from 9,060 follower ratings has found that servant leadership is positively correlated with a variety of measures of job satisfaction and with several measures of job performance.

Servant leadership is negatively correlated with follower stress, burnout, disengagement and turnover intentions.

Servant Leadership

Research Results

Servant Leadership and Organizational Outcomes

Strongly - Correlated	Moderately - Correlated	Weakly - Correlated
-1 to -.50	-.49 to -.30	-.29 to -.10

Weakly + Correlated	Moderately + Correlated	Strongly + Correlated
.10 to .29	.30 to .49	.50 to 1

Outcome	Follow-	
Weakly, Positively Correlated		
Procedural Justice Climate (F)	815	.17
Moderately, Positively Correlated		
Team Performance (H)	191[d]	.38
Sales Performance (R)	40	.38
Service Climate (F)	815	.45
Sales Behavior (R)	245	.49
Strongly, Positively Correlated		
Organizational Justice (I)	187	.51
OCB - Conscientiousness (E) [b]	249	.55
OCB - Helping (E) [b]	249	.60
Team Performance (D)	71[a]	.60
Organizational Commitment (M)	501	.67
Procedural Justice Climate (E)	249	.72
Organizational Trust (A)	69	.72

Note. a Teams consisting of 304 employees and 60 managers. b Employee-rated. c Manager-rated. d 191 teams consisting of 999 participants. OCB = Organizational Citizenship Behavior. RSLP-S = Revised Servant Leader-ship Profile for Sport. e Nine items from Jacobs' instrument. OCB-I = OCB directed toward co-workers.

Research from 3,681 follower ratings has found that follower ratings of servant leadership are moderately to strongly, positively correlated with several measures of performance, and strongly, positively correlated with several measures of justice, commitment and performance.

Servant Leadership

Research Results

Servant Leadership and Leader Outcomes

Strongly - Correlated	Moderately - Correlated	Weakly - Correlated	Weakly + Correlated	Moderately + Correlated	Strongly + Correlated
-1 to -.50	-.49 to -.30	-.29 to -.10	.10 to .29	.30 to .49	.50 to 1

Outcome	Followers	
Weakly, Positively Correlated		
Role Inversion Behavior (K)	210	.17
Leader Trust (A)	69	.19
Initiating Structure (L)	250	.19
Moderately, Positively Correlated		
Leader Integrity (C)	283	.37
Cognition-Based Trust (H)	191[b]	.37
Leader Trust (B)	555	.39
Leader Effectiveness (P)	97[c]	.39
Leader Empathy (C)	283	.42
Transformational Leadership (Q)	155	.42
Affect-Based Trust (H)	191[b]	.47
Strongly, Positively Correlated		
Leader Agreeableness (C)	126	.57
Leader Competence (C)	283	.59
Transformational Leadership (H)	191[b]	.67

In empirical studies on leading as a servant leader, and ratings of a second aspect of leadership, analyses from 2,884 follower ratings of servant leadership have found that being a servant leader is moderately correlated with trust in the leader and ratings of leader effectiveness and competence.

Ratings of servant leadership are strongly, positively correlated with transformational leadership and leader competence.

Servant Leadership
Discussion

The empirical research to date generally shows positive relationships between servant leadership and leader outcomes, follower outcomes and organizational outcomes. Until more research is conducted, it remains unclear how unique what is being measured as servant leadership truly is.

For example, there is likely a great deal of overlap between servant leadership and consideration measured by the *LBDQ-XII*, agreeableness measured by a big five assessment of personality, individual consideration measured by the *MLQ 5X* and so forth.

The movement toward providing more measureable structure to the servant leadership philosophy, however, is a valuable contribution to the field of leadership research.

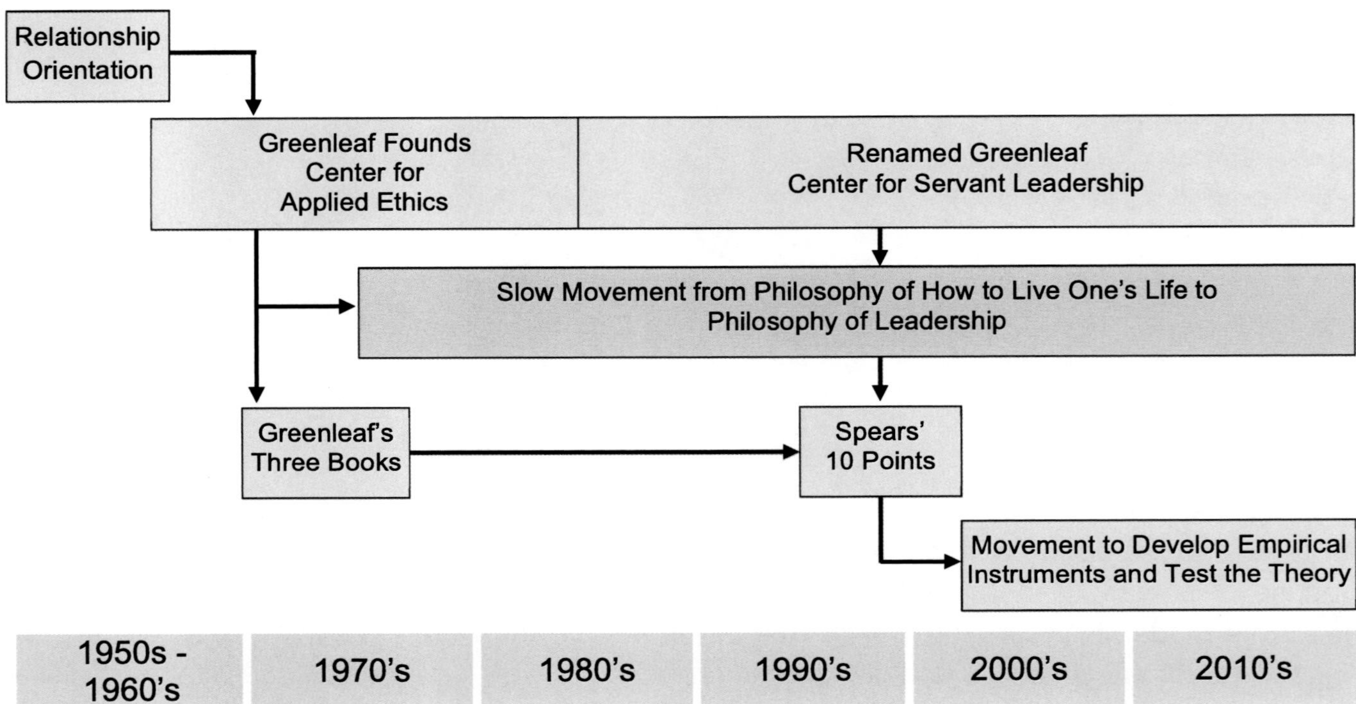

Servant Leadership

Summary

Servant leadership is slowly moving from a philosophy to a theory with measureable components. There is no widely accepted model, yet, of exactly what constructs comprise servant leadership. Seventeen of the aspects from Spears' 1998 model and four emerging instruments are similar to elements of the full range model of leadership or authentic leadership. The other seventeen components, however, don't readily map to areas of the full range model of leadership or authentic leadership.

These somewhat unique aspects can be grouped into the six categories below. We notice that two aspects – spirituality and altruism - are primarily characteristics or behaviors related to the leader. Two aspects – healing and empowerment – are generally related to the relationship between the leader and a follower(s). The final two aspects – stewardship and building community - are related to the leader and larger groups than just a few followers.

Related to the Leader	Related to the Follower	Related to the Community
Spirituality	Healing	Stewardship
Altruism	Empowerment	Building Community

Servant leadership is positively correlated with a variety of measures of job satisfaction and with several measures of job performance.

Servant leadership is negatively correlated with follower stress, burnout, disengagement and turnover intentions.

Servant leadership is moderately to strongly, positively correlated with several measures of performance, and strongly, positively correlated with several measures of justice, commitment and performance.

In empirical studies on leading as a servant leader, and ratings of a second aspect of leadership, we see that being a servant leader is moderately correlated with trust in the leader and ratings of leader effectiveness and competence.

We also see that being a servant leader is correlated with being a transformational leader and with the use of initiation of structure.

Finally, we see that being a servant leader is correlated with measures of trust that followers have in the leader and the belief that the servant leader has integrity.

Servant Leadership

Studies References

Studies Referenced

A. Joseph and Winston (2005)
B. Senjaya and Pekerti (2010)
C. Washington et al. (2006)
D. Hu and Liden (2011)
E. Ehrhart (2004)
F. Walumbwa et al. (2010)
G. Irving and Longbotham (2007)
H. Schaubroeck et al. (2011)
I. Mayer, Bardes and Piccolo (2008)
J. Cerit (2009)
K. Jenkins and Stewart (2010)
L. Neubert, Kacmar, Carlson, Chonko and Roberts (2008)
M. Jaramillo, Grisaffe, Chonko and Roberts (2009)
N. Rieke, Hammermeister and Chase (2008)
O. Babakus, Yavas and Ashill (2011)
P. Hale and Fields (2007)
Q. Choudhart, Akhtar, and Zaheer (2012)
R. Hunter, Neubert, Perry, Witt, Penney and Weinberger (2012)
S. Cerit (2010)
T. Chatbury, Beaty and Kriek (2010)

Servant Leadership

Notes

[1] There is an instrument associated with Laub's model. Laub developed the *Organizational Leadership Assessment* for his doctoral dissertation. He first developed a pool of questions based on his review of the literature on servant leadership. He then had between 14 and 25 experts who had written on or taught servant leadership at the university level participate in a three step *Delphi* process in order to add to the original pool of items and then rate those items' importance. At the conclusion of the third iteration of the *Delphi* process, 74 potential items had been developed.

Eighty items were then tested with 828 participants. Laub performed a series of exploratory factor analyses (EFA) on these data. Laub found that 27 items loaded on a single component called *Organizational Assessment* and 53 items loaded on a single component called *Leadership Assessment.*

The eigenvalues from the exploratory factor analysis were not provided. The 23 items that loaded on Organizational Assessment had factor loadings between .40 and .71. The 57 items that loaded on Leadership Assessment had factor loadings between .46 and .73.

No factor analytic evidence was provided to support unique subscales (first order) within the factor called Leader-ship Assessment. It is unclear how the items for each first order scale were assigned to each scale. After the EFA, the instrument was reduced from 74 to 60 questions to decrease the time it took to complete the instrument. No additional details were provided on how the 60 questions were selected.

[2] There is an instrument associated with Ehrhart's model. Based on his review of the literature, Ehrhart hypothesized the seven aspects of servant leadership shown in the table. He developed 14 questions based on those seven aspects. Ehrhart administered the *Servant Leadership Scale*, the *LMX-7* and the *MLQ 5X* to 254 employed university students. He conducted a confirmatory factor analysis (CFA) that included all three measures. The results of the CFA found that the three instruments loaded on three different factors (X^2 = 429, *df* = 167, *CFI* = .95, *SRMR* = .04, *RMSEA* = .08).

[3] McSherry, W., & Cash, K. (2004). The language of spirituality: an emerging taxonomy. *International Journal of Nursing Studies, 41,* 2, 151-161

[4] One does not necessarily have to fall in just one of these areas, this is simply a chart to envision different conceptualizations of spirituality.

[5] Fry, L., & Cohen, M. (2009). Spiritual Leadership as a Paradigm for Organizational Transformation and Recovery from Extended Work Hours Cultures. *Journal of Business Ethics, 84,* 265-278.

[6] Batson, C., Ahmad, N. & Lishner, D. *Empathy and altruism*, in Snyder, C. R., & Lopez, S. J. (2005). *Handbook of positive psychology*. Oxford: Oxford University Press.

[7] Ibid.

[8] Lindenfield, G. (2008). *The emotional healing strategy: A recovery guide for any setback, disappointment or loss*. London: Michael Joseph.

[9] Spreitzer, G. M. (1995). Psychological empowerment in the workplace: Dimensions, measurement, and validation. *Academy of Management Journal, 38,* 5, 1442.

Spreitzer built his four aspects on work done by 10 previous authors.

[10] The terms shown in the bark blue boxes are Spreitzer's terms. The light blue boxes capture Spreitzer's definitions of the terms. I added the beige boxes as a learning aid.

[11] Davis, J. H., Schoorman, F. D., & Donaldson, L. (1997). Toward a Stewardship Theory of Management. *The Academy of Management Review, 22,* 1, 20. I have paraphrased some of the terminology they used to make it more understandable to non-economists. For space reasons, the table provided here doesn't include all of the contrasts provided by the authors.

[12] Podsakoff, P. (2000). Organizational citizenship behaviors: a critical review of the theoretical and empirical literature and suggestions for future research. *Journal of Management, 26,* 3, 513-563.

Podsakoff, N. P., Whiting, S. W., Podsakoff, P. M., & Blume, B. D. (January 01, 2009). Individual- and organizational-level consequences of organizational citizenship behaviors: A meta-analysis. *The Journal of Applied Psychology, 94,* 1, 122-41.

[13] Schein, E. H. (1985). *Organizational culture and leadership*. San Francisco: Jossey-Bass Publishers.

[14] The information on this page came from Laub, J. A. (1999). *Assessing the servant organization: Development of the servant organizational leadership assessment (SOLA) instrument.* (9921922, Florida Atlantic University). *ProQuest Dissertations and Theses.*

[15] The eigenvalues from the exploratory factor analysis were not provided. The 23 items that loaded on *Organizational Assessment* had factor loadings between .40 and .71. The 57 items that loaded on *Leadership Assessment* had factor loadings between .46 and .73.

No factor analytic evidence was provided to support unique subscales (first order) within the factor called Leadership Assessment. It is unclear how the items for each first order scale were assigned to each scale.

[16] Liden, R., Wayne, S., Zhao. H. and Henderson, D. (2008). Servant leadership: Development of a multidimensional measure and multi-level assessment. *Leadership Quarterly*, 19(2), 161.

[17] Sendjaya, Sen, Sarros, James and Santora, Joseph. (2008). *Defining and measuring servant leadership behaviour in organizations*. (Wiley-Blackwell Publishing Ltd.) Wiley-Blackwell Publishing Ltd.

[18] Letts, L., Wilkins, S., Law, M., Stewart, D., Bosch, J. and Westmorland, M. (2007). Critical review form: Qualitative studies (version 2.0). Retrieved from

http://www.sph.nhs.uk/sphfiles/caspappraisaltools/Qualitative%20Appraisal%20Tool.pdf

[19] Institute for Public Health Sciences. (2002). 11 questions to help you make sense of descriptive/cross-sectional studies. New York: Yeshiva University.

[20] Stoltz, P., Ude´n, G. and Willman, A. (2004). Support for family careers who care for an elderly person at home - A systematic literature review. *Scandinavian Journal of Caring Sciences*, 18, 111–118.

[21] The exact boundary between weak, moderate and strong correlations is not universally agreed upon. The definitions used are based on Cohen, J. (1992). A power primer. *Psychological Bulletin, 112,* 1, 155-9.

Chapter 10
Authentic Leadership

Authentic Leadership

Introduction

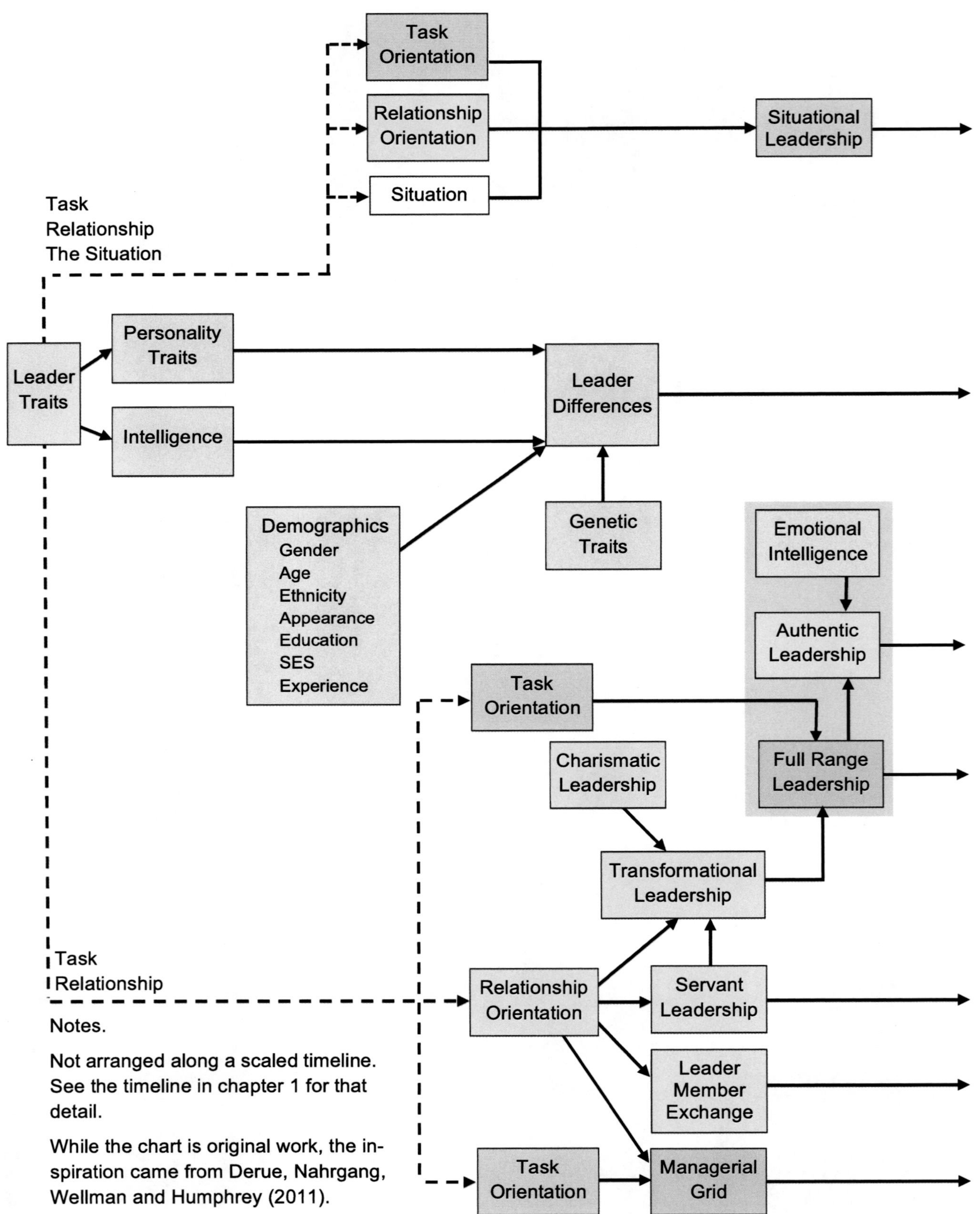

Notes.

Not arranged along a scaled timeline. See the timeline in chapter 1 for that detail.

While the chart is original work, the inspiration came from Derue, Nahrgang, Wellman and Humphrey (2011).

Authentic Leadership

Introduction

The idea of the authentic self has a long history. Academic areas such as philosophy, theology, drama, poetry and, more recently, psychology all explore what it means to be an authentic person.

Within the area of leadership, a both specific and popular theory of authentic leadership began to take shape in the early 2000's.

While certainly influenced by millennia of discussion of authenticity in individuals, the leadership aspects of authentic leadership built on the foundations of transformational leadership as well as emotional intelligence.

The theory of authentic leadership is so new, that there have yet to be any meta-analyses published on the theory. There have been, however, a number of empirical studies done with the currently popular instrument – the *Authentic Leadership Questionnaire.*[1]

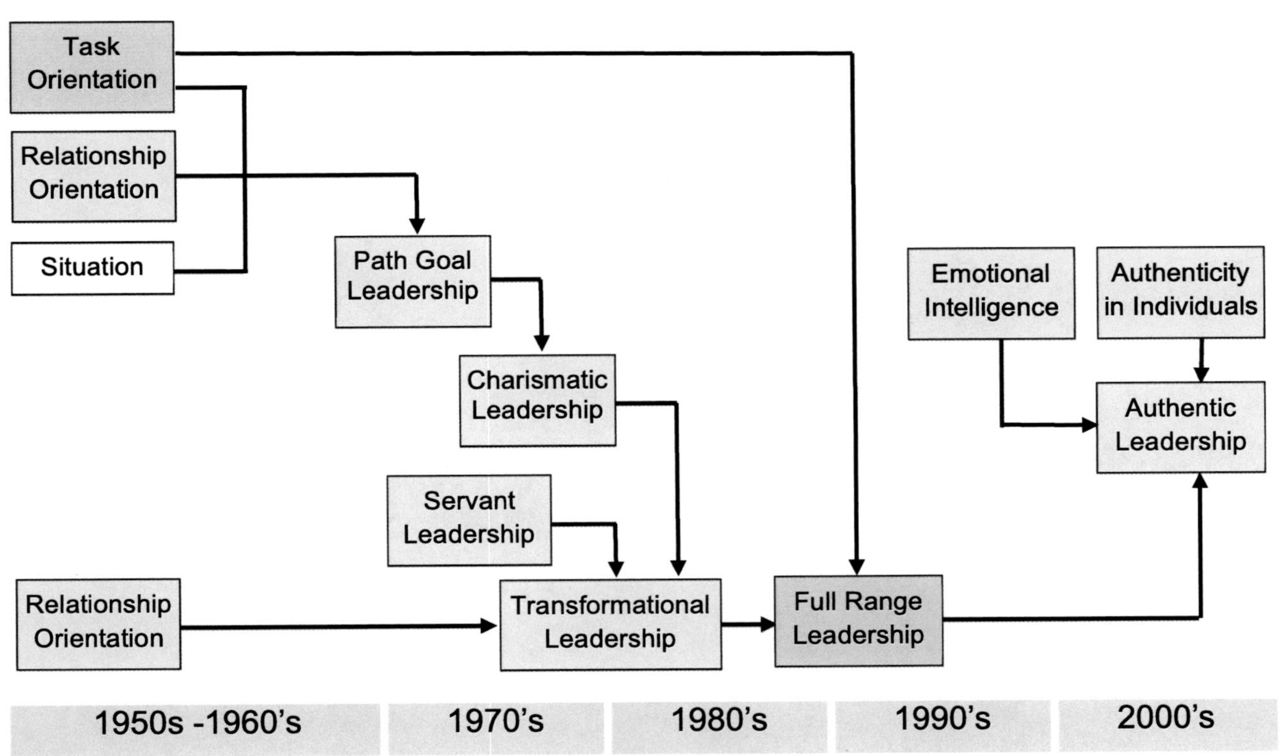

Authentic Leadership

Early Models

Authentic leadership has undergone several iterations of development. One of the important foundations for our current theory of authentic leadership was work done by Kernis and Goldman on the general concept of authenticity in individuals. In 2003, and again in 2006, Kernis and Goldman developed a model of authenticity that consisted of four aspects.

At about the same time, George, in his 2003 book, and George and Sims in their 2007 book, described three aspects of authentic leadership that are congruent with three of the four aspects from Kernis and Goldman: purpose with passion, enduring relationships and solid values.[2]

The dimension George described, called self-discipline, is similar to the dimension of self-regulation described a few years later by Avolio and Gardner (2005). While George's fifth aspect, called heart, is likely infused within most models of leadership, it doesn't specifically align with other high-level aspects of popular authentic leadership models.

Early Models of Authenticity and Authentic Leadership

Authentic Leadership Constructs	Kernis, (2003) Kernis and Goldman (2003, 2004, 2006)	George, (2003) George and Sims, (2007)
Self-Awareness	Awareness	Purpose with Passion
Relational Transparency	Relationship Orientation	Enduring Relationships
Internalized Moral Perspective	Authentic Behavior	Solid Values
Balanced Processing	Unbiased Processing	
Positive Moral Perspective		
Psychological Capital		
Self-Regulation		Self-Discipline
Merged into Other Constructs		Heart

Authentic Leadership

Kernis (2003), Kernis and Goldman (2003, 2004, 2006)

Kernis (2003) and Kernis and Goldman (2003, 2004, 2006) developed a model of authenticity. Their model was not specifically about authentic leadership, but rather about authenticity in individuals.

As part of their model of authenticity, they developed the four components shown below, as well as a 45-item instrument called *The Authenticity Inventory* that measures those four concepts.

Those four aspects of authenticity in individuals have influenced several subsequent theories of authentic leadership.

Kernis (2003) Authenticity Components[3]	
Awareness 	Awareness, Knowledge of and Trust in One's Motives, Feelings, Desires and Self-Relevant Cognitions Awareness of One's Strengths and Weaknesses, Dominant-Recessive Aspects of Personality, Powerful Emotions and Their Roles in Behavior
Relational Orientation 	Value and Make Efforts to Achieve Openness and Truthfulness in Close Relationships Allow Those Close to You to See the Real You, Those Deep, Dark, or Potentially Shadowy Self-aspects That Are Not Routinely Discussed Relational Authenticity Means Being Genuine and Not "Fake" in One's Relationships with Others
Authentic Behavior 	Acting in Ways Congruent with One's Values, Preferences, and Needs Rather than Acting Merely to Please Others or to Attain Rewards or Avoid Punishments
Unbiased Processing 	Minimal, if Any, Denial, Distortion, Exaggeration or Ignoring of Private Knowledge, Internal Experiences and Externally Based Self-Evaluative Information Objectivity and Acceptance with Respect to One's Strengths and Weaknesses

Authentic Leadership

George (2003)
George and Sims (2007)

George (2003) and George and Sims (2007) wrote two very popular books on authentic leadership, in which they posited that authentic leadership is comprised of five aspects. George interviewed 125 individuals who had been leaders (most typically CEO's) of large organizations, and who had reputations as being authentic leaders. The leaders were selected from six different age strata, ranging from 23-29 to 70-93. Based on his interviews, George posited five aspects of authentic leadership.

George (2003) and George and Sims (2007) Aspects of Authentic Leadership	
Pursuing Purpose with Passion	Understanding Ourselves as Leaders Understanding Our Passions as Leaders Using Those Passions to Understand the Purpose of Our Leadership
Establishing Enduring Relationships	Followers Want Personal Relationships with Their Leaders Before They Will Give Themselves Fully to Their Jobs Followers Insist on Access to Their Leaders, Knowing That Trust and Commitment Are Built on the Openness and Depth of Relationships
Practicing Solid Values	Integrity Is the One Value Required of Every Authentic Leader Values Are Shaped by Our Personal Beliefs and Developed Through Study, Introspection, Consultation with Others and Years of Experience
Leading with Heart	Authentic Leaders Lead with Their Hearts as Well as Their Heads Leading with the Heart Means Having Passion for Our Work, Compassion for the People We Serve, Empathy for the People With Whom We Work and the Courage to Make Difficult Decisions
Demonstrating Self-Discipline	Authentic Leaders Set High Standards for Themselves and Others Authentic Leadership Requires Accepting Full Responsibility for Outcomes and Holding Others Accountable for Their Performance Self-Discipline Should Be Reflected in Their Personal Lives as Well

Authentic Leadership

George (2003)
George and Sims (2007)

Based on his interviews with authentic leaders, George also developed a list of bad leader archetypes that prevent leaders from being authentic.

George (2003) and George and Sims (2007) Bad Leader Archetypes	
Imposters	Imposters Rise Through the Ranks by Using Cunning and Aggression They Understand the Politics of Getting Ahead by Eliminating Competitors They Have Little Appetite for Self-Reflection or for Developing Self-Awareness
Rationalizers	To People Outside of Their Organizations, Rationalizers Always Appear on Top of the Issues When Things Don't Go Their Way, They Blame External Forces or Subordinates or Offer Facile Answers to Their Problems They Rarely Step up and Take Responsibility Themselves
Glory Seekers	Define Themselves by Acclaim of the External World Money, Fame, Glory and Power are Their Goals Often It Seems More Important to Them to Appear on Lists of the Most Powerful Business Leaders than It Does to Build Organizations of Lasting Value
Loners	Loners Avoid Forming Close Relationships, Seeking out Mentors or Creating Support Networks Not to Be Confused with Introverts, Loners Often Have a Myriad of Superficial Relationships and Acolytes, but They Do Not Listen to Them They Reject Honest Feedback, Even from Those Who Care about Them
Shooting Stars	Shooting Stars Focus Entirely on Their Careers They Rarely Make Time for Family, Friendships, Communities or Themselves They Move up so Rapidly in Their Careers That They Never Have Time to Learn from Their Mistakes A Year or Two into Any Job, They Are Ready to Move on, Before They Have Had to Confront the Results Of Their Decisions

Although George posits that authentic leaders engage in all five aspects of authentic leadership described on the preceding page, he provided a developmental path for poor leaders who fall into one of the five bad archetypes shown above. In the table below, for example, a poor leader who falls into the imposters category would need to spend significant time working on self-awareness to determine her/his true passion and purpose as a leader.

Bad Archetype	Needed Work	To Become More Authentic In This Area
Imposters	Self-Awareness	Pursuing Purpose with Passion
Rationalizers	Developing Values and Principles	Practicing Solid Values
Glory Seekers	Clarifying Motivations	Leading with Heart
Loners	Developing and Listening to Support Team	Establishing Enduring Relationships
Shooting Stars	Developing a More Integrated Life	Demonstrating Self-Discipline

Authentic Leadership

Avolio, Gardner, Walumbwa, Luthans and May, 2004

In 2004, Avolio, Gardner, Walumbwa, Luthans and May provided a model, not of dimensions of authentic leadership, but on the direct and indirect outcomes of authentic leadership. The indirect follower outcomes in their model included hope, trust, positive emotions and optimism. These ideas would influence subsequent refinements of conceptions of authentic leadership.

Avolio, Gardner, Walumbwa, Luthans and May, 2004				
Authentic Leadership	Direct Follower Outcomes	Indirect Follower Outcomes	Follower Work Attitudes	Follower Behaviors
➡	Personal Identification with the Leader Social Identification with the Group ➡	Hope Trust Positive Emotions Optimism ➡	Commitment Job Satisfaction Meaningfulness Engagement ➡	Job Performance Extra Effort Withdrawal Behaviors

Authentic Leadership Constructs	Kernis[a] 2003	George[b] 2003	Avolio[c] 2004
Self-Awareness	Awareness	Purpose with Passion	
Relational Transparency	Relationship Orientation	Enduring Relationships	
Internalized Moral Perspective	Authentic Behavior	Solid Values	
Balanced Processing	Unbiased Processing		
Positive Moral Perspective			
Psychological Capital			Hope, Trust Positive Emotions Optimism
Self-Regulation		Self-Discipline	
Merged into Other Constructs		Heart	Personal and Social Identification

Authentic Leadership

Avolio and Gardner, 2005

In 2005, Avolio and Gardner discussed eight high-level aspects of authentic leadership. Self-awareness is similar to previous concepts by Kernis as well as George. Self-regulation is similar to George's concept of self-discipline. Within the idea of self-regulation, Avolio and Gardner included balanced processing, relational transparency and internalized regulation.

Avolio and Gardner also added three additional considerations. Positive moral perspective would remain in several subsequent theories of authentic leadership. Psychological capital became a popular theory in its own right, and has also been described as an outcome of authentic leadership. Finally, Avolio and Gardner also described a set of leader behaviors and processes believed to be related to authentic leadership beyond self-awareness, balanced processing, relational transparency and internalized regulation.

Authentic Leadership Constructs	Kernis[a] 2003	George[b] 2003	Avolio[c] 2004	Avolio[d] 2005
Self-Awareness	Awareness	Purpose with Passion		Self-Awareness
Relational Transparency	Relationship Orientation	Enduring Relationships		Relational Transparency
Internalized Moral Perspective	Authentic Behavior	Solid Values		Internalized Regulation
Balanced Processing	Unbiased Processing			Balanced Processing
Positive Moral Perspective				Positive Moral Perspective
Psychological Capital			Hope Trust Positive Emotions Optimism	Confidence Optimism Hope Resiliency
Self-Regulation		Self-Discipline		Self-Regulation
Merged into Other Constructs		Heart	Personal Identification Social Identification	Personal Identification Social Identification Positive Modeling Emotional Contagion Supporting Self-Determination Positive Social Exchanges

Authentic Leadership

Avolio and Gardner, 2005

The table contains the definitions of the various constructs used by Avolio and Gardner (2005).

Avolio and Gardner, 2005[4]	
Self-Awareness	Self-Awareness Occurs When Individuals Are Cognizant of Their Own Existence, and What Constitutes That Existence Within the Context Within Which They Operate over Time. The Leader Understands His or Her Unique Talents, Strengths, Sense of Purpose, Core Values, Beliefs and Desires
Self-Regulation[5]	Self-Regulation Is the Process Through Which Authentic Leaders Align Their Values with Their Intentions and Actions
Relational Transparency	Relational Authenticity Means Being Genuine and Not "Fake" in One's Relationships with Others (Kernis, 2003)
Internalized Regulation	Acting in Ways Congruent with One's Values, Preferences, and Needs Rather than Acting Merely to Please Others or to Attain Rewards or Avoid Punishments (Kernis, 2003)
Balanced Processing	Minimal, If Any, Denial, Distortion, Exaggeration, or Ignoring of Private Knowledge, Internal Experiences, and Externally Based Self-Evaluative Information (Kernis, 2003)
Positive Moral Perspective	An Ethical and Transparent Decision Making Process Whereby Authentic Leaders Develop and Draw upon Reserves of Moral Capacity, Efficacy, Courage, and Resiliency to Address Ethical Issues and Achieve Authentic and Sustained Moral Actions. (May et al., 2003)
Psychological Capital	Confidence, Optimism, Hope and Resilience are Personal Resources of the Authentic Leader. They Help Heighten Self-Awareness and Self-Regulatory Behavior as Part of the Process of Self-Development
Hope	A Positive Motivational State that Is Based on an Interactively Derived Sense of Successful Goal-Directed Energy and Planning to Meet Goals (Snyder, Irving, and Anderson, 1991)
Trust	A Psychological State Comprising the Intention to Accept Vulnerability Based upon Positive Expectations of the Intentions or Behavior of Another (Rousseau, Sitkin, Burt and Camerer, 1998)
Positive Emotions	Authentic Leaders Through Their Positive Emotions Influence Followers and Their Development
Optimism	A Cognitive Process Involving Positive Outcome Expectancies and Causal Attributions That Are External, Temporary, and Specific in Interpreting Bad or Negative Events and Internal, Stable, and Global for Good or Positive Events (Seligman, 1998)
Personal and Social Identification	Followers Come to Identify with Authentic Leaders and Their Values

Authentic Leadership

Gardner, Avolio, Luthans, May and Walumbwa, 2005

In 2005, Gardner, Avolio, Luthans, May and Walumbwa provided a model of authentic leadership with two major parts: self-awareness and self-regulation. Self-awareness is similar to Kernis and Goldman's concept of awareness, George's concept of purpose with passion and Avolio and Gardner's concept of self-awareness.

Self-regulation is similar to George's construct of self-discipline, but contained subcategories. Three important subcategories were balanced processing, relational transparency and internalized regulation. These are consistent with those concepts discussed by Avolio and Gardner (2005).

Similar to Avolio, Gardner, Walumbwa, Luthans and May (2004), Gardner, Avolio, Luthans, May and Walumbwa (2005) included a series of follower outcomes and performance in their model. They also introduced the idea of authentic followership.

Authentic Leadership	→	Authentic Followership	→	Follower Outcomes	→	Follower Performance
Self-Awareness Values Identity Emotions Motives Self-Regulation Internalized Regulation Balanced Processing Relational Transparency Authentic Behavior	→	Self-Awareness Values Identity Emotions Motives Self-Regulation Internalized Regulation Balanced Processing Relational Transparency Authentic Behavior	→	Trust Engagement Workplace Well-Being	→	Sustainable Verifiable

	Kernis[a] 2003	George[b] 2003	Avolio[d] 2005	Gardner[e] 2005
Self-Awareness	Awareness	Purpose with Passion	Self-Awareness	Self-Awareness
Relational Transparency	Relationship Orientation	Enduring Relationships	Relational Transparency	Relational Transparency
Internalized Moral Perspective	Authentic Behavior	Solid Values	Internalized Regulation	Internalized Regulation
Balanced Processing	Unbiased Processing		Balanced Processing	Balanced Processing

Authentic Leadership

Walumbwa, Avolio, Gardner, Wernsing and Peterson, 2008

By 2008, Walumbwa, Avolio, Gardner, Wernsing and Peterson (2008) elevated balanced processing, relational transparency and internalized regulation to separate aspects of authentic leadership, and added a fifth aspect called positive moral perspective.

When conducting content validity for the *Authentic Leadership Questionnaire*, however, Walumbwa, Avolio, Gardner, Wernsing and Peterson (2008) combined the two categories of internalized regulation and positive moral perspective into a single domain called internalized moral perspective.

The chart on the opposite page doesn't endeavor to capture all of the nuances of the many contributions to authentic leadership. Rather, it provides a sense of the progression of ideas that have lead to the four dimensions measured by the *Authentic Leadership Questionnaire* as well as the *Authentic Leadership Inventory*.

Several observations are instructive.

First, self-awareness has been consistent in most models of authentic leadership.

Relational transparency and balanced processing have also been consistent in most models. In some models, these aspects were treated as primary dimensions. In other models, the concept of self-regulation was a primary dimension and balanced processing and relational transparency were contained within the dimension of self-regulation.

Internalized regulation is conceptually similar to what Kernis (2003) called authentic behavior and George (2003) called solid values.

Positive moral perspective was a primary dimension in several models. When the *Authentic Leadership Questionnaire* was developed, however, it was combined with internalized regulation to create the current dimension of internalized moral perspective.

Self-regulation was included in several models as a higher-order construct, typically including the dimensions of balanced processing, relational transparency and internalized regulation. Self-regulation dissipated as a higher order dimension and balanced processing, relational transparency and internalized regulation became first-order dimensions.

Finally, psychological capital was included in several models as a primary dimension. It likely is infused in the current model, but did not remain as a unique dimension. It has, however, become a separate, stand-alone theory with an attendant instrument.

Authentic Leadership

Historical Overview

	Kernis[a] 2003	George[b] 2003	Avolio[c] 2004	Avolio[d] 2005	Gardner[e] 2005	Walumbwa[f] 2008(a)	Walumbwa[g] 2008(b)
Self-Awareness	Awareness	Purpose with Passion		Self-Awareness	Self-Awareness	Self-Awareness	Self-Awareness
Relational Transparency	Relationship Orientation	Enduring Relationships		Relational Transparency	Relational Transparency	Relational Transparency	Relational Transparency
Balanced Processing	Unbiased Processing			Balanced Processing	Balanced Processing	Balanced Processing	Balanced Processing
Internalized Moral Perspective	Authentic Behavior	Solid Values		Internalized Regulation	Internalized Regulation	Internalized Regulation	Internalized Moral Perspective
Positive Moral Perspective				Positive Moral Perspective		Positive Moral Perspective	
Psychological Capital			Hope Trust Positive Emotions Optimism	Confidence Optimism Hope Resiliency			
Self-Regulation		Self-Discipline		Self-Regulation	Self-Regulation		
Merged into Other Constructs or Dissipated		Heart	Personal and Social Identification	Personal Identification Social Identification Positive Modeling Emotional Contagion Supporting Self Determination Positive Social Exchanges			

a. Kernis, 2003, Kernis and Goldman 2003-2006
b. George, 2003, George and Sims, 2007
c. Avolio, Gardner, Walumbwa, Luthans and May, 2004
d. Avolio and Gardner, (2005)
e. Gardner, Avolio, Luthans, May and Walumbwa, (2005)
f. Walumbwa, Avolio, Gardner, Wernsing and Peterson (2008a)
g. Walumbwa, Avolio, Gardner, Wernsing and Peterson (2008b)

Authentic Leadership

Current Dimensions

As of 2015, the predominant model of authentic leadership used the four dimensions below.

Walumbwa, Avolio, Gardner, Wernsing and Peterson, 2008[6]	
Self-Awareness 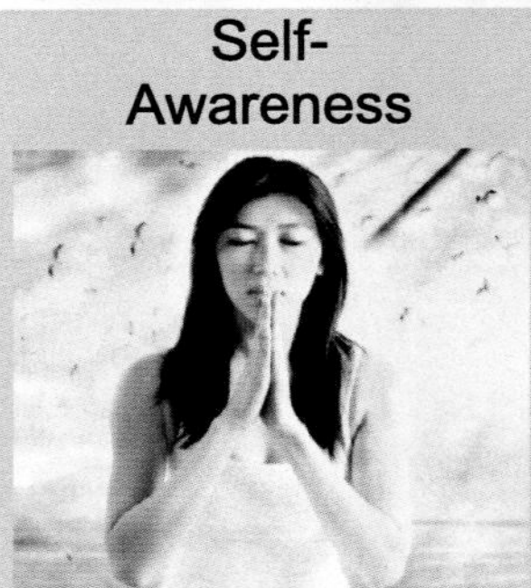	Demonstrating an Understanding of How One Derives and Makes Meaning of the World and How That Meaning-Making Process Impacts the Way One Views Himself or Herself over Time Showing an Understanding of One's Strengths and Weaknesses and the Multifaceted Nature of the Self, Which Includes Gaining Insight into the Self Through Exposure to Others, and Being Cognizant of One's Impact on Other People
Relational Transparency 	Presenting One's Authentic Self (as Opposed to Fake or Distorted Self) to Others Such Behavior Promotes Trust Through Disclosures That Involve Openly Sharing Information and Expressions of One's True Thoughts and Feelings While Trying to Minimize Displays of Inappropriate Emotions
Balanced Processing 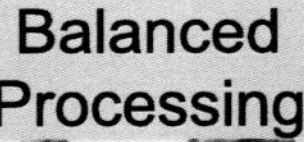 	Leaders Objectively Analyze All Relevant Data Before Coming to a Decision Leaders Solicit Views That Challenge Their Deeply Held Positions
Internalized Moral Perspective 	An Internalized and Integrated Form of Self-Regulation. This Sort of Self-Regulation is Guided by Internal Moral Standards and Values Versus Group, Organizational and Societal Pressures It Results in Expressed Decision Making and Behavior That is Consistent with These Internalized Values

Authentic Leadership

Seminal Definitions

There are numerous definitions of authentic leadership. The following four, however, provide a sense of the evolution of those definitions.

Henderson and Hoy (1983, pp. 67–68)
Leadership authenticity is therefore defined as the extent to which subordinates perceive their leader to demonstrate the acceptance of organizational and personal responsibility for actions, outcomes, and mistakes; to be non-manipulating of subordinates; and to exhibit salience of self over role. Leadership inauthenticity is defined as the extent to which subordinates perceive their leader to be 'passing the buck' and blaming others and circumstances for errors and outcomes; to be manipulative of subordinates; and to be demonstrating a salience of role over self.

George (2003, p. 12)
Authentic leaders use their natural abilities, but they also recognize their shortcomings and work hard to overcome them. They lead with purpose, meaning and values. They build enduring relationships with people. Others follow them because they know where they stand. They are consistent and self-disciplined. When their principles are tested, they refuse to compromise. Authentic leaders are dedicated to developing themselves because they know that becoming a leader takes a lifetime of personal growth.

Luthans and Avolio (2003, p. 243)
Authentic leadership [is] a process that draws from both positive psychological capacities and a highly developed organizational context. This results in both greater self-awareness and self-regulated positive behaviors on the part of leaders and associates, fostering positive self-development. The authentic leader is confident, hopeful, optimistic, resilient, transparent, moral/ethical, future-oriented and gives priority to developing associates into leaders themselves. The authentic leader does not try to coerce or even rationally persuade associates, but rather the leader's authentic values, beliefs and behaviors serve to model the development of associates.

Walumbwa, Peterson, Avolio, Wernsing and Peterson (2008, p. 94)
Authentic leadership is a pattern of leader behavior that draws upon and promotes both positive psychological capacities and a positive ethical climate, to foster greater self-awareness, an internalized moral perspective, balanced processing of information, and relational transparency on the part of leaders working with followers, fostering positive self-development.

Authentic Leadership

Becoming a More Authentic Leader

Becoming a More Authentic Leader
The following four pages will discuss ways to increase your authenticity as a leader. The pages will provide a bit of detail on each of the unique aspects of authentic leadership, and offer some practical suggestions.

Transparency is related to openly sharing information and expressing our true thoughts and feelings.

Self-Awareness is related to gaining a better understanding of our strengths and weaknesses and how our behaviors impact others.

Balanced Processing occurs when we objectively analyze all relevant data before coming to a decision and solicit views that challenge our deeply held positions.

Internal Moralized Perspective is a form of self-regulation in which we are guided by internal moral standards and values versus group, organizational and societal pressures.

Authentic Leadership

Becoming More Transparent

Transparency

When we look at the leader to the left, his expression tells us that he likely "holds his cards close to his chest." He likely provides followers with dribbles of information in order to maintain power. This is the opposite of transparency.

Although the idea of being a transparent leader encompasses many aspects, two aspects help capture what it means to be a transparent leader.

Ideas for Becoming a More Transparent Leader

Allow Followers to Be Forthcoming with Their Ideas

An important aspect of allowing followers to be forthcoming with their ideas is to withhold your opinion until followers have had a chance to express their thoughts.

As an example, imagine that a leader said "I think this new project is pretty risky. What do you all think?" By expressing her or his opinion first, the leader has reduced the likelihood that she or he will get honest input.

A better approach might be to say something such as "I've thought about this project but haven't been able to organize my thoughts. It would be really helpful if I could hear from each of you. I need to hear the good and bad aspects of the project and you all are the experts."

Tell Followers What You Believe, Even if it is Hard Truth

An old joke is "how do you know when politicians are lying…their lips are moving." This aptly captures the idea of avoiding hard truths. Part of leader transparency is telling our followers hard truths.

Providing our followers the hard truth is, of course, difficult to do. It is much easier, however, to give our followers difficult feedback in smaller, regular doses that in infrequent large doses.

One way to structure this sort of difficult feedback is through the creation of a joint development plan. This sort of plan accomplishes several things. First, it identifies areas in which the follower needs to grow. Second, it outlines behaviors and possible training to assist the follower in those changes. Third, if there are regularly scheduled review sessions, we have a chance to positively reinforce the changes the follower is making. Finally, the hard truth isn't provided all at once, but in smaller increments that the follower can better absorb without becoming defensive.

Authentic Leadership

Becoming More Self Aware

Self-Awareness

In his book *True North*, George provided an analogy that becoming more self-aware as a leader resembles layers of an onion. We need to continually peel away our layers in order to understand our true inner selves.

George argues that our outer layers are our public leader persona. These consist of things such as how we talk and dress, our routine facial expressions and our body language. Beneath these outer layers are things that are a bit less obvious to both our followers and to us. These are things such as our values and motivations. The center of the onion is our true, authentic self.

Ideas for Becoming a More Self-Aware Leader

The Johari Window A famous model for thinking about self-awareness is the Johari Window.[7] The X axis in the model consists of the degree to which we are aware of ourselves. The Y axis consists of the degree to which we share our true selves with others.

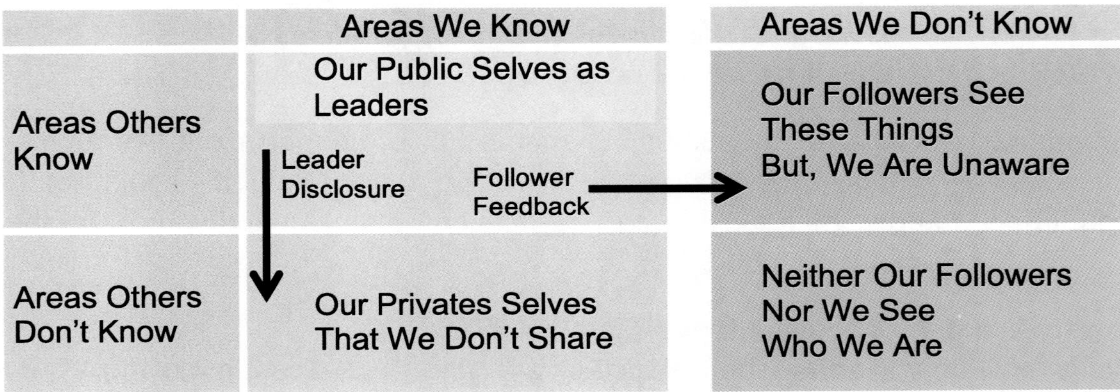

In the model above, the light blue quadrant is the part of ourselves that we share with others (the outside of the onion). The grey quadrant represents aspects of ourselves that we know, but are unwilling to share with others. The purple quadrant represents aspects of who we are to which we are blind (a layer down in the onion). Others see these aspects but we don't. The pink quadrant represents aspects of who we are that are hidden from both ourselves and others (the center of the onion).

As leaders, we would like the purple quadrant to be as small as possible. These are often called our blind spots – aspects of who we are and how we lead that others observe, but for which we are oblivious. The leader action to decrease this quadrant is being willing to receive feedback from others.

We may also want to decrease the size of the grey quadrant. This is related to being more transparent. Here the required behavior is to increase the amount of personal information we are willing to share with others.

Authentic Leadership

Increasing Balanced Processing

Balanced Processing refers to how we solicit sufficient opinions and viewpoints prior to making important decisions. An important aspect of balanced processing is to analyze all relevant data before we reach a decision.

Included in balanced processing is seeking opinions from other stakeholders who may not agree with us.

Ideas for Increasing Our Balanced Processing

Be Aware of the Time Versus Quality Aspects of Decisions Volume 1 of this series discussed the idea of satisficing. As leaders, we rarely have all of the time we would like to devote to making a "perfect" decision. There are simply too many decisions and deadlines to allocate all of our time to one decision. Consequently, we often search for the first solution that will work for a problem, and then move to the next challenge.

A nuance of increasing our balanced processing when making decisions is to determine how important a variety of perspectives are for any particular decision. While there are many aspects that can contribute to the complexities of a decision, one that works in tandem with balanced processing is the amount of uncertainty involved in a decision. The more uncertainty there is surrounding a leadership challenge, the more important it is to solicit input from a variety of sources.

Solicit Different Points of View For decisions with a great deal of uncertainty, we will want colleagues and followers to feel at ease contributing to the decision. One way to do this is to first organize the issues related to the challenge. A good first step is to clearly write the goal on a sheet of paper. Next, write down how the organization will know if the goal has been achieved.

After those foundational aspects are clear, next create a column labeled constraints and a column labeled resources. Constraints are things that might assist in solving the problem but are "off the table," at the present decision-making point. Examples often include the timeframe in which the decision must be made, the budget available and so forth.

In the column labeled resources, list what available resources are currently available. These are often things such as the number of workers available for the project or other organizational resources. Once we as leaders have gotten some structure on paper, the next step is to solicit input from a variety of people on what other resources we might have, or how to reduce the constraints we perceive.

Once those contributions are added to our sheet, we can generate options for solving the problem. An important point is that we didn't start with solutions. That technique tends to frustrate followers who proposed solutions that weren't selected. Rather, we involved followers in the foundational discussions about the problem. Usually, once people understand the timeframe, constraints and resources, they are more accepting of whatever final solution was chosen.

Authentic Leadership

Demonstrating Our Internalized Moral Perspective

Internalized Moral Perspective refers to an internalized and integrated form of self-regulation.[8] Internalized moral perspective is related to having high ethical standards. There are, however, two broad and often competing ways to decide what is ethical.

One ethical view advocates following a certain moral code regardless of the outcomes. The other ethical view evaluates possible outcomes and argues that the ethical choice is the one that produces the greatest good for the greatest number of people.[9]

To envision this, lets imagine that the Chief Financial Officer (CFO) discovered that a vice president of a company was embezzling funds. Only the CEO and CFO know about the embezzlement. Both following principles as well as the greatest good for the greatest number can be used to argue either prosecuting the vice president or allowing her or him to resign quietly. In any of the four examples below, the leader who chose that action would likely believe that she or he made an ethical decision.

Follow Principles	Greatest Good for the Greatest Number
Prosecute the Vice President	**Prosecute the Vice President**
The principles being followed include being transparent and upholding the law.	Society rests on a set of laws. Allowing the powerful to escape justice sends a message to others that crime is acceptable. The greatest good is to send a clear message to all of the organization and society.
Allow the Vice President to Quietly Resign	**Allow the Vice President to Quietly Resign**
The principle being followed is to never make the company look bad publicly.	Publicly prosecuting the vice president would likely lower the organization's stock price, which may require layoffs and also hurt all stockholders – the greatest good is a quiet resignation.

Ideas for Demonstrating Our Internalized Moral Perspective

Set High Ethical Standards The table above reminds us that there will be different opinions on what is "ethical." When we are grappling with an ethical decision it can be helpful to create a table with headings similar to those in gold above and then fill in the light blue boxes for the possible decisions. This is very helpful as a way to explain to others why we selected the course we did. It demonstrates that we contemplated multiple ethical and moral aspects of the situation prior to reaching a decision.

Think About Your Ideal Leader Once we have clarified how all four possible actions could be deemed ethical or unethical by others, how do we decide which course to take? Hopefully, one of the four quadrants will resonate with you much more than others. For some decisions, however, we remain torn even after organizing our thoughts.

One technique for selecting your action relates to your image of the ideal leader you would like to be. It can be helpful to metaphorically "step outside of yourself" for a few moments. Imagine yourself not as you currently are, but as the ideal you would like to be. Now ask "which of the four quadrants would the ideal me select?"

Authentic Leadership

The Authentic Leadership Inventory

As of 2015, the primary research instrument to measure authentic leadership was the *Authentic Leadership Questionnaire*. In 2011, however, Neider and Schriesheim developed different questions (items) to measure the four aspects of authentic leadership of self-awareness, relational transparency, balanced processing and internalized regulation. Their instrument is the *Authentic Leadership Inventory*.[10]

Development of the *Authentic Leadership Inventory*

Item Development

The authors first pilot tested the development of 16 possible authentic leadership questions with a sample of undergraduate and graduate students. Following the pilot test, the 16 questions were administered to 499 undergraduates. This analysis was done in 2008, and students were asked to rate presidential candidates John McCain or Barak Obama as authentic leaders. These data were analyzed using confirmatory factor analysis (CFA). CFA's were run for ratings of Senator McCain and also for ratings of President Obama. The best fitting CFA for Senator McCain was a four-factor model, but a one-factor model was the best fitting model for ratings of President Obama.

Confirmatory Factor Analyses

Based on the discrepancies between the two CFA's, the authors removed two of the 16 questions. The 14-question model produced a sufficient four-factor fit for ratings of Senator McCain (X^2 = 238.13, *df* = 71, *CFI* = 0.95, *RMSEA* = 0.07), and President Obama (X^2 = 262.47, *df* = 71, *CFI* = 0.95, *RMSEA* = 0.07). The difference between the two models was non-significant.

The 14-question model was then tested with 229 respondents who rated their immediate supervisors. The 14 questions produced a good fit for a four-factor model. (X^2 = 154.97, *df* = 71, *CFI* = 0.94, *RMSEA* = 0.07).

Reliability

The Cronbach Alpha scores for the final, 14-question version of the *ALI* ranged from .70 to .82 for the four subscales.

Predictive Validity

The four components of the *ALI* were correlated with general satisfaction (*r* = .39 to .48) and supervisor satisfaction (*r* = .58 to .62) measured by the *Minnesota Satisfaction Questionnaire* as well as organizational commitment measured by the *Organizational Commitment Questionnaire* (*r* = .28 to .33).

Acquiring the *Authentic Leadership Inventory*

As of 2015, researchers wishing to use the *Authentic Leadership Inventory* should contact Dr.'s Linda L. Neider or Chester A. Schriesheim in the School of Business Administration at the University of Miami.[11]

Authentic Leadership

The Authentic Leadership Questionnaire

Development of the *Authentic Leadership Questionnaire*

Item Development

Walumbwa, Avolio, Gardner, Wernsing and Peterson (2008) began by reviewing the literature on ethical and transformational literature. Based on that literature review, they developed 35 potential questions (items). They then reduced those 35 items to 22 that they felt best described the four content areas.

These 22 items were then subjected to a content validity assessment by faculty members and doctoral students. The reviewers were provided with a brief description of the four dimensions of authentic leadership and asked to assign each of the 22 items to one of the four content areas. Sixteen of the 22 items were assigned by the reviewers to the correct category more than 80% of the time. Six items were not sufficiently classified into the correct content area, and were eliminated from the question set. The sixteen items retained from the content validity analysis were: self-awareness (4 items), relational transparency (5 items), internalized moral perspective (4 items) and balanced processing (3 items).

Confirmatory Factor Analyses

In addition to the confirmatory factor analyses conducted during the development of the *Authentic Leadership Questionnaire*, several peer-reviewed articles have also reported CFA results. The table below provides a summary of CFA's on the *ALQ* as of 2015. A general sense is that scoring the four subscales, then creating an overall authentic leadership score from those four subscales results in the best model fit.

Models with All Questions Loading on a Single Factor					
Study	X^2	*df*	*CFI*	*GFI*	*RMSEA*
A	69.79	33	.92		.07
C	133.41	100	.95		.08
E			.95		.09
I	353.21	306	.90	.86	.09
M	705.20	10	.98	.92	.08
T			.96	.95	.06
Models with Four First-Order Factors					
H	240.53	100		.88	.08
I	227.24	306	.95	.92	.07
Models with Four First-Order Factors, Then Loading on a Single, Second-Order Factor					
B	234.70	98	.97		.05
B	176.03	98	.95		.06
H	233.21	98	.94		.08
I	251.15	306	.94	.91	.07

Study details are provided at the end of the chapter.

Authentic Leadership

The Authentic Leadership Questionnaire

Internal Reliability

Internal reliability is explained in greater detail in chapter 2. Generally, the idea is that if a certain number of questions indicate they measure a construct, such as self-awareness, we would like the responses to those questions to be highly consistent or correlated.

High Reliability	Low Reliability
Question 1: 4	Question 1: 4
Question 2: 5	Question 2: 1
Question 3: 4	Question 3: 3
Question 4: 5	Question 4: 5
Question 5: 4	Question 5: 2

In the example on the left, if a very self-aware leader was being rated on self-awareness, we would anticipate that the rater would generally rate that leader high (4's and 5's) on the questions.

If, on the other hand, the ratings were similar to the *low reliability* example, we would be concerned about the internal consistency or reliability of the scale. The internal reliability is typically explained by a score between 0 and 1. The closer the score, called an *Alpha* score, is to 1, the more internally reliable the scale.

Multiple studies have reported the internal reliability of the *Authentic Leadership Questionnaire.*

***Authentic Leadership Questionnaire* Internal Reliability**

Study	Self-Awareness	Relational Transparency	Internalized Moral Perspective	Balanced Processing	Overall Authenticity
B	.92	.87	.76	.81	
C					.95
F	.88	.71	.83	.69	.91
G					.80
H	.84	.87	.86	.81	
I	.86	.81	.85	.78	.94
J	.88	.80	.81	.83	.95
K					.88
M	.91	.84	.88	.81	.96
P					.94
Q	.80	.93	.83	.83	.88
U					.94

Authentic Leadership

The Authentic Leadership Questionnaire

Discriminant Validity

Discriminant validity broadly asks whether an instrument is measuring something "different" from constructs measured by other instruments. A good metaphor is asking whether the two different instruments are "apples and oranges."

In this case, can the *ALQ* discriminate between the construct of authentic leadership (an apple) and other, related constructs such as transformational or ethical leadership (oranges)? The table below indicates that, as of 2015, studies of the *ALQ* indicate that it is moderately correlated with the five "I's" from the *MLQ 5X* and with scores on the *Brown Ethical Leadership Scale*.

The *ALQ*, however, is somewhat strongly correlated with other measures of leader integrity, transformational leadership, leader predictability and leader-member relationships.

Discriminant Validity						
Variable	Instrument	SA	RT	IMP	BP	AUTH
Correlated Less Than .60						
Ethical Leadership (B1)	*Brown Ethical Leadership Scale*	*r* = .58**	*r* = .53**	*r* = .55**	*r* = .51**	
Idealized Influence (B2)	*Multifactor Leadership Questionnaire*	*r* = .58**	*r* = .45**	*r* = .49**	*r* = .54**	
Individualized Consideration (B2)	*Multifactor Leadership Questionnaire*	*r* = .54**	*r* = .56**	*r* = .58**	*r* = .53**	
Inspirational Motivation (B2)	*Multifactor Leadership Questionnaire*	*r* = .51**	*r* = .42**	*r* = .52**	*r* = .47**	
Intellectual Stimulation (B2)	*Multifactor Leadership Questionnaire*	*r* = .59**	*r* = .47**	*r* = .54**	*r* = .55**	
Correlated Greater Than .60						
Leader Integrity (C)	*Perceived Behavioral Integrity*					*r* = .66**
Transformational Leadership (J)	*Global Transformational Leadership Scale*	*r* = .85**	*r* = .79**	*r* = .78**	*r* = .79**	
Leader Predictability (I1)	Ambivalence Dimension of the *Questionnaire on Trust in the Leader*	*r* = .60**	*r* = .69**	*r* = .60**	*r* = .56**	*r* = .69** β = .69**
Leader-Member Relationship (N)	*LMX-7*					*r* = .66** β = .53**

The second instrument in each study was the *Authentic Leadership Questionnaire*. SA = Self-Awareness, RT = Relational Transparency, IMP = Internal Moral Perspective, BP = Balanced Processing, AUTH = Overall Authentic Leadership Score. *** $p < .001$, ** $p < .01$, * $p < .05$, NS = Not Significant

Authentic Leadership

The Authentic Leadership Questionnaire

Convergent Validity

To some degree, convergent validity asks the inverse of discriminant validity. If the *ALQ* indicates that it measures self-awareness, balanced processing, relational transparency and internalized moral perspective (red apples), is it reasonably correlated with other instruments that measure similar constructs (green apples).

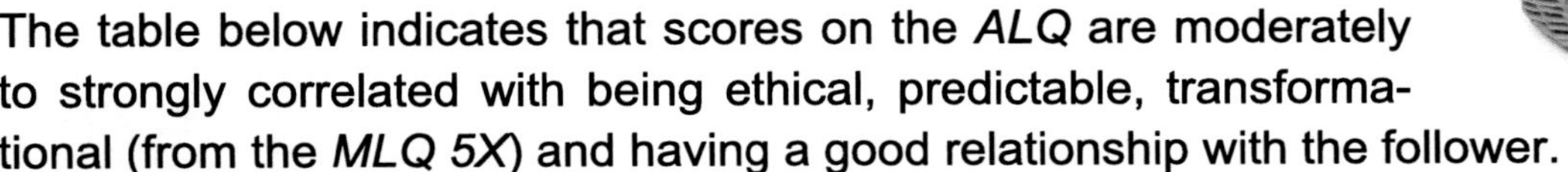

The table below indicates that scores on the *ALQ* are moderately to strongly correlated with being ethical, predictable, transformational (from the *MLQ 5X*) and having a good relationship with the follower.

Convergent Validity

Variable	Instrument	SA	RT	IMP	BP	AUTH
Ethical Leadership (B1)	*Brown Ethical Leadership Scale*	*r* = .58**	*r* = .53**	*r* = .55**	*r* = .51**	
Leader Integrity (c)	*Perceived Behavioral Integrity*					*r* = .66**
Leader Predictability (I1)	Ambivalence Dimension of the *Questionnaire on Trust in the Leader*	*r* = .60**	*r* = .69**	*r* = .60**	*r* = .56**	*r* = .69** β = .69**
Transformational Leadership (J)	*Global Transformational Leadership Scale*	*r* = .85**	*r* = .79**	*r* = .78**	r = .79**	
Leader-Member Relationship (N)	*LMX-7*					r = .66** β = .53**
Idealized Influence (B2)	*Multifactor Leadership Questionnaire*	*r* = .58**	*r* = .45**	*r* = .49**	*r* = .54**	
Individualized Consideration (B2)	*Multifactor Leadership Questionnaire*	*r* = .54**	*r* = .56**	*r* = .58**	*r* = .53**	
Inspirational Motivation (B2)	*Multifactor Leadership Questionnaire*	*r* = .51**	*r* = .42**	*r* = .52**	*r* = .47**	
Intellectual Stimulation (B2)	*Multifactor Leadership Questionnaire*	*r* = .59**	*r* = .47**	*r* = .54**	*r* = .55**	

The second instrument in each study was the *Authentic Leadership Questionnaire*. SA = Self-Awareness, RT = Relational Transparency, IMP = Internal Moral Perspective, BP = Balanced Processing, AUTH = Overall Authentic Leadership Score. *** $p < .001$, ** $p < .01$, * $p < .05$, NS = Not Significant

.

Authentic Leadership

The Authentic Leadership Questionnaire

Predictive Validity

Predictive validity is often an area of great interest for leadership researchers. This type of validity asks whether scores on an instrument predict some phenomenon of which we are interested. In organizational leadership, these phenomena are often things such as follower motivation, satisfaction, commitment, citizenship and performance.

The table below indicates that ratings of the leader's authentic leadership are weakly to moderately associated with follower job satisfaction.

Job Satisfaction						
Variable	Instrument	SA	RT	IMP	BP	AUTH
Job Satisfaction (X)	*Global Job Satisfaction Survey*	$r = .32^{**}$	$r = .32^{**}$	$r = .34^{**}$	$r = .31^{**}$	$r = .35^{**}$ $\beta = .16^{**}$
Job Satisfaction (B4)	*Brayfield Rothe Scale*	$r = .15^{*}$	$r = .23^{**}$	$r = .17^{**}$	$r = .14^{*}$	$\beta = .19^{*}$
Overall Job Satisfaction (J)	*Job Diagnostic Survey*	$r = .52^{**}$	$r = .50^{**}$	$r = .46^{**}$	$r = .44^{**}$	
Work Satisfaction (F)	*Index of Work Satisfaction Scale*	$r = .25^{**}$	$r = .26^{**}$	$r = .31^{**}$	$r = .17^{**}$	$r = .29^{**}$ $\beta = .22^{**}$

The second instrument in each study was the *Authentic Leadership Questionnaire.* SA = Self-Awareness, RT = Relational Transparency, IMP = Internal Moral Perspective, BP = Balanced Processing, AUTH = Overall Authentic Leadership Score. *** $p < .001$, ** $p < .01$, * $p < .05$, NS = Not Significant

Authentic Leadership

The Authentic Leadership Questionnaire

Predictive Validity

The table below and on the following page summarizes results for ratings of the leader's authenticity and a second aspect of leadership. Generally, we see that there are moderate to strong correlations between ratings on the *Authentic Leadership Questionnaire* and these dimensions of leadership.

Leadership						
Variable	Instrument	SA	RT	IMP	BP	AUTH
Idealized Influence (B2)	*Multifactor Leadership Questionnaire*	r = .58**	r = .45**	r = .49**	r = .54**	
Individual Consideration (B2)	*Multifactor Leadership Questionnaire*	r = .54**	r = .56**	r = .58**	r = .53**	
Inspirational Motivation (B2)	*Multifactor Leadership Questionnaire*	r = .51**	r = .42**	r = .52**	r = .47**	
Intellectual Stimulation (B2)	*Multifactor Leadership Questionnaire*	r = .59**	r = .47**	r = .54**	r = .55**	
Interpersonal Leader Trust (T)	*Interpersonal Trust Scales*					β = .80**[12]
Leader Consistency (I1)	*Self-Consistency*	r = .62***	r = .63***	r = .69***	r = .59***	r = .71*** β = .38***
Leader Self-Knowledge (I1)	*Self-Knowledge*	r = .73***	r = .64***	r = .69***	r = .64***	r = .76*** β = .52***
Leader Predictability (I1)	*Ambivalence Dimension of the Questionnaire on Trust in the Leader*	r = .60**	r = .69**	r = .60**	r = .56**	r = .69** β = .69**
Leader Benevolence (T)	*Interpersonal Trust Scales*	r = .56**	r = .56**	r = .56**	r = .56**	
Leader Competence (T)	*Interpersonal Trust Scales*	r = .47*	r = .62*	r = .58*	r = .57*	
Satisfaction with Supervision (B1)	*Job Descriptive Index*	r = .49**	r = .44**	r = .33**	r = .41**	β = .26**
Satisfaction with Supervision (R)	*Job Descriptive Index*	r = .58**	r = .55**	r = .50**	r = .52**	β = .32**

Authentic Leadership

The Authentic Leadership Questionnaire
Predictive Validity

Leadership (Continued)						
Variable	Instrument	SA	RT	IMP	BP	AUTH
Leader Reliability (T)	*Interpersonal Trust Scales*	*r* = .47*	*r* = .60*	*r* = .56*	*r* = .57*	
Leader-Member Relationship (N)	*LMX-7*					*r* = .66** β = .53**
Satisfaction with the Leader (Supervisor) (I1)	*Multifactor Leadership Questionnaire*	*r* = .77***	*r* = .76***	*r* = .68***	*r* = .67***	*r* = .81*** β = .69***
Satisfaction with the Leader (Supervisor) (I2)	*Multifactor Leadership Questionnaire*					*r* = .59*** β = .66***
Transformational Leadership (J)	*Global Transformational Leadership Scale*	*r* = .85**	*r* = .79**	*r* = .78**	*r* = .79**	
Trust in Leader (M)	*Workplace Trust Survey*					*HLM Path Coefficient* = .89*
Trust in Management (E)	*Trust in Management*					β = .21**

The second instrument in each study was the *Authentic Leadership Questionnaire*. SA = Self-Awareness, RT = Relational Transparency, IMP = Internal Moral Perspective, BP = Balanced Processing, AUTH = Overall Authentic Leadership Score. *** $p < .001$, ** $p < .01$, * $p < .05$, NS = Not Significant

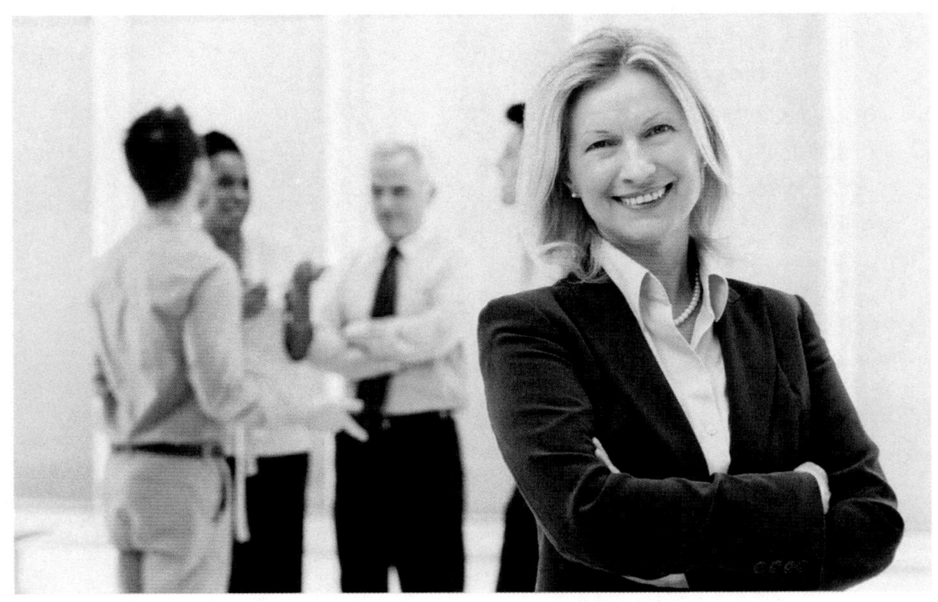

Authentic Leadership

Research on Authentic Leadership

Understanding the Research Results for Authentic Leadership

There has not been sufficient research on authentic leadership to conduct meta-analyses. There are, however, results from 24 empirical studies of authentic leadership. Chapter 2 explained both correlations and meta-analyses. The table below, however, provides a quick review of how the research results will be presented in this chapter.[13]

Example - Authentic Leadership and Follower Engagement

In the example below, one of the studies published was on the relationship between leaders' authentic leadership behaviors and followers' engagement. The study referenced (T) is described at the end of the chapter. The finding was a strong, positive correlation (.60). The more authentic leader behaviors used, the higher the follower engagement.

Strongly - Correlated	Moderately - Correlated	Weakly - Correlated	Weakly + Correlated	Moderately + Correlated	Strongly + Correlated
-1 to -.50	-.49 to -.30	-.29 to -.10	.10 to .29	.30 to .49	.50 to 1

Outcome	
Follower Engagement (T)	.60

Authentic Leadership

Research on Authentic Leadership

Authentic Leadership and Follower Satisfaction[14]

The table below indicates that ratings of the leaders' authentic leadership are weakly to moderately associated with follower job satisfaction.

Strongly - Correlated	Moderately - Correlated	Weakly - Correlated	Weakly + Correlated	Moderately + Correlated	Strongly + Correlated
-1 to -.50	-.49 to -.30	-.29 to -.10	.10 to .29	.30 to .49	.50 to 1

Outcome	
Weakly, Positively Correlated	
Job Satisfaction (B4)	.19
Work Satisfaction (F)	.29
Moderately, Positively Correlated	
Job Satisfaction (X)	.35
Overall Job Satisfaction (J)	.48

Authentic Leadership

Research on Authentic Leadership

Authentic Leadership and Ratings of Leadership

The table below highlights that authentic leadership is positively related to an array of ratings of leadership.

Strongly - Correlated	Moderately - Correlated	Weakly - Correlated	Weakly + Correlated	Moderately + Correlated	Strongly + Correlated
-1 to -.50	-.49 to -.30	-.29 to -.10	.10 to .29	.30 to .49	.50 to 1

Outcome	
Weakly, Positively Correlated	
Trust in Management (E)	.21
Satisfaction with Supervision (B1)	.26
Moderately, Positively Correlated	
Inspirational Motivation (B2)	.48
Strongly, Positively Correlated	
Idealized Influence (B2)	.52
Leader Reliability (T)	.53
Intellectual Stimulation (B2)	.54
Satisfaction with Supervision (R)	.54
Individual Consideration (B2)	.55
Leader Benevolence (T)	.56
Leader Competence (T)	.56
Satisfaction with the Leader (Supervisor) (I2)	.59
Leader-Member Relationship (N)	.66
Leader Predictability (I1)	.69
Leader Consistency (I1)	.71
Leader Self-Knowledge (I1)	.76
Interpersonal Leader Trust (T)	.80
Satisfaction with the Leader (Supervisor) (I1)	.81
Transformational Leadership (J)	.81
Trust in Leader (M)	*.89*

Authentic Leadership

Research on Authentic Leadership

Authentic Leadership and Ethics, Integrity and Trust

The table below highlights that authentic leadership is positively related to multiple measures of ethics, integrity and trust.

Strongly - Correlated	Moderately - Correlated	Weakly - Correlated	Weakly + Correlated	Moderately + Correlated	Strongly + Correlated
-1 to -.50	-.49 to -.30	-.29 to -.10	.10 to .29	.30 to .49	.50 to 1

Outcome	
Weakly, Positively Correlated	
Follower Moral Courage (K)	.18
Trust in Management (E)	.21
Trust in Management (E)	.21
Follower Ethical Behavior (K)	.29
Moderately, Positively Correlated	
Follower Pro-Social Behavior (K)	.32
Idealized Influence (B2)	.49
Strongly, Positively Correlated	
Ethical Culture (C)	.51
Leader Reliability (T)	.52
Ethical Leadership (B1)	.54
Leader Competence (T)	.54
Leader Benevolence (T)	.56
Team Virtuousness (H)	.57
Procedural Justice (N)	.63
Leader Integrity (C)	.66
Trust in Manager (W)	.69
Affective Trust (Q)	.70
Cognitive Trust (Q)	.79
Employee Trust (P)	.80
Overall Trust (Q)	.80
Interpersonal Leader Trust (T)	.80
Trust in Leader (M)	.89

Authentic Leadership

Research on Authentic Leadership

Authentic Leadership and Organizational Citizenship, Organizational Climate

The tables below highlight that authentic leadership is positively related to multiple measures of organizational citizenship, organizational climate and team outcomes.

Strongly - Correlated	Moderately - Correlated	Weakly - Correlated	Weakly + Correlated	Moderately + Correlated	Strongly + Correlated
-1 to -.50	-.49 to -.30	-.29 to -.10	.10 to .29	.30 to .49	.50 to 1

Outcome	
Weakly, Positively Correlated	
Organizational Climate (B4)	.18
Organizational Citizenship Behavior (B1)	.29
Organizational Citizenship Behavior Toward Individuals (O)	.29
Moderately, Positively Correlated	
Organizational Citizenship Behavior (B2)	.30
Organizational Citizenship Behavior Toward the Organization (O)	.44
Strongly, Positively Correlated	
Ethical Culture (C)	.51
Positive Work Climate (U)	.64

Authentic Leadership and Team Outcomes

Strongly - Correlated	Moderately - Correlated	Weakly - Correlated	Weakly + Correlated	Moderately + Correlated	Strongly + Correlated
-1 to -.50	-.49 to -.30	-.29 to -.10	.10 to .29	.30 to .49	.50 to 1

Outcome	
Weakly, Positively Correlated	
Team Potency (H)	.27
Group Productivity (A)	.27
Moderately, Positively Correlated	
Team Virtuousness (H)	.30
Unit Sales Performance (E)	.30
Teamwork Behavior (A)	*.31*
Follower Pro-Social Behavior (A)	*.32*
Team Affective Commitment (H)	.40
Strongly, Positively Correlated	
Team Effectiveness (I2)	.53
Positive Team Affective Tone (V)	.68

Authentic Leadership

Research on Authentic Leadership

Authentic Leadership and Follower Engagement, Commitment

The tables below highlight that authentic leadership is positively related to multiple measures of follower engagement, follower commitment and follower performance.

Strongly - Correlated	Moderately - Correlated	Weakly - Correlated	Weakly + Correlated	Moderately + Correlated	Strongly + Correlated
-1 to -.50	-.49 to -.30	-.29 to -.10	.10 to .29	.30 to .49	.50 to 1

Outcome	
Weakly, Positively Correlated	
Work Engagement (F)	.21
Organizational Commitment (C)	.25
Organizational Commitment (B1)	.28
Moderately, Positively Correlated	
Organizational Commitment (B2)	.34
Team Affective Commitment (H)	.40
Strongly, Positively Correlated	
Employee Engagement (P)	.58
Follower Engagement (T)	.60
Organizational Commitment (I1)	.65
Follower Extra Effort (I1)	.65
Follower Psychological Capital (S)	.65
Employee Engagement (M)	.76

Authentic Leadership and Follower Performance

Strongly - Correlated	Moderately - Correlated	Weakly - Correlated	Weakly + Correlated	Moderately + Correlated	Strongly + Correlated
-1 to -.50	-.49 to -.30	-.29 to -.10	.10 to .29	.30 to .49	.50 to 1

Outcome	
Weakly, Positively Correlated	
Work Role Performance (C)	.22
Career Performance (Self-Assessed) (Q)	.27
Moderately, Positively Correlated	
Unit Sales Performance (E)	.30
Team Performance (Self-Assessed) (Q)	.34
Group Job Performance (L)	.35
Innovative Performance (Self-Assessed) (Q)	.35
Job Performance (B4)	.44
Overall Performance (Self-Assessed) (Q)	.49
Strongly, Positively Correlated	
Job Performance (Self-Assessed) (Q)	.53

Authentic Leadership

Summary

Currently, the conceptualization of authentic leadership consists of four aspects: being self-aware, being transparent in our relationships with others, engaging in balanced processing whereby we consider a range of opinions before making important decisions, and having a consistent, internalized moral perspective.

Studies using the *Authentic Leadership Questionnaire* have found that authentic leadership is positively related to follower satisfaction, ratings of leadership ethics, integrity and trust, organizational citizenship, organizational climate, team outcomes and follower performance.

Retracted Articles since the Second Edition

Since the second edition of *Graduate Leadership*, two articles included in the research results in the second edition have been retracted by their respective journals. Articles removed from the third edition are:

Article D: Walumbwa, F. O., Wang, P., Wang, H., Schaubroeck, J., & Avolio, B. J. (2010). Psychological processes linking authentic leadership to follower behaviors. *The Leadership Quarterly*, 21(5), 901-914. doi:10.1016/j.leaqua.2010.07.015

Article L: Walumbwa, F. O., Luthans, F., Avey, J. B., & Oke, A. (2011). Authentically leading groups: The mediating role of collective psychological capital and trust. *Journal Of Organizational Behavior*, 32(1), 4-24. doi:10.1002/job.653

Authentic Leadership

Studies Reviewed

A. Hannah, Walumbwa and Fry, (2011). The sample consisted of 217 soldiers, representing 47 teams from intact military squads attending a training program at a major Army training base in the eastern United States.

B. Walumbwa, Avolio, Gardner, Wernsing and Peterson, (2008). The sample was (B1) 178 working MBA and evening adult students; (B2) 236 adult evening students with full-time jobs, (B3) both samples; (B4) 478 employees in multinational companies operating in Kenya, Africa.

Participants rated their leaders' authentic leadership and their satisfaction with their supervisor, leaders' ethical leadership, leaders' transformational leadership, their organizational citizenship, their organizational commitment and their job satisfaction. The leader rated the follower's job performance.

C. Leroy, Palanski and Simons, (2012). The sample consisted of 252 followers from 25 small-to medium- sized service organizations in Belgium.

Participants rated their leaders' authentic leadership and behavioral integrity, their own affective organizational commitment and assessed the organization's ethical climate. The leaders rated their follower's work role performance.

D. **Retracted:** Walumbwa, Wang, Wang, Schaubroeck and Avolio, (2010). The sample consisted of 129 supervisors and 387 immediate direct reports from two telecom firms that were each located in a separate major city in China.

Followers rated their identification with their supervisor and empowerment. Leaders rated their followers' work engagement and organizational citizenship.

E. Clapp-Smith, Vogelgesang and Avey, (2009). The sample consisted of 89 employees at 26 small retail stores in the US Midwest.

Followers rated their leaders' authentic leadership and their trust in management.

F. Giallonardo, Wong and Iwasiw, (2010). The sample consisted of new graduate nurses with less than or equal to 3 years of nursing experience.

Followers rated their leaders' authentic leadership and rated their own work engagement and work satisfaction.

G. Bird, Wang and Murray, (2009). The sample consisted of 224 superintendents in six southeastern states.

Superintendents self-assessed their authentic leadership and their budget processes.

Authentic Leadership

Studies Reviewed

H. Rego, (2013). The sample consisted of 212 participants from a Portuguese university. The 212 participants were members of 51 teams.

Participants rated their leaders' authentic leadership and their team's virtuousness, affective commitment and potency.

I. Peus, Wesche, Streicher, Braun and Frey, (2012). (I1) The sample consisted of 157 individuals from a broad range of branches of industry in Germany. (I2) The sample consisted of 86 individuals from a broad range of branches of industry in Germany.

Participants rated their leaders' authentic leadership and their leaders' self-knowledge, self-consistency and predictability. They rated their own satisfaction with their leader, extra effort and organizational commitment.

J. Tonkin, (2013). The sample consisted of 129 employees working in an organization within a publicly held, large Fortune 100 software company.

Participants rated their leaders' authentic leadership and transformational behaviors. They rated their own job satisfaction and altruism.

K. Hannah, Avolio and Walumbwa, (2011). The sample consisted of 162 soldiers attending a training program at a major U.S. Army school in the United States.

Soldiers rated their squad leaders' level of authentic leadership and were rated by multiple peers on their moral courage, ethical behavior and pro-social behavior.

L. **Retracted:** Walumbwa, Luthans, Avey and Oke, (2011). The sample consisted of 146 intact (existing) work groups (526 employees and their immediate supervisors) of a large bank located in the Southwest United States.

Participants rated their leaders' authentic leadership and their work group's collective psychological capital and work group's trust. Leaders rated their group's group citizenship behavior and group performance.

M. Wang, (2011). The sample consisted of 917 teachers who rated 60 principals.

Participants rated their leaders' authentic leadership, their trust in the leader and their own engagement.

Authentic Leadership

Studies Reviewed

N. Hsiung, (2012). The sample consisted of 404 salespersons from 70 work groups in real estate, in China.

Participants rated their leaders' authentic leadership and their own positive affect/mood, the quality of the leader-follower relationship, their own sense of the procedural justice climate and their own sense of the degree to which they were listened (voice).

O. Valsania, Leon, Molero, Alonso and Cantisano, (2012). The sample consisted of 227 employees who worked in 40 groups who belonged to 22 organizations in the region of Madrid, Spain.

Participants rated their leaders' authentic leadership and their own organizational citizenship towards their organization and other individuals.

P. Wang and Hsieh (2013). The sample consisted of 386 employees in the top 1,000 manufacturing companies and the top 500 service companies in Taiwan.

Participants rated their leaders' authentic leadership, their trust in the leader and their own engagement.

Q. Zamahani, Ghorbani and Rezaei, (2011). The sample consisted of 200 employees from an international telecommunication company in Iran.

Participants rated their leaders' authentic leadership, psychological capital, their performance and their trust in the leader.

R.

S. Rego, Sousa, Marques and Cunha, (2012). The sample consisted of 201 employees, working in 33 commerce organizations operating in Portugal.

Participants reported their own psychological capital, as well as their supervisors' authentic leadership. Supervisors described the employees' creativity.

T. Hassan, (2011). The sample consisted of 395 employees from seven banks and their branches located around Kuala Lumpur, Malaysia.

Participants rated their leaders' authentic leadership and their own trust in leadership and work engagement.

Authentic Leadership

Studies Reviewed

U. Woolley, Caza and Levy, (2011). The sample consisted of 828 New Zealand adults based on archival survey data collected by the New Zealand Leadership Institute of the University of Auckland Business School.

Participants rated their leaders' authentic leadership and their work climate. Participants rated their psychological capital.

V. Hmieleski, Cole and Baron. (2012). The sample consisted of participants from 179 firms.

Participating firms rated their shared (team) authentic leadership and positive team affective tone. Firm performance was measured by lagged (one-year) performance data on revenue growth and employment growth obtained from Dun and Bradstreet.

W. Wong and Giallonardo, (2013). The sample consisted of a secondary analysis of data collected in a cross-sectional survey of 280 registered nurses working in acute care hospitals in Ontario.

Participants rated their leaders' authentic leadership and the trust in their leaders. Participants self-rated in the areas of work life and their perceptions of the incidence of common adverse patient outcomes over the past year.

X. Wong and Laschinger (2013). The sample consisted of 280 registered nurses working in acute care hospitals across Ontario in Canada.

Participants rated their leaders' authentic leadership. Participants rated their job satisfaction and performance as well as their perception of structural empowerment.

Authentic Leadership

Instruments Used in Studies Reviewed

Used In Study	Instrument
R	3-item scale to assess external peer ratings of moral courage (Hannah, Avolio and Walumbwa, 2011)
S	4-item scale (Zhou and George, 2001)
R	5-item standardized military institutional measure of ethical behavior
R	5-item standardized military institutional measure of pro-social behavior
C	*Affective Organizational Commitment Scale,* (Meyer, Allen and Smith, 1993)
A	*Authenticity Strength,* the coefficient of variation for individual team member authentic leadership ratings (Hannah, Walumbwa and Fry, 2011)
B	*Benevolence Dimension Scale,* (Victor and Cullen, 1988)
B	*Brayfield Rothe Scale*, (Brayfield and Rothe, 1951)
B	*Brown Ethical Leadership Scale,* (Brown, Treviño and Harrison, 2005)
G	*Budget-Building Practices Questionnaire,* (Bird, Wang and Murray, 2009)
M	*Employee (Teacher) Engagement,* (Buckingham and Coffman, 1999)
P	*Employee Trust*, (McAllister, 1995)
N	*Employee Voice (Does my Leader Listen to Me), (*Van Dyne and LePine, 1998)
C	*Ethical Culture,* (Kaptein, 2008)
X	*General Performance Scale*, (Roe, Zinoviera, Dienes and Ten Horn, 2000)
X	*Global Job Satisfaction Survey,* (Quinn and Shepard, 1974)
J	*Global Transformational Leadership Scale,* (Carless, Wearing and Mann, 2000)
O	*Group Citizenship Behavior,* (Lee and Allen, 2002)
F	*Index of Work Satisfaction Scale,* (Stamps, 1997)
J	*Job Diagnostic Survey, (*Hackman and Oldham, 1975)
B	*Job Performance* a 10-item measure of job performance, including personal initiative, self-direction and innovation. (Bono and Judge, 2003; Stewart, Carson and Cardy, 1996; Welbourne, Johnson and Erez, 1998)
V	*Job-Related Affective Well-Being Scale*, (Van Katwyk, Fox, Spector, and Kelloway, 2000)
N	*LMX-7*, (Graen and Uhl-Bien, 1995)
W	Modified *American Nurses Association Nursing Quality Indicators Scale,* (Sochalski, 2001)
B, I	*Multifactor Leadership Questionnaire 5X, (*Bass and Avolio, 2004)
D	*Organizational Citizenship Behavior Scale,* (Podsakoff, MacKenzie, Moorman and Fetter, 1990)
B	*Organizational Citizenship Behavior,* (Wayne, Shore and Liden, 1997)
J	*Organizational Citizenship Behavior Altruism Scale,* (Smith, Organ and Near, 1983)
B, I	*Organizational Commitment Questionnaire,* (Mowday, Steers, and Porter, 1979)
Q	*Organizational Trust Inventory*, (Cummings and Bromiley, 1996)

Authentic Leadership

Instruments Used in Studies Reviewed

K	*Peer Moral Courage*, (Hannah, Avolio and Walumbwa, 2011)
K	*Peer Pro-Social Behavior*, (Hannah, Avolio and Walumbwa, 2011)
C	*Perceived Behavioral Integrity,* (Simons and McLean-Parks, 2007)
U	*Positive Work Climate,* (Avolio and Luthans, 2006)
N	*Procedural Justice Climate, (*Niehoff and Moorman, 1993)
U	*Psychological Capital Questionnaire,* (Luthans, Avolio, Avey and Norman, 2007)
Q	Psychological Capital Questionnaire, (Luthans, Avolio, Norman and Avey, 2007
I	*Questionnaire on Trust in the Leader*, (Kopp and Schuler, 2003)
Q	Role-Based Performance Scale, (Welbourne, Johnson, Erez and Amir, 1998)
B	Satisfaction with Supervisor, *Job Descriptive Index*, (Smith, Kendall, and Hulin, 1969)
I	Self Consistency, The German *Inventory On Self-Concept And Self-Confidence* (ISS: Inventar zu Selbstkonzept und Selbstvertrauen, (Fend, Helmke and Richter, 1984)
I	Self Knowledge, The German *Inventory On Self-Concept And Self-Confidence* (ISS: Inventar zu Selbstkonzept und Selbstvertrauen, (Fend, Helmke and Richter, 1984)
H	*Team Affective Commitment* Four items taken from the *Affective Organizational Commitment Scale,* (Meyer, Allen and Smith, 1993)
A	*Team Authenticity*, an index created by calculating the mean levels of authenticity, representing the general leadership style of team members and the level of variance or authenticity strength across the team (Hannah, Walumbwa and Fry, 2011)
H	*Team Potency,* Six items taken from (De Jong, Ruyter and Wetzels, 2005)
A	*Team Productivity*, three items from Nyhan's (2000) *Group Productivity Scale* plus an additional item
H	*Team Virtuousness, (*Cameron, Bright and Caza, 2004)
I	*Teamwork Assessment Questionnaire,* (Borrill and West, 2000)
A	*Teamwork Behavior,* a standardized institutional 24-item instrument
W	*The Areas of Worklife Scale* (AWS) (Leiter and Maslach, 2002)
X	*The Conditions of Work Effectiveness Questionnaire II,* (Laschinger, Finegan, Shamian and Wilk, 2001)
N	*The Positive and Negative Affect Schedule Scale, (Watson, Clark and Tellegen, 1988)*
E, W	*Trust in Management,* (Mayer and Gavin, 2005)
M	Trust in Principal, nine items taken from the *Workplace Trust Survey, (*Ferris and Travaglione, 2003)
E	*Unit Sales Performance* was calculated as the difference in (unit sales divided by the square feet of the unit) between the two points of time measured in the study, (Clapp-Smith, Vogelgesang and Avey, 2009).
F	*Utrecht Work Engagement Scale,* (Schaufeli and Bakker, 2003)
P	*Work Engagement Scale*, (Schaufeli, Bakker and Salanova, 2006)
C	*Work Role Performance*, (Griffin, Neal and Parker, 2007)

Authentic Leadership

Notes

[1] As of 2015, there were a few more peer-reviewed studies that used the *ALQ* than are reported in this chapter. A few studies that only used "traditional" undergraduate students for the sample were not included.

[2] In 2003, Luthans and Avolio were writing about authentic leadership development. In this chapter's effort to simplify the evolution of authentic leadership, their 2005 article was used rather than their 2003 chapter: Luthans, F. and Avolio, B., (2003). Authentic Leadership Development, in Cameron, K. S., Dutton, J. E., and Quinn, R. E. (2003). *Positive organizational scholarship: Foundations of a new discipline*. San Francisco, CA: Berrett-Koehler.

[3] Kernis, M. H. (2003). Toward a conceptualization of optimal self-esteem. *Psychological Inquiry, 14, 1–26.*

[4] The concepts of positive modeling, emotional contagion, supporting, self-determination and positive social exchanges are described in the article, but for space reasons were not included in the table provided.

[5] The three constructs of relational transparency, internalized regulation and balanced processing are presented in the model as dimensions of self-regulation.

[6] These definitions can be found in Walumbwa, Avolio, Gardner, Wernsing and Peterson, 2008, pp. 95-6.

[7] Luft, J. and Ingham, H. (1955). "The Johari window, a graphic model of interpersonal awareness". *Proceedings of the western training laboratory in group development* (Los Angeles: UCLA).

[8] Ryan, R. M., & Deci, E. L. 2003. On assimilating identities to the self: A self-determination theory perspective on internalization and integrity within cultures. In M. R. Leary & J. P. Tangney (Eds.),*Handbook of self and identity*: 253-272. New York: Guilford.

[9] The more academic names for these two ideas are deontological (rule based) and teleological (outcomes based).

[10] As of late, 2013, no peer-reviewed articles using the *Authentic Leadership Inventory* were located.

[11] The development of the instrument is provided in Neider, L. L., Schriesheim, C. A. and Leadership Quarterly Yearly Review. (December 01, 2011). *The Authentic Leadership Inventory* (ALI): Development and empirical tests. *The Leadership Quarterly, 22,* 6, 1146-1164.

Notes

[12] The beta weight reported was a result of a structural equation model.

[13] The exact boundary between weak, moderate and strong correlations is not universally agreed upon. The definitions used are based on Cohen, J. (1992). A power primer. *Psychological Bulletin, 112,* 1, 155-9.

[14] For studies in which the four sub-scales were reported but no overall authentic score was reported, the mean of the correlations for the four sub-scales is shown.

Subject Index

Subject Index

Subject Index

Subject Index

Subject Index

Subject Index

Subject Index

Subject Index

Subject Index

Subject Index

Author Index

Author Index

Author Index

Author Index

Author Index

Author Index

Credits

Front Cover
Business Woman Leading A Team - Licensed from andres through Bigstock.com
Preface
Praying Woman - Licensed from Subbotina Anna through Bigstock.com
Team Meeting In Creative Office - Licensed from Cathy Yeulet through Bigstock.com
Explanation - Licensed from Dmitriy Shironosov through Bigstock.com
Woman sitting at study desks - Licensed from Wavebreak Media Ltd through Bigstock.com
Student In Library - Licensed from Jean-Marie Guyon through Bigstock.com
College Student Studying In The Library - Licensed from Arekmalang through Bigstock.com
Books - Licensed from Ghenadii Boico through Bigstock.com
Hands on Computer - Licensed from Ratchanida Thippayos through Bigstock.com
Man Doing Homework - Licensed from Diego Cervo through Bigstock.com
Paperwork - Licensed from Erol Berberovic through Bigstock.com
Mature students sitting at the library - Licensed by Wavebreak Media Ltd through Bigstock.com
In the library- pretty female student with laptop and books- Licensed by Lightpoet through Bigstock.com
Chapter 1
Business woman - Licensed from andres through Bigstock.com
Stack of plates - Licensed from montego6 through Bigstock.com
Dishwashing - Licensed from alexraths through Bigstock.com
Large ethnic group - Licensed from Rawpixel through Bigstock.com
Happy librarian with stack of books - Licensed from Wavebreak Media Ltd through Bigstock.com
Group of business people - Licensed from Kurhan through Bigstock.com
Group of business people in a row - Licensed from michaeljung through Bigstock.com
Student in library - Licensed from stokkete through Bigstock.com
Professional landscaping - Licensed from essa667 through Bigstock.com
Female scientist - Licensed from Wavebreak Media Ltd through Bigstock.com
Bachelors Students - Licensed from Viktor Cap through Bigstock.com
Graduate Students - Licensed from Lisa F. Young through Bigstock.com
Doctoral Students - Licensed from Zsolt Nyulaszi through Bigstock.com
Books on Sale - Licensed from Rafal Olkis through Bigstock.com
Close-Up of businessman pointing with pen – Licensed from Dmitriy Shironosov through Bigstock.com
Portrait of a Businessman – Licensed from Minerva Studio through Bigstock.com
Businesswoman Talking to Her Team - Licensed from Wavebreak Media Ltd through Bigstock.com
Business Women Talking - - Licensed from MonkeyBusiness Images through Bigstock.com
Over the Shoulder Notebook Computer – Licensed from Sean Nel through Bigstock.com
Work on desk - Licensed from Sergey Nivens through Bigstock.com
Magazines – Licensed from Raga Irusta through Bigstock.com
Pills - Licensed from Steve Van Horn through Bigstock.com
Businessman Workplace with Papers - Licensed from Sergey Nivens through Bigstock.com
Finger Touching Slime - Licensed from Sergey Likov through Bigstock.com

Credits

Successful Woman - Licensed from Dmitriy Shironosov through Bigstock.com
Man standing in front of flat panels - Licensed from Photosani through Bigstock.com
Secrets – Licensed from Edyta Linek through Bigstock.com
Asian Woman in library - Licensed from Sung Kuk Kim through Bigstock.com
Senior woman reading - Licensed from Wong Szefei through Bigstock.com
Man Holding Tablet in Library - Licensed from Wavebreak Media Ltd through Bigstock.com
Afro-American Young Woman Reading - Licensed from Pablo Calvog through Bigstock.com
Young woman writing– Licensed from Artemis Gordon through Bigstock.com
Angry Boss– Licensed from Core Pics through Bigstock.com

Chapter 2

Hispanic Baseball Boy– Licensed from Nicholas Burningham through Bigstock.com
Businessman relaxing – Licensed from Kati Neudert through Bigstock.com
Confused man– Licensed from Abbas Saigara through Bigstock.com
Teacher– Licensed from Michele Piacquadio through Bigstock.com
Woman Carrying Books– Licensed from Jason Stitt through Bigstock.com
Business Man Smiling– Licensed from Andres Rodriguez through Bigstock.com
Business Woman with Broken Down Car– Licensed from Norman Pogson through Bigstock.com
Files– Licensed from Aaron Amat through Bigstock.com
Inside Modern Closet– Licensed from Dimitry Kultlayev through Bigstock.com
High School Baseball Pitcher– Licensed from Glenn Nagel through Bigstock.com
Pitcher Windup– Licensed from Leigh Folds through Bigstock.com
Bachelors Students - Licensed from Viktor Cap through Bigstock.com
Graduate Students - Licensed from Lisa F. Young through Bigstock.com
Doctoral Students - Licensed from Zsolt Nyulaszi through Bigstock.com
Adelie Penguin– Licensed from Moritz Buchty through Bigstock.com
Row of Business People at Lecture– Licensed from Dmitriy Shironosov through Bigstock.com
Businessman facing a Blackboard– Licensed from Viorel Sima through Bigstock.com
Eye– Licensed from Johanna Goodyear through Bigstock.com
Mathematics– Licensed from Inga Nielsen through Bigstock.com
Taking a Test – Licensed from Kostyantine Pankin through Bigstock.com
Businesswoman extending a Handshake– Licensed from Stephanie Bidouze through Bigstock.com
Businesswoman Signing a Contract– Licensed from Andrey Malinkin through Bigstock.com
Elite Business People– Licensed from Edhar Yuualaits through Bigstock.com
Written Work– Licensed from Dmitriy Shironosov through Bigstock.com
Manger Meeting with an Employee– Licensed from Wavebreak Media Ltd through Bigstock.com
Crowd of People Walking– Licensed from Rafael Ramirez Lee through Bigstock.com
Smiling Business Man– Licensed from Andres Rodriguez through Bigstock.com
Smiling Businesswoman with Arms Crossed– Licensed from Phil Date through Bigstock.com
Workplace with Red Lamp– Licensed from Dmitriy Shironosov through Bigstock.com
Heap of magazines- Licensed by BooblGum through Bigstock.com
Filing Cabinet- Licensed by Badboo through Bigstock.com
Hands of accountant with calculator and pen- Licensed by Kurhan through Bigstock.com

Chapter 3

Clapping business people - Licensed from stokkete through Bigstock.com
Businessman with thumb up - Licensed from cristovao through Bigstock.com
Colorful binders - Licensed from heiko 119 through Bigstock.com
Business people laughing - Licensed from zurijeta through Bigstock.com
Business women talking - Licensed from Wavebreak Media Ltd through Bigstock.com
Businessman in empty office – Licensed Blend Images from through Bigstock.com
Excited businessman - Licensed from Dragon Images through Bigstock.com
Two businessmen interacting - Licensed from pressmaster through Bigstock.com
Businessmen looking at smart phone - Licensed from Rido81 through Bigstock.com
Happy factory worker - Licensed from Minerva Studio through Bigstock.com
Businessman in from of blurred team - Licensed from Bigedhar through Bigstock.com
Business group smiling - Licensed from andres through Bigstock.com
Business woman - Licensed from Andres through Bigstock.com
College graduates - Licensed from Blend Images through Bigstock.com
Successful meeting presentation - Licensed from Andres through Bigstock.com
Job interview - Licensed from Ambrophoto through Bigstock.com
Surprised businesswoman using her laptop computer - Licensed from Dolgachov through Bigstock.com
Two Businesswomen Meeting In Office - Licensed from Monkeybusinessimages through Bigstock.com
Two Students having coffee - Licensed from Wavebreak Media Ltd through Bigstock.com
Secretary having bad day - Licensed from Stokkete through Bigstock.com
Business Woman Handshake - Licensed from Nruboc through Bigstock.com
Female office worker on phone- Licensed from Michaeljung through Bigstock.com
Business Team - Licensed from Dean Drobot through Bigstock.com
Business woman handshake – Licensed from Andres Rodriguez through Bigstock.com
Young man carrying box – Licensed from Franck Boston through Bigstock.com
Blank Business Diagram – Licensed from Steve VanHorn through Bigstock.com
Files– Licensed from Aaron Amat through Bigstock.com

Credits

United Team of Doctors Embracing – Licensed from Blaj Gabriel through Bigstock.com
Businesswoman Multitasking– Licensed from Core Pics through Bigstock.com
Office worker sleeping on her desk– Licensed from Michal Kowalski through Bigstock.com
Businessman relaxing – Licensed from Kati Neudert through Bigstock.com
Happy young business woman– Licensed from Edhar Yuualaits through Bigstock.com
Creative Team - Licensed from Wavebreak Media through Bigstock.com
Multitasking– Licensed from Core Pics through Bigstock.com
Boss yelling at employee– Licensed from Auremar through Bigstock.com
Young attractive business people– Licensed from Edhar Yuualaits through Bigstock.com
Adult student in class– Licensed from Cathy Yeulet through Bigstock.com
Woman studying at library– Licensed from Andres Rodriguez through Bigstock.com
Business man sleeping– Licensed from Petr Kurgan through Bigstock.com
Excited business woman– Licensed from Ryan Jorgensen through Bigstock.com
Business woman applauding– Licensed from Andres Rodriguez through Bigstock.com
Business woman with red file folder– Licensed from Jaimie Duplass through Bigstock.com
Minority Businessman– Licensed from Rob Marmion through Bigstock.com
Survey and pen– Licensed from Ryan Fox through Bigstock.com
Doctoral Students - Licensed from Zsolt Nyulaszi through Bigstock.com
Woman in Library - Licensed from Wavebreak Media through Bigstock.com

Chapter 4

Industrial engineer workers - Licensed from kadmy through Bigstock.com
Two architects at drawing board - Licensed from Nyul through Bigstock.com
Businesswomen talking on sofa - Licensed from Wavebreak Media Ltd through Bigstock.com
Business people at table - Licensed from Nosnibor137 through Bigstock.com
Young females having coffee on sofa - Licensed from lightwavemedia through Bigstock.com
Businesswoman working on computer - Licensed from iofoto.com through Bigstock.com
Businesswoman reading - Licensed from Ammentorp through Bigstock.com
Smiling business woman - Licensed from Odua Images through Bigstock.com
Work colleagues arguing - Licensed from Zinkevych through Bigstock.com
Business graphs and charts - Licensed from Alina Khalchenko through Bigstock.com
Rural road in autumn - Licensed from nature78 through Bigstock.com
Sad woman - Licensed from pressmaster through Bigstock.com
Happy business people applauding - Licensed from pressmaster through Bigstock.com
Business people standing at table - Licensed from zurijeta through Bigstock.com
Business people in huddle - Licensed from mangostock through Bigstock.com
Muslin business woman - Licensed from Distinctive Images through Bigstock.com
Happy business group in office - Licensed from andres through Bigstock.com
Group of people by escalator - Licensed from Kurhan through Bigstock.com
Smiling business woman - Licensed from Kurhan through Bigstock.com
Counting bank notes - Licensed from AndreyPopov through Bigstock.com
Women talking on sofa - Licensed from Monkeybusinessimages through Bigstock.com
Summer studying - Licensed from slackmeister through Bigstock.com
Group of people in business people - Licensed from shock through Bigstock.com
Blank Business Diagram – Licensed from Steve VanHorn through Bigstock.com
Survey and pen– Licensed from Ryan Fox through Bigstock.com
Files– Licensed from Aaron Amat through Bigstock.com
Happy Multiracial Businesswoman with Hands Crossed– Licensed from M Sorensen through Bigstock.com
Businessman relaxing – Licensed from Kati Neudert through Bigstock.com
Senior and junior businessmen - Licensed from Michal Kowalski through Bigstock.com
Weekly Time Sheet - Licensed from John Kwan through Bigstock.com
MLADA BOLESLAV – Licensed from Nataliya Hora through Bigstock.com
Teamwork– Licensed from Dmitry Shironosov through Bigstock.com
Man giving lecture to three people– Licensed from Cathy Yeulet through Bigstock.com
Man with Money with Glasses - Licensed from Paul Paladin through Bigstock.com
Manager pointing at Computer with Secretary- Licensed from Wavebreak Media Ltd through Bigstock.com
Mature Businessman in Front of Team– Licensed from Wavebreak Media Ltd through Bigstock.com
Business woman in a Wheelchair at Meeting– Licensed from Wavebreak Media Ltd through Bigstock.com
Frightened Man Behind Computer – Licensed from azxAXe through Bigstock.com
Anguish Expressive Man – Licensed from Franck Camhi through Bigstock.com
Elite Business People– Licensed from Edhar Yuualaits through Bigstock.com
Happy Office Workers- Licensed from Scott Griessel through Bigstock.com
Female Hands Reviewing Documents - Licensed from Karel Noppe through Bigstock.com
Man in Library - Licensed from Viktor Cap through Bigstock.com

Chapter 5

Business people in elevator - Licensed from Nosnibor137 through Bigstock.com
Business men talking - Licensed from Minerva Studio through Bigstock.com
Three people in library - Licensed from Monkeybusinessimages through Bigstock.com
Woman in wheel chair - Licensed from michaeljung through Bigstock.com
Business woman with arms crossed - Licensed from Wavebreak Media Ltd through Bigstock.com
Blurred businessmen - Licensed from Nosnibor137 through Bigstock.com

Credits

Production workers - Licensed from Kasia Bialasiewicz through Bigstock.com
Woman with mask - Licensed from Poslovni-svet through Bigstock.com
Colleagues gossiping behind man - Licensed from lightwavemedia through Bigstock.com
Industrial robot - Licensed from Vinne through Bigstock.com
Sleeping office worker - Licensed from ronstik through Bigstock.com
Smiling woman with thumbs up - Licensed from AntonioGuillem through Bigstock.com
Sheet of paper and pen - Licensed from Di Studio through Bigstock.com
Young man drawing flowchart - Licensed from gualtiero boffi through Bigstock.com
Corporate woman presenting - Licensed from Goodluz through Bigstock.com
Businessmen shaking hands in meeting - Licensed from Bigedhar through Bigstock.com
Business woman reading - Licensed from racom through Bigstock.com
Job interview two men - Licensed from auremar through Bigstock.com
Discussion with tablet - Licensed from Bloomua through Bigstock.com
Colleagues gossiping behind woman - Licensed from Lightwavemedia through Bigstock.com
Business People working on table - Licensed from Dean Drobot through Bigstock.com
Deliveryman carrying parcel - Licensed from Franck Boston through Bigstock.com
Smiling business team - Licensed from Goodluz through Bigstock.com
Business Woman talking - Licensed from Odua Images through Bigstock.com
Four Professions planning- Licensed from Kzenon through Bigstock.com
Blank Business Diagram – Licensed from Steve VanHorn through Bigstock.com
Survey and pen– Licensed from Ryan Fox through Bigstock.com
Female Student Reading Book- Licensed from Dzmitry Stankevich through Bigstock.com
Elite Business People– Licensed from Edhar Yuualaits through Bigstock.com
Files– Licensed from Aaron Amat through Bigstock.com
Two Business Women Talking- Licensed from Daniel Hurst through Bigstock.com
Three Road Construction Workers- Licensed from Dmitry Kalinovsky through Bigstock.com
Test - Licensed from Jason Stitt through Bigstock.com
Happy young business woman– Licensed from Edhar Yuualaits through Bigstock.com
Businesswomen Laughing in Alley- Licensed from Scott Griessel through Bigstock.com
Smiling Young Businesswoman in Meeting- Licensed from Zsolt Nyulaszi through Bigstock.com
Business People Arriving in Elevator- Licensed from Zsolt Nyulaszi through Bigstock.com
Sheet of Paper- Licensed from Aleksandr Sokolov through Bigstock.com
Business Woman Writing - Licensed from Rob Marmion through Bigstock.com
Man in Library - Licensed from Blend Images through Bigstock.com

Chapter 6

Elite business people - Licensed from Bigedhar through Bigstock.com
Happy senior citizens - Licensed from style-photographs through Bigstock.com
Handhelp - Licensed from ion_plus through Bigstock.com
Business team hands in - Licensed from chagin through Bigstock.com
Two business people meeting - Licensed from Ambrophoto through Bigstock.com
Pile of books - Licensed from Sabphoto through Bigstock.com
Purple onion - Licensed from Aaron Amat through Bigstock.com
Happy business people standing in a row - Licensed from michaeljung through Bigstock.com
Group of doctors and a nurse - Licensed from Marmion through Bigstock.com
Blank Business Diagram – Licensed from Steve VanHorn through Bigstock.com
Survey and pen– Licensed from Ryan Fox through Bigstock.com
Files– Licensed from Aaron Amat through Bigstock.com
Meeting of Support Group – Licensed from Cathy Yeulet through Bigstock.com
Beautiful Woman Praying – Licensed from Jaimie Duplass through Bigstock.com
Young Muslim Woman Praying – Licensed from Hongqi Zhang through Bigstock.com
Businesswoman with Date Book – Licensed from Jaimie Duplass through Bigstock.com
Portrait of a Businessman in Front of Team – Licensed from Luca Bertolli through Bigstock.com
Beautiful Woman with Business People in Back – Licensed from Konstantin Chagin through Bigstock.com
Woman with Open Hand for Handshake – Licensed from Lev Dolgachov through Bigstock.com
Businesswoman With Date Book – Licensed from Jaimie Duplass through Bigstock.com
Two Women Smiling – Licensed from Cathy Yeulet through Bigstock.com
Daughter Comforts Mother – Licensed from Martin Novak through Bigstock.com
Two Women Talking in Living Room – Licensed from Cathy Yeulet through Bigstock.com
Woman Praying in Church – Licensed from R. Eko Bintoro through Bigstock.com

Chapter 7

Senior Businessman - Licensed by Pressmaster through Bigstock.com
Produce Apples and Oranges Woman - Licensed by Dgilder through Bigstock.com
Basket full with different types of apples full frame - Licensed by Picturepartners though Bigstock.com
Serious middle aged businessman - Licensed by Nosnibor137 through Bigstock.com
Young businesswoman sitting at her desk- Licensed by Blend Images through Bigstock.com
Clapping Business People- Licensing by Stokkete through Bigstock.com
Pretty African American businesswoman- Licensed by Michaeljung through Bigstock.com
Coworkers having financial meeting in conference room- Licensed by Pictrough through Bigstock.com
Woman in wheelchair with laptop computer- Licensed by Auremar through Bigstock.com
Group of happy business people with arms up- Licensed by Goodluz through Bigstock.com

Credits

Young female doctor portrait- Licensed by Minerva Studio through Bigstock.com
Business group in a meeting- Licensed by Andres through Bigstock.com
Beautiful modern Middle Eastern office worker- Licensed by Michaeljung through Bigstock.com
Smiling business team looking at camera- Licensed by Goodluz through Bigstock.com
Construction roofer carpenter worker- Licensed by Kadmy through Bigstock.com
Business team in an office- Licensed by Andres through Bigstock.com
Senior businessman isolated on white background by Rido81 through Bigstock.com
Successful business woman at the office with her team - Licensed from andres through Bigstock.com
Group of doctors and a nurse - Licensed from Marmion through Bigstock.com
Student - Young Asian man in library with laptop - Licensed from Kzenon through Bigstock.com
Business, education, people and office concept – Licensed from dolgachov through Bigstock.com
Getting The Book - Licensed from andykaziethrough Bigstock.com
Successful Motivated Multiethnic Business Team - Licensed from Racorn through Bigstock.com
Close-up of Business people discussing a financial plan- Licensed from Chagin through Bigstock.com
Group portrait of multiethnic business people smiling in office - Licensed from Nosnibor137 through Bigstock.com
Two Business Woman Analyzing Balance Sheet - Licensed from Imagesbavaria through Bigstock.com
Business Conference Meeting - Licensed from iofoto.com through Bigstock.com

Chapter 8

Blank Business Diagram – Licensed from Steve VanHorn through Bigstock.com
Survey and pen– Licensed from Ryan Fox through Bigstock.com
Businessman Designing a Plan – Licensed from Edhar Yuualaits through Bigstock.com
Factory Workers on Production Line – Licensed from Cathy Yeulet through Bigstock.com
Firefighters by Fire Engine – Licensed from Cathy Yeulet through Bigstock.com
Two Women Smiling – Licensed from Cathy Yeulet through Bigstock.com
Woman with Handmade Accessory – Licensed from Anna Omelchenko through Bigstock.com
Islamic Young Woman with Diverse Group – Licensed from Anna Omelchenko through Bigstock.com
Business People Meeting Green Chairs in Back – Licensed from Cathy Yeulet through Bigstock.com
Young Man Raising Whiskey Glass – Licensed from Wavebreak Media Ltd through Bigstock.com
Rodeo Cowboy Silhouette – Licensed from Sascha Burkard through Bigstock.com
Confident businesswoman with coworkers in Background – Licensed from Artemis Gordon through Bigstock.com
Happy Diverse Group of Volunteers – Licensed from Mauricio Jordan through Bigstock.com
Confident Business People – Licensed from Cathy Yeulet through Bigstock.com
Boardroom – Licensed from Bill Howe through Bigstock.com
Brainstorming – Licensed from Andres Rodriguez through Bigstock.com
Hands – Licensed from Andres Rodriguez through Bigstock.com
Profit Dynamics – Licensed from Dinis Tolipov through Bigstock.com
Limo by Executive Jet – Licensed from Alan Crosthwaite through Bigstock.com
Young Tired, Overworked Female Office Worker – Licensed from Michal Kowalski through Bigstock.com
Boss Yelling at Employee – Licensed from auremar through Bigstock.com
Team Meeting in Creative Office – Licensed from Cathy Yeulet through Bigstock.com
Portrait of Mature Businessman Pointing – Licensed from Andres Rodriguez through Bigstock.com
Business Team with Arms up at Office – Licensed from Andres Rodriguez through Bigstock.com
Dwelling on Idea – Licensed from Andres Rodriguez through Bigstock.com
Businessman Relaxing – Licensed from Kati Neudert through Bigstock.com
Business Partner Deal – Licensed from Andres Rodriguez through Bigstock.com
Planet Earth – Licensed from Johan Swanepoel through Bigstock.com
Arabic Businesswoman with Team in Back – Licensed from Greg Crawford through Bigstock.com
Uncertain Young Businesswoman – Licensed from Michal Kowalski through Bigstock.com
Angry Boss – Licensed from Core Pics through Bigstock.com
Woman in Library – Licensed from Yatigra through Bigstock.com
Business team in an office- Licensed by Andres through Bigstock.com
Senior businessman isolated on white background by Rido81 through Bigstock.com
Beautiful business woman walking outside her office- Licensed by Yo-ichi through Bigstock.com
Factory Worker Welding- Licensed by ChrisAlleaume through Bigstock.com
Factory worker processing roll of steel sheet- Licensed by Uwphotographer through Bigstock.com
Happy young business woman standing in front of her team- Licensed by Bigedhar through Bigstock.com
Is there a problem?- Licensed by Starfotograf through Bigstock.com
Group of happy young business people in a meeting at office-Licensed by .Shock through Bigstock.com
Closeup of a hand giving female employee loyalty card- Licensed by Nosnibor137 through Bigstock.com
Mature businessman showing growing chart- Licensed by Rido81 through Bigstock.com
Mature businessman showing growing chart- Licensed by Rido81 through Bigstock.com
Mature business man- Licensed by ZM Photography through Bigstock.com
Young man doing homework and studying- Licensed by Diego Cervo through Bigstock.com
Man writing on a blackboard- Licensed by Minerva Studio through Bigstock.com
Successful young business woman with hands folded- Licensed by Tatsianama through Bigstock.com
Glad businesswoman talking to her team- Licensed by Wavebreak Media Ltd through Bigstock.com
Portrait of happy young business woman isolated on white background- Licensed by Kurhan by Bigstock.com
Young smiling executives shaking hands in front - Licensed by Wavebreak Media Ltd by Bigstock.com
Portrait of happy female colleagues accounting in office- Licensed by Pressmaster through Bigstock.com
United Flags- Licensed by Zhaoliang through Bigstock.com

Credits

Portrait of team in creative office- Licensed by Monkeybusinessimages through Bigstock.com
Student doing the notes- Licensed by Kasia Bialasiewicz through Bigstock.com
Pretty young college student in a library- Licensed by Lightpoet through Bigstock.com
Business Woman- Licensed by Kurhan through Bigstock.com
Smiling Business Woman- Licensed by Kurhan through Bigstock.com

Chapter 9

Blank Business Diagram – Licensed from Steve VanHorn through Bigstock.com
Survey and pen– Licensed from Ryan Fox through Bigstock.com
Files– Licensed from Aaron Amat through Bigstock.com
Meeting of Support Group – Licensed from Cathy Yeulet through Bigstock.com
Beautiful Woman Praying – Licensed from Jaimie Duplass through Bigstock.com
Young Muslim Woman Praying – Licensed from Hongqi Zhang through Bigstock.com
Businesswoman with Date Book – Licensed from Jaimie Duplass through Bigstock.com
Portrait of a Businessman in Front of Team – Licensed from Luca Bertolli through Bigstock.com
Beautiful Woman with Business People in Back – Licensed from Konstantin Chagin through Bigstock.com
Woman with Open Hand for Handshake – Licensed from Lev Dolgachov through Bigstock.com
Businesswoman With Date Book – Licensed from Jaimie Duplass through Bigstock.com
Two Women Smiling – Licensed from Cathy Yeulet through Bigstock.com
Daughter Comforts Mother – Licensed from Martin Novak through Bigstock.com
Two Women Talking in Living Room – Licensed from Cathy Yeulet through Bigstock.com
Woman Praying in Church – Licensed from R. Eko Bintoro through Bigstock.com

Chapter 10

Senior Businessman - Licensed by Pressmaster through Bigstock.com
Produce Apples and Oranges Woman - Licensed by Dgilder through Bigstock.com
Basket full with different types of apples full frame - Licensed by Picturepartners though Bigstock.com
Serious middle aged businessman - Licensed by Nosnibor137 through Bigstock.com
Young businesswoman sitting at her desk- Licensed by Blend Images through Bigstock.com
Clapping Business People- Licensing by Stokkete through Bigstock.com
Pretty African American businesswoman- Licensed by Michaeljung through Bigstock.com
Coworkers having financial meeting in conference room- Licensed by Pictrough through Bigstock.com
Woman in wheelchair with laptop computer- Licensed by Auremar through Bigstock.com
Group of happy business people with arms up- Licensed by Goodluz through Bigstock.com
Young female doctor portrait- Licensed by Minerva Studio through Bigstock.com
Business group in a meeting- Licensed by Andres through Bigstock.com
Beautiful modern Middle Eastern office worker- Licensed by Michaeljung through Bigstock.com
Smiling business team looking at camera- Licensed by Goodluz through Bigstock.com
Construction roofer carpenter worker- Licensed by Kadmy through Bigstock.com
Business team in an office- Licensed by Andres through Bigstock.com
Senior businessman isolated on white background by Rido81 through Bigstock.com

References

Alarcon, G., Eschleman, K., & Bowling, N. (2009). Relationships between personality variables and burnout: a meta-analysis. *Work & Stress*, 23(3), 244-263.

Anderson, L. W., & Krathwohl, D. R. (2001). *A taxonomy for learning, teaching, and assessing: A revision of Bloom's taxonomy of educational objectives*. New York: Longman.

Antonakis, J., Avolio, B. J., & Sivasubramaniam, N. (2003). Context and leadership: an examination of the nine-factor full-range leadership theory using the Multifactor Leadership Questionnaire. *The Leadership Quarterly, 14,* 3, 261.

Argyris, C. (1957). *Personality and organization*. New York: Harper.

Argyris, C. (1962). *Interpersonal competence and organizational effectiveness*. Homewood, IL: Irwin-Dorsey.

Argyris, C. (1964). *Integrating the individual and the organization*. New York: Wiley.

Argyris, C. (1973). Personality and Organization Theory Revisited. *Administrative Science Quarterly, 18,* 2, 141-167.

Argyris, C. (1983). Action science and intervention. *Journal of Applied Behavioral Science*, 19, 115– 140.

Arvey, R. D., Rotundo, M., Johnson, W., Zhang, Z., & McGue, M. (2006). The determinants of leadership role occupancy: Genetic and personality factors. *The Leadership Quarterly*, 17, 1–20.

Atinc, G., Darrat, M., Fuller, B., & Parker, B. W. (2010). Perceptions of organizational politics: a meta-analysis of theoretical antecedents. *Journal of Managerial Issues : Jmi, 22,* 4, 494-512.

Aupperle, K. E., Acar, W., & Booth, D. E. (1986). An empirical critique of 'in search of excellence': how excellent are the excellent companies?. *Journal of Management*, 12(4), 499.

Avolio, B. J. (1990). Transactional leadership: Viewed as an organizational development process. In C. N. Jactions & M. R. Manning (Eds.), Organizational Development Annual, 3. Arlington, VA: American Society for Training and Development.

Avolio, B. J. (1995). Integrating transformational leadership and afro-centric management. Human Resource Management Journal, 11(6), 17-21.

Avolio, B. J. & Bass, B.M. (1995). Individual consideration viewed at multiple levels of analysis: A multi-level framework for examining the diffusion of transformational leadership. *Leadership Quarterly*, 6, 199-218.

Avolio, B. J., & Bass, B. M. (1988). An alternative strategy for reducing biases in leadership ratings. Paper, Academy of Management, Anaheim, CA.

Avolio, B. J., & Bass, B. M. (1991). *The full range leadership development programs: basic and advanced manuals.* Binghamton, NY: Bass, Avolio & Associates.

References

Avolio, B. J., & Bass, B. M. (1994). Evaluate the impact of transformational leadership training at individual, group, organizational, and community levels. Final report to W. K. Kellogg Foundation. Binghamton: State University of New York, Center for Leadership Studies.

Avolio, B. J., & Bass, B. M. (1996). You can drag a horse to water, but you can't make it drink: Evaluating a full range leadership model for training and development (CLS Report 96- 4). Binghamton: State University of New York, Center for Leadership Studies.

Avolio, B. J., & Bass, B.M. (1998). You can drag a horse to water, but you can't make it drink except when it's thirsty. *Journal of Leadership Studies, 5,* 1-17

Avolio, B. J., & Gardner, W. L. (2005). Authentic leadership development: Getting to the root of positive forms of leadership. *Leadership Quarterly*, 16, 3, 315-338.

Avolio, B. J., & Gibbons, T. C. (1988). Developing transformational leaders: A lifespan approach. In J. A. Conger & R. N. Kanungo (Eds.), Charismatic leadership: The elusive factor in organizational effectiveness (pp. 276–308). San Francisco: Jossey-Bass.

Avolio, B. J., & Howell, J. M. (1990). The effects of leader-follower personality congruence: Predicting follower satisfaction and business unit performance. Paper, International Association of Applied Psychology, Kyoto, Japan.

Avolio, B. J., & Howell, J. M. (1992). The impact of leader behavior and leader-follower personality match on satisfaction and unit performance. In K. E. Clark, M. B. Clark, & D. R. Campbell (Eds.), Impact of leadership. Greensboro, NC: The Center for Creative Leadership.

Avolio, B. J., & Yammarino, F. J. (1997). Leadership and organizational culture in TQM. In S. B. Krause (Ed.), Human resource management issues in total quality management. Washington, D. C.: ASQC Press.

Avolio, B. J., Bass, B. M., & Jung, D. (1996). Construct validation of the multifactor leadership questionnaire MLQ-Form 5X (CLS Report 96-1). Binghamton: State University of New York, Center for Leadership Studies.

Avolio, B. J., Bass, B. M., & Jung, D. I. (1995). *MLQ multifactor leadership questionnaire: technical report.* Redwood City, CA: Mindgarden.

Avolio, B. J., Bass, B. M., & Jung, D. I. (1999). Re-examining the components of transformational and transactional leadership using the Multifactor Leadership Questionnaire. *Journal of Occupational and Organizational Psychology*, 72, 441–462.

Avolio, B. J., Gardner, W. L and Walumbwa, F. O. (2007). *The Authentic Leadership Questionnaire.* Mindgarden.com

Avolio, B. J., Waldman, D. W., & Yammarino, F. L. (1991). Leading in the 1990's: towards understanding the four I's of transformational leadership. *Journal of European Industrial Training*, 15(4), 9–16.

Avolio, B.J. (1994). The "natural" leader: Some antecedents to transformational leadership. *International Journal of Public Administration, 17*, 1559-1581.

Avolio, B.J. (1999) *Full Leadership Development: Building the Vital Forces in Organizations*. Thousand Oaks, CA: Sage.

Avolio, B.J. (2004). *Leadership Development in Balance: Made/Born.* NJ: Erlbaum.

Avolio, B.J. & Bass, B.M. (1988) Transformational leadership, charisma and beyond. In J.G. Hunt, B.R. Baloga, H.P. Dachler, & C. Schriesheim (Eds.). *Emerging leadership vistas* (pp. 29-50). Emsford, NY: Pergamon Press.

Avolio, B.J., & Bass, B.M. (1991). *The full-range of leadership development*. Center for Leadership Studies, Binghamton, NY.

Avolio, B.J., & Yammarino, F.J. (2003). Transformational and charismatic leadership: The road ahead. Oxford: Elsevier Press.

Avolio, B.J., Jung, D.I., Murry, W., Sivasubramaniam, N., & Garger, J. (2003). Assessing shared leadership: Development of a Team Multifactor Leadership Questionnaire. In C.L. Pearce & Jay A. Conger (Eds.), Shared leadership: Reframing the hows and whys of leadership. (pp. 143-172). Thousand Oaks: Sage.

Babakus, E., Yavas, U., & Ashill, N. J. (2011). Service worker burnout and turnover intentions: Roles of person-job fit, servant leadership, and customer orientation. *Services Marketing Quarterly*, 32(1), 17–31.

Bar-On, R. (1997). *The Emotional Quotient Inventory* (*EQ-i*): *A test of emotional intelligence*. Toronto, Canada: Multi-Health Systems, Inc.

References

Bar-On, R. (2000). *The Emotional Quotient Inventory (EQ-i): Technical manual.* Toronto, Canada: Multi-Health Systems, Inc.

Bar-On, R. (2004). The Bar-On Emotional Quotient Inventory (EQ-i): Rationale, description, and summary of psychometric properties. In Glenn Geher (Ed.), *Measuring emotional intelligence: common ground and controversy*. Hauppauge, NY: Nova Science Publishers, pp. 111-142.

Bar-On, R. (2006). The Bar-On model of emotional-social intelligence (ESI). *Psicothema, 18*, 13-25.

Barbuto Jr., J. E., & Wheeler, D. W. (2006). Scale development and construct clarification of servant leadership. *Group & Organization Management*, 31(3), 300-326.

Barnard, C. I. (1938) *The functions of the executive*. Cambridge, Mass: Harvard University Press.

Barrick, M. R., Mount, M. K., & Judge, T. A. (2001). The FFM personality dimensions and Job performance: meta-analysis of meta-analyses. *International Journal of Selection and Assessment,* 9, 9-30.

Bass, B. M. (1985). *Leadership and performance beyond expectations*. New York: Free Press.

Bass, B. M. (1985). Leadership: Good, better, best. *Organizational Dynamics,* 13(3), 26-40.

Bass, B. M. (1985). *The multifactor leadership questionnaire: Form 5*. Binghamton: State University of New York.

Bass, B. M. (1987). Charismatic and inspirational leadership: what's the difference? *Symposium, Charismatic Leadership in Management*. Faculty of Management, McGill University, Montreal, QU.

Bass, B. M. (1988). Transformational leadership and coping with crisis and stress conditions. *International Congress of Psychology*, Sydney, Australia.

Bass, B. M. (1989). The inspirational processes of leadership. Journal of Management Development, 7(5), 21–31.

Bass, B. M. (1989). The two faces of charismatic leadership. *Leaders Magazine,* 12 (4), 44– 45.

Bass, B. M. (1990). *Bass and Stogdill's handbook of leadership.* New York: Free Press.

Bass, B. M. (1990). From transactional to transformational leadership: Learning to share the vision. *Organization Dynamics*, 18(3), 19–36.

Bass, B. M. (1995). The universality of transformational leadership. Distinguished Scientific Contributors Award Address, Society for Industrial/Organizational Psychology, Orlando, FL.

Bass, B. M. (1995). Transformational leadership redux. Leadership Quarterly, 6, 463–477.

Bass, B. M. (1996). *The ethics of transformational leadership.* College Park: University of Maryland, Leadership Studies Group, Center for Politics and Participation.

Bass, B. M. (1997) Does the transactional/transformational leadership paradigm transcend organizational and national boundaries? *American Psychologist, 52*, 130-139.

Bass, B. M. (1998). The ethics of transformational leadership. In J. B. Ciulla (Ed), *Ethics, the heart of leadership*. Westport, CT: Praeger.

Bass, B. M. (1998). *Transformational leadership: Industrial, military, and educational impact*. Mahwah, NJ: Lawrence Erlbaum & Associates.

Bass, B. M. (1999) Two decades of research and development in transformational leadership. European Journal of Work and Organizational Psychology, 8(1), 9-32.

Bass, B. M. (1999). Current developments in transformational leadership: Research and applications. *Psychologist-Manager Journal*, 3, 5– 21.

Bass, B. M. (2000). The future of leadership in the learning organization. *Journal of Leadership Studies*, 7(3), 18–38.

Bass, B. M. & Bass, R. (2009). *The Bass handbook of leadership: Theory, research, and managerial applications*. New York: Simon & Schuster, Inc.. Kindle Edition.

Bass, B. M., & Avolio, B. J. (1989). Potential biases in leadership measures: How prototypes, leniency, and general satisfaction relate to ratings and rankings of transformational and transactional leadership constructs. Educational Tests and Measurement, 49, 509–527.

Bass, B. M., & Avolio, B. J. (1995) *Manual for the Multifactor Leadership Questionnaire.* Redwood City, CA: Mind Garden.

Bass, B. M., & Avolio, B. J. (1996). *Multifactor leadership questionnaire feedback report.* Palo Alto, CA: Consulting Psychologists Press.

Bass, B. M., & Avolio, B. J. (1996). *Transformational leadership development: manual for the multifactor leadership questionnaire.* Palo Alto, CA: Consulting Psychologists Press.

References

Bass, B. M., & Avolio, B. J. (1997). *Full range of leadership: Manual for the Multifactor Leadership Questionnaire.* Redwood City, CA: Mind Garden.

Bass, B. M., & Avolio, B. J. (2004). *Multifactor leadership questionnaire: Manual leader form, rater, and scoring key for MLQ (Form 5x-Short*). Redwood City, CA: Mind Garden.

Bass, B. M., & Avolio, B. J. (Eds.) (1994). *Improving organizational effectiveness through transformational leadership*. Thousand Oaks, CA: Sage Publications.

Bass, B. M., & Avolio, B. J. (undated). Intuitive-empirical approach to biodata analysis. Binghamton: State University of New York, Center for Leadership Studies.

Bass, B. M., & Bass, R. (2008). *The Bass handbook of leadership: Theory, research, and managerial applications*. New York: Free Press.

Bass, B. M., & Seltzer, J. (1990). Transformational leadership: Beyond initiation and consideration. Journal of Management, 16, 693–703.

Bass, B. M., & Steidlmeier, P.A. (1999) Ethics,character, authenticity, and transformational leadership. Leadership Quarterly, 10, 181-217.

Bass, B. M., & Yammarino, F. (1989). Transformational leaders know themselves better (Tech Rep. No. ONR-Tr-5). Alexandria, VA: Office of Naval Research.

Bass, B. M., & Yammarino, F. J. (1991). Congruence of self and others' leadership ratings of naval officers for understanding successful performance. Applied Psychology: An International Review, 40, 437–454.

Bass, B. M., & Yokochi, N. (1991). Charisma among senior executives and the special case of Japanese CEO's. Consulting Psychology Bulletin, Winter/Spring, 1, 31–38.

Bass, B. M., Avolio, B. J., & Atwater, L. (1996). The transformational and transactional leadership of men and women. International Review of Applied Psychology, 45, 5-34.

Bass, B. M., Avolio, B. J., Jung, D. I., & Berson, Y. (2003). Predicting unit performance by assessing transformational and transactional leadership. *Journal of Applied Psychology*, 88 (2), 207– 218.

Bass, B. M., Avolio, B.J., & Atwater, L. (1996). The transformational and transactional leadership of men and women. *Applied Psychology: An International Review*, 45,5-34.

Bass, B. M., Avolio, B.J., Jung, D.I., & Berson, Y. (2003). Predicting unit performance by assessing transformational and transactional leadership. *Journal of Applied Psychology*, 88, 207-218.

Bass. B. M., Avolio, B. J., & Jung, D. I. (1999). Reexamining the components of transformational and transactional leadership using the Multifactor Leadership Questionnaire (Form 5X). *Journal of Organizational and Occupational Psychology*, 72, 441– 462.

Batson, C. D. (1991). The altruism question: Toward a social psychological answer. Hills-dale, NJ: Erlbaum.

Batson, C., Ahmad, N. & Lishner, D. *Empathy and altruism*, in Snyder, C. R., & Lopez, S. J. (2005). *Handbook of positive psychology*. Oxford: Oxford University Press.

Bennis, W. G., & Nanus, B. (1985). *Leaders: The strategies for taking charge*. New York: Harper & Row.

Bernard, L. L. (1926). *An introduction to social psychology.* New York: Holt.

Bingham, W. V. (1927). Leadership. In H. C. Metcalf, *The psychological foundations of management*. New York: Shaw.

Bird, C. (1940). *Social psychology.* New York: Appleton-Century.

Bird, J., Wang, C., & Murray, L. (2009). Building budgets and trust through superintendent leadership. *Journal of Education Finance* 35 (2), 140-156.

Blake, R. R., & McCanse, A. A. (1991). *Leadership dilemmas--grid solutions*. Houston: Gulf Pub. Co.

Blake, R. R., & Mouton, J. S. (1964). *The managerial grid*. Houston, TX: Gulf.

Blake, R. R., & Mouton, J. S. (1965). A 9, 9 approach for increasing organizational productivity. In E. H. Schein & W. G. Bennis (eds.), *Personal and organizational change through group methods*. New York: Wiley.

Blake, R. R., & Mouton, J. S. (1972). The managerial grid: Key orientations for achieving production through people. Houston, TX: Gulf.

Blake, R. R., & Mouton, J. S. (1978). *The new managerial grid*. Houston, TX: Gulf.

Bloom, B. S., Engelhart, M. D., & Committee of College and University Examiners. (1956). *Taxonomy of educational objectives: The classification of educational goals*. London: Longmans.

Bono, J. E., & Judge, T. A. (2003). Self-concordance at work: Toward understanding the motivational effects of

References

transformational leaders. *Academy of Management Journal, 46: 554-571.*

Bono, J. E., & Judge, T. A. (2004). Personality and transformational and transactional leadership: a meta-analysis. *The Journal of Applied Psychology, 89,* 5, 901-10.

Bowden, A.O. (1927), A study on the personality of student leadership in the united states, *Journal of Abnormal Social Psychology,* Vol. 21, pp. 149-60.

Bowers, D. G., & Seashore, S. E. (1966). Predicting organizational effectiveness with a four-factor theory of leadership. *Administrative Science Quarterly*, 11, 238– 263.

Bowling, N. (2010). A meta-analysis of the predictors and consequences of organization-based self-esteem. *Journal Of Occupational & Organizational Psychology*, *83*(3), 601. doi:10.1348/096317909X454382

Brackett, M., & Mayer, J. (2003). Convergent, discriminant, and incremental validity of competing measures of emotional intelligence. *Personality & Social Psychology Bulletin*, 9(9), 1147-1158.

Brayfield, A. H., & Rothe, H. F. (1951). An index of job satisfaction. *Journal of Applied Psychology, 35: 307-311.*

Brown, M. E., Trevino, L. K., & Harrison, D. A. (2005). Ethical leadership: A social learning perspective for construct development and testing. *Organizational Behavior and Human Decision Processes*, 97, 117–134.

Burke, C. S., Stagl, K. C., Klein, C., Goodwin, G. F., Salas, E., & Halpin, S. M. (2006). What type of leadership behaviors are functional in teams? A meta-analysis. *The Leadership Quarterly, 17,* 3, 288.

Burns, J. M. (1978). *Leadership*. New York: Harper & Row.

Burns, T., & Stalker, G. M. (1961). *The management of innovation.* Chicago: Quadrangle Books.

Bycio, P., Hackett, R. D., & Allen, J. S. (1995). Further assessments of Bass's (1985) conceptualization of transactional and transformational leadership. *Journal of Applied Psychology*, 80, 468–478.

Cameron, K. S., Bright, D., & Caza, A. (2004). Exploring the relationships between organizational virtuousness and performance. *American Behavioral Scientist*, 47(6), 1–24.

Campion, M. A., Medsker, G., & Higgs, C. (1993). Relations between work group characteristics and effectiveness: Implications for designing effective work groups. *Personnel Psychology*, 46, 823–850.

Caplow, T., Hicks, L., & Wattenberg, B. J. (2001). *The first measured century: An illustrated guide to trends in America, 1900-2000*. Washington, D.C: AEI Press.

Carless, S. A., Wearing, A. J., & Mann, L. (2000). A short mesure of transformation leadership. *Journal of Business and Psychology,* 14(3), 389-406.

Carlyle, T., Goldberg, M. K., Brattin, J. J., & Engel, M. (1888; Republished in1993). *On heroes, hero-worship, & the heroic in history*. Fredrick A. Stokes & Brother, New York, 1888; Berkeley: University of California Press., 1993.

Carson, P., Carson, K. D., & Roe, C. (1993). Social power bases: A meta-analytic examination of interrelationships and outcomes. *Journal of Applied Social Psychology*, 23(14), 1150-1169.

Cartwright, D., Zander, A. F., & Harold D. Lasswell Collection (Yale Law Library). (1960).*Group dynamics: Research and theory. Ed. by Dorwin Cartwright [and] Alvin Zander*. New York: Harper & Row.

Caruso, D. (Date Unknown) *All About the Mayer-Salovey-Caruso Emotional Intelligence Test* (MSCEIT) downloaded from http://www.calcasa.org/sites/default/files/ msceit_white_paper.pdf

Cattell, H. B. (1989). *The 16PF: Personality In Depth*. Champaign, IL: Institute for Personality and Ability Testing, Inc.

Cattell, R. B. (1946). *Description and measurement of personality*. Yonkers-on-Hudson, N. Y: World book company.

Cerit, Y. (2009). The effects of servant leadership behaviors of school principals on teachers' job satisfaction. *Educational Management Administration & Leadership*, 37(5), 600–623.

Ceruzzi, P. E. (2012). *Computing: A concise history*. Cambridge, Mass: MIT Press.

Chandler, A. D., Hikino, T., & Von, N. A. (2008). *Inventing the electronic century: The epic story of the consumer electronics and computer industries*. New York: Free Press.

Chaturvedi, S., Arvey, R., Zhang, Z., & Christoforou, P. (2011). Genetic underpinnings of transformational leadership: the mediating role of dispositional hope. *Journal of Leadership & Organizational Studies, 18,* 4, 469-479.

References

Chiaburu, D., Oh, I., Berry, C., Li, N., & Gardner, R. (2011). The five-factor model of personality traits and organizational citizenship behaviors: A meta-analysis. *Journal Of Applied Psychology*, 96(6), 1140-1166.

Cialdini, R. B., Trost, M. R., & Newsom, J. T. (1995). Preference for consistency: The development of a valid measure and the discovery of surprising behavioral implications. *Journal of Personality and Social Psychology*, 69(2), 318–328.

Clapp-Smith, R., Vogelgesang, G. R., & Avey, J. B. (2009). Authentic leadership and positive psychological capital: The mediating role of trust at the group level of analysis. *Journal of Leadership and Organizational Studies*, 15, 227–240.

Collins, J. C. (2001). *Good to great: Why some companies make the leap--and others don't*. New York, NY: HarperBusiness.

Collins, J. C., & Porras, J. I. (1994). *Built to last: Successful habits of visionary companies*. New York, NY: HarperCollins.

Collins, J. C., & Porras, J. I. (1996). Building your company's vision. *Harvard Business Review, 74,* 5, 65-78.

Collins, M. D. (2007). Understanding the relationship between leader-member exchange (LMX), psychological empowerment, job satisfaction, and turnover intent in a limited-service restaurant environment. *Unpublished doctoral dissertation, The Ohio State University*.

Colquitt, J. A., Scott, B. A., Rodell, J. B., Long, D. M., Zapata, C. P., Conlon, D. E., & Wesson, M. J. (January 01, 2013). Justice at the millennium, a decade later: A meta-analytic test of social exchange and affect-based perspectives. *The Journal of Applied Psychology, 98,* 2, 199-236.

Conger, J. A., & Kanungo, R. N. (1997). Measuring charisma: Dimensionality and validity of the Conger-Kanungo scale of charismatic Leadership. *Canadian Journal Of Administrative Sciences (Canadian Journal Of Administrative Sciences), 14* (3), 290.

Costa, P. T., McCrae, R. R., & Dye, D. A. (January 01, 1991). Facet scales for agreeableness and conscientiousness: A revision of the NEO personality inventory. *Personality and Individual Differences, 12,* 9, 887-898.

Costa, P. T., McCrae, R. R., & Psychological Assessment Resources, Inc. (1992). *Revised NEO Personality Inventory (NEO PI-R) and NEO Five-Factor Inventory (NEO-FFI)*. Odessa, Fla. Psychological Assessment Resources.

Cyert, R. M., & March, J. G. *A behavioral theory of the firm*. Englewood Cliffs, N. J.: Prentice Hall, 1963.

Daft, R. L. (2004). Theory Z: Opening the corporate door for participative management. *The Academy of Management Executive, 18,* 4, 117.

Dansereau, F., Graen, G. B., & Haga, W. J. (1975). *A vertical dyad linkage approach to leadership within formal organizations: A longitudinal investigation of the role making process*. Champaign, Ill: Institute of Labor and Industrial Relations, University of Illinois at Urbana-Champaign.

Dansereau, F., Graen, G., & Haga, W. (1975). A vertical dyad approach to leadership within formal organizations. *Organizational Behavior and Human Performance*, 13, 46– 78.

Davis, J. H., Schoorman, F. D., & Donaldson, L. (1997). Toward a Stewardship Theory of Management. *The Academy of Management Review, 22,* 1, 20.

Dawda, D., & Hart, S. D. (2000). Assessing emotional intelligence: reliability and validity of the Bar-On Emotional Quotient Inventory (EQ-i) in university students. *Personality and Individual Differences, 28,* 4, 797-812.

De Jong, A., de Ruyter, K.,&Wetzels, M. (2005). Antecedents and consequences of group potency: A study of self-managing service teams. *Management Science*, 1(11), 1610–1625.

DeGroot, T., Kiker, D. S., and Cross, T. C. (2009). A Meta-Analysis to Review Organizational Outcomes Related to Charismatic Leadership. *Canadian Journal of Administrative Sciences / Revue Canadienne Des Sciences De L'administration*, 17, 4, 356-372.

Deming, W. E. (1986). *Out of the crisis*. Cambridge, Mass: Massachusetts Institute of Technology, Center for Advanced Engineering Study.

Deming, W. E. (1994). *The new economics for industry, government, education*. Cambridge, Mass: M.I.T. Press.

Den Hartog, D. N., Van Muijen, J. J., & Koopman, P. L. (1997). Transactional versus transformational leadership: an analysis of the MLQ. *Journal of Occupational and Organizational Psychology*, 70, 19–34.

Den Hartog. D. N., House, R. J., Hanges, P. J., Ruiz-Quintanilla, S. A., Dorfman, P. W., Brenk, K. M., Konrad, E., Sabadin, A. (1999). Culture specific and cross culturally generalizable implicit leadership theories: Are

References

attributes of charismatic/transformational leadership universally endorsed?. *The Leadership Quarterly, 10,* 2, 219-256.

Derue, D. S., Nahrgang, J. D., Wellman, N., & Humphrey, S. E. (2011). Trait and behavioral theories of leadership: An integration and meta-analytic test of their relative validity. *Personnel Psychology, 64,* 1, 7-52.

Digman, J. M. (1997). Higher-order factors of the Big Five. *Journal of Personality and Social Psychology*, 73, 1246–1256.

Dorfman, P., Javidan, M., Hanges, P., Dastmalchian, A., House, R. (2012). GLOBE: A twenty year journey into the intriguing world of culture and leadership. *Journal of World Business, 47,*4, 504-518.

Downton, J. V. (1973). *Rebel leadership: Commitment and charisma in the revolutionary process*. New York: Free Press.

Drucker, P. F. (1946). *Concept of the corporation*. New York: John Day.

Drucker, P. F. (1954). *The practice of management*. New York: Harper & Row.

Druskat, V. U. (1994). Gender and leadership style: transformational and transactional leadership in the Roman Catholic Church. The Leadership Quarterly, 5, 99–119.

Dulebohn, J. H., Bommer, W. H., Liden, R. C., Brouer, R. L., & Ferris, G. R. (November 01, 2012). A Meta-Analysis of Antecedents and Consequences of Leader-Member Exchange: Integrating the Past With an Eye Toward the Future. *Journal of Management,38,* 6, 1715-1759.

Dulewicz, V., Higgs, M., & Slaski, M. (2003). Measuring emotional intelligence: content, construct and criterion-related validity. *Journal of Managerial Psychology*, 18(5), 405.

Eagly, A. H. (2005). Achieving relational authenticity in leadership: Does gender matter? *Leadership Quarterly,* 16, 459– 474.

Eagly, A. H., Johannesen-Schmidt, M. C., & van Engen, M. L, (2004). Transformational, transactional, and laissez-faire leadership styles: A meta-analysis comparing women and men. *Psychological Bulletin, 129,* 4, 569-91.

Edú Valsania, S., Moriano León, J., Molero Alonso, F., & Topa Cantisano, G. (2012). Authentic leadership and its effect on employees' organizational citizenship behaviours. *Psicothema*, *24*(4), 561-566.

Ehrhart, M. G. (2004). Leadership and procedural justice climate as antecedents of unit level organizational citizenship behavior. *Personnel Psychology*, 57(1), 61–94.

Eisenberg, N. (2000). Emotion, regulation, and moral development. Annual Review of Psy-chology, 51, 665–697.

Eisenberger, R., Armeli, S., Rexwinkel, B., Lynch, P. D., & Rhoades, L. (2001). Reciprocation of perceived organizational support. *Journal of Applied Psychology,* 86, 42–51.

Eisenberger, R., Karagonlar, G., Stinglhamber, F., Neves, P., Becker, T. E., Gonzalez-Morales, M. G., & Steiger-Mueller, M. (2010). Leader–member exchange and affective organizational commitment: The contribution of supervisor's organizational embodiment. *Journal of Applied Psychology,* 95, 1085–1103.

Ensari, N., Riggio, R. E., Christian, J., Carslaw, G., & Digit Ratio (2D:4D) and Individual Differences Research. (September 01, 2011). Who emerges as a leader? Meta-analyses of individual differences as predictors of leadership emergence. Personality and Individual Differences, 51, 4, 532-536.

Epstein, D. (2001). *20th century pop culture*. Philadelphia: Chelsea House.

Evans, M. G. (1970). The effects of supervisory behavior on the path-goal relationship. *Organizational Behavior and Human Performance*, 5, 277– 298.

Eysenck, H. J. (1997). Personality and experimental psychology: The unification of psychology and the possibility of a paradigm. *Journal of Personality and Social Psychology, 73*, 1224–1237.

Fayol, H, (1916), *Administration industrielle et générale; prévoyance, organisation, commandement, coordination, controle* (in French), Paris, H. Dunod et E. Pinat

Fayol, H. (1949). *General and industrial management*. London: Pitman.

Fend, H., Helmke, A., & Richter, P. (1984). *Inventar zu Selbstkonzept und Selbstvertrauen*. Konstanz: Univ. Konstanz.

Ferres, N., & Travaglione, T. (2003). The development and validation of the workplace trust survey: Combining qualitative and quantitative methodologies. Paper presented at the 9th Asia Pacific Researchers in Organization Studies Conference, Oaxaca, Mexico.

References

Ferster, C. B., Skinner, B. F., Harvard University., & United States. (1957). Schedules of reinforcement: By C.B. Ferster and B.F. Skinner. New York: Ap-pleton-Century-Crofts

Fiedler, F. E. (1964). A contingency model of leadership effectiveness. In L. Berkowitz (ed.), *Advances in experimental social psychology*, vol. 1. New York: Academic Press.

Fiedler, F. E. (1966). The effect of leadership and cultural heterogeneity on group performance: A test of the contingency model. *Journal of Experimental Social Psychology*, 2, 237– 264.

Fiedler, F. E. (1967). *A theory of leadership effectiveness.* New York: McGraw–Hill.

Fiedler, F. E. (1971). *Leadership*. New York: General Learning Press.

Fiedler, F. E. & Garcia, J. E. (1987). *New approaches to effective leadership: Cognitive resources and organizational performance.* New York: Wiley.

Fiedler, F. E., & Chemers, M. M. (1974). *Leadership and effective management*. Glenview, IL: Scott, Foresman.

Fiedler, F. E., & Mahar, L. (1979). A field experiment validating contingency model leadership training. *Journal of Applied Psychology*, 64, 247– 254.

Fiedler, F. E., & Mahar, L. (1979). The effectiveness of contingency model training: Validation of leader match. *Personnel Psychology*, 32, 45– 62.

Fiedler, F. E., Chemers, M. M., & Mahar, L. (1976). *Improving leadership effectiveness: The leader match concept.* New York: Wiley.

Fisher, B. M., & Edwards, J. E. (1988). Consideration and initiating structure and their relationships with leader effectiveness: A meta-analysis. *Academy of Management Best Papers Proceedings, 8,* 1, 201-205.

Fleishman, E. A. (1989). *Leadership Opinion Questionnaire (LOQ) examiner's manual.* Park Ridge, IL: Science Research Associates.

Fleishman, E. A. (1989). *Supervisory Behavior Description Questionnaire (SBD) examiner's manual.* Park Ridge, IL: Science Research Associates.

Fleishman, E. A., Harris, E. F., & Burtt, H. E. (1955). *Leadership and supervision in industry.* Columbus: Ohio State University, Bureau of Educational Research.

Fleishman, E. A., Mumford, M. D., Zaccaro, S. J., Levin, K. Y., Korotkin, A. L., & Hein, M. B. (1991). Taxonomic efforts in the description of leader behavior: A synthesis and functional interpretation. *The Leadership Quarterly, 2,* 4, 245-287.

Fleishman, E.A. (1953). The description of supervisory behavior. *Personnel Psychology, 37,* 1-6.

French, J. R. P. (1950). Field experiments: Changing group productivity. In J. C. Miller (ed.), Experiments in social process. New York: McGraw-Hill.

French, J. R. P. (1956). A formal theory of social power. *Psychological Review*, 63, 181– 194.

French, J. R. P. and Raven, B.H. (1959), "The Bases of Social Power", in Cartwright, D. (Ed.),*Studies of Social Power,* Institute for Social Research, Ann Arbor, Michigan.

Fry, L., & Cohen, M. (January 01, 2009). Spiritual Leadership as a Paradigm for Organizational Transformation and Recovery from Extended Work Hours Cultures. *Journal of Business Ethics, 84,* 265-278.

Gardner, W. L., Avolio, B. J., & Walumbwa, F. O. (2005). Authentic Leadership Theory and Practice: Origins, Effects and Development. *Monographs in Leadership and Management, Volume 3*. Emerald Group Publishing.

George, B. (2003). *Authentic leadership: Rediscovering the secrets to creating lasting value*. San Francisco: Jossey-Bass.

George, B., & Sims, P. (2007). *True north: Discover your authentic leadership*. San Francisco, Calif: Jossey-Bass/John Wiley & Sons.

Georgesen, J. C., & Harris, M. (1998). Why's my boss always holding me down? A meta-analysis of power effects on performance evaluations. *Personality & Social Psychology Review* (Lawrence Erlbaum Associates), 2(3), 184

Gerstner, C. R., & Day, D. V. (January 01, 1997). Meta-Analytic review of leader-member exchange theory: correlates and construct issues. *Journal of Applied Psychology, 82,* 6, 827.

Geyer, A. L. J., & Steyrer, J. M. (1998). Transformational leadership and objective performance in banks. *Applied Psychology: An International Review,* 47, 397–420.

Giallonardo, L. M., Wong, C. A., & Iwasiw, C. L. (2010). Authentic leadership of preceptors: Predictor of new

References

graduate nurses' work engagement and job satisfaction. *Journal of Nursing Management*, 18, 993–1003.

Gilbreth, L. M., & Witzel, M. (2001). *The psychology of management*. Bristol: Thoemmes.

Goethals, G. R., Sorenson, G. J., & Burns, J. M. G. (2004). *Encyclopedia of leadership*. Thousand Oaks, Calif: Sage Publications.

Goldberg, L. R. (January 01, 1990). An alternative "description of personality": the big-five factor structure. *Journal of Personality and Social Psychology, 59,* 6, 1216-29.

Goleman, D. (1995). *Emotional intelligence*. New York: Bantam Books.

Goleman, D. (1998). What makes a leader. *Harvard Business Review*, *76*(6), 92-102.

Gowing, M. K. (2001). Measurement of individual emotional competence. In C. Cherniss, & D. Goleman (Eds.), *The emotionally intelligent workplace: How to select for, measure, and improve emotional intelligence in individuals, groups, and organizations* (pp. 83–131). San Francisco, CA: Jossey-Bass.

Graeff, C. L. (1997). Evolution of situational leadership theory: A critical review. *Leadership Quarterly*, 8(2), 153-170.

Graen, G. B. (1976). Role-making processes within complex organizations. In M. D. Dunnette (Ed.), *Handbook of industrial and organizational psychology* (pp. 1202– 1245). Chicago: Rand McNally.

Graen, G. B., & Cashman, J. (1975). A role-making model of leadership in formal organizations: A developmental approach. In J. G. Hunt & L. L. Larson (Eds.), *Leadership frontiers* (pp. 143– 166). Kent, OH: Kent State University Press.

Graen, G. B., & Scandura, T. A. (1987). Toward a psychology of dyadic organizing. In B. Staw & L. L. Cumming (Eds.), *Research in organizational behavior* (Vol. 9, pp. 175– 208). Greenwich, CT: JAI.

Graen, G. B., & Uhl-Bien, M. (1991). The transformation of professionals into self-managing and partially self-designing contributions: Toward a theory of leadership making. *Journal of Management Systems*, 3 , 33–48.

Graen, G. B., & Uhl-Bien, M. (1995). Relationship-based approach to leadership: Development of leader–member exchange (LMX) theory of leadership over 25 years: Applying a multi-level, multi-domain perspective. *Leadership Quarterly*, 6(2), 219– 247.

Graen, G.B., Novak, M., and Sommerkamp, P. (1982). The effects of leader-member exchange and job design on productivity and satisfaction: Testing a dual attachment model. *Organizational Behavior and Human Performance*, 30, 109-131.

Graham, J. (1991). Servant-leadership in organizations: Inspirational and moral. *Leadership Quarterly*, 2(2), 105–119.

Green, M. (2012). *Visualizing Transformational Leadership*. North Charleston, SC.

Greenleaf, R. K. (1970). *The servant as leader*. Cambridge, Mass: Center for Applied Studies.

Greenleaf, R. K. (1972). *The institution as servant*. Cambridge, Mass: Center for Applied Studies.

Greenleaf, R. K. (1974). *Trustees as servants*. Cambridge, Mass: Center for Applied Studies.

Greenleaf, R. K. (1977). *Servant leadership.* Essay, Robert K. Greenleaf Center, Indianapolis, IN.

Greenleaf, R. K. (1979). *Servant leadership: A journey into the nature of legitimate power and greatness*. New York: Paulist Press.

Griffin, M., Neal, A., & Parker, S. (2007). A new model of work role performance: Positive behaviors in uncertain and interdependent contexts. *Academy of Management Journal*, 50, 327–347.

Hackman, J. & Oldham, G. (1975). Development of the Job Diagnostic Survey. *Journal of Applied Psychology*, 60, 1975, 159-170.

Hackman, M. & Johnson, C. (2009). *Leadership: A communication perspective*. Long Grove, IL: Waveland Press, Inc.

Hale, J. R., & Fields, D. L. (2007). Exploring servant leadership across cultures: A study of followers in Ghana and the USA. *Leadership*, 3(4), 397–417.

Halpin, A. W. (1957). *Manual for the Leader Behavior Description Questionnaire*. Columbus, OH: Bureau of Business Research, Ohio State University.

Halpin, A.W. & Winer, B.J. (1957). A factorial study of the leader behavior descriptions. In R.M. Stogdill and A.E. Coons (eds), *Leader behavior: Its description and measurement*. Columbus, OH: Bureau of Business Research, Ohio State University.

References

Hamel, G., & Prahalad, C. K. (1994). Competing for the Future. *Harvard Business Review*, *72*(4), 122.

Hamel, G., & Prahalad, C. K. (1996). *Competing for the future*. Boston, Mass: Harvard Business School Press.

Hammer, M., & Champy, J. (1993). Reengineering the corporation: A manifesto for business revolution. New York, NY: HarperBusiness.

Hammer, M., & Champy, J. (1993). *Reengineering the corporation: A manifesto for business revolution*. New York, NY: Harper Business.

Hannah S.T., Walumbwa F.O., & Fry L.W. (2011). Leadership in action teams: Team leader and members' authenticity, authenticity strength, and team outcomes. *Personnel Psychology*. 64, 771-802.

Hannah, S. T., Avolio, B. J., & Walumbwa, F. O. (2011). Relationships between Authentic Leadership, Moral Courage, and Ethical and Pro-Social Behaviors. *Business Ethics Quarterly*, *21*(4), 555-578.

Hannah, S., Avolio, B. and Walumbwa, F. (2011). Relationships between Authentic Leadership, Moral Courage, and Ethical and Pro-Social Behaviors. *Business Ethics Quarterly*, *21*(4), 555-578

Harms, P. D., & Credé, M. (2010). Emotional Intelligence and Transformational and Transactional Leadership: A Meta-Analysis. *Journal of Leadership & Organizational Studies* (Sage Publications Inc.), 17(1), 5-17.

Hassan, A., & Ahmed, F. (August 01, 2011). Authentic leadership, trust and work engagement. *Proceedings of World Academy of Science, Engineering and Technology,80,* 750-756.

Hater, J. J., & Bass, B. M. (1988). Superiors' evaluations and subordinates' perceptions of transformational and transactional leadership. *Journal of Applied Psychology*, 73, 695–702.

Hatfield, E., Cacioppo, J. T., & Rapson, R. L. (1994). Emotional contagion. New York, NY: Cambridge University Press.

Helms, M. M. (2000). *Encyclopedia of management*. Detroit, [Mich.: Gale Group

Hemphill, J. K., & Coons, A. E. (1957). Development of the Leader Behavior Description Questionnaire. In R. M. Stogdill & A. E. Coons (eds.), *Leader behavior: Its description and measurement*. Columbus: Ohio State University, Bureau of Business Research.

Herman, R. D. (1994). *The Jossey-Bass handbook of nonprofit leadership and management*. San Francisco: Jossey-Bass.

Hersey, P., & Blanchard, K. H. (1969). Life cycle theory of leadership. *Training & Development Journal*, 23, 26–34.

Hersey, P., & Blanchard, K. H. (1969). *Management of organizational behavior.* Englewood Cliffs, NJ: Prentice-Hall.

Hersey, P., & Blanchard, K. H. (1973). *Leader effectiveness and adaptability description– self*. Escondido, CA: Center for Leadership Studies.

Hersey, P., & Blanchard, K. H. (1977). *Management of organizational behavior: Utilizing human resources.* Englewood Cliffs, NJ: Prentice-Hall.

Herzberg, F. (1959). *The motivation to work*. New York: Wiley.

Herzberg, F. (1966). *Work and the nature of man*. Cleveland: World Pub. Co.

Herzberg, F. (1976). *The managerial choice: To be efficient and to be human*. Homewood, Ill: Dow Jones-Irwin.

Hiebert, M., & Klatt, B. (2001). *The encyclopedia of leadership: A practical guide to popular leadership theories and techniques*. New York: McGraw-Hill.

Hinkin, T. R., & Schriesheim, C. A. (2008). A theoretical and empirical examination of the transactional and non-leadership dimensions of the Multifactor Leadership Questionnaire (MLQ). *Leadership Quarterly, 19,* 5, 501-513.

Hinkin, T. R., Tracey, J. B., & Enz, C. A. (1997). Scale construction: developing reliable and valid measurement instruments. *Journal of Hospitality and Tourism Research,* 21, 100–120.

Hmieleski, Cole and Baron. (2012). Shared authentic leadership and new venture performance. *Journal of Management*, 38(5), 1476-1499

Hofstede, G. (1980). *Culture's consequences: International differences in work-related values.* London: Sage.

Hofstede, G. (2001). *Culture's consequences: Comparing values, behaviors, institutions and organizations across nations,* (2nd edition). Thousand Oaks, CA: Sage.

Hollander, E. P. (1958). Conformity, status, and idiosyncrasy credit. *Psychological Review*, 65, 2, 117-27.

References

Hollander, E. P. (1961). Emergent leadership and social influence. In L. Petrullo & B. M. Bass (Eds.), *Leadership and interpersonal behavior* (pp. 30 – 47). New York: Holt, Rinehart, and Winston.

Hollander, E. P. (1964). *Leaders, groups, and influence*. New York: Oxford University Press.

Hollander, E. P., & Kelly, D. R. (1990). *Rewards from leaders as perceived by followers*. Paper presented at the meeting of the Eastern Psychological Association, Philadelphia, PA.

House, R. J. (1971). A path goal theory of leader effectiveness. *Administrative Science Quarterly*, 16, 321– 338.

House, R. J. (1977) A 1976 theory of charismatic leadership. In J. G. Hunt & L. L. Larson (eds.), *Leadership: The cutting edge*. Carbondale, IL: Southern Illinois University Press.

House, R. J. (1996). Path-goal theory of leadership: Lessons, legacy, and a reformulated theory. *Leadership Quarterly*. p. 323 - 340.

House, R. J., & Global Leadership and Organizational Behavior Effectiveness Research Program. (2004). *Culture, leadership, and organizations: The GLOBE study of 62 societies*. Thousand Oaks, Calif: Sage Publications.

House, R. J., & Shamir, B. (1993). Towards the integration of transformational, charismatic, and visionary theories. In M. M. Chemers & R. Ayman (eds.), *Leadership theory and research: Perspective and directions. New* York: Academic Press.

House, R. J., Howell, J. M., Shamir, B., et al. (1992). Charismatic leadership: A 1992 theory and five empirical tests. Unpublished manuscript.

House, R. J., Woycke, J., & Fodor, E. M. (1988). Charismatic and non-charismatic leaders: Differences in behavior and effectiveness. In J. A. Conger & R. N. Kanungo (eds.), *Charismatic leadership: The elusive factor in organizational effectiveness.* San Francisco: Jossey-Bass.

Howell, J. M., & Avolio, B. J. (1992). Charismatic leadership: Submission or liberation? Academy of Management Executive, 6(2), 43-53.

Howell, J. M., & Avolio, B. J. (1993). Transformational leadership, transactional leadership, locus of control, and support for innovation: Key predictors of consolidated business business-unit performance. *Journal of Applied Psychology*, 78, 891–902.

Hsiung, H. (2012). Authentic leadership and employee voice behavior: A multi-level psychological process. *Journal Of Business Ethics, 107*(3), 349-361.

Hu, J., & Liden, R. C. (2011). Antecedents of team potency and team effectiveness: An examination of goal and process clarity and servant leadership. *Journal of Applied Psychology* 1–12.

Ilies, R., Nahrgang, J. D., & Morgeson, F. P. (January 01, 2007). Leader-member exchange and citizenship behaviors: a meta-analysis. The Journal of Applied Psychology, 92, 1, 269-77.

Ilies, R., Nahrgang, J. D., & Morgeson, F. P. (January 01, 2007). Leader-member exchange and citizenship behaviors: a meta-analysis. *The Journal of Applied Psychology, 92,* 1, 269-77.

Indvik, J. (1986a). Path-goal theory of leadership: A meta-analysis. *Proceedings, Academy of Management*, Chicago, 189– 192.

Institute for Public Health Sciences. (2002). *11 questions to help you make sense of descriptive/cross-sectional studies.* New York: Yeshiva University.

Irving, J. A., & Longbotham, G. J. (2007). Team effectiveness and six essential servant leadership themes: A regression model based on items in the organizational leadership assessment. *International Journal of Leadership Studies*, 2(2), 98–113.

Jackson T, Meyer J, Wang X. Leadership, commitment, and culture: A meta-analysis. *Journal Of Leadership & Organizational Studies* [serial online]. February 2013;20(1):84-106. Available from: PsycINFO, Ipswich, MA. Accessed May 1, 2015.

Jackson, T. A., Meyer, J. P., & Wang, X. (2013). Leadership, commitment, and culture: A meta-analysis. *Journal of Leadership & Organizational Studies, 20*(1), 84-106.

Jacobs, T. O., & Jaques, E. (1990). Military executive leadership. In K. E. Clark and M. B. Clark (Eds.), *Measures of leadership*. West Orange, New Jersey: Leadership Library of America, pp 281-295.

Jaramillo, F., Grisaffe, D. B., Chonko, L. B., & Roberts, J. A. (2009). Examining the impact of servant leadership on sales force performance. *Journal of Personal Selling & Sales Management,* 29(3), 257–275.

References

Jenkins, M., & Stewart, A. C. (2010). The importance of a servant leader orientation. *Health Care Management Review,* 35(1), 46–54.

Jensen, J. L., Olberding, J. C., & Rodgers, R. (1997). The quality of leader-member exchange (LMX) and member performance: A meta-analytic review. *Academy of Management Best Papers Proceedings, 8,* 1, 320-324.

Jensen, S. M., & Luthans, F. (2006). Relationship between Entrepreneurs' Psychological Capital and Their Authentic Leadership.*Journal Of Managerial Issues*, *18*(2), 254-273.

Johnson, A. M., Vernon, P. A., McCarthy, J. M., Molso, M., Harris, J. A., & Jang, K. J. (1998). Nature vs nurture: Are leaders born or made? A behavior genetic investigation of leadership style. *Twin Research*, 1, 216–223.

Joseph, D., Newman & D. A., (2010). Emotional Intelligence: An Integrative Meta-Analysis and Cascading Model. *Journal of Applied Psychology, 95*(1), 54-78.

Joseph, D., Newman, D. A., & Sin, H. (2011), Leader–Member exchange (LMX) measurement: evidence for consensus, construct breadth, and discriminant validity, in Donald D. Bergh, David J. Ketchen (ed.) *Building Methodological Bridges (Research Methodology in Strategy and Management, Volume 6)*, Emerald Group Publishing Limited, pp.89-135

Joseph, E. E., & Winston, B. E. (2005). A correlation of servant leadership, leader trust, and organizational trust. *Leadership & Organization Development Journal*, 26(1), 6–22.

Judge, T. A., & Ilies, R. (2002). Relationship of personality to performance motivation: A meta-analytic review. *Journal Of Applied Psychology*, 87(4), 797-807.

Judge, T. A., & Piccolo, R. F. (2004). Transformational and transactional leadership: A meta-analytic test of their relative validity. *The Journal of Applied Psychology, 89,* 5, 755-68.

Judge, T. A., Bono, J. E., Ilies, R., & Gerhardt, M. W. (January 01, 2002). Personality and leadership: a qualitative and quantitative review. *The Journal of Applied Psychology, 87,* 4, 765-80.

Judge, T. A., Heller, D., & Mount, M. K. (2002). Five-factor model of personality and job satisfaction: A meta-analysis. *The Journal of Applied Psychology, 87,*3, 530-41

Judge, T. A., Piccolo, R. F., & Ilies, R. (2004). The forgotten ones? The validity of consideration and initiating structure in leadership research. *The Journal of Applied Psychology, 89,* 1, 36-51.

Kanste, O., Miettunen, J., & Kyngäs, H. (2007). Psychometric properties of the Multifactor Leadership Questionnaire among nurses. *Journal of Advanced Nursing, 57,* 2, 201-212.

Kanungo, R. B. & Conger, J. (1989) Dimensions of executive charisma, *Perspectives*, Vol.14, No 4, 1-8.

Kaptein, M. (2008). Developing and testing a measure for the ethical culture of organizations: The corporate ethical virtues model. *Journal of Organizational Behavior*, 29, 23–947.

Kark, R., Shamir, B., & Chen, G. (2003). The two faces of transformational leadership: empowerment and dependency. *The Journal of Applied Psychology, 88,* 2, 246-55.

Katz, D. & Kahn, R.L. (1952). Some recent findings in human relations research, In E. Swanson, T. Newcombe and E. Hartley (eds), *Readings in social psychology,* NY: Holt, Reinhart and Winston.

Katz, D., & Kahn, R. L. (1966). *The social psychology of organizations.* New York: Wiley.

Katz, D., & Kahn, R. L. (1978). *The social psychology of organizations.* New York: Wiley.

Kaye, B. L., & Giulioni, J. W. (2012). Help them grow or watch them go: Career conversa-tions employees want. San Francisco: Berrett-Koehler Publishers, Inc.

Kellerman, B. (2008). *Followership: How followers are creating change and changing leaders*. Boston, Mass: Harvard Business School Press.

Kelley, R. E. (1992). *The power of followership: How to create leaders people want to follow, and followers who lead themselves*. New York: Doubleday/Currency.

Kernis, M. H. (2003). Toward a conceptualization of optimal self-esteem. *Psychological Inquiry*, 14, 1–26.

Kernis, M. H. and Goldman, B .M. (2006) A multicomponent conceptualization of authenticity: research and theory. *Advances in Experimental Social Psychology*, 38, 284–357.

Kernis, M. H. and Goldman, B. M. (2005) Authenticity: a multicomponent perspective, in Tesser, A., Wood, J. and Stapel, D. (eds) O*n Building, Defending, and Regulating the Self: A Psychological Perspective*, Psychology Press, New York, pp. 31–52.

References

Kerr, S., & Jermier, J. (1978). Substitutes for leadership: Their meaning and measurement. *Organizational Behavior and Human Performance*, 22, 374– 403.

Kilbourne, C. E. (1935). The elements of leadership. *Journal of Coast Artillery*, 78, 437– 439.

Kinicki, A. J., McKee-Ryan, F. M., Schriesheim, C. A., & Carson, K. P. (2002). Assessing the construct validity of the Job Descriptive Index: A review and meta-analysis. *Journal of Applied Psychology*, *87*(1), 14-32

Koh, W. L., Steers, R. M., & Terborg, J. R. (1995). The effects of transformational leadership on teacher attitudes and student performance in Singapore. *Journal of Organizational Behavior*, 16, 319–333.

Kopelman, R. L. (2008). Douglas McGregor's Theory X and Y: Toward a Construct-valid Measure. *Journal of Managerial Issues,* 20(2), 255-271.

Kopp, T., & Schuler, H. (2003). Vertrauen gegenu¨ber Vorgesetzten und Akzeptanz von Entgeltsystemen. *Zeitschrift fu¨r Personalpsychologie*, 2(4), 182–192.

Kotter, J. P. (1990). What leaders really do. *Harvard Business Review, 68,*3.

Kotter, J. P. (1996). *Leading change.* Boston, Mass: Harvard Business School Press.

Kotter, J. P. (1999). *John P. Kotter on what leaders really do.* Boston: Harvard Business School Press.

Kouzes, J. M., & Posner, B. Z. (2002). *The leadership challenge*. San Francisco: Jossey-Bass.

Kouzes, J. M., & Posner, B. Z. (2007). *Leadership Is everyone's business*. San Francisco, Calif: Jossey-Bass.

Kurtz, J. E., & Parrish, C. L. (2001). Semantic response consistency and protocol validity in structured personality assessment: the case of the NEO-PI-R. *Journal of Personality Assessment, 76,* 2, 315-32.

Lapierre, L. M., & Hackett, R. D. (2007). Trait conscientiousness, leader-member exchange, job satisfaction and organizational citizenship behaviour: A test of an integrative model. *Journal of Occupational and Organizational Psychology, 80,* 3, 539-554.

Laub, J. A. (1999), *Assessing the servant organization: development of the Servant Organizational Leadership Assessment (SOLA) instrument*, Dissertation Abstracts International, UMI No. 9921922.

Lee, K., & Allen, N. J. (2002). Organizational citizenship behavior and workplace deviance: The role of affect and cognitions. *Journal of Applied Psychology*, 87, 131–142.

Leister, A., Borden, D., & Fiedler, F. E. (1977), Validation of Contingency Model Leadership Training: Leader Match, *Academy of Management Journal,* Vol. 20, No. 3, pp. 464-470.

Leroy, H., Palanski, M., & Simons, T. (2012). Authentic Leadership and Behavioral Integrity as Drivers of Follower Commitment and Performance. *Journal Of Business Ethics*, *107*(3), 255-264.

Letts, L., Wilkins, S., Law, M., Stewart, D., Bosch, J., & Westmorland, M. (2007). Critical review form: Qualitative studies (version 2.0).

Li, W. D., Arvey, R. D., Zhang, Z., & Song, Z. (2011). Do leadership role occupancy and transformational leadership share the same genetic and environmental influences?. *The Leadership Quarterly.*

Liden, R. C., & Graen, G. B. (1980). Generalizability of the vertical dyad linkage model of leadership. *Academy of Management Journal,* 23, 451–465.

Liden, R. C., & Maslyn, J. M. (1998). Multi-dimensionality of leader–member exchange: An empirical assessment through scale development. *Journal of Management*, 24, 43–72.

Liden, R. C., Wayne, S., Zhao. H. & Henderson, D. (2008). Servant leadership: Development of a multidimensional measure and multi-level assessment. *Leadership Quarterly*, 19(2), 161.

Lievens, F., Van Geit, P., & Coetsier, P. (1997). Identification of transformational leadership qualities: an examination of potential biases. *European Journal of Work and Organizational Psychology,* 6, 415–530.

Likert, R. (1961). *New patterns of management*. New York: McGraw-Hill.

Likert, R. (1967). *The human organization: Its management and value*. New York: McGraw-Hill.

Likert, R., & Likert, J. G. (1976). *New ways of managing conflict*. New York: McGraw-Hill.

Lindenfield, G. (2008). *The emotional healing strategy: A recovery guide for any setback, disappointment or loss.* London: Michael Joseph.

Loehlin, J. C., McCrae, R. R., Costa, P. T., & John, O. P. (1998). Heritabilities of common and measure-specific components of the big five personality factors. *Journal of Research in Personality*, 32, 431– 453.

Lord, R. G., de Vader, C. L., & Alliger, G. M. (1986). A meta-analysis of the relation between personality traits and leadership perceptions: An application of validity generalization procedures. *Journal of Applied Psychology, 71,* 3, 402-410.

References

Lowe, K. B., Kroeck, K. G., & Sivasubramaniam, N. (1996). Effectiveness correlates of transformational and transactional leadership: A meta-analytic review of the MLQ literature. *The Leadership Quarterly*, 7(3), 385-415.

Luft, J. and Ingham, H. (1955). "The Johari window, a graphic model of interpersonal awareness". *Proceedings of the western training laboratory in group development* (Los Angeles: UCLA).

Luthans, F. and Avolio, B., (2003). Authentic Leadership Development, in Cameron, K. S., Dutton, J. E., & Quinn, R. E. (2003). *Positive organizational scholarship: Foundations of a new discipline*. San Francisco, CA: Berrett-Koehler.

Luthans, F., Avolio, B., Avey, J., & Norman, S. (2007). Psychological capital: Measurement and relationship with performance and satisfaction. *Personnel Psychology*, 60, 541–572.

Lytle, R. S., Hom, P. W., & Mokwa, M. P. (1998). SERV_OR: A managerial measure of organizational service-orientation. *Journal of Retailing*, 74, 455–489.

Mackey, J. D., Frieder, R. E., Brees, J. R., & Martinko, M. J. (March 03, 2015). Abusive Supervision: A Meta-Analysis and Empirical Review. Journal of Management.

March, J. G., & Simon, H. A. (1958). *Organizations*. New York: Wiley

Martins, A., Ramalho, N., & Morin, E. (2010). A comprehensive meta-analysis of the relationship between emotional intelligence and health. *Personality & Individual Differences*, *49*(6), 554-564.

Maslow, A. H. (1954). *Motivation and personality*. New York: Harper.

Maslow, A. H. (1965). *Eupsychian management: A journal.* Homewood, IL: Dorsey.

Maslow, A. H. *Toward a psychology of being.* Princeton, N. J.: Van Nostrand, 1962.

May, D. R., Chan, A. Y. L., Hodges, T. D., & Avolio, B. J. (2003). Developing the moral component of authentic leadership. *Organizational Dynamics*, 32, 247–260.

Mayer, D. M., Bardes, M., & Piccolo, R. F. (2008). Do servant leaders help satisfy follower needs? An organizational justice perspective. *European Journal of Work and Organizational Psychology*, 17(2), 180–197.

Mayer, J. D., Caruso, D., & Salovey, P. (2000). Selecting a measure of emotional intelligence: the case for ability scales. In R. Bar-On, & J. D. Parker (Eds.), *Handbook of emotional intelligence* (pp. 320–342).New York: Jossey-Bass.

Mayer, J. D., Roberts, R. D. and Barsade, S. G. (2008). Human abilities: Emotional intelligence. *Annual Review of Psychology*, 59, 507–536. p. 511.

Mayer, J. D., Salovey, P., & Caruso, D. R. (2004). Emotional Intelligence: Theory, Findings, and Implications. *Psychological Inquiry, 15,* 3, 197-215.

Mayer, J. D., Salovey, P., Caruso, D. R., & Sitarenios, G. (2003). Measuring emotional intelligence with the MSCEIT V2.0. *Emotion*, 3, 97–105.

Mayer, R.C., Davis, J.H., and Schoorman, F.D. (1995), "An Integration Model of Organizational Trust," *Academy of Management Review*, Vol. 20, 709-729.

Mayo, E. (1933). *The human problems of an industrial civilization*. New York: Macmillan.

Mayo, E. (1945). *The social problems of an industrial civilization*. Boston, MA: Harvard University, Graduate School of Business Administration.

McCrae, R. R., & Costa, P. T. J. (1987). Validation of the five-factor model of personality across instruments and observers. *Journal of Personality and Social Psychology, 52,* 1, 81-90.

McCrae, R. R., & Costa, P. T., Jr. (1997). Personality trait structure as a human universal. *American Psychologist*, 52, 509– 516.

McCrae, R. R., & Costa, P. T., Jr., (1990). *Personality in adulthood*. New York: Guilford.

McCrae, R. R., & Costa, P. T., Jr., (1992). Discriminant validity of NEO-PIR facet scales. *Educational & Psychological Measurement*, 52 (1), 229.

McCrae, R. R., & Costa, P. T., Psychological Assessment Resources, Inc. (2010). *NEO inventories for the NEO Personality Inventory-3 (NEO-PI-3), NEO Five-Factor Inventory-3 (NEO-FFI-3), NEO Personality Inventory-Revised (NEO PI-R): Professional manual.* Lutz, FL: PAR.

References

McCrae, R., Zonderman, A. B., Costa, P. T. Jr., Bond, M. H., & Paunone, S. V. (1996). Evaluating replicability of factors in the revised NEO personality: Confirmatory factor analysis versus Procrustes rotation. *Journal of Personality & Social Psychology*, 70 (3), 552– 566.

McGregor, D. (1960). *The human side of enterprise*. New York: McGraw-Hill.

McGregor, D. (1966). *Leadership and motivation*. MIT Press.

McSherry, W., & Cash, K. (January 01, 2004). The language of spirituality: an emerging taxonomy. *International Journal of Nursing Studies, 41,* 2, 151-161

Meyer, J. P., Allen, N. J., & Gellatly, I. R. (1990). Affective and continuance commitment to the organization: Evaluation of measures and analysis of concurrent and time-lagged relations. *Journal of Applied Psychology*, 75, 710–720.

Meyer, J. P., Allen, N. J., & Smith, C. A. (1993). Commitment to organizations and occupations: Extension and test of a three-component conceptualization. *Journal of Applied Psychology,* 78(4), 538–551.

Miner, J. B. (2006). *Organizational Behavior 3: Historical origins, theoretical foundations, and the future.* Armonk, NY: Sharpe.

Miner, J. B., (2003). The rated importance, scientific validity, and practical usefulness of organizational behavior theories: a quantitative review. *Academy of Management Learning and Education, 2,* 3, 250-268.

Mitchell T, Biglan A and Fiedler F (1970), The contingency model: criticism and suggestions, *Academy of Management Journal*, Vol. 13, No. 3, pp. 253-267.

Moosa, K., & Sajid, A. (2010). Critical analysis of six sigma implementation. *Total Quality Management & Business Excellence*, 21(7), 745-759

Mowday, R. T., Steers, R. M., & Porter, L. W. (1979). The measurement of organizational commitment. *Journal of Vocational Behavior,* 14: 224-247.

Neider, L. A. (2011). The Authentic Leadership Inventory (ALI): Development and empirical tests. *Leadership Quarterly*, *22*(6), 1146.

Neubert, M. J., Kacmar, K. M., Carlson, D. S., Chonko, L. B., & Roberts, J. A. (2008). Regulatory focus as a mediator of the influence of initiating structure and servant leadership on employee behavior. *Journal of Applied Psychology,* 93(6), 1220–1233.

Newsome, S., Day, A. L., & Catano, V. M. (2000). Assessing the predictive validity of emotional intelligence. *Personality and Individual Differences*, 29(6), 1005–1016.

Ng, T. H., Eby, L. T., Sorensen, K. L., & Feldman, D. C. (2005). Predictors of objective and subjective career success. A meta-analysis. *Personnel Psychology,* 58(2), 367-408.

Nielson, L. (2011). *Computing: a business history*. New York. New Street Communication.

Noel, C., John, U. F., James, M. H., & David, L. (1991). In search of excellence ten years later: strategy and organization do matter. *Management Decision, 29,* 4

Nohria, N., & Khurana, R. (2010). *Handbook of leadership theory and practice: An HBS centennial colloquium on advancing leadership*. Boston, Mass: Harvard Business Press.

Northouse, P. (1999). *Leadership : theory and practice*. Sage Publications.

Northouse, P. (2013). *Leadership : theory and practice*. Sage Publications.

Nwogu, O. G. (2004). Servant leadership model: The role of follower self-esteem, emotional intelligence, and attributions on organizational effectiveness. Paper presented at the *Servant Leadership Roundtable*, Regent University.

Nyhan R. (2000). Changing the paradigm: Trust and its role in public sector organizations. *American Public Review of Administration,* 30, 87–109.

O'Boyle, E. H., Humphrey, R. H., Pollack, J. M., Hawver, T. H., & Story, P. A. (July 01, 2011). The relation between emotional intelligence and job performance: A meta-analysis. Journal of Organizational Behavior, 32, 5, 788-818.

Ouchi, W. (1981). Going from A to Z: Thirteen steps to a Theory Z organization. Management Review, 70(5), 8.

Ouchi, W. G. (1981). *Theory Z: How American business can meet the Japanese challenge*. Reading, Mass: Addison-Wesley.

Ouchi, W. G. (1984). *The M-form society: How American teamwork can recapture the competitive edge*. Reading, Mass: Addison-Wesley.

References

Ouchi, W. G., & Jaeger, A. M. (1978). *Type z organization: A better match for a mobile society*. Stanford, Calif.: Graduate School of Business, Stanford University.

Ouchi, W. G., & Jaeger, A. M. (1978). Type z organization: stability in the midst of mobility. *Academy Of Management Review*, 3(2), 305-314. doi:10.5465/AMR.1978.4294895

Page, D. P. (1935). Measurement and prediction of leadership. *American Journal of Sociology*, 41, 31– 43.

Page, D., & Wong, T. P. (2000). A philosophy conceptual framework for measuring servant leadership. In S. Adjibolosoo (Ed.), *The Human factor in shaping the course of history and development.* Lanham, MD: University Press of America.

Parris, D. L., & Peachey, J. W. (2013). A systematic literature review of servant leadership theory in organizational contexts. *Journal of Business Ethics, 113,*3, 377-393.

Patterson, K. (2003). *Servant leadership: A theoretical model*. Dissertation Abstracts International, 64(2), 570 (UMI No. 3082719).

Paustian-Underdahl, S. (2012). *A meta-analysis of gender differences in leadership effectiveness* (Order No. 3539035). Available from ProQuest Dissertations & Theses Global. (1071705758).

Peters, T. J., & Waterman, R. H. (1982). *In search of excellence: Lessons from America's best-run companies*. New York: Harper & Row.

Peterson, K., Malouff, J., & Thorsteinsson, E. B. (2011). A meta-analytic investigation of emotional intelligence and alcohol involvement. *Substance Use & Misuse*, *46*(14), 1726-1733.

Piccolo, R. F., Bono, J. E., Heinitz, K., Rowold, J., Duehr, E., & Judge, T. A. (June 01, 2012). The relative impact of complementary leader behaviors: Which matter most?. The Leadership Quarterly, 23, 3, 567-581.

Podsakoff, N. P., Whiting, S. W., Podsakoff, P. M., & Blume, B. D. (January 01, 2009). Individual- and organizational-level consequences of organizational citizenship behaviors: A meta-analysis. *The Journal of Applied Psychology, 94,* 1, 122-41.

Podsakoff, P. (January 01, 2000). Organizational citizenship behaviors: a critical review of the theoretical and empirical literature and suggestions for future research. *Journal of Management, 26,* 3, 513-563.

Podsakoff, P. M., Bommer, W. H., Podsakoff, N. P., & MacKenzie, S. B. (2006). Relationships between leader reward and punishment behavior and subordinate attitudes, perceptions, and behaviors: A meta-analytic review of existing and new research. *Organizational Behavior and Human Decision Processes, 99,* 2, 113-142

Rafferty, A. E., & Griffin, M. A. (2004). Dimensions of transformational leadership: Conceptual and empirical extensions. *The Leadership Quarterly*, 15, 329–354.

Randolph-Seng, B., & Gardner, W. L. (2013). Validating Measures of Leader Authenticity: Relationships Between Implicit/Explicit Self-Esteem, Situational Cues, and Leader Authenticity. *Journal Of Leadership & Organizational Studies* (Sage Publications Inc.), 20(2), 214-231.

Rauch, C. F., & Behling, O. (1984). Functionalism: Basis for an alternate approach to the study of leadership. In J. G. Hunt, D. M. Hosking, C. A. Schriesheim, and R. Stewart (Eds.), *Leaders and managers: International perspectives on managerial behavior and leadership.* New York: Pergamon Press, pp. 45-62.

Rego, A. (2013). Are authentic leaders associated with more virtuous, committed and potent teams?. *Leadership Quarterly, 24*(1), 61-79.

Rego, A., Sousa, F., Marques, C., & Cunha, M. (2012). Authentic leadership promoting employees' psychological capital and creativity. *Journal Of Business Research*, *65*(3), 429-437

Richards, D. & Engle, S. (1986). After the vision. In *Transforming leadership*, J.D. Adams (Ed), Alexandria, VA. Miles River Press.

Rieke, M., Hammermeister, J., & Chase, M. (2008). Servant leadership in sport: A new paradigm for effective coach behavior. *International Journal of Sports Science & Coaching*, 3(2), 227–239.

Riggio, R. E., Chaleff, I., & Lipman-Blumen, J. (2008). *The art of followership: How great followers create great leaders and organizations*. San Francisco, CA: Jossey-Bass.

Roberto, M. A. (2005). Why great leaders don't take yes for an answer: Managing for conflict and consensus. Upper Saddle River, N.J: Wharton School Pub.

Rost, J. C. (1991). *Leadership for the twenty-first century.* New York: Praeger.

References

Rousseau, D. M., Sitkin, S. B., Burt, R. S., & Camerer, C. (1998). Not so different after all: A cross-discipline view of trust. *Academy of Management Review*, 23, 393–404.

Russell, R., & Stone, A. G. (2002). A review of servant leadership attributes: Developing a practical model. *Leadership and Organizational Development Journal*, 23(3), 145–157.

Ryan, R. M., & Deci, E. L. 2003. On assimilating identities to the self: A self-determination theory perspective on internalization and integrity within cultures. In M. R. Leary & J. P. Tangney (Eds.), *Handbook of self and identity*: 253-272. New York: Guilford.

Salovey, P. & Mayer, J. D. (1990). Emotional intelligence. *Imagination, Cognition, and Personality*, *9*, 185-211.

Scandura, T. A., & Graen, G. B. (1984). Moderating effects of initial leader-member exchange status on the effects of a leadership intervention. *Journal of Applied Psychology*, 69, 428–436.

Schaubroeck, J., Lam, S. S. K., & Peng, A. C. (2011). Cognition based and affect-based trust as mediators of leader behavior influences on team performance. *Journal of Applied Psychology*, 96(4), 863–871.

Schaufeli W.B. & Bakker A.B. (2003) *Utrecht Work Engagement Scale (UWES) Preliminary Manual.* Occupational Health Psychology Unit, Utrecht University, ND.

Schein, E. H. (1985). *Organizational culture and leadership*. San Francisco: Jossey-Bass Publishers.

Schein, E. H. (1992). *Organizational culture and leadership*. San Francisco: Jossey-Bass.

Schlaerth, A., Ensari, N., & Christian, J. (2013). A meta-analytical review of the relationship between emotional intelligence and leaders' constructive conflict management. *Group Processes & Intergroup Relations*, *16*(1), 126-136.

Schriesheim, C. A., & Cogliser, C. C. (2009). Construct validation in leadership research: Explication and illustration. *The Leadership Quarterly*, 20, 725–736.

Schriesheim, C. A., Castro, S. L., & Cogliser, C. C. (1999). Leader-member exchange (LMX) research: A comprehensive review of theory, measurement, and data-analytic practices. *The Leadership Quarterly, 10,* 1, 63-113

Schriesheim, C. A., Tepper, B. J., & Tetrault, L. A. (1994). Least Preferred Co-Worker Score, situational control, and leadership effectiveness: A meta-analysis of contingency model performance predictions. *Journal Of Applied Psychology,79*(4), 561-573.

Schutte, N. S., Malouff, J. M., Hall, L. E., Haggerty, D. J., Cooper, J. T., Golden, C. J., & Dornheim, L. (1998). Development and validation of a measure of emotional intelligence. *Personality and Individual Differences*, *25*(2), 167-177.

Schutte, N. S., Malouff, J. M., Thorsteinsson, E. B., Bhullar, N., & Rooke, S. E. (2007). A meta-analytic investigation of the relationship between emotional intelligence and health. *Personality & Individual Differences*, *42*(6), 921-933.

Schyns, B., & Schilling, J. (February 01, 2013). How bad are the effects of bad leaders? A meta-analysis of destructive leadership and its outcomes. The Leadership Quarterly, 24, 1, 138-158.

Seligman, M. E. P. (1998). *Learned optimism*. New York: Pocket Books.

Sendjaya, S., & Pekerti, A. (2010). Servant leadership as antecedent of trust in organizations. *Leadership & Organization Development Journal*, 31(7), 643–663.

Sendjaya, S., Sarros, J., & Santora, J. (2008). Defining and measuring servant leadership behavior in organizations. *Journal of Management Studies*, 45(2), 402–424.

Senge, P. M. (1990). *The fifth discipline: The art and practice of the learning organization*. New York: Doubleday/Currency.

Simon, H. A. (1947). *Administrative behavior: A study of decision-making processes in administrative organization*. New York: Macmillan Co.

Simons, T. L., & McLean-Parks, J. (2000). The sequential impact of behavior integrity on trust, commitment, discretionary service behavior, customer satisfaction and profitability. Paper presented at the annual *Academy of Management Conference*, Toronto, ON.

Skinner, B. F. (1972). Cumulative record: A selection of pa-pers. New York: Appleton-Century-Crofts.

Smircich, L., & Morgan, G. (1982). Leadership: The management of meaning. *Journal of Applied Behavioral Science*, 18, 257–273.

Smith, C. A., Organ, D. W., & Near, J. P. (1983). Organizational citizenship behavior: Its nature and antecedents.

References

Journal of Applied Psychology, 68(4), 653-663.

Smith, P. C., Kendall, L. M., & Hulin, C. L. (1969). *The measurement of satisfaction in work and retirement.* Chicago: Rand-McNally.

Snyder, C. R., Irving, L., & Anderson, J. R. (1991). Hope and health: Measuring the will and the ways. In C. R. Snyder, & D. R. Forsyth (Eds.), *Handbook of social and clinical psychology* (pp. 285–305). Elmsford, NY, Pergamon.

Snyder, T. D., & National Center for Education Statistics. (1993). *120 years of American education: A statistical portrait*. Washington, D.C: U.S. Dept. of Education, Office of Educational Research and Improvement, National Center for Education Statistics.

Spears, L.C. (1994). Servant leadership: Quest for caring leadership. *Inner Quest*, 2, 1-4.

Spears, L.C. (1995). (Ed.). *Reflections on leadership: How Robert K. Greenleaf's theory of servant-leadership influenced today's top management thinkers.* New York: John Wiley & Sons, Inc.

Spears, L.C. (Ed.). (1998). *Insights on leadership: Service, stewardship, spirit and servant-leadership.* New York, NY: John Wiley & Sons.

Spreitzer, G. M. (1995). Psychological Empowerment in the Workplace: Dimensions, Measurement, and Validation. *Academy of Management Journal, 38,* 5, 1442.

Stamps P.L. (1997) *Nurses and Work Satisfaction: An Index for Measurement, 2nd ed.* Health Administration Press, Chicago, IL.

Stewart, G. L., Carson, K. P., & Cardy, R. L. 1996. The joint effects of conscientiousness and self-leadership training on employee self-directed behavior in a service setting. *Personnel Psychology*, 49: 143-164.

Stodgill, R.M., Goode, O.S. and Day, D.R. (1962). New leader behavior description subscales. *Journal of Psychology, 54*, 259-269.

Stogdill, R. M. (1948). Personal factors associated with leadership: A survey of the literature. *Journal of Psychology*, 25, 35– 71.

Stogdill, R. M. (1963). *Manual for the Leader Behavior Description Questionnaire Form XII.* Columbus: Ohio State University, Bureau of Business Research.

Stogdill, R. M. (1963). *Team achievement under high motivation.* Columbus, Ohio: Ohio State University, Bureau of Business Research, College of Commerce and Administration.

Stogdill, R. M. (1974). *Handbook of leadership: A survey of theory and research*. New York: Free Press.

Stoltz, P., Ude´n, G., & Willman, A. (2004). Support for family careers who care for an elderly person at home - A systematic literature review. *Scandinavian Journal of Caring Sciences*, 18, 111–118.

Taylor, F. W. (1911). *The principles of scientific management*. New York: Norton.

Tead, O. (1935). *The art of leadership*. New York: McGraw-Hill.

Tepper, B. J., & Percy, P. M. (1994). Structural validity of the multifactor leadership questionnaire. *Educational and Psychological Measurement,* 54, 734–744.

Toor, S., & Ofori, G. (2009). Authenticity and its influence on psychological well-being and contingent self-esteem of leaders in Singapore construction sector. Construction Management and Economics, 27, 299–313

Tracey, J. B., & Hinkin, T. R. (1998). Transformational leadership or effective managerial practices? *Group and Organization Management*, 23, 220–236.

Trice, H. M., & Beyer, J. M. (1986). Charisma and its routinization in two social movement organizations. *Research in Organizational Behavior,* 8, 113– 164.

United States, & U.S. Census Bureau. (1878). *Statistical abstract of the United States*. Washington: U.S. G.P.O.

Van Dierendonck, D. (2011). Servant leadership: A review and syntheses. *Journal of Management*, 27(4), 1228–1261.

van Dierendonck, D., & Nuijten, I. (2011). The Servant Leadership Survey: Development and Validation of a Multidimensional Measure. *Journal Of Business And Psychology*, *26*(3), 249-267.

van Dyne, L. V., Graham, J. W., & Dienesch, R. M. (1994). Organizational citizenship behavior: Construct redefinition, measurement, and validation. *Academy of Management Journal*, 37, 765–802.

Van Rooy, D. L., & Viswesvaran, C. (2004). Emotional intelligence: A meta-analytic investigation of predictive validity and nomological net. *Journal Of Vocational Behavior*, 65 (1), 71-95.

References

Van Seters, D. & Field, R. (1990). The evolution of leadership theory. *Journal of Organizational Change Management, 3,* 3, 29-45.

von Collani, G., & Blank, H. (2003). Perso¨nlichkeitsmerkmale, soziale U¨ berzeugungen und politische Parteienpra¨ferenzen: Eine Internetbefragung zur Bundestagswahl 2002. Zeitschrift fuer Politische Psychologie, 11(4), 307–324.

Vroom, V. H., & Jago, A. G. (1978). On the validity of the Vroom-Yetton model. *Journal of Applied Psychology,* 63, 151– 162.

Vroom, V. H., & Jago, A. G. (1988). *The new leadership: Managing participation in organizations*. Englewood Cliffs, NJ: Prentice-Hall.

Vroom, V. H., & Yetton, P. W. (1973). *Leadership and decision-making*. Pittsburgh: University of Pittsburgh Press. New York: Wiley.

Walumbwa, F. O., & Lawler, J.J. (2003). Building effective organizations. Transformational leadership, collectivist orientation, work-related attitudes, and withdrawal behaviors in three emerging economies. *International Journal of Human Resource Manage*ment, 14, 1083-1101.

Walumbwa, F. O., Avolio, B. J., Gardner, W. L., Wernsing, T. S., & Peterson, S. J. (2008). Authentic leadership: Development and validation of a theory-based measure. Journal of Management, 34, 89–126.

Walumbwa, F. O., Avolio, B., Gardner, W., Wernsing, T., & Peterson, S. (2008). Authentic Leadership: Development and Validation of a Theory-Based Measure. *DigitalCommons@University of Nebraska - Lincoln.*

Walumbwa, F. O., Hartnell, C. A., & Oke, A. (2010). Servant leadership, procedural justice climate, service climate, employee attitudes and organizational citizenship behavior: A cross-level investigation. *Journal of Applied Psychology,* 95(3), 517–529.

Walumbwa, F. O., Lawler, J.J., Avolio, B.J., & Wang, P. (2003). *Relationship between transformational leadership and work-related attitudes: The Moderating effects of collective and self-efficacy across cultures*. Working paper, University of Nebraska, Lincoln.

Walumbwa, F. O., Wang, P., Lawler, J. J., & Shi, K. (2004). The role of collective efficacy in the relations between transformational leadership and work outcomes. *Journal of Occupational and Organizational Psychology, 77,* 4, 515-530.

Walumbwa, F. O., Wu, C., & Ojode, L. (2004). Gender and instructional outcomes: The mediating effects of leadership styles. *Journal of Management Development*, 23, 2.

Wang, C & Bird, J. (2011). Multi-level modeling of principal authenticity and teachers' trust and engagement Academy of Educational Leadership Journal, Volume 15, Number 4, 2011

Wang, D., & Hsieh, C. (2013). The effect of authentic leadership on employee trust and employee engagement. *Social Behavior And Personality,* 41(4), 613-624.

Wang, G., Courtright, S. H., Colbert, A. E., & Oh, I. (2011). Transformational leadership and performance across criteria and levels: A meta-analytic review of 25 years of research. *Group and Organization Management, 36,* 2, 223-270.

Washington, R. R., Sutton, C. D., & Feild, H. S. (2006). Individual differences in servant leadership: The roles of values and personality. *Leadership & Organization Development Journal*, 27(8), 700–716.

Wayne, S. J., Shore, L. M., & Liden, R. C. (1997). Perceived organizational support and leader-member exchange: A social exchange perspective. *Academy of Management Journal,* 40: 82-111.

Weber, M. (1924/1947). *The theory of social and economic organization* (Trans. T. Parsons). New York: Free Press.

Welbourne Theresa, M., E. Johnson Diane, Erez Amir, 1998. The Role-based Performance Scale: Validity Analysis of a Theory-based Measure. *Academy of Management Journal*, 415: 540-555.

Welbourne, T. M., Johnson, D. E., & Erez, A. 1998. The role-based performance scale: Validity analysis of a theory-based measure. *Academy of Management Journal*, 41: 540-555.

Williams, L. J., & Anderson, S. E. (1991). Job satisfaction and organizational commitment as predictors of organizational citizenship and in-role behaviors. *Journal of Management*, 17, 601–617.

Witzel, M. (2011). *A history of management thought*. Milton Park, Abingdon, Oxon: Routledge.

Wofford, J., Liska, L. (1993). Path-goal theories of leadership: A meta-analysis. *Journal of Management, 19,* 4, 857-87

References

Wong and Giallonardo, (2013). Authentic leadership and nurse-assessed adverse patient outcomes. *Journal of Nursing Management*, 21, 740-752.

Wong, C. A., & Cummings, G. G. (2009). The influence of authentic leadership behaviors on trust and work outcomes of health care staff. Journal of Leadership Studies, 3(2), 6–23

Wong, C. A., & Laschinger, H. S. (2013). Authentic leadership, performance, and job satisfaction: the mediating role of empowerment. Journal Of Advanced Nursing, 69(4), 947-959.

Woodward, J. (1965). *Industrial organization: theory and practice*. London: Oxford University Press.

Woodward, J. (1970). *Industrial organization: behavior and control*. London: Oxford University Press.

Woolley, C. and Levy, F. (2011). Authentic leadership and follower development: Psychological capital, positive work climate, and gender. *Journal of Leadership & Organizational Studies*. 10 (5), 1-11.

Wren, D. A (2005). *The history of management thought*. Hoboken, N.J: Wiley.

Wren, J. T. (1995). *The leader's companion: Insights on leadership through the ages*. New York: Free Press.

Yammarino, F. J., Spangler, W. D., & Bass, B. M. (1993). Transformational leadership and performance: a longitudinal investigation. *The Leadership Quarterly*, 4, 81–108.

Yukl, G. A. (2012). *Leadership in organizations*. Boston: Pearson.

Yukl, G., Gordon, A., & Taber, T. (2002). A Hierarchical Taxonomy of Leadership Behavior: Integrating a Half Century of Behavior Research. *Journal of Leadership & Organizational Studies*, 9, 1, 15-32.

Zamahani, M., Ghorbani, V., & Rezaei, F. (2011). Impact of Authentic Leadership and Psychological Capital on Followers' Trust and Performance. *Australian Journal Of Basic & Applied Sciences*, *5*(12), 658-667.

Zhao, H., & Seibert, S. E. (2006). The Big Five Personality Dimensions and Entrepreneurial Status: A Meta-Analytical Review. Journal of Applied Psychology, 91(2), 259-271.

Zimmerman, R. D. (2008). Understanding the impact of personality traits on individuals' turnover decisions: a meta-analytic path model. *Personnel Psychology*, 61(2), 309-348.